Paul and the Jewish Law

Compendia Rerum Iudaicarum ad Novum Testamentum

SECTION III

JEWISH TRADITIONS IN EARLY CHRISTIAN LITERATURE

Volume 1

Published under the auspices of the
Foundation Compendia Rerum Iudaicarum ad Novum Testamentum
Amsterdam

Peter J. Tomson

Paul and the Jewish Law: Halakha in the Letters of the Apostle to the Gentiles

1990

Van Gorcum, Assen/Maastricht
Fortress Press, Minneapolis

© 1990 Van Gorcum & Comp. b.v., P.O.Box 43, 9400 AA Assen,
The Netherlands

CIP-DATA KONINKLIJKE BIBLIOTHEEK, DEN HAAG

Tomson, Peter J.

Paul and the Jewish law: Halakha in the Letters of the Apostle to the Gentiles/Peter J. Tomson. -
Assen [etc.]: Van Gorcum; Minneapolis: Fortress Press. - (Compendia Rerum Iudaicarum ad
Novum Testamentum. Section three, Jewish traditions in early christian literature; [1])
With index, bibliography.
SISO 213 UDC 296.5 NUGI 633
Subject headings: jewish religion.

ISBN 90 232 2490 6 (Van Gorcum)
ISBN 0 8006 2467 x (Fortress Press)

The research project resulting in this publication was supported by a subvention of the Ministry of
Science and Research of Nordrhein-Westphalen, Federal German Republic.

Printed in The Netherlands by Van Gorcum, Assen

לדוד פלוסר
ושמואל ספראי
בני השבעים

οἷς οὐκ ἐγὼ μόνος εὐχαριστῶ
ἀλλὰ καὶ πᾶσαι αἱ ἐκκλεσίαι τῶν ἐθνῶν
(Rom 16:4)

Indem ich das Verhältnis des Paulus zum Judenchristentum und Judentum untersuche, bin ich mir bewußt, einen Punkt ins Auge zu fassen, der mit dem ganzen Ernst des Protestantismus und mit Eifersucht von der Kritik behütet wird.

(A. von Harnack, *Beiträge*, 28)

Die Lösung kann also nur darin liegen, daß man ...die Einseitigkeit wagt, die Lehre des Heidenapostels ausschließlich aus dem Jüdisch-Urchristlichen begreifen zu wollen.

(A. Schweitzer, *Geschichte*, 187)

Foundation's Preface

The Board of the *Compendia Rerum Iudaicarum ad Novum Testamentum* Foundation is proud to present the first volume of Section III of the series. A central aspect of the project, which was conceived in 1964 and began to take shape with the appearance of the first volume in 1974, is now nearing its fulfilment. The basis was laid by the volumes of Sections I and II which deal with the history and culture of Judaism as it existed around the beginning of the common era, and which formed the matrix within which Christianity was born and took shape. Section III, on the other hand, will deal with the cross-fertilization of ancient Jewish and early Christian thinking. Here the form of 'compendia' which would compound the subject matter into overcomplicated volumes is inadequate. The rest of the series will be made up of monographs.

The *Compendia* Foundation is justly proud of this fact. The present stage could not have been reached, if it had not been for the assistance of a great number of outstanding scholars. Their names figure in the volumes published so far and in the list of the Editorial Board of Section III. Amongst those names we find that of Professor Heinz Kremers whose sad and untimely death two years ago was announced in volume II/1. At this moment we also have to mourn the death of the former chairman of the Board, Professor H. van Praag. It is in large measure due to his creative and innovative mind that our project got actually started a quarter of a century ago (cf Preface in volume I/1). At that time, hardly anyone recognized the necessity of such an endeavour, let alone considered it possible. Likewise, we mourn the tragic death of a former co-editor and one of the great scholars in the field of Judaism in the Greco-Roman world, Professor Menahem Stern.

The previous volumes could not have been published without material support from many quarters. To all those, scholars and supporters alike, we owe a great debt of gratitude.

It seems fitting that the author of the first volume to appear in Section III should be Dr. P.J. Tomson. Dr. Tomson has for many years been closely connected with the publication of earlier volumes. Without his learning and his perseverance the *Compendia* series would not be where it stands today.

Finally a word of thanks is due to the publishers of the *Compendia*, both in the Netherlands and in the United States of America, whose co-operation has made it possible for an ambitious plan to become a book.

R.A. Levisson, chairman.
Y. Aschkenasy, H. de Bie, L. Dequeker, J. van Goudoever (secretary), A. van der Heide, Th.C. de Kruyf, Mrs. R.C. Musaph-Andriesse, H.E. Oving (treasurer), H. Sysling.

Editors' Preface

The aim of the COMPENDIA RERUM IUDAICARUM AD NOVUM TESTAMENTUM is to present a comprehensive picture of ancient Judaism, particularly in relation to the earliest stages of Christianity, and to describe the history and literature of both religious traditions in their developing interrelationship.

Obviously, Jewish-Christian cooperation is an essential prerequisite. The resources of Jewish and Christian scholarship, which for so long have been developing separately, have to be fused and applied to the gamut of extant Jewish and Christian sources. This does not simply require an application of established insights to well-known documents. What is needed is almost the opposite: a process of re-interpretation which involves continuous questioning of accepted principles and starting points. This is particularly pressing in view of discoveries, such as the Qumran scrolls, which reveal hitherto unknown aspects of ancient Judaism and put long-known texts in a different perspective. Moreover the very ideas we have of ancient Judaism and earliest Christianity and of the demarcation lines between them often prove inadequate when confronted with the sources thus studied. In this process of re-reading and reinterpreting, both Jewish and Christian scholars have to transcend conventional boundaries and conceptions.

From the start, the editors have been aware of the complexity of this task. It was decided to devote Section I of the series tomore external, 'objective' aspects: historical geography, political history, and social, cultural and religious life and institutions. Nevertheless, even the presentation of these so-called *realia* involves many interpretative intricacies. This is even more so the case in Section II, which describes the various branches of ancient Jewish literature: Scripture, apocryphal and pseudepigraphic writings, the Qumran scrolls, Greek Jewish works and Rabbinic literature. In the original design this section included the Jewish stratum of early Christian literature, but the interpretative problems proved so large that this difficult field of study had to be relegated to a separate section.

Thus Section III aims at describing the presence of Jewish traditions within early Christian literature. This is a phenomenon which has a multiple significance and is invested with central interests of the *Compendia* project as a whole. First, the presence of Jewish traditions in early Christian literature, which may not have been preserved elsewhere, is of direct relevance to the history of Jewish literature. Second, this testifies to the general continuity of early Christianity vis-àvis Judaism. Third, the specific form in which these traditions were incorporated is in itself a highly informative source for the development of the attitude of early Christians towards Judaism and its literature.

IX

In fact the various branches of ancient Christianity served as the archivists of otherwise forgotten Jewish documents and traditions. The whole corpus of biblical Apocrypha, Jewish Pseudepigrapha and Hellenistic Jewish writings, including the Septuagint, Philo and Josephus, was preserved and transmitted not by Jews but by learned Christian bishops, monks and sectaries. Many documents were lost and only emerged into daylight in the nineteenth century. As a result, for instance, scholars began to re-discover the apocalyptic element in the early Christian writings. The discovery of the Dead Sea Scrolls not only amplified this wealth of ancient sources but revealed the extent to which esoteric apocalypticism could coexist with life according to the Jewish Law. This makes the questions about the relationship of these writings to the contemporary forms of Rabbinic tradition all the more pressing. What gradually emerges is a revolutionized picture of ancient Judaism and consequently of the matrix of earliest Christianity.

When seen in this perspective, however, the Christian texts are more than just depositories of Jewish literary sediments. They are in themselves historical sources of prime importance which reflect additional varieties of pluriform Second Temple Judaism. But as we have stated, an assessment of this fact requires careful analysis in the perspective of the developing relationship of early Christianity to Judaism. In fact, this involves a further step in a process of study and research which has only just begun. It seems no coincidence that the revised edition of Schürer's *History*, an excellent handbook which supplies much information not offered in this series, does not include the earliest Christian writings in its description of the relevant sources, despite the adjunct with the re-editors chose to maintain in its title: '...in the age of Jesus Christ'. Thus the present section is not only crucial to the *Compendia* as a whole, but it also aims at breaking new ground. The editors are well aware that as well as this being tremendously exciting there are also risks involved.

In order to get to grips with the subject matter, the editors made a provisional division between the incorporation into early Christian documents of written Jewish sources and the preservation of oral literary traditions. Examples of the first category are found in the Sibylline Oracles and the Testaments of the Twelve Patriarchs, the Didache, and the Christian reception of the works of Philo and Josephus. The second category is represented by the presence of midrash, halakha and aggada in early Christian literature, as also of certain ethical teachings, prayers and mystical traditions. Often however, both categories may be found side by side in the same Christian source. An additional difficulty is that in some cases treatment will most naturally follow the traces of the Jewish sources, while in others it is more appropriate to take a Christian document for a frame of reference.

As a result Section III appears in a new format. Comprehensive handbooks presenting all aspects in a more or less coherent way are no longer possible here. The editors opted for a series of monographs each of which will explore one aspect of the field in their own way and will in that respect be independent studies. Accordingly, the list of planned volumes does not pretend to provide full coverage of all the aspects in the field, nor can it predict the order of publication. Due shortly are volumes on Jewish traditions in early Christian art and literature; Philo in early Christian literature; Jewish apocalyptic in early Christian literature; and Jewish esoteric traditions in the New Testament.

It is our hope that this section will not only contribute to our knowledge of Jewish-Christian relations in the distant past but will also foster understanding between Jews and Christians in a generation which has witnessed both a profound crisis within both religions and unprecedented horror in their mutual relationship.

Y. Aschkenasy, T. Baarda, W.J. Burgers, D. Flusser, P.W. van der Horst, Th.C. de Kruyf, S. Safrai, P.J. Tomson, B.H. Young

Foreword

In a way, it all started in Jerusalem. While studying for a year at the Hebrew University, eleven years ago now, I also attended the meetings of the Ecumenical Theological Research Fraternity. Toward the end of that year Coos Schoneveld, the Fraternity's study secretary, invited me to present my views on Paul in a paper which was not to exceed 20 minutes. Although I failed to meet that requirement, the occasion stimulated me to integrate my involvement in Jewish studies with my interest in the Apostle to the gentiles. A process got under way which was eventually to result in the present book. The original paper has not only grown in size but hopefully in clarity and accuracy too. At any rate, a 20 minute talk on 'Paul and the Jewish Law' would no longer seem to be a problem.

My interest in Paul first developed in Amsterdam, particularly during a seminar on Galatians with Ben Hemelsoet. At that time I also got to know two works which were to decide my later course in this field: K. Stendahl's *Paul among Jews and Gentiles* and E.P. Sanders' *Paul and Palestinian Judaism*. I should also mention one other important though rather unknown book: J. Meuzelaar, *Der Leib des Messias*. Meuzelaar belonged to a circle around K.H. Kroon, a pioneer of Christian-Jewish relations in Amsterdam who inspired a fresh and passionate interest in Paul, the Jewish Apostle to the gentiles. It is through Hemelsoet that I came under the influence of Kroon's approach.

But most of my energy in those years was spent on Jewish studies. I am very grateful for the inspiration I gained from Yehuda Aschkenasy, already from the beginning of my studies, as well as the encouragement he gave me to find my own way in the world of Jewish learning. He also organized the yearly seminars in which Shmuel Safrai and David Flusser made us participate in their learning. In retrospect, that was where my basic approach took shape. It was to grow in depth and scope during my year in Jerusalem.

The setting of my Jerusalem paper on Paul also illuminates the final result of this book. It is a Paul revisited after years of work in Jewish studies. At this stage I could also say: it represents an approach on the Pauline letters as if they were another area of the study of ancient Judaism. Whether this description is acceptable depends not only on one's views on Paul but also on one's definition of 'ancient Judaism'. The study of the introvert apocalyptics of the Qumran sect has acquired its place among the disciplines of Judaic scholarship. Study of the intellectual adventures of Philo, Spinoza and Shabtai Tswi has also long been accepted. Rabbinic mysticism is recently enjoying a growing popularity. I see no sound reason to disregard the passionate dialectics of the 'Apostle to the gentiles'.

There are those who draw lines to separate, and those who do so to connect. Aware that both kind of people are needed, I cannot help but belong to the second. It has always been obvious to me that demarcations between scholarly disciplines can only be provisional. They are like divisions in a library, which in my experience are so often arbitrary. Or as Albert Schweitzer put it: they are no more than conveniencies which help draw up a nice division of academic courses. Yet time is short and one must choose while being in the library. As to bibliography, students of the New Testament will find many important studies and even some standard works missing. Judaic scholars might wish to add references in the field of textual criticism, as well as certain specialized studies. Being a layman in Hellenistic studies, my references in this field are only through secondary literature. Patristic literature comes off little better. But I am well aware that the Pauline branch of Judaic study is still *in statu nascendi*. Drawing lines is a preliminary to building.

On the other hand, Paul is the leading Apostle of gentile Christianity. Indeed 'Paul and the Law' has been a major theme in Christian theological discussions for centuries, and is increasingly so. Readers may wonder: what has become of this pillar of Christian doctrine here? My question in response is: is there necessarily a contradiction here? Does a Jewish Paul exclude the pioneer of Christian theology? I am convinced he does not. In the first place, the Jewish Paul who emerges shows a surprising affinity with the tradition of the original Apostles of Jesus. A study of Paul's Jewish antecedents reveals his indebtedness to the teacher of Nazareth. This may seem disconcerting to the guardians of academic and ecclesial theology, but it is a relief to those who wish to follow Jesus. Moreover, my explorations of the roots of Paul's teaching in the halakha, the legal tradition of Judaism, eventually led to a better insight into the structure of his thought. What emerges, especially in the concluding chapter, is a description of the main contours of that structure. The blank which so to say is left in the middle is open to theological re-assessments in depth and detail. Main subjects here are Paul's christology and doctrine of the Law.

But Paul's significance transcends theology. Combining elements of Jewish apocalyptic, Jewish-Christian midrash and Hellenistic humanism, he envisaged a 'church of God', a 'body of Christ' which encompassed both 'Jew and Greek, slave and free, male and female'. Remarkably, this vision of apocalyptic humanism both radically transcended the immutable social order of his day and presupposed it as a matter of fact. Those who cherished and preserved Paul's letters throughout the ages could hardly have been able to grasp the dynamic and compass of this vision. Today, on the other hand, we live in a world transformed by Enlightenment and revolution to a degree we can only begin to realize. A Copernican shift vis-à-vis the relationship of religion and society has determined our perception of history, politics and human relations in a way which makes it very difficult really to understand the ideas and world view of the ancients. Thus paradoxically, if we wish to understand Paul within the framework of his generation, beyond the barriers which separate it from ours, we need to adopt some of the humanist-apocalyptic power of his thought. And in turn, such a post-revolutionary understanding of Paul may inspire us in our struggle against the intolerable obstacles on the road towards one just and peaceful world embracing many tongues and cultures. He is still there, awaiting us now as then: Paul, the Apostle of Jesus to the gentiles.

It remains for me to fulfil the pleasant and honourable duty of thanking those whose names are not mentioned elsewhere in the book for their contributions toward its realization. I am grateful to the Board of the Compendia Foundation, in particular to its chairman R.A. Levisson, for their support and their patience whenever time schedules turned out to be wishful thinking. I would like to thank G. Kramer and D.C.J. Bakkes of Van Gorcum's and S.A. Herman, corrector, for taking their share of the unavoidable stress at the printing stage. I feel indebted to P.W. van der Horst for a critical reading of parts of the manuscript, to G. Muussies for correcting Greek orthography and especially to W.J. Burgers for his stimulating and critical support in the initial stages. Discussions with students both in university and in church have given me invaluable insights. H. Kremers procured the necessary research grant and inspired me as a profound and visionary scholar; his memory will always be associated with this book. I am unable to express my indebtedness to Christien, all those years.

Amsterdam
Palmarum, anno Domini 1990

Peter Tomson

Contents

CONCLUSION: *The Nexus of Halakha and Theology*

Introduction

How to Approach Paul and the Law

Three Traditional Assumptions

Scholarship on Paul has been based on three traditional assumptions: (1) the centre of his thought is a polemic against the Law; (2) the Law for him no longer had a practical meaning; and (3) ancient Jewish literature is no source for explaining his letters. In order to be fully conscious of the significance of our main task, the study of halakha in Paul, it is necessary to take a closer look at these assumptions, their development and their influence.

The three assumptions have, in varying forms and combinations, been guiding the perception and judgment of scholars from the beginnings of historical criticism to the present day. Each of these has to do with the way Christianity views its Jewish background and each is somehow rooted in Christian tradition. But they are very different, originating as they do in historical periods centuries apart.

The assumption of the centrality of the Law polemic in Paul is not the oldest of the three, but it is the most conspicuous in scholarly literature. In recent years its correctness is increasingly being questioned, but it has also found gallant defenders. It originated during the Protestant Reformation, crystallizing around the conviction that a Christian is saved 'by faith alone,[1] without works of the Law'. Significantly this had nothing to do with the Jewish Law proper, which for the Reformation leaders was not really a problem.[2] The thrust of their polemic was against prevailing Roman Catholic theology with its emphasis on pious deeds as a means of obtaining salvation. In that situation Paul's theology of justification by faith as expressed in the Epistles to the Romans and the Galatians gained acute importance.[3] Indeed to the extent that the concept of justification by faith became the nerve of Reformation theology it came to serve

---

[1] David Flusser points out that the word μόνον, typical of the Protestant catch phrase, is absent in Rom 3:28 (and Gal 2:16), but is found early on with the Church fathers; it probably derives from the polemical phrase Jas 2:24 οὐκ ἐκ πίστεως μόνον.

[2] Only in the 1530's, rumours on massive sabbatizing and judaizing may have hardened Luther's position on Jews and Judaism, but this position in itself did not change; thus Oberman, *Antisemitismus*, 157f.

[3] Cf Oberman, *Luther*, 159-63, 171-7 on Luther's struggle concerning the meaning of the phrase 'righteousness of God' (Rom 1:17).

1

as the key to all of Paul's writings and, by implication, all of the New Testament.[4]

This resulted in the paradoxical situation that on the one hand Paul's Law polemic acquired new actuality, while on the other hand there was, unlike Paul's situation, no longer a direct relation to Judaism. In other words the polemic on the Jewish Law was abstracted from its original context, and 'The Law' was generalized into a theoretical concept associated with degenerated, organized religion.[5] But to the extent that at the same time the Law was still felt to be 'Jewish', 'Jew' evolved into an equally theoretical concept denoting religous man in general.[6] Both 'the Law' and 'the Jew' became mere theological terms in an inner-Christian polemic with only an accidental relation to actual Judaism.[7] Nonetheless this implied a re-affirmation, albeit on the theoretical level, of the negative verdict on the Jewish Law inherent in ancient Christian tradition. Thus the Protestant assumption of the centrality of the Law polemic may be viewed as a spiritualization of the much older second assumption: for Paul, the Jewish Law has no practical significance. This insight explains a typically Protestant phenomenon which endures to our day: the unmistakable yet barely palpable character of 'introjected' anti-Judaism.[8]

The second assumption has to do with the actual observance of the Jewish Law. As distinct from the Reformation leaders this was a serious problem for the Church Fathers, especially those residing in areas with a prominent Jewish community such as Antioch.[9] According to Josephus the liturgical ceremonies of the Jewish community there were attracting numerous non-Jews by the middle of the first century CE.[10] And apparently, this remarkable gentile interest in Jewish ritual did not stop at the Church doors, for other sources inform us that the Church leaders felt the need for radical counter-measures. In plain words, written by Ignatius, bishop of Antioch around the end of the first century CE: practice of the Jewish Law is forbidden to Christians, and a Jew becoming Christian should stop living as a Jew.[11] The prohibition against

---

[4] In this connection Hübner, *Gesetz*, 77 notes: 'Käsemann kann also mit genau denselben Worten über Paulus und Jesus sprechen'.

[5] Similarly Stendahl, *Paul*, 5f, 85f. This is carried to an extreme by Karl Barth's rendering of the Law in Romans as 'Religion überhaupt': *Römerbrief*, ch7.

[6] This is pointed out by Watson, *Paul*, 1-10; see also my 'Paulus und das Gesetz'.

[7] On 'Jews' as a theological term in Luther's polemic see Oberman, *Antisemitismus*, 135-43. While Oberman's distinction between Luther's anti-Judaism and modern 'anti-Semitism' is correct, he overlooks the negative potential of 'theoretical' anti-Judaism, cf ib 155f, 163-5 (cf remarks on Luther's fictional anti-zionism, *Luther*, 70-2).

[8] Hence 'the Jew in us' as a negative category in Christian theology independently found in two dialectic theologians: Käsemann (above n6) and Miskotte (see my 'K.H. Miskotte'). Correspondingly Protestant exegetes find it difficult to see through the anti-Jewish character of the gospel of John.

[9] On the phenomenon in general see Simon, *Verus Israel*, 356-93; especially on Antioch see Meeks-Wilken, *Jews and Christians*, introductory essay, 1-52.

[10] War 7:45; cf Ag Ap 2:282f.

[11] 'If we live till now according to Judaism, we confess that we did not receive grace. ...(we should live) not sabbatizing, but keeping the Lord's day. ...It is unworthy to speak of Jesus Christ and to live

participation in Jewish ritual was declared official canon law at the Councils of Antioch (341 CE) and Laodicea (c. 360 CE).[12] All of this was to stress the fundamental view of Jewish tradition as being inherently evil, obsolete, and, needless to say, irrelevant for practical Christian life. In this situation, when Paul says that in Christ there is 'neither Jew nor Greek', this was taken to mean that both are to desist from the Jewish Law and should become Christian, that is, non-Jewish, Greeks.[13] By consequence the Church did not recognize such practical distinctions between Jews and gentiles as created and maintained by the halakha.[14]

This was summarized in the Patristic concept of the Church as a uniform 'Third Race' distinct both from Judaism and paganism.[15] It implied a view of 'Christianity' as an axiomatically non-Jewish religious community.[16] It was probably this vigorous assertion of a non-Jewish identity which generated classical Christian anti-Judaism. It is a far cry from Paul. Although today this axiomatically un-Jewish and thus anti-Jewish character of the Church is increasingly being questioned, the assumption that the Jewish Law for Paul had lost its practical meaning has remained practically unchallenged in New Testament scholarship. One result is that hardly any scholar has given attention to the possible existence of practical distinctions between 'Jews and Greeks' in Paul's reasoning.

The third traditional assumption is of more recent date and presupposes the axioms of historical criticism. In this discipline, the interpretation of Paul is not considered to be scientific until it relies on what Ferdinand Christian BAUR, founder of the Tübingen school of New Testament historical criticism, termed – itself a historical event – 'a reliable historical point'.[17] This implied a funda-

---

Jewish...' (Magn 8:1, 9:1, 10:3; cf Phil 6:1).

[12] See Parkes, *Conflict*, 175f, 381f; Simon, *Verus Israel*, 382ff.

[13] Chrysostom (Antioch, late 4th century), commenting on Galatians, preached against those 'who, even if not circumcised, today observe the fastings and the sabbath with those', whereas obedience to Christ implies 'to become a tresspasser of the Law ...for He absolved the Law, and absolve He commanded'; 'Become followers of the Lord, who Himself, being a Jew, lived like a gentile' (cf Gal 2:14!; Hom in Gal, MPG 61, 642-44). On Chrysostom see Simon, *Verus Israel*, 256-63.

[14] Stendahl, *Paul* again called attention to the distinction. His observation (p16) that the Church Fathers knew Paul talked about the practical relation of Jews and gentiles but themselves did not have this problem, is not quite correct. They knew and faced the problem. But in effect, as Stendahl correctly goes on to say, they rejected Paul's solution, and this meant opting for anti-Judaism. An Augustine could observe in a matter-of-fact way that his Church no longer consisted of Jews and gentiles; see below p184.

[15] The post-Pauline genesis both of this conception and the explicit phrase have been set forth by Harnack, *Mission*, 259-81. See also the important studies of Richardson, *Israel*, esp 22ff; and De Lange, *Origen*, esp 75-87.

[16] Χριστιανισμός as a separate movement directly opposed to 'Ιουδαϊσμός, and χριστιανοί as its members, are first documented in the letters of Ignatius bishop of Antioch (Magn 10:1, 3; Phil 6:1). Χριστιανοί is also found in Acts and called Antiochene in origin (11:26; cf 26:28); it has no anti-Jewish meaning. Hence χριστιανισμός is not inherently anti-Jewish but can be made so. Paul does not use the word χριστιανοί but speaks of πίστοι vs ἄπιστοι.

[17] Title and subtitle are programmatic: 'Über Zweck und Veranlassung des Römerbriefs und die damit zusammenhängenden Verhältnisse der römischen Gemeinde. Eine historisch-kritische Stu-

mental departure from the tradition of reading Paul in the framework of Christian and especially Protestant doctrine.[18] In other words Paul's teaching on the Law is to be explained within the religious and social context of his own time as revealed in contemporary sources. But curiously enough, Greek rather than Hebrew and Aramaic sources were thought really relevant, and halakhic sources least of all.

This is all the more striking in view of the lively interest in Rabbinic literature as a source for understanding the New Testament in the seventeenth and eighteenth centuries. That was a different age in scholarship, in which religious exposition was predominant and polemic pervasive.[19] With the rise of historical scholarship the Jewish sources were forgotten, as was the possibility of recognizing their relevance for Paul. More precisely, a curious cleavage appeared in scholarship, which somehow relates to social developments in post-revolutionary Europe; its results are still felt in our day. Historic-critical study of the Hebrew and Aramaic sources, neglected by Christian scholars, was initiated by Jews. The 'Wissenschaft des Judentums', 'science of Judaism', was created by men like Leopold ZUNZ and Zacharias FRANKEL and for a century developed totally separate from Christian historical scholarship. Only in recent generations is this curious, sad and counterproductive dichotomy being overcome and have scholars of Christian provenance started to draw on the resources of modern Jewish scholarship, the great centres of which have since moved outside of Europe: to Israel and North America.

Behind the irrational selectivity regarding the sources of nascent Christian historical criticism, implicit theological premises may be suspected. The influence of religious tradition easily extends beyond the boundaries of consciousness, even that of a scholar. It is obvious to surmise a connection with the traditional assumptions about Paul and the Law. This would explain the specific character of the third assumption of Pauline scholarship. It would be a modern assumption in that it is expressed not in theological doctrine, but in a historical conception and a concomitant selectivity about the sources. Put in other terms, it would be a secular 'operationalization' of traditional religious views.

Once this intuition is aroused, it appears possible to identify secularized forms of the Patristic and Protestant assumptions behind the methods of historical criticism. Baur stated frankly that Paul was the only early Christian really to advocate 'a total renunciation of the compulsoriness of the Mosaic Law' and reveal the fundamental 'antithesis between Judaism and Pauline Christianity'.[20] This throws theological light on Baur's novel historical conception of the fundamental antithesis between Pauline and 'Petrine', i.e. Jewish, Christianity

---

die.' Referring to the opposition by the Jewish-Christian party in the Roman church he writes ib p141: 'Hiermit haben wir nun erst einen festen historischen Punkt...'

[18] Schweitzer, *Geschichte*; cf Watson, *Paul* (below).

[19] See the first section of Moore, 'Christian Writers', 216-22. He does not connect this with the subsequent eclipse of the Hebrew and Aramaic sources.

[20] Baur, 'Christuspartei', 49, 74f. The radical significance of these words was emphasized by Harnack, see below n44.

as the driving force of earliest Christian history. On the philosophical level, it is not difficult today to detect the Hegelian dialectics at work in Baur's conception. What is important to us is that the novel scholarly approach of historical criticism, priceless in itself, also became the vehicle of ancient theological prejudice. Apart from the neglect of ancient Jewish sources in general, a far-reaching consequence of Baur's approach was the assumption of an absolute rupture between Paul and the Jewish-Christian tradition of Jesus and his Apostles.

A different scholarly re-affirmation of the ancient assumptions appeared by the late nineteenth century in historical accounts of Judaism by Protestant scholars. What was new now was the interest in religions as coherent phenomena with their own development, to be studied in their historical background. Unlike the previous period, cultic and ritual elements were now perceived as essential. In this 'history-of-religions' approach Rabbinic literature including the halakha did come within view, only in a negative sense. Like in the theological polemics of old, Jewish religiosity was portrayed as the dark foil against which the light of Christian freedom from the Law was made to shine out, this time in the language of historical description. Jesus was a Jew, but one who fundamentally criticized Judaism and especially the Law. In order to make this plausible, a conceptual model was needed which could describe Jewish religious life as the ideological antipode of Jesus' message. The Protestant justification doctrine served this aim. What resulted was the historiographic stereotype of Judaism as a religion tainted by petrification and formalism.[21]

For the purpose of this discussion the secularized versions of both assumptions are viewed together as fundamentally one modern scholarly assumption: when writing his letters, Paul's historical background was no longer in Judaism, and by consequence ancient Jewish literature is no source for explaining his teaching.

Historical Scholarship and Theology

The rise of modern scholarship is tantamount to its emancipation from organized religion. But outward emancipation does not equal inner freedom. Scholars, however alienated from the Church's jurisdiction, have consciously or unconsciously been carrying its traditional ideas with them. Thus it appears, and this is only logical, that it is very difficult to read Paul independently of the interpretations offered by Christian tradition. Yet it is the essential task of scholarship to interpret texts preserved within a religious tradition in an adequate, reflected distance from that tradition itself.

Mutatis mutandis this equally regards the interpretation of Pharisaic and other ancient Jewish elements contained within Rabbinic literature. The continuous verification of the form and contents of early Tannaic traditions as against the various interpretative frameworks, especially those of the revered

---

[21] Moore, 'Christian Writers'; see below.

Babylonian schools, is part of the main task of present-day Judaic scholarship. On the other hand the discovery of the Damascus Covenant and later of other Essene texts presented scholarship with a very different situation. In this intriguing situation the absence of a transmissional framework created an irresistible interpretative vacuum which keeps inspiring phantasy.[22]

By implication, objectivity in reading Paul necessitates critical reflection of the position of the reading subject vis-à-vis Christian and Protestant theological tradition. In other words we are confronted with the hermeneutical question in a most fundamental way. Historical observation and judgment vis-à-vis Paul and Judaism can never be seen separately from the historian's theological conceptions. As in modern physics the optimum of objective observation requires continuous integration of the observer's own position and motion. This does not only apply to scholars with a Christian upbringing. What typifies traditional interpretative frameworks is the apparent self-evidence of the interpretations they offer. Therefore modern Jewish interpreters of Paul can hardly be thought immune to the influence of Christian and Protestant tradition.[23]

Thus the desired optimum of objectivity lies not only beyond traditionalism but also beyond agnosticism. Sheer agnosticism, or the decision to be ignorant about theology, which is typical of positivist historiography, is bound to overlook or misjudge vital elements of the post-Pauline Christian tradition and their subconscious influence on one's own observations. The concomitant pretense of detached 'objectivity' may impress the naive but quickly proves superficial. What is needed is a qualified distance, or in other words a critical subjectivity which includes conscious and recurring reflection on the substance of Christian tradition. In order to be able to approach the 'real Paul', one has to get to know his important ancient and recent interpreters. The critical historian who wants to study Paul has no choice, he must become a self-critical student of Pauline theology.[24]

But reflected subjectivity for the sake of optimal objectivity is not only required in order to study Paul. A historical conception giving central and indiscriminate importance to the Pauline polemic against the Law is bound to have hermeneutical problems with Judaism as well. The incorrect historical portrayal of Judaism as a religion of petrified legalism is best viewed as a projection of implicit Christian ideas. Its conceptional opposite, characteristically expressed in German as a 'gesetzesfreies Evangelium', has an unmis-

---

[22] See Schürer, *History* 2, 583-5, esp n40-44 for the various identifications offered. Add Leszynsky, *Sadduzäer* (CD = Sadducee) and Ginzberg, *Jewish Sect* (CD = Pharisee in origin). For fundamentals of the study of Rabbinic literature see below.

[23] The assumption of the centrality of the Law polemic and the abrogation of the practical commandments for Jewish Christians is variously combined with the assumed presence of Jewish traditions in Paul's theology and ethics by Löwy, 'Paulinische Lehre'; Baeck, 'Romantic Religion'; Buber, *Zwei Glaubensweisen*; Klausner, *Von Jesus zu Paulus* (see below); Schoeps, *Paulus*; Sandmel, *Genius*.

[24] I am indebted to Anne Marie Reynen for enhanced comprehension of the hermeneutical question.

takable rigidity which is reminiscent of the suppression of disconcerting elements.[25] The correlated spectres of suppressive legalism and unconscious antinomianism, so often supposed to be haunting Paul as remnants from his Jewish past, may perhaps be sought first of all between the lines of Christian, and especially Protestant, scholarship. A particularly revealing projection is Wellhausen's phrase decribing Paul as 'the great pathologist of Rabbinic Judaism'.[26]

In other words: an adequate reading of Paul requires a correct approach of ancient Judaism; and both presuppose a reflected distance towards Christian tradition. This desideratum implies nothing less than a paradigmatic shift in the basic perceptions, aims and methods of established Christian scholarship. Yet contrary to what one might be inclined to think, this is not completely new. Already two generations ago it was placed on the agenda by two remarkable Christian scholars.

In 1921 George Foot MOORE published his study 'Christian Writers on Judaism' which gave a fundamental criticism of the description of ancient Judaism which was especially typical of German historians. These scholars portrayed Judaism as a religion marked by the constant and depressive need to earn salvation by observing commandments of the Law.[27] Moore observed that this emphasis, which was new in modern scholarship, was motivated by the apologetical need to differentiate between the religion of the historical Jesus, now percieved as the authentic core of Christian belief, and his Jewish background.[28] The traditional Protestant-Paulinist colouring of this antithesis is evident. Some years after his critical review Moore's own historical synthesis of ancient Rabbinic Judaism followed, very different and much more adequate: *Judaism* (1927-30). Life under the Law is merely one aspect in this presentation, and it is described with the objectivity and sympathy worthy of a historian-of-religions. A significant feature of Moore's approach as a Christian scholar is his openness towards the works of Jewish scholars or in other words his integrating the results of the tradition of the 'Wissenschaft des Judentums'.

The other scholar we will mention here is Albert SCHWEITZER. His penetrating critique of Pauline research (1911) and his own positive interpretation (1930) represent a fundamentally new approach. His works will be dealt with extensively below.

It is remarkable that neither Moore's hermeneutically astute presentation of ancient Judaism nor Schweitzer's original and coherent rendering of Paul's complex thought have won much appreciation, least of all in the traditional

---

[25] One example of technically excellent scholarship which is nonetheless informed by this rigid Lutheranism is Strobel, 'Aposteldekret': (What Paul has in mind is) 'ein Evangelium ohne jede Verbindung mit dem mosaischen Gesetz', 'ein radikal-gesetzesfreies Evangelium' (180, 188). But Catholic exegetes can come to similar caricatures: cf Fitzmeyer, 'Paul and the Law', 194, Paul's conception of the Law opposes 'Mosaic law with its Pharisaic interpretation and casuistry'; Murphy O'Connor, 'Freedom or the Ghetto' [sic], 557f on 'Paul's radical antinomianism'.

[26] Noted in 1914 by Montefiore, *Judaism*, 21 and again in 1987 by Gaston, *Paul*, 16.

[27] Weber, *System*; Schürer, *Geschichte*; Bousset-Gressmann, *Religion*. The excursions in Strack-Billerbeck's *Kommentar* 4/1-2 may readily be added.

[28] Moore, 'Christian Writers', 252f.

7

centres of Protestant learning. Schweitzer became famous for his critique of the quest for the historical Jesus of Protestant liberal theology, but his study on Paul, which must be considered his major work,[29] passed relatively unnoticed.[30] Moore was criticised for underrating apocalypticism, which is partly correct but does not sufficiently explain the neglect he met,[31] especially so since Bousset and Schürer whom he so justly criticised came to be considered standard works. Speaking again in Kuhnian terms their approach on Paul and Judaism apparently involved a paradigm incompatible with 'normal' theological and historical scholarship. But more than half a century later[32] the time seems ripe for wider acceptance.[33] A new generation of Christian scholars is becoming aware that Paul and Judaism cannot be treated as diametrical opposites and each require a more subtle approach.[34]

Meanwhile scholarship on Paul and Judaism has reached a fundamentally new hermeneutical situation. Unlike the ideological complexities mentioned above this extends at the human level and is both inescapable and morally indispensible.[35] To all our knowledge the so-called Holocaust has brought Jews and Christians together more than ever before. At least it made Christians realize that as humans they share the world with those Jews who, thank God, survived. A basic urge towards a re-evaluation of inherited theological and scholarly conceptions and hence towards a new approach on Paul and the Jewish Law springs from grief over what happened, joy over new developments in relations of Jews and Christians, and hope for what we all believe will happen.

[29] Cf Stendahl, *Bible*, 2 n10 (Schweitzer's *Mystik* is 'less well-known but ...more significant' than his *Leben Jesu Forschung*); Davies, 'Paul and Judaism since Schweitzer', in *Paul*, vii-xv; Kümmel, 'Einführung', i, xiiif.

[30] The Bultmann school could use Schweitzer's *Leben Jesu Forschung* in its struggle (along with dialectical theology) against liberal theology, but regarding Paul was committed to Bousset's theory of the 'hellenistische Urgemeinde'; see below.

[31] This criticism should not be exaggerated. A similar criticism concerns his 'invention' of 'normative Judaism'. While discussion rightly continues, it is no reason to ignore Moore either. As indicated by the sub-title his work aims at describing Tannaic religion. Tannaic tradition hardly betrays traces of esoteric teaching and presents itself as normative Judaism.

[32] Cf Kuhn, *Structure*; on similar time lags in natural science ib section XII. Gager, *Origins*, 198-204 rightly applies Kuhn's observations on 'paradigm shifts' to the work of Stendahl, Sanders, Gaston and others. But a more comprehensive perspective of research history is appropriate.

[33] Hübner, 'Paulusforschung' gives the impression that since 1945 Bultmannian historical criticism is unchallenged. The thematic overview starts, after a section on Paul's biography, with 'Das Gesetz' and 'Die Gerechtigkeit Gottes'. Parenesis is not dealt with, the Law is only theory. The criticism of Sanders and Räisänen on the Bultmann school is in 'the wrong direction' and gives no new information on Paul (2653-5).

[34] A renewed attempt was made by Sanders, *Paul* (1977), see below. Similar in aim and conclusions is Hoheisel, *Judentum* (1978).

[35] A suitable hermeneutic conceptualization may be found in the 'inter-subjective historical criticism' designed from a feminist perspective by Schüssler Fiorenza, *Bread*, chs 5-6. With others she perceives a hopeful convergency at the inter-subjective level between feminist, liberational and 'post-Holocaust' theology.

We shall now review a number of important studies which mark the successive steps taken towards the desired new approach on Paul, as well as some which typically resist it or reveal significant anomalies in the traditional approaches.[36] If it is true that a shift of paradigm is required in scholarship on Paul and the Jewish Law,[37] we are in the situation that anomalous results which disharmonize with in the established paradigm are essential indicators as well as starting points towards a more adequate paradigm.

We begin our survey with a most remarkable chapter written by the great Adolf von HARNACK. Apparently it did not have great consequences in his theory or that of others and was deposited like an erratic block alongside the glacier of his gigantic oeuvre. In the framework of a discussion on the authorship of Acts he wrote a section called 'Paul the Apostle's Attitude towards Judaism and Jewish Christianity according to his Letters; His Jewish Constraints' (1911).[38]

Harnack thinks it incorrect to interpret Paul from Galatians only and consider his saying that 'to the Jews I became a Jew' (1Cor 9:20) a mere accomodation. Things are more complicated. Certainly the position of Galatians was no accidental polemic but the main principle of Paul's religious thought:[39] the Law had been abrogated from a religious and ethical point of view both for Jew and gentile. But remarkably, his antagonists in Galatia say he still preaches circumcision (Gal 5:11). This is confirmed by his own statements elsewhere: 1Cor 7:18, μὴ ἐπισπάσθω, means that Jewish believers should remain faithful to their ancestral traditions; Gal 5:3 states that he who is circumcised should keep the whole Law; and Rom 9-11 expresses wholehearted adherence to Paul's own people, Ἰσραὴλ κατὰ σάρκα, and belief in the irreversible promises made to them. What does this mean? Harnack concludes that Paul only painfully conceded to sacrifice his cherished Jewish belonging (2Cor 11:22; Rom 11:1; Phil 3:4f) for the sake of the gospel (Phil 3:7ff). Gal 2:11ff indicates that Jewish Christians must be ready to neglect purity laws only to accomodate with gentiles. It was this 'Jewish constraint' (jüdische Schranke) of Paul, 'the Jew in him',[40] which prevented him from taking the full consequence of his otherwise

---

[36] For previous or more exhaustive bibliographies on Pauline study see Schweitzer, *Geschichte* (1911); Bultmann, 'Geschichte' (1929); Metzger, *Index* (up to 1956); Ellis, 'Pauline Studies' (1961); Rigaux, *Saint Paul*, 13-51 (1962); Räisänen, *Paul*, 270-97 (up to 1983); Hübner, 'Paulusforschung' (basically up to 1980; see above n33).

[37] Above n32.

[38] 'Die Stellung des Apostels Paulus zum Judentum und Judenchristentum nach seinen Briefen; seine jüdischen Schranken', in *Beiträge*, 28-47.

[39] p29. Here Harnack obviously rejects Wrede's thesis, later re-stated by Schweitzer (see below), thereby confirming the first traditional assumption and blocking his way towards a coherent understanding of the Jewish Paul.

[40] ib 43f; cf the remarkable expression also in Käsemann, above n8.

9

'progressive religious thinking'. The really consistent 'Pauline' position had to be formulated by Apostolic Fathers like Justin.

The last sentences reflect Harnack's avowed predilection for the 'ultra-Paulinism' of Marcion, who severed all ties with Judaism and the Old Testament.[41] In our terminology, Harnack radically endorsed the first two traditional assumptions, but he struck on the inadequacy of the third. With his uncanny acumen he had recognized the Jewish Paul from his own letters, criticizing, incidentally, the explanation from Hellenism by Reitzenstein and others;[42] but he could not accomodate what he read.[43] The Jewish Paul did not fit in and was an obstacle to the 'true Paulinism' he favoured. Hence this evidence from Paul's letters should be considered a major anomaly vis-à-vis the paradigm utilized by the leading scholar of his generation.[44]

Of lasting importance for both the study of early Christianity and of ancient Judaism is Wilhelm BOUSSET, a main representative of the powerful 'religions-geschichtliche Schule'. He wrote influential works in both fields which not only are complementary but also reveal the same bias. One is his description of ancient Judaism, *Die Religion des Judentums* (first edition 1903). While rightly criticised by Moore for treating Rabbinic Judaism as a petrified religion of works-righteousness, it contains profound insights into the apocalyptic and mystical aspects of ancient Judaism. The other work, *Kyrios Christos* (1913), offers a novel history of early christology paying special attention to its cultic function; Paul plays a central role. One of its basic theories gained lasting influence through its adoption by Bultmann. Assuming a fundamental dichotomy between the Jewish church in Jerusalem and its gentile counterpart at Antioch, Bousset hypothesized the cradle of Paul's theology to have been in the latter. Thus he sees traditions as in 1Cor 15:1ff and 11:23-25 as deriving from the gentile Hellenistic church. In effect Paul's letters present a refined revision of that tradition, and at the same time are a major source for studying it.[45] Obviously Bousset used the inherited opposition between Paul and Judaism as

---

[41] Harnack, *Marcion*, 235: unlike the Church's 'paulinische Halbheit' in maintaining, with Judaism and Jewish Christianity, the authority of the OT, Marcion was a real 'Religionsstifter', 'ein wirklicher Reformator, ...der erste Protestant' (iv, 231).

[42] 'Die Kritik, die heute mehr als je geneigt ist, ihn zum Hellenisten zu machen, ...täte gut, sich zuerst den Juden und den Christen Paulus zu sicherer Erkenntnis zu bringen...' (p42f n1). This was noted by Schweitzer, see *Leben und Denken*, 94.

[43] Cf below p35 for his earlier simplified view on Paul. He seems to have been half-conscious of the anomaly vis-à-vis his paradigm; cf the saying of Franz Overbeck which he liked to quote: 'Niemand hat Paulus je verstanden und der einzige, der ihn verstand, Marcion, hat ihn mißverstanden' (see Schweitzer, *Mystik*, 39). Clearly Harnack requires much further study.

[44] The importance of Harnack's flirtation with Marcion should not be underestimated. He gave expression to a fundamental but usually invisible motivation of Christian historiography: the mythical antithesis between Judaism and (European) Christianity (above n20; below p32 n1). Marcion chose Galatians as the starting point for his teaching 'mit sicherem Griff', like in his day ...*F.C. Baur!* Indeed, 'die Übereinstimmung zwischen M. und den Tübingern ist sehr groß' (239f).

[45] See devastating and ironic criticism by Schweitzer, *Mystik*, 27-34.

a working principle in both works, and they are a clear example of the secular-ization of the traditional assumptions about Paul and the Law.[46]

In several repects Albert SCHWEITZER's approach is diametrically opposed to that of Bousset. His main work, *Die Mystik des Apostels Paulus*, appeared in 1930 but was planned to appear soon after his preliminary study. This work, *Die Geschichte der paulinischen Forschung* (1911), expresses the stature of his endeavour, giving a critical account of previous scholarship as it developed from historical criticism since Baur, and subsequently outlining his own meth-od.[47] Although Baur's answers proved inadequate, his challenge was left unan-swered. Baur abandoned the tradition of using Paul to uphold Protestant theology, and launched the first historical explanation of the growth of gentile Christianity out of its Jewish matrix and of Paul's share in the process. Adopting and developing this critical starting point, Schweitzer formulated what was to become the popular phrase of his interpretation.[48] Unlike the traditional Pro-testant assumption, he did not view the teaching of 'justification by faith' as the centre of Paul's thought but as a mere 'subsidiary crater' of his volcanic thought.[49] It appears distinctly in Galatians and Romans, in specific contexts 'where the controversy over the Law' is at stake.[50]

As to the actual historical background of Paul's teaching, Schweitzer depart-ed radically from the direction chosen by Baur and his school and further developed by contemporaries such as Bousset. Rather than try to explain Paul from a Hellenistic or Hellenistic-Jewish perspective, we should not shrink from the 'one-sidedness' to understand him exclusively in the light of his Jewish and Jewish-Christian background.[51] This was another very unusual viewpoint at the time, but the question is of course, what Jewish sources qualify as Paul's background. Unable to to recognize more in Rabbinic literature than 'unpro-ductive commenting on the Law',[52] Schweitzer opted for Jewish apocalyptic tradition as Paul's historical background. On that basis he designed his concep-tion of Paul's thought as a Jewish, mystic-apocalyptic re-interpretation of primeval Apostolic christology; the teaching of 'justification by faith' is ex-plained from the same background.

---

[46] In his lecture *Der Apostel Paulus* Bousset calls Paul's gentile gospel 'die recht eigentliche Fortsetzung des Werkes Jesu'; it puts his churches before 'das große Entweder-Oder: Christus oder Moses, Gesetz oder Evangelium' (p11). Related in spirit is Windisch, *Paulus und das Judentum*. It is an apology of Paul over against the 'Deutsche Christen' (1935!) which evinces a comprehensive scholarly approach but in effect saves Paul by sacrificing Judaism (p56, 'die Aufhebung des Judentums').

[47] He followed this method of scholarly self-criticism, today called hermeneutics, also for his Jesus studies. He learned it from Aristotle, see Schweitzer, *Leben und Denken*, 91.

[48] See Sanders, *Paul*, 434-42.

[49] *Mystik*, 220f. Schweitzer was the first to state this insight in the framework of a major scholarly presentation, but actually was preceded by Wrede, *Paulus* (1904); see Schweitzer, *Geschichte*, 130-4.

[50] *Mystik*, 216; I quote from the German original in my own translation.

[51] *Geschichte*, 187.

[52] *Geschichte*, 38.

11

A third original element was Schweitzer's theory of Paul's *status quo* teaching of pluriformity as regards Law observance; in spite of its importance it passed hardly noticed.[53] Interestingly it converges with Harnack's 'anomaly', but there is no apparent connection; it seems both scholars independently arrived at the same insight.[54] Paul's contribution was to make the mission to the gentiles *qua* gentiles into a necessary requirement as distinct from the existence and propagation of Jewish Christianity. The secret of Paul's novel teaching lay in his apocalyptic Christ-mysticism. 'In Christ' the Law is abolished, and inasmuch as all believers are 'in Christ', there are no distinctions between them. But as far as believers still live 'in the flesh', in the world where the Law applies, the Law is still in force. Paul, who apparently lived as an observant Jew himself and expected other Jewish believers to do the same, summarized this *status quo* teaching in 1Cor 7:17, 20: 'Let everyone walk as the Lord has assigned to him, everyone as the Lord has called him... Let everyone remain in that calling in which he was called.'[55]

In sum, Schweitzer's presentation paved the way towards an approach no longer based on the three traditional assumptions. In contrast, he assumed that comparison with ancient Jewish literature was needed to explain Paul's letters, notably the apocalyptic writings; that Paul expected Jewish Christians to observe the Law; and that his justification doctrine had a limited, specific purpose. Several recent authors whose work shows affinity to this approach also display Schweitzer's influence, direct or indirect, and explicitly or not. In that sense it is justified to speak of 'Pauline study since Schweitzer'.[56]

There are some basic criticisms to be made regarding Schweitzer's uncompromising rejection of Hellenistic parallels, which is understandable in view of the situation he faced but really is a 'one-sidedness'.[57] There is also a curious dichotomy between his exposition of Paul's teaching on the Law and on justification.[58] Quite serious from the perspective of the present study is Schweitzer's rejection of Rabbinic literature in favour of apocalyptic literature; in that respect he conformed completely to established Christian scholarly opinion.[59] But undoubtedly the pervasive apocalyptic trend in ancient Judaism constituted an important element of Paul's cultural background. The Qumran scrolls have proved that once and for all.

Unfortunately the work of Rudolf BULTMANN must be mentioned here mainly for negative reasons; a discussion of his form-critical approach is beyond

---

[53] Davies, *Paul*, 71 picks up this item but unconvincingly rejects the explanation from eschatology.
[54] As noted Schweitzer's work incurred much delay; his medical work prevented him from reading any amount of research literature later than his *Geschichte*.
[55] *Mystik*, 178-99. I follow Schweitzer's own literal translation.
[56] Cf critical assessment by Davies, 'Paul and Judaism since Schweitzer'. Similarly Ellis, 'Pauline Studies'.
[57] See Davies, *Paul*, 1-8; 'Paul and Judaism'; and below ch 1.
[58] *Mystik*, 178-214. This anomaly must relate to Schweitzer's prejudice against the Jewish Law or in other words the halakha.
[59] Significantly Schweitzer *Geschichte*, 38 n1 here refers to Bousset (as noted also by Sanders, *Paul*, p39 n22f).

the limits of this study.[60] As stated it was through Bultmann that Bousset gained decisive and lasting influence, especially in German research. This extended to both elements of Bousset's work: (1) the priority of the primitive Hellenistic church and of Hellenistic sources for explaining Paul,[61] and (2) its corollary: the idea of Judaism as a petrified works-religion.[62] If caricature can enhance insight we might call this hermeneutical compound the *interpretatio Graeco-Lutherana*. It gained a strategic function in Bultmann's *Theologie des Neuen Testaments*, both in the pages about Paul's historical background and in the section explicitly dealing with the teachings of the primitive Hellenistic church. The exposition of Paul's theological anthropology turns on the axis of Law and justification, so that the essence of the gospel can be summarized as 'justification by faith'.[63] Ancient Jewish sources were no priority in explaining Paul. The fascinating discovery of the Qumran scrolls indirectly proved the apocalyptic Jewish background of many Pauline ideas; but this connection presented Bultmann with an anomaly which he was forced to play down.[64] Similarly Bultmann expressed the conviction, inherited from Bousset and as we have seen ultimately also from Baur, that Paul practically does not relate to the Jewish Apostolic tradition.[65]

In contrast, the discovery of the Dead Sea scrolls confirmed the work of W.D. DAVIES in a way he could have never dreamt of; it happened in the same year that his *Paul and Rabbinic Judaism* was published (1947).[66] Avoiding a one-sided dismissal of Hellenism, Davies followed Schweitzer's main interest in explaining Paul using contemporaneous Jewish sources. But, again correcting Schweitzer, he argued that Rabbinic literature had definitely to be included. Hellenistic influence in Palestine and close ties with the diaspora cannot be denied, nor can the Pharisaic-Rabbinic movement be isolated from the strong apocalyptic vein in Second Temple Judaism or the mystical undercurrent evident in Rabbinic literature. The bulk of Davies' book consists of a detailed comparison of Pauline concepts with Rabbinic and other Jewish sources. The lack of a historical framework is a major setback, as is the dogmatic phraseology used in the chapter titles without apparent connection to the respective phil-

---

[60] Cf Davies, 'A Quest to be Resumed in NT Studies', in id, *Christian Origins*, 1-17, esp 3-10 on the formcritical and kerygmatic approaches.

[61] Bultmann was among the re-editors of *Kyrios Christos*, see preface to 2nd ed, xv; and cf Bultmann's own preface to the 5th ed of 1964.

[62] On the important influence of Bousset's *Religion des Judentums* via Bultmann see Sanders, *Paul*, 39-47.

[63] Bultmann, *Theologie*, 260-83.

[64] See *Theologie*, preface 5th ed ('Analogiebildungen'). On p235f (mentioning Kuhn and Davies) the Qumran evidence forces him to accept that Pauline σάρξ has a Jewish background, while Bousset saw it as a prime example of Paul's Hellenism (*Kyrios Christos*, 129ff). The 2nd ed is identical here; I was unable to get hold of the first edition of Bultmann's *Theologie* in which I suspect to find Bousset's view.

[65] *Theologie*, 190, 475. On p473 Bultmann terms 1Cor 11:23-25 and 15:3f 'Hellenistic cult myths', apparently implying the same opposition between the gentile Hellenistic church and Jerusalem.

[66] See also his important studies 'Apocalyptic and Pharisaism' and 'Paul and the Dead Sea Scrolls: Flesh and Spirit', in *Christian Origins*, 19-30, 145-77.

ological studies. Three insights of immediate importance to our study result from Davies' approach and also reveal his affinity with Schweitzer: Paul remained true to Jewish tradition and observance; he had a positive relationship with the tradition of the Jewish Apostles; and the doctrine of justification was not central to his thought nor was it directed against Judaism as such.[67]

A singular place is taken by Joseph KLAUSNER, *Von Jesus zu Paulus* (1950). In contrast to what Christian scholars are used to, Klausner draws naturally from the resources of Jewish aggadic and halakhic study and reveals many important convergencies between Paul and Rabbinic tradition.[68] He even estimates that 'Paul's ethics ... is based almost completely on Jewish morality ...(and) differs less from it than the teaching of Jesus'.[69] Nor is Klausner blind to the marked influence of Stoic traditions, a feature Paul shares with Rabbinic Judaism.[70] The influence of the Christian tradition of interpretation is felt when Klausner nevertheless assumes without discussion that 'the Tora, the Teaching of Israel, had been abolished along with all its commandments'. As a result 'all distinctions between Jews and non-Jews' and in fact 'the Jewish nation' are dissolved.[71] In the perspective of this survey it is remarkable that Klausner, while adopting the first and second traditional assumptions, naturally ignores the third which is the secularized, scholarly version of the former two. In other words he rejects Christian scholarly prejudice but adopts Christian theological prejudice. That the result is chimaeric is fully understandable, considering the inherent connection between the theological assumptions and their secularized form.[72]

Johannes MUNCK is especially important for his clear-minded critique of Baur's Tübingen school. Their literary-historical theories were all laid to rest, but their hermeneutic principles remain very active in ever new combinations. They are rooted in the trend to isolate Paul both from his wider surroundings, contemporaneous Judaism, and his immediate context: the Apostolic Church and its Jesus traditions. Thus Paul's letters are read as the documents of an irredeemable polemicist. In this analysis it is not difficult to recognize the Bultmann school as a modern version of the Tübingen principles. Munck summarized these ideas in his *Paulus und die Heilsgeschichte* (1954), in which he also investigates Paul's call as a missionary to the gentiles and his positive relations with the Jerusalem church.[73]

---

[67] Davies, *Paul*, 69-84, 136-45, 221-3.

[68] See important passages on women, marriage and divorce, and slavery, 523-33.

[69] Klausner, *Von Jesus zu Paulus*, 509, my translation.

[70] ib 517, cf 420-34.

[71] ib 479, 492, 494.

[72] A more astonishing combination is found in Schoeps, *Paulus*. While explaining many motifs of Paul's theology from Jewish sources and also supposing, like Klausner, the abrogation of Law and commandments, in addition Schoeps assumes profound *pagan Hellenistic* influence on Paul's christology. Inconsistency is also expressed in the combined reliance on Schweitzer, Bousset and Reitzenstein.

[73] Cf also his SBL lecture 'Pauline Research since Schweitzer', a title which evidently was not his idea and does not cover the contents of his paper.

The importance of Krister STENDAHL's *Paul among Jews and Gentiles* is inversely proportional to its size. Stating indebtedness to Schweitzer and especially Munck, this small collection of papers centres on a lecture given to an audience of psychologists in 1961, 'Paul and the Introspective Conscience of the West'. With great hermeneutic acumen and interpretative creativity this seminal paper distinguishes three or four strata of communication between Paul and his present-day readers; moreover it does not address exegetes but psychologists who are more interested in what one might call the side-effects of theology. In a nutshell, it describes the interpretative process outlined in our previous section, i.e. a self-critical study of Paul's recent and ancient interpreters as a prerequisite to studying Paul in his historical context. The message is that the 'introspective conscience', conventionally ascribed to Paul, originated in Protestant religion which in turn was a reaffirmation of Augustine's interpretation. Paul himself had a 'robust conscience' and knew nothing of the pangs of conscience of Lutheran and Calvinist piety. Indeed, for him the Law had the specific connotation of practical commandments. Paul had to deal with the concrete relationship of Jews and gentiles. Through a stratified process of generalization, his letters addressing this specific situation were read as expressing a timeless message about man and his religious problems.

Judging by the vigorous reaction of Ernst KÄSEMANN, Stendahl's hermeneutical miniature hit the mark. This reaction was also curiously self-contradictory. In an overtly polemical public lecture, Käsemann stated both that Stendahl had struck a very dangerous blow to Protestantism and the heritage of the Reformation, and that his view of justification theology as a 'subsidiary crater' in Paul's thought was nothing new but had been existing since Wrede and Schweitzer.[74] Käsemann sees irony in the fact that the Bultmann school, heir to radical historical criticism, now finds itself defending the Reformation: justification by faith is its essence and should not be reduced to specific historical or salvation-historical situations. Clearly Käsemann is a devoted defender of the first traditional assumption on Paul and the Law. He also exemplifies the tendency to spiritualize 'the Jew' and 'the Law' into negative categories of Protestant theology (above p2). This leads him to a series of militant antitheses. Justification is not just the core of Paul's letters but of the entire Bible and salvation history. It parallels the antithesis between flesh and Spirit which has three dimensions: anthropological, eschatological and ecclesiological, the last of which secures the separation of the Church from the Synagogue.[75] Thus Käsemann's defense of the first traditional assumption implies affirmation of the second.

E.P. SANDERS' *Paul and Palestinian Judaism* (1977) is an energetic contribution towards the demolishment of Protestant prejudice regarding Paul and Judaism. Explicitly following Moore and Schweitzer, Sanders writes fascinat-

---

[74] 'Justification and Salvation History in the Epistle to the Romans', in *Paulinische Perspektiven*, 108-39. I quote from the German in my translation.
[75] *Paulinische Perspektiven*, 131, 135, 281f.

15

ingly on 'the view of Rabbinic religion as a religion of legalistic works-righteousness' and Paul with his justification gospel as its declared adversary.[76] A fundamental innovation of the book is that in its study of the ancient Jewish sources it refers extensively to modern Jewish research, studies written in Hebrew included. The extended expositions of ancient Jewish theological concepts are a treasure of learning. The book also offers a 'comparison of patterns of religion'. The 'pattern' of Judaism, summarized as 'covenantal nomism', emerges from independent study of the Jewish sources. In Paul's case source study is restricted and relies heavily on Schweitzer and Bultmann.[77] A more serious drawback, contrasting sharply with the new approach aspired to elsewhere, is that Paul is studied as though separate from Judaism, without reference to ancient Jewish sources.[78] Although a tendency to the contrary is felt, the third traditional assumption regarding Paul and the Law is effectively maintained. The analysis of Jewish sources in the first part serves to enhance Paul's opposition to Jewish 'covenantal nomism'.

In contrast Sanders' next book, *Paul, the Law and the Jewish People* (1983) views Paul against his Jewish background.[79] Some highly relevant issues for the present study are discussed, especially concerning the validity of the Law as it appears in Romans and Galatians. Galatians is not about theological anthropology but about 'the condition on which Gentiles enter the people of God', and in that sense circumcision and the Law are 'not an entrance requirement'.[80] This starting point is enlightening and is reminiscent of Stendahl.

The book then carries on to discuss practical instruction. Paul 'had definite ideas of correct behavior' which relate to the Law and Jewish tradition.[81] This leads to the essential question whether Paul's instruction can be termed halakha. The answer is negative but somewhat vague, and it is re-phrased several times. Paul creates 'no full halakhic system'; his teachings show 'lack of halakhic precision'; and 'there is virtually no systematic halakah in his letters'.[82] For some reason Sanders does not undertake a real comparison with the halakha, all except for one footnote.[83] Correspondingly the halakhic character of specific Pauline teachings is overlooked, again except for one hesitating footnote: Paul's discussion of marriage in 1Cor 7 'is close to halakha'.[84] On the other hand Sanders takes it that Paul dispensed with Jewish commandments such as circumcision, the sabbath or food laws, and concludes on Paul's 'de facto reduction of the law'. The reason is that these ritual commandments govern the

---

[76] *Paul*, 33-59, 434-42. Sanders does not seem aware of the intrinsic correlation between the approaches of Moore and Schweitzer.

[77] Sanders, *Paul*, 434-42, 481ff. This ignores the contradictions between both approaches.

[78] This seems implied by Dunn, 'New Perspective', 100: '(Sanders) remained more impressed by the *difference* between Paul's pattern ...and that of first-century Judaism'.

[79] Admitted in preface, ix.

[80] Sanders, *Paul, the Law*, 18-20.

[81] ib 94f. Curiously the teaching in 1Cor 6:15ff; 7:10f is not considered 'Jewish'.

[82] ib 95, 106, 107.

[83] p56 n58 on Gal 5:3. Sanders overlooks its importance; see below p88f.

[84] ib 119 n46. But see above n81.

social distinction between Jews and gentiles and prevent the unity of the church. Paul knew that these laws are rooted in the Bible and may not have been conscious of the reduction. But there remains a paradox, formulated in 1Cor 7:19, 'one of the most amazing sentences he ever wrote: "Neither circumcision nor uncircumcision counts for anything, but keeping the commandments of God"'.[85] Sanders senses the different atmosphere in First Corinthians where Paul speaks of transgression, punishment and atonement 'in a thoroughly Jewish way'. He even concedes that 'in the Corinthian correspondence we see aspects of a new "covenantal nomism"'.[86]

In effect Sanders ignores the specific view proposed by Schweitzer, Davies and Stendahl, namely that Paul envisaged a pluralism in which only Jewish Christians keep all commandments of the Law. Instead Sanders sticks to the classical conception of a uniform church. This leads him to the absurd hypothesis that Paul unwittingly discarded crucial biblical commandments. He even introduces the Patristic idea of 'Christianity' as a 'third race' into his interpretation of Paul.[87] The different language in First Corinthians and the verse in 1Cor 7:19 remain unexplained anomalies. In spite of these contradictions the book really takes us into the heart of the matter.

Of particular importance to our endeavour is J.D.G. DUNN's study, 'The Incident at Antioch' (1983). While the Antioch incident will be fully discussed in chapter six, Dunn's approach is relevant here. His study lines up with other recent publications in drawing inspiration from Stendahl's 'famous essay', adding Sanders' insights on Jewish 'covenantal nomism'.[88] Dunn's contribution is firstly that he works out a highly interesting historical, socio-political setting for the incident. Secondly, and most important, he adduces a lot of information from the halakhic sources which helps explain both Paul's stance and that of his opponents. In other words he transcends the magic boundary of the third traditional assumption. To the extent that he conceives of Paul as propagating a mitigated observance by Jewish Christians, he also does away with the second. But he reverts to the first assumption when, following Sanders, he interprets Jewish 'covenantal nomism' as the fundamental counterpart of Paul's theology, of which justification is the central concept.

Heikki RÄISÄNEN's *Paul and the Law* (1984) emphasizes tension, development and contradiction in Paul. A range of statements against the practice of the Law conflict with appeals to fulfil the Law, and this should not be harmonized but taken to reflect internal difficulties. According to Räisänen the Antioch incident took Paul by surprise and forced him to do away with the Law – a decision he never could really integrate in his thought. The value of this book is in pointing out the anomalies in current interpretations of Paul. 1Cor 7:19

---

[85] ib 100-105, 161f.
[86] ib 107-113, 208. This refutes the whole design of his previous book, although he believes the opposite to be true, p154.
[87] ib 171-9. Sanders is conscious that the concept is definitely post-Pauline as demonstrated by Harnack, see p171 n1 and p173.
[88] Dunn, 'Incident', 5.

remains a 'surprising statement' in its 'very much Jewish' stress on keeping the commandments of God (p67f).

Paul, Judaism and the Gentiles by Francis WATSON (1986) follows Stendahl and Sanders in viewing Paul as being first of all concerned with relations between Jews and gentiles. This contrasts with the Luther-Bultmann-Käsemann tradition where Paul is turned into a 'quasi-mythological figure' and 'the Jew' is spiritualized into an anthropological concept.[89] On the other hand Watson rejects the view of Stendahl and Davies concerning Paul's Jewish observance and returns to Baur's solution. What Paul was after is a church 'in sharp separation from the Jewish community' (19). Thus while resolutely departing from the first traditional assumption Watson goes on to embrace the second. The third is implicit: Jewish sources are not taken into consideration. An entirely correct and fruitful point of view is that Rom 14f offers a clue to the letter as a whole.[90]

Two recent authors with related approaches are Lloyd GASTON, *Paul and the Torah* (1987) and Peter von den OSTEN-SACKEN, *Evangelium und Thora* (1987) and *Die Heiligkeit der Thora* (1989). Both explore Paul's positive attitude towards the Tora on the theological, rather than the practical level. Emphasis is on passages from Romans and Galatians;[91] Jewish sources are referred to, but no halakhic sources. The first and third assumptions are abandoned here, but the second one, concerning the practical significance of the Law, is not yet called fully into question.

To sum up, a new direction in Pauline study appears to have been developing for two or three generations. For a long time it has represented a minority as compared with the scholarly tradition of Bousset-Bultmann-Käsemann which vigorously adheres to all three assumptions. However judging by most recent publications the interest in it is growing. It was in Schweitzer's approach that the three traditional assumptions were seriously questioned for the first time. His work underwent important correction by Davies, and in turn this indirectly influenced Stendahl, Sanders and others in various ways. Munck belongs somewhere on the margins of this development. We also noted that Klausner and Dunn undertook successful comparisons with halakhic sources. 1Cor 7:17ff presented an anomaly for Harnack in his day, and, on different premises, for Sanders and Räisänen; it was recognized as an essential expression of Paul's practical attitude towards the Law by Schweitzer and Davies.

Adopting and modifying the new approach, the following chapters will study Paul on the threefold assumption, in effect a re-arranged inversion of the tradional assumptions, that his historical background was in Judaism as represented in the ancient Jewish sources; that the Law polemic was not his constant concern; and that the Law retained a practical function. As far as method is

---

[89] Watson, *Paul*, 7f; cf above p2.
[90] See further ch 6 below.
[91] Von der Osten-Sacken's study on 1Cor 10:1-13 (*Heiligkeit*, 60-86) stresses Paul's positive affirmation of the Tora in a practical context.

concerned this means that we shall study Paul (1) comparing him throughout with ancient Jewish sources (which will not exclude Hellenistic influences); (2) considering his justification theology as a specific doctrine not to be read in where it is not written; and (3) investigating with special interest those passages where the practical implications of the Law are evident.

And where practical implications of the Jewish Law are involved, we might as well say 'halakha'. In the concluding chapter we shall deal with two 'theological' passages which involve Paul's practical attitude to the Law, including the 'anomaly' 1Cor 7:17-24. But the main emphasis of this study is on the halakhic element in Paul's letters. Therefore we shall now elaborate on our approach to this subject.

The Study of Halakha in Ancient Writings

It is not necessary here to dwell on the fundamentals of the study of ancient Jewish literature. As stated, a first decisive step towards integration of the results of Christian and Jewish scholars was made by MOORE; it was further elaborated by SANDERS and others. Our focus is on halakha.

The study of halakha in the letters of Paul is new only in the choice of material and the way it is viewed, not in the literary and historical approach to be taken. Study of halakha in ancient Jewish and other writings is well-established, especially among scholars of the 'Wissenschaft des Judentums' tradition who have worked in North America and the land of Israel since the first World War. A glance into this branch of research will be helpful in further defining our own objects, aims and methods; these will be made explicit in the next section.

A number of parameters will first be defined. Halakha may be described as the tradition of formulated rules of conduct regulating life in Judaism.[92] It has a literary, a legal and a social aspect: halakha is, besides midrash and aggada, one of the classic literary genres of Rabbinic literature; it is also a legal system which develops in comparable ways to other systems yet distinct from them; and it is the whole of traditional behavioural rules of the Jewish people. The three aspects are always interconnected and the student of halakha or associated literature should be conscious of this. The organic interconnection is expressed in the description of halakha as 'the tradition of formulated rules regulating life'. It is a 'tradition' because it is the creation of a community of scholars who were in many ways ordinary members of society, and for centuries they transmitted their tradition orally.[93] The implication is that when studying a halakhic detail one should bear in mind that it concerns not only an element of a body of literature, but that it also reflects a living society and is a fragment of an ever developing legal system.[94] Approached from this angle, the ancient halakha is also a historical source of prime importance.

---

[92] For definitions and description cf Safrai, 'Halakha'; Urbach, *Ha-halakha*.
[93] For a description of these aspects see Safrai, 'Oral Tora'.
[94] For the significance of the minor quantity of 'theoretical' halakha see Safrai, 'Halakha', 130-2.

19

As such halakha plays a central role in the main documents of classic Rabbinic literature, Mishna, Tosefta and the Talmudim. Together with the ongoing relevance of halakha for Jewish life in gaonic, medieval and modern times, its central role in Rabbinic literature has inspired a great and sustained interest. The study of halakhic elements in ancient Jewish writings such as the Apocrypha and Pseudepigrapha and Hellenistic Jewish writings has not been as popular among scholars; the same holds true for the Qumran writings. This is undoubtedly due to the non-legal character of most of these documents, as well as the fact that they were transmitted outside the traditional frameworks of Rabbinic Judaism, where halakhic interest and expertise are traditionally concentrated. Nevertheless it is remarkable that while these works have been recognized as important sources for Jewish history since the nineteenth century, disproportionally little attention has been paid to the halakhic aspect. This illustrates the level of disinterest in halakha among scholars and the degree to which its significance to Judaism in past and present is underestimated.

The following survey does not pretend to be representative. Neither is it chronological; it follows the nature of the documents, that is to say: Apocrypha, Pseudepigrapha, Greek Jewish writings, Qumran, early Christian writings.

Because of its importance as a historical source, an interest in traces of halakha in non-halakhic Second Temple writings is likely to be found in studies on ancient Rabbinic halakha.[95] The focus of such works being on the halakha as it is extant in Tannaic literature, their aim is to elucidate its antecedents by means of comparison with earlier extraneous sources. This is legitimate in itself, but our immediate interest here is in studies which focus on halakha as it appears in the non-Rabbinic documents themselves.

In 1927 Ralph MARCUS published a small monograph called *Law in the Apocrypha* based on the following premise. Both Christian and Jewish scholars, their interest being restricted to theology or history, 'have somewhat neglected (the apocryphal books) as sources of knowledge of the legal aspect of Hellenistic Judaism, as a literature, tho [sic] only incidentally, bearing on those subjects of religious and ceremonial law which were known to the rabbis as halakah' (xi). This work is an initial systematic study. The survey is restricted to the Apocrypha, Aristeas and the Testaments of the Twelve Patriarchs, with occasional reference to Philo. Subjects covered are ceremonial observances such as sabbath, festivals, temple, sacrifice and offerings. There is a lot of detailed information, but no theory and hardly any conclusions are made.

The book of Judith reveals a number of interesting halakhic traditions which, when their provenance is examined, may offer a clue to the historical background of the work. This is the argument of Adolph BÜCHLER in a study which despite its title, 'Hearot we-haarot al matsav ha-isha be-Sefer Yehudit' (Notes and Remarks on the Position of the Woman in the Book of Judith; 1926), offers us little about the position of women but much about the specifically pious

---

[95] Albeck, *Introduction*, 1-24 (on LXX, Jub, Sir, 1Macc, Jdt, Arist); Safrai, 'Halakha', 133-46 (on Jdt, LXX, Jub and 1Macc).

halakha ascribed to the heroine and her town, Bethulia. Examples are her unmarried state as a widow, and young and beautiful at that; her sustained fasting in mourning, except on shabbat and feast days; her praying outside the camp in ritual purity, and her eating in purity; and the custom of her town not to touch tithes.

Halakha in the book of Ben Sira is the subject of a brief study by L.I. RABINOWITZ, 'The Halakha as Reflected in Ben-Sira' (1967). The author seeks to demonstrate continuity between Ben Sira, earliest Tannaic halakha and the activities of the 'Men of the Great Synagogue'. Ben Sira belongs to the genre of wisdom writings, in which halakha is found only incidentally and indirectly. The most prominent are a group which the author terms 'ethical halakha', i.e. rules regarding גמילות חסד, 'deeds of loving kindness'. Except for honouring one's parents, the halakhot concerned are all post-biblical. Other halakhot mentioned here concern mourning rituals and, depending on text-critical considerations, ritual slaughter. The specific details of these cases are typical of post-biblical Jewish law and reflect Rabbinic halakha.

Halakha in Josephus' expositions of biblical law is the subject of Bernard REVEL's study, 'Some Anti-Traditional Laws of Josephus' (1924). Referring to earlier studies on the halakha in Josephus,[96] the author describes nine halakhot which do not agree with any of the Rabbinic sources and in his opinion cannot be explained as earlier versions of the halakha contained in those sources. They coincide, however, with the halakha found in early Karaite sources. The author's conclusion is that the separation from Palestinian tradition forced Josephus, as was the case with the Karaites, to follow the literal meaning of biblical verses.

The halakha in Philo is dealt with in chapter 1 because of its special significance in that context.

The book of Jubilees displays a clear halakhic interest and has received ample attention. Louis FINKELSTEIN, 'The Book of Jubilees and the Rabbinic Halaka' (1923) discusses the following halakhic areas found in this work: calendar, shabbat, festivals, tithes and fourth year's fruit, sacrifices and priests, covering of blood, marriage and sexuality, impurity, circumcision, retaliation, Noachian laws. The article restricts itself to pointing out parallels mainly with the Babylonian Talmud and only occasionally does it enter into the historical relationship.

The discussion about Jubilees was brought to another level in Chanoch ALBECK's monograph, *Das Buch der Jubiläen und die Halacha* (1930). In addition to an extensive analysis of the various halakhot in comparison with Rabbinic literature, Albeck endeavours to describe its social provenance. It being clear that his halakha is stricter on many counts than Pharisaic tradition, the author must have belonged to some sectarian movement. From comparison with other ancient writings Albeck concluded that there must have been an 'Enoch circle' in which not only Jubilees but also the Enoch apocalypses and the Damascus Covenant originated. This theory gained additional significance with

---

[96] p293 n1f (Ritter, Weyl, Olitzki).

the subsequent discovery of the Dead Sea scrolls. The Essene literature shows characteristic features reminiscent of Jubilees and the Enoch apocalypses and should be looked on as a specific outgrowth from the 'Enoch circle'.

Yet another study on Jubilees is Hayim KAPLAN, 'Halakha be-Sefer ha-Yovelot' (1934). Dealing first with the idea of Jubilees of 'eternal laws' as distinct from the 'book of Tora' which was given only later to Moses, the author proceeds to describe the various clusters of halakhot implied in these laws. Only description is given on the basis of comparison with the Babylonian Talmud.

The importance of the halakhic section of the Damascus Covenant for the discussion about its historical background was stressed early on by Louis GINZBERG, *Eine unbekannte jüdische Sekte* (1922, integral publication in English in 1976: *An Unknown Jewish Sect*). Ginzberg formulated some critical fundamentals: '...For the correct understanding of the circle in which the fragments ...originated, the Halakah contained in them is much more important than their theological position.' '...Not every variation in law is to be taken as an indication of sectarianism;' and it is incorrect to operate with a concept of 'standard Halakah' (105f). Pharisaic halakha went through a considerable development and many halakhot which differ from Rabbinic literature can be identified as early in that development. Ginzberg went to great lengths to demonstrate the basic Pharisaic character of the document, isolating the prohibition of marrying the brother's daughter as the only really un-Pharisaic halakha (23f). Subsequent study especially of the Qumran scrolls made this position untenable, but both Ginzberg's principles and his analyses remain important.[97]

The large amount of halakha contained in the Temple Scroll has opened up a new field of study and in the view of J.M. BAUMGARTEN its publication is a 'watershed in our knowledge of pre-rabbinic religious law'. In a recent publication on 'The Laws of 'Orlah and First Fruits in the Light of Jubilees, the Qumran Writings, and Targum Ps. Jonathan' (1987) he uses the Temple Scroll to answer old questions on the history of the halakha. His conclusion is that 'the spectrum of halakhic interpretation in the Second Temple period was wider and more complex than previously supposed'.[98]

Halakha in early Christian literature was put on the agenda of Judaic studies by Solomon ZEITLIN, 'The Halaka in the Gospels' (1924). Two issues are treated: baptism and the washing of hands before meals. On the basis of rather imprecise analysis the author posits that both customs were non-existent in Jesus' day and that the gospels reflect later circumstances.[99]

Although the title 'Rabbinic Studies in the Synoptic Gospels' suggests otherwise, this study by Jacob MANN (1924) deals with a fair number of halakhot as reflected in popular customs described by the gospels. In a comprehensive and

---

[97] Recent studies on Qumran halakha are Baumgarten, *Studies*; Schiffman, *The Halakha*.

[98] Baumgarten, 'Laws of 'Orlah', 195, 202.

[99] p373. The author takes baptism for proselytes to be meant, although John the Baptist baptized only Jews; the connection with the טובלי שחרית and Essenes (p359) is missed. As to the uncleanness of hands the erroneous basic explanation of the Bavli is followed.

accurate analysis the following issues are covered: circumcision and naming; redemption of first-born and pilgrimage; marriage and table customs; the 'last supper' and the *Pesah* meal; funerals and tombs. The focus is on these customs as they appear in the texts; the method is a systematic comparison with Rabbinic and contemporary sources. Mann offers the following programmatic considerations: '...It is proposed to deal with a number of popular Jewish rites and customs as far as they are enumerated, often only casually, in the Gospels. In using Rabbinic literature for this purpose special care has to be taken to adduce, as much as possible, contemporary evidence. The material contained in the *Talmud* covers a period of several centuries and in applying it great caution as well as critical acumen have to be exercised' (323).

Gedalyahu ALON revolutionized the study of halakha in ancient writings in two respects: he expanded the field to include post-canonical Apostolic writings and he created a theoretical framework enabling one to explain the existence of halakha in them. His two studies, 'Ha-halakha be-Torat 12 ha-Shelihim' (The Halakha in the Didache, 1940) and 'Ha-halakha be-Iggeret Bar Nava' (The Halakha in the Epistle of Barnabas, 1941), were not included in the translation of his *Studies*; therefore a more extensive summary follows here. We will start with the article on Barnabas because of its interesting theoretical observations.[100]

Jewish halakha was preserved in early Christian writings in four different ways: (1) in the teachings ascribed to Jesus, his disciples and others including Paul – a unique category since these were all Jews who remained within the boundaries of Judaism, even though many of these sources were eventually written or edited by non-Jews; (2) in fragments of halakhic collections which in themselves may have been insignificant for the author but which he copied for other reasons; (3) in testimonies on the behaviour of Jews and Jewish Christians; (4) in Christian halakhot which in effect are consonant with Judaism. In distinguishing the halakhot from their redactional context, one must often neutralize the element of polemic against Judaism. Sources of the second type are rare but extremely interesting for the history of the halakha, since they give us information about the nature and form of Jewish sources used by the Christian authors. The Epistle of Barnabas belongs to this type.

The Epistle of Barnabas, written around the end of the first century CE, is a letter only in form. In fact it is a theological tract against 'judaizing' which make extensive use of allegoric-typological expositions to demonstrate the obsolescence of ceremonial commandments from the Tora. Alon isolates halakhot in the following areas from this fundamentally anti-Jewish treatise: the red heifer ceremony (Barn 8:1-4); the scape goat and connected ritual of the Day of Atonement (7:3-8); and shabbat (6:1).

---

[100] The paragraph in *Studies* 1, 295f gives the impression that Alon intended this article as the first instalment of a larger study, probably to be followed by the Didache study and others which remained unwritten. On Alon's work see biographical note in his *The Jews* 2, introduction.

Most important in all these halakhic areas is the literary method of the author: he interweaves halakhot into the biblical text, in a similar way to certain ancient Jewish sources. In fact he naively quotes halakhic interpretations which he takes to belong to the biblical text, at the same time as he tries to demonstrate the voidness of the literal meaning of that text.[101] When added to the obvious mistakes stemming from his misunderstanding of the source, we are led to conclude that the author of Barnabas used some ancient paraphrastic commentary to the Tora text, and that it was in Greek.[102] Alon comes to the final conclusion that the author of Barnabas used a Greek midrash compilation which interweaved brief expository phrases, halakhic or aggadic, in the biblical text. This is an ancient type of midrash which is also preserved in Jubilees and the Biblical Antiquities (Pseudo-Philo), as well as in the Targum Pseudo Yonatan and fragments of halakhic midrash found in the Mishna;[103] this type, we can now add, is also found in the Temple Scroll from Qumran. Thus the study of halakha in an Apostolic writing has lead to the re-discovery of a previously lost type of literature: Greek halakhic midrash.

The Didache, a hortatory work from about the turn of the first century CE, contains many halakhot which were adapted to the aims of the community for which it was written: a Christian community which identified itself as being opposed to the Jewish community with its Rabbis. However chapters 1-6 as a whole contain many halakhot in pure Jewish form. This section, which from its opening words may be called the 'Two Ways', differs in contents and language from the rest, and has a remarkable parallel in the Epistle of Barnabas, chapters 19-20. It is reasonable to assume that this Jewish source existed in written form before the destruction of the Temple. Its aim is to exhort the reader towards the ethics and monotheism of Judaism, as opposed to pagan culture. In this respect it somewhat parallels the source which is integrated in Josephus' Against Apion and Philo's Hypothetica,[104] but even more so the sentences contained in Pseudo-Phocylides.

The halakhot contained in the first, Jewish section of the Didache are: a prohibition against abortion (2:2), against sorcery and incantation (3:4), against rudeness to slaves (4:10); and a general adhortation to 'flee from anything bad' (3:1). In each case the Didache supports isolated halakhic opinions or an otherwise unknown halakha. In the second part of the Didache the following Christian halakhot are found: prayer three times a day (8:3); blessing after meals (ch 9); fasting on Mondays and Thursdays (8:1); sprinkling water instead of real baptism (6:23); 'first fruits' of money and textiles (13:3). Each of these Apostolic halakhot also illuminates obscure details or supports minority opinions in Tannaic halakha.

---

[101] Alon differs with Güdemann (*Religionsgeschichtliche Studien*) who without knowledge of the halakha concludes on the author's expertise in the Hebrew scriptures.

[102] Alon refers e.g. to the misreading ῥαχός (some herb, Barn 7:8) for more probable ῥάχη or ῥάχις = Hebr רכב, rock or ridge, see mYom 6:6 (*Studies* 1, 305, 310).

[103] mMSh 5:13; mSot 8:1-2; Alon, *Studies* 1, 311 n39, following a comment of J.N. Epstein.

[104] On that hypothesis see also Belkin, *Alexandrian Halakah*.

With the preceding review in mind we now proceed to describe our aims, our methods, and our materials or in other words the object of our study.

Several possibilities could be formulated as to the aim of studying halakha in an ancient document. One is to focus on the development of Rabbinic halakha and to use the evidence of the document to that aim. Another is to use the halakhic evidence arising from the document to elucidate its historical background and to compare this with others. A third option is to analyse the halakhic evidence in the document with the aim of improving one's understanding of the document itself. The details of halakhic analysis will not differ much between these options; this always consists of a comparison of the document with Rabbinic halakha and other ancient sources. Rather the aim of any study is revealed in its focus and editorial framework, and in some of the reviewed studies one can observe that the various aims overlap. Historical presentation requires literary analysis and vice versa. The present study follows a similar mediatory path: a historical analysis of the halakha reflected in Paul's letters as a contribution to a more adequate interpretation.

As to method, the halakha contained in the main Rabbinic collections is a primary frame of reference in all studies reviewed. It is with an eye trained in the subject matter, literary form, technical terminology, and theoretical conceptions specific of Rabbinic halakha that one is best able to recognize and identify halakhot in non-halakhic contexts. This is explained by the fact that the Rabbinic collections are simply the most comprehensive and coherent source of halakha (see below). An additional, more complex explanation is that the halakha preserved in the Rabbinic collections appears to reflect the various traditions followed in one or another way by a large majority of Jews in antiquity.[105]

A second methodical element is the need to approach Rabbinic halakha through the perspective of its historical development. This involves the careful assembling of cumulative evidence as pioneered by classic historic-critical study. Continuous cross-reference should be made to extra-Rabbinic literary and archeological sources. One must also be continually alert on the textual criticism of Rabbinic literature. The production of basic critical editions for the halakhic collections is still in the initial stages.[106] Furthermore one should learn to differentiate between the specific contributions of the various generations of Tannaim and Amoraim,[107] and to appreciate the value of Babylonian as against

---

[105] This issue is fraught with hermeneutic difficulties. Two fundamental arguments are the smoothness and the wide support of the Pharisaic take-over after the Great War against Rome, and the large spread of parallels to Rabbinic traditions over the whole gamut of non-Rabbinic Jewish writings.

[106] Basic is Epstein, *Nosah*. The desiderata stated in his inaugural lecture at the Hebrew University, 'Ha-madda ha-talmudi' (1925) are still unfulfilled.

[107] See the literary theory of redactional layers in Mishna and Tosefta of Abraham Goldberg, 'Mishna' and 'Tosefta'.

Palestinian traditions. A hermeneutic problem of the first magnitude is the significance of the shift from what we know as the Pharisaic movement to Rabbinic Judaism as it emerged from the debris of the Great War against Rome.[108]

A third methodical requirement is the ability to view Rabbinic literature as the depository of a tradition which, in its Second Temple phase, outwardly contrasted with different traditions such as those of Sadducees and Essenes and in itself consisted of various strands. While a major division was between the schools of Shammaites and Hillelites, other variants existed at the fringes of the Pharisaic movement, notably the ancient hasidim.[109] A difficult hermeneutic question in this respect is to what extent the apocalyptic interest found in the various Second Temple writings was rooted in Pharisaic Judaism. That mysticism was an esoteric tradition passed on by leading Sages has already been emphasized. Another religio-cultural strand which is difficult to locate in the groups known to us is represented by writings such as the Testaments of the Twelve Patriarchs, and which David Flusser has termed 'semi-Essene'.[110] It is in these surroundings, finally, that the core of the early Christian movement may have originated. Except where the sources indicate sharp divisions, as in the case of the Essenes and Sadducees, all these movements should be seen as being in touch with what we may consider to be the polymorphous tradition carried on by the Pharisaic Sages.

A fourth pre-condition of method lies at the basis of all the preceding ones: the various bodies of literature should be looked at from an overall historical perspective in which no watersheds exist, certainly not along the boundaries between the established disciplines of scholarship. Not only does the fortuitous constellation and the nature of the extant sources condition our information on the actual historical situation in antiquity, but they tend to generate scholarly specialisms separate from others. But lack of knowledge should not be a criterion in scholarship. It is better to risk making a misjudgment in a field which is outside one's specialism but appears to be important for the problem at hand, than to stay safely within the bounds and maintain the false impression of unfailing scholarship.[111] Rabbinic literature in its various elements and historical phases is as relevant as the Qumran writings, Greek Jewish literature, Apocrypha and Pseudepigrapha or, last but not least, early Christian literature. Finally, in view of our limited knowledge, historical imagination is indispensible for discovering previously unnoticed elements, especially when it concerns sources we have come to know like the back of our hands.

---

[108] See n105.

[109] On these see the studies by Safrai, 'Teaching' and 'Hasidim'.

[110] The Jewish source of Did 1-6 belongs with this type.

[111] Cf Schweitzer, *Geschichte*, vii: 'Die Wissenschaft, die ...in dieser Teilung beharrt, als ob es sich dabei um mehr als eine Abmachung für das Vorlesungsverzeichnis handelt, gesteht damit ihre Ohnmacht ein... Die ihrem Eigendasein überlassenen Einzeldisziplinen ...leben geradezu davon, daß sie ihre Behauptungen nie über die klüglich abgesteckten Grenzen hinaus zo verfolgen brauchen...'

A more general observation concerns nomenclature. There are several ways

h traditions are preserved in early Christian sources. The ques-
ich sources should be termed 'Jewish', 'Christian' or 'Jewish-
owing for situations where it is not possible to make an un-
..nction, the criterion here proposed is social belonging. A source
which has any part of the Jewish people or community as its social environment
is termed 'Jewish'. Conversely, 'Christian' is the accepted indication for a
source reflecting allegiance to any type of community professing messianic
belief in Jesus. It must be used with care for earliest Christian history, for as far
as Paul is concerned it is an anachronism.[112] We shall nevertheless use the term
for lack of a better one. A source which combines both social belongings can be
termed 'Jewish-Christian'. Hence Barnabas is a Christian document, not Jewish, although it uses a Jewish source, but the Didache is a Jewish-Christian text
apparently incorporating a pre-Christian Jewish source. According to the conclusions of the present work Paul's letters could be termed Jewish-'Christian' as
far as their author is concerned, notwithstanding the gentile audience they
appear to be addressing.[113]

We must now define our material according to its quality as a source for
halakha. Our study is restricted to the letters of Paul and does not deal with Acts
in view of the ongoing methodical discussion on its actual relationship with the
Pauline corpus. Systematic comparison with Acts is postponed to a later occasion. Halakha is preserved in ancient Jewish and Christian writings in various
ways, and a comparative overview will help us imagine how we may expect to
find it in Paul's letters.

The halakhic collections of Rabbinic literature stand out. This is in the first
place due to their aim and organizing principle. The Mishna intends to offer the
standard formulation of Tannaic halakha, the Tosefta presents a collection of
'additional' halakhot following the Mishna's organization, and in structure the
Palestinian and Babylonian Talmud comment on the Mishna. In the second
place these 'halakhic collections', as distinct from the midrash collections,
contain independent or pure halakha, i.e. not based on texts from the Bible or
other sources of authority. They represent the first mode in our overview: direct
formulation of pure halakha. In the third place these works stand out by
contents: the 63 tractates of the six 'Orders' of Mishna and Tosefta cover all
aspects of life according to Jewish tradition; the Talmudim comment on most of
these. Fourthly, they embody the halakhic traditions apparently followed by a
large majority – certainly in Amoraic times an overwhelming majority – of
Jews. Thus the main Rabbinic collections are the principal halakhic sources by
aim, organization, form, contents and social background.

Closely related by form, though not in content, is the halakhic section in the
Damascus Covenant (CD 9:1-16:19). Halakha in pure form, direct and un-

---

[112] See above n16.
[113] The addressees of Paul's letters are discussed in ch 2.

related to the Bible, is formulated regarding several distinct areas of Jewish life: purity, shabbat, relations with gentiles; many other halakhot regarding specific conditions of the sect. This is a very important source for historical comparison for the development of the halakha; it is also the earliest witness to the genre of halakha in its pure form. A section in the Rule of the Community (1QS 5:1-9:11) contains halakhot regarding admission and exclusion and other aspects of community life, again without continuous reference to the Bible, but in a less concentrated form. In both documents, however, the halakhic section is embedded in lengthy hortatory and expository passages. Formulating halakha is but one of their various aims.

Another direct mode of formulating halakha is by way of midrash. Foremost by scope here are the Tannaic midrash collections which are in aim halakhic: Mekhilta, Sifra and Sifrei.[114] Though not excluding all intermediate narrative parts, they largely concentrate on the legislative parts of the Tora; thus Genesis is excluded and the Mekhilta starts with Exod 12.[115] These works do not formulate halakha in its pure form but develop it by means of set techniques and terminology from the biblical text. In principle the same halakhot can be found here as in the halakhic collections. This is characteristically expressed in formulae like מכאן אמרו *mikan amru*, 'hence they said...', whereupon a halakha taken from Mishna or Tosefta follows.[116] Again the Rabbinic collections are the largest of this sort of halakhic material.

The older form of midrashic halakha consists of continued citation of the biblical text with interwoven brief interpretative and specifying phrases. This form is preserved in some parts of the Mishna[117] but most extensively in the Essene Temple Scroll; it is also found in the Palestinian Targumim.

These are the two direct forms of formulating halakha: pure halakha and midrashic halakha. Both are already in evidence in Qumran. The question as to which is older is complex.[118] While the Qumran texts are very important sources for the historical development, the Rabbinic collections are the largest, most complete and most coherent sources of direct halakha.

The remaining sources were not written to formulate halakha; their organization, form and content reveal other aims. This includes most of the ancient Jewish writings: Apocrypha and Pseudepigrapha, Greek Jewish writings including Philo and Josephus, and most of the Qumran writings. We must also add the remaining Rabbinic documents, especially the various Amoraic collections of aggadic midrash. Thus when halakha occurs in these works, it is largely in an indirect form. Halakha may be mentioned in the course of a narrative, apocalypse or biblical exposition, or a certain behaviour or custom reflecting

---

[114] The common designation 'Halakhic Midrashim' is confusing since a considerable amount of aggadic material is included.

[115] The Mekhilta de-R.Shimon ben Yohai starts in Exod 3.

[116] In fact this formula indicates the priority of mishnaic formulation at the time and that 'halakhic midrash' had become a secondary mode of formulating halakha.

[117] Above n103.

[118] See Safrai, 'Halakha' 146-55, in discussion with Urbach.

28

one or more halakhot may be described. Halakha may appear to be paraphrased in somewhat more direct form, especially in hortatory works such as testaments and letters, and in certain expository works (especially Jubilees). Yet there are also rare instances where fragments of formulated halakha are quoted directly in these documents; a sure indication is the typical style of direct halakha in pure or midrash form.[119]

In these instances the incidental occurrence of halakhic content or form can be adequately identified only when the requirements already mentioned are fulfilled: a trained eye and a broad knowledge of halakha; a critical approach toward the halakha in its development and varied social background; and an overall view of the history of ancient Judaism. This is true for halakhot of which parallels can be found in the extant sources of direct halakha. It is even more true when it concerns halakhic contents or formulations which are not preserved elsewhere, whether they belong to the Pharisaic-Rabbinic tradition or others.

It remains to locate the early Christian writings in this framework. Obviously no extant Jewish-Christian collection of pure or midrashic halakha has as yet been discovered. Extant early Christian literature belongs in the category of non-halakhic writings. What we have are indirect reflections and quotations, fragments in direct quotation, or redactional adaptations within the framework of gospels, narratives, letters or apocalypses. Dependent on where in ancient Jewish society Jesus and his earliest followers must be located, we may expect to find halakhot representative of the Pharisaic-Rabbinic tradition or those which are not. It may be possible to find reflections of halakha not otherwise preserved.

Rearranging Alon's categories and adapting them to our focus, we list the following modifications of halakha in early Christian literature: (1) halakha reflected in the behaviour or speech of Jews within a narrative (e.g. gospels, Acts); (2) halakha cited in support within a hortatory writing (e.g. Didache); (3) halakha contained in a Jewish source used for his own rhetorical purpose by a Christian author or editor, on the premise that the Law should no longer be observed (e.g. Barnabas).

Adhortation or parenesis being predominant in Paul's letters, category (1) will not be much in evidence. In view of the hortatory purpose category (2) could be found more often. Nor can we exclude category (3).

We can further develop this distinction into a theory of literary significance. The categories have a very different literary effect. This is produced by the specific relation between the purpose of the author and the halakha he uses. Halakha reflected in a narrative (category 1) does not inform us directly on the author's own attitude towards it. It can signify anything from tacit support to implicit rejection, depending on its rhetorical function in the work as a whole.

---

[119] One example is Josephus, AgAp 2:201; see below. A special case is presented by the *Yelamme-deinu* midrash, a fixed aggadic expositional form which starts out by asking the reason for some halakha quoted explicitly.

In contrast, halakha cited to support an adhortative passage (no. 2) by definition reflects the author's positive relationship towards it. Category (3) presupposes an author who is separated from Judaism yet still uses halakhic traditions for a different purpose; this contrast is also highly informative.

Literary significance yields historical and theological meaning. This most directly regards categories (2) and (3). Category (2), if found, will present us with a Paul who positively relates to Jewish traditional law. But if we find category (3) it will confirm the traditional view: an Apostle using Jewish tradition, or even accomodating to it, on the premise that Law observance is fundamentally obsolete. Hence we may expect that an analysis along these lines will offer conclusive evidence about the traditional assumptions on Paul and the Law.

Chapter One

The Quest for Paul's Historical Background

The object in this chapter is to discuss the general cultural situation in which Paul wrote his letters. The aim is not a portrait of first century Judaism in all its diversity but is restricted to aspects which directly concern these documents. Thus we shall not speculate, for example, about literary phenomena he might have been familiar with but does not employ in his letters, such as Jewish parables or Greek philosophical writings.

Intricate hermeneutic questions are involved here as elsewhere. We need not repeat those raised in the introduction. What must be emphasized here is the general observation that we are able to gain an adequate view on Paul's historical background only in the course of a hermeneutical process of reading his letters in comparison with contemporaneous sources and with continuous feedback to our own interpretative categories. In fact the verification of the observations made in this chapter will be found in the subsequent chapters, or in other words in the account of our reading; conversely an appreciation of the present chapter may require reading the chapters that follow. Insight, for example, into the relevance of the position of halakha in diaspora Judaism correlates with one's awareness of the presence of halakha in Paul's letters. And vice versa. Those who fail to see here more than circularity might be wise to re-evaluate their own procedures of literary interpretation and historical representation.

By implication a survey of the historical problems involved in Paul's cultural background also requires a critical review of previous research. Some elements from the discussion in the introduction on that aspect return, but here with the focus on ancient Judaism at large.

Judaism and Hellenism

The debate on the relationship of Judaism and Hellenism is genetically related to Pauline study but has a significance which far transcends it. This does not only mean the fields of research it touches such as New Testament and Judaic studies, but also the intellectual climate in which it originated. It may be seen as another expression of the titanic wrestling of European intellectuals with their religious and philosophical heritage in an age of alternating enlightenment, revolution and restauration. The challenge was, and is, to view and describe the history of mankind and human culture as an immanent process while integrating the development of one's inherited religion. The difficulty is that while events may seem easily transferable from a theological to a historical frame of reference, the historiographic conceptions in which these 'events' are couched are not. Was the severing of the bonds connecting Christianity to Judaism really a progress towards a higher stage, from particularistic bondage to fearless universalism, from the arid desert of legalism to the fertile plains of living culture? And if it was, could it be a return to a more authentic and purer level of human development at the same time?[1]

The interest in Hellenism as a political and cultural phenomenon was a novel feature of nineteenth century historical scholarship. Its immediate importance for the development of gentile Christianity was emphasized in several ways. The way was paved by F.C. BAUR's theory about the historical confrontation of 'Petrine', Jewish Christianity and Pauline universalism, first published in the year 1831.[2] According to the fashion of the day gentile Christianity was here presented as a synthesis between particularistic Judaism and the universal human Spirit.[3] In the same year, his former student A.F. GFROERER emphasized, in what has been considered the first modern Christian history of Judaism, the decisive influence of Greek-speaking Alexandrian Judaism on nascent Christianity.[4] Also in that year, J.G. DROYSEN took the early existence of Greek-speaking Christians (Acts 6:1!) to imply the closeness of Christianity to pagan Greek rather than Jewish thought. Finally then, some years later Droysen coined the historiographic concept *Hellenism* to denote the process of cultural fusion stamped by Greek political theory, language, culture and religion and generated in the wake of Alexander the Great's conquests.[5] Towards the end of the century the interest in Hellenism was modified and intensified in the much more adequate history-of-religions approach.[6] In particular Hellenistic syncretism was stressed, among others by Wilhelm BOUSSET. The result was an explanation of Paul's universalism from Hellenistic rather than Jewish religiosity.

This novel historical interest involved a special use of the ancient Greek word 'Hellenism'. In general ancient usage it meant nothing more than an the elegant command of the Greek language. Accordingly in Acts 6:1 and 9:29 ἑλλη-

---

[1] Related to our problem is the mythical antinomy of 'Aryans' and 'Semites' in nineteenth century generative linguistics as described by Olender, *Les Langues du paradis*. As stressed in J. Starobinski's review (*Liber; revue européenne des livres* [*Le Monde* supplement] 2/1, March 1990, p14f) this must be seen as a pseudo-scientific translation of an inherited theological conception which also took on such forms as the antithesis 'Athens-Jerusalem' (cf 'Babel und Bibel', 'Jesus und Paulus'). The 'arid desert' of Judaism figures prominently in E. Renan's *Vie de Jésus*, see Olender p95-103. An excellent discussion of these problems in classical historiography is found in Hoffmann, *Juden*.
[2] 'Christuspartei'. See introduction.
[3] On Baur's *interpretatio Hegeliana* see Bultmann, 'Geschichte', 307-9.
[4] On Gfroerer see Moore, 'Christian Writers', 223-8.
[5] See Hengel, *Judaism*, 2f.
[6] Cf Momigliano, 'Hellenism'.

νιστής means 'Greek-speaker'.[7] Remarkably it was the Greek-writing Jewish author of Second Maccabees who originally, and very unusually in his day, employed 'Hellenism' as a polemical term aimed against Greek religion and culture. In his description of the heroic affirmation by Jewish martyrs and warriors of their Ἰουδαϊσμός – the Greek-Jewish indication for Jewish tradition – he perceived the intrusion of certain Greek customs as a symbol of heathendom and called this, strikingly, Ἑλληνισμός.[8]

The debate surrounding the impact of 'Hellenism' on ancient Judaism, and by implication on earliest Christianity, has never ceased.[9] It is certain that Greek names and terminology, as well as the Greek language and popular Hellenistic motifs, found their way into Palestinian Jewish culture and literature early on. The question is precisely when, in what circles, to what extent, and with what implication.[10] Another specific question which must be clearly distinguished from the one just raised is the actual influence of 'Hellenistic' religion, i.e., syncretistic paganism, on early Judaism, either in Palestine,[11] or in the diaspora. In connection with the debate on Judaism and Hellenism it has correctly been stressed that ancient Judaism was no monolythic entity and consequently was receptive to foreign influences in varying degrees and intensities. But neither was 'Hellenism' a coherent phenomenon or 'Hellenistic Judaism' an unequivocal entity.[12] As long as the linguistic and the religio-cultural aspects of 'Hellenism' are not consciously distinguished,[13] the use of this historical term is often quite problematic.[14]

---

[7] See Bauer, *Wörterbuch* s.v.; Hengel, 'Zwischen Jesus und Paulus', 157-69.
[8] 2Macc 4:12f, 2:21, 14:38. See Amir, 'Ioudaismos', esp 38f; Hengel, *Judaism*, 2.
[9] Linguistic and conceptuologic discussion was triggered by Lieberman, *Greek*; id, *Hellenism*. See criticism by Alon, *Studies* 2, 248-77; Lieberman (later) 'How much Greek?'; and Lifshitz, 'L'Hellénisation'. On languages see further Rabin, 'Hebrew and Aramaic'; Muussies, 'Greek'; Rosen, 'Sprachsituation'; Schürer, *History* 2, 20-28. Cultural items are surveyed in Schürer, *History* 2, 29-80. For broad cultural study see Tcherikover, *Hellenistic Civilization* (criticizing Bickermann); Baer, *Israel*; and Flusser, 'Motsa ha-Natsrut' (criticizing Baer); id, 'Paganism'. Mention must be made of Goodenough, *Symbols*; one reaction is Urbach, 'Rabbinical Laws' (below ch 4). Thorough and provocative is Hengel, *Judaism* (see below). See criticism by Stern, 'Hengel'; Momigliano, 'Judentum'; Millar, 'Background'; Herr, 'Ha-hellenismus'; Goldstein, 'Jewish Acceptance'; Feldman, 'How much Hellenism'. Ever-important are 'grass-root' studies of literary and cultural 'congruencies' between Hellenism and Judaism: see Flusser, *Gleichnisse*, 141-60; and, with care as regards Rabbinics, Fischel (below p53 n107; p216f).
[10] See Gafni, 'Background', in Compendia II/2, 1-9. Herr's analysis ('Ha-hellenismus') is that, while Hellenistic (= Greek language) influence is in evidence from the Maccabean period onwards, only in the Byzantine period can large-scale influence be documented.
[11] See the interesting study by Flusser, 'Paganism', who concludes that even the religious helllenization of Christianity started only in the third century and coincided with the syncretistic revival of paganism. Schürer, *History* 2, 81-4 presupposes the distinction here advocated.
[12] Thus also Goodenough, *Introduction*, 75f; Hengel, 'Zwischen Jesus und Paulus', 173.
[13] Cf critical comments by Hengel, 'Zwischen Jesus und Paulus', 166-8.
[14] A striking example of such terminological syncretism is Schoeps, *Paulus* with often equivocal use of 'hellenistisch', 'jüdisch-hellenistisch' and 'pagan-hellenistisch'.

In antiquity it was perfectly possible to speak or write fluent Greek and at the same time be a zealous and self-confident Jew. It was precisely that position which was eloquently defended by the Greek-writing author of 2 Maccabees.[15] Some two centuries later, the self-confidence of diaspora Jews in oppressed circumstances in Northern Africa was even able to result in outright military revolt, the so-called Quietus war.[16] Similarly Paul, of a prominent diaspora family, writes, in Greek, about his past life in Judaism as being 'exceedingly zealous for my ancestral traditions' (Gal 1:14). Apart from all its other implications, this verse excludes the *a priori* assumption of a religious predominance of 'Hellenism' in its coexistence with Judaism. The presence of Greek-speaking synagogues in Jewish Palestine including Jerusalem (Acts 6:1, 9) is another case in point.[17] Rather than the pervasive religious influence of Hellenism this indicates the power of Judaism to express itself – and if necessary to defend itself (Acts 9:29!)[18] – in Greek. Apparently participation in a supra-Jewish language system did not impair the coherence of the Jewish community.[19] Undoubtedly a major factor in creating and maintaining that coherence was the halakha, referred to in Greek-Jewish usage as the 'ancestral traditions'.[20] We shall turn our attention to the place of halakha in diaspora Judaism in the next section.

In view of all this it is curious to see nineteenth century historians explain the rise of gentile Christianity by means of a linguistic concept which the ancient Greek-Jewish author applied in the context of religio-cultural polemic: 'Hellenism' as opposing Judaism. In order to explain the emergence of Christianity on the historical level, the creative socio-cultural forces were no longer sought in Judaism, but in its theoretical opposite, Hellenism. Significantly both this interest in Hellenism and the creation of the term did not come about without a marked religious bias. DROYSEN, it is reported, 'regarded Hellenism as the "modern period of antiquity", which found its goal and climax in the rise of Christianity'.[21] In other words the theological concept of Christianity as the supersession of Judaism was transposed to the level of historical description, somewhat updated according to the modern idea of social emancipation, and thus transformed became in turn a prejudice in historical observation and judgment.

These considerations reveal the importance of Albert SCHWEITZER's decision, announced in 1911, to depart from the course Baur had taken in historical

[15] Thus also Hengel, *Judaism* 2, 98f, 104.
[16] See Alon, *The Jews* 2, 382-405; Smallwood, *The Jews*, 389-427.
[17] Cf mSot 7:1; mMeg 2:1; tMeg 4:13. Cf also the Greek votive inscription by Theodotos son of Vettenus for a synagogue in Jerusalem, *CII* no 1404.
[18] Cf Hengel, 'Zwischen Jesus und Paulus', 173f, 182-5.
[19] Closely related is the alternating use by ancient Jews of the names 'Israel' and 'Jews', expressing socially distinct modes of Jewish identity, which operates in all languages; see Tomson, 'Names'.
[20] See below n65.
[21] Hengel, *Judaism*, 2. Hengel seems to express sympathy for Droysen's motivation in the use of the term 'radical reform Judaism' (292; cf Stern's review 96f) for the Hellenistic reform under Antiochus Epiphanes. See below.

criticism and to explain Paul through contemporaneous Judaism. Not only did this change of perspective gradually prove more fruitful in exegesis but it received unexpected confirmation from archeology. His decision was not arbitrary, nor did it result from a narrow view of culture (a criticism he ironically rejected, calling it 'one-sided') but from the insight that the 'Hellenistic' explanations of Paul offered in his day were defective, vague and insufficient.[22] This was no common view. Around the turn of the century the prior relevance of Hellenistic sources for Pauline Christianity was as undisputed as the hellenization of Christianity was positively acclaimed. We need only refer to the theological best-seller of one of the greatest scholars of the day, Adolf von HARNACK's *Wesen des Christentums*: with Hellenistic Judaism as his herald, it was Paul who liberated the gospel from its Jewish constraints and brought it in the open air of Greco-Roman culture.[23] This both explains the success in subsequent scholarship of Wilhelm BOUSSET's theory of the early gentile Hellenistic church ('hellenistische Urgemeinde') and the relative neglect of Schweitzer's interpretation through Jewish apocalyptic.

The relevance of the debate on Judaism and Hellenism for the history of Christianity is as evident as theological alertness in this field remains necessary. In other words it remains essential to question the extent to which interest in the debate is informed and motivated by implicit theological convictions, connected especially with traditional Paulinism. One cannot avoid doing this when reading Martin HENGEL's impressively erudite study, *Judaism and Hellenism*. While its introduction explicitly stresses the importance of Hellenism for the study of the New Testament, the conclusions unashamedly express a view on Judaism and its Law basically consonant with traditional Paulinism. In this view, Paul effected the breakthrough of the 'true national self-surrender [of Judaism] for the nations of the world' which was prepared by the Hellenistic Reform under Antiochus Epiphanes but came to an untimely halt thanks to the typically Pharisaic 'zeal for the Law'.[24] In a later study Hengel takes a more sober stance, indicating that the concept of 'hellenization' is extremely complex and contradictory, and that in Egypt and Syria 'Hellenistic culture' remained a

---

[22] *Geschichte*, 50-78, 141-84; *Mystik*, 27-37. See especially the critique of Bousset, 30-4: the hypothesis of a pre-Pauline syncretist-Hellenistic Kyrios-cult fails on two counts. The evidence on Hellenistic mystery cults is centuries later than Paul, and the supposedly hellenized Christians at Antioch had good relations with the Palestinian churches (Jerusalem's influence was greater than Paul's: Gal 2:11-13! cf Acts 11:19-30, 15:22-39).

[23] Harnack, *Wesen*, 109ff. Hellenistic Judaism outside Palestine had, by its symbolical explanation, 'die partikularen und statutarischen Bestimmungen des Gesetzes ...beseitigt' and can be considered 'eine Vorstufe des Christentums'. But 'Paulus ist es gewesen, der ...das Evangelium sicher als etwas Neues beurteilt hat, das die Gesetzesreligion aufhebt; ...(er) hat ...das Evangelium ...vom Judentum auf den griechisch-römischen Boden hinübergestellt'. Cf however Harnack's anomalous findings published ten years later, above p9f.

[24] *Judaism*, 1-5, 169-75, 303-14; cf reviews by Stern, 'Hengel'; Momigliano, 'Judentum'; and Millar, 'Background'. The idea of Paul's mission as occurring in the 'fulness of time' (Gal 4:4) is a revealing commonplace, cf von der Osten-Sacken, *Evangelium*, 162-72. Interesting (though tainted with the same dogmatic views) is Hengel's 'Zwischen Jesus und Paulus', positing the existence of a Greek-speaking Jewish Church in Jerusalem which first translated the Aramaic Jesus traditions into Greek.

phenomenon of the urban elite.[25] Another influential scholar whose remarkable interest in Hellenism and Hellenistic Judaism was motivated by a personal interest in Christianity was GOODENOUGH; his views will be discussed below in the section on diaspora Judaism.

As stated, Hellenistic influence on first century Judaism is undeniable, not only in the diaspora, but also in Palestine. The question is: what is its significance in comparison with other facets of Jewish existence? A lucid summary of the problem is found in the lecture which the great scholar of Jewish law and lore, Louis GINZBERG, delivered to Harvard Divinity School in 1920, 'The Religion of the Jews at the Time of Jesus'. He describes his historical perspective in the following words: 'Christianity saw the light in Palestine and the given elements from which it was created must be looked for in the religious thoughts of Palestinian Jewry and not in the Alexandrian Hellenism of the Diaspora Jew. Even granted that Hellenism was not without influence upon Palestinian Judaism – and this influence is to my mind of a very problematic nature, – we must not forget that the Jew always had a genius for assimilating foreign matter by impressing upon it his own individuality. Hence it is Judaized Hellenism that might have had its share in the mental makeup of the Palestinian Jew, and not Hellenism, pure and simple. The Hellenism of the Diaspora Jew may have been of great importance for the development of Christianity of the second century, but it can be disregarded in the study of the rise of Christianity.'[26]

Ginzberg's perspective is remarkable for his day. Yet the question is whether the antithesis he uses between Palestinian and diaspora Judaism is correct. In other words is his view of diaspora Judaism, a view he shared with his Christian colleagues and is still widely held, adequate? Would the diaspora Jew not, like his brother in Palestine, have been able to 'assimilate foreign matter by impressing upon it his own individuality' – as a Jew?

Halakha in Diaspora Judaism

While it is accepted that halakha occupied a central place in hebraizing Palestinian Judaism, its function in diaspora Judaism is not so clear. This affects our view on Paul. Was he not born in Tarsus and did he not write letters in Greek, so how could we deny him the illustrious epithet of being a 'Hellenistic diaspora Jew'? The point is, what entity do we indicate by 'Hellenistic diaspora Judaism'?[27] A very important aspect, which is not often discussed, is the actual place of halakha in that branch of Second Temple Judaism. In looking for answers to this question we shall in effect continue our review of research on halakha in ancient writings in the introduction.

[25] *Juden*, 104-115.
[26] p308f. A passage on apocalyptic follows which underestimates its importance for mid-first century Pharisaism. Without that flaw Flusser, 'Motsa ha-Natsrut' brilliantly argues and documents the same basic position.
[27] Cf Momigliano's *bon mot* (in 'Judentum') about 'Hellenism and Judaism' as the comparison of two unknown quantities.

Let us first of all deal with Philo, that prominent Alexandrian Jew famous for his large output of philosophical expositions of the Law written in sophisticated Greek. More than anywhere else the obvious question is how did Hellenistic and Jewish elements go together in Philo's mind. It is equally clear that tensions are most likely to exist around the Law. Understandably then, the theme 'Philo and the halakha' occasioned a debate which has been going on for over a century – intermittently, that is, for the subject has never been popular among Philonists.[28]

In 1879 Bernard RITTER published *Philo und die Halacha*. The inspiration to this work came from his teacher Zacharias FRANKEL, a founding father of the 'Wissenschaft des Judentums', where the interest in Philo was one of the features.[29] It coincided with the interest in Philo in Christian historical theology as represented by GFROERER. Referring to previous research Ritter expresses the essence of his contribution in the following words about the place of halakha in Philo: '...Precisely because Philo is considered *only* an allegorizing exegete, his actual legal expositions are left unstudied. ...Philo's indulgence in allegoric exegesis does not signify that he did not pay homage to the Law as such, but that he considered Scripture a divine revelation from which he could retrieve anything of worth he had assimilated from Greek thinkers and poets.'[30] As for method, Ritter compares Philo's legal explanations with Rabbinic halakha preserved in Mishna and Talmud and with Josephus. Major agreement with Rabbinic sources shows that Philo was largely dependent on the Palestinian halakha; discrepancies that he drew on the independent jurisprudence of Alexandrian Jewish courts.

The brief encyclopedia article by J.Z. LAUTERBACH, '[Philo] – His Relation to the Halakah' (1905), marks a next step in the discussion. Apart from summarizing the results of Ritter and others he wrote: 'The most important feature of Philo's relation to the Halakah is his frequent agreement with an earlier halakah where it differs from a later one. This fact has thus far remained unnoticed' (16). The point is that Philo's halakha often reflects an earlier stage and offers an interesting comparison with Tannaic halakha. This desideratum was fulfilled later.

A very important contribution was made by Isaak HEINEMANN, *Philons griechische und jüdische Bildung* (1929-32).[31] Heinemann's ultimate aim was a balanced evaluation of Philo's dependency on Greek and Jewish intellectual traditions, or in other words his specific situation in the cultural context of

---

[28] Cf Cohen, 'Jewish Dimension', 166 ('neglected facet'). The section on Philo in Schürer, *History* 3/2, 809-89 devotes one sentence to the subject (p874); P. Borgen, 'Philo' (in *Compendia* II/2, 233-82) one or two more. The volume on Philo of *ANRW*, II/21.1, contains nothing on halakha; Sandmel's article (3-46) only spends some pages on the general theme, 'Jew or Greek'. For bibliography on Philo up to 1937 see Goodenough, *Politics*; from 1937 till 1986 Runia – Radice, *Philo*.

[29] On Ritter and Frankel see Heinemann, *Bildung*, 8f; Belkin, *Philo*, viii. For a brief review of Jewish Philo study see Amir, *Hellenistische Gestalt*, 3f.

[30] Ritter, *Philo*, 11f (my translation).

[31] The following summarizes the Heinemann's chapter 'Aufgabe und Methode', *Bildung*, 5-15.

Alexandrian Hellenistic Judaism. But as long as apart from Philo nothing is known of that context, any element of his writings may arbitrarily be assigned to Hellenistic or Jewish traditions. Parallels with Rabbinic halakha do not prove Philo's dependence, for Palestinian tradition may also have assimilated Hellenistic elements, in which case parallels indicate convergency within a larger cultural context. Heinemann demonstrated this comprehensive approach in other areas as well.[32] Thus the cultural background of Philo, our main source for Alexandrian Judaism, can be approached only by means of a careful analysis of his writings in comparison with both classical Greek and Hellenistic and with ancient Jewish sources.

For an area of comparison Heinemann chose Philo's exposition of the Law, because here the clearest differentiation between both cultural traditions would be visible. He did not elaborate on the fundamental significance of this point of departure, but it may be gathered from scattered remarks and from another publication.[33] Philo spent all his energy in explaining his religious thought in terms of his Hellenistic context, but his place was within Jewish tradition. He presupposed the practical commandments and their observance, and on that basis he proceeded to produce his voluminous work, summarized by Heinemann as 'the first attempt at a systematic answer to the problem of the motivation behind the commandments'.[34]

Thus Heinemann's work consists of a comparative analysis of Philo's exposition of the practical commandments, 'On the special laws'. Philo's explanations are continuously checked against Rabbinic halakhic literature and especially against the Mishna. Caution is needed here, according to Heinemann, because the halakha contained in these sources is not always identical with that used by Philo. While this stated aim is impeccable, we shall see that Heinemann did not fully achieve it.[35] A similarly critical approach is necessary regarding Greek literature, Heinemann's actual expertise. Thus methodically armed, Heinemann sets out to analyse the sucessive halakhic topics in Philo's 'Special Laws'. Whenever Philo's dependency on sources reflected in Rabbinic literature is inconclusive in Heinemann's analysis, as is often the case, he adduces a wealth of Greek and Hellenistic parallels. This is what makes the book invaluable. However Heinemann curiously gives precedence to Hellenistic material even where a number of Jewish parallels from different quarters are available.[36]

---

[32] Heinemann, 'Herakleitos' assigns the marked criticism of idol worship in the letters of Pseudo-Heraclitus not to a Jewish provenance, as maintained by Bernays, but to the Cynic-Stoic tradition which ancient Judaism shared with the Hellenistic world at large. He was recently followed by Attridge, *Cynicism*.

[33] *Taamei ha-mitswot* ('The motivation of the commandments'), ch4 on Hellenistic Judaism. Cf *Bildung*, 484, 510, 557, 566, 570-2.

[34] *Taamei ha-mitswot*, 40.

[35] Heinemann (*Bildung*, 11f) rejects the term 'halakha' used in Ritter's title, equating it with the systematic study of Jewish religious law. This displays a rigid, un-historical view of halakha. See below.

[36] See esp p261-77 on sexual ethics; cf below ch3.

Indeed his treatment gives the overall impression of overemphasizing the value of Philo's Hellenistic education.[37]

Heinemann's final conclusion is that Philo did not know Hebrew, had had only partial knowledge of the various sacred scriptures, and had at most a fragmentary acquaintance with the halakhic tradition contained in Rabbinic literature. Jewish tradition was known to him from actual practice, not the Hebrew oral tradition transmitted by the Sages. The end result is both a hellenization of Judaism and a judaization of Hellenism. Philo the Jew offered an explanation of Jewish existence using an eclectic application of Greek and Hellenistic thought patterns. This is important: while the sources are mainly of Hellenistic provenance, their selection and organization are, still according to Heinemann's conclusion, those of a pious Alexandrian Jew.[38] Inevitably Philo's adaptation procedure must have caused deformation of central Jewish conceptions. Here Heinemann saw a tragic side to Philo: a more adequate knowledge of Jewish tradition would have made Philo's historic attempt at a rational explanation of Judaism more successful.[39]

In the years 1933-35 Gedalyahu ALON published a Hebrew study called 'On the study of Philo's halakha' which responds to Heinemann but does not enter into his overall endeavour.[40] Alon restricts himself to demonstrating that the analysis of the halakha contained in Philo requires a more adequate historic-critical approach. It appears that a number of Philo's explanations which Heinemann could not fit in with Tannaic halakha and therefore ascribed to Philo's Hellenistic education,[41] in fact reflect halakhic traditions older than those preserved in the Mishna and other Rabbinic collections. In Heinemann's historical evaluation Philo's halakha gives at most secondary support to the evidence of the Rabbinic collections.[42] But Alon shows that Philo's explanations bear witness to the prehistory of the extant Tannaic halakha.[43] Conversely, while Philo's indebtedness to Hellenistic thought is undisputed, he was much closer to Palestinian halakha in its ancient form.

---

[37] The abstract emphasis on Hellenism is striking in his interpretation of Philo's famous passage on the literal observance of the commandments, Migr 89ff; see below n63f. Similarly Cohen, 'Jewish Dimension'.

[38] See final summary, Bildung, 557-73.

[39] Taamei ha-mitswot, 45f.

[40] Tarbiz vols 5-6 (1933-5); repr Studies 1, 83-114; ET with less outspoken title, 'On Philo's Halakha': Jews, Judaism, 89-137. Alon also takes Heinemann's annotated translation of the Special Laws into account (ed L. Cohn).

[41] In a footnote (p102 n2) Heinemann shows he is conscious of different halakhic traditions in Jub and CD, but denies a parallel with Philo's halakha.

[42] Bildung p41, criticizing Schürer.

[43] Alon elaborates 4 of Philo's explanations: (1) priestly dues must always be brought to Jerusalem (Heinemann, trans. Spec leg, p53 n1; cf Bildung, 34-7); (2) the sota must first be tried in the Jerusalem court (Bildung, 22-24, p24 explicitly rejecting the possibility that the mishnaic halakhot are younger!); (3) the rightfulness of execution by zealot lynching (Bildung, 123-30, opposing Goodenough, Politics who here establishes Philo's Hellenistic Jewish background); (4) the shofar may be blown only in the Temple (Bildung, 99, 536).

The correction of Heinemann's approach was amplified in Samuel BELKIN's monograph, *Philo and the Oral Law* (1940). Unlike the classical scholar and philosopher Heinemann, Belkin was a specialist in halakha. On the other hand this book ignores Heinemann's comprehensive ambition and gives no comparison with Greek and Hellenistic traditions but restricts itself to early Rabbinic halakha. Its strength is in the extensive and detailed halakhic analysis of all issues covered by Heinemann. Although with less erudition and historical acumen than Alon, Belkin demonstrates agreement between Philo and the halakha, especially the earlier or non-Pharisaic, in many cases where Heinemann only referred to Hellenistic sources. He also accepts Ritter's thesis of a relatively independent Alexandrian halakhic tradition. In an earlier publication, Belkin gives a very interesting comparative analysis of the halakha contained in some of Philo's works and in Josephus' 'Against Apion'. The conclusion is that Josephus, who was no great expert in halakha, here probably depended on Philo.[44]

A recent study by Naomi COHEN, 'The Jewish Dimension of Philo's Judaism' (1987), concludes with the methodological observation that 'in order to gain a valid conception of Philo's spiritual world we must keep in mind at one and the same time his "Traditional-Jewish-Hellenistic" and his "Hellenistic-Philosophic" frames of reference'. Allowing for Philo's freely eclectic assimilation of Greek philosophic traditions, the author emphasizes a 'neglected facet': 'the content of Philo's traditional Jewish frame of reference, which probably did come, as Heinemann put it, from practice'.[45] Close and comprehensive study of a passage in Philo's Special Laws reveals that he presupposed 'normative' Hellenistic Jewish rules regarding the *Shema* (followed by the Ten Commandments according to the usage in his day), *tefillin*, *mezuza*, the precept to teach one's children Tora, and the commandment derived from the Tora to keep the 'unwritten laws' too.[46] This reveals Philo's socio-cultural background: a Hellenistic thought structure erected on the halakhic substructure of Jewish community life.

Pending further study,[47] the debate on Philo's relation to the early Palestinian halakha as part of his intellectual background remains open. What is important for our discussion is that even Heinemann admits Philo's unrelenting loyalty to the practice of Jewish life. At this point it would be right to refer to the conclusions drawn from the debate by GOODENOUGH, a Philo scholar who openly avowed both his lack of halakhic training[48] and his interest, following

---

[44] *Alexandrian Halakah* (published in part in *JQR* 1936), esp 68f. On the extensive section on marriage law p37-53, which is better than that in his book, see below ch3.

[45] Cohen, 'Jewish Dimension', 186, 168.

[46] The last connection was strongly combatted by Heinemann, but Cohen (174-80) adduces much evidence to demonstrate the rigidity of Heinemann's approach and the probability that such Hellenistic terms were commonly used in a non-philosophic way.

[47] Runia-Radice, *Philo*, index sv 'Halachah' mention no fundamentally new positions. Add note in Safrai, *Wallfahrt*, 286f; Amir, *Die hellenistische Gestalt*, 33f, 37-51 (no halakhic analysis but discussion of principles).

[48] *Introduction*, 12f, feeling Heinemann to be 'closer to the truth' than Belkin, and not having read

Heinemann but for different reasons, in emphasizing Philo's Greek education. In his *Introduction to Philo Judaeus* (1940),[49] a little book of great wisdom and beauty, he wrote: 'However much Philo may have enriched the meaning of the laws and customs with Greek metaphysics, science, and ethics, ideas for him could not take the place of active observance'. 'Indeed it is the final test of Philo's Jewish loyalty that, however dualistic he may actually have been, the whole labour of his literary life was prompted by Jewish loyalty.'[50] Goodenough in fact endorses Heinemann's view of Philo's eclectic freedom vis-à-vis Hellenistic thought patterns by a life of Jewish observance. Incidentally this also confirms Ritter's observations on the place of halakha in Philo's thought.

Indeed Goodenough's stance is instructive both for its contents and its outspoken theological motivation. His earlier major work, *By Light, Light* (1935), which carries the revealing sub-title, 'the Mystic Gospel of Hellenistic Judaism', is an extended endeavour to demonstrate not just Philo's indebtedness to Hellenism, but his far-reaching reformulation of Jewish piety in terms of Hellenistic mystery religion. While the exaggeration inherent in this approach need not detain us here, it is important that even here Goodenough recognized the importance of Jewish observance, or in other words of halakha, in Philo.[51] Although pressing Philo's affinity to the idiom of Hellenistic mystery religion, Goodenough recognized Philo's disdain and hatred for actual idolatry and mystery cults.[52] With Heinemann, he emphasized Philo's potential undermining of Jewish observance by his extensive use of allegory. But unlike Heinemann, here lies his positive interest.[53] In Goodenough's opinion, the allegorization of Philo and other Alexandrian Jews formed the bridge towards the development of... gentile Christianity, with Paul exemplifying allegorical antinomianism![54] In viewing Paul's letters, the earliest Christian documents, as 'completely oriented to Hellenism', Goodenough plainly follows the basic Tübingen approach.[55] Significant for us is that Goodenough nevertheless sees

---

Alon's Hebrew study.

[49] Goodenough had read Belkin's study in manuscript.

[50] *Introduction*, 78, 88. Similarly (but superficially) Sandmel, *Philo's Place*, 24f; *Philo*, 133f.

[51] *Light*, ch3 (p72-94) esp p72, 81-4.

[52] Cf *Introduction*, 68-74, 80-85.

[53] See revealing statement, *Introduction*, 90: 'As one who has approached Philo more from the Greek than the Jewish point of view, I have ...hitherto stressed the Greek more than the Jewish... I have allowed myself to do so because I have always frankly written as a gentile scholar... In this (Introduction) the Jewish side must be emphasized as I have never had occasion to do before.'

[54] The exploration of Hellenistic Judaism was only a transitory phase in Goodenough's life project. See *Light*, 9; *Introduction*, 73f and final pages. And cf Sandmel, *Philo*, 140-7: 'Goodenough on Philo'. Goodenough's ultimate aim is represented by 'Paul and the Hellenization', but it remained a torso, posthumuously edited by A.T. Kraabel.

[55] *Symbols* 1, p3, the opening sentence of that monumental work having stated its purpose: to contribute to 'the problem in the origin of Christianity' presented by 'its rapid hellenization'. To this corresponds his view of Romans as the ποὺ στῷ for explaining Paul (and hence justification as the centre of his thought): 'Paul', 34. While Goodenough's work remains invaluable for its erudition and utmost clarity, in these basic aspects it is an americanized version of the *interpretatio Graeco-Lutherana*.

41

reason to state that 'no more patent fact springs out of the pages of Philo than his loyalty to Judaism, ...most of all ...to the Jewish Law'.[56]

Leaving Goodenough's intriguing interests in Paul, Hellenism and Judaism for what they are,[57] his description of Philo's complex mind is illuminiating. He calls it Philo's 'duality': his ability to combine freedom of (Hellenistic) thought with fixity in (Jewish) practice. For all the vagueness typifying Hellenistic Judaism in its adapting foreign thought patterns, '...this adaptation remained Jewish ...because it insisted upon keeping Judaism and the Jewish people distinct and separate from gentiles. ...The basis of differentiation had to be a distinct group of customs, ways of living. ...From this point of view Philo was a Jew of the Jews.'[58] A modern-day intellectual believer can truly admire this: 'To hold to an inspiring cultus while one's mind is open to philosophical speculation is one of the most sensible of dualistic solutions of life.'[59] Suffice it to observe that this flexible 'dualism' of liberal thought and observant practice may be considered typical of mainstream Judaism, from Hillel the Elder to Moses Mendelssohn.

Meanwhile Goodenough has reminded us of the question: what is 'Jewish'? How and when can one define something or somebody as Jewish?[60] This perennial question transcends the case of Philo. It would also be easier not to pose it first of all in relation to metaphysics and mysticism but, bringing the high-minded reader back down to earth, to ask it in relation to food. This is not just a matter of taste but, from the perspective of Judaism, it represents a no less important object of intellectual reflection. What makes a dish 'Jewish'? Perhaps it is only the absence of certain ingredients or of combinations of them which makes *kugel*, *blintshes* and *borshtsh*, *falafel*, *shoarma* or *shashlik* 'Jewish'; otherwise they are just Eastern-European or Middle-Eastern. Still Jews and non-Jews recognize these as conveying an unmistakable taste of Ashkenazi or Israeli Jewishness. Likewise while the origin of *matsos* and *haroset* is probably hard to find, the definitely Hellenistic-Roman provenance of reclining at banquets and having a 'dip-dish' for an *hors d'oeuvre* identifies these crucial elements of the *seder* meal (*ma nishtana?!*) as originally non-Jewish customs assimilated into something unmistakably Jewish. Apparently there is some socio-religious mechanism which identifies assimilated outside elements as 'Jewish', which can be understood by Jews and non-Jews alike.

Judging from the example of food, the secret of 'Jewishness' is not in the substance itself, but in its specific selection, its combination, its structure. Judaism articulates itself in form, not matter.[61] This is what Heinemann's systematic comparison comes down to: if the subject matter of Philo's exposi-

---

[56] *Light*, 72.
[57] See also below ch4 for Urbach's critique of Goodenough's basic theory.
[58] *Introduction*, 77.
[59] Goodenough, *Introduction*, 84.
[60] cf *Introduction*, 77.
[61] Cf Heinemann, *Bildung*, 79: Philo's exposition of temple laws expresses 'jüdische Form in griechischer Formel'.

tions is borrowed from a range of Greek and Hellenistic sources, its organization is Jewish. This is stating the primary significance of the halakha.
Halakha organizes and structures life into Jewish life. Structuring Philo's life, it
stamped his Hellenistic philosophy as being Jewish.[62]

A well-known passage from Philo's allegorical expositions will serve to
conclude this part of our argument. The fact that all major discussions of the
subject quote it *in extenso* should not deter us from doing so too.[63] In his
'Migration of Abraham' Philo derives five spiritual gifts from the divine promise made to the archetype of all true believers, Abraham (Gen 12:1-4). They are
prefaced by the command 'to depart from country, kindred and father's house',
which Philo interprets as the divine 'stimulus towards full salvation' of the soul,
realized in its removal from 'body, sense-perception, and speech' (Migr 1f).
Quintessential allegory: the bodily, visible and speakable must be left behind,
and the soul is to ascend to the green pastures of eternal truth. But the fourth
gift, reflected in the words 'I will magnify thy name', signals a constraint on the
soul's journey. If eternal truth is the goal, why should one care for a name in
society at all?

> In my opinion this means the following. As it is profitable to be good and
> noble (ἀγαθὸν εἶναι καὶ καλόν), so it is to be reputed such. And, while
> reality (ἀλήθεια) is better than reputation (δόξα), happiness comes
> from both (ἀμφοῖν). (ib 86)

Thus Philo sets out to delineate the vital connection of the soul with life in the
body. A recurring phrase is that true happiness comes from 'both' (ἀμφότερα):
being virtuous and being reputed such (ib 88), visible and invisible virtue (89);
in other words: both fulfilling the actual commandments and their true spiritual
intention.[64]

> He on whom God has bestowed both – being good and noble and having
> the reputation to be so – he is in truth happy and his name is great in
> reality. We should consider fair fame a great matter and very useful for
> the life in the body. And it is obtained by almost all who cheerfully and
> eagerly refrain from interfering with the established laws, but observe
> their ancestral constitution (τὴν πάτριον πολιτείαν) not without
> care. (ib 88)

'Ancestral constitution' describes what a hebraizing Jew could call 'halakha'.
Faithfulness to one's 'ancestral laws' (πάτριοι νόμοι) was a virtue praised by

---

[62] Once again Heinemann ib 572: 'Die nivellierende Wirkung des Hellenismus hatte im Judentum
ihre Schranke gefunden an den festen Formen des jüdischen Gemeinschafslebens. Aus ihm stammte
jenes Urerlebnis, das Philons Ekloge innerhalb des griechischen Geisteslebens bestimmt...' It is
intriguing that Harnack used the same term, 'jüdische Schranke', negatively of Paul; above p9f.
[63] Most adequate to the literary context is Amir, *Die hellenistische Gestalt*, 47-50. See also Belkin,
Philo, 11f; Goodenough, *Introduction*, 78-80; *Light*, 80-94. Heinemann, *Bildung*, 464f (cf 565) is
curiously off the mark in his emphasis on public opinion as Philo's main argument (the phrase
concerned is introduced πρὸς τῷ, Migr 93, indicating a secondary argument); see also next n.
[64] This refutes Heinemann's interpretation, see previous n. Similarly Cohen, 'Jewish Dimension',
172.

Jews, Greeks and Romans alike.[65] However this insight was not shared by the radical allegorists, Jews or others pretending to dispense with the bodily and literal and feeding on eternal truth only, and against whom Philo now turns.

> For there are some who, while regarding the formulated laws as symbols for intellectual matters (ῥητοὺς νόμους σύμβολα νοητῶν πραγμάτων), are very careful about the latter but light-heartedly neglect the former. …Thus, as though living in a desert alone by themselves or already being disembodied souls, who know neither city, village, or household, nor any human company at all, they overlook all that the majority of men regard and try to approach truth in its naked self. These the sacred word teaches to be thoughtful about a good reputation and undo nothing that is part of the traditions (ἔθεσι) defined by inspired and greater men than those of our time. (ib 89f)

Philo then argues that the insight that the symbolical meaning of sabbath, festivals, circumcision or pilgrimage to the Temple represents the real, spiritual content of these commandments, should not prevent us from actually observing them, and continues:

> No, one must regard these (commandments) as resembling the body, and those (inner meanings) as the soul: just as one must consider the body because it is the soul's home, one must pay attention to the formulated laws. For observing them will give a much clearer understanding of what they symbolize – besides avoiding the criticism and calumny of the public. (ib 93)

Philo is clearly addressing the elect who strive for the highest aim: spiritual salvation beyond the bodily, visible and speakable. It is they who need his advice, not the uneducated mass who are happy with the sensuous and take tradition for granted. The advice is that even the enlightened must consider the body. These true children of Abraham cannot ignore what connects them with the body of society: ancestral traditions and formulated laws. The inclusive use of the word 'body', a common Hellenistic topic,[66] is obvious. The soul's consideration with the 'body' not only avoids outward misunderstanding, but leads to clearer inner light. For Philo, observance of the Jewish Law is a prerequisite to true illumination. While a rejection of extreme monachism is implicit, his words are reminiscent of his admiration for the Essenes and especially the Therapeutae.[67] Comparing them to pagan Hellenistic moral abuse, he presents these groups as exemplary in spiritual piety and discipline. It is clear that they also exemplify total devotion to that which inspired all of his writings: the Jewish Law.

---

[65] Heinemann, *Bildung*, 470-3; Kippenberg, 'Die jüdischen Überlieferungen'. The autonomous significance of the concept of אבות / אבותינו found in the OT, Rabbinic tradition, and the New Testament (Rom 9:5!) must be added. This is another convergence between Hellenistic and biblical-Jewish concepts.
[66] See below p79.
[67] Vit cont; Quod omn 75-91; Hypoth 11:1-18.

The image we gain from Philo is that of enlightened piety, freely enriched with numerous elements from Hellenistic intellectual tradition, but organized along the lines of Jewish life. This image is enhanced by information from other sources.

Tannaic literature contains a fair amount of scattered references to Alexandria, most of them halakhic in nature. Mention is made of synagogues of Alexandrians in Jerusalem[68] and of several high-priestly families who immigrated from Alexandria.[69] We hear of halakhic questions advanced by Alexandrians before R. Yoshua,[70] and, apparently in Jerusalem, before Hillel.[71] Conversely, requests for priestly expertise went to Alexandria.[72] Other passages give halakhic specifics pertaining to Alexandrians or Alexandrian circumstances such as their offerings in the Temple, their ships, the typical Egyptian water-pump, and the court which once existed in Alexandria.[73] One exclamation of R. Yehuda is remarkable: 'He who has not seen the double-colonnaded building (διπλόστωον)[74] of Egyptian Alexandria, never saw the glory of Israel in his life;'[75] he goes on to describe the large basilica synagogue in which the golden seats of the 71 elders were to be seen. Quite likely he had not seen the magnificent community centre himself and was transmitting an earlier testimony.[76]

The conclusion must be that at least one part of Alexandrian Jewry, once the greatest diaspora community, was in open communication with the Palestinian Sages on halakhic matters. If Philo did not belong to this group, he could well have been in contact with it, as appears from his visit to Jerusalem and the detailed knowledge of the Temple ritual he appears to have acquired then.[77]

Indeed there is every reason to suppose that not only Alexandrian Jewry but all diaspora communities were in close communication with Palestine, and that this involved many aspects in which halakha played an important role.[78] Reli-

---

[68]   Acts 6:9; tMeg 2:17.

[69]   For a broader account on Alexandria see Stern, 'Diaspora', 122-33; on relations with Jerusalem the brief note by I. Gafni in *EJ* 2, 590; on courts Belkin, *Philo*, 6-8 (not his conclusion, p6, that Philo wrote his 'Special Laws' supervised by Palestinian Sages!).

[70]   mNeg 14:13; tNeg 9:9; and the fuller account bNid 69b.

[71]   tKet 4:9; yKet 4, 29a; yYev 15, 14d. 'A case came before the Sages' seems to imply that the Palestinian Sages were consulted. On the issue itself, which was connected with Roman law, see Belkin, *Alexandrian Halakah*, 52f.

[72]   tYom 2:5f; tAr 2:4.

[73]   mHal 4:10; mBekh 4:4; mKel 15:1; mOh 8:1; mNeg 14:13; tPea 4:6 = tKet 3:1 (bKet 25a); tShab 2:3; tMakh 3:4 (cf tMikw 4:2); bYev 80a.

[74]   Lieberman, *Tosefta ki-Fshutah* 4, 889f.

[75]   tSuk 4:6; bSuk 51b.

[76]   ySuk 5, 55a-b gives the same tradition, adding its destruction by Trajan. This refers to the 'Quietus war' 115-117 CE, see Smallwood, *The Jews*, 389-427, esp 399. Cf Goodenough, *Symbols* 2, 84-88; and vol 12, 191ff on the Sardis synagogue.

[77]   See Heinemann, *Bildung*, 16ff; Belkin, *Philo*, 49ff.

[78]   See Alon, *The Jews* 1, 234-52 (esp 236 on R. Akiva's travels); ib 2, 325-46 (on Alexandrian Jewry); Safrai, 'Relations'; id, *Wallfahrt*, chs 2 and 4 (pilgrimage); and Schürer (F. Millar), *History* 3/1, 138-49, esp the emphasis p140 (religion and law).

gious life in the diaspora was in constant touch with the Temple and the Great Court. Directed towards Jerusalem were the half-shekel for the Temple service yearly paid by a major part of diaspora Jewry, and the pilgrimage to the Temple was made by many. Conversely, envoys and letters were issued from Palestine for calender matters, halakhic instruction and collections.[79] Synchronization of calendars was considered vital for the correct celebration of the festivals, which must have been an important factor in uniting Jews all over the inhabited world. The books of Second Maccabees and the Greek Esther encourage the celebration of the minor festivals, Hanukka and Purim in the diaspora; the major festivals most probably needed no such stimulus. In short, religious life and liturgy which, granted the many local differences, united the Jews in time if not in space, also vitalized a common pattern of halakha.

Nor was Jewish life in the diaspora restricted to religious affairs. Diaspora communities were organized around the 'synagogue', a building which not only served for prayers and festivities but also for study, administration, law courts, meetings, welfare work and other communal affairs. In other words all aspects of the life of Jews centred on the 'synagogue'.[80] It fits perfectly in the political and social structure of the Hellenistic world that Jewish diaspora communities lived in relative independence among their non-Jewish fellow-townsmen. A Hellenistic political concept applied in many cases is πολίτευμα. As such, Jewish communities often acquired special privileges which allowed them to live according to their 'religion'. These included exemption from military conscription, exemption from appearance in court or distribution of grain and money on sabbath, and payment in cash instead of oil distributed free by the city administration.[81] In all, it is clear that the diaspora communities stood for their religion, that is, the νόμος τῶν Ἰουδαίων, 'Law of the Jews'. It was precisely because they were a minority thoroughly exposed to non-Jewish ways of life, cultures and religions, that communities of exiles would stick together and keep to their tradition. One may even suppose a degree of anxious conservatism,[82] as shown by the aggressive 'Hellenists' mentioned in Acts (6:9; 9:29). An unimpeachable witness to the central value of the halakha for diaspora Judaism is Augustine, who expresses wonder at the ability of the Jewish people to retain its own character under whatever rule, by faithfullness to their Law.[83]

Finally, a Greek synagogue inscription from the 2nd-3rd century CE, found at the ancient site of Aphrodisias in Asia Minor and published recently, shows in some details the degree to which the halakha formulated in Palestine obtained among Hellenistic diaspora Jews.[84] Apart from an interesting list of 'God-

---

[79] On envoys see also below p147.
[80] On the organization of diaspora communities see Applebaum, 'Organization', esp 490ff; Schürer, *History* 3/1, 87-137; Tcherikover, *Civilization*, 296-332: 'Jewish Community and Greek City'. In Northern Africa the term προσευχή prevailed.
[81] Tcherikover ib; Applebaum ib 488; Schürer, *History* 2, 120-5 (F. Millar).
[82] As mentioned also by Heinemann, *Bildung*, 566, 570.
[83] Contra Faustum (MPL 42, 261); cf Urbach, *Ha-halakha*, 7.
[84] Reynolds-Tannenbaum, *Jews and Godfearers*. Cf Schürer, *History* 3/1, 25f.

fearers', which illustrates the attractive power of Judaism in the Hellenistic world,[85] most important to our discussion are Greek technical terms pertaining to the communal and social function of the synagogue and strongly reminiscent of the terminology of Tannaic halakha.[86] In the view of its editors the historical significance of the inscription is in the 'institutional parallelism between the Greco-Roman diaspora and Palestine ...as to the requirements of the Law'.[87]

The halakha, we may safely conclude, was a vital element of ancient Judaism, in the diaspora at least as much as in Palestine. In contrast to what is generally supposed Philo, the proverbial representative of Hellenistic diaspora Judaism, appeared to be one of our more significant witnesses. It would seem to follow that unless it appears that Paul effectively departed from the ways of Judaism, halakha must have remained a central factor in his life and thought.

Apocalyptic, Midrash and Love of Mankind

The relationship of Judaism and Hellenism is not the only problem fraught with hermeneutical questions; there are also a number of other essential aspects of first century Judaism. Lively debates concern themes such as the relationship of Pharisaism and apocalyptic, the existence of a 'normative' Jewish tradition, the measure of pluriformity within Pharisaism, and the receptivity of Palestinian Jewry towards universal trends of thought.

In each of these issues, the difficulty is in the gaps between the preserved sources and in the varying uncertainty as to what social groups they represent. The corollary is that this combination of physical discontinuity and social anonymity must be assessed by people equipped with sets of theological and historical conceptions immediately related to their own position vis-à-vis some of these documents. Some interpretative short circuiting is inevitable, but it is it not totally incurable. One detached thought suffices to grasp that the rise of Hellenism does not equal the spread of Enlightenment; nor does the relation between Pharisaism and Hellenistic Judaism resemble that between modern Jewish Orthodoxy and Reform, or Jewish life under the British Mandate that under Roman rule. Or, to turn to some other sets of pre-conceptions, the Pharisees were no Jesuite clerics, or the Scribes Calvinist theologians; nor was Jesus a semi-literate, proletarian revolutionary. Yet it is also true that such comparative images stimulate the imagination and may motivate the search for more information. The feedback into these interpretative images of the in-formation emerging from the sources is all-important: at that critical moment anomalies and exceptions to the familiar image become the key to better understanding.

---

[85] This is elaborated on by Van der Horst, 'Jews and Christians'. On 'God-fearers' see below.

[86] πατελλα for תמחוי and δεκανια for מניך; see Reynolds-Tannenbaum, *Jews and Godfearers*, 26-30.

[87] ib p78.

Thus if we are to believe Paul that his background was in Pharisaism (Phil 3:5; Gal 1:14) the question is: what kind of Judaism was that? Albert SCHWEITZER, we recall, emphasized the apocalyptic element, excluding both the influence of Hellenism and of Rabbinic tradition. While correcting this double one-sidedness, W.D. DAVIES adopted Schweitzer's main point and accepted apocalyptic mysticism as a basic part of Paul's thought. The term 'mysticism' as used by Schweitzer, admittedly with a rather off-handed definition, attracted much criticism in his day, but appears justified today.[88] What he meant is the intense, direct, apocalyptic and supra-personal relation of the Christian to the reality of the dead and risen Christ. In short: his existence 'in Christ', which implies his existence as 'a new creation' and his share in the resurrection into the world-to-come. Schweitzer further describes this mysticism as 'eschatological', 'cosmic-historic', 'predestinarian', 'sacramental', 'collectivist' and 'activist'.[89] All of this may be taken to emphasize, not that Paul was not a mystic at all,[90] but that his was a *Jewish* mysticism.

The discovery of the Qumran scrolls, a watershed in Judaic and New Testament scholarship, confirmed Schweitzer's basic intuition beyond all theoretical discussion: apocalyptic theology and esoteric mysticism did co-exist in Second Temple Judaism. Since then no study of Paul can ignore the Qumran scrolls and other extant apocalyptic writings.[91]

But Schweitzer incorrectly assumed that this excludes Rabbinic literature. As noted already by DAVIES, reflections of mysticism are also found in many Tannaic traditions.[92] The fact that R. Akiva, the leading Tanna, emphatically advocated the reading of the Song of Songs should be seen together with the report that he was also a highly respected mystic; moreover he was certainly not the only one.[93] The reading of the Song of Songs implied a typological interpretation of those nuptial hymns in the light of the Exodus, the Sinai covenant and the messianic redemption.[94] This is what one might call a historic-eschatologic mysticism,[95] which in view of the obvious connection with Pesah

---

[88] *Mystik*, 1. See Schoeps, *Paulus*, 37; Kümmel, 'Einführung', xif; Sanders, *Paul*, 434 n19 for criticisms cited. Sanders, *Paul*, 440 avoids Schweitzer's 'mystical' and instead speaks of 'participationist' vocabulary.

[89] *Mystik*, 18-26; *Geschichte*, 188.

[90] Thus H. Groos, quoted by Kümmel, 'Einführung', xi.

[91] Cf Ellis, 'Pauline Studies', 28: Schweitzer's intuition, as opposed to Bousset-Bultmann, 'was more than fulfilled by the discovery of the Dead Sea scrolls'. Inspired by Käsemann, Stuhlmacher, *Gerechtigkeit Gottes* emphasizes apocalyptic in Paul in view of Qumran without recognizing Schweitzer's contribution. Similarly Beker, *Paul*, with due reference to Schweitzer. A most important comparison of Qumranic and Pauline elements is Flusser, 'Dead Sea Sect'.

[92] Davies, *Paul*, ix; 13-15.

[93] On R. Akiva's mysticism and his predilection for the Song of Songs see mYad 3:5; tSan 12:10; ARN a 36 (54b-55a); tHag 2:2-4.

[94] For Amoraic examples see PesRK 6-10 (p88-99) and parallels indicated there. Jesus' saying Mark 13:28 and parr proves the early existence of these midrashim. In general, the bridegroom topos in the NT can only be understood against this background.

[95] The term 'sacramental mysticism ' can hardly be used in connection with rabbinic Judaism. Flusser, 'Motsa ha-Natsrut', also rejects it for Essenism on the grounds that baptism presupposed

has its genetic context or 'Sitz im Leben' in the liturgy.[96] Gershom SCHOLEM has established once and for all the existence of Jewish mysticism from the talmudic period onwards, and the presence of mystical traditions under the surface of Rabbinic literature is indisputable. On the other hand the existence of mysticism in Hellenistic Judaism was emphasized by GOODENOUGH; it involved no special rites, but gave a mystic illumination to standard Jewish ritual.[97] However Goodenough's theses are to be judged, it is indisputable that mysticism was pervasive in ancient Judaism. Another conclusion is that the nature of Pharisaic Judaism must have been different from the impression one gains from the surface of Rabbinic literature. Thus while there is every reason to suppose that Paul's Pharisaism included an apocalyptic-mystic strand, there is no reason whatsoever to exclude Rabbinic literature from comparison with Paul.

The relevance of Rabbinic literature for Pauline study extends to many other areas, though not all of them are of central importance to this study. At least of indirect importance is the phenomenon of midrash or biblical interpretation. The nature of midrash is not exegesis proper, and even less so systematic thinking, but the creation of connections between the written verses on the one hand and actual life or thought on the other. Its emphasis is either aggadic, i.e. homiletic, aiming at the imaginative illumination of life and Scripture – or halakhic, i.e. expounding the practical implications of Scripture in the details of daily life. In effect the scriptural verses serve as crystallization points which allow traditional or novel patterns of thought and behaviour to be connected with the world of Scripture in ever changing constructions. Midrash might be called an activity,[98] an active relation towards Scripture rather than a method of exegesis. This explains its diversified and dynamic character. Its coherence is not in a logical system but in the set parameters of the written Tora and the life of the community. This is important for understanding Paul's way of reasoning.

But the sources indicate more. If apocalyptic was prominent in Qumran, halakha was no less important. Similarly R. Akiva's mystic inclination did not in any way interfere with his activity as a leading teacher and redactor of halakha and halakhic midrash. Hence in the Rabbinic and Essene branches of ancient Judaism apocalyptic and mysticism could intimately co-exist with halakha. We also saw how halakha remained basic to Hellenistic diaspora Judaism at the selfsame time as sophisticated esoterical systems were developed. Thus it is hardly likely that halakha was excluded from Paul's background, and the failure hitherto to include it seems to be due to convention and disinformation. But we

---

repentance. But Qumran liturgy certainly had sacramental aspects, see 4QFlor and discussion by Dimant, '4QFlorilegium', 187.

[96] While the reading of the Song of Songs at Pesah is first documented in Sofrim 14:3, 18 (a Gaonic source) the connection of the content of these midrashim with Pesah is evident. The midrashim were collected in MidrCant.

[97] See *Introduction*, 134-60.

[98] As the verbal noun מדרש indicates; cf מקרא and משנה as nouns denoting other literary 'activities'.

cannot press the argument here. The presence of halakha in Paul must appear from the evidence in his letters, and must for the time being remain a supposition.

Granted the imaginary presence of halakha in Paul, one aspect of it would have been crucial both for him and and his addressees, and that is the position of gentiles vis-à-vis the halakha. The practical relevance of Jewish Law for gentiles was an issue which involved both variety of opinion and a degree of development within ancient Judaism. The commandments assumed to be imposed on the sons of Noah, the so-called 'Noachian commandments' are important here.[99] The idea is ancient and is already found in an elementary form in the book of Jubilees, where it is developed from certain verses in the Tora text. Other traditions reduce these commandments to Adam in the creation narrative. Around the beginning of the first century three such universal commandments seem to have been accepted: the prohibition of idolatry, sexual abuse and bloodshed. We shall deal with the first two items in chapters three, four and five below. Later traditions mention four, six, seven or more items. The fundamental point is that only a restricted number of Jewish commandments apply to the rest of mankind; these could be seen as a universal code of morality. The relevance of this idea was rediscovered by Christian scholars in England in the sixteenth and seventeenth centuries who studied Rabbinic literature.[100]

It is usual to associate the Noachian laws with the phenomenon of gentile sympathisers with Judaism known as 'Godfearers': יראי אלוהים, σεβόμε-νοι or φοβούμενοι τὸν θεόν, or *metuentes*.[101] The practical relevance of the phenomenon was recently confirmed by the Aphrodisias inscription mentioned above (p47). The inscription contains a long list of persons explicitly named as 'Godfearers', which conclusively proves the actual existence of that category of sympathizing gentiles in antiquity.[102] While the precise relation between both phenomena need not detain us here, the existence of this category of sympathizing gentiles implies that the idea of universal moral laws such as that embodied in the concept of the Noachian commandments had actual relevance. This is confirmed by the prominence of 'God-fearers' in the larger historiography of Luke-Acts – a conclusion we can draw without prejudicing our study of Paul.

---

[99] See Flusser-Safrai, 'Aposteldekret'. There seems to be a convergence with the concept of *jus gentium* in Roman law, see Cohen, *Jewish and Roman Law*, 338-43, 380. Cohen considers it an 'international private law code'. Indeed discussions in Rabbinic literature specifically mention proselytes, i.e. cases crossing the borderlines between Jews and gentiles; see below p99f. Gaston, *Paul*, 23f has correctly noted the relevance of this issue but is too schematic.

[100] John Selden (1584-1654), see Cohen *Jewish and Roman Law*, 380; and John Toland (1670-1722), see Flusser-Safrai, 'Aposteldekret', 192.

[101] See Stern, *Greek and Latin Authors* 2, 103-107; id in *Compendia* I/2, 1158f.

[102] This disproves the renewed argument to the effect that the term 'God-fearer' was a theological invention without real existence, as maintained by Kraabel, 'Greeks, Jews' and MacLennon-Kraabel, 'God-Fearers'. *Contra*: Gager, 'Jews, Gentiles'; Tannenbaum, 'Jews and God-Fearers'; Feldman, 'Omnipresence'.

The relationship with gentiles also has an important ethical dimension. Early Tannaic tradition, as preserved in Rabbinic literature, displays a touch of humanism which corresponds to a receptivity towards universal ethics and wisdom. Remarkable examples are ascribed especially to Hillel, and there are indications that humanity and universal love of mankind was characteristic of the Hillelite tradition. Some of the evidence appears in chapter 6 below. We shall see that at this level there is a convergence with Cynico-Stoic traditions, or in other words that Hellenistic trend of thought to which Pharisaic-Rabbinic tradition proved especially receptive. To be sure there was also an opposite current. In times of political and religious crisis Judaism, both in antiquity and later, shows a tendency to emphasize elements symbolising identity and nationality and to develop a measure of seclusion otherwise dormant. In chapter 4 we shall see a striking example from the beginning of the Roman war and be able to observe that the Shammaites were especially inclined to take this attitude. It certainly was in the air in Paul's time too.

Paul, a Hellenistic Pharisee?

We now approach the main objective of this quest for Paul's historical background. It remains to ask what his place was in Hellenistic and other ancient 'Judaisms'. Since the following chapters will analyse a major aspect of that problem, the halakhic one, here we shall merely arrange some external details pertaining to his life and person. The ongoing discussion on the relationship of Paul to Acts makes it wise to leave the latter work largely out of consideration.

In view of the open relationship between Palestine and the diaspora especially as regards festivals it is revealing to hear Paul mention the feast of 'Pentecost' which he wants to celebrate in Ephesus (1Cor 16:8). Even if he were to celebrate it with specifically Christian liturgical additions, this is no reason to deny the probability that he intended to celebrate the Jewish festival of Weeks, probably with his fellow-Jews Prisca and Aquila among others (1Cor 16:19). Equally significant is the energy he spent on the collection for the Jewish Christian church in Judea,[103] as well as his repeated visits to Jerusalem and the official commission conveyed to him and Barnabas by the Jerusalem Apostles.[104] On another level we may add the special attention Paul gives to his fellow-Jews in Rome, Prisca and Aquila again figuring prominently (Rom 16:3; below p61). It appears that the parameters of Paul's social and geographical mobility were congruent with those of Jewish existence in the Land and the diaspora.

We have studied the case of Philo and concluded that being a Hellenistic philosopher in a Northern African metropole did not prevent him from being an active and faithful member of the Jewish community there. Halakha played a vital role in his existence. This may offer us a helpful parallel for imagining

---

[103] See below p80f.
[104] Gal 1-2.

51

Paul's place in Judaism. A number of well-known basic facts indicate that Paul had a much closer affinity with Palestinian Jewry than Philo. As distinct from Philo, Paul had an openly avowed knowledge of Hebrew and of Pharisaic tradition; the complexity of his statements about his relationship to the latter need not detain us here.[105] In glaring contrast to Philo, but without such complexity, Paul displays a natural familiarity with the language and imagery of apocalyptic, which may have come to him either through the mediation of Apostolic tradition or through his own education. It extends not only to eschatology but demonology and angelology. Again as opposed to Philo, Paul does not just draw on the Hebraist Jewish tradition of midrash but proves an independent and creative master of the genre, as we shall have occasion to observe below. If Paul, unlike Philo, shared these elements of Palestinian Jewish tradition, could halakha, *kal wa-homer*, not be expected to play an important role in his life and thought?

The comparison with Philo has more to teach us. In Philo's case the importance of halakha remains largely implicit and appears to exist relatively independently to the intricacies of his philosophic-exegetical system. The quintessential allegory of Abraham's spiritual ascent appeared to be founded on the conformity of the mystic sage to the ancestral traditions of his community, in other words Jewish halakhic tradition. This is essential: esoteric teaching and halakha in no way exclude each other, but on the contrary presuppose each other even if they do not appear simultaneously. *Mutatis mutandis* the same pattern is found in the case of Rabbinic Judaism or Qumran: the basic matrix of community life in the tradition of halakha allowed for a blossoming outgrowth of midrash, aggada, eschatological speculations, apocalyptic, astrology and physiognomy. In the case of Qumran this resulted in a highly characteristic, 'one-dimensional' doctrine, while Rabbinic tradition intently displays an uninhibited multiformity. A similar relative independence of theological teaching and halakhic adherence should be quite plausible in the case of Paul.

Despite the contrast with Philo, we have to assess the significance of Paul's 'Hellenism'. SCHWEITZER's emphasis may serve to open our eyes to the importance of Palestinian Judaism, but should not induce us to suport his one-sidedness. Paul was a hellenizing Jew to the extent that he lived among Greek-speaking communities of Jews and gentiles, wrote letters to them in Greek, and in doing so employed both Hellenistic literary conventions and motifs from popular Stoic and Cynic wisdom. This is only remotely reminiscent of Philo. Scholars agree that apart from such minor and superficial parallels Paul shows no interest in Greek philosophy as such.[106] On the other hand elements from

---

[105] Gal 1:13f; Phil 3:4-6; 2Cor 11:22f. On Paul as a ἑβραῖος = Hebrew/Aramaic-speaker (Phil 3:5; 2Cor 11:22) cf Hengel, 'Zwischen Jesus und Paulus', 169f.

[106] Cf Pohlenz, *Paulus und die Stoa* (as opposed to Philo, Paul's knowledge of Greek philosophy superficial, but affinity with Stoicism); Sevenster, *Paul and Seneca* (same); Koester, 'Paul and Hellenism' (Cynic-Stoic rhetorics but no evidence of philosophy; Hellenistic syncretism); Flusser, 'De Joodse en Griekse vorming van Paulus' (Stoic and Cynic influences but prior affinity with Palestinian Judaism); Stanley Jones, *Freiheit* (reflections of Cynic-Stoic concept of freedom). Cf also

popular Hellenistic and especially Stoic-Cynic tradition are found in Rabbinic literature; but again no interest in philosophy.[107] When the amounts of the authentic and the foreign are weighed up one sees that as far as these Hellenistic motifs are concerned Paul is rather much at one with Palestinian, Pharisaic-Rabbinic Judaism.

Thus Paul's was a specifically Jewish Hellenism. Although apparently descending from a prominent diaspora family who had acquired Roman citizenship,[108] his mother tongue, quite probably,[109] was not Tarsean Greek but the Hebrew and Aramaic of Jerusalem. The element of apocalyptic has been pointed out above. Furthermore scholars argue a close material relationship between elements of Paul's teaching and Pharisaic-Rabbinic tradition.[110] In view of all this – and pending the results of our investigation of the crucial halakhic element – we could call Paul a Hellenistic Pharisee.

Finally one element of Paul's background which to his own mind was undoubtedly decisive has not even been mentioned yet: Apostolic tradition. The reason is clear: in line with the Tübingen approach, a dominant opinion in New Testament exegesis is that Paul drew his inspiration from elsewhere than the Apostolic Jewish church. As noted in the introduction this became a methodical principle, via BOUSSET, in the BULTMANN school. In itself it is only another consequence of an approach which traditionally separates Christianity from Judaism and then on the historical level is forced to seek its sources elsewhere. Thus either Apostolic tradition was not perceived as basically Jewish or Paul was viewed as fundamentally opposing it. This criticism was formulated most clearly by Johannes MUNCK. Others, notably A. RESCH, and later C.H. DODD, W.D. DAVIES and other Anglo-Saxon and Scandinavian scholars, started sorting out and listing the parallels between the synoptic gospels and Paul's letters and concluded on Paul's dependence on Apostolic tradition.[111] In the next chapter we shall do something similar and list the probable sources of one major letter, First Corinthians. The outcome will not confirm the Tübingen principle.

Chadwick, 'St. Paul and Philo'.

[107] Lieberman, 'How Much Greek' gives a sober evaluation. Useful bibliography and a number of studies in Fischel, *Essays*. A profound synthetic approach on fables and parables is Flusser, *Gleichnisse*, 141-60. For some other material see Fischel, *Rabbinic Literature*, 35-89. See also below ch6, p246f.

[108] Mommsen, 'Rechtsverhältnisse'. In this context we may rely on the Acts tradition.

[109] Van Unnik, *Tarsus or Jerusalem*; see previous n.

[110] Basic are still Davies, *Paul*; Daube, *New Testament*. Cf discussion on Paul's affinity with Shammaite vs Hillelite elements: Townsend, 'I Corinthians 3:15' (interesting); Jeremias, 'Paulus als Hillelit' (enlightening but somewhat imprecise) and *contra* Haacker, 'War Paulus Hillelit?' (rather atomistic); Hübner, 'Gal 3,10' (important material).

[111] See below p81 n113, p144-9.

Chapter Two

Halakha in Paul's Letters

The aim of the present chapter is to sound out if and where halakha is to be found in Paul's letters; later chapters will offer more detailed analysis. But before setting out on our survey some theoretical questions will have to be considered. Could it be imaginable that elements of the Jewish Law co-existed with Paul's theology of 'justification by faith without works of the Law'? And if it is, how would this effect the relative validity of the theology of justification? Obviously the answers to these questions must be sought in Paul's letters themselves. In order to be able to judge adequately we must first consider the more elementary question of what kind of documents Paul's letters actually are. What is the purpose they were written for, by what kind of author, and for what sort of audience?

Purpose and Character of Paul's Letters

It is generally accepted that in his Letter to the Romans Paul offered a well-balanced presentation of his thought. Indeed here, taking the concept of justification by faith as his starting point, he sets forth his one gospel both for Jew and Greek, discusses their respective place in the history of salvation and gives instruction on their fellowship at the one table within the church. But the question is, how are we to evaluate the seemingly universal conception expressed in Romans?

Traditionally the balanced argument of Romans is taken to signify a systematic way of thinking. And by implication both this way of thinking and the ideas involved are presupposed also in the other letters. In effect Paul's letters are read as the successive chapters of a systematic theology, with the first and largest, Romans, as the centerpiece. Classically formulated, Romans is the *compendium doctrinae christianae*.[1] This interpretation is found not only in traditional exegesis, especially of Protestant vintage, but is shared by influential modern scholars.[2] In general all those considering the justification doctrine to

---

[1] Melanchthon (commentary on Romans) quoted by Beker, *Paul*, 59.

[2] The power of tradition is seen in Bultmann, *Theologie*, who, admitting that Paul's thought is not speculative but responds to practical situations, yet assumes all letters to be based on the theo-anthropological position of Romans, and bases the exposition of his thought on its specific terminology. Cf also Goodenough, above p41 n55.

be the centre of Paul's thought belong in this category. The fact is that the 'justification' theme which is seen as the heart of this systematic reading of Paul, features in Galatians in a quite different way than in Romans, and in the other letters it is hardly found at all.

More attentive to the diversity of Paul's letters, other modern commentators have hypothesized a development in Paul's theological views on justification and the Law. An earlier, 'Jewish' and legalistic attitude is thought to have been gradually replaced by a more universal approach without much questioning. While First Thessalonians is evidently early and Romans late, Galatians and First and Second Corinthians must be placed somewhere in the middle.[3] However this theory is equally hard to reconcile with the sources, since the four 'major letters' apparently all belong to the same period in Paul's life.[4] But more fundamental is the objection that this approach is only a more sophisticated variant of the systematic reading of Paul: apparent tensions and contradictions are found improper for a real theologian and hence they must reflect an evolution of his thought.[5]

A more plausible assumption is that Paul's letters should not be read as disparate chapters of dogma or as milestones in a moving theological biography, nor indeed that Paul was a systematic theologian at all. This insight was stated fundamentally by Albert SCHWEITZER,[6] and argued at length more recently by J. Christiaan BEKER.[7] Paul's epistles display a logic which seems homiletical and pastoral rather than systematic, and they read most naturally as *ad hoc* letters written to various communities in different situations. Obviously these situations involved not only theological issues, but all kinds of practical questions reflecting the vicissitudes of daily life. In view of Paul's Jewish background we may even suspect that his concern with such practical questions was at least as important as his theological expositions.

If we focus on the purpose of Paul's correspondence, a perusal of his letters reveals such phrases as: 'My little children, ...I could wish to be present with you now and to change my tone, for I am perplexed about you' (Gal 4:19f); or, 'I write this while I am away from you, in order that when I come I may not have to be severe' (2Cor 13:10); and, 'For though absent in body I am present in spirit, and as if present, I have already pronounced judgment' (1Cor 5:3). These quotations not only express Paul's acute concern with practical issues but show that his letters are intended as a substitute for his personal presence.[8] We find passionate expressions of his longing to see his addressees 'face to face' (1Thess

---

[3] E.g. Wilckens, 'Entwicklung'; Drane, *Paul*, and id, 'Tradition'. See below.

[4] See Räisänen, *Paul*, 8-10.

[5] Räisänen actually bases his own approach on the assumption of a systematic logic in Paul, and explains the contradictions which emerge from psychological tensions. See above, Introduction.

[6] *Paulus*, 44; and see the first part of his *Geschichte*.

[7] *Paul*; cf 'Paul's Theology': Paul's thought was basically contingent, and his letters should each be read in view of their specific occasion; on the other hand there is a basic consistency in the apocalyptic dimension.

[8] Similarly R. Funk, referred to by Beker, *Paul*, 23.

2:17-3:10) and to regain an untroubled relationship with them (2Cor 6:11-13; 7:2-3). Indeed one entire letter was apparently written because a much hoped-for and long-announced personal visit had to be cancelled (see 2Cor 1:15-2:11). Another letter appears to have been written in order to pave the way for a first visit to a distinguished church founded by other Apostles (Rom 15:14-29; 1:10-17; see below).

The historical purpose of these ancient documents must be read from their *Sitz im Leben*: the vital relationship of an Apostle with churches depending on his authoritative teaching. Hence the recurring appeal to instruction given during previous visits or in earlier correspondence. Indeed Paul exorcized any doubt as to the actual instructional authority of his letters *expressis verbis*: 'I would not seem to be frightening you with letters; for they say, "His letters are weighty and strong, but his bodily presence is weak, and his speech is of no account" – let such people understand that just as we appear in written words when absent, thus we are in behaviour (τῷ ἔργῳ) when present' (2Cor 10:9-11).

A letter remarkable for its parenetical character is First Corinthians. This is readily seen from the headings which introduce sections on specific issues, often extending over one or more chapters: 'Now concerning the matters about which you wrote...' (7:1), 'Now concerning the unmarried...' (7:25), 'Now concerning food offered to idols...' (8:1), 'Now concerning spiritual gifts...' (12:1), 'Now concerning the contribution for the saints...' (16:1), and 'Now concerning our brother Apollos...' (16:12). Moreover these headings indicate that the issues were discussed in earlier correspondence.[9] The Corinthians seem to have written a letter, probably in reaction to Paul's previous oral and written in-struction (5:9), requesting explanation on a number of practical issues. In the present letter Paul responds in his capacity as Apostle of Jesus Christ. Other issues are introduced with a reference to oral reports (1:11; 5:1; 11:18). Some-times Apostolic 'traditions' the Corinthians had already received are expound-ed without apparent reason (11:2ff; 15:1ff). All of this is extremely important for the present study, and First Corinthians will be looked at in detail further on.

It has been emphasized correctly that the parenetical parts should not be viewed as mere appendices to theological tracts but are integral to the letters as intended by Paul.[10] Such practical issues were even recognized as being decisive in determining the actual historical background to each letter, and hence as crucial for their interpretation. One example is Romans in which the section 14:1-15:13 on common meals of Jews and gentiles is surely of more than

---

[9] The best discussion of 1Cor and its possible pre-history is Hurd, *Origin*.

[10] Schrage, *Einzelgebote*, in a systematic-theological treatment. The author's sustained contrasting Paul's parenesis with Jewish Law precludes deeper insight into the importance of his thesis. It is no surprise that he maintains the justification doctrine as the centre of Paul's thought ('Die Frage nach der Mitte', 440).

accidental importance.[11] Interpretations which overlook this are bound to miss at least part of the point.[12]

In sum, Paul's letters are real letters written to various communities in rather different situations. Their purpose is to respond to specific questions arising out of those situations. Hence they contain both theological and practical instruction. But there is another aspect. Paul was a former Pharisee, and while his background has been recognized in elements of his exegesis, it has not been sufficiently considered in connection with his way of thinking as such.[13] Whereas the purpose of instruction could be called an external factor, Paul's way of thinking may be seen as an internal factor determining the non-systematic nature of his letters.

Paul's theological and practical instruction evolves around two centres: continuous reference to Scripture and consistent concern for the actual situation of his readers. The basic structure of this mediating, interpretative way of thinking is reminiscent, among other phenomena, of Rabbinic midrash. Many examples are put forward in the following pages, sometimes with far-reaching implications. Midrash involves creative thought in a way very different from that of systematic theology and exegesis, and this is without doubt one of the reasons for the 'systematic' misunderstanding of Paul. This is reflected, among other things, in a characteristic coagulation of biblical verses and interpretative conceptions into rather flexible units which, when appearing in different letters, varies in form; the very doctrine of justification will offer an example below. A 'systematic' approach here tends to focus on common materials and ignore the specific significance they acquire in context. Another case in point is found in two sections treated extensively below, 1Cor 8-10 and Rom 14f. As we shall see the concern for 'the weak' and other concepts used by the Apostle has a rather different practical implication in both passages. Although in different circumstances, a similar 'unsystematic' way of thinking, here involving creative association of biblical verses with philosophical concepts, is found in Philo.[14] Philo will again serve us for comparison later.

A last basic question about Paul's letters concerns the character of the adressees. Of utmost importance for our further deliberations is whether they were Jews, gentiles, or both; we must also ask whether this was the same for all the letters. Paul's letters contain a number of explicit indications in this direction, which we shall now examine.

---

[11] Watson, *Paul*, following Baur, 'Über Zweck und Veranlassung'. Watson calls his 'a sociological approach', although no attempt is made at the difficult discipline of ancient social history (cf M. Rostovtzeff).

[12] Käsemann, *Römer*, 351ff considers the section as 'Spezielle Paränese', in contrast to chs 12-13 which are directly connected with the main theological part, chs 1-11.

[13] Räisänen, *Paul*, 15, 176 hints in this direction without exploring it.

[14] Runia, 'Naming and Knowing'. He calls Philo's method that of correlation, i.e. he relates biblical words and concepts to acceptable philosophical ideas (90). One could say that Philo uses the dynamic method of midrash in relating to Greek philosophy.

The non-Jewish status of Paul's readers is specifically referred to in 1Cor 12:2, 'You know that when you were heathen (ἔθνη), you were drifting towards the dumb idols'.[15] This corresponds to the discussion of the consumption of idol food offerings (1Cor 8-10), which could hardly have been a question for Jewish Christ-believers. Another letter obviously addressed to non-Jews is First Thessalonians: 'They report ... how you turned to God from the idols, to serve the living God and the True One' (1Thess 1:9).[16] The same holds for the Galatians to whom Paul wrote: 'Formerly, when you did not know God, you were in bondage to beings that by nature are no gods' (Gal 4:8). The non-Jewish status of the Galatian church members corresponds with the main message of the letter, which is to disclaim obligatory circumcision for gentile believers. Judging from the vehement attack against circumcision in view of the readers we may assume the same for the letter to the Philippian church: '...Look out for the mutilation (κατατομή); for we are the true circumcision, who worship God in spirit, ...and put no confidence in the flesh. Though I myself have reason for confidence in the flesh also: ...circumcised on the eighth day...' (Phil 3:2-5). Accepting Pauline authorship for Colossians,[17] we can say the same about this letter (Col 1:27; 2:11-13). The Second Letter to the Corinthians, finally, seems to have been written shortly after the First (2Cor 9:2), and if we are to consider it an integral letter,[18] it appears to address the same non-Jewish church.[19]

The impression we gain is that Paul's letters were exclusively addressed to non-Jews. If this is so, it would reflect Paul's faithfulness to the agreement with the Jerusalem Apostles, according to his own statement: Paul 'had been entrusted with the gospel to the uncircumcised, just as Peter with that of the circumcised' (Gal 2:7). In other words Paul wrote the extant letters[20] within the boundaries of his specific mission to the gentiles and did not interfere with Peter's mission to the Jews.[21]

An intriguing question is the extent to which this also holds true for the letter to Rome.[22] In one passage Paul explicitly addresses non-Jews and also identifies

---

[15] ἔθνη is an ambivalent concept in Paul.

[16] A non-Jewish audience is also supposed in the much-disputed text, 1Thess 2:14-16.

[17] I do not consider Ephesians authentic.

[18] In favour of the integrity of 2 Corinthians is the use throughout the letter of four key words: παρακαλέω / παράκλησις (comfort), συνίστημι / συστατικός (recommend), καυχάομαι / καύχησις / καύχημα (boast) and θλίβω / θλῖψις (suffer). The frequent use of these words is in clear contrast to Paul's other letters. The famous passages 3:3-5:10 (next n) and even more so 6:14-7:1 (below p198f) read as independent literary units but are not un-Pauline by content nor is their digressive function alien to Paul's rhetorical style.

[19] The well-known section about the Old and the New Covenant 3:3-5:10, which is framed between statements containing the key words συνίστημι and καυχάομαι (5:12 and 3:1-3, συστατικῶν ἐπιστολῶν!), appears to combat Jewish or Jewish-Christian missionary attempts and hence addresses non-Jews. Paul's defensive 'boasting' of his Jewishness 11:22 indicates (as in Phil 3:5) that his readers were not Jewish.

[20] Whether or not Philemon was a Jew is unclear; see below.

[21] Similarly Gaston, *Paul*, 21-23.

[22] This is a crucial aspect of the 'Romans debate' carried on ever since Baur's 'Zweck und Veranlassung', for which see Donfried, *Romans Debate*. Fundamental is Bruce, 'Romans Debate'

himself as their special missionary: 'I am speaking to you, gentiles: inasmuch as I am an Apostle to the gentiles, I magnify my ministry in order to make my flesh (i.e. my fellow Jews) jealous, and thus save some of them' (Rom 11:13). This statement conforms to the Apostolic agreement. Paul does not say that he intends to preach to the Roman Jews, but that his work among the gentiles may impress itself on them. Likewise the opening section refers to Paul's 'apostle-ship ...among all the gentiles,[23] including yourselves' (1:5f); and when he comes to Rome he hopes to 'reap some harvest among you as among the rest of the gentiles: to Greeks and barbarians ...I am obliged: so I am eager to preach the gospel to you also who are in Rome' (1:13-15).[24] The impression one gets is that, as in his other letters, Paul is addressing the gentiles in the Roman church.

On the other hand there are also strong indications of a serious concern with Jews and Jewish members of the Roman church:

(1) The opening of the letter emphasizes continuity with the people and tradition of Israel: '...the gospel of God which he promised beforehand through his prophets in the holy scriptures, concerning his Son who was descended from David according to the flesh...' (Rom 1:1-3; cf 9:5).

(2) Throughout the letter, starting with the opening motto 1:16f, Paul emphasizes that his gospel concerns 'every one who has faith, the Jew first and also the Greek',[25] and in that respect 'there is no distinction'.[26]

(3) The letter envisages a church which consists of the circumcised and the uncircumcised, i.e. in Paul's terminology those who keep the Jewish Law and those who do not.[27]

(4) The letter confronts 'people who slanderously charge us with saying: Let us do evil that good may come', or in other words those who suspect Paul of antinomism.[28]

(5) The expression μὴ γένοιτο, 'by no means!', occurs throughout in answer to rhetorical questions doubting the justice of God,[29] the holiness of the Tora and 'the commandment',[30] and the eternity of Israel's election.[31]

(6) Chapter seven, which deals with life under the Law, in v7-12 refers to ἡ ἐντολή, 'the commandment', in a way which would probably sound unfamiliar to non-Jews.[32]

(see below).

[23] RSV translates here, in contrast to v13, 'nations'.

[24] There is a tension here with Paul's 'non-interference policy' (Rom 15:20); see von der Osten-Sacken, *Evangelium*, 119-30.

[25] Rom 1:16; 2:9f; cf 3:29; 9:24.

[26] Rom 3:22; 10:4, 12; cf 2:11.

[27] See the rhetorical climax Rom 3:29; the midrash conclusion 4:11f; and the hymnic conclusion 15:7-9.

[28] Rom 3:8, cf 6:1. And cf Acts 21:21.

[29] Rom 3:5f; 9:14.

[30] Rom 3:31; 6:1, 15; 7:7, 13. Cf 7:12 ὁ νόμος ἅγιος καὶ ἡ ἐντολὴ ἁγία; 7:14 ὁ νόμος πνευματικός; 7:16 ὁ νόμος καλός. And cf 7:22-24; 8:2.

[31] Rom 3:3f; 11:1, 11.

[32] Cf Rom 7:1-6 (v1: γινώσκουσιν γὰρ νόμον λαλῶ!), a section replete with allusions to Jewish

(7) The election of Israel, as compared with the calling of the church, is the subject of the famous chapters 9-11.[33]

(8) In this context the reference to those Roman Christians who observe certain days and a particular diet seems to indicate Jews.[34]

(9) Paul makes a special point of the collection he is organizing in Macedonia and Asia for 'the poor among the saints in Jerusalem', and of which he hopes 'that it may be acceptable to the saints' (15:25-31).[35]

(10) Paul sends greetings to fellow-Jews explicitly indicated as such.[36]

All this makes Romans stand out among Paul's letters. While formally remaining within the boundaries of his 'apostleship to the gentiles', Romans in effect addresses a church in which Jews have an important place. It is also remarkable that Paul uses that self-designation, 'Apostle to the gentiles', precisely in a passage (11:13) which by exception singles out the gentiles among his readers. Equally remarkable is the expression (16:4) that 'not only I but *all the churches of the gentiles* give thanks' – namely to Prisca and Aquila, the two prominent Jewish Christians from Rome and 'co-workers' of Paul.

The church in Rome was evidently not Paul's own foundation. Indeed he had never been there (Rom 1:13), and this adds to the exceptional character of the letter. Superficially it reads as an elaborate self-introduction to the established and distinguished church in Rome in order to preach to the gentiles there (1:13-15). Another and probably more substantial motive is the wish to acquire a base for his planned expedition to Spain (15:24). The remarkable attention paid to the cause of the Jews cannot be fully explained from the assumption, in itself likely, that the Roman church contained many Jewish members. A more specific cause may be sought in a measure taken by Claudius somewhere in the forties, the nature of which is not quite clear but in any case effected the departure of Christ-believing Jews.[37] After his decease the decree must have relaxed, and the return of Jewish Christians after years of absence may well have caused problems of re-integration in the church. Paul, whose friends and co-workers Prisca and Aquila had meanwhile returned (Rom 16:3, cf Acts 18:2), may have heard about these problems and this could explain his plea for wholehearted acceptance of the Jewish brothers and sisters.[38] If this is so, it

---

tradition, see Str-B.

[33] Remarkably, these chapters mostly use the inner-Jewish self-designation 'Israel'; see Tomson, 'Names', 284-6. At the time of writing, I had not yet recognized the Jewish-Christian aspect of Romans.

[34] Rom 14:1-6; cf 15:8f, περιτομή and ἔθνη.

[35] See below n112.

[36] συγγενεῖς Rom 16:7, 11, 21; cf 9:3! The word is not found elsewhere in Paul. And cf Prisca and Aquila 16:3 (Acts 18:2; 1Cor 16:19).

[37] On the episode, including the seemingly exaggerated statement in Acts 18:2 that 'Claudius had commanded all the Jews to leave Rome', see Smallwood, *Jews*, 210-6; Stern, 'Diaspora', 180-3; Schürer, *History* 3/2, 77f.

[38] Thus Bruce, 'Romans Debate'. The evidence of Rom 14f if correctly assessed corroborates this explanation, but unfortunately Bruce (p348f) here follows traditional lines.

helped make it such a dignified and balanced letter. In sum, Romans addresses gentiles with unusual attention to issues concerning Jews.

In conclusion, Paul's extant letters respond to actual practical and theological questions of churches in varying circumstances. They do this using a midrash-like way of thinking with a dynamic interaction of exegetical, practical and theological elements. They address gentile churches and their specific problems; this also holds for Romans although here the specific situation necessitated an unusual concern for Jewish church members. The adequate approach is to read each letter in the context of the specific practical problems presented by its situation. Priority should be given to the specific significance which recurring concepts and rules have in any particular context; a priori generalizations from one letter to another should be avoided.

Justification Theology and Halakha

Let us now turn to the theoretical questions referred to the beginning of this chapter. Could elements of Jewish traditional law exist side by side with the theology of justification in Paul's mind? And if so, what would that imply for the relative validity of these?

Clearly we are dealing with two entities here, one of which is all too familiar in Christian theology whilst the other is not. In order to be able to discuss them, we must consider their place in Paul's letters and determine their character. Obviously the theology of justification figures mainly in Romans and Galatians. The presence of halakha in Paul's letters is what is to be established here; at this preliminary stage we should ask ourselves if it is imaginable at all. Where should we look? Halakha consists of formulated rules of behaviour. Hence the most likely place to look for it is in the parenetical parts of Paul's letters, where he gives his own rules of conduct. The more practical Paul becomes, the greater the possibility of finding traces of halakha. Given the instructional, situation-bound purpose of Paul's letters and the relative importance of parenesis in them, this possibility would seem considerable.

It is in this connection that we must consider one important consequence of the non-Jewish status of Paul's adressees. As set forth in the previous chapter (p50) the relevance of Jewish traditional law for gentiles was restricted to the assumed validity of a few universal commandments. Basically this was an accepted tradition; discussion went about precisely which commandments were involved. It is reasonable to assume that Paul, a former Pharisee, used that same basic tradition. Thus when writing for gentiles he will only have used halakha to the extent that it applied to gentiles in his opinion. Only when Jews or Judaism were involved, he may have been thinking of other commandments. We may think of dietary rules involved in table fellowship or other customs affecting Jewish-gentile relationships. In those cases indirect reference may be made to halakha applying only to Jews.

Here however we come face to face with the ancient Christian dispute in which Paul represented one of the outspoken parties: which halakhic rules apply to gentiles, inasmuch as they wish to be true Christian believers? Paul's violent defense against fellow Christians who adviced observance of sacred days and dietary laws or even circumcision to gentile believers (Gal 4-5; Phil 3:2-21; Col 2:16-23) reveals a lack of consensus here. This Apostolic dispute can even be understood as a specific expression of the general Jewish discussion on this matter. Where these problems are at stake we may find a decidedly negative way of referring to halakha: halakha of which Paul maintains that it does *not* apply to gentiles.

Having theorized about the possible location and nature of the two entities we are dealing with: halakha and Law theology, our next question regards their interdependence. What we must ask is if it is possible to study Paul's parenesis, where halakha may be expected, as an entity relatively independent of the justification doctrine. Can we establish such a relative independence in Paul's letters? To the extent that Paul when writing his letters was a Jew like any other, we might expect something similar to the relative independence of speculative theology and practical instruction explored in the previous chapter. But for the clarity of the discussion we shall here ignore the relation with Philo and other contemporary Jews. The question is: do Paul's letters justify an approach which compares them with Jewish traditional law without referring to his theology of justification?

We must consider this question from either direction: practical parenesis and justification theology. Does Paul's parenesis involve his justification doctrine? Is the theology of justification connected with practical problems?

Let us first consider Paul's parenesis. A cursory review of some of the problems to be studied in later chapters will not impair the theoretical purity of the present argument. One of the main practical issues which was obviously connected with the Jewish Law is that of idol food offerings in 1Cor 8-10. Is there any connection between Paul's discussion of this issue and the theology of 'justification by faith without works of the Law'? A simple but effective criterion is his use of the specific terminology pertaining to that theology. Do those chapters contain the words δικαιόω, πίστις, ἔργον and νόμος, and if so, in what sense? The concordance reveals that δικαιόω and πίστις are not found at all. ῎Εργον is found once (1Cor 9:1), but in an affirmative sense: Paul boasts that the Corinthians are his 'workmanship in the Lord'. Νόμος is found several times in ch 9. Twice it has a positive, authoritative function (1Cor 9:8f): 'Does not the Law say...?' For the rest the word is used in one brief and very dialectical passage (1Cor 9:20), which does in fact relate to the justification theology. However it is not necessary to assume that this passage has a direct, practical bearing on the problem under discussion, the eating of idol offerings. The whole of chapter 9 is a digression within the argument which has a supportive aim: to argue for self-restraint in accordance with the Apostle's own example. On the other hand, in the actual discussion on idol food the specific 'justification terminology' is not used. On the contrary, as we shall see, one important argument Paul adduces is the narrative of the Israelites in the desert, where the

63

sin of idolatry was punished as a severe transgression of the Law (1Cor 10:1-13).

Another important parenetic section to be dealt with below is the discussion of common meals of Jews and non-Jews in Rom 14:1-15:13. In view of the fact that both 'the circumcised' (15:8) and dietary and other laws are mentioned (14:1ff, 14) it seems evident that the Jewish Law is involved. Now the word νόμος which is typical of Romans, occurring 74 times as against 44 times in the rest of Paul's letters, is not found once in these chapters. Ἔργον is found once, but referring to the church as 'God's work' (14:20). Δικαιοσύνη is also found once, but in a way different from its specific meaning in the justification theology: 'For the kingdom of God is not food and drink but righteousness and peace and joy' (14:17). Finally πίστις, typical also of Romans (40 times as against 56 mentions in the rest of Paul), is found here four times (14:1, 22f). The question is however whether its use is specific of the justification theology.[39] Πίστις can have a different connotation when it is combined with ἀγάπη, which is not at all untypical of Paul.[40] In such cases it is an attribute of human conduct, rather than the typically religious attitude of dependence on God's grace. Correspondingly it is entirely possible to translate Rom 14:1, 'As for the weak, welcome him in faith, not for disputes over opinions.'[41] This connotation is not intended in 14:22f. There, as we shall see in a moment, it has a meaning which even when related to the justification theme does not represent a full diametrical opposite to ἔργα νόμου. Under certain circumstances πίστις and ἔργα can go together. At any rate the absence of the other specific terms, δικαιοσύνη and νόμος, makes the use of πίστις in these two verses hardly specific of justification theology. Hence the discussion on common meals in Rom 14f has at the most a tenuous connection with justification theology.

Thus in two important parenetic passages touching on the Jewish Law the typical aspects of justification theology do not actually occur. But let us assume for a moment they did occur. Would it not have been only too natural for Paul to have written: 'Eat whatever is sold in the meat market without raising any question on the ground of conscience, for you are not under the Law but under grace;' or, 'Why should my liberty be determined by another man's scruples, for I am justified not by works but by faith' (cf 1Cor 10:25, 29).[42] Or again: 'I am convinced in the Lord that nothing is unclean in itself, for you were called to freedom; do not submit again to a yoke of slavery' (cf Rom 14:14). Paul wrote no such things, and this should be taken utterly serious. When writing those verses of practical instruction which are traditionally taken to prove his dis-

---

[39] πίστις as meaning 'faithfulness' even in 'justification' contexts is maintained by Gaston, *Paul*, 12f and *passim*.

[40] 1Cor 13:13; Gal 5:6, 22; 1Thess 5:8; Phlm 5.

[41] Connecting τῇ πίστει not with the preceding noun, but with the verb, in contrast to the negation which follows.

[42] For the argument's sake I have used RSV's incorrect translation of κρίνεται and συνείδησις, especially in 1Cor 10:29; see below.

regard for the Jewish Law, Paul did not apply the ideas typical of his justification theology.

Let us now turn to the other aspect: that of the justification theology itself. There are no problems finding it: it is a basic theme in Romans and Galatians, and appears momentarily in Philippians 3; we shall also meet some furtive references in First Corinthians. Our question is, again: are we justified in approaching Paul's parenesis, and the halakha which it may contain, without referring to his justification theology?

We shall start by considering the character of justification theology. As we have already said, Paul was no systematic thinker, but a former Pharisee who responded to practical and theological issues in his gentile churches with a midrashic way of thinking. In fact the very concept of 'justification by faith' offers us an outstanding example of this way of thinking, even though it has since become typical of the 'systematic' misunderstanding of Paul. Rather than being the centre of a theological system, the concept of justification by faith functions within a midrash in which Paul brilliantly combined his gospel for Jew and Greek, the spiritual descendance of Abraham and the share in the world to come inherent in it, and the central concept of faith.[43] The midrash turns on two verses from Tora (Gen 15:6) and prophets (Hab 2:4) which involve the key terms 'faith' and 'righteous(ness)': πίστις or אמונה, and δίκαιοσ(υνη) or צדיק/צדקה. This midrash appears in different forms, combined with various other verses, in two contexts, Gal 3 and Rom 1-4, according to the need of the argument.

In Gal 3:6-14 the midrash serves the argument of the letter against the obligation for gentiles to accept circumcision and the other commandments of the Law as a condition for them to become true Christians.[44] Firstly Abraham's faith (Gen 15:6) is presented as the fulfilled condition for the blessing to all gentiles (Gen 12:3). Secondly the dispensation of the Law which came after is described as secondary and involving a curse (Deut 27:26). Finally life comes through having faith (Hab 2:4), not through doing the Law (Lev 18:5). In Romans on the other hand Paul argues for equal rights of Jews and gentiles within the church.[45] Hab 2:4 appears first (Rom 1:17), underlining the proclamation of the one gospel for Jew and Greek. In view of the deplorable state of both gentiles and Jews and their need of the one gospel (chs 2-3), the faith of Abraham 'confirms' what is written in the Law (3:31).[46] By having faith even while still uncircumcised (Gen 15:6; 17:10!) Abraham could become 'the father of all those who have faith but are not circumcised', as well as 'of those who are not only circumcised but also follow the footsteps of Abraham's faith' (Rom 4:11f).

---

[43] Thus the basic emphasis of Stendahl, *Paul*, inspiringly developed recently by Gaston, *Paul*. But see Schweitzer in his day, *Mystik*, 204-10; and cf Beker, *Paul*, 47.

[44] See the emphasis in Gal 2:3, 7f; 5:2f, 6, 11; 6:12f, 15.

[45] On the purpose of Romans see above p61.

[46] The phrases 'absolve' and 'confirm the Law' are Tannaic technical terms, see Bacher, *Terminologie* 1, 170f.

Thus while in Romans the argument is that both the circumcised and uncircumcised are sinners but become justified children of Abraham in faith, in Galatians the emphasis is that for gentiles to become Abraham's children faith alone is sufficient and circumcision is not needed. The application differs, but the pivotal insight in both letters is that the actual participation in Abraham's salvation, i.e. 'justification' which is in faith, stands independent of the practical commandment of circumcision. It seems that for Paul 'faith' and 'commandments' are so to say on a different level and that the emphasis on faith need not exclude the observance of commandments.

This same situation is found in ancient Jewish literature. The concept of 'faith' in connection with 'salvation' or 'righteousness' was no monopoly of Paul's; it also figures in Qumran and in Rabbinic literature.[47] Of great significance are two Qumran texts. While expounding Hab 2:4, the Rule of the Community refers to כול עושי התורה ...אשר יצילם אל ...בעבור אמלם ואמנתם במורה הצדק, 'all those who do the Law... whom God will save ...because of their effort and their faith in the Teacher of Righteousness'.[48] Furthermore an as yet unpublished letter from Qumran calls the halakhic instruction contained in it מקצת מעשי התורה, 'some works of the Law', and in encouraging the reader to obey them uses the expression ונחשבה לך לצדקה, 'and it will be counted for you as righteousness'.[49] These passages, which clearly expound the words אמונה and צדקה from Gen 15:6 and Hab 2:4, signal a theology of 'justification' connected with 'faith' towards the Teacher of Righteousness and expressly implying 'works of the Law' to be done.[50] In this context the honorific title, 'Teacher of *Righteousness*', even appears to have a soteriological connotation.[51]

As we have said the concept of 'faith(fulness)' is also stressed in Tannaic literature. Not only do we find it in the context of a discussion about the grounds for Israel's redemption,[52] it even appears in the form of an extended 'eulogy on faith' which seems to represent a dominant line of thought in the same discussion.[53] The great number of Sages involved, extending over many generations, shows the importance of the discussion. The eulogy emphasizes not only

[47] *Pace* Hahn, 'Taufe', 121 n106. Bousset, *Religion*, 195 correctly recognized this fact, but on the traditional premise that Paul's innovative contribution was 'in der kraftigen Entgegensetzung' of law and faith.

[48] 1QpHab 8:1. The phrase might throw light on what Josephus writes about the Essenes: 'After God they hold most in awe the name of the lawgiver' (War 2:145). Rather than Moses this special νομοθέτης may be the Teacher of Righteousness. See also n51 below.

[49] See text of a fragment in Flusser, *Judaism*, 722; for a first report on the letter see Qimron-Strugnell, 'Halakhic Letter'.

[50] The terminology, so well-known from Paul, was common in Qumran and other ancient Jewish writings; for references see Flusser, 'Paul's Jewish-Christian Opponents', p83 n20.

[51] The name itself is a midrash on two prophetic texts combining spiritual and material salvation, Hos 10:12 and Joel 2:23. And see above n48.

[52] Mekh Beshallah Wayehi 3 (p97-100); MekhRSbY p57-59. The oldest partners in the discussion are Shemaya and Avtalyon, Hillel's teachers, who emphasize Abraham's faith (Gen 15:6) or Israel's own faith as the grounds of redemption (Exod 4:31); ib p99 and p58, respectively.

[53] גדולה האמונה, Mekh Beshallah Wayehi 6 (p114f); MekhRSbY p70.

66

that it was faith which made Abraham worthy to inherit both this world and the world to come, but also that it made Israel worthy to receive the Holy Spirit. Hab 2:4 and especially Gen 15:6 figure prominently, and, although less emphatically than in the Qumran text, the words צדקה and צדיק are also expounded, being associated with 'salvation in the world to come' in the footsteps of Abraham.[54]

The emphasis on faith in these texts does not preclude observance of the commandments. In the eulogy on faith R. Nehemia states that 'he who accepts one commandment in faith before Him who created the world by his word, is worthy to receive the Holy Spirit'.[55] Thus while making a different emphasis, he does not fundamentally disagree with his colleague Shimon ha-Timni, who in the discussion we have been referring to emphasizes that redemption happened on account of Israel's faithfulness to the 'covenant of circumcision', i.e. the covenant with Abraham.[56] The theme of 'justification by faith' could function perfectly well in the framework of Tannaic teaching, along with other themes. While R. Nehemia flourished a century after Paul, the existence of the theme at Qumran two or three centuries earlier shows that it is likely to have been well known throughout the period.

Significantly, apart from the more common term for 'faith', אמונה, the related אמנה (amana) is also used in these Tannaic texts, where it has the connotation of 'trustworthiness'. אמנה in biblical Hebrew means 'trustworthy agreement',[57] a connotation still found in Rabbinic usage. In one interesting legal expression in the Palestinian Talmud, we seem to find parallel terms for 'a deed of trust' involving both Hebrew and Greek: שטר אמנה ושטר פיסטיס (shtar amana we-shtar pistis). Both אמנה and πίστις here mean 'trustworthiness'.[58] This rather more active use also underlines the fact that 'faith' does not exclude obeying the commandments.

Thus neither in Rabbinic tradition nor in Qumran 'salvation' or 'justification by faith' excluded obeying commandments. The same appears to hold true for Paul.[59] Especially remarkable is his mention of 'those who not only are circumcised but also follow the footsteps of Abraham's faith' (Rom 4:12), i.e. Jews who have both Law and faith, the emphasis being that faith and not the commandments are decisive. This is understandable in Romans which argues for equal rights for Jews and gentiles. In the large treatise on Law and justification (Rom 1-8), Paul metaphorically uses a halakha which elsewhere he appears

[54] Apart from Gen 15:6 and Hab 2:4 this appears from the reference to Ps 118:20 and Isa 26:2.
[55] Ib p114/p70; cf the emphasis bPes 117a, '...the Shekhina descends ...only upon (experiencing) the joy of a commandment'.
[56] ib p98/p57f. They flourished after the Bar Kokhba war; both opinions may reflect the view that observance of circumcision or other essential commandments in defiance of Hadrian's decrees (see Herr, 'Persecutions', 93-8), was an act of 'faith' in God's promise comparable to Abraham's faith when facing a difficult situation.
[57] Neh 10:1; 11:23.
[58] yKet 2, 26b bot.; cf bKet 19b; see Sperber, Dictionary, 145-7.
[59] Cf Gaston, Paul, esp 123f and 45-63 on Rom 4; and following him Gager, Origins, esp 217-20 (Rom 4), 249-52 (righteousness, faith).

to apply in a literal sense (Rom 7:2f; 1Cor 7:39, see below p121f). But surprisingly something similar is found in Galatians. In the heat of his argument against forced circumcision of gentile Christians, Paul suddenly takes recourse to a rule which is actually known from Pharisaic-Rabbinic tradition: 'I testify again to every man who receives circumcision that he is bound to keep the whole Law' (Gal 5:3, see below p88f). The argument is about justification by faith both for gentiles and Jews (2:15!), but it is supported with the rule that Jews and proselytes must observe 'the whole Law'. This can only mean that the rule is thought to be in force. We see that in both examples justification theology is supported by a reference to a halakha which for Paul appears to be in force. Justification theology and halakha exist independently in Paul and do not exclude one another.

We have argued that it is reasonable to assume that Paul's parenesis is developed without reference to his justification theology, inasmuch as the latter does not explicitly appear in its characteristic terminology. On the other hand justification theology itself appears to have the character of a midrash which appears distinctly in Romans and Galatians; furthermore it does not preclude observance of the commandments *per se*. This means that it is theoretically legitimate to treat the halakha in Paul's parenesis as being independent from his justification theology. This is not to deny that there was some relation between justification theology and halakha in Paul's thought. We have seen some of it here; it will be dealt with again in the concluding chapter.

The Significance of First Corinthians

Our image of Paul, as of other ancient personalities and groups, is not only determined by the availability of sources but also by the way we interpret them. In the last analysis it is our perception which is decisive: newly discovered sources are easily fitted into familiar frameworks, whilst awkward aspects and elements remain unnoticed. What we cannot imagine, we are unable to discover in the sources. We might well regret that we possess no other Pauline letters than those he addressed to gentile churches and that those he apparently wrote to the brethren in Jerusalem (1Cor 16:3) have been lost.[60] But suppose these possibly Aramaic letters were to be discovered by archeologists, whom would we perceive? The Apostle of the gentiles who, as we all know, was putting on in order to appease the Jewish brethren? Or a Law-abiding Paul, who in those letters reveals another aspect of his flexible mind hitherto unknown? The point of this imaginary discovery is that while archeologists do their work trying to discover new sources, let us do ours and take a fresh look at those we already have.

---

[60] RSV connects δι' ἐπιστολῶν with δοκιμάσητε and not with πέμψω, translating 'I will send those whom you accredit by letter' instead of the more usual interpretation, 'I will send those you accredit, with letters'.

First Corinthians has a number of remarkable features as compared with the other letters of Paul. As noted above and emphasized by others, practical parenesis has a prominent place.[61] Some have even described its character as rather 'legal' or 'Jewish', trying to explain this by means of development theories.[62] Attention has also been drawn to the expression ἔννομος Χριστοῦ (1Cor 9:21) which somehow suggests a positive attitude towards the Law; this was associated with the remarkable presence of traditions from Jesus in the same letter.[63] As we have noted earlier (above p17f), the saying that 'circumcision nor foreskin are anything, but keeping God's commandments' (1Cor 7:19), has been signalled as 'most remarkable' or even contradictory with regard to the rest of Paul's teachings. Finally, as we shall see in a moment, justification theology is not a theme, but on the contrary, Paul's parenesis is full of positive appeals to 'the Law' and 'tradition'. Here all these features are viewed together in relation to Paul's Jewish background. The theoretical considerations in the previous section should lead us to expect to find traces of a relatively large amount of halakha in this letter.

Other general features have special significance in this context. Pauline authorship of First Corinthians has never been disputed. Furthermore while today it is a rather inconspicuous Pauline letter, this has not always been the case. In ancient traditions First Corinthians enjoyed pride of place,[64] and it was apparently felt to be an important and authoritative letter. Internal features support this observation. It is a letter involving hardly any polemics against rival preachers. Paul conveys practical instruction quietly and calmly on a number of crucial issues to a church he himself founded and whose members he considers his own spiritual children. In short: First Corinthians is not only remarkable among Paul's letters for its 'legal' and 'Jewish' character, but it appears very much to reflect Paul's own thinking and was recognized as such in the early church. Evidently this letter should be especially significant for the present study.

Moreover it is useful to study the occurrence in First Corinthians of words otherwise typical of Paul's justification theology. We have already seen that the usage in chapters 8-10 indicates that the practical instruction there was developed independently of the justification theology. This conclusion holds for the letter as a whole.[65] In the first place not only is the word νόμος scarcely used, but

---

[61] Schrage, *Einzelgebote*, 62. On the significance of 1Cor cf also Davies, 'Paul and the Law', 9.

[62] Drane (*Paul*; 'Tradition') remains within the theological sphere and fails to do justice to the specific questions underlying the various letters. Wilckens, 'Entwicklung', 157-61 considers 1Cor early; its striking emphasis ('ungeschützt jüdisch'; 'derselbe Paulus?') is explained from the serious ethical problems (6:9-11) but must be understood in the light of the later (!) justification doctrine (!). Law polemic is implicit in 9:19-23 (ἔννομος Χριστοῦ being anti-Jewish polemic) and explicit in 15:56 which also stems from anti-synagogue polemic. Thus Wilckens 'explains' this 'early, legalistic' stage by (1) positing the implicit presence of 'later, justificational' concepts; (2) reducing explicit Law theology to anti-Jewish polemic. See also below n66.

[64] The Canon Muratori, lines 50-54 (end 2nd cent; see Schneemelcher, *Apokryphen* 2, 20f, 29) lists 1 Corinthians first and Romans last among Paul's letters.

[65] Schrage, 'Frage nach der Mitte', 440 maintains that 1Cor 1-2 'sachlich weitgehend die Erörterung

69

in a number of cases it has a remarkably affirmative sense. Νόμος is found nine times in the whole of First Corinthians, as against 74 times in Romans and 31 in Galatians. By contrast in four cases νόμος denotes the Law as an authoritative source of practical instruction. Twice, as already noted above, this happens in the passage where Paul, discussing his authority as an Apostle, refers to his right of being sustained by the Corinthians. In support he quotes a Tora verse with the following words: 'Do I say this on human authority? Does not *the Law say* the same? For *it is written in the Law of Moses...*' (1Cor 9:8f). Another instance is found in the discussion of glossolalia. Paul pleads for reason and control and quotes a supporting verse (Isa 28:11f) with the introduction: '*In the Law it is written...*' (1Cor 14:21); the use of 'Tora' to include the prophets is not uncommon in Jewish literature. In the same chapter women are commanded to be silent during worship services according to the custom 'in all the churches of the saints' and 'as also *the Law says*' (1Cor 14:34).

Such explicit mentions of 'the Law' as a positive source of instruction are not found in other Pauline letters. Yet, however unusual, they need not be considered un-Pauline. The case seems to be that 'the Jewish Law' was no problem in the Corinthian church at the time of writing of this letter. Indeed it is quite clear that, unlike Romans and Galatians, the Law polemic is not a main theme in First Corinthians. And it must have been precisely this that made such uncomplicated and unpolemical appeals to 'the Law' possible.[66]

A crucial passage which supports this point without using the word νόμος is the one where Paul appeals to the narrative of Israel in the desert in support of his teaching regarding the idol food offerings (1Cor 10:1-14).[67] The events that befell 'our fathers' who were 'baptized unto Moses' yet fell into idolatry and fornication, and thus out of the covenant, were 'examples (τύποι) for us' (v6). 'Therefore, my beloved ones, flee from idolatry' (v14). An implicit link is made with chapter six which deals with the sin of πορνεία, 'unchastity', and where a similar exclamation follows: 'Flee from πορνεία' (6:18). The connection is further borne out in sacramental language concerning the congregation (6:15, 19; 10:17f; cf 3:16). Participation in 'Christ', i.e. the messianic community, precludes participation in idolatry and unchastity.[68] The significance of this sacramental language shall be dealt with below. What is important now is this uncomplicated appeal to the Law.

This does not mean that the theology of justification did not yet exist in Paul's mind. First Corinthians contains three isolated verses which show it did. 1Cor

über die Rechtfertigung im Römer- und Galater-brief entspricht'. The methodical problem is in the 'sachlich weitgehend'. Δικαιοσύνη as used in 1Cor 1:30 teaches a completely different message (see below).

[66] Wilckens, 'Entwicklung', 158 runs into contradiction by supposing (1) that in Corinth the 'Gesetzesfreiheit' and the distance towards the synagogue were sufficiently safe and (2) that this talk of the Law and the commandments (7:17ff) is abnormal for Paul (above n62).

[67] Cf elaboration on this passage by von der Osten-Sacken, *Die Heiligkeit der Tora,* 60-86.

[68] Closely related is the passage 2Cor 6:14-7:1, 'We are the temple of the living God' (ib 6:16). Note also δικαιοσύνη as opposed to ἀνομία (6:14), and ἁγιασμός (7:1). See below p198f.

9:20, which contains the word νόμος four times, has been mentioned already. 7:18f does not contain νόμος but περιτομή and ἀκροβυστία which obviously denote observance or non-observance of the Jewish Law. Both passages are crucial for understanding Paul's actual attitude towards the Jewish Law and will be dealt with in detail in the concluding chapter. What concerns us now is their place in context. As we have stated, 1Cor 9:20 occurs in a digression which demonstrates Paul's selfless behaviour as an Apostle, the main argument being about the consumption of idol food offerings. However important in itself, the passage is one element among others in a digression from that main theme. The same holds true for 1Cor 7:18f, which is located in a brief digression within a chapter devoted to practical teaching on celibacy, marriage and divorce.

The third reflection of the Law polemic is also the remaining passage in First Corinthians in which νόμος occurs. It is found at the end of the resurrection chapter, and seemingly out of context (1Cor 15:54-56). In this hymnic perora-tion, Paul quotes two verses from the prophets, adds a brief expositional phrase, and ends with a benediction. The important parts are the following: 'Then the word will happen that is written: "Death is swallowed up in victory" (Isa 25:8); "Death, where is thy sting? grave, where is thy victory?" (Hos 13:14) – The sting of death is sin, and the strength of sin is the Law.' The abrupt reference to the connection Law-sin-death, a train of thought developed at length especially in Romans 7, has been 'explained away' as a gloss,[69] but is viewed more adequately as a 'flash-like', habitual association.[70] This is all the more obvious if the parallel in the Rabbinic Targum to Hosea is taken into account. The Hebrew דבריך *devoreikha*, 'thy sting', is read there as *devareik-ha*, 'thy words'. Hence in the context of Hosea's prophetic admonition, the 'sting of death' which comes to punish Ephraim for its sins is interpreted as God's word, the Tora.[71] It follows that Paul here makes use of a traditional Jewish interpretation.

This passage has a multiple significance for our discussion. In the first place it is a nice example both of Paul's unsystematic and dynamic way of thinking and of the direct relationship this has to Pharisaic-Rabbinic tradition. In the second place this, together with the passages 1Cor 7:17-24 and 9:19-23, is the only indication that the Law polemic existed in the Apostle's mind at all when writing First Corinthians. In the third place it is precisely the furtive character of these references which signifies that while the Law theology was there in his mind, he saw no reason to develop it in this letter. In the fourth place this rules out the explanation of the 'legal' character of First Corinthians as an early development in Paul's thought, as compared with Galatians and Romans. Finally this shows that indeed the theology of the Law and justification was not

---

[69]   See Nestle-Aland ad loc and Räisänen, *Paul*, 143.

[70]   Räisänen ib, without noting the Targum.

[71]   Tg Hos 13:14, 'Now, My word shall be among them to kill, and my saying to destroy; because they violated my Tora אוריתא I shall remove my Presence from among them.' Cf Str-B 3, 483.

the essential core of Paul's thought but could be applied or not, just as the situation required.

The absence of the Law polemic from First Corinthians is all the more striking if we take the other 'justification' terms into account. The words δικαιοσύνη and δικαιόω are used three times, in a way untypical of justification theology.[72] In 1:30 Paul refers to the Corinthians with the words: 'But ...you are in Christ Jesus, who was made ...for us wisdom, and justification, and sanctification, and redemption.' Similarly, 'But you were washed, but you were sanctified, but you were justified in the name of the Lord Jesus Christ and in the Spirit of our God' (6:11). Tradition criticism recognizes these texts as elaborations of baptismal traditions.[73] The association is with repentance and redemption in view of God's future judgement. Similarly Paul refers to himself as a faultless messenger of Jesus, yet adds: 'But that is not what I am justified by, for He that judges me is the Lord; therefore judge nothing before the time, until the Lord comes...' (4:4).

Πίστις as used in First Corinthians denotes active confidence in view of the future resurrection (15:14, 17; cf 16:13) or God's power (2:5), and is a gift of the Spirit (12:9, 13:2). In 13:13 it is juxtaposed to hope and love, a usage we have already noted. This aspect of πίστις agrees with the Rabbinic אמונה as ascribed to Abraham while still a childless sojourner and to Israel when subjugated in Egyptian slavery (above p66f). Ἔργον in First Corinthians denotes 'the work' of building the community, which will be judged in the Day of the Lord, and, accordingly, one 'will receive a reward' (3:13-15). Similarly Paul states, referring to Timothy, 'he is doing the work of the Lord as I am' (16:10), and to the Corinthians themselves, 'be steadfast, immovable, always abounding in the work of the Lord' (15:58).[74] Nor is this 'moralist' use of ἔργον untypical of Paul.[75] Thus the use made in First Corinthians of νόμος, δικαιόω, πίστις, and ἔργον is quite untypical of justification theology.

Another remarkable aspect of First Corinthians is its use of traditions and tradition terminology related to Judaism and Apostolic, Jewish Christianity. In 1Cor 11:2 Paul writes: 'I praise you, brethren, that you ...keep the traditions as I handed them down to you'. There follows an exposition of two traditions touching on the liturgy which apparently derive from the Apostolic church: the head-covering of women during prayer and the eucharist tradition. Another important tradition is the resurrection narrative (15:3). The introductory phrases are revealing: '...the traditions even as I have delivered them to you' (11:2);

---

[72] Similarly Stendahl, *Paul*, 25f on the occurrence of δικαιοσύνη and its significance for the essence of Paul's theology.

[73] See e.g. Hahn, 'Taufe'. That being accepted, the baptismal, 'purificational' connotation does exist in Paul's speech.

[74] Ἔργον τοῦ κυρίου/Χριστοῦ in Paul denotes the building of the church: Rom 14:20; 1Cor 15:58; 16:10; Phil 2:30.

[75] Reward according to work is stressed in Rom 2:6; exhortations to do 'good works' are heard (2Cor 9:8; Col 1:10). Thus the usage in Ef 2:10 and the Pastorals is not post-Pauline per se, but a standardisation of Paul's usage.

'For I received of the Lord what I also delivered to you...' (11:23); 'For I delivered to you ...what I also received' (15:3). We shall explore the Jewish background of this terminology at the end of chapter 3. Among these traditions, those attributed to Jesus stand out. Only five times in the extant letters does Paul explicitly quote a saying of 'the Lord', i.e. Jesus. One is the eschatological tradition in 1Thess 4:15f. The others are all in First Corinthians: 'To the married I give charge, not I but the Lord...' (7:10); 'In the same way, the Lord commanded...' (9:14); 'For I received from the Lord what I also delivered to you...' (11:23); '...what I am writing to you is a command of the Lord' (14:37). More than anything else the explicit use of Jesus traditions demonstrates Paul's dependence on Apostolic tradition.

As we have seen First Corinthians was described as a 'Jewish' and 'legal' letter. This assessment is further strengthened by a passage which expresses Paul's sacramental and covenantal conception of the community of Christ. It comments on the eucharist tradition just mentioned. Someone who fills his stomach at 'the Lord's supper' while others are still hungry, 'eats the bread and drinks the cup of the Lord in an unworthy manner', for 'the Lord Jesus ...said: ...this cup is the New Covenant in my blood'; he is 'guilty of profaning the body and blood of the Lord', and 'that is why many of you are weak and ill, and some have died' (11:20-34).[76] Nor is this passage an exception. We must add those where the sins of unchastity and idolatry are condemned in sacramental language (1Cor 6 and 10). From these passages it is evident that what E.P. SANDERS outlined as the main characteristic of Palestinian Judaism is a vital element of Paul's instruction to the Corinthians. Rather than the decisive division between Paul and Judaism, 'covenantal nomism' is here found to indicate a common heritage.[77]

To summarize, in First Corinthians, a letter replete with practical instruction, justification theology is not a theme; the Law is affirmed as an authoritive source of practical teaching; Jewish-Christian traditions are explicitly used, four of them deriving from Jesus; and the conception of the church parallels Jewish covenantal nomism. All of this makes it a letter eminently suitable for the study of Jewish traditions in Paul, and especially halakha.

Traditions in First Corinthians

The presence of Jewish traditional law in First Corinthians must be viewed in a correct perspective. First, there are many non-legal Jewish traditions and second, there are also traditions which are not typically Jewish. Therefore we shall now make a survey of the letter and note the traditions it contains.[78] In so

---

[76] On the 'New Covenant' and entrance into it in Qumran and early Christianity see Flusser, 'Dead Sea Scrolls', 236-46. The 'sacramental' and 'physical' aspect was rightly stressed by Schweitzer, *Mystik*, 18-22, 273-8.

[77] Above, p16f. Sanders, *Paul, the Law*, 107-114, 208 concedes that in 1 Corinthians a 'beginning covenantal nomism' exists. Cf also Hooker, 'Covenantal Nomism'.

[78] Cf Ellis, 'Traditions'. On Paul and Apostolic tradition in general see the end of ch 3.

doing, we shall try to describe their distinct cultural provenance and, for reasons which will become increasingly clear, the authority they are given. Passages of the letter to which no reference is made in later chapters will receive some additional attention here. This having been done, the results will be registered in a classified inventory. It will show us a rough, preliminary religio-cultural portrait of First Corinthians and its author.

The first larger section, **1:10-4:21**,[79] although not directly parenetic, refers to the practical problem of factions (σχίσματα) which exist in the Corinth church according to oral reports from 'those of Chloe' (1:10-12). Prominent names mentioned are 'Apollos' and 'Cephas'. Making a link with Gal 2 one might hypothesize that 'Cephas' stood for an anti-Pauline Jewish-Christian party in Corinth;[80] however this is overstressing the few but honourable appearances of 'Cephas' in First Corinthians.[81] By contrast Apollos seems a real cause for Paul's extended admonition, the problem being 'jealousy and strife' between fans of 'Paul' and 'Apollos' (3:3f; 4:6).

There is a remarkable congruence here with information from Acts. Acts 18:24-19:1 describes Apollos as a brilliant Alexandrian Jewish exegete and rhetor. While residing in Ephesus he appeared in need of additional instruction about the gospel; having received it he went to Corinth. At about that time Paul arrived in Ephesus. From First Corinthians we learn that it was while here that he got his news from Corinth, apparently also about Apollos, and that he wrote the present letter to Corinth when Apollos had left (1Cor 1:11; 16:8; 16:12). Working behind the scenes in Ephesus were Paul's companions Aquila and Prisc(ill)a, according to both sources: it was they who taught Apollos 'more accurately' (Acts 19:26) and sent greetings to the Corinthians (1Cor 16:19). Seen in this light 1Cor 1-4 reads as a prudent warning against the superficial rhetorics Apollos had displayed in Corinth. Paul's language supports that impression.[82] He stresses his authority as the Apostle who first conveyed revelations of God's hidden wisdom to the Corinthians (2:1, 6-16; 4:1) and spiritually fathered their church (3:6; 4:15).[83] 1Cor 16:12 informs the Corinthians that Paul urged Apollos to return to them 'with the other brethren', but

[79] Wuellner, 'Greek Rhetoric' considers 1:3 and 6:11 a chiasm marking off a first rhetoric unit; however 6:12-20 continue on πορνεία, and the 'schism' theme is restricted to chs 1-4.

[80] Classical is Baur, 'Christuspartei'.

[81] See Barrett, 'Cephas and Corinth', who sees a difference with 2Cor. Cephas appears again in 1Cor 3:22 (with Apollos), 9:5 (with 'the brethren of the Lord', possibly including James) and 15:5 (along with the other apostles and James). He is never connected explicitly with practical issues such as in 1Cor 8-10. Nor can 'the weak' there be Jewish Christians, see below.

[82] 1Cor 1:20, 'the wise, the scribe, the disputer'; 1:17, 'empty speech of wisdom'; 2:4, 'enticing words of wisdom'; 4:19, 'not puffed-up words, but power'; 3:12, not 'wood, hay and straw' but 'gold, silver and gems'.

[83] Interestingly, Acts 19:1-7 refers to people in Ephesus baptized with the baptism of John and ignorant about the Spirit. Exactly this was Apollos's deficiency (ib 18:25). This throws light on Paul's reference to his baptisms in Corinth (1Cor 1:13-17) and his 'manifestation of Spirit and power' (ib 2:4, 10-16).

that the latter did not want to. Thus it was the form, not the contents of Apollos' appearance which troubled Paul. There are no indications of a direct relation with the chapters of parenesis which follow; Apollos's rhetorics do not seem to have undermined Paul's practical instructions.[84] If this would have been the case, Paul's verdict would have been less moderate.

Sources of authority quoted in 1Cor 1-4 are primarily five scriptural verses, four of which are formally introduced: (καθὼς) γέγραπται (1:19, 31; 2:9, 16; 3:19f). An implicit source of authority, recurring elsewhere in the letter, is the idea of the church as a temple of the Spirit which suffers no violation (3:16f). The appeal to follow the speaker's own example, a common device in Hellenistic rhetoric,[85] is also included (4:16).

From now on practical instruction dominates First Corinthians. 5:1-6:20 deals in the gravest terms with the sin of πορνεία, 'forbidden sexual relationships'; this concept and the specific case involved will be discussed in the next chapter. Unlike later sections Paul does not respond here to written questions but to oral reports. Although he wisely avoids identifying his informants (5:1, ἀκούεται), a link with 'those of Chloe' seems obvious (1:11; cf 11:18). In fact the previous section which is a direct reaction to their news from Corinth, links closely with this one. 4:14-21 is a preparation for the severe language of 5:1ff, the connection becoming explicit in the expression πεφυσιωμένοι ἐστέ, 'you are puffed up' (5:2; 4:18f; cf 4:6), and the combination ἔρχομαι, 'I am coming' (4:18f) and ἐγω...ἀπὼν...παρὼν, 'I, being absent/present' (5:3).

The variety among the sources of authority in this section is interesting. The absolute prohibition of marrying one's stepmother (5:1) implicitly relates to the Jewish halakha, as will be shown in the next chapter. In the second place Paul refers to two Tora verses. Deut 17:7 (and parallels), 'Drive out the wicked person from among you', underlines the appeal for the Corinthian church to try its own cases of unchastity (1Cor 5:13); Gen 2:24, speaking of man and woman as one flesh, is summoned in order to denounce sexual relations with a prostitute (1Cor 6:16). Underlying these quotations are two interpretative concepts: sexuality as having sacramental implications, and the church as the body of Christ and a temple of the Spirit precluding communion with unchastity (6:19).

Another source of support is the Jewish wisdom tradition. Twice in First Corinthians Paul quotes the saying: Πάντα ἔξεστιν ἀλλ᾽ οὐ πάντα συμφέρει, 'all things are lawful, but not all things edify' (6:12; 10:23). This may well have echoed popular Stoic ethics and sounded familiar in Corinthian ears,[86] but its origin seems to be in Ben Sira: Οὐ γὰρ πάντα πᾶσιν συμφέρει, καί οὐ πᾶσα ψυχὴ ἐν παντὶ εὐδοκεῖ (Sir 37:28). The connection is even closer with the

---

[84] A relation with the γνῶσις which 'puffs up' (8:1) is a mere guess; on the other hand there is a direct connection with 5:1ff, see below. But there might be some connection with the resurrection chapter (15:51, μυστήριον; cf 2:1, 7).

[85] See Wuellner, 'Greek Rhetoric', 184. The Apostolic, halakhic dimension (see below) must be added.

[86] Räisänen, Paul, 48f; but he overlooks the Ben Sira connection and Paul's subtle criticism.

Hebrew which reads: כי לא הכל לכל טוב, לא כל נפש כל זן תבחר, 'For not all is good for all; nor do all souls prefer all foods.' The play on the word כל, 'all' is significant, as is the reference to food. Ben Sira is known to have circulated in Rabbinic circles in widely varying forms, and Paul may have used or freely quoted one such version.[87] In the discussion on idol meat the variety of diets receives a special sting. Here an intermediate term is needed in order make the connection with πορνεία: 'Foods are for the belly and the belly is for foods, and God shall cause both to decay; but the body is not for πορνεία, but for the Lord...' (1Cor 6:13).

Finally Paul draws from what seems to be general Jewish or Jewish-Christian ethical tradition. The adhortation, 'flee from unchastity' (φεύγετε τὴν πορνείαν, 6:18) corresponds to the motto, 'flee from idolatry' (φεύγετε ἀπὸ τῆς εἰδωλολατρίας, 10:14). Not only are these mottos clearly related but they have Jewish and Jewish-Christian parallels.[88] Similarly the almost parallel vice lists cited in 5:10f and 6:9f, including the sequence πόρνοι... εἰδωλολάτριαι... μοιχοί..., clearly indicates a Jewish and Hellenistic-Jewish background.[89] The association of idolatry and unchastity is basic to biblical tradition and common in post-biblical Judaism.[90]

Chapter 7 starts with the heading dealt with above, 'Now concerning the things about which you wrote.' While this indicates a new section in reply to the Corinthian's own letter, the mention of πορνεία (v2) connects it with the preceding section. These topics had apparently been recurring in Paul's correspondence with Corinth: we hear of Paul's earlier letter in this context (5:9), the Corinthians' letter (7:1), and rumours (5:1). This corresponds to the stern emphasis in both sections. Chapter 7 is one of the most 'legal' chapters in First Corinthians and in all of Paul's letters. It is almost entirely devoted to a discussion of various marriage laws: marital intercourse, divorce, mixed marriage, celibacy and re-marriage. Although again not referred to such, these important matters all relate to the halakha; they will be dealt with in the next chapter.

Remarkably, Paul explicitly cites several distinct sources of authority here: 'I say this by way of concession, not of command (κατὰ συγγνώμην, οὐ κατ' ἐπιταγήν)' (v6); 'To the unmarried... I say' (v8); 'To the married I give charge (παραγγέλλω), not I but the Lord' (v10); 'Thus I ordain (διατάσσομαι) in all

[87] On the Rabbinic use of Ben Sira and the various Hebrew-Aramaic versions see Segal, *Ben Sira*, 37-42. It is clear that various Greek versions circulated too.
[88] TReub 5:5, φεύγετε ...τὴν πορνείαν; ib 6:1 φυλάσσεσθε ἀπὸ τῆς πορνείας; TBenj 7:1 φεύγετε τὴν κακίαν τοῦ Βελιάρ; Did 3:1, φεῦγε ἀπὸ παντὸς πονηροῦ; Ps-Phoc 146 φεῦγε κακὴν φήμην. Cf Alon, *Studies* 1, 283-5 on this tradition.
[89] See Flusser, *Jewish Sources*, 235-52. Cf the 'way of death' Did 5:1-2 and the negative of the 'way of life' ib 3:2-6; and the parallels in 'the way of darkness' and of 'light' Barn 20:1-2 and 19:2-6. Most important is the Qumran parallel 1QS 3:13-4:1.
[90] See also Wis 14:12, Ἀρχὴ γὰρ πορνείας ἐπινοία εἰδωλῶν.

the churches' (v17); 'Concerning the unmarried, I have no command of the Lord (ἐπιταγὴ κυρίου), but I give my opinion (γνώμη)' (v25); '...in my opinion (γνώμη)' (v40).[91]

Non-explicit authority sources are also involved. In v3f a rule is implied which states the right of married partners to each other's body, which conforms to Jewish halakha; v39 quotes an unidentified rule which also relates to halakhic traditions.

Finally the chapter contains a passage reflecting the Law polemic (7:17-24) including the remarkable appeal to keep 'the commandments of God' (v19). A fundamental rule is referred to which appears to be typical of Paul and has a halakhic edge (v17). In itself this is a digression of the sort found throughout First Corinthians; it is dealt with in the last chapter.

Chapters 8 – 10, 'Now concerning food offered to idols (εἰδωλόθυτα)', apparently are another response to a written question from Corinth. Obviously it is directly concerned with Jewish Law and its validity; we shall devote chapters 4 and 5 to the subject. The relationship to Jewish halakhic traditions which will be established there remains implicit. While the issue itself is tackled in 8:1-13 and again 10:23-33, the parts in between are a rhetorical digression giving moral examples from life and from biblical history. This reflects a Hellenistic rhetoric device.[92]

1Cor 9 presents Paul's performance as an Apostle working unselfishly for the good of all as an example to be followed by the Corinthians (see 9:19-23 and 10:31-11:1). A little further Paul urges the Corinthians in plain words: 'Become my imitators, as I am of Christ' (11:1). Paul the Apostle represents Christ. Hence the immediate source of authority here is Paul's own Apostolic example. This explains the elaboration on 'apostleship', a matter which as we shall see in the next chapter has important halakhic implications. The sources of authority on which it is based have already been noted: repeated explicit appeals to 'the Law (of Moses)' (9:8f) and a highly significant tradition from Jesus (9:14).

The other sources Paul to which appeals add an interesting degree of variety. First he uses an example from the Greek world, the training of an athlete (9:24-27); it resembles adaptations from popular Greek wisdom found in Hellenistic Jewish traditions[93] and in Rabbinic literature.[94] A second authority source has already been mentioned: a compelling appeal to the Tora narrative of Israel in the desert (10:1-13). But it should not be overlooked that Paul's

---

[91] Daube, *New Testament*, 205-23 compares with the rabbinic categories רשות, מצוה, חובה; similarly Löwy, 'Paulinische Lehre' II, 410, following Lightfoot. But these terms are unspecific and flexible even in later Tannaic traditions; see Alon, *Studies* 2, 111-9. There may have been divergent traditions existing side by side early on, one of which was somehow reflected in Paul; but this requires further study.

[92] Wuellner, 'Greek Rhetoric'.

[93] See Philo, Hypoth 11:6-7 (of the Essenes) and Vit cont 42; and what may be a Hellenistic Jewish prayer preserved in the Apostolic Constitutions, identified as such by Bousset and quoted in Goodenough, *Light*, 316 (cf ib 306 for discussion).

[94] Str-B 3, 401ff.

77

exposition includes a paraphrase (10:1-4) and other interpretative references which directly relate to Jewish targumic and midrashic tradition both in form and in substance (see ch 5 below). Thirdly, in parallel with chapter 6 Jewish wisdom (10:24) and ethical traditions (10:14) are used. Finally we find here the union with the body of Christ which excludes communion with sin, in this case idolatry (10:14-22); the underlying sacramental conception has already been pointed out.

Chapter 11, as we have already seen, specifically refers to 'traditions'. They have to do with the liturgy: the headcovering of women (11:3-16) and procedures at the eucharist (11:17-34). The second issue is raised by Paul in response to oral reports from Corinth about divisions and misdemeanours (11:18; cf 1:11; 5:1). The reason for the exposition on the first tradition is not given here but may also have been in the oral reports. These are Jewish-Christian traditions which have clear halakhic implications; they are dealt with in the next chapter.

We find three sources of authority: (1) Apostolic tradition which includes Jesus traditions and is indicated by the transmission terms παράδοσις, παραδίδωμι, and παραλαμβάνω and by the reference to the 'custom' (συνηθεία) of the 'churches of God'; (2) reason and the evidence of 'nature' (11:13f), which is reminiscent of the common Hellenistic motif, 'the law of nature';[95] and (3) an implicit Tora reference (v8f).

Chapters 12-14: 'Now concerning the spiritual matters' (πνευματικά). Elsewhere Paul calls these χαρίσματα, 'gifts' (12:4; 1:7).[96] Χάρισμα is synonymous with another word found in early Christian tradition, δόμα; both have a Hebrew background.[97] Paul discerns a range of χαρίσματα including teaching, prophesying, tongues and healing (12:28-31).[98] In view of their community function and the connection with the Pentecost story (Acts 2), their background in Jewish tradition is evident.[99] In Corinth the spiritual gifts tended to lead their own life, resulting in vain pride and a 'confusion of tongues'. This was apparently another practical question the Corinthians had written about.

Paul pleads for order (cf 14:33, 40) and mutual tolerance. The rhetorical structure is similar to that of chs 8-10: a more general introduction is followed by a digression calling on moral arguments (12:12-13:13), whereupon the main argument resumes with detailed teaching. The first part of the digression

---

[95] Below p85.
[96] Some interpret, 'spiritual persons'. But cf 14:1, τὰ πνευματικά as a generic concept.
[97] See Matt 7:11 and Luke 11:13, heavenly 'gifts', i.e. (Luke) πνεῦμα ἅγιον. Similarly Eph 4:8 quoting Ps 68:19, 'Having ascended on high, he ...gave gifts unto men'; the Hebrew here has מתנות. Rabbinic tradition expounds this in view of Sinai: the Tora is a מתנה, i.e. free, brought by Moses 'from on high' and given 'unto men', in 70 tongues. See Tg Ps 68; and MidrPs 68,5 (159a); ib 68,11 (160a); bShab 88b; cf connection with Exod 20:19, TanhB Shemot 22 (7a). The connection with Acts 2 is important for the history of the tradition. For the plain meaning 'gift' cf χάρις for the collection for Jerusalem (1Cor 16:3, 2Cor 8:4, 6f, 19, etc).
[98] Cf Rom 12:3-8; Eph 4:11. Cf also the very general meaning 1Cor 1:7, 7:7.
[99] On Pentecost and Tora see Weinfeld, 'Pentecost'.

consists of the well-known Hellenistic fable of the body and the limbs (12:12-27).[100] The fable, which adds a touch of graceful humour to Paul's otherwise austere letter,[101] is also reflected in many variations in Rabbinic literature.[102] The second part of the excursion is Paul's famous 'Canticle' which shows 'a still more excellent way': love (ch 13). Whoever may have contributed to this beautiful spiritual hymn, its (Hellenistic-)Jewish materials cannot be over-looked.[103] The section continues with detailed instruction on an orderly community worship (14:1-33).[104]

An explicit appeal to 'the Law' (Isa 28:11f, 1Cor 14:21) for authoritative support was mentioned already. The instruction to translate prophecies so that the community may answer 'Amen' (14:16) reflects a halakha known from Rabbinic tradition. Another tradition teaches the silence of women during the worship service (14:34-36; cf 11:3-16). This is a Jewish-Christian halakha explicitly supported by various sources of authority: the custom of the 'churches of the holy' (v34), 'the Law' (ib) and, more generally and probably covering the whole preceding section, 'a commandment of the Lord' (v37). These halakhot will also be dealt with in the next chapter.

Chapter 15 suddenly introduces a renewed proclamation of Paul's resurrection gospel. Remarkable again is the explicit mention of sources of authority. The basis is Apostolic, Jewish-Christian tradition: 'I handed down to you ...what I also received...'; there follows the narrative of apparitions to the Apostles and, 'last of all, as to one untimely born', to Paul himself (v3-8). Formal appeals to 'the Scriptures' are also included (v3f).

The issue is apparently that in Corinth 'some say ...that there is no resurrection of the dead' (v12). There is no indication how that information had reached Paul; oral reports seem the most obvious way. Paul starts his positive argument from Jesus' resurrection as 'the first fruit' (v20)[105] and from there develops the general eschatological plan (vv23-28). He also appeals to the curious practice of 'baptism for the dead', which indicates his realistic conception of the sacraments.[106] Next is the question of how the resurrection 'works'; the similes Paul adduces in order to stimulate the imagination (vv35-49) resemble Rabbinic traditions. Discussions on resurrection were prominent in Second Temple

---

[100] For discussion and sources see Meuzelaar, *Leib*, esp 149-55.

[101] It is noted as such by Jónsson, *Humour*, 232f. On humour in ancient Judaism and Christianity see also my 'Oud-Joodse humor'.

[102] See Str-B 3, 446-8. Not mentioned there is its significant application in the midrash of the 613 mitswot: the '248 limbs of the body' rival each to do a positive commandment, while all commandments are one organic whole. PesRK 12 (p203); cf bMak 23b; bShevu 29a; bYev 47b; bNed 25a. On the relations between Rabbinic parables and popular Hellenistic fables see Flusser, *Gleichnisse*, 141-60.

[103] See Str-B 3, 449-54; cf Gerhardsson, 'I Kor 13'.

[104] Interesting is the connection between the tongues and Num 11:25, the inspiration of the seventy elders leading the community; see Weinfeld, 'Pentecost', 16.

[105] Cf Rom 8:29; Col 1:15, 18.

[106] This was stressed by Schweitzer, *Mystik*, 276-8; cf 252-6, 18-22.

Judaism, and various sources testify that belief in resurrection was considered a typically Pharisaic tenet.[107] Paul imparted it to his gentile churches.

The chapter ends with the revelation of a 'mystery' concerning the actual order of the resurrection; it includes the targumic peroration discussed above (vv50-57).[108] The word μυστήριον represents a hidden universe of sacred knowledge and ritual firmly rooted in Hellenistic religious thought and found as such, typically, in Philo.[109] In this context however it functions as an apocalyptic concept denoting the revelation of a hidden insight into the process of redemption; it has distinct equivalents in Essene and Rabbinic usage which should be distinguished from the Hellenistic usage of the word.[110] The concluding sentence (1Cor 15:28) draws the lesson: 'be steadfast, ...abounding in the work of the Lord'. Truly Jewish and Pharisaic, Paul's apocalyptic faith is consummated in active life.[111]

Chapter 16, 'Now on the collection'. The collection is destined for 'the holy', which may have been a special appellation of the Jerusalem church (16:1, 3).[112] Paul 'orders' the same procedure to be followed as in the Galatian churches: 'On the First after the Sabbath, each of you is to put something aside' (v2). This

---

[107] Mark 12:18-27 and parr; Acts 23:1-10; Josephus, War 2:162-66; Ant 18:12-17; mSan 10:1 (a very old tradition, cf 1En 60:6); bSan 90b-92b (exegetical arguments and similes). See Str-B 1, 885-97. The second benediction of the daily prayer, תחית המתים, reflects the importance of this belief in the ancient period. On its development and versions see note by Ginzberg, *Commentary* 4, 148-268.

[108] A connection with chs 1-4 may be reflected; see above n84.

[109] E.g. Cher 14, 48. Goodenough, *Light*, ch 9 and, somewhat more balanced, *Introduction* ch 7 elaborately describes Philo's thought as a Hellenistic mystic representation of Judaism; cf *Light*, 268ff on the term in the Wisdom of Solomon. Not basically different Wolfson, *Philo* 1, 24f discerns two basic meanings in Greek usage: secret rites and esoteric teachings, the second meaning being adopted by Hellenistic Judaism to indicate revealed divine Wisdom, i.e. the Tora.

[110] Cf 1Cor 2:7-11; Rom 11:25; Eph 3:3f, 9. This may also be the more original background of the synoptic μυστήριον τῆς βασιλείας τοῦ θεοῦ Mark 4:11 parr. The concept relates to the Qumran רזי אל, mysteries of God connected with the doctrine of the קצים, end-times; see Flusser, 'Motsa ha-Natsrut', 437; cf Dimant, 'Qumran', 507f, 536. The milieu of these concepts is in apocalyptic and dream interpretation of typically Iranian and Chaldean provenance. For a Rabbinic parallel see TanhB Wayehi 8 (108b): Isaac and Jacob on their deathbeds (Gen 27:1, 49:1) wishing to 'reveal the מסתורין' of God and 'reveal the קץ'. See also Str-B 1, 659f; good discussion in Knox, *Church of the Gentiles*, 227f (involving the duality מסטורין / מסתורין); Brown, *Semitic Background*. Both in Rabbinic and early Christian literature the concept also had a non-apocalyptic esoteric meaning closer to general Hellenistic usage. See Str-B ib; Eph 1:9; 5:32; 6:19; 1Tim 3:9, 16. 1Cor 2:1 (but see textual variants) and 4:1 would fit in here.

[111] This insight is central to Schweitzer's *Mystik*. See below p281.

[112] Cf gifts for 'the holy' Rom 12:13; 15:31; 2Cor 8:4; 9:1, 12. On 1Cor 14:33 see below. This theory was developed by Cerfaux, *Théologie*, 113-7, 219-21. But there are objections. The name is used without any hesitation for all other churches, 1Cor 1:1; 6:1f; 2Cor 1:1; Col 1:1; Phil 1:1; Phlm 5, 7; and, outside Paul, Ef 1:1; Acts 9:13, 32. See Bauer, *Wörterbuch* sv ἅγιος 2,d,β. It may originally have been a special indication for the Jerusalem church. Interestingly, Hegesippus reports the piety of James, its leader (Eusebius, Hist eccl 2:23). But soon, the name may, certainly in Paul's spirit, have been extended to all churches; cf Ef 2:19. Paul would have then used the older meaning when referring to the collection. – There is a late 2nd cent CE parallel in the pious Rabbinic order in Jerusalem called עדה קדושה or קהילא קדישא; its spiritual father was probably R. Meir who was called 'holy'; see Safrai, 'Holy Congregation'.

order is apparently given on his own Apostolic authority. The letters he will send to Jerusalem to accompany the 'gift' (χάρις, v3) have, alas, been lost. Paul himself was also planning to leave but decided to stay in at least until 'Pentecost', i.e. the Jewish Festival of Weeks (vv5-9). Another answer to a question from the Corinthians appears to be included: 'Now concerning our brother Apollos...' (v12). Last assignments and greetings follow, as well as a salutation 'in my own hand' containing the Aramaic liturgical exclamation: 'Maranatha' (vv10-23). The presence of Jewish customs and traditions in all these details is evident and natural.

The above survey enables us to draw up a provisional inventory of the various sources and traditions Paul draws on in First Corinthians; some elements not mentioned in the survey are added here. Incidentally, the idea of an inventory of sources in Paul was suggested already by Alfred RESCH, in the framework of his investigation into the connections between Paul and the synoptic tradition.[113]

A basic distinction to be made is between traditions which are explicitly cited as authorities and those which are not. An explicit citation, characteristically introduced with a specific formula, signals that a tradition is thought to be recognized by all and can be formally appealed to; this may be termed a formal source of authority. A tradition used without such signalization remains as it were anonymous. No appeal is made to its status, and it can generally be categorized as an informal authority. But the absence of an introductory formula does not always signify an informal source: Bible verses may be used or alluded to without a formula.

These two main categories can be further divided. Formal sources of authority in First Corinthians are of three kinds: (1) Scripture; (2) Apostolic tradition; (3) Paul's own Apostolic teaching. We may also distinguish three types of informal authority sources: (4) Jewish tradition; (5) popular Hellenistic wisdom; (6) informal elements of Christian tradition.

A problem arises with the distinction between 'Apostolic' and 'Jewish' elements. For clarity's sake we shall use the conventional distinction between 'Jewish' i.e. non-Christian and Apostolic traditions. The same holds true for Hellenistic and Hellenistic-Jewish materials, which moreover sometimes are dressed in Christian garb. As to such cultural borderlines, inventories like the one following below involve an inevitable degree of arbitrariness. We should recall that 'Jewishness' is not defined by the materials themselves but by the form or function they have. And this may well be a more general principle. Nevertheless sorting out the materials by basic categories yields interesting information.

---

[113] Resch, *Paulinismus*, 603-28 lists the following sources of 'Paulinism' (which in his terminology includes the Deutero-Paulines): 1) OT; 2) Apocrypha; 3) 'Jewish theology'; 4) Hellenistic diaspora tradition; 5) gentile Hellenistic thought; 6) Apostolic tradition. Resch's ambivalence towards Judaism is expressed in his reservation as regards Rabbinic literature (609-13), while welcoming the work on the Hebrew original of the Jesus *logia* (623-8).

1. *Scripture*. Second Temple Jews accepted Scripture both as the basis of practical life and thought; so did Paul. Scriptural verses are generally introduced with quotation formulae such as: '...as it is written', as is common in Hebrew, Aramaic and Greek Jewish works. Often short explanatory phrases are inserted or, as in 1Cor 10:1-4, a paraphrase is given. This usage is in line with ancient Jewish targumic and midrashic tradition: quotation which includes interpretation.[114]

1.1 The formula 'it is written (in the Law)':
9:9 ἐν γὰρ τῷ Μωϋσέως νόμῳ γέγραπται (Deut 25:4);
14:21 ἐν τῷ νόμῳ γέγραπται (Isa 28:11f);
1:19 γέγραπται γάρ (Isa 29:14); id 3:19f (Job 5:12f; Ps 94:11);
1:31 καθὼς γέγραπται (Jer 9:22f); id 2:9 (source unknown);[115]
10:7 ὥσπερ γέγραπται (Exod 32:6);
15:45 οὕτως καὶ γέγραπται (Gen 2:7).

1.2 Cases citing 'the Law' for general support:
9:8 καὶ ὁ νόμος ταῦτα λέγει (see 9:9; Deut 25:4);
14:34 καθὼς καὶ ὁ νόμος λέγει (no quotation given; but cf 11:8f).

1.3 Formulae referring to a paraphrase:
10:6 ταῦτα δὲ τύποι ἡμῶν ἐγενήθησαν;
10:11 ταῦτα δὲ τυπικῶς συνέβαινεν ἐκείνοις, ἐγράφη δὲ πρὸς νουθεσίαν ἡμῶν (10:6-13).

1.4 Scriptural verses cited without an introductory formula, or even by way of a paraphrase:
5:13 (Deut 17:7); 6:16 (Gen 2:24); (11:8f, Gen 2:18).

2. *Apostolic tradition*. This category contains traditions which are neither found in Scripture nor derive from Paul's own authority. They consist of:

2.1 Traditions explicitly referred to as descending from 'the Lord', i.e. words of Jesus; as we saw there are four instances, three of which have parallels in the extant gospels:
7:10 παραγγέλλω, οὐκ ἐγὼ ἀλλὰ ὁ κύριος (cf Mark 10:11f and parr.);
9:14 ὁ κύριος διέταξεν (cf Matt 10:10 and par.);
11:23 παρέλαβον ἀπὸ τοῦ κυρίου (cf Mark 14:22ff and parr.);
14:37 κυρίου ἐστὶν ἐντολή (no extant gospel parallel).

---

[114] An ancient example of interpretative glossing is found in the Temple Scroll.
[115] Isa 52:15 and 64:3 can be termed similar at the most. Origen, Jerome and other church Fathers disputed a reference to an Apocalypse of Elijah here; see Str-B 3, 327f and Charlesworth, *OTP* 1, 728.

2.2 Other traditions of the Jewish-Christian church cited with explicit reference to their authority; they consist of gospel tradition, formulated halakhic rules, and custom. They are the following:

11:3-15, the headcovering of women (referred to as παράδοσις in 11:2 and as συνήθεια (τῶν ἐκκλησιῶν) in 11:16);

14:34ff, the prescription of silence of women 14:34 ὥς ἐν πάσαις ταῖς ἐκκλησίας;

15:3ff, the gospel tradition concerning Jesus's resurrection announced as παρέδωκα ...ὃ καὶ παρέλαβον.

3. *Paul's Apostolic teaching* is repeatedly emphasized as being a separate source of instruction. It includes the following items:

3.1 Traditions, instruction, mysteries, and revelations:
2:1, 6 καταγγέλλω τὸ μυστήριον τοῦ θεοῦ (2:1-16);
11:2 παρέδωκα τὰς παραδόσεις (11:2-33);
15:1 γνωρίζω ...τὸ εὐαγγέλιον (15:3-8); cf 15:3;
15:51 ἰδοὺ μυστήριον ...λέγω (15:51-57).

3.2 The pronunciation of Apostolic judgment:
1:10 παρακαλῶ ...ὑμᾶς ...διὰ τοῦ ὀνόματος τοῦ κυρίου ἡμῶν Ἰησοῦ Χριστοῦ;
4:16 παρακαλῶ ὑμᾶς, 5:3 ἐγὼ ...ἤδη κέκρικα ...ἐν τῷ ὀνόματι τοῦ κυρίου Ἰησοῦ (4:14-5:13).

3.3 The promulgation of ordinances and opinions:
7:6 τοῦτο δὲ λέγω κατὰ συγγνώμην οὐ κατ' ἐπιταγήν;
7:8 λέγω τοῖς ἀγάμοις ...καλόν;
7:12 τοῖς δὲ λοιποῖς λέγω ἐγὼ οὐχ ὁ κύριος (cf 7:10);
7:25 περί τῶν παρθένων ἐπιταγὴν κυρίου οὐκ ἔχω, γνώμην δίδωμι;
7:40 κατὰ τὴν ἐμὴν γνώμην (widows);
11:33 διατάξομαι (traditions);
16:1 διέταξα (the collection).

3.4 The Apostle's exemplary and normative conduct, a motive which is found elsewhere in Paul's parenesis, but also relates to Hellenistic rhetoric:[116]
4:16, 11:1 μιμηταί μου γίνεσθε;
9:1-23, an extended appeal to Paul's example (cf 10:31-33).

4. *Jewish tradition.* Non-biblical traditions are referred to here, also known from or closely paralleling ancient non-Christian Jewish sources. We may discern the following elements:

---

[116] 1Thess 1:6 (cf 2:14); Phil 3:17; 4:9. Cf above n85; Stanley Jones, *"Freiheit"*, 48.

4.1 Wisdom. This category contains sayings related to known wisdom writings, especially Ben Sira:

6:12 and 10:23, an adaptation of Sir 37:28;

7:19, an expression related to Sir 32:23 and Prov 19:16 (below p272);

9:10, an unidentified quotation which much resembles Sir 6:18f (below p129).

4.2 Targum, midrash and aggada. Only a few examples are listed; this category could be easily expanded and invites much further study.[117]

1Cor 10:1-13, Exodus midrashim and targumim;

15:35-49, similes explaining resurrection;

15:54f, a targumic exposition.

4.3 Apocalyptic. This is a vague category, but clearly present. The line between Jewish and Jewish-Christian (Apostolic) elements is hard to draw here (cf resurrection images, ch 15).

15:50 (cf 2:1, 6): the term μυστήριον as referring to salvation history.

5:5; 11:10, Satan and 'the angels' (i.e. fallen angels).

4.4 Ethical traditions. These also tend to transcend the borderlines between the various groups and movements (above p76).

5:10f; 6:9f, lists of vices.

6:14 and 10:24, 'flee from unchastity / idolatry'.

4.5 Hellenistic Jewish tradition.

1Cor 13, the spiritual hymn. Its status is not formally announced, nor does it contain any specific Christian element. It seems to draw on Hellenistic Jewish conventions.

4.6 Halakha. Apart from the formally introduced Apostolic traditions mentioned above the following halakhot may also be mentioned. The list is based on the results of the analysis in chapters 3, 4 and 5.

5:1, a halakha prohibiting non-Jews from cohabiting with their step-mother.

7:3f, halakhot regarding marital obligations.

7:39, three halakhot concerning remarriage of widows.

9:9f, a reflection of halakhot concerning the wages of field labourers.

10:24-29, a halakha permitting Christ-believing gentiles to eat food of unknown status vis-à-vis idol offerings when sold or offered to them.

14:16, a halakha regarding community benedictions.

---

[117] Conspicuous is the use of Jewish traditions in 9:7-13 (see ch 3 below). Similarly, the imagery of 'milk' and 'solid food' in 3:2b relates to Jewish tradition (see YalkShim p581f; bEr 54b), as well as that of 'planting' and 'watering' in 3:6-9 (cf tSot 7:11; ARN b34; 4Ezra 4:28-32; 8:41-44; 9:17, 30-37; and cf the parables about 'sowing' in the gospels).

5. *Popular Hellenistic wisdom.* In three clear instances Paul informally cites elements from popular wisdom which may have been quite familiar for his Greek readers. They remind one of popular Hellenistic philosophy, particularly the Stoic-Cynic tradition, elements of which were also assimilated into Rabbinic tradition.

9:24-27, the exemplum of the athlete and his training;[118]

11:13f, an appeal to reason and 'nature' in support of the prescription of headcovering for women in church: ἐν ὑμῖν αὐτοῖς κρίνατε ...οὐδὲ ἡ φύσις αὐτὴ διδάσκει.[119]

12:12-27, the famous fable of the body and its limbs.[120]

6. *Informal elements of Christian tradition.* Two elements stand out:

4:16f; 6:12-20; and 10:14-23 (cf 11:20-29): the concept of the church as a temple of the spirit or the body of Christ. This involves two cultural backgrounds, the 'temple' relating to apocalyptic traditions and the 'body' to Stoic-Cynic thought.

7:19, 22; 11:11f; 12:13, quasi-ceremonial formulae expressing the equality of social classes, probably with a baptismal background (12:13; cf Gal 3:27f). As with the 'body of Christ', a relationship with Stoic-Cynic wisdom is unmistakable (see below, Conclusion). These ideas may have their milieu in Hellenistic Judaism.

Some concluding remarks.

The listing of informal elements is not exhaustive. This certainly regards elements from Pharisaic-Rabbinic and other Jewish traditions. As we have indicated a systematic search will reveal many more midrashic and aggadic parallels; Strack-Billerbeck is a good start, but by no means exhaustive and devoid of historical comparison. The same holds true for Hellenistic elements, where we must depend on specialists in the field. The examples given show that Paul, while rooted in apocalyptic and Pharisaic-Rabbinic tradition, could use common Hellenistic ideas quite naturally. This should be emphasized precisely because the focus of this study is on Jewish and especially halakhic elements.[121]

Practical instruction, and more specifically: halakha is conspicuous in First Corinthians. It might seem that halakha is poorly represented with only six relevant passages (5:1; 7:3; 7:39; 9:9f; 10:24-29; 14:16). But this concerns only halakhot from informal sources. The importance of practical instruction is

---

[118] Above p77.

[119] On the complexities of 'the law of nature' in Philo, general Greek philosophy and Paul see Goodenough, *Light*, 50f; Pohlenz, *Paulus*, 75-7; cf also Conzelmann p190. Paul's appeal to 'nature' is unsophisticated as compared with Philo. For the appeal to reason cf דין in Tannaic literature and סברא in the Babylonian Talmud.

[120] Above p79.

[121] Cf above p31-36 on 'Judaism and Hellenism'. Some further thought follows in ch 5 below.

visible especially among the formal sources; it is emphasized by the explicit appeal to their authority. All of the four Jesus traditions are practical (7:10; 9:14; 11:23; 14:37), and the same holds true for three of the four Jewish-Christian church rules (11:3-15; 17-34; 14:34f; there is a partial overlap here with the Jesus traditions). Moreover of the ten formal appeals to Scripture, five are part of direct practical instruction (9:8, 9; 10:7; 14:21, 34; cf also 10:6, 11). And although they are not traditions in the strict sense, the practical orders in Paul's own teaching may be added (7:6, 8, 12, 25, 40; 16:2; cf 11:33). Many of the informal traditions also have a practical aim. The 'informal' halakhot stand out.

On the whole, the authoritative, halakhic character of First Corinthians is striking. In a way the letter reminds one of the *responsa*, letters written in answer to halakhic questions typical of medieval Judaism. But there are parallels closer in history. Tannaic literature reports that halakhic letters were written by Paul's reputed teacher, Gamliel the Elder, as also by Shimon ben Gamliel, his son, and Yohanan ben Zakkai, about the laws of first fruits and intercalation of the calendar.[122] Similar halakhic letters are referred to many times in the Talmud.[123] Another example is from the New Testament: even if the story of the letter to the Antioch church about the commandments for gentile believers (Acts 15) is not fully historical, it does testify to the phenomenon of letters with 'legal instruction' in Apostolic Christianity. Finally archeology provided us with a halakhic letter from Qumran which contains a number of sectarian halakhot and must have been written in ca. 150 BCE.[124]

This is not to overlook the degree to which First Corinthians reflects Hellenistic rhetorical and epistolary conventions. The letter presents a characteristic blend of Jewish-Christian halakhic material in Hellenistic parenetic form.

The question of why First Corinthians has this remarkably halakhic character must be approached soberly. Halakhic elements can also be found in other Pauline letters, most strikingly in First Thessalonians, Paul's earliest letter (see below). On the other hand the Second Letter to the Corinthians, written only one or two years after the First, hardly contains any halakha or practical instruction. Therefore to explain the character of First Corinthians from the specifically immoral situation in Corinth,[125] or from a 'legalistic' intermezzo in Paul's development, is unsatisfactory. Much more probable is that earlier correspondence on practical matters led to this letter. Its halakhic character does not contradict the different emphasis in Second Corinthians or in other letters of Paul; nor does the scarcity of halakha in some other letters diminish the significance of its presence in First Corinthians.

Finally, the numerous elements of Jewish tradition in First Corinthians, halakhot included, remain 'anonymous'. They are never introduced with for-

---

[122] tSan 2:6; ySan 1, 18d; bSan 11b; MidrGad Deut 26:1 (p597f). Büchler, 'Igarot' considers these two separate sets of letters.
[123] See list in Epstein, *Nosah*, 699f.
[124] See Qimron-Strugnell, 'Halakhic Letter'. It was quoted above p66.
[125] Corinth was a harbour city with loose morals, see e.g. Sellin, 'Hauptprobleme', 2995f.

mulae comparable to those signalling Scripture verses, Apostolic traditions or the Apostle's own teaching. Again the question is, what does this signify? Introductory formulae and appeals to authority are absent not only in the references to popular Hellenistic wisdom but also in those to informal Christian tradition. The formal affirmation of the authority of Scripture and Apostolic tradition merely emphasizes the ideology of the Apostolic church. Next to these, the informal sources are simply there; their authority is neither emphasized nor disputed.

Halakha in the Remaining Letters

The purpose here is to outline the spread of halakha in the rest of the Pauline corpus. Only one larger issue from Galatians and Romans will be elaborated on further (chapter 6, table fellowship). The other topics will not, even though some may be very interesting; they receive cursory attention here.

Second Corinthians, which can be read as an integral Pauline letter,[126] has no parenetic section. The only practical question discussed is the collection (2Cor 8f); what Paul writes there can best be read as a fund-raising sermon. There is a remarkable section containing polemic over the reading of the Law, 2Cor 3-5.[127] While these chapters are replete with midrashic traditions adapted to serve Paul's own purposes, they reflect serious tension with the Synagogue. One expression even seems to contradict Paul's adherence to Apostolic tradition as documented in First Corinthians. In 2Cor 5:16 he writes: 'From now on, therefore, we know no one according to the flesh; even if we once knew Christ according to the flesh (ἐγνώκαμεν κατὰ σάρκα Χριστόν), we do not know him any longer.'[128] But proposing that κατὰ σάρκα modifies ἐγνώκαμεν rather than Χριστόν we may maintain a non-docetic reading: 'once our knowledge of Christ was according to the flesh'. Nevertheless the contrast between First and Second Corinthians seems to indicate that meanwhile a judaizing development had arisen in Corinth.[129]

Galatians is remarkable because it is totally devoted to polemic on the Law. From 1:13 to 6:15 the argument is over circumcision and the practice of the Jewish Law. The specific terms appear throughout, and mostly in the 'characteristic' sense: νόμος (31 mentions), ἔργον (8), δικαιόω and derivatives (12), and πίστις (22). Indeed along with Romans, Galatians is the classical document for Paul's theology of 'justification through faith without works of the Law' (Gal 2:16). The expression that 'in Christ there is neither Jew nor Greek...' appears no less than three times in various forms (3:28; 5:6; 6:15) and

---

[126] See above p59 n18f.
[127] The use of δικαιοσύνη in 3:9 and 5:21 is specific to the justification theology; but not so in 6:7, 14; 9:9f (!); 11:15. The contrast is significant.
[128] RSV nicely interprets: 'We regard him thus no longer'.
[129] See Barrett, 'Cephas and Corinth'.

must be recognized as being a characteristic formula which seems to reflect the main interest of the letter.

Paul writes his letter in opposition to 'those ...that would compel you to be circumcised' (6:12); evidently Jewish Christian missionaries following a different policy from Paul's are involved here. As against such efforts to 'compel the gentiles to judaize' (2:14; cf 2:3),[130] Paul stands up for 'the truth of the gospel' (2:14; cf v5). Galatians is about the obligation for gentile Christians to take the Jewish Law and its commandments upon themselves. Paul's gospel of 'justification by faith' liberates them from that obligation.

Meanwhile circumcision obviously has to do with halakha. We can leave the ins and outs of justification theology for the moment and look at what is relevant from the viewpoint of halakha: Paul is concerned with people who are not Jewish and indeed he wishes them to remain such (4:8). This confirms the theoretical principle stated above: in Paul's letters to gentiles we can expect only those halakhot to be affirmed which he deems applicable to them.

This is what appears to be meant by Paul's sarcasm about the observance of 'days, and months, and seasons, and years' (Gal 4:10). Although he explains these customs to his gentile readers as re-enslavement to 'the weak and beggarly elemental spirits' (4:8f), the point seems to be that they 'desire to be under the Law' (4:21). There are two distinct aspects here: the theme of enslavement and freedom vis-à-vis the Jewish Law which runs all through chs 4 and 5, and the theological disapproval of this enslavement as a form of angel worship. The latter aspect is expressed more fully in Colossians (see below).

Circumcision obviously has to do with halakha. Therefore it is significant that it is in Paul's polemic against circumcision of gentile Christians that we find a halakha reflected. It appears to be the only explicit halakhic reference in Galatians. In Gal 5:2-3 we read: 'Now I, Paul, say to you that if you have yourself circumcised, Christ will be of no advantage to you. I testify again[131] to every man who is circumcized that he is bound to keep the whole Law.' The remarkable repetition of content between these two sentences is balanced by a difference in form: the first is a personal statement and refers to Christ, whereas the second is an impersonal statement of principle. This gives the impression that the second sentence states some accepted rule.

This is confirmed by comparison with Rabbinic literature. In the first place the introductory phrase μαρτύρομαι, 'I testify', parallels a technical term in Hebrew: העיד, 'testify', which means to quote formally an oral tradition, usually a halakha.[132] In the second place a Tannaic halakha states: 'A proselyte who accepts all commandments of the Tora except for one is not accepted; R. Yose son of R. Yehuda says: even (if it concerns) a detail of the niceties of the

---

[130] This use of ἀναγκάζω is typical for Gal; the only other occurrence in Paul is 2Cor 12:11 with a different application.

[131] If πάλιν is not meant to repeat and clarify v2, it refers to an unclear precedent; it is absent in D*, F, G, 1881 et al, it, Ambst.

[132] e.g. mEd 1:3; 2:1, 3. Albeck, *Mishna* 4, 277 thus explains the accepted name of the entire tractate: Eduyot.

Scribes.'[133] Thus it seems that Paul quotes and applies a halakha regarding proselyting in his polemic against circumcision of gentile Christians. The Rabbinic halakha just quoted makes the impression of being ancient.[134] This is confirmed by a similar statement in the Letter of James, evidently referring to an accepted rule: 'For whoever keeps the whole Law but fails in one point has become guilty of all of it' (Jas 2:10).[135]

Paul's use of a halakha to prove his point against circumcision of gentile Christians has much to teach us. Halakha supports theological Law polemic. This proves that the argument against circumcision, in other words the Law polemic, is not directed against the validity of the halakha. Both this halakha and the Law polemic are auxiliaries in the case against circumcision of gentile Christians. Once again this confirms the theoretical principle proposed earlier: halakha and Law polemic exist independently and are not mutually exclusive.

A reflection of halakha is found in 2:11-14, in the famous and extremely important dispute over table fellowship of Jews and gentiles within the Antiochene church. The same problem is seen in Rom 14f, and we shall return to both passages in chapter 6. Gal 4:1-7 adduces the law of inheritance merely for theological purposes, and 5:16-23 has a list of virtues and vices which is in the category of moral parenesis.

Gal 6:6 refers to the rule that evangelists are entitled to sustenance from their hosts: 'Let him who is taught (κατηχούμενος) the word share all good things with him who teaches (κατηχοῦντι).' The rule is well-established in early Christianity and appears in various forms in Paul's letters;[136] it relates directly to the Jesus tradition cited in 1Cor 9:14. There follow some verses elaborating on well-doing and its future reward remeniscent of 2Cor 8.

Philippians, chapter 3 has another passage reflecting the Law theology.[137] Once again tension with Jews or Jewish Christians about the issue of circumcision is evident, although here it is not the main theme of the letter. On the one hand Paul emphasizes that he, no less than his opponents, was circumcised on the eighth day (3:5); on the other, he emphatically maintains that 'we', the church of Christ, 'are the circumcision, who worship God in Spirit ...and put no confidence in the flesh' (3:3). The implication again is that non-Jewish church

---

[133] tDem 2:5 (absent in ms B by *homoioteleuton*); Sifra, Kedoshim 8 (91a), introduced מכאן אמרו; bBekh 30b; Tanh Wayikra 2 (1b); TanhB Wayikra 3 (2a).

[134] Sanders, *Paul, the Law*, 27-29 and 56 n57-58 underestimates the force of these data. The rules in question do not appear to be 'later instructions' (Sanders ib n58); the conjuction with the דברי חברות (on which in later redactional layers R. Meir, R. Yose be-R. Yehuda and others dispute) points to Second Temple traditions. Parallels with the Essene community code corroborate this; see Lieberman, 'Discipline'; Licht, *Rule Scroll*, 294-303.

[135] See close parallels in tDem 2:3-4; bBekh 30b.

[136] Smit, *Opbouw*, 120 curiously isolates this sentence from the parenetical section 5:13-6:10, which in his analysis is not authentic, and ascribes it to the later editor.

[137] See δικαιοσύνη in 3:6; 3:9 (opposed to πίστις).

members need not be circumcised. Apart from a general reference to financial support (4:15-19), no other practical issues are mentioned in Philippians.

Circumcision is at stake also in **Colossians** and here Paul develops his idea in a remarkable way: 'In him also you were circumcised with a circumcision made without hands, by putting off the body of flesh in the circumcision of Christ' (Col 2:11). While a discussion of this curious passage transcends the limits of this study, we note that Paul implies that the non-Jewish Colossian Christians were not and should not be circumcised.[138]

Very specific is the passage which follows: 'Therefore let no one pass judgment on you in questions of food and drink or with regard to a festival or a new moon or a sabbath. ...If with Christ you died to the elemental spirits of the universe, ...why do you submit to regulations "Do not handle, Do not taste, Do not touch"?' (2:16-23). Clearly the observance of Jewish customs was at stake here, although they appear to have been couched in some doctrine of esoteric angelology (2:18); less emphatically something similar was observed in Galatians. It is not necessary to work out the provenance of this doctrine or to specify the actual halakhot involved here. What is decisive is that in Paul's opinion the non-Jewish Colossian Christians should not be subservient to the doctrine and should not observe the halakhot. An important element however is the rationalism Paul expresses vis-à-vis the halakhot: 'These are only a shadow of what is to come' (2:17). This rationalism also comes to expression in Romans 14, and we shall discuss it when treating that passage.

It is worth remarking that Paul, in pleading against circumcision and Jewish observance for his non-Jewish spiritual children, only partly deploys his justification theology in Colossians. The 'characteristic' terms, νόμος, ἔργον, δικαιοσύνη, and πίστις, do not occur. What we find is the sentence: 'And you, ...God made alive together with him, having forgiven us all our tresspasses, having cancelled the bond which stood against us with its legal demands...' (Col 2:13f).[139] The emphasis is not on justification through faith without works, but on the cosmic shift of power: 'He disarmed the principalities and powers..., triumphing over them in him' (2:15).

The second part of Colossians (chs 3-4) is devoted to parenesis. Paul urges his readers to put away all kinds of unworthy behaviour and put on the new humanity which is continually being renewed in the image of the Creator, and '...in which there is no Greek and Jew, circumcised and uncircumcised, barbarian, Scythian, slave, free man, but Christ is all and in all' (Col 3:10f). While in Galatians and elsewhere this idea functions in the context of justification theology, here it offers basic ethics. After additional ethical parenesis there follows a 'Haustafel' listing mutual duties within the larger family. While all of

---

[138] Cf 4:10f where Paul expressly mentions the only three of his fellow workers (at that moment, cf Rom 16:3) who are 'of the circumcision'. Cf also Phlm 23.

[139] τοῖς δόγμασιν absent in ms 1881, a minuscule with more remarkable variants. The imagery (see Str-B 3, 628) and the 'we' used suddenly (v13!) suggest that Paul engages the Colossians in a Jewish speech situation.

this parenesis is very practical and has obvious relevance for the halakha it remains primarily ethical; reflections or implications of actual halakha do not appear.

Such reflections are to be found in **First Thessalonians**. Interestingly they are, as in First Corinthians, connected with authoritative instructions and apparently also traditions handed down by the Apostle. The last, parenetical part of the letter begins with the words: '...We exhort you ...that as you learned from us how you ought to walk... you do so more and more; for you know what instructions (παραγγελίας) we gave you through the Lord Jesus' (1Thess 4:1f). There follows a brief section framed in 'sanctification' language reminiscent of First Corinthians: 'For this is the will of God, your sanctification... For God has not called us for uncleanliness, but in sanctification' (1Thess 4:3, 7). From these expressions we may conclude that the commandments which follow were part and parcel of Paul's initial Apostolic instruction and probably connected with baptism.[140]

The brief section within the *inclusio* contains three general commandments: '...that you abstain from unchastity; that each one of you know how to acquire a woman for himself in sanctity and honour, not in the passion of lust like the pagans who do not know God; that one is not to overreach and wrong one's brother in business...' (4:3-6). First is the general prohibition of πορνεία which is stressed also in 1Cor 6-7; it was one of the Noachian commandments also reputed to have been part of the Apostles' decree (see below chapter 3). The second commandment is apparently directed against undecorous ways of contracting marriage; the terminology (σκεῦος κτᾶσθαι) reflects Rabbinic usage.[141] Third is a general commandment against wrongdoing in business which resembles the Rabbinic prohibition of הונאה, *honaa*.[142] In other words we have here three halakhot from what we may call Paul's catechism to the gentile church of Thessalonici.

Diplomatically Paul goes on to remind his readers of another basic instruction. He begins (4:9) by mentioning a commandment about which the Thessalonians do not need additional instruction: brotherly love (φιλαδελφία), a matter which is apparently not as unspecific as it seems at first sight. Something practical seems to be involved, since on this item the Thessalonians had not only been long 'taught by God' (θεοδίδακτοί) but they also had a good reputation 'throughout Macedonia' (v10). Paul then exhorts his brethren 'to go beyond that (περισσεύειν μᾶλλον): to aspire to live quietly, to mind your own affairs and to work with your own hands, as we instructed (παρηγγείλαμεν) you, that you may walk respectfully before the outsiders

---

[140] See 1Cor 6:11; 1:30; above p72.

[141] σκεῦος parallels the Hebrew כלי, 'vessel' or 'wife' (see Str-B 3, 632f), and in this sense appears to have been Jewish and Christian Greek usage (see Bauer, *Wörterbuch* sv); κτᾶσθαι corresponds to לקנות, cf mKid 1:1, etc (Str-B ib).

[142] See mBM ch 4; tBM 3:13-29. The prohibition is rooted in the biblical imperative, לא תונו (Exod 22:20; Lev 19:33; 25:14, 17; etc.).

and be dependent of nobody' (v11f). This seems to be the real substance: a re-emphasis of the basic instruction, 'to work with your own hands' and 'be dependent on nobody'. The urge to work for one's own living, including Tora scholars, was prominent in early Rabbinic Judaism, and what we have here is an early Christian parallel. The same conception, connected with Paul's own personal example and with clear halakhic implications, is found in 1Cor 9:4-14; we shall deal with this whole complex in the next chapter.

A general reminder to 'admonish the idlers' follows in the second parenetic section concluding the letter. No additional halakhic material seems to be in evidence. Even so First Thessalonians turns out to be an important document. While it is Paul's earliest letter it turns out to contain, like First Corinthians, affirmative references to halakha connected with Paul's Apostolic instruction.

While Pauline authorship of **Second Thessalonians** is doubtful, the letter contains additional exposition on the commandment to earn one's own living (2Thess 3:6-12). Not only is it emphatically connected with a reference to 'the tradition that you received from us' (3:6) but with the exhortation to follow the Apostle's own example (v7, 9). Again this refers us 1Cor 9:4ff, to be dealt with in chapter 3.

The precious little letter written by Paul to **Philemon** deals with the latter's runaway slave Onesimus who was sent back to him by Paul. This was a matter of strong financial and legal implications which was bound to have a bearing on the halakha. An additional reason to suppose a connection with the halakha is the biblical prohibition of returning a runaway slave: 'You shall not deliver to his master a slave who has escaped from his master to you; he shall dwell with you...' (Deut 23:16f). However it is not clear whether this prohibition applied in Onesimus's case.

Ancient Jewish literature, taking it for granted that the verse was concerned with a gentile slave, was divided on the interpretation of the verse.[143] The difficulty was that a slave was considered his master's possession and must be returned to his owner;[144] this also followed from biblical law (Deut 22:1-3).[145] One answer was that the slave might be escaping from an idolatrous master and in that case should not be forced to return.[146] It must be noted that a slave in a Jewish household was considered a Jew in most respects and upon manumission a Jew in all respects.[147] More difficult to uphold was the literal meaning of the

---

[143] Str-B 3, 668-70 offers some sources, but in a misleading interpretative framework; the same holds for the excursus on slavery Str-B 4, 698-744.

[144] Thus a Tannaic midrash in MidrGad Deut 23:16 (p524); cf the words, 'Can a slave possibly escape from his master?' i.e. without formal manumission. More briefly the midrash appears as a baraita bGit 45a.

[145] Thus Rav Hisda, bGit 45a, quoted also MidrGad ib p525; and anonymously yGit 4, 46a.

[146] Thus the Tannaic midrash, MidrGad ib, pointing to Exod 23:33 for the reason for the commandment; cf TgPs-Yon, and apparently also TgOnk, ad loc. Philo in Leg all 3:194 reflects this interpretation (but cf n148).

[147] See on the status of slaves in ancient Jewish society Stern, 'Aspects', 624-30 (literature p624 n1,

verse.[148] Palestinian Amoraic Sages plainly ruled that it was permitted to return a runaway slave to his master.[149] However discussion evolved around the issue of selling a slave to a non-Jew or to a master outside the Land. An Essene halakha ruled that it was simply forbidden; this is quite probably a reflection of ancient measures against supporting idolatry.[150] According to Tannaic halakha a Jew who sold his slave to a non-Jew or outside the Land was obliged to emancipate the slave.[151] Tannaic midrash connected this ruling with biblical law, interpreting לא תסגיר 'you shall not deliver', as 'you shall not sell'.[152] This interpretation appears to be ancient since it is also found in the same Essene halakha, and apparently it lay at the root of the Tannaic halakha on selling slaves. In the last analysis Amoraic discussion revolved on whether or not a Jew was entitled to sell his runaway slave to a non-Jew, thus regaining his money but relinquishing his slave's adherence to Judaism.[153]

What was Onesimus' status precisely? Most important, it remains unclear whether Philemon was a Jew or not and hence whether the Jewish Law ever applied to start with.[154] In any case Paul, while sending Onesimus back (ἀνέπεμψά, v12), does not turn him over to an idolatrous home but to a Godfearing, Christian household (v1-2). But Paul goes beyond that. He writes to Philemon that he returns Onesimus 'no longer as a slave but more than a slave: as a beloved brother' (v16). The question is whether this remains restricted to Paul's christological pluralism in which 'there is neither slave nor free' (Gal 3:28; Col 3:11). Paul even writes a formal declaration to the effect that any debts Onesimus may have incurred must be payed: 'I, Paul, write this with my own hand, I will repay it' (v18f). This is not suggestive of the position of a slave. Moreover he writes, 'if you consider me your partner (κοινωνόν), receive him as you would receive me' (v17). Again this suggests some financial agreement. The implication seems to be that in Paul's view Onesimus's 'temporary absence' (v15) in principle set him free. This appears to mean that while Paul could 'command' (διατασσεῖν, cf above p83) Philemon to effect Onesimus's

---

p628 n7, p629 n6); on rules and customs applying to them Safrai, 'Home', 750-52; and on ancient Jewish and Hellenistic law Falk, 'Private Law', 509-11 and Wolff, 'Private Law', 542f. Gayer, *Stellung* reviews pagan and non-Rabbinic Jewish sources and all but (p148) ignores Rabbinic sources, which may be caused by the supposed 'Antithese von Gesetz und Evangelium' (p146f). For a survey of research literature see Bartchy, *Mallon chrêsai*, 29-35.

[148] Philo stresses the literal meaning of Deut 23:16 in his apology for the humanity (φιλανθρωπία) of Mosaic Law, Virt 124, but significantly, in his exposition appeals to to Attic law (see note Colson ad loc and appendix p447).

[149] yGit 4, 46a.

[150] CD 12:10f, prohibiting the sale of a slave to gentiles because he is a partner in Abraham's Covenant.

[151] mGit 4:6, supplemented tAZ 3:16, 18-19. And see baraitot and subsequent discussion yGit 4, 46a; bGit 43b-45a; and note by Albeck, *Mishna* 4, 400.

[152] SifDeut 259 (p282), apparently quoting the tradition in MidrGad Deut 23:16 (p525) as a דבר אחר.

[153] tAZ 3:18; yGit 4, 46a (on R. Ammi's teaching cf Sperber, *Dictionary*, 47); bGit 45a.

[154] Therefore Str-B's conclusion ib 670 is unwarranted.

manumission as an Apostle of Christ (v8), he urges him to do so of his own free will (v14, cf 21).[155]

Finally there is the letter to the **Romans**. As outlined above (p59-61) it is exceptional among the Pauline letters in that it addresses a church which seems to include a prominent Jewish-Christian segment, rather than one of the 'churches of the gentiles' (cf Rom 16:4). It pays correspondingly more attention than the other letters to the problems of Jewish-gentile co-existence within the framework of the church and especially the Jewish side of the issue. This is reflected among other features in the elaborate theological discussion on the Jewish Law and the Jewish people which occupies most of the letter (chs 1-11): although 'there is no distinction' the motto is 'the Jew first, and also the Greek'.[156]

In this theological discussion there is little actual halakha. Two basic commandments are referred to in order to point out the sinful state of the pagans: the prohibitions regarding idolatry (1:22-25) and unchastity (1:26f).[157] The ensuing list of vices (1:28-31), while related to the halakha, belongs in the category of moral parenesis. Likewise the sinfulness of Jews is demonstrated from the supposed transgression of the main commandments against theft, adultery and involvement with idolatry (2:21f). These halakhot are viewed as basic to human conduct; a relation with the Noachian commandments is obvious.[158] In Paul's theological argument they represent both the universality of the Tora and of human sin against it. Precisely this rhetorical utilization of halakhot gives the passage its theological and non-halakhic character.[159] Other reflections of halakha in chs 1-11 are restricted to the symbolical and theological. In Rom 2:25-3:9 another theological discussion on circumcision appears; 7:1-3 refers to several halakhot for comparison with salvation through the death of Christ.[160]

---

[155] This conclusion bears on the crux interpretum in 1Cor 7:21, μᾶλλον χρῆσαι. In view of Phlm it is preferable to translate 'but if you can become free, use the opportunity!' Cf Bartchy, *Mallon chrêsai*, chs 4-5.

[156] See above n25f.

[157] Two prohibitions seem included: 'unnatural' intercourse χρῆσις παρὰ φύσιν of women with men, in the halakha called שלא כדרכה, and male homosexuality ἄρσενες ἐν ἄρσεσιν; see sources Str-B 3, 64-74 (but the commentary there is inexact and arbitrary). The explicit mention of male homosexuality seems to ignore lesbianism among the 'unnatural intercourse' of females.

[158] See above p50. See Flusser, *Judaism*, 508.

[159] The reference to Jews robbing pagan temples may reflect some actual event; their other iniquities sound rather unspecific. Gentile morality rated low in Jewish eyes, but the vice list seems to be rhetorical. Sanders, *Paul, the Law*, 123-32 is an interesting discussion of the passage, although the correct conclusion that it 'cannot be fitted into a category otherwise known from Paul's letters' (p132) is not brought to its full significance.

[160] Rom 7:1 in conjunction with 6:7 reflects the Rabbinic principle that 'when dead, man is free from the commandments'; it was connected in the first place with halakha, but of course also had theological significance. Highly relevant for comparison with Paul are the themes of slavery/freedom vis-à-vis the mitswot and their annullment in the age to come. See mKil 9:4; tKil 5:26 (the 'clothes of the high priest' suggest antecedents contemporaneous with Paul); yKil 9, 32a; yKet 12, 34d; bNid

Rom 12-13 contains moral parenesis full of parallels with Jewish teachings; Paul's use of traditional material is obvious here. Especially interesting is 12:9-21 for its connections with ancient Jewish piety, including the teaching of Jesus preserved in Matt 5:44-48. The only specific commandment is to love one's neighbour, which is presented as the summation of the Tora (Rom 13:8-10; cf Gal 5:14 and Matt 7:12).[161] All this is within the sphere of the ethical and homiletical.

Rom 14:1-15:13 forms a contrast. The reference is no longer to general moral examples but to actual problems troubling the Roman church. They concern differences in diet (14:2) associated with purity and impurity (v14, 20) and over the observance of days somehow connected with biblical tradition (v5f). 15:8f shows beyond doubt that these are divergencies in life style between 'the circumcised' and 'the gentiles', or in other words social tensions between Jewish and non-Jewish church members.[162] Here Paul clearly touches on an issue which, in comparison with the preceding theological considerations, had a direct and vital relevance for the Roman church. The style is that of practical parenesis found also in 1Cor 8-10, for example. Relations with Jewish dietary laws are also evident. The remarkable degree of consideration shown for the Jewish side in the conflict illustrates the general attitude of the letter. Thus what we have here is not only a piece of practical parenesis with social implications essential to the historical situation and the interpretation of Romans.[163] We have here a vital document on Paul's attitude towards the Jewish Law in the practical sense, or in other words a crucial text on Paul and the halakha. Along with Gal 2:11-14, Rom 14f will be dealt with in chapter 6 below.

The remainder of Romans is devoted to messages and greetings. Practical topics are the collection for Jerusalem (15:25-32), the help due to deaconess Phoebe from Cenchreae (16:1f), and a warning against strife and dissent (16:17-20). We may surmise that certain halakhot were involved both in the collection for the poor and in the material support for those doing the 'work of the Lord',[164] interestingly in this case a woman, but the references are too general to allow any conclusions as to which halakhot.

61b; bShab 151b; ib 30a; PesRK Acharei mot (p450); TgYon Ps 88:6; cf Str-B 3, 232. – Rom 7:2ff symbolically uses the halakha appearing also 1Cor 7:39, see below ch 3.

[161] See Flusser, 'New Sensitivity', 121-6 for a discussion of these and similar connections. To the sources must be added Sefer Pitron Tora p79f, a Rabbinic version of the double love commandment. The publication in 1978 of this hitherto unknown midrash collection miraculously proved the correctness of Flusser's judgment ten years earlier: '...we deem it incidental that although this dual commandment is found in contemporary extra-Rabbinical Jewish sources, it is wanting in the Rabbinic sources that have been preserved' (ib p113 at n7).

[162] See above p61.

[163] Thus correctly Watson, *Paul*, rejuvenating Baur's interpretation (above p18). But their solution that Paul envisaged a de-judaized church, although supported by theological tradition, is the opposite of Paul's intentions as understood here.

[164] See above n74.

Chapter Three

The Halakha in First Corinthians

The previous chapter described First Corinthians as unique among Paul's letters for its relatively large amount of practical instruction, the positive significance it gives to the Law and the use it makes of Jewish and Jewish-Christian halakhic traditions. This uniqueness does not signify contradiction in Paul, rather it shows his flexibility in responding to very different situations. First Corinthians shows us an aspect of Paul hardly known from the other letters. The present study focuses on that aspect and therefore gives much attention to First Corinthians. The crucial problem of idol food, 1Cor 8-10, requires two separate chapters: chapter 4 discusses the relevant Jewish and Patristic evidence and chapter 5 the passage itself. The present chapter deals with the rest of the halakhic material found in First Corinthians.

Illicit Sexuality (1Cor 5-6)

The series of practical questions which form the main body of First Corinthians starts with the case of a man 'living with his father's wife' (1Cor 5:1). Paul, who considers this a cardinal sin, includes it under the category of πορνεία, best translated 'prohibited sexual relations'. Adhortations against πορνεία occur in most of Paul's letters but are especially prominent in First Corinthians.[1]

The admonition that follows extends for over two chapters. While its contents and sources of authority were dealt with above (p75f), some observations on its structure are in place here. The theme is clearly πορνεία, the word and its cognates recurring throughout the two chapters. But there is a middle section, extending from 6:1 (or 5:12) to 6:11, which deals with a different subject: 'going to law before the unrighteous' (6:1). Paul goes into some detail, reproaching the Corinthians for their lawsuits against each other (v4, 7). But this is clearly of secondary importance; its message supports that of the section as a whole: 'Do you not know that the saints will judge the world?'[2] (v2). The Corinthians, although the behaviour of some of them had not been fitting to the kingdom of God, are 'washed, ...sanctified ...justified' (v11). They are 'called

---

[1] πορνεία 5:1; 6:13, 18; 7:2; πόρνη 6:15f; πόρνος 5:9, 10, 11; 6:9; πορνεύω 6:18; 10:8. πορνεία further 2Cor 12:21; Gal 5:19; Col 3:5; 1Thess 4:3; cf Ef 5:3.
[2] The typical rhetoric formula, οὐκ οἴδατε recurs in this section: 5:6; 6:2, 3, 9, 15, 16, 19. It appears also 3:16; 9:13, 24; and Rom 6:16.

to be the saints' (cf 1:2) who are to judge the outside world. In other words the middle section is a digression which serves to remind the Corinthian Christians of their position and their moral standards. Similar digressions from the main argument appear elsewhere in the letter (above, p77f).

Thus the line of Paul's argument becomes clear. 5:1-13 forcefully presents the law case and the sentence (v1-5), and the command to execute it: 'Drive out the wicked person from among you' (v13). v6-8 remind the Corinthians of their position, comparing it with unleavened Paschal bread; v9-13 re-emphasize what Paul had written in his previous letter: your concern should not be not the immorality of those outside but that of those among you, and this you should do something about. Then follows the digression (6:1-11) on the Corinthian church having its own moral standards and not needing legal assistance in its internal affairs. The final part (6:12-20) returns to the main theme, πορνεία, developing the concept of the 'body'. It starts out from the Ben Sira allusion (above p75f) connecting body, diet and sexuality. The bodies of Christians are 'members of Christ' (v15) and cannot become 'one body' with a prostitute (v15f); they are a 'temple of the Holy Spirit' and should be used for glorifying God (v19f). The motto, which suggests a traditional formula, is: 'Flee from πορνεία!' (v18).[3]

The concept of πορνεία as used by Paul has a Jewish and Jewish-Christian background. Its meaning is rather vague and in that sense parallels the Hebrew זנות, 'unchastity, fornication', a word found already in biblical usage.[4] A more formal equivalent exists in Rabbinic usage, which in certain cases is preferable,[5] as also here: עריות (גלוי), (giluy) arayot, literally 'uncovering nakednesses', i.e. intercourse with near relatives, adultery, homosexuality and bestiality. This is a post-biblical development from the usage in Lev 18 and 20, in particular from the expression לגלות ערוה, 'to uncover nakedness'.[6] Correspondingly Rabbinic tradition calls these chapters in Leviticus עריות, '(the passage on) forbidden degrees',[7] which is also the name of the collection of pertinent halakhot counted among the 'substance of the Tora'.[8]

---

[3] See above ch2 n88.

[4] A prophetical metaphor suggesting the link with idolatry: Num 14:33; Jer 3:2, 9; 13:27; Ezek 23:27; 43:7, 9. It is also used in Qumran, e.g. 1QS 4:10 (in a vice list) and CD 4:17, 20 (see below p111). זנות is proposed as the equivalent of πορνεία in Str-B 3, 342.

[5] In Matt 19:9 and 5:32 πορνεία renders ערוה (Deut 24:1 – see below p110f). Fitzmeyer, 'Matthean Divorce Texts', 88f lists interpretations of πορνεία in Matthew but does not mention the Rabbinical עריות; Luz, Matthäus, 273f disqualifies the link with Lev 18 without necessity.

[6] Lev 18:6. The plural עריות is not found in the Bible. The singular ערוה is found Ezek 16:7, 22; 23:29; and in Rabbinic literature mBek 6:5; yKid 1, 58c line 12f.

[7] עריות: mHag 2:1 (thus Albeck a.l.; cf next n; the verb דורשין and the juxtaposition of עריות, מעשה בראשית and מרכבה indicate that study of the respective biblical sections is meant); פרשת עריות: LevR 24,6 (p559f); yYev 2, 3d.

[8] mHag 1:8; tHag 1:9. In basic form it dates at least from before the common era; see Epstein, Tannaitic Literature, 47. For the precise meaning of עריות here see Epstein ib; Albeck, Mishna 2, 510. 'Perek arayot' designates a post-talmudic tract of sexual halakhot contained in DER ch 1; see M.B. Lerner in Compendia II/3a, 384f.

The prohibition of certain types of sexual relationships both for Jews and gentiles is considered fundamental in the various domains of ancient Jewish literature. Pharisaic-Rabbinic tradition includes גלוי עריות among the three commandments which Jews may never violate, even under threat of death.[9] Similarly the Testaments of the Twelve Patriarchs stress the danger of πορ-νεία throughout and see it as 'the mother of all wickedness'.[10] According to a tradition at least as ancient as the Book of Jubilees (7:20) it was a universal commandment conveyed by Noah to his children. In Rabbinic literature it is associated with the Genesis narrative.[11] Stressing the universal implication of the word 'man' the Rabbis explain:[12] 'How do we know that Noahides are admonished for prohibited sexual relations like Israelites? "(Therefore a man leaves his father and mother and) cleaves to his wife" (Gen 2:24) – and not to another's wife, a male, or a beast.'[13] A prohibition of πορνεία is also contai-ned in the 'Apostolic Decree' (Acts 15) which defined the basic commandments to be observed by all.[14] Hence Paul's emphasis on the prohibition of πορνεία as a 'cardinal sin' for gentiles too is in agreement with the Jewish and Jewish-Christian background of the term.[15]

There was discussion on precisely what degrees of affinity were to be conside-red prohibited for gentiles. The Rabbinic sources distinguish between degrees of affinity forbidden to gentiles and Jews.[16] Forbidden to Jews are those enumerated in the Tora (Lev 18 and 20) plus an additional number of 'degrees forbidden on the authority of the Scribes' עריות מדברי סופרים.[17] The latter could hardly be thought applicable to gentiles,[18] but discussion remained on the biblical prohibitions. This was not a purely theoretical discussion. One ques-tion, for example, was whether or not a proselyte could marry a woman of a degree of affinity forbidden to a Jew either before or after his conversion.[19]

---

[9] The others are idolatry and bloodshed. bSan 74a; ySan 21b; yShev 4, 35a. See Safrai, 'Kiddush ha-Shem'.

[10] TSim 5:3; cf TReub 4:6; TBenj 10:10.

[11] See for this whole complex tAZ 8:4-6; GenR 16,6 (p151); ib 18,24 (p165f); yKid 1, 58b-c; yYev 11, 12a; bSan 56a-58b; bYev 97b-98b; MidrGad Gen 2:16 (p83); ib 2:24 (p91f); YalShim Gen 2:16 (p77f); ib 2:25 (p86-88). The singular tradition ascribed to R. Yehuda must not be overlooked, however: 'Adam [as distinct from Noah] was commanded regarding idolatry only' (bSan 56b).

[12] Another implication was perceived in the verse, which was also utilized by Jesus and Paul; see below p115f.

[13] Thus brief summary GenR 18,6 (p167); ib 16,6 (p150); yKid 1, 58c; cf bSan 58a. The universality was also connected with the repeated איש איש in Lev 18:6, Sifra Aharei 85d; yKid 1, 58b; bSan 57b.

[14] See above p50.

[15] Cohen, *Jewish and Roman Law*, 338, 380 compares with the Roman concept of *jus gentium*. For our subject see ib 338-43.

[16] yKid 1, 58a-b (cf yYev 11, 12a); bSan 57a-b (cf bYev 97b-98b).

[17] mYev 2:4 (ms K and piska in yYev 2, 3d). Other Mishna versions and tYev 2:4, שניות מדברי סופרים. They are listed in the Talmudim, yYev 2, 3d; bYev 21a; and DER 1 (= 'Perek arayot', above n8).

[18] The gemara bYev 22a makes this conclusion explicit.

[19] Sources in n22. Another discussion concerned the categories for which a gentile was actually considered punishable according to Jewish but not gentile law. The conclusion was that only one category came into account: the betrothed girl; yKid 1, 58b-c; bSan 57b. Cf tAZ 8:4 (mutilated); GenR 18,5 (p166).

Accepted rules of thumb were that 'a gentile [i.e. a proselyte] has no father'[20] and 'a gentile become proselyte is like a newborn child'.[21] In principle this meant that the mother's relations were forbidden but not the father's; however the exact consequences were a matter of discussion.[22]

Among the categories discussed was one which we shall discuss here: 'the father's wife'. In the Tora this category is juxtaposed to the physical 'mother' (Lev 18:7), which indicates that the stepmother is meant.[23] This is also the case in the halakha.[24] The question was whether this category was among the sexual prohibitions for gentiles mentioned in the verse, 'Therefore a man leaves his father and mother' (Gen 2:24); 'man' taken to indicate the universal implication. The Babylonian Talmud preserves a discussion in which R. Eliezer explains 'father and mother' as prohibiting both 'his father's and mother's sister'. On the other hand the more moderate R. Akiva explains:[25] '"his father" – his father's wife; "his mother" – his real mother'.[26] According to a tradition cited in Palestinian sources, R. Meir prohibited sexual relations between proselytes and their step-sisters either by their father or their mother and their mother's sister, though allowing their father's sister; while R. Yehuda allowed a step-sister by the father and only prohibited step-sisters by the mother and the mother's sister by her mother.[27] This tradition also appears in the Babylonian Talmud, but in a conflicting version from which it is concluded that both R. Meir and R. Eliezer allowed the father's wife.[28] However a comparison with the Palestinian sources reveals that R. Eliezer was the most restrictive and R. Akiva the most lenient regarding sexual prohibitions for gentiles, while the latter's pupils, R. Meir and R. Yehuda, were somewhere in the middle. It should also be noted that intercourse with the father's wife was among the gravest sins for Jews, ultimately punishable by stoning.[29] The Babylonian solution notwithstanding, the conclusion must be that all agreed on the prohibi-

---

[20] GenR 18,5 (p165).

[21] bYev 22a; 48b; 97b; bBekh 47a.

[22] See extended discussion between R. Meir and R. Yehuda, yYev 11, 12a and related fragments GenR 18,5 (p165); bSan 57b-58a; bYev 97b-98b. The Babylonian baraitot do not seem fully authentic, see below.

[23] See Str-B 3, 343f. On Str-B's further comments see below. The prohibition is reiterated in Lev 20:11; Deut 23:1; 27:20; cf Gen 25:22; 49:4; 2Sam 16:21f.

[24] mSan 7:4; mKer 1:1; tSan 10:1.

[25] See also R. Akiva, bYev 98a, 'A proselyte may marry the wife of his brother by mother' (qualifying Lev 18:16).

[26] bSan 58a. The wording of MidrGad Gen 2:24 (p91) reflects Maimonides, Hilkhot Melakhim 9:5.

[27] yYev 11, 12a; GenR 18,5 (p165, see comments).

[28] bSan 57b-58a; bYev 98a-b: R. Meir allows his sister by father and prohibits the father's sister by his mother; only in the third clause which allows the mother's sister by her father but not by her mother is there agreement with the Yerushalmi. Thus the Bavli ascribes the rule of affinity by mother to R. Meir instead of R. Yehuda, stresses it as an absolute principle and in consequence manipulates the baraita.

[29] Along with intercourse with the mother and daughter-in-law, idolatry, homosexuality and bestiality: mSan 7:4.

tion of the father's wife for gentiles.[30]

A word must be said here on STRACK-BILLERBECK's *Kommentar* which has some remarkable comments to make on this issue. It offers an unusual amount of halakhic material, including extensive quotations from Rashi, the Tosafot and even the Shulhan Arukh. Neglecting the Palestinian sources, however, it bases its presentation on the forced conclusion of the Babylonian Talmud to the effect that R. Eliezer, although prohibiting the father's and mother's sister, allowed marriage with the father's wife.[31] The commentary declares this to be 'the older opinion' and arbitrarily concludes: 'We can be certain that in New Testament times the majority of Jewish Sages would not object to a gentile's or proselyte's marrying his stepmother.' Furthermore such Rabbinic lenience is thought to have been far from helpful in redressing the moral laxity of the Corinthian church. One can be critical about the commentary's literary and historical judgment, but the final conclusion is surprising: 'At any rate we have an example here of how utterly meaningless the Jewish halakha had become for Paul, the Rabbinic-educated Apostle, in assessing serious moral questions.'[32] It appears that Billerbeck, in spite of his sustained effort, had not succeeded in understanding the spirit of the ancient halakha here and withdrew to the safe ground of Protestant doctrine. More serious is that his conclusions prevent the reader from grasping the halakhic background of Paul's teaching.

Returning now to Paul we are able to reconstruct the case he is dealing with: this is someone living with 'his father's wife', as distinct from his physical mother. This, prominent Tannaim agreed, also is prohibited for gentiles. It is a sin, Paul states, which is 'unheard of' even among gentiles (1Cor 5:1). This information is interesting enough, but it only functions as an additional argument.[33] We can safely assume that the Apostolic Jewish church fully agreed with the fundamental renunciation of the act. 'Though absent in the body' Paul condemns the perpetrator 'in the name of the Lord Jesus', declaring that the congregation should solemnly 'deliver him to Satan for the destruction of the flesh, that his spirit may be saved in the Day of the Lord'[34] (v3-5). Instruction given in his previous letter (v9) is made more specific here: Christians are 'not to associate with anyone who, bearing the name of brother, has prohibited sexual relations, is greedy, or practices idolatry, slander, drunkenness, or robbery – not even to eat with such a one' (v11). In other words the perpetrator is excommunicated and, by human standards, excluded from salvation.

It is interesting to compare Paul's solemn judgment with the category of punishment in ancient Jewish law called 'death at the hands of Heaven'.[35] In

---

[30] I am indebted to Shmuel Safrai for basic hints in this complicated matter.

[31] bSan 58a; bYev 98b. See previous notes.

[32] Str-B 3, 358.

[33] See Conzelmann p123 n29 on incest prohibitions in Roman law.

[34] Omitting 'Ἰησοῦ Χριστοῦ with P46, B, some minuscles, Tertullian and Ephiphanius. Cf Acts 2:20; 2Pet 2:10 for this prophetic expression (Isa 2:12; 13:6, 9; Joel 2:11; 3:4; Mal 3:23[22], etc).

[35] I am indebted to David Flusser for this suggestion.

theory, as in biblical law, the principal cases of prohibited sexual relations were ultimately punishable by execution.[36] But in practice Jewish courts mostly delivered those convicted to 'extirpation' כרת *karet*,[37] explained as heavenly punishment in the form of an untimely death.[38] This punishment reflects a lesser degree of severity.[39] A death sentence was possible only when the act was done in conscious neglect of explicit, repeated warnings by the witnesses.[40] The requirements imposed on the testimony made execution according to Pharisaic-Rabbinic criminal law practically impossible.[41] In addition the Roman government monopolized the power to try capital cases.[42] In terms of criminal law 'extirpation' was mostly executed by way of disciplinary flogging, aimed not only at deterring the perpetrator from recidivism but at his repentance and eternal salvation.[43]

It seems that, apart from flogging, these elements were also found in the sentence pronounced by Paul in his letter. Flogging was a prerogative of the Jewish communities[44] for which the church in Corinth would hardly qualify. What Paul does mention is the punishment of a case of illicit sexual relations גלוי עריות, as applying to gentiles, by excommunication and 'delivery to Satan for the destruction of the flesh' כרת, 'that his spirit may be saved in the Day of the Lord'.

The previous chapter focused on the two biblical verses which function as sources of authority in this section (p75). It is interesting to examine the halakhic implications attached to them in Rabbinic literature. Gen 2:24 was seen as representing the prohibition of certain sexual relations for all human-kind, exemplified in cohabitation with a prostitute (below p115). These are the exact same elements in Paul's admonishment of gentile Christians in Corinth: 'Do you not know that he who cleaves to a prostitute becomes one body with her? For, he says, 'The two shall become one flesh'' (1Cor 6:16).

The other verse quoted is Deut 17:7, 'Drive out the wicked person from among you' (1Cor 5:13). The quotation occurs in the digression on going to law with 'outsiders' (5:12-6:11), the implication being that the Corinthians themselves must try their own internal cases. Now in view of the above observations the context of the verse quoted is highly relevant. It comes at the end of a passage which states that an accusation of a capital sin (in this case idolatry) must be

---

[36] mSan 7:4 (punished by stoning); 9:1 (burning); 11:1 (strangulation). The list is continued in mMak 3:1 with those forbidden degrees punishable by flogging.

[37] mKer 1:1 includes all categories (previous n) among the 36 acts punishable by כרת.

[38] See Albeck, *Mishna* 5, 243f.

[39] mSan 9:6; 11:5; cf 7:8; mYev 4:13; mMeg 1:5.

[40] mSan 5:1; tSan 9:1; ib 12:7; ySan 5, 22d top. And see the rule yKid 1, 58c top: 'with two witnesses and 23 judges, with previous warning and stoning'.

[41] mSan 4:5-5:5; cf ib 6:5; mMak 1:10 for the intentional discouragement of capital punishment.

[42] Cf the tradition that '40 years before the destruction of the Temple the power to judge capital cases was taken from Israel', ySan 7, 24b; ib 1, 18a; cf bSan 41a. See M. Stern, in *Compendia* I/1, 336-40; S. Safrai, ib 397-400; H.H. Cohn – L.I. Rabinowitz, 'Capital Punishment' (*EJ* 5, 142-7; bibl.).

[43] mMak ch 3. See I. Ta-Shma, 'Karet' (*EJ* 10, 788f); H.H. Cohn, 'Divine Punishment' (*EJ* 6, 120-22).

[44] mMak 3:12 mentions the חזן הכנסת (overseer of the community) as supervising its execution.

'inquired into diligently', that the sentence must be based 'on the evidence of two or three witnesses', and that when the convicted person is stoned 'the hand of the witnesses shall be first against him' (Deut 17:4-7). These are cornerstones in the Tannaic halakha for procedures in capital cases.[45] Here Paul is not arguing for capital punishment but for something like the lesser punishment of 'extirpation', and his verdict evidently relates to Pharisaic-Rabbinic criminal law. Significantly, the same holds true for the early Christian disciplinary procedure seen in Matt 18:15-17, which mentions the need for two or three witnesses and a final conviction by a solemn congregation.[46]

This having been stated, the wording of Paul's sentence of 'extirpation' offers us other possible associations. He pronounces that the convicted must be 'delivered to Satan for the destruction of the flesh'. In the Testaments of the Twelve Patriarchs and related literature, Satan or Beliar (cf 2Cor 6:15) is a common name for the Ruler of evil,[47] who sometimes seems especially connected with prohibited sexual relations.[48] The association appears to be with the fallen angels who defiled themselves with the 'daughters of man' (Gen 6:1-4), an idea prominent in the Enoch tradition.[49] What Paul apparently means is that Heaven leaves the execution of 'extirpation' to Satan;[50] this also reminds one vaguely of Job 1:6-12. This passage is one of those which gives us a glimpse of Paul's realistic angelology.[51]

Celibacy, Marriage and Divorce (1Cor 7)

The practical teaching contained in 1Cor 7 presents us with an unusual convergency between Paul, Jesus and ancient Jewish law.[52] Apart from Paul's parenesis and the synoptic Gospels, our sources include Rabbinic literature, the Qumran scrolls and various other Hebrew and Greek Jewish writings. Our investigation will not only reveal a degree of variety and development within Pharisaic-Rabbinic halakha but also the existence of a distinct halakhic tradition more severe than that of the Pharisaic Sages. This is of interest not only for the history of Paul and early Christianity, but that of ancient Judaism and its halakha in general.

---

[45] mSan ch 5-6, esp 6:4; tSan ch 9; SifD 149 (p203f); MidrGad Deut 17 (p282-6).

[46] The quote there is from Deut 19:15. On the repeated warning (by the witnesses!) cf tSan 12:7. Incidentally, Str-B 1, 787 found here another opportunity for expressing anti-Jewish views.

[47] See notes in Charlesworth, *OTP* 1, 782f. Souls are 'taken captive' by Beliar, TIss 7:7; TZeb 9:8; TDan 5:11. Cf CD 12:2; 1QS 1:18, 23f.

[48] See esp TReub 4:7, 11; 6:3; CD 4:15-17 (referring to a Testament of Levi).

[49] 1En ch 6-12; 69:4f; 2En 31:3-6; Jub 4:21f, cf 10:5; TDan 5:6 (cf TSim 5:3f; TJuda 18:1; TNaft 4:1; TBen 9:1). And cf the NT letter of Jude v6-8, 14.

[50] See also the long note in Weiss, *Korintherbrief*, 129-33.

[51] Esp 1Cor 11:10, below p136.

[52] Yarbrough, *Not Like the Gentiles*, stressing Paul's assimilation to Stoic marriage conceptions, misses these connections. There is also a theological motive. Having correctly considered the rabbinic *nidda* and levirate laws hardly relevant to (mainly) gentile Corinth, he declares: 'More important, however, Paul himself doubtless considered niddah and levirate marriage issues which, like circumcision, had nothing to do with believing the gospel' (28f).

The practical, normative character of the chapter has already been noted. Urgent advice, direct instruction and brief explanation prevail; there is no exposition of Scripture. In a way this is one of the most 'un-theological' chapters of First Corinthians and of Paul's letters. The one exception is 7:17-24 which briefly refers to the Law theology and makes a furtive reference to sacred Writings. That passage will be dealth with in the concluding chapter.

Let us analyse the contents of the chapter with reference to its aim:

vv1-9 deal with celibacy and sexual abstinence in marriage. Although preferring celibacy Paul thinks it wise that everyone be married; and married partners must be moderate as regards abstinence.

vv10-16 prohibit divorce except where an unbelieving partner wishes to separate.

vv17-24, the theological digression of the chapter, argues for pluriformity. It is a fragment of the Law theology used here as a digression in the discussion on marriage and celibacy.

vv25-38 resume the question of celibacy, for virgins. Paul personally prefers celibacy 'because of the present distress', but for others considers it 'no sin' to marry.

v39f define the conditions for remarriage of widows, repeating the preference for celibacy.

The theme of celibacy is prominent: it appears in v1, 7-9, 25-38, and 40. Moreover the introduction in v1, 'Now concerning the matters about which you wrote', announces a discussion of written questions. But in v25 another introduction follows: 'Now concerning the virgins'. Given the prominence of the celibacy theme this reads as a further specification of the former introduction. Thus the chapter appears to respond to a specific question about the desirability of celibacy. The theme of divorce fits in; it seems to reflect the question whether married couples should separate or divorce and live as celibates. The way in which Paul indicates his distinct source of authority in each case (above p76f) gives us the impression that the Corinthians had asked about the degree to which these requirements were obligatory.

This reveals the function of another literary aspect: Paul addresses various distinct groups in succession. After a general treatment of celibacy and sexual abstinence three groups are addressed: 'To the unmarried and the widows I say...' (v8); 'To the married I give charge...' (v10); 'To the others I say...' (v12). Then after the theological intermezzo to stress pluralism the theme of celibacy returns with regard to yet another group: 'Now concerning the virgins' (v25). Finally a rule about marriage and divorce is given which in effect concerns widows (v39f). The emphasis in each case is summarized with the phrase: 'He who marries... does well and he who does not marry will do better' (v38).

In short, the chapter answers the Corinthians' request for clarification about the desirability of celibacy and sexual abstinence, or even divorce, for the sake of a sanctified life. In the course of his treatment Paul touches on a range of subjects which not only clearly relate to the halakha but also involve the direct implementation of halakhic elements. These will concern us here.

1Cor 7:1f introduces the theme and immediately states Paul's dual approach: 'Now concerning the matters about which you wrote: it is well for a person (ἀνθρώπῳ) not to touch a woman; but in view of the danger of unchastity (πορνεία), each man should have his own wife and each woman her own husband.' The opening phrase 'not to touch a woman' encompasses both celibacy and sexual abstinence within marriage. In vv2-7 Paul goes on to limit such abstinence within reasonable boundaries.

Paul expresses his preference for celibacy briefly in v1, 7-9 and 40, and gives a longer exposition in v25-38. He gives two motivations. The first is eschatological: 'In view of the present distress it is well for a person to remain as he is... the appointed time has grown short... for the form of this world is passing away' (v26, 29, 31). This motif has received ample attention in the wake of SCHWEITZER's eschatological interpretation.[53] The second motif, that of expediency and devotion, must be seen separately. 'I want you to be free from worry': the unmarried person 'worries about the things of the Lord' only and 'can be holy both in body and in spirit', but someone who is married 'worries about the things of the world', how to please one's partner, and 'is divided' (v32-34). On the other hand this teaching unmistakably reflects a negative view of sexuality.

It is illuminating to compare Paul's attitude towards marriage and celibacy with Second Temple Judaism. A rejection of marriage by the Essenes is reported by both Josephus and Philo. They did not condemn it on principle but shunned pleasure, strove for self-control and avoided contact with female 'wantonness' and 'egoism'.[54] Josephus adds that one branch of Essenes held procreation in higher esteem and allowed marriage as long as it resulted in childbirth.[55] This is echoed by both Philo and Josephus themselves, who also considered marriage necessary and in accordance with nature, but only for the sake of procreation; sexual relations are not defensible as such.[56]

The idea of marriage as a concession to human nature in order to check unchastity, and hence the view of sexual relations as inherently negative, is variously reflected in Rabbinic and other ancient Jewish literature.[57] The unavoidable corollary in a patriachal society – the prototypical male projection –

---

[53] Schweitzer, *Paulus*, 303.

[54] Josephus War 2:120f; Philo Hypoth 11:14-17.

[55] War 2:160f. This is confirmed by CD 7:6-9 = 19:2-5. On female remains at Qumran cemeteries see references given by Dimant, 'Qumran', 484 n8. According to Josephus the Essenes allowed a three years' probation, which is much stricter than the minimum term of ten years prescribed by the Tannaim for an unfruitful marriage to be dissolved, mYev 6:6.

[56] See Heinemann, *Bildung*, 261-77, pointing out also Greek parallels; Belkin, *Alexandrian Halakah*, 37-42; id, *Philo*, 219-22.

[57] TLevi 9:9f. The same idea arises from the *derasha* on Gen 2:24 as formulated in GenR 16,6 (p150), see above. Cf the practice of the 'Early Hasidim' as opposed to the majority of Tannaim (bNid 38a-b; see Safrai, 'Mishnat hasidim', 144f), and the chaste behaviour of some of the Tannaim (R. Eliezer, see Gilat, *Eliezer*, 277f; R. Yose, see Belkin, *Alexandrian Halakah*, 38).

was the view of woman as the embodiment of earthly passion.[58] More positively both Shammaites and Hillelites, while disagreeing on specifics, agreed that marriage and procreation are major divine commandments: 'No one should abstain from "being fruitful and multiplying" unless he has children.'[59] In addition, as we shall see, Rabbinic tradition acknowledged marital sexual relations even as independent from the aim of procreation. References to celibacy as a sacred aim are rare in Rabbinic tradition.[60] Celibacy of widows is a separate phenomenon which seems to reflect a specific, pious tradition.[61]

As to the benefits of marriage Paul appears to vacillate between the negative view of the Essenes and and the more positive view of mainstream Jewry. Repeatedly stressing his personal preference for celibacy, he concedes in each case that marriage is beneficial (v1f, 7-9, 27f, 36-38, 39f). He summarizes this dual approach several times: 'I wish that all persons were as I am; but each has his own gift χάρισμα from God, one such and another such' (v7); 'he who marries his virgin does well and he who does not marry does better' (v38). The reasons for marriage are negative: 'In view of the dangers of unchastity διὰ τὰς πορνείας, each man should have his own wife and each woman her own husband' (1Cor 7:2). The same idea, connected with a divine commandment, is expressed in 1Thess 4:3f, 'This is the will of God, …that you abstain from unchastity; that each one of you know how to acquire a woman for himself in sanctity and honour.'[62]

Paul's preference for celibacy reminds one of the attitude which Matthew ascribes to Jesus (Matt 19:10-12)[63] and which certain circles associated with John the Baptist.[64] Paul argues for celibacy in view of 'the things of the Lord' (1Cor 7:32); similarly the Matthean Jesus, in view of 'the Kingdom of Heaven' (Matt 19:12). Hence marriage and sexual intercourse are considered remote from the Kingdom. This view coincides with that of pious Jewish circles. But it should be noted that according to Paul's testimony (1Cor 9:5) both Jesus' brothers (James and others) and his most important disciple, Cephas, were married. Therefore if Jesus had a preference for celibacy it was purely personal and not obligatory for others. In addition Paul states he has 'no command of the

---

[58] The 'Gospel of Truth' 45:23-46:15 derives sexual desire from Eve's sin with the serpent, a tradition found also in the Adam and Eve narratives: Life of Adam and Eve 18:1-4; Apoc Mos 19:3; and see wealth of material in Ginzberg, *Legends* 5, 133f. TReub ch 5 (cf TJuda 15:5f) presents women as the seducers even of angels (Gen 6:1-4) and therefore prescribes a modest dress and hair style. This reminds of 1Cor 11:10.

[59] mYev 6:6; tYev 8:4-7 (cf previous n); bYev 61b-64a. See Safrai, 'Home', 748.

[60] Interesting is the explanation Ben Azzai gives for his unmarried state: 'My soul lusts for Tora' (tYev 8:7; GenR 34,14, p326f). See Safrai ib n5 for other sources.

[61] Safrai, 'Home', 788f.

[62] Above p91.

[63] Flusser, 'Montages', 45 n10 considers this solely Matthean passage spurious on linguistic and conceptual grounds and doubts Jesus' preference for celibacy.

[64] John the Baptist apparently was a lifelong *nazir* who abstained from wine (Matt 11:18; Luke 1:15, 7:33). According to some traditions Elijah, with whom John was identified (Matt 11:14; 17:11-13) was a celibate, see Ginzberg, *Legends* 6, 316. The 'Gospel of Truth' from Nag Hammadi associates John with celibacy (cod IX, 30:24-31:5; 45:6-22).

Lord' about the virgins (1Cor 7:25). This means he did not possess the celibacy teaching attributed to Jesus and considered it a personal opinion (γνώμη, 7:25, 40). This is expressed positively in his teaching on sexual relations.

This is what Paul has to say on abstinence by married couples:

> The husband should give to his wife the conjugal rights, and likewise the wife to her husband. For the wife does not rule over her own body, but the husband does; likewise the husband does not rule over his own body, but the wife does. Do not refuse one another except [perhaps][65] by agreement for a period, in order to devote yourselves to prayer, but then come together again, lest Satan tempt you through lack of self-control. (1Cor 7:3-5)

Here Paul moves along the lines of the Tannaic halakha. Rabbinic tradition stressed the rights of the wife on the basis of Exod 21:10, 'He shall not diminish her food, her clothing, or her marital rights' שארה, כסותה ועונתה. While the Tannaim disputed the precise meaning of these ancient terms, the right to sexual intercourse was understood to be included.[66] Paul's term for 'conjugal right': ἡ ὀφειλή, 'what is due', may reflect any of those interpretations.[67] As to periodic abstinence for prayer, general references to it occur in early Jewish writings.[68] Tannaic halakha defined the maximum period for which a married man was allowed to abstain in various specified circumstances, and if he exceeded it, his wife had the right to divorce. Tora study, for example, allowed him a period of 30 days separation 'without [her] consent'.[69] On the same level Paul stressed mutual consent as a condition for abstinence.

The idea that in marriage one's body belongs to the partner is also found in a Rabbinic tradition which praises 'him who loves his wife as his own body and honours her more than his own body'.[70] This is a humane definition of the right of the woman to her own body and that of her partner; yet she remains a subordinate partner within a patriarchal system. A closer parallel to the same tradition appears in a letter of some associate of Paul's: 'Even so men should love their wives as their own bodies; he who loves his wife loves himself' (Ef 5:28). The verses following refer to Gen 2:24, 'the two shall become one flesh', and it is clear that the writer simply draws on Jewish tradition, patriarchy included. Here we perceive a certain contrast with Paul. His definition of the partners' right to each other's body has a remarkable reciprocity which transcends both the accepted Rabbinic conception and that of his associate. Its emancipatory potential should be gladly welcomed, even though it is not immediately clear what circumstances or sources inspired him to this. As we shall have occasion to observe below, Paul's actual conception of women was

[65] Lacking in P46, B, r.

[66] שארה and עונתה were alternately interpreted as 'money' and 'intercourse'; see mNed 5:6; Mekh p258f; MekhRSbY p167f; TgOnk and Ps-Yon Exod 21:10; and other sources in Str-B 3, 368-72. Cf also Daube, *New Testament*, 365.

[67] Cf LXX Exod 21:10, τὰ δέοντα καὶ τὸν ἱματισμὸν καὶ τὴν ὁμιλίαν.

[68] TNaft 8:8; cf Eccl 3:5.

[69] mNed 5:6 (see Albeck a.l.); tNed 5:6.

[70] bYev 62b.

not much different from his contemporaries either.

Various other questions remain as to the background of Paul's teaching. His personal preference for celibacy, independent of the tradition of Jesus, points to somewhere in Essene surroundings. But the acceptance of marriage as a necessary and legitimate option for others coincides with mainstream Judaism. Quite in line with Pharisaic-Rabbinic tradition is his humane stance on the sexual relationship of married partners. In short the usual demarcations of 'Pharisaism' and 'Essenism' seem inadequate to locate Paul.

DIVORCE IN RABBINIC HALAKHA AND QUMRAN

In the course of his treatise on the desirability of celibacy Paul also touches on divorce. This is an important subject which, more than celibacy, has wide ramifications in ancient Jewish an Jewish-Christian tradition. For a correct assessment we must compare Paul's teaching with the synoptic Jesus tradition, and both must be viewed in the light of the ancient Jewish halakha in its various forms. We shall start with ancient Judaism, then study the synoptic tradition and finally we shall turn to Paul himself.

A mishnaic halakha defines the establishment of the marriage bond and its legal termination, i.e. divorce, as follows:[71]

> The woman is acquired by three means and acquires herself (i.e. her freedom) by two means: she is acquired by money or by writ or by intercourse... And she acquires herself by a divorce bill or by death of the husband. (mKid 1:1)[72]

While Rabbinic halakha did a great deal to secure the rights of women, ancient Jewish marriage law was based structurally in biblical patriarchal society.[73] In accepted practice the woman's consent in the marriage was a necessary condition and she could also demand divorce in certain circumstances.[74] Formally the man remained the one who effected marriage and divorce, the woman being 'acquired' or 'sent away'. Similar terminology applied to the acquisition and manumission of slaves mentioned in the same context (mKid 1:2-3).

On the other hand Hellenistic law, which operated with a much more individualized personality concept, allowed divorce at the wife's initiative.[75] As we shall see, this situation is of direct relevance to 1Cor 7. While in Hellenistic legal usage formal marriage remained a possibility especially in conservative circles, a legal marriage bond could be established informally by the conjugal union.

---

[71] See introduction and additional note by Albeck, *Mishna* 3, 265f, 407f; Falk, *Introduction* 2, 276-316; general survey in Moore, *Judaism* 2, 119-27; material in Str-B 1, 312-20. Lucid in its compactness is Blau, *Ehescheidung*, covering biblical, ancient Jewish and early Christian divorce law.

[72] See Epstein, *Tannaitic Literature*, 52-4. The antiquity of the tradition was posited by the Savoraim on the grounds of the use of the verb קנה i.e. buy, as against קידש used in ch2. The discussion of Beit Shammai and Beit Hillel on the amount of 'money' presupposes existence of the halakha itself.

[73] For more on the position of women see below p133-5.

[74] Cf Safrai, 'Home', 790f.

[75] Divorce at the woman's initiative is in evidence also in the Elephantine papyri, see Blau, *Ehescheidung*, 15-20. This seems to reflect Egyptian circumstances.

However in this situation 'the husband had no conjugal power over his wife. ...Both spouses could dissolve the marriage at will and without formality, by mutual agreement, or by expelling or deserting the partner...' This was contrary to Jewish law but in a different way also to ancient Greek and Roman law, in which the power (κυριεία, *manus*) of the husband was essential.[76] This then was the apparent background of three cases of women from the Herodian family who 'departed from' their husbands for another marriage which, as Josephus comments, was contrary to the Law of the Jews.[77] It seems that execution of marriage or divorce according to Hellenic law was a possibility open to certain Jewish aristocratic circles,[78] which of course drew criticism from other Jews.[79]

Here we are concerned with the legal means by which in ancient Jewish law the woman 'acquires herself' and thus becomes free to re-marry: i.e. divorce and death of the husband. Divorce was legally executed by handing the woman a bill which stipulated her freedom to remarry. This was according to biblical usage as referred to in the Tora verse. '...And if she is disgraceful in his eyes and he finds in her a thing of shame, and he writes a bill of divorce, puts it in her hand and expels her from his house...' (Deut 24:1). The verse introduces a more complicated case and hence simply presupposes the possibility of divorce with a bill. The Mishna preserves two versions of the essential divorce formula, one in Hebrew and the other, quoted by R. Yehuda, in Aramaic: '"Lo, you are permitted to any man." R. Yehuda says: "Let this be from me your bill of divorce, ...that you may go and be married to any man you want."'[80]

What were the possible grounds for divorce? There was a protracted discussion on this issue which, as we shall see below, seems to have originated in the earlier Second Temple period. The discussion turned on the meaning of the

[76] Wolff, 'Hellenistic Private Law'; quote p540. Wolff, *Written and Unwritten Marriages* investigates Hellenistic papyri and concludes that there is no basic difference between the ἄγραφος γάμος, which allowed dissolution by either partner, and a 'written marriage'. Cf now GenR 18,5 (p166) and yKid 1, 58c: 'Either they (= non-Jews) have no divorce or both partners divorce each other; R. Yohanan says: his wife can divorce him and give him a ריפודין' (= *repudium*, see Cohen, *Jewish and Roman Law*, 384-6; Sperber, *Dictionary*, 88f). See also below n109.

[77] According to Ant 15:259 Salome issued her own divorce bill 'not in accordance with Jewish law' since a woman who has 'departed' (διαχωρισθείση) is not allowed to remarry until the husband 'sends her away' (ἀφίεντος, as in most mss), i.e. gives her a divorce bill. Similarly Ant 18:136, 'Herodias, choosing to flout ancestral custom (ἐπὶ συγχύσει φρονήσασα τῶν πατρίων), married Herod (Antipas) after having parted (διαστᾶσα) from her husband, that one's brother by the same father, while he was still alive'. Finally in Ant 20:142f Drusilla was convinced by Felix to 'leave her husband' (τὸν ἄνδρα καταλιποῦσαν) and marry him, thus 'transgressing the ancestral laws' παραβῆναί τε τὰ πάτρια νόμιμα).

[78] Cf the Greek marriage contract from the archives of the Jewish matron Babata stating that it was drawn up 'according to Hellenic law' (Yadin, *Bar Kochba*, 246); cf Tomson, 'Names', 268-72. Unconvincingly Brooten, 'Frauen im alten Judentum' maintains that the three cases in Josephus indicate the alternative possibility within Jewish law that women initiate divorce.

[79] Well known is John the Baptist's reprimand of Herodias and Herod Antipas, Mark 6:18f parr; the issue is, as Josephus' complicated sentence Ant 18:136 indicates (above n77), both illegal divorce by Herodias and illegal marriage by Herod. On the confusion of names see Schürer, *History* 1, 344.

[80] mGit 9:3.

phrase 'a thing of shame' עָרְוַת דָּבָר in Deut 24:1. In Deut 23:15 the same expression is used referring to desecration of the encampment by nocturnal pollution or excrement. This would imply the general meaning 'anything shameful' or 'disgraceful'. But the Sages differed on the precise meaning. Two directly related passages preserved in different collections give the various opinions:

> Beit Shammai say: A man should not divorce his wife except if he found in her unchastity עֶרְוָה, for it is said: "...if he found in her 'shame'" (Deut 24:1). But Beit Hillel say: Even if she spoilt his dish – for it is said: "...if he found in her 'a thing' דָּבָר". R. Akiva says: Even if he found another more beautiful than her, as it is said: "...and if she is disgraceful in his eye..." (ib).[81]

> R. Yishmael says: ...Even as there (Deut 23:15)[82] "a thing of shame" means unchaste and idolatrous ideas הִרְהוּר עֶרְוָה וַעֲבוֹדָה זָרָה, so here (24:1) "a thing of shame" means unchaste and idolatrous ideas. Rabbi says: ...Even as there "a thing of shame" implies anything disgraceful מְשׁוּם בִּזָּיוֹן, so here "a thing of shame" implies anything disgraceful.[83]

The difference between Beit Shammai and Beit Hillel in interpreting עָרְוַת דָּבָר was in their respective view on the sanctity of the marriage bond. Beit Shammai took a strict view and emphasized the word עֶרְוָה, which in Rabbinic Hebrew denotes sexual abuse and unchaste behaviour.[84] Beit Hillel, emphasizing דָּבָר, accepted 'anything' i.e. including non-sexual motives as a ground for divorce. These views received several later elaborations. R. Yishmael, staying rather close to the spirit of the written text and its Shammaite interpretation, compared both passages and emphasized דָּבָר in the sense of impious or immoral 'words' or 'thoughts'. In a free interpretation R. Akiva stressed the woman's 'grace', expounding the word חֵן. Rabbi (Yehuda the Prince) summed up the dicussion and explained the expression as meaning any disgrace affecting the husband's honour, thus definitely endorsing the Hillelite position.[85] Incidentally, R. Akiva's view should not be seen to imply that a man could change wives whenever he saw a more beautiful woman. Elsewhere he expresses a moving concern for emotional warmth between married partners.[86] Hence his exposition, as that of Beit Hillel in general, should be understood as a

---

[81] mGit 9:10, according to the uncorrected ms K and other versions, and SifDeut 269 (p288). See Albeck, *Mishna* 3, 407.

[82] The original context of this discussion is undoubtedly the divorce question (Deut 24:1) and not, as in the present text, the purity of the encampment (23:15); thus D. Hoffmann, *Midrash Tannaim* 2, 148 n1.

[83] MidrGad Deut 23:15 (p522f).

[84] For the wider definition cf ySot 1, 16b; yGit 9, 50d; and cf mKet 7:6. Cf Belkin, *Philo*, 230: 'anything that shows immodesty and that indirectly leads to a suspicion of adultery'. Similarly Matt 5:27-30. But Blau, *Ehescheidung*, 34 considers this a late mitigation of the Shammaite position.

[85] Cf Blau, *Ehescheidung*, 39: mGit reflects R. Akiva's halakha and the dispute with the Shammaites appears as an appendix.

[86] Sifra Metsora 79c. See Safrai, 'Halakha', 205; id, *Akiva*, 34-36.

strictly legal definition: even if someone divorces his wife on these grounds, the divorce should be recognized and the woman is free to remarry.[87]

An altogether different opinion on marriage and divorce appears to be reflected in the Qumran scrolls. It seems even possible to detect outright opposition to the divorce practice of the Pharisees. The Essenes cherished a what may be called sacramental idea of the unbreakable sexual union between man and woman, which apparently excluded divorce as a legal option. A crucial passage in the Damascus Covenant reads:

> The Builders of the Wall ...are caught in fornication זנות, taking two wives in their lifetime; but the foundation of creation is: "Male and female he created them" (Gen 1:27); and those who went into the ark, went two by two; and about the Prince it is written, "And he shall not multiply wives for himself" (Deut 17:17). But David had not read in the sealed Book of the Law which was in the ark, for it had not been opened in Israel since the day Eleazar died ...But it remained hidden and was not revealed until the appearance of Zadok. (CD 4:19-5:5)

The expression 'Builders of the Wall' seems to refer to the Pharisees or their predecessors,[88] and the passage may reflect a polemic against their flexible divorce law. In the eyes of the author of the Covenant, the Genesis verse teaches that 'the foundation of creation' implies one should not take 'two wives in their lifetime', i.e. before the first one has died. This is confirmed by a passage in the Temple Scroll: 'And he shall not take another wife apart from her, for she alone shall be with him all the days of her life; but if she dies he may marry another one...'[89] The passage expounds Lev 18:18, 'And you shall not take a woman as a rival wife to her sister ...while her sister is yet alive.' As long as the 'sister', i.e. the first wife, is still alive he cannot marry another one. The implication of both passages is a prohibition not only of polygamy but also of divorce.[90] It was not only meant to apply to the king, since his case is cited as one among many.

What also strikes one in the passage in the Damascus Covenant is the conviction that its opinion is on the one hand a 'foundation of creation' but that on the other it was known neither to King David of old nor to the 'Builders of the Wall', obviously because they explained the Law differently. The correct insight was revealed only through 'Zadok', evidently an important person in the history of the Sect.

---

[87] My student Annemieke van der Veen suggests that the aim of R. Akiva's ruling was to avoid adultery.

[88] Cf CD 4:12. They are also called 'vipers' (5:14) and 'whitewashers' (9:12, 17; 19:24f, 31). Their exegesis is liberal (5:12). All this reminds one of the דורשי החלקות who, as Flusser, 'Pharisäer' demonstrated, are identical with the Pharisees. See esp ib 151-4, 'the Builders'.

[89] 11QTemp 57:17-19.

[90] Thus already Blau, *Ehescheidung*, 59-61, with important remarks also about CD 8:4-7 = 19:17-19. See Yadin, *Temple Scroll* 1, 270-4; Fitzmeyer, 'Matthean Divorce Texts', 92-7. Underestimating the Temple Scroll Vermes, 'Sectarian Matrimonial Halakha' in CD 4:20f reads a prohibition of polygamy only.

The teaching on divorce in the synoptic tradition is highly complicated.[91] This is due not only to the inherent processes of the synoptic tradition but apparently also to the interaction of two opposed halakhic traditions. The material consists of two literary elements: a halakhic saying about divorce and remarriage attributed to Jesus, and the narrative of a discussion with some Pharisees on the durability of the marriage bond. These elements appear in various combinations. The discussion narrative is found in Mark 10:2-9 and Matt 19:3-8; the saying appears both by way of conclusion to the same narrative in Mark (10:11f) and Matthew (19:9), and in the form of a separate saying in Luke (16:18) but, surprisingly, it reappears in Matthew (5:31f).

Thus the saying appears twice in Matthew (5:32 and 19:9) and seems to represent an important issue there. In addition, in both cases it is markedly different from the Markan and Lukan versions. The difference is fundamental when viewed within the framework of the ancient halakha. It may be noted that the separate appearance of the saying in Matt 5:32 differs in character from its immediate context – the antitheses of the Sermon on the Mount – and reads as a redactional addition.[92] Thus it appears that Matthew emphasizes a special tradition on divorce which differs from the tradition found in Mark and Luke.

Let us first look at the saying. In its simplest form it is found in Luke, where it is found disconnected after sayings about John the Baptist and the eternity of the Tora:

> Everyone who divorces his wife and marries another commits adultery; and he who marries a woman divorced from her husband commits adultery (Luke 16:18).

Here we have a straightforward denial of the possibility of divorce, i.e. legal termination of the marriage bond which allows the woman to remarry. This possibility is excluded in the second clause, which is apparently meant to make the prohibition of divorce clear beyond doubt. The phrase, which is variously rendered in the synoptics, looks like a popular inverted version of the official divorce formula, 'you are free to be married to anyone'. A divorced woman is not free to be married to anyone: there is no such thing as divorce!

The same is found in Mark, but there are interesting elaborations:

> Whoever divorces his wife and marries another, commits adultery against her; and if she, having divorced her husband, marries another, she commits adultery (Mark 10:11-12).

---

[91] See especially Luz, *Matthäus*, 268-79. See also Fitzmeyer, 'Matthean Divorce Texts' (though unclear on the Jewish background of Matthew); and Bockmuehl, 'Matthew 5.32' (stressing adultery as defilement in view of 1QapGen 20:15).

[92] Unlike the other 5 antitheses this is no 'pious radicalisation' of a Tora commandment to the effect that even the 'smallest' commandments are weighty in the eyes of Heaven; it lacks the hyperbolic effect of the others and in fact is a plain halakha. Moreover in the introductory formula the characteristic ἠκούσατε ὅτι is absent. See Blau, *Ehescheiding*, 51f (referring to the contradiction with Matt 5:27-30); Flusser, 'Die Tora', 21; Luz, *Matthäus*, 269.

The first clause is more explicit than that of Luke. It stipulates that he who divorces and remarries commits adultery against his first wife.[93] The implication is twofold: not only is the possibility of divorce excluded, but the marriage with the second woman violates the first marriage. In other words a fundamental rejection of polygamy is included. Upon closer inspection these implications also appear to be present in Luke. The sentence, 'Everyone who divorces his wife and marries another commits adultery', not only excludes divorce but presupposes monogamy. Thus the extant Mark adds an explanatory gloss to the first clause as found in Luke. In the end both Mark and Luke show us Jesus teaching absolute, life-long monogamy.[94]

The second clause in Mark turns the issue around and proclaims that a woman who divorces and remarries also commits adultery against her original partner. This formulation transcends the limits of Jewish law which only accepts the man as the acting legal person in marriage and divorce.[95] As we have seen the possibility of divorce by the woman existed in contemporary Hellenistic law. This indicates that the Gospel, in its present form,[96] addresses the problems of non-Jews.[97] It prescribes lifelong monogamy both for the man and the woman.

Let us now turn to Matthew. The version of the saying attached to the discussion with the Pharisees (19:9) is similar to the first half of the version in Mark, where it appears in the same context.[98] On the other hand the separate appearance in 5:32 bears particular similarities to both Luke[99] and Mark.[100]

In both cases Matthew has a revolutionary addition as compared with Mark and Luke:

> And I say to you: Whoever divorces his wife except for unchastity (μὴ ἐπὶ πορνείᾳ) and marries another, commits adultery.[101] (Matt 19:9)
> But I say to you: Everyone who divorces his wife except on the ground of unchastity (παρεκτὸς λόγου πορνείας) makes her an adulteress; and

[93] Luz, *Matthäus*, 269 n6.
[94] Cf Luz's comments, ib 271f.
[95] Daube, *New Testament*, 365 rejects the Markan version as spurious for this reason. Incidentally ms D and some others have a version of Mark 10:12 which conforms to Jewish law: ἐὰν αὐτὴ ἐξέλθῃ ἀπὸ τοῦ ἀνδρός. Ἐξέρχομαι corresponds to διαχωρίζω used by Paul and Josephus, see below p117.
[96] The second clause in Mark is an elaboration of the version found in Luke 16:18 and Matt 5:32. Hence positing the extant Mark as a source for Matthew is simplistic. The elaborated form of the second clause in Mark 10:12 (grafted on Luke, possibly) and its absence in the parallel in Matthew 19:9 may indicate the greater authenticity of Matthew here.
[97] Another indication is Mark 7:3-4 which explains 'traditions' of 'the Pharisees and all the Jews' – obviously to non-Jews.
[98] The formulations ὃς ἂν and γαμήσῃ ἄλλην are identical, as against πᾶς ὁ and γαμῶν ἑτέραν in Luke. The additional clause about the woman's divorce of course is absent in Matthew.
[99] The formulation πᾶς ὁ (see previous n); and the second clause stipulating the prohibition to marry an ἀπολελυμένην.
[100] The explanatory expression, ποιεῖ αὐτὴν μοιχηθῆναι formally (not materially) resembles Mark 10:11, μοιχᾶται ἐπ' αὐτήν.
[101] A majority adds, following the parallel in Matt 5:32 and Luke: καὶ ὁ ἀπολελυμένην γαμῶν μοιχᾶται, but not so Sinai ms, D and others.

113

whoever marries a divorced woman commits adultery. (Matt 5:31f)
In these versions unchastity is the explicit ground for legal divorce. This, as we can see now, conforms to the Shammaite opinion regarding divorce. Its repeated addition indicates emphatic opposition to the tradition that Jesus did not accept the legality of divorce.

A similar Matthean revision can be perceived in the other element, the narrative of the discussion with the Pharisees on the durability of the marriage bond. In Mark 10:2-9 the narrative has an uninterrupted flow. The discussion is triggered by the Pharisees' question, 'Is it lawful for a man to divorce his wife?' Thus the issue is whether divorce is allowed at all. When asked what the Law prescribes the Pharisees quote Deut 24:1. In response Jesus expounds Gen 1:27 and 2:24[102] to mean that divorce was not intended by the Law 'from the beginning'[103] but was allowed 'for your hardness of heart', and comes to the final pronouncement: 'What therefore God has joined together, let not man put asunder.' This comes down to a fundamental suppression of the possibility of divorce as based on Deut 24:1. The narrative ends with the disciples' request for more explanation when 'in the house'[104] and Jesus' saying against divorce quoted above. Thus in Mark the discussion narrative supports and illustrates the saying against divorce.

Let us now review the version in Matt 19:3-9:

> And Pharisees came up to him and tested him by asking, Is it lawful to divorce one's wife for any cause? He answered, Have you not read that He who created them from the beginning, "male and female He made them" (Gen 1:27); and said he,[105] "For this reason a man shall leave his father and mother and cleave to his wife, and the two shall become one flesh" (Gen 2:24)? So they are no longer two but one flesh. What therefore God has joined together, let not man put asunder.
>
> They said to him, Why then did Moses order to give her a bill of renunciation and send her away? (Deut 24:1). He said to them, For your hardness of heart Moses allowed you to divorce your wives, but from the beginning it was not so.
>
> And I say to you: Whoever divorces his wife except for unchastity and marries another, commits adultery.

We see that in Matthew the Pharisees' question is not about the possibility of divorce. They implicitly accept it but ask about its legal grounds: 'Is it lawful to divorce one's wife for any cause κατὰ πᾶσαν αἰτίαν?' In this version there

---

[102] καὶ κολληθήσεται τῇ γυναικὶ αὐτοῦ is absent in Mark according to mss Vatican, Sinai, Athos, some minuscles and sy^s. It may have been too plastic for Roman ears.

[103] The word ἀπὸ δὲ ἀρχῆς (κτίσεως) is absent in D and some other mss as well as in the parallel in Matthew and is explanatory.

[104] Mark 10:10-12. A similar procedure is recorded several times of Tannaic Sages: 'When the man was gone, the disciples asked: Master, him you did send away with a superficial answer, but to us, what do you say?', e.g. PesRK Para 7 (p74). Cf Bacher, Tannaiten 1, 40.

[105] καὶ εἶπεν. Very likely this is an incorrect rendering of ויאמר, which refers to Scripture, as in Rabbinic literature and in Paul (who cites the same midrash 1Cor 6:16); see Str-B 3, 365f. It is absent in Mark in most mss.

follows the explanation of the Genesis verses and the concluding principle that 'what God has joined together, let not man put asunder'. Only when the Pharisees object that Deut 24:1 implies the possibility of divorce, does Jesus give his reply that this was a concession not meant 'from the beginning'. The narrative culminates in the rule excluding divorce except on the grounds of unchastity.

The emphasis is clear: to the question whether divorce is allowed 'for any cause', Jesus replies that it is allowed only on the grounds of unchastity. The Matthean version of the question clearly reflects the Hillelite formulation of the grounds for divorce, and in response Jesus emphasizes the Shammaite opinion. In other words in Matthew the discussion is between Hillelite Pharisees and Jesus as a representative of the Shammaite divorce tradition.

Furthermore the exposition of the Genesis verses in this version of the narrative is awkward. As in Rabbinic midrash, Jesus could have based his opinion that only adultery permits divorce on Deut 24:1, without referring to Genesis. Moreover the statement that 'it was not so from the beginning', which in Matthew appears at the end, actually refers to the Genesis discussion at the beginning. While the Markan version is coherent, the Matthean narrative encompasses two conflicting traditions: (1) divorce is not allowed in view of Gen 2:24; (2) divorce is allowed only on the ground of unchastity in view of Deut 24:1.[106]

We are forced to conclude that that while using traditional material found also in the other Gospels, Matthew presents Jesus as adhering to the Shammaite tradition on divorce. On the other hand Mark and Luke reveal a different, stricter tradition. A historical explanation may be found by studying Jesus' midrash on the marriage bond more closely.

The conclusion Jesus draws from Gen 2:24, 'the two shall be into one flesh', is based on a very specific idea: sexual union constituting an undissolvable marriage bond. This is an ancient tradition, as appears from the emphatic paraphrase of Gen 2:24 in Jub 3:3-7.[107] We also found it in Paul's adhortation against prohibited sexual relations: 'Do you not know that he who cleaves to a prostitute becomes one body with her? For, he says, "The two shall become one flesh"' (1Cor 6:16). And the same tradition, also mentioning a prostitute, is found in Rabbinic literature with explicit reference to Noachides.[108] What is important now is that the conclusion drawn there is that the biblical divorce commandment was given to Israel and that 'gentiles have no divorce'.[109] While the immediate application is to the case of proselytes, this suggests the view that

---

[106] Blau, *Ehescheidung*, 52-55. The same duality in Matt 5:32, where the first clause allows divorce on the ground of unchastity but the second clause, similar to Luke, stipulates that even 'he who marries a divorced woman commits adultery'. The redactor of course meant the second clause to include the condition παρεκτὸς λόγου πορνείας, but his material shows the uniformity with Luke.

[107] As pointed out by Blau, *Ehescheidung*, 63f.

[108] GenR 18,5 (p166) (version YalkShim Gen no. 18, p88: ואפילו לא נתבון); similarly yKid 1, 58b bottom.

[109] yKid 1, 58c; GenR 18,5 (p166); the connection was seen already by Blau, *Ehescheidung*, 56f, mentioning additional sources. Cf also above n76.

divorce was a later concession to the human condition. By contrast Rabbinic halakha, rather than stressing this literal interpretation of 'one flesh', emphasizes the clause 'he leaves his father and mother' as referring to the categories of prohibited sexual relations.[110] The Tannaim stated, apparently implying rape: 'Any intercourse ...not for the sake of marriage – (the result is that) she is not married.'[111] As to polygamy, which involves sexual union with more than one wife, this was avoided in practice but remained legally possible.[112] Thus the idea shared by Jesus and Paul was not typical of Pharisaic-Rabbinic Judaism at large.[113]

Moreover we have seen that the idea of the undissolvable sexual union is found in the the Qumran scrolls, with explicit reference to the other Genesis verse quoted by Jesus, and we noted the striking fact that the Damascus Covenant terms this a 'foundation of creation' unknown to a majority of Jews. This strongly reminds one of the words of Jesus: marriage was intended as life-long monogamy 'from the beginning' until Moses made a concession to man's hardness of heart. The conclusion is obvious: the teaching of Jesus here displays 'Qumran-like features'.[114] The same idea is attributed to John the Baptist; one may surmise that he was typical of non-Essene circles who followed Essene views on marriage, and from whom Jesus took his inspiration.[115]

If this is so only Matthew's position remains to be explained. It would seem that, unlike to the Essenish marriage teaching of Jesus as contained in Luke and Mark – and, as we shall see, in Paul – the Matthean community held Rabbinic and specifically Shammaite views.[116] Judging from the repeated emphasis, it must have been an urgent matter. This indicates that at some stage in its history the gospel of Matthew functioned in circles markedly closer to Rabbinic Judaism than Paul and other Apostles.

PAUL'S DIVORCE HALAKHA

Paul's chapter on celibacy goes on to deal with divorce in various situations. v11f are addressed 'to the married' and v12-16 'to the others', the question in both cases being whether one may leave one's partner in order to live the more saintly life of a celibate. At the end of the chapter v39f address the specific question whether widows may remarry or not. All cases turn on two separate problems: the theological and ethical problem of the desirability of celibacy, which have been discussed above, and the halakhic problem of the termination of the marriage bond. Paul was conscious of this distinction, as we saw: while

---

[110] See above on πορνεία, p99. See further Str-B 1, 802f (add Targumim).

[111] tKid 1:3.

[112] See Safrai, 'Home', 748-50.

[113] Cf Ben Sira, below p123.

[114] This conclusion was already drawn 'audaciously' by Flusser, 'Motsa ha-Natsrut', 425 and n20. Similarly Luz, *Matthäus*, 272: 'Ein qumranisch anmutender Zug scheint hier vorzuliegen.'

[115] David Flusser orally. See Mark 6:17f; Matt 14:3f; Josephus, Ant 18:113. And see Schürer, *History* 1, 344.

[116] Similarly Blau, *Ehescheidung*, 55; Luz, *Matthäus*, 275f.

stating general rules on divorce and marriage in each case, he also gives his own opinion on celibacy. Here we shall discuss the halakhic problem specifically in connection with the three successive cases.

> To the married I command – not I but the Lord: the wife should not depart from her husband, and if she depart, she must either remain unmarried or be reconciled with her husband; and the man should not send away his wife. (1Cor 7:10f)

A most remarkable feature here is that Paul explicitly relies on a commandment of 'the Lord'. This contrasts with what he has to say 'to the others' (v12) and 'about the virgins' (v25). It is clear that it refers to the divorce law of Jesus preserved in the synoptic gospels. Paul cites Apostolic, Jewish-Christian tradition as his source of authority.

Furthermore Paul refers to the woman's 'departing' (χωρισθῆναι) as opposed to the 'sending away' by the man (ἀφιέναι). This terminology corresponds to the distinct legal position of man and woman in Jewish law.[117] It is striking that attention is given to the woman's action first, and that her 'departing' from her husband is disencouraged. As we saw above (p108) Hellenistic law allowed the legal initiative towards divorce to be taken by the woman. This is another indication that Paul is addressing non-Jews here. Hence while quoting an Apostolic tradition 'of the Lord' he adapts it to the situation of Corinthian non-Jews who were not married, with the classic formula, 'according to the Law of the Jews'.[118] The closest actual parallel is the Markan version of Jesus' saying: 'Whoever divorces his wife and marries another, commits adultery against her; and if she, having divorced her husband, marries another, she commits adultery' (Mark 10:11f, above p113).

The conclusion is that, on the authority of Jesus, v10f prohibits men and women married either under Jewish or other law from divorcing. Even if the wife has 'departed' the marriage bond remains in force and she is not free to remarry; likewise the man is not allowed to divorce his wife and re-marry.[119] Paul supports the Markan and Lukan version of Jesus' teaching, rather than Matthew's: there is no divorce.

Now let us read the next section:

> To the others I say – I, not the Lord: if any brother has a wife who is unbelieving, and she consents to live with him, he should not send her away. And a woman, if she has an unbelieving husband, and he consents to live with her, she should not send away the husband. For the unbelieving man is sanctified in the woman, and the unbelieving woman is sanctified in the brother; otherwise, the children would be unclean, but now they are holy. But if the unbeliever departs, the partner may depart

---

[117] Cf Daube, *New Testament*, 362-72, 'Terms for Divorce'. Fitzmeyer, 'Matthean Divorce Texts', 89-91 gives papyrological data on the divorce terms.

[118] The standard phrase, see Tomson, 'Names', 268-72.

[119] Blau, *Ehescheidung*, 62f reads in 1Cor 7:10f that Paul allowed the man to remarry in accordance with Pharisaic halakha. But this is not conclusive and moreover contradicts the Jesus tradition which Paul explicitly quotes.

too;[120] in such cases the brother or sister is not under bondage, for God has called you[121] to peace. For how do you know, woman, if you will save your husband? or how do you know, man, if you will save your wife? (1Cor 7:12-16)

Paul here addresses 'the others'. What was their precise situation? It is worth repeating that 1Cor 7 is remarkable for its specified practical instruction, given in combination with appeals to formal sources of authority; hence some halakhic clarification is needed. Let us outline the differences with the categories of the 'unmarried' and the 'married'.

Here Paul emphasizes the woman as the active legal person partner more than in the case of married partners, and thus unequivocally presupposes Hellenistic law: 'she should not send away away her husband' (μὴ ἀφιέτω, v13). But this difference is not specific: 'the married' were not necessarily Jews, nor would their marriage conform to Jewish law. A specific difference is contained in the fact that 'the others' were called neither 'unmarried' (ἄγαμοι) nor 'married' (γεγαμήκοι) and evidently presented a category in between. The implication is that they were married informally, which as we have seen was a widely used option in Hellenistic law. There is an additional difference: the partners were non-believers, i.e. non-believing gentiles.[122] Paul's gentile readers could hardly have been married to Jews since Jewish law prohibited mixed marriages; moreover Jewish law did not recognize informal marriage.[123] But this is not a fundamental difference either. Paul's prohibition of divorce does not distinguish between believing or unbelieving partners. Apparently he did not a consider a formal marriage terminated even if the partner were a non-believer and had 'departed', since its legal status was distinct from informal marriage.[124]

In Paul's view the attitude of the non-believing partner was decisive.[125] If he or she consented to remain living with the Christian partner, the latter could not dissolve their informal marriage since the non-believer is 'sanctified' (ἡγίασ-

[120] Paul seems to imply 'mutual divorce' according to Hellenistic law.

[121] Sinai', A and others, ὑμᾶς; P46, Sinai² and majority: ἡμᾶς.

[122] ''Απιστος as a term for 'pagan' is common in 1Cor: it occurs also in 6:6; 10:27; 14:22. Similarly in 2Cor 6:14f. In 2Cor 4:4 the meaning is not distinct but may include Jews. See Bauer, *Wörterbuch* s.v. In 7:12-15 this does not seem to imply someone who actively participated in pagan worship; it is even unlikely in view of their relation with the 'body of Christ' via the believing partner (see below). Hence I translate 'non-believer'.

[123] mKid 1:1 (above) counts sexual union as one of the legal means of establishing the marriage bond.

[124] This differs from Hellenistic law, see above n76. It seems that Paul, in line with Jewish law and the teaching of Jesus, took formal marriage very seriously. The situation endured into late Imperial times: cf Augustine's Confessions 6:13 and 15 on his concubines as opposed to a 'wife'. On Augustine's high ideal of formal marriage and its influence on the remarkable development of Byzantine legislation towards 'written marriages' see Wolff, *Written and Unwritten Marriages*, 97-100.

[125] Hence Daube's interesting note on our passage ('Onesimos', 41) to the effect that the neophyte is halakhically 'a newborn' like a proselyte (see above n21) whence the marriage is dissolved, is not decisive. The same holds in case the pagan partner wishes to stay together. Nor do converted couples seem to have needed re-marriage.

ται) in marriage with the Christian (vv12-14). Apparently *de facto* union with a Christian constituted *de facto* union with the body of Christ. But if the non-believer wished to 'depart' (χωρίζεται) the Christian 'is not bound' (οὐ δεδούλωται v15), i.e. in Paul's eyes there is no longer a legal marriage bond. In this case not the conjugal union but the union with Christ was apparently of decisive importance. The unwilling non-believer is not 'sanctified' here: 'For how do you know, woman, if you will save your husband? or how do you know, man, if you will save your wife?' (v16). This seems to imply that by 'departing' from an informal Christian partner the non-believer rejected the *de facto* union with Christ.

Thus Paul acknowledged legal termination of an informal marriage with a non-believing partner at the latter's initiative. The importance of this acknow-legment should not be overlooked; he generally held the conjugal union in highest esteem and refused to recognize divorce. Nor would the case have been provided for in Apostolic tradition. As stated, neither informal marriage nor marriage with a gentile was possible in Judaism.[126] This underlines Paul's words he himself teaches here and 'not the Lord' (v12).

All this raises the question whether Paul would not implicitly have acknow-ledged divorce in the event of adultery, in line with the Shammaites. If 'departu-re' of the non-believing partner constituted termination of informal marriage, would not adultery do so too? Paul specifically states that πορνεία and union with Christ are mutually exclusive (1Cor 6:15-18) and that those who commit πορνεία should be excommunicated (1Cor 5:9-13). Logically an adulterous partner should equally well be excluded from married life. But the question is whether this implied divorce, i.e. legal termination of the marriage bond enabling living partners to re-marry. This is precisely what is prohibited in an apocryphal apocalypse of the Apostolic period, the Pastor of Hermas. In a passage dealing with repentance the question is asked what to do when an adulterous wife refuses to mend her ways. The answer is: 'He should send her away, said (the Lord), and the husband must stay alone; for if he, having sent his wife away, marries another, he commits adultery himself.'[127] Adultery does not terminate the marriage bond. This document is a strong indication that Paul's silence on this matter may not be interpreted to mean that he implicitly accepted divorce in the event of adultery.

Our last passage in connection with divorce addresses the question of remar-riage by a widow:

> A woman is given (δέδεται) for all the time her husband lives; but if the man passes away, she is free to be married to whom she wants, only in the Lord. But she is more blessed if she remains as she is, in my opinion; and I think that I also have the Spirit of God. (1Cor 7:39f)

---

[126] mGit 9:2 counts the non-Jew among those who have no 'right of betrothal' with a Jewish woman. See below p121.

[127] Herm 29:6 (Mand 4:1:6). This document is dated first half second cent CE (Dibelius, *Hirt des Hermas*, 422) and associated with the Roman Church: see Canon Muratori lines 73-77.

v39 comes separately after the preceding passage about virgins. By literary form it is a legal rule, as distinct from the following verse which is a personal opinion. We have seen the distinction Paul makes in the chapter between commands 'of the Lord', instruction of his own and his 'opinion' (γνώμη), the term which appears in v40. Here as elsewhere Paul offers his preference for celibacy as a personal opinion. The preceding verse however appears to be citing an accepted rule.

Part of the same rule is paraphrased in Rom 7:2. There however it is used as a metaphor in view of the abrogation of the Law by death, i.e. the death of Christ. It is this difference which enhances its function as a legal rule here.[128] In short, Paul sums up his argument regarding widows using an accepted rule supplemented with his own opinion.

These conclusions from literary analysis are confirmed when compared with Rabbinic halakha. We have seen that marriage is legally terminated either by divorce or by the death of a partner. The latter case needs little explanation; it is based on Deut 24:3, '...if the latter husband dies...'[129] This is the halakha used by Paul when speaking of the widow's right to remarry. As we shall see he uses formulations directly related to Rabbinic halakha.[130] In fact this rule presents us with the purest formulation of halakha in First Corinthians and in the whole of Paul's writings.

1Cor 7:39 contains three distinct halakhot: (1) the death of the husband terminates the marriage bond; (2) a widow may marry whomever she wants; (3) re-marriage excludes non-believers.

(1) 'The wife is given for all the time her husband lives; but if the man passes away, she is free to be married...' As stated this first element conforms to the last part of the mishna, 'the woman acquires herself by divorce and the death of her husband' (mKid 1:1). The strictly halakhic implication is clear from comparison with Rom 7:2. What is more, the fact that Paul cites this rule in letters to two different churches suggests that this halakha was part and parcel of his basic parenesis.[131] Meanwhile his one glaring omission is the other legal means of terminating the marriage bond: divorce. As we have seen divorce by means of a bill was a biblical institution and well established in Second Temple practice. Paul's omission appears to be intentional and underlines what we concluded earlier: he supports the tradition of Jesus that marriage is life-long and is terminated only by the death of a partner. Similarly the Temple Scroll only recognizes of the wife's death as allowing re-marriage.[132] Thus the first element in 1Cor 7:39 is dissenting Jewish halakha which relates to the tradition of Jesus:

[128] The majority version γυνὴ δέδεται (νομῷ) 1Cor 7:39 (not in P46, Sinai, A, B, D˙ et al.) would seem to underline the halakhic meaning here, but may be safely considered a secondary addition from Romans.

[129] Explicitly so yKid 1, 58d explaining mKid 1:1, ובמיתת הבעל.

[130] This was noticed in part by Str-B 3, 377.

[131] Cf Rom 7:1, 'I am speaking to those who know the Law'. This may be an address to Jewish co-readers (above p61) but includes gentiles. The marriage halakha 1Cor 7 addresses gentile believers and is included in the 'commandments of God' 1Cor 7:19.

[132] 11QTemp 57:18 (above p111).

it coincides with the 'command of the Lord' in v10, although it is not attributed to him.

(2) '...she is free to be married to any man she wants...' This second element is similar to the 'essential formula' of the divorce bill as formulated in the mishna quoted above: 'Lo, you are permitted to any man; You may go and be married to any man you want' (mGit 9:3). Indeed, Paul's formulation is one of the early sources testifying to the existence of that formula. The literary similarities indicate that Paul used standard halakhic formulas.

(3) '......any man she wants, if only in the Lord'. The third element is very interesting for the history of the halakha and its relevance in early Christianity. If the widow is free to marry anyone except a non-believer, she is not absolutely free. Similar restrictive clauses added to the essential divorce formula were known in the more ancient halakha.[133] Subsequently the question was asked whether such a condition did not conflict with the legal concept of divorce and in effect invalidate it. The older halakha was taught, as usual, by R. Eliezer the conservative Shammaite:[134]

> If a man divorced his wife and said:[135] Lo, you are permitted to any man, except NN – R. Eliezer approves, but the Sages prohibit. After R. Eliezer's death, four elders gathered to respond to his words... R. Tarfon responded... Said R. Yose from Gelil... Said R. Elazar ben Azarya... R. Akiva says... Hence we learned that such is no divorce.[136]
> (If he said:) Lo, you are permitted to any man, except to my father or your father, to my brother or your brother, to a slave or a non-Jew, or to anyone who has no right of betrothal קדושין with her – it is valid.[137]

The Sages who, around 100 CE, gathered to discuss R. Eliezer's halakha concluded that a clause excluding a specific person or group of persons from the woman's future marriage partnership invalidates the divorce. They conceded however that a clause excluding persons who have no legal title to marry her in the first place – such as close relatives, slaves or non-Jews – is formally superfluous but does not invalidate the divorce bill. A divorce deed written in the early second century CE and discovered in Bar Kokhba surroundings confirms the historical usage of these specifications. At the 'essential formula' it reads: '...you may go and be married to any Jewish man you want'.[138]

Paul's teaching parallels the older halakha represented by R. Eliezer: the widow is 'free' to marry 'anyone except' a non-believer. The final clause may

---

[133] Cohen, *Jewish and Roman Law*, 406 refers to a Roman parallel and explains the phenomenon from the husband's revenge.

[134] On R. Eliezer see Safrai, 'Halakha', 186, 198-200.

[135] Albeck, *Mishna* 3, 300 explains that it concerns an oral, not a written stipulation. In the continuation the Mishna lays down that the same bill should be handed over once more with the correct oral formula. However 'if he wrote this in the bill – even if upon reconsideration he erased it, (the divorce) is invalid'. The Bar Kokhba *get* (see below) has a similar formula, but it is in the category that does not contradict the halakha of the Sages.

[136] tGit 7:1-5; SifDeut 269 (p289); cf mGit 9:1.

[137] mGit 9:2.

[138] *DJD* 2 no 19. See Tomson, 'Names' 271f.

even be a similar superfluous condition if we suppose that Paul opposed marriage with a pagan to start with.[139] If so, this throws additional light on his acceptance of divorce in the case of an informal marriage with a pagan wishing to separate. We have seen that in this case, as distinct from the cases of formal marriage with a pagan and informal marriage with a pagan who consents to remain together, he recognized no legal marriage bond. The unwillingness of the pagan partner to live with a believer determined the non-existence of a legal marriage bond.

The halakha in 1Cor 7:39 summarizes Paul's formal halakhic stance on divorce. As long as the partner is alive the marriage bond remains in force (v10f); only where a pagan partner in an informal marriage departs does the marriage bond end (vv12-16); hence if the partner dies the surviving partner is free to remarry anyone except a non-believer (v39). Alongside this formal position Paul's repeated recommandation of celibacy has the status of an informal, personal preference.

HISTORICAL PERSPECTIVE

All this leads us to try to place Paul's teaching in the development in ancient Jewish divorce law. The relevance of Hellenistic and Roman marriage law is only indirect: Paul has to face up to the wish of the woman to divorce her partner. In any case he follows the authority of the Apostolic Jewish halakha.

The antiquity of the divorce issue as disputed between Essenes, Shammaites and Hillelites is evident from a range of sources. The Damascus Covenant and the Temple Scroll are evidence of the existence of the idea of life-long monogamy at least as far back as the second century BCE.[140] The polemics against the more liberal divorce law of the 'Builders of the Wall' give the impression that the general Pharisaic principle of divorce was well established by that time. This assumption is confirmed by other sources.

The vague expression ערות דבר in Deut 24:1 is translated similarly in the Septuagint: ἄσχημον πρᾶγμα, 'an unworthy deed'; similarly, in Deut 23:15, ἀσχημοσύνη πράγματος, 'shamefulness of deeds'. This rather literal translation resembles the Hillelite view. However this does not give us a clue to its date since dating any particular Septuagint version is difficult.[141] Josephus gives an outspoken Hillelite rendering, presenting it as established practice: καθ' ἀσδη-ποτοῦν αἰτίας, 'for whatever cause'.[142] So does Philo: καθ' ἥν ἄν τύχῃ πρόφασιν, 'for any cause whatever'.[143] This brings us as far back as the first half of the first century CE. However evidence definitely from the early second

---

[139] See 2Cor 6:14f. Davies, *Setting*, 344 concludes from this verse (without referring to 1Cor 7:39) on Paul's prohibition against marrying an unbeliever.

[140] See Schürer, *History* 3/1, 415-7 on the date of the Temple Scroll.

[141] For accounts of the literary history see Tov, 'Septuagint', 161-8; Schürer, *History* III/2, 474-87.

[142] Ant 4:253. Cf ib 4:247, 16:198; Life 426. See Daube, *New Testament*, 371.

[143] Spec leg 3:30. Belkin, *Philo*, 229-31 interprets this as not being Philo's own opinion. Cf Colson's note a.l.

century BCE is found in Ben Sira: '...A wicked wife... if she does not walk following your hand, cut her off from your flesh, give (a divorce bill) and send (her away).' The reference is not to unchastity but to bad behaviour in general.[144] It seems that there existed a continuous and widespread tradition since biblical times which interpreted ערות דבר literally as a vague and comprehensive ground for divorce.

Thus the Hillelite tradition not only seems to represent the more widespread but also the more ancient idea which is also closer to the plain meaning in Deuteronomy.[145] This is unusual since in most topics the Shammaites preserved the older tradition and the more literal interpretation, while the Hillelites usually represent the more innovative and rational point of view. In this case the more liberal tradition of the Hillelites seems to be the more ancient, while the Shammaite opinion must reflect a peculiar, strict and pious tradition which originated during the Second Temple period. An ancient Rabbinic tradition emphasizes that 'in days of old' divorce was taken lightly and that even the Pharisees took measures to curb this;[146] it is possible that pious circles wanted to go further. This seems to be confirmed by the passage in the Damascus Covenant which polemicizes against the flexibility of Pharisaic marriage law. We can assume that this particular tradition developed in the larger pious movement from which first the Essene sect and later the movement of Jesus and his disciples originated. In this perspective the Shammaite tradition represents a reflection within the Pharisaic-Rabbinic movement of that more pious tradition. At its centre lay a very high regard for the sexual union.

In Ben Sira we see the contrast. Representing the broader and more ancient tradition which was to be carried on later by the Hillelites, he considered the 'fleshly union' terminated by divorce even if the grounds were not unchastity but a defect in the partner's character. Similarly, he saw cohabitation with prostitutes as morally bad but not as repetitive adultery.[147] This must have been inconceivable for the Essenes and Jesus. In their view, the 'fleshly union' existed as long as both partners lived (CD 4:21; Luke 16:18 and parallels). In other words, the essence of this Essene and Jesuanic tradition was a sacramental view of sexuality, comparable to the sacramental idea of baptism and other rites developed in both movements.[148]

It is this more pious tradition which Paul follows: the marriage bond is terminated only by the death of a partner (1Cor 7:39; Rom 7:2). While he calls himself a former Pharisee (Phil 3:5; cf Acts 22:3) he formally transmits a halakha not supported either by the Hillelite or the Shammaite wing of Pharisaism. He explicitly ascribes it to a commandment of Jesus (1Cor 7:10f). This

---

[144] Sir 25:29f(25f). See Segal a.l. תן ושלח is absent in the Greek version. Some version of this passage is referred to in the Talmud, stressing the right to divorce a 'bad wife', bYev 63b.

[145] Safrai, 'Home', 790; Moore, *Judaism* 2, 124.

[146] tKet 12:1; yKet 8, 32b-c, commenting on the ordainment (i.e. emendation, see Lieberman a.l.) of the *ketubba* by Shimon ben Shetah.

[147] Sir 19:2, using the biblical expression דבק בזונות, LXX κολλώμενος πόρναις (Gen 2:24!) but not stressing 'one flesh'.

[148] See above p48f, 75.

means that here Paul is dependent on Apostolic halakha which is at variance with his own Pharisaic background. The exactness of the halakhic formulations in 1Cor 7:39 give the impression that it is a direct quotation. It follows that these Pauline passages are first-rate evidence for the existence of a distinct, more or less dissident tradition within Second Temple halakha: the halakha of the Jewish church which ascribed highest authority to the halakhic teachings of Jesus. That it is formulated in Greek adds to its historical interest; other indications of halakhic traditions in Greek will be discussed later.

Alongside his formal halakhic teaching on marriage and divorce, Paul repeatedly expresses a personal preference for celibacy. This sustained duality of general rule and personal preference is remarkable. It may be that the situation in Corinth induced him to take this dual stance; it may have been, for example, that his personal preference for celibacy collided with a quite different view on sexuality in Corinthian society. Other explanations need not be excluded. A distinction between the halakha accepted by all and the specific behaviour of the pious was common in ancient Judaism. The Sages called such 'extra' pious deeds commandments 'beyond the strict line of the Law'[149] and sometimes identified them as coming from a distinct tradition known as 'the teaching of the Hasidim'.[150] The teaching of Jesus, exemplified by his demand of 'righteousness exceeding that of scribes and Pharisees' (Matt 5:17-48), may be viewed in this light. Hence it appears not only that Paul shared a similar tradition in the form of his preference for celibacy, but was conscious of its distinction from the accepted halakha as it applied to society at large.

Thus we face a very complex situation. We have both Paul's 'Essenish' opinion on celibacy, for which he had no Jesus tradition, and his more humane, 'Pharisaic' stance on sexual abstinence. In addition there is Matthew's Shammaite revision of Jesus' divorce halakha. The conclusion is that early Jewish-Christian halakha was far from monolithic on the questions of celibacy, marriage and divorce. So this was very likely to be the case on other issues too. Nevertheless the strict opinion on divorce was widely shared and, together with the preference for celibacy, rose to become official law in later Christianity. Strikingly, the Roman Catholic *Codex juris canonici* preserves the remnants of the ancient Essene and Jewish-Apostolic tradition in the clear and distinct formulations of latinized halakha: 'Matrimonium ratum et consummatum nulla humana potestate ullaque causa, *praeterquam morte*, dissolvi potest.'[151]

This does not help Paul's modern interpreters in answering moral and pastoral questions on marriage and divorce.[152] It helps them appreciate his position in a distinct halakhic tradition in Second Temple Jewry.

---

[149] See Urbach, *Sages*, 330-3.
[150] Safrai, 'Mishnat hasidim'.
[151] Libreria Editrice Vaticana 1983, canon 1141.
[152] For modern developments and implications see Luz, *Matthäus*, 276-9; Tomson, 'Paulus'.

The Apostles' Right (1Cor 9)

1Cor 9 is a digression in Paul's discussion on the important practical question of the consumption of food sacrificed to idols; this larger context is discussed in chapter 5 below. The digression functions as an adhortation to follow the Apostle's own example and renounce one's rights if the brother's interest so requires. The right Paul renounced while residing in Corinth was an Apostle's privilege to be materially supported by the churches he visits. This right is based on a teaching of Jesus which in turn relates to ancient Jewish ideas regarding 'wages' for 'labourers'. The passage in question contains an interesting halakhic core which again evinces a continuous connection between Paul, Apostolic tradition, Jesus and the larger Jewish tradition.

Before analysing the elements relevant to this study in detail let us look at the argument about the rights of the Apostles.[153] After an introduction (9:1-3) which establishes Paul's apostleship (see last section of this chapter) the fundamental Apostolic right is posited in a series of rhetorical questions. The change in the formal argument is indicated by the shift from 'you' and 'I' to 'we', i.e. the Apostles, in v4.

> Do we not have the right (ἐχουσία) to our food and drink? Do we not have the right to bring along a wife who is also a sister, as the other Apostles and the brothers of the Lord and Cephas? Or do only I and Barnabas not have the right to be exempt from working? (1Cor 9:4-6)

Apostles were entitled to board and lodging along with their wives who were also sisters and, possibly, 'workers in the Lord'.[154] The fundamental opening statement is explained in a series of consecutive arguments. It opens (v7) with three examples which in their popular appeal relate both to Stoic-Cynic and Rabbinic tradition: mercenaries sent to war are entitled to the king's payment;[155] labourers working the wineyard may eat of its fruits; and shepherds may drink from the sheep's milk.[156] Then the argument is given another dimension by stating that the examples do not reflect mere human principles but confirm what the divine Law says: 'You shall not muzzle a threshing ox' (Deut 25:4). This rule is evidently meant not for oxen but for men, i.e. field labourers (v8-10). A provisional conclusion follows: if the right to reap implied in the Tora verse applies to labourers who sow actual seed, it must apply to Apostles as well: Paul has sown 'things of the Spirit' and has a right to 'reap fleshly things'

---

[153] The commentary of Weiss is most fruitful here; I disagree only on the *a minori* argument v8-10. Willis, 'Apostolic Apologia' gives a good analysis of the argument of the chapter and its relation with the context.

[154] Partners in such Apostolic couples were not only Jesus' brothers and disciples, but also Prisca and Aquila (Rom 16:3f) and others. See Schüssler Fiorenza, *Memory*, 47f, 168-75 on such couples and on female functionaries in general.

[155] Ὀψωνία, cf Rom 6:23; see Str-B 3,233 on its Rabbinic use. Cf Sevenster, *Paul and Seneca*, 160-2 on common Stoic use of military metaphor.

[156] The shepherd who may drink of the milk is among the types of labourers mentioned in the halakhic sources, tBM 8:7; MidrGad Deut 25:4 (p660); on field labourers see below.

(v11-12a). But he has 'not made use of this right' (v12b), which is the point of the chapter as a whole. Then another dimension is added using a popular simile which refers to the Jewish and to any other sacrificial cult: 'those working in the holy things' partake in the sacrifices while officiating (v13). This leads to the final argument: 'In the same way the Lord commanded that those who proclaim the gospel should earn their living by the gospel' (v14).

This is therefore the Apostles' right. The main argument is that Paul, as did Barnabas, waived his right and earned his own living while in Corinth. This is reiterated in v6, 12, 15 and 18. The passages on Paul's unselfish apostleship (v19-23) and the athlete's training (v24-27) round up the argument.

The following elements will be analysed in detail here: (1) the halakhic implications of the Apostles' right; (2) the halakhic midrash from Deut 25:4; (3) the imagery derived from agricultural labour. The significance of the Jesus tradition involved will be dealt with in the last section of the chapter.

(1) The connection between the 'command of the Lord' quoted by Paul and a synoptic Jesus logion has long been recognized, but not so the halakhic connotations of both passages.[157] The saying is transmitted in two versions: 'The labourer is worthy of his food' (Matt 10:10); 'The labourer is worthy of his wages' (Luke 10:7). The context in both versions is the narrative of the dispatch of the Apostles by Jesus. The narrative contains a number of key words which also appear in Paul's argument; this points to a common tradition which was most probably oral.[158] The halakhic intention is clear: Jesus actually orders his Apostles (Matt 10:5) not to take money or food along but to enjoy the hospitality offered to them.[159] The immediate connection with our passage in Paul is obvious: he claims the fundamental right to board and lodging as an Apostle of Jesus.

The function of the saying in its synoptic context is to underline Jesus' command by appealing to an apparently well-known rule: 'Take no gold, nor silver, nor copper in your belts, no bag for your journey, nor two tunics, nor sandals, nor a staff; for the labourer is worthy of his food' (Matt 10:9f). It seems that we have here a traditional saying with halakhic implications, which is applied to the livelihood of the Apostles.

This being the case it is not immediately clear how the terminology of the saying which itself refers to 'labourers' and 'wages' or 'food' actually applies to the Apostles. Remarkably, in this case it is Paul who offers us the key with which we are able to understand a synoptic logion. It is found in his Tora quotation: 'You shall not muzzle the threshing ox.' Interpreted literally, one

---

[157] Barrett p208 states in passing that Paul is far 'from taking the teaching of Jesus as a new *halakah*'. By contrast Weiss 238f sees a parallel with Rabbinic legislation, as in 1Cor 7:10, with significant terms διατάσσω and ἐπιταγή here and elsewhere.

[158] See Fjärstedt, *Synoptic Tradition*. On p73 he points out the 'word cluster' ἀπόστολος – ἔργον-ἐχουσία – ἐσθίω – πίνω – μισθός – εὐαγγλίζομαι. Related thematic appears in 1Cor 3:6-9 (below).

[159] Matt 10:9-13; Luke 10:4-8; cf Luke 9:3-5; Mark 6:8-11. Interestingly my student Hans Timmerman proposes to view 'belt' and 'bag' in Matt 10:9f as a halakhic extension of the 'utensil' כלי of Deut 23:25f.

126

imagines the good ox taking a mouthful of the corn ears as he threshes away. This moving example of humanity towards animals is naturally extended to humans, and that is what we find in Rabbinic literature.[160] The extension is all the more logical since biblical law allows a person passing through the others' fields to eat of their fruit' (Deut 23:24f). Rabbinic tradition restricted this, apparently in accordance with a different sense of justice due to changed circumstances, to mean not everyone but only labourers.[161] Indeed the Mishna and related literature define the rights of labourers to eat of the fruits of the field or orchard they are working in detail,[162] taking into account different local customs.[163] The main tradition appears to be well established by the middle of the first century CE.[164]

It would seem that the synoptic saying, 'The labourer is worthy of his food', is a proverbial summation of these halakhic rules. This is confirmed in Rabbinic literature. A similar saying is contained in a tradition of R. Shimon ben Yohai who expresses amazement about the fact that although the Tora prohibits theft even in the smallest details, the rule is: 'A labourer while working may eat and is innocent of theft.'[165] Both sayings are not just related in subject matter but give a proverbial summation of a halakhic principle which may be termed a 'halakhic saying'.

It seems that in the halakha the labourer's right to eat while working was seen as an additional right not included in his wages, unless otherwise agreed; some landowners would even offer rich meals.[166] This would indicate that the Matthean version of the synoptic saying, 'The labourer is worthy of his food', stays closer to the halakha on field labour, while Luke's version, 'The labourer is worthy of his wages', is a more remote generalization.[167] This is confirmed by R. Shimon ben Yohai's parallel saying which stresses the labourer's right to 'eat'. And this is precisely the implication of the words which precede the saying in Luke and in Matthew: 'Remain in the same house, eating and drinking what they provide, for the labourer...' (Luke 10:7); 'You received without paying, give without pay' (Matt 10:8).

On the other hand this also also parallels the Tannaic view that Tora teaching is not a trade: Tora is a free gift and studying and teaching it is a selfless aim for

---

[160] SifDeut 287 (p305); MidrGad Deut 25:4 (p560f); yMaas 2, 50a; bBM 58b-59a. On the rights and status of (mainly agricultural) labourers in ancient Judaism cf Ayali, *Poalim we-omanim*; for our problem ib 58-61 and selection of sources 153-5.

[161] See TgY Deut 23:24f; SifDeut 266f (p286f) and MidrGad Deut 23:24f (p533-5). Issi ben Akavya maintains the literal sense, everyone being meant: yMaas 2, 50a. In bBM 92a Rav calls him Issi ben Yehuda and states he found his tradition in 'the hidden scroll of R. Hiya'. This may indicate a hasidic background; see Safrai, 'Mishnat hasidim' at n55f.

[162] mBM chap 7; tBM chap 8; yBM 7, 11b (cf yMaas 2, 50a); bBM 87a-93a. The passages in SifDeut and MidrGad mentioned in the previous notes also belong here and contain the same material.

[163] mBM 7:1; yBM 7, 11a, including the rule: 'Custom overrules halakha'.

[164] Akavya ben Mahalalel adds a detail, MidrGad 23:25 (p533).

[165] yMaas 2, 50a. Cf MidrGad 23:25 (p534), 'a labourer eats and is innocent'.

[166] mBM 7:1, 6 (Albeck a.l.); tBM 8:7; SifD 266 (p286); bBM 52a, R. Elazar Hisma and the Sages. And see the section on 'food of labourers' in Ayali, *Poalim we-omanim*, 58-61.

[167] Thus also David Flusser orally.

which one should not receive payment.[168] Working for one's living was held in high regard by the Sages, indeed most of them actually worked for their living, except when they were traveling around and were offered free hospitality out of respect for the Tora.[169]

With this information we will now be able to explain Paul's argument more fully. He points out that he did have the right to be sustained as an Apostle but renounced it so as to remain independent of the Corinthians. Paul chose to consider his extended stay there[170] not as that of a traveling Apostle but as that of any Tora teacher who had to work for his own living. From a parallel passage in Paul's earliest letter (1Thess 4:11, see below) it would seem that the reason for Paul's behaviour was to set an example of financial independence by working. This is indeed what he writes: he taught the gospel 'free' (ἤκὼν) and his 'reward' (μισθός) was precisely this: a gospel 'free of charge' (ἀδάπανος) (1Cor 9:17f). Thus while renouncing the formal right established by the command of the Lord, Paul made sure the intention of Jesus' instruction was kept: 'You received without paying, give without pay'. Paul's behaviour as an Apostle of Jesus here coincided with the fundamentals of Rabbinic Judaism.

(2) As shown, the Tora verse about the threshing ox and its interpretation are crucial to in Paul's argument. Paul asks rhetorically: 'Is it for oxen that God is concerned? Does he not speak entirely for our sake? It was written for our sake...' (1Cor 9:9f). This can be seen as the sarcastic form of a *kal wa-homer* argument.[171] This type of argument on issues like these are common in Rabbinic and Apostolic tradition, not only in the sphere of aggada but also of halakha. The aggadic *kal wa-homer* on this matter is well known from the gospel but is also found in Rabbinic literature: if God feeds the fowl of the air who neither sow nor reap, and dresses the lilies of the field like Solomon in all his glory – 'how much more you, o men of little faith?' (Matt 6:26-30).[172] As for the halakha, the Babylonian Talmud explicitly refers to a 'קל וחומר from the

---

[168] mAv 4:5; 5:22f; 6:1; Mekh Yitro (p205); SifD 48 (p111); MidrPs 68,11 (160a). See Safrai 'Education', 956f and id, 'Oral Tora', 105f.

[169] See Safrai ib 964-6 and sources mentioned there.

[170] According to Acts 18:1-11 Paul lived in Corinth for a year and a half and worked as a tent maker with Prisca and Aquila.

[171] The μὴ... ἤ..; here (as in v8) is a sarcastic rhetorism. Appealing to Philo, Weiss 235f; Conzelmann 183 n38; Barrett 206 (but not Robertson-Plummer) consider this a Hellenistic allegory radically different from a *kal wa-homer*. This is a theorizing exaggeration. Philo Mig 89ff (above p43f) shows consciousness to the distinct value of the literal and spiritual meaning, and Virt 145f maintains the literal sense as an example of the Tora's humane attitude towards animals. Here we have a theoretical *a minori* argument. If Philo, the philosophizing preacher, upheld the literal sense, Paul, steeped in Pharisaic-Rabbinic tradition, would refrain from radical allegorization. His sentiment rather resembles Arist 144. On the other hand Rabbinic halakha allowed the muzzling of a threshing ox as against the literal meaning of the verse, but not without tying a basket with fodder to its mouth and thus fulfilling the intention of the verse: tBM 8:10-12 (see Lieberman a.l.); bBM 89b-90a; cf yTer 9, 46c.

[172] Cf image of שלומו בשעתו for field labourers' meals, mBM 7:1; and *kal wa-homer* about beasts and fowl, mKid 4:14. See related *kal wa-homer* of Jesus in context of despatch narrative, Matt 10:29-31, 'Are you not more than many sparrows?'

128

ox',[173] but in doing so merely applies the technical term to a widespread Tannaic tradition which defines the rights of labourers on the basis of Deut 25:4.[174] The basic tradition, attested in mid-first century, already contains a halakhic *kal wa-homer* from the ox on man.[175]

The halakhic connotation is also implied in the similes of the labourer in the vineyard and the shepherd (v7); they directly relate to the Tannaic halakhic midrash tradition just mentioned.[176] The same holds true for the unidentified verse Paul quotes (v10)[177] to illustrate that the law of the oxen was written 'for our sake': 'Indeed for our sake it was written: "In hope should the plougher plough, and so the thresher, in hope of partaking".' This is not a verse from the Masoretic Bible but seems to reflect a verse of Ben Sira, which work is known to have circulated in Rabbinic circles in various forms and is quoted several times as though it were Scripture.[178] Another almost formal *kal wa-homer* argument serves to draw the lesson (v11): 'If we have sown the things of the Spirit for you, is it a great thing if we reap the things of the flesh from you?' It becomes obvious here that there is a double argument *a minori*: one from the ox on man and another from field labourers on preachers. The common element transferred from one category to another is the right to eat while working. Thus Paul utilizes a halakhic midrash tradition related to a saying of Jesus.

(3) Paul's application of the rule for field labourers to Apostles, which apparently derives from Apostolic tradition,[179] is more than a metaphor because of its halakhic stratum. Yet it also implies a metaphor, and one which is pervasive in Second Temple Judaism: the imagery of agricultural labour, of sowing and harvesting, as representing the Kingdom of Heaven. It is prominent both in the synoptic tradition and in the gospel of John, found in Rabbinic and other Jewish literature, and it also figures in Paul's letters. Let us look at this more closely.

At the beginning of the despatch narrative in Matthew and Luke a Jesus logion is quoted: 'Then he said to his disciples: the harvest is plentiful, but the labourers are few; pray therefore the lord of the harvest to send out labourers into his harvest' (Matt 9:37f; Luke 10:2). A different but related version of this tradition which also has a clear halakhic stratum is found in the gospel of John: 'I tell you: ...see how the fields are already white for harvest; he who reaps

---

[173] bBM 88b.

[174] See sources above n160-2, esp tBM 8:7.

[175] MidrGad 23:25 (p533), Akavya ben Mahalalel.

[176] See the same sources (previous n). The similes of the mercenaries (v7) and the priests (v13) also relate to Rabbinic literature, see Str-B 3, 233 (ὀψωνία) and 400f.

[177] It has poetic quality (Weiss 237) and introduces the new notion of 'hope'; thus it cannot be seen as an interpretation.

[178] Sir 6:18f (Hebr), 'My son, take instruction when young, and in your grey age you shall attain wisdom. Approach her like one who ploughs and reaps [LXX: sows], and you may hope for a rich harvest. For if in her labour you labour little, tomorrow you will eat her fruits.' On Ben Sira see above p75f, 84.

[179] Cf Gal 6:6; 2Tim 2:3-7. See also Jas 5:4 which is restricted to the agricultural context.

129

receives wages, and gathers fruit for eternal life, so that sower and reaper may rejoice together; …I sent you to reap that for which you did not labour…' (John 4:35-38).[180] Note the key words 'harvest', 'labourer', 'sow', 'reap', and 'wages' as distinct from 'fruit unto life eternal'.[181] The metaphor of man as a labourer in God's Kingdom is in evidence in Judaism at least as early as the second century BCE, and shows interesting parallels with the Hippocratic saying *ars longa, vita brevis*.[182] The sayings of R. Tarfon are also revealing: 'The day is short, the work is plentiful, the labourers are indolent, the reward is great and the landowner is urgent. …It is not incumbent on you to finish the work, but neither are you free to abandon it…'[183]

The related metaphor of the seed as denoting the word of God or Tora is basic to a number of Jesus' parables[184] and is also found in the Apocalypse of Ezra[185] and Rabbinic literature.[186] In a wider perspective both Rabbinic aggada and liturgy view the earthly blessing of a rich harvest within the context of the covenant relationship which extends to resurrection into the world to come.[187]

As stated these metaphors appear in Paul's letters too, and not only in the present passage. The applications vary. 1Cor 3:6-9 compares Paul and Apollos as preachers of the gospel with labourers who plant and water and will 'each receive reward according to his own labour', while it is God who gives the increase; this directly relates to the tradition of Apostles as workers in God's harvest in 1Cor 9 and to the synoptic despatch narrative.[188] In 1Cor 15:36-44 Paul uses the simile of the seed to explain the resurrection into the world to come, a simile also attributed to Jesus (John 12:24). Faintly related is Gal 6:7-9 which juxtaposes 'sowing' and 'reaping on the flesh' to the same 'on the Spirit'. Finally 2Cor 9:6, 10 apply 'sowing' and 'reaping' to charity connected with the collection for Jerusalem. In this connection 2Cor 9:10 uses a remarkable expression which does not fit in traditional Paulinism: 'He Who supplies seed to

---

[180] The talk of food v31-34 also relates to this complex and its halakhic stratum. But for the extant gospel halakhic connotations seem to have become meaningless.

[181] Cf fruits in this world vs main reward in the world to come, in return for exemplary good deeds (mPea 1:1); treasures gathered in heaven by loving kindness (tPea 4:18; yPea 1, 15a; Matt 6:19 par; Luke 12:16-21; Matt 19:21 parr).

[182] See Flusser, *Gleichnisse*, 141-58: *ars* = τέχνη, 'craft'. See his important remarks on the wider implications of such relationships between Rabbinic parables and popular Greek ethics. Cf Jesus' parables of labourers and tenants, Matt 20:1-15; Matt 21:33-39 parr.

[183] mAv 2:15f.

[184] Matt 13:3-8 parr; Matt 13:24-30; Mark 4:26-29. See Flusser, *Gleichnisse*, 122-8 on 'allegory' in these parables.

[185] 4Ezra 4:28-32; 8:41-44; 9:17, 30-37.

[186] tSot 7:11, Tora a plant which multiplies; ARN b 34 (38a-b), good deeds as roots of a plant. Both are attributed to R. Elazar ben Azaria. – The λόγος σπερματικός seems another stray seed blown away by the spirit.

[187] On rain, childbirth and resurrection see GenR 13,3-6 (p115-7); MidrGad Deut 28:12 (p610-3); and parr indicated there. On liturgy see prayer for rain and fasts for drought, mTaan chs 1-2. In one Palestinian version of *birkat ha-shanim* (9th benediction of the *Shemone Esrei*) the prayer for a good harvest is directly associated with the coming of the 'end': קיץ (Elbogen, *Gottesdienst*, 49); the play is on the word קיץ (summer).

[188] See Fjärstedt (above n158).

the sower and bread for food (Isa 55:10) ...will increase the revenues of your charity (δικαιοσύνης).'[189]

Summing up we can state that Paul expounds his rights as an Apostle in connection with a halakhic saying of Jesus, developing the halakhic midrash on which the latter is based. Such connections were quickly and completely lost from Christian tradition, with the result that today they have to be 'discovered' anew. The development was facilitated by the rapid influx of gentile Christians, stimulated by Paul himself, and is already reflected in the New Testament. One of the deutero-Pauline letters supports the call to honour preachers and teachers as follows: 'For the scripture says: "You shall not muzzle the ox when it is treading out the grain", and, "The labourer deserves his wages" (1Tim 5:18). The Jesus logion is quoted, in its secondary Lukan form, as though it were Scripture. The author shows no awareness that it concerns a halakhic saying expounding the verse just quoted; he purports to be quoting two independent, authoritative sayings each supplementing the other. The loss of distinction between 'Scripture' and gospel, between Written Tora and midrash, suggests we are confronted here with an early, canonized example of the *de facto* hellenization and de-judaization of Pauline tradition.[190] It reminds us that it was Paul's fate to be read and preserved in later history – on the basis of being misunderstood.[191] And unfortunately, this is not restricted to the concern for oxen either.

Worship and Liturgy (1Cor 11-14)

Chapters 11-14 of First Corinthians are wholly devoted to worship and liturgy. It is a weighty subject which sometimes involves appeal to doubled or even tripled formal sources of authority. The section is introduced as being about 'traditions' taught by Paul (11:2). Other explicit designations used are the 'practice' of the 'church of God' (11:16); that which Paul 'received from the Lord and also delivered to you' (11:23); that which is 'written in the Law' (14:21); and that which is customary 'in all the churches of the saints... as even the Law says', and which moreover 'is a command of the Lord' (14:34, 37).

PARTICIPATION OF WOMEN

The liturgical section contains two instructions regarding the participation of women during worship: their headcovering (11:3-16) and their silence (14:33-36). These commandments have a multiple interest for present-day study into Paul and the Jewish Law.

In the first place the two passages stand out remarkably in First Corinthians and particularly here. The other subjects treated are practical procedures at the eucharist (11:17-34) and, in a complex argument, the spiritual gifts of speaking

---

[189] This relates to the material mentioned above n181.
[190] De-judaization does not of necessity imply anti-Judaism, but has no defense against it.
[191] Cf Overbeck's saying, above p10 n43.

in tongues and prophesying (12:1-14:33). While the concluding instruction on female silence apparently refers to the public activities of female prophets, the one concerning the headcovering prefaces the adhortation for decency during the sacred community meals. In effect the two laws on women open and close the entire section on worship. This can hardly be considered co-incidental and signifies special emphasis.

In the second place, as we shall see below, the traditions involved are closely related to ancient Jewish custom. As has been stated they are explicitly introduced as 'traditions' (παραδόσεις) and 'custom' (συνήθεια) followed by all 'churches of God' or 'churches of the holy' (1Cor 11:3, 16; 14:34). The authoritative, Jewish-Christian character of such formal ascriptions has been outlined in the previous chapter. Indeed these passages well illustrate that Paul is no exception to the general affirmation of patriarchy in antiquity and in this sense he appears to be firmly rooted in ancient Jewish tradition.

In the third place these passages have been used in the framework of Christian social teaching to support the subjugation of women even in cultural situations where such did not or no longer corresponded to women's self-awareness.[192] Historical criticism, which originated in a post-revolutionary climate of profound social and religious transformation, by nature must face up to the various interests reflected in and projected into these texts and try to decode the distinct messages they imply.

In the perspective of a feminist-oriented historical criticism,[193] Elisabeth SCHÜSSLER FIORENZA emphasizes the strategic function of these laws in First Corinthians, making a link with with the prominence of Chloe in 1Cor 1:11 and the crucial role of women in the marriage instructions in ch 7. She also interprets Paul's authoritative language in First Corinthians as a repressive reaction to the more liberal position of women in the Corinthian church.[194] As such it would indicate Paul's regression from an original Christian egalitarianism.[195] This is a compelling analysis, but one important aspect of historical criticism is not taken into account: the genetic relation of early Christianity to Judaism.[196]

---

[192] For this perspective see Stendahl, *Bible*.

[193] For a thorough theoretical discussion see Schüssler Fiorenza, *Bread*, esp chs 5-6 (recognizing a hopeful solidarity both with liberation and 'post-holocaust' theology, p114f).

[194] Schüssler Fiorenza, 'Rhetorical Situation'; less radical in *Memory*, 226-33. There is some exaggeration here. Authoritative speech is densest in 1Cor 14:34-37 which directly relates to female silence, but aims also at spiritual gifts and the eucharist. But stronger language is used for the idol offerings (1Cor 10:1-23) and especially the incest case (5:1-6:20), in which women's rights are not emphasized.

[195] This projects Enlightenment rationalism into Paul (cf 'the abolition of the religious distinctions between Jew and Greek'; *Memory*, 210, 213). Correspondingly the author rejects the pluralist interpretation of Paul's ecclesiology ironically as 'the "equal but different assumption" ' (p207) and takes 1Cor 7:17-21 to mean that 'Paul clearly does not [sic] advise the former Jew or the former gentile to remain in their Jewish or pagan state' (p221). More moderate is 'Die Frauen', 129.

[196] Jewish feminist criticism applies, see Plaskow-Daum, 'Blaming Jews', 11 (mentioning Fiorenza, ib 13); cf also Brooten, 'Jewish Women's History'. While aware of this criticism (*Memory*, 105-7), Schüssler Fiorenza's description of the 'Jesus Movement' as a 'Renewal Movement Within Judaism' (ib ch4) is inadequate. The idea of Jesus as 'the woman-identified man' (p154) and of his followers as 'the discipleship of equals' (p107) is a romanticism in view of the massive patriarchalism of Jewish

An adequate assessment of Paul's stance on the rights of women, which is incumbent on his modern interpreters,[197] requires a historic-critical evaluation of (1) his relation to contemporary Jewish and Jewish-Christian traditions and (2) the attitudes towards women in those traditions. While Paul's relationship to Jewish tradition is the main subject of the present study, some words about the place of women in ancient Jewish society and worship are relevant here.

Apparently quite in line with contemporary Mediterranean culture,[198] Josephus summarized the position of women in ancient Judaism: 'The woman, says [the Law], is in all things inferior to the man; let her therefore be submissive, not for her humiliation, but that she may be directed; for the authority (κράτος) has been given by God to the man.'[199] While later Tannaic halakha as reflected in the Mishna gave the woman legal power, the ancient conception reflected in Philo and Josephus her permanent subordination, if not to her father or brother, then to her husband.[200] This social inferiority was expressed in the woman's dress. While in general women were supposed to appear in public as little as possible,[201] an unmarried girl could occasionally go out with her hair uncovered,[202] but the headcovering of the married woman when appearing in public was an essential feature of the 'Law of the Jews', violation of which was considered very serious: 'These (women) are divorced without their *ketuba* (marriage contract stating the divorce fee): if she transgresses the Law of Moses and the Jews דת משה ויהודים. ...What (is a transgression of) the Law of the Jews? If she goes out with her hair unbound, or spins in the street, or talks to everyone...'[203] Conversely, men did not cover their head as a rule: 'Why does the woman cover her head and does the man not cover his head?'[204] The reason given in the latter tradition is Eve's sin – an answer commensurate with that of common male Jewish opinion of the day, like the one expressed by Paul that woman was created second (1Cor 11:8), or Philo, that womanhood is inferior and sense-directed.[205] Greek and Roman head covering fashions were different. Roman men apparently used to wear veils during religious ceremonies,[206] while

and Apostolic tradition.

[197] An admirable endeavour, though practically excluding Rabbinic literature, is Küchler, *Schweigen*.

[198] See Heinemann's unsparing and passionate analysis, *Bildung*, 231-53, placing Philo in general Hellenistic and Jewish perspective. Only some Cynics seem to have been an exception, ib 233. Heinemann's more positive impression about the Mishna (e.g. p240) does not hold for mid-first century halakha, certainly not in Alexandria; see above p38f.

[199] Ag Ap 2:201. 'The Law' (ὁ νόμος ib 199) refers not to the written Law but to the halakha.

[200] See Belkin, *Alexandrian Halakah*, 53-55; id *Philo*, 225-8; Heinemann, *Bildung*, 302-9.

[201] Cf Philo, Spec leg 3:169-172.

[202] mKet 2:1; yKet 2, 26b. Even girls often remained inside the house in Jewish and general Hellenistic custom: Heinemann, *Bildung*, 234f.

[203] mKet 7:6; cf mBK 8:6; mShab 6:1, 5. See Str-B 3, 423-35. See Lieberman, *Texts*, 54-56 on pious Jewish women even covering their faces.

[204] ARN b 9 (13a); according to the parallel GenR 17 (p159) the author of the derasha is R. Yoshua. See Str-B 3, 423-6 for later traditions indicating occasional headcovering by males in the talmudic period. The standard Jewish scullcap is a medieval innovation.

[205] Above n54, 58. See Spec leg 3:169-180.

[206] Oster, 'Veils'.

in certain Hellenistic cult rites, which may have been familiar to Corinthian gentiles, women participated with hair unbound.[207]

As to community worship, the participation of women was generally accepted in Judaism as a matter of course. While the majority of Essenes shunned the presence of women,[208] in other pious circles the presence of men and women during worship, even though seated separately, was apparently well established.[209] The evidence of literary and archeological sources is that female attendance in synagogue was a regular practice. Women used to pray along with the men in the main room, and only in the middle ages did the women's gallery become a standard part of the synagogue.[210] Combined evidence also suggests that women played prominent roles: many extant inscriptions mention female 'leaders', 'elders' and 'mothers of synagogues'.[211] While the impression is that these were not mere honorific titles, they may have been related to any of the various social and religious functions of the ancient synagogue and not necessarily have indicated a liturgical function.[212] On the other hand, the Tannaim held that women should not officiate during community prayers: 'One does not invite women to read out before the community'.[213] In other words they are not accepted as 'deputy of the community' שליח ציבור (shaliah tsibbur) to pray or read in the name of the community.[214] In view of the more general subordination of women,[215] this must have been common practice. Thus women attended synagogue but prayed silently and did not officiate.

For Paul too, female participation in community worship was self-evident. Elsewhere, he advocates the participation of women in an interesting midrashic tradition. Using the verse in which God promises David that his son shall build a temple (2Sam 7:14) he continues: 'For we are the temple of the living God, as God said: ..."I will be a father to you, and you shall be sons and daughters to Me, says the Lord Almighty"' (2Cor 6:16-18). The verse reads, 'I will be a to him, and he shall be a son to Me'; hence Paul not only changes to the plural

---

[207] See references in Schüssler Fiorenza, *Memory*, 227.

[208] Above n55.

[209] TReub 6:1f suggests separation of men and women 'in order to purify their minds'. Similarly the Therapeutes worshipped while men and women could not see each other, Philo, Vit cont 32f; but cf ib 83-89.

[210] For sources and treatment see Safrai, 'Women's Gallery', and 'Synagogue', 919-21 and, following him, Brooten, *Women Leaders*, 103-47.

[211] Brooten, *Women Leaders*; Kraemer, 'A New Inscription'.

[212] See vague evidence adduced by Brooten ib. On the function and organisation of the diaspora synagogue see Applebaum, 'Organization'; on Palestinian city leadership Safrai, 'Self-Government', 412-7.

[213] tMeg 3:11, see Lieberman a.l.!; bMeg 23a.

[214] The Bavli gives as basic explanation 'respect for the community'. Other commentaries point out that a woman does not have the biblical obligation to read and therefore cannot fulfil the obligation of the community (cf mRH 3:8); see Lieberman, *Tosefta Ki-fshutah* 5, 1176-8; cf Albeck, *Mishna* 2, 366 (on mMeg 4:6). SifDeut 235 (p269) cites the rule, 'Women have no authority (רשות) to speak in the name of men', in connection with the woman's testimony (Deut 22:16), which suggests that women could not officiate because of legal incompetence.

[215] See mAv 1:5, summary of halakhot tSot 2,7-9, and cf mKet 4:4 and mSot3:8.

'sons' but adds 'and daughters'.[216] While the context of the exposition emphasizes Christian separation from paganism by means of dualistic language reminiscent of Essenism,[217] the targumic inclusion of the 'daughters' points toward Pharisaic mainstream Judaism. Paul's exposition also seems to draw on Isa 43:6, 'Bring my sons from afar and my daughters from the end of the earth', which apart from the daughters also suggests the inclusion of gentiles in the church.[218]

Now we turn to Paul's instruction about the headcovering of women during worship. In the light of the above, it is in no way remarkable for its own time. The argument opens with a statement which leaves no doubts about the Apostle's view:[219]

> The head of every man is Christ, but the head of woman is the man, and the head of the Christ is God. Any man who prays or prophesies with his head covered dishonours his head, and any woman who prays or prophesies with her head unveiled dishonours her head. (1Cor 11:3-5a).

Reason is selective: a woman praying bareheaded dishonours her 'man', but a man when praying should uncover his head in honour of Christ. Paul further develops the idea of 'dishonour' by stating that a woman who prays bareheaded might as well have her head shaven, which in his eyes is equally disgraceful (1Cor 11:5b-6). In ancient Judaism a shaven woman was repugnant and could be divorced.[220] Another connotation which is directed more at the readers may be that in the Isis cult, which was present in Corinth, male initiates had their hair shaven.[221]

Then another element is introduced: 'A man is not obliged to cover his head, since he is the image and glory of God, but the woman is the glory of a man' (v7). This continues the usage of man as 'the head' in v3, but involves a biblical allusion. In fact it is an androcentric midrash which expounds the words 'in the image of God he created him' (Gen 1:27) as separate from the clause immediately following, 'male and female he created them' and hence as referring to man only. The insinuation is that woman was not created in the image of God.[222] Another biblical allusion is added: 'Indeed a man was not created for the woman but a woman for the man; therefore a woman is obliged to have an

---

[216] Attention to this passage is also drawn by Schüssler Fiorenza, *Memory*, 194-6.

[217] 4Qflor 1:1-13 views the community as a spiritual temple on the basis of 2Sam 7 (Flusser, 'Two Notes'; Dimant, 'Qumran', 518-21). TLev 19:1 uses related dualistic language including the name of Beliar. The possibility of a Qumranic interpolation was raised by Fitzmeyer, 'Qumran'; Betz, '2 Cor 6:14-7:1' sees cultic and anti-gentile anti-Paulinism. Positions are summarized by Thrall, 'Problem'.

[218] Another parallel is Ps 107:3. This midrash seems also reflected in Matt 8:11, but in an un-Pauline, anti-Jewish revision (see Flusser, 'Two Anti-Jewish Montages').

[219] I am indebted to Jaap van der Meij for his perceptive comments on the structure of 1Cor 11:2-16.

[220] mNaz 4:5; tNez 3:12-14; cf Str-B 3, 434f. The main spokesman is R. Akiva. See Lieberman, *Tosefta Ki-fshutah* 7, 531-3 on the complicated explanation in the Bavli; and note by Albeck, *Mishna* 4, 374. Later Jewish and Christian sources mention shaving the head as a punishment for indecency: Lieberman, *Texts*, 53f.

[221] See reference in Schüssler Fiorenza, *Memory*, 227.

[222] More positively Schüssler ib 229.

authority (ἐξουσία) her head, because of the angels' (1Cor 11:9f). Ἐξουσία equals Hebrew רשות: authority, power.[223] What appears to be meant is the veil precisely as a sign of woman's subordination to man.[224] The clause mentioning 'angels' sounds incidental but may actually explain the main statement: the 'angels' should be reminded that the woman is under authority. It connects with ancient traditions about the seduction of angels by women,[225] and incidentally this gives us another glimpse of Paul's realistic angelology. Thus Paul's midrash demonstrates the subordination of women from the biblical perspective.

At this point Paul's rhetorical sensitivity seems to lead him to introduce a quite different line of thought, which even runs against the grain of his argument: 'At any rate, woman is not apart from man nor man from woman, in the Lord; for as the woman is from the man, so the man is through the woman; and all is from God' (v11f).[226] The mood here is one of tolerance and equality and of the relativity of all human positions. It is reminiscent of Stoic-Cynic ideas more clearly expressed in other passages,[227] as well as of the ecclesial christology expressed by Paul especially in Galatians.[228]

This leads us to the final phase of the argument. It begins by reiterating the theme of shamefulness (v13; cf v5) and then adds a new aspect apparently meant to be irresistible to the Corinthians: 'Does not nature itself teach you that for a man to wear long hair is degrading to him, but if a woman grows long hair it is her glory? For her hair is given to her for a covering' (11:14f). The reference to nature is another typical feature of the Cynico-Stoic tradition (above p85) and may have been placed at the end, after the biblical motive, because of its universal appeal. What it also shows is that 'nature' could refer to such obvious cultural features as hair-styling.

An authoritative statement, stressing the 'custom' recognized by the Apostle and the 'churches of God', closes the discussion (v16).[229] In line with Jewish practice, women must cover their heads at least when praying.

The question remains as to what situation Paul's command concerning female headcovering during worship refers to. It is often thought to contradict the

---

[223] See below n283. G. Kittel and before him Herklotz (BZ 10 p 154) supposed a more direct connection with שלטונ(י)א (yShab 6, 8b) = 'head-band', but lit. 'authority'. See Str-B 3, 436; Klausner, Von Jesus zu Paulus, 524 n27; and the rich note in Weiss 274f.

[224] Schüssler Fiorenza, Memory, 227 reads 11:15 ἀντὶ as 'instead' (of a head-covering) and on that basis rejects a parallel with the Jewish custom. Unconvincingly she proposes to interpret Paul's teaching as a positive affirmation of 'bound-up hair as the symbol of women's prophetic-charismatic power' (230). This overlooks (in spite of ib p229) the link with v7 where the woman, including her hair, is the husband's glory (in Paul's view). 'Decency' forbade Jews except the husband to look at a woman's hair, cf mSot 1:5. See below.

[225] Above at n58; cf Küchler, Schweigen, 89-110.

[226] Schüssler Fiorenza ib 229 reads this as Paul's assurance that he maintains sex equality in the church. The atmosphere here is very similar to R. Yoshua's derasha, see n204.

[227] See below ch 6.

[228] E.g. 3:28; see Conclusion below.

[229] It is less reasonable to associate the 'custom' with 'being contentious', but the net result is the same.

prohibition for women to speak up during worship.[230] But there is no reason to suppose that prayer and prophecy should always be aloud when practised in the community. The headcovering of married women would naturally apply both in private and public worship, irrespective of their speaking or being silent. It should not be confused with the issue of female officiating.

The silence of women in church (1Cor 14:33-38) is emphasized by Paul according to ancient Jewish traditions: 'For they are not permitted to speak but should be subordinate, as also the Law says' (1Cor 14:34). The reference to 'the Law' apparently needed no explanation, but again may be assumed to refer to the Genesis narrative.[231] At any rate it seems that Paul, in line with Tannaic tradition, opposes the idea that women be allowed to speak in the name of the congregation or in other words that they should not be allowed to officiate as *shaliah tsibbur*. This interpretation seems confirmed by the halakhic implications of 1Cor 14:16 (below). Opposition to public performance by women was also found in Roman circles.[232] A further specification by Paul which apparently no longer refers to actual worship is remarkable: 'If they want to be informed about anything, let them ask their own men at home' (v35). This opinion seems to reflect the more restrictive and conservative trend in ancient Judaism. There are reports of women bringing their questions to the Houses of Study, but not all Sages welcomed this, notably R. Eliezer the Shammaite.[233] It is remarkable that this opinion is represented in Apostolic Christianity.

Judging from the textual variants, resistance to the accumulated authority of the commandment is ancient; modern exegetes are also inclined to radical solutions.[234] A number of manuscripts place v34f after v40 and in v37 omit the word ἐντολή.[235] The effect is that not only does the silence of women become a secondary appendix but the rhetorical unity is broken. 14:39f clearly give a concluding rule: 'So, my brethren, be zealous to prophesy and do not prevent speaking in tongues, but do everything decently and in order.' Another solution is offered by the manuscripts which read a plural in v37, 'commandments of the Lord',[236] to the effect that female silence would be one item among many. The question then comes down to where the actual summary of the chapter begins: in v39 or earlier. But this is no real problem. As usual, Paul comes up with an important subject at the end. Even if the summary were to start at v36 and the accumulation of authority sources were to refer to the chapter as a whole, the words on female silence would resound poignantly in the reader's ears. As they

---

[230] Schüssler ib 230f takes 14:33-36 to refer to wives and 11:2-16 to unmarried women. See above.

[231] The parallel in 1Tim 2:13f suggests Gen 1:27 and 2:18-23. Str-B 3, 468 also propose Gen 3:16.

[232] Schüssler Fiorenza, *Memory*, 231f adduces a striking parallel from Livy. Sevenster, *Paul and Seneca*, 192-6 describes Seneca's view of women as rather lowly with occasional exceptions.

[233] Safrai, 'Oral Tora', 68f. See mSot 3:4; mNed 4:3; ySot 3, 18d-19a; yHag 1, 75d.

[234] Conzelmann p298f considers the passage an interpolation since it contradicts 11:2ff, deviates in vocabulary and reflects post-Pauline bourgeois consolidation. He fails to refer to 11:16 (but cf his sceptical treatment there, p233f).

[235] D*, F, G, b, Ambst; Dodd, 'Ennomos', 105 n1 (below n239) adds Origen.

[236] D², Athos ms, Byzantine majority, lat, sy, sa.

seem to be meant to do.

The accumulation of formal authority sources in this instance is unmistakably emphatic: the appeal is to the custom of the 'congregations of the Holy' (v33b); to 'the Law' (v34); and to a 'commandment of the Lord' (v37). If we add the strategic position of the two women's commandments in the letter, the impression is that Paul must have come against fundamental resistance here. One is reminded of the possibility of active participation of women in non-Jewish cult societies.[237] Inscriptions indicate that even the θεολογία, the festive speech at a banquet in honour of the gods, could be delivered by a woman.[238] Paul's instruction regarding his gentile sisters on this point appears to have implied that they should assimilate to Jewish custom; and to a stricter variant in fact, one which even excluded asking questions.

Most intriguing is Paul's appeal to a Jesus tradition: 'If anyone thinks that he is a prophet, or spiritual, he should acknowledge that what I am writing to you is a commandment of the Lord (Κυρίου ἐντολή, 14:37). If this reading is acceptable, as seems confirmed by the undisputed Pauline ἐπιταγή Κυρίου in 1Cor 7:25,[239] it is unique in the New Testament. While parallel phrases are found in the Johannine tradition,[240] the word ἐντολή otherwise generally refers to a commandment of the Tora. The expression ἐντολή Κυρίου however is attested in the later Apostolic writings.[241] First Corinthians apparently reveals its Apostolic origin.

The precise contents of this 'commandment of the Lord' are not clear. As we have seen, the solution of reading it as referring to the Apostolic authority of Paul's teaching in general does not suffice. Moreover such appeals are made in a much more specific sense elsewhere in First Corinthians.[242] In this case the extant gospel tradition does not help us out; Paul is our only source for this sort of teaching of Jesus. The combination with the equally obscure appeal to 'the Law' leads us to hypothesize some midrash on the creation story which figures elsewhere in Paul's other instruction as well as in Jesus' teachings.[243]

Apparently Paul's reference to Jesus cannot easily be dismissed on literary grounds. This raises the historical question about Jesus' attitude towards women. While women are prominent in many gospel stories, an openness towards women also seems to be typical of the hasidic personalities who figure in ancient Rabbinic literature.[244] But the question is whether this necessarily implies a more liberal stance on public offices held by women. Jesus' strong emphasis on modesty and decency towards the opposite sex (Matt 5:27-30) and, as in ancient

---

[237] See Moffatt, xxi, 149; and references by Schüssler Fiorenza, *Memory*, 229f.

[238] Poland, *Geschichte*, 268. See also ib 289ff on the position of women.

[239] See above n235. Dodd rejects ἐντολή in view of the ms evidence, and because he cannot see how the rule can follow both from 'the Law' and a 'commandment of the Lord'.

[240] John 13:34; 14:15, 21; 15:10, 12; 1John and 2John *passim*.

[241] Did 4:13 and Barn 19:2, both in the catechism of the Two Ways; cf Ign Eph 9:2, Tr 3:1 (cf Sm 8:1); Polyc Phil 4:1.

[242] Cf 9:4-14; 3:6, 10f, 4:15; and, especially, 7:6-12, 25, 40.

[243] 1Cor 11:8f; Mark 10:6f; cf 1Cor 6:16.

[244] Safrai, 'Hasidim', 141-4.

hasidic tradition, on inwardness and concentration in prayer (Matt 6:5f), suggests a more complex situation.[245] It is of course thinkable that on certain details the early Apostolic church headed by James the brother of the Lord was stricter than Jesus himself, but this should not be assumed automatically. At any rate Paul draws on a custom which Apostolic tradition ascribed to Jesus.

Each generation takes its own message from sacred texts. Traditionally the stress is laid on the element of patriarchy in these passages. A generation which has become sensitive to the value of social equality and conceives social change as a human activity has no choice but to focus on the aspect of equality which is explicit in other texts:[246] 'There is neither Jew nor Greek, there is neither slave nor free, there is neither male nor female; for you are all one in Christ Jesus' (Gal 3:28); 'At any rate, woman is not apart from man nor man from woman, in the Lord; for as the woman is from the man, so the man is through the woman; and all is from God' (1Cor 11:11f). As in other passages, this theoretical egalitarianism is of Cynico-Stoic provenance.[247]

THE EUCHARIST

The section on the eucharist (1Cor 11:17-34) involves a number of halakhic elements. Paul calls it κυριακὸν δεῖπνον 'supper of the Lord' (1Cor 11:20), apparently because of the tradition 'from the Lord' (v23) which is at its centre. It appears to be meant as a community meal, the decorous character of which was blurred in Corinth. Quite bluntly Paul reprimands his church: 'In giving you this instruction I do not commend you...; Shall I commend you in this? No, I will not' (v17, 22; cf v2!). In reaction Paul most formally presents the 'tradition':[248]

> For I received from the Lord what I also delivered to you, that the Lord Jesus on the night when he was betrayed took bread, and having said a benediction broke it and said, This is my body for you; do this in order to remember me. In the same way also the cup, after supper, saying, This cup is the new covenant in my blood; do this, as often as you drink it, in order to remember me. ...Whoever, therefore, eats the bread or drinks the cup of the Lord in an unworthy manner will be guilty of (profaning) the body and blood of the Lord. (1Cor 11:23-26)

The tradition was already well-known to the Corinthians, and for some reason the Apostle repeats it word by word in his instructional letter. Paul adds at the end of the section: 'About the other things I will give instructions διατάξομαι when I come' (v34). The atmosphere is that of practical instruction and involves halakha.

---

[245] Cf mBer 5:1, 5 (on which see Safrai, 'Mishnat hasidim', 147-50). On 'snakes and scorpions' cf Luke 10:19; 11:12.

[246] Thus with admirable frankness Stendahl, *Bible*.

[247] Cf indications in Heinemann, *Bildung*, 233 and Conclusion below. Nevertheless it is striking that in both parallels in 1Cor (7:17-24; 12:13) the male-female binary is lacking.

[248] Following the text in the major mss, including P46.

139

Communal meals were a common phenomenon in the Hellenistic world. Their counterparts in Pharisaic-Rabbinic Judaism were known as *havura*-meals.[249] These had an elaborate liturgical order which differed according to custom, as appears from an extended halakhic disputation between Shammaites and Hillelites regarding the correct sequence of the various ritual elements and corresponding benedictions.[250] Similarly the Qumran scrolls contain rudimentary indications of a decorous liturgy at table. Among the participants, who are seated by rank, the priest is always first to say the blessing and partake of 'bread and wine' (the importance of this order will be apparent below).[251] Josephus and Philo refer to the communal meals of the Essenes and Therapeutae. In the case of the Essenes they are surrounded with intricate purity rituals, and the participants, dressed in white and seated in hierarchical order, attended silently, listening to sermons or chanting sacred songs.[252]

Comparison of liturgical meals mentioned in the Didache with Jewish literature shows that the early Christian community meal developed from the *havura* meals.[253] Characteristic elements are the benedictions preceding and concluding the meal, and the language used.[254] The very expressions εὐχαριστέω and εὐλογέω which are used alternately reflect the language of Jewish 'benedictions':[255] לברך or להודות.[256] In the same way εὐχαριστία equals ברכה or הודאה in 1Cor 14:16 (see below).

Thus it appears that the 'supper of the Lord' was a sacred meal of the community of Christ and that it was to have a decorous liturgical order, which began and ended with a festive blessing in which a commemoration of the Lord was included. From oral reports (1Cor 11:18) it had transpired to Paul that at Corinth the liturgical order, which he considered essential, did not function: 'It is not the Lord's supper that you eat; for in eating each one goes ahead with his own meal, and one is hungry and another is drunk' (v21). This implied a violation of the 'body', i.e. the body of Christ (v27, 29, cf 24), for it enhanced

[249] See Lieberman, *Texts*, 200-7 (= *JBL* 71 [1951] 199-206); Neusner, 'Fellowship'.
[250] mBer 8; and esp tBer 5-6.
[251] 1QS 6:4-6; 1QSa 2:17-22.
[252] War 2:129-133; Vit cont 66-82.
[253] Alon, *Studies* 1, 286-91 (above p24). Alon rejects the artificial distinction scholars make between the 'real Eucharist' on Sundays in Did 14:1 and ἀγαπή meals on other days in 9:1, pointing out that one basic liturgical form is involved which developed from the חבורה meals.
[254] The expressions ἁγία ἄμπελος connected with the cup (Did 9:2), and even more γένημα τῆς ἀμπέλου (Matt 26:29; Mark 14:25; Luke 22:18), directly remind of the פרי הגפן of the Jewish benediction upon wine, mBer 6:1. Cf also κλάσματος Did 9:3 ms H ἄρτου in other mss).
[255] Both words indiscriminately in 1Cor 14:16f. For benediction on regular bread: εὐλογέω in Matt 14:19 parr and Acts 24:30; but εὐχαριστέω Matt 15:36 parr. In connection with the last supper: εὐλογέω in Matt 26:26 and Mark 14:22 on bread, in 1Cor 10:16 on wine; εὐχαριστέω in Luke 22:19 and 1Cor 11:24 on bread, in Matt and Mark ib on wine. In Did 9:1-5 and Justin, Apol 1:66,3 only εὐχαριστέω which may be on the way towards εὐχαριστέω as a specific term for 'Eucharist' i.e. sacred Christian meal. Cf 1Cor 10:16 ποτήριον τῆς εὐχαριστίας (instead of εὐλογίας) in some later mss. Cf Conzelmann p290 and ib n58-60 on Hellenistic-Jewish usage.
[256] לברך became the standard Rabbinic term, while להודות remained in use (cf the 18th benediction of the *Shemone Esrei*); in Qumran להודות was current, see the 'Hodayot', but לברך was also used, e.g. at table: 1QS 6:5; 1QSa 2:19, 21.

the contrast between the poor and the rich: 'Or do you despise the church of God and humiliate those who have nothing?' (v22). It also involved a serious violation of the liturgical order: 'when you come together to eat, wait for one another' (v33). What Paul appears to imply is that the church members should await the festive blessing before starting to eat, just as at the meals of the Pharisaic *havurot* and at Qumran, and probably also that they should not eat after the final cup.

This implication may explain an intriguing question: why does Paul quote the entire 'eucharist' tradition, since we may suppose that the Corinthians knew it by heart? What Paul seems to mean by quoting the eucharist tradition is that the last supper of the Lord involved the same decorous order. As has been indicated, thematic words from the eucharist tradition like the 'body' also play a role, but what Paul seems to need here specifically is to stress 'that the Lord Jesus ...took bread, and having said a benediction broke it and said... in the same way also the cup, after supper...'. In other words Paul repeats the well-known eucharist tradition in order to teach the correct beginning and ending of the 'supper of the Lord'. As in Qumran and Rabbinic tradition, this belongs in the genre of halakha.

Incidentally the Apostolic *havura* meal seems to include a halakhic variation which is reminiscent of the controversies on the table liturgy between Shammaites and Hillelites, and of which our text is a part.[257] Other important documents are the synoptic eucharist tradition and the Qumran Community Rule. The issue is which comes first: bread or wine. One synoptic version has the order 'bread-wine' which, as we saw, is also found in the Qumran scrolls; it appears in Matt 26:26-29 and Mark 14:22-25 and, judging by the manuscript evidence in the Lukan parallel, came to be considered official by the Church. On the other hand Did 9:1-4 and some versions of Luke 22:15-20 preserve the order 'wine-bread' which may be considered the more general contemporary Jewish usage.[258] The version found in most other manuscripts in Luke is composite and apparently, in line with the official Church order, involves a secondary addition from the present text in Paul,[259] the result being that Jesus pronounces both on a cup before and after the meal.[260]

Thus the official order, which happens to conform to the Essene tradition, is reflected in what Paul here formally transmits as being Apostolic tradition: 'I received from the Lord what I also delivered to you, that the Lord Jesus ...took bread... In the same way also the cup, after supper...' (1Cor 11:23-25). The words 'after supper' μετὰ τὸ δειπνῆσαι remarkably indicate the cup introducing a blessing *after* meal, an element not found in Mark and Matthew. It

---

[257] This issue was raised by Flusser, 'Last Supper'.
[258] Flusser seems to be right in concluding that Luke 22:19b-20 is an awkward harmonization. The words are absent in D and most old Latin mss. Adapting this apparently more original version to the 'official' order, the old Latin mss b and e and the Syrian mss in various combinations place v19 (bread) first and omit the additional cup of v20. The language is decisive, see next n.
[259] See characteristic expressions τοῦτο ποιεῖτε εἰς τὴν ἐμὴν ἀνάμνησιν and μετὰ τὸ δειπνῆσαι.
[260] In turn some other versions cure this difficulty by radically omitting v17-18 (first cup).

would seem obvious to think here of an expression Paul uses in passing in his discussion of idol offerings: 'the cup of blessing which we bless' (ποτήριον τῆς εὐλογίας ὃ εὐλογοῦμεν 1Cor 10:16). The expression has a direct Hebrew parallel, כוס של ברכה, which in Rabbinic literature denotes the cup after meal.[261] But the situation is more complex. In 1Cor 10:16 the expression occurs quite unemphatically *before* the mention of the eucharist bread and hence refers to the common Jewish order: 'the cup of blessing which we bless... the bread which we break...' An explanation could be that in Paul's day the expression was not fixed and could be used to refer to the opening cup.

In any event it is most interesting to note that in 1Cor 10:16, where Paul does not formally quote Apostolic tradition, he follows the more common Jewish order. Hence the phrase 'after supper' in 1Cor 11:25 is remarkable in view of two other facts: even though the order in the synoptic parallels is also bread-wine, this phrase is absent; and in 1Cor 10:16 Paul inadvertently follows the order wine-bread. It may well be that the phrase is an explanatory addition which, in line with the rhetorical purpose of the eucharist quotation, serves to emphasize the decorous table liturgy: the 'cup after supper' concludes the meal with a festive blessing. It would be unrealistic to consider this an incidental invention; it must reflect an actual custom. This adds to our information about Christian diversity on the eucharist order. We already had the Essenish order of 'bread and wine' at the beginning of the meal, as in the synoptics, as well as the more common Jewish order wine-bread found in the Didache, the shorter version of Luke and in 1Cor 10:16. In addition we now have the option of bread at the beginning and a cup of blessing at the end of the meal. This may seem to be a compromise between the Apostolic order and Pharisaic tradition, whether or not initiated by Paul, but at any rate it does not conform to the regular Jewish order.[262]

In view of Paul's Pharisaic background, from which he certainly inherited this common order, this contrast has a double significance. It enhances the Essene colouring of the Apostolic tradition, and it underlines that it is some version of this tradition which Paul is formally transmitting in 1Cor 11:23-25. A similar contrast between Paul's supposed Pharisaic tradition and the Essenish Apostolic tradition was found in his teaching on divorce (1Cor 7:10, 39).

COMMUNITY BENEDICTIONS

Chapters 12-14 of First Corinthians give instruction, as the headline indicates: 'About the gifts of the spirit'. The problem is again disorder in the service, especially in connection with the gift of 'speaking in tongues' i.e. 'pneumatic prayer' (14:14-16). As indicated earlier the structure is similar to that in chap-

---

[261] bBer 51a, involving a tradition called מתניתא i.e. baraita. The *sugya* takes the cup of the *birkat ha-mazon* to be meant, thus also Rashi; and see other references Str-B 3, 419; ib 4, 628-31.

[262] Flusser ib 25f considers the phrase μετὰ τὸ δειπνῆσαι Paul's personal explanation of the inverse order, and points to the notion of 'covenant' as another semi-Essene element lacking in the original version of Luke.

ters 8-10. The subject is introduced in a general way; a digression leads on to edifying images, examples or other imaginative material; and the third part offers practical instruction. In this case Paul gets down to real issues in 14:13, 'Therefore let he who speaks in a tongue pray for the power to interpret.' The aim is that the community be edified, in accordance with the 'more excellent way' of love (12:31-14:12).

In the ensuing exposition Paul uses an argument which contains several halakhic elements. These are the words of a Jewish Apostle to his gentile church: 'Otherwise, if you bless with the spirit, how can he who represents the congregation respond the Amen to your blessing, since he does not know what you are saying?' (1Cor 14:16). The significance of the words εὐλογέω (v16) and εὐχαριστέω (v16-18) have been pointed out in the preceding section.

First, we have here the custom of responding 'Amen' to a benediction. It is well rooted in biblical usage (Deut 27) and basic to post-biblical Judaism,[263] from where it spread to Christianity and Islam.

Second, the expression ὁ ἀναπληρῶν τὸν τόπον τοῦ ἰδιώτου, hardly understandable in Greek,[264] seems to be an equivalent of the Hebrew שליח ציבור shaliah tsibbur, 'representative of the community'. In Rabbinic literature this term indicates a person who prays aloud in front of the congregation and thereby vicariously fulfils the duty of those unable to pray.[265] This function could be exercized by any member except a minor and, as we have seen, a woman.[266] The congregation members confirm his prayer in their name by responding 'Amen'.[267] Something similar it seems to be the situation here. The word ἰδιώτης means 'commoner' and here seems to indicate 'one unable to pray'.[268] In v23f it designates the inexperienced who, as the 'unbelieving', cannot follow the uninterpreted pneumatic prayer. 'Αναπληρεῖν τὸν τόπον means 'taking the place', 'representing' someone.[269] It seems to stand for the Hebrew term שליח, 'legal agent' or 'representative' (see below p147). A peculiar circumstance here is that the 'representative' apparently responds 'Amen' to pneumatic blessings said by other community members in the name of the 'commoners', who probably cannot follow such prayer. At any rate the similarity is such that we seem to be faced with a grecized halakhic term.

The apparent translation of a halakhic expression into Greek is reminiscent of the Apostolic halakha in Greek concerning remarriage of widows (1Cor 7:39). Together with two recently excavated examples of grecized halakhic

---

[263] See Elbogen, *Gottesdienst*, 496f; Schürer, *History* 2, 450 n108.

[264] Cf RSV 'any one in the position of an outsider', or alternatively 'him that is without gifts'.

[265] mBer 5:3-5 (the more usual expression being העובר לפני התיבה); mRH 4:9 (see Albeck *Mishna* 2, 491). And cf Elbogen, *Gottesdienst*, 494-7.

[266] mMeg 4:6; tMeg 3:11.

[267] mBer 5:4-5; bBer 53b.

[268] Bauer, *Wörterbuch* s.v. ἰδιώτης no. 1; in Rabbinic usage the word, hebraized הדיוט, has the same meaning, see Str-B 3, 454-6.

[269] Bauer ib s.v. ἀναπληρόω. There is no necessity, nor does it seem to make sense, to interpret this spatially (unlike Bauer ib and s.v. ἰδιώτης no. 2, following Weiss and Heinrici).

concepts[270] and other literary evidence[271] these instances indicate the one-time existence of 'halakhic Greek'.

Incidentally, the expression allows a further insight into the halakhic nature of the commandment in 1Cor 14:34 demanding the silence of women during worship. Our explanation of the rule was that women should not be allowed to officiate as representative of the community. The situation presupposed in that explanation appears to be confirmed in the present text. The implication is that women should not partake in the freely rotating function of 'representative of the community'.

Third, Paul's argument presupposes that one who responds 'Amen' must have heard and understood the blessing. This is exactly what is stated in a halakha in the Tosefta, as explained in the Palestinian Talmud:[272]

> One should not answer with an "orphanized Amen" אמן יתומה, nor a "snatched" Amen... What is an "orphanized Amen"? Rav Huna said: Someone obliged to say a blessing who responds [Amen] without having heard what he is responding to.

This halakha is given an aggadic explanation by Ben Azzai, early second century CE, which allows a late first century dating. 1Cor 14:16 brings us back another century.

Here we see Paul applying a set of halakhot regarding benedictions to the gentile church. As we shall see later the possibility of this application to gentiles is already present in the Rabbinic halakha and in itself no invention of Paul's. This insight will serve us well in connection with the blessing upon enjoying food hinted at in 1Cor 10 and Rom 14-15 (p257f).

Conclusion: Paul and the Apostolic Tradition

Apostolic tradition, which includes Jesus traditions, was mentioned in the previous chapter (p82f) among the explicit sources of authority in First Corinthians. The following Apostolic halakhot have been discussed in the present chapter: (1) the Lord's command concerning divorce (7:10); (2) the Lord's command concerning the Apostles' sustenance (9:14); (3) the 'tradition' or 'custom' of the headcovering of women (11:5); (4) the 'tradition' of eucharist procedures which includes a Jesus tradition (11:23-26); (5) the custom in 'all churches of the holy' of the silence of women during worship services, based on an otherwise unknown 'commandment of the Lord' (14:34-37). A sixth, non-halakhic tradition is about the resurrection (15:3-8). These six traditions and their their unmistakable function as authority sources in Paul's teaching testify to his positive relationship towards the Apostolic tradition of the Jewish church.

---

[270] See above p47 n 86.

[271] Alon, *Studies* 2, 295-312 ('Ha-halakha be-Iggeret Bar-Nava') concluded on Barnabas' use of a Greek 'halakhic midrash' comparable to the Tannaic midrash collections.

[272] tMeg 3:27; yBer 8, [12]c; ySuk 3, 54a; yMeg 1, 72a; cf bBer 47a. For text and explanation see Lieberman, *Tosefta ki-Fshutah* 5, 1208f. Cf Str-B 3, 456-61.

That these Apostolic traditions derive from the Jewish church is indicated by the other halakhot which the Apostle adduces informally: on πορνεία (5:1); marital relations (7:3f); remarriage of widows (7:39); wages of field labourers (9:9); idol offerings (10:25-29; below chapter 5); and community benedictions (14:16). Except for the halakhic midrash on wages which is merely adduced as an example, in the eyes of the Apostle these halakhot should also be followed by gentiles or at least gentile Christians. They signify the relevance of Jewish-Apostolic tradition for gentile believers.

The importance of the Apostolic tradition in First Corinthians is even more obvious if we study the terminology Paul uses. Two concepts and related terms come to the fore: παράδοσις and ἀποστολή.

The word παράδοσις is used three times in the authentic Pauline letters. In Gal 1:14 Paul remembers how 'extremely zealous' he was 'for the traditions of my fathers πατρικῶν παραδόσεων'. While the full implication of this passage can only be devined from the specific purpose and content of Galatians this much is clear: παράδοσις is a standard phrase for 'tradition' and refers here to the traditions of the Jewish Sages; similar terms are found in other sources.[273] A polemical usage appears in Col 2:8 where Paul, writing to gentile Christians, refers to specifically Jewish halakhot (cf 2:11, 16) as 'the tradition of men παράδοσις τῶν ἀνθρώπων'. A different phrasing further on in the chapter shows that there is also a link with a synoptic tradition: '...all of which ...is according to the precepts and doctrines of men' (Col 2:22).[274] Interestingly, this tradition which elaborates the tension between human legalism and divinely-inspired piety is also found in a source related to ancient hasidism.[275] It appears that Paul utilized this inner-Jewish motif in his polemic against the forced observance of the Jewish Law by gentile Christians.

In view of the preceding paragraph the positive, non-polemic use of παράδοσις in the remaining passage, 1Cor 11:2, is remarkable: 'I commend you because you ...maintain the traditions as I handed them down to you' (1Cor 11:2).[276] The reference is to the headcovering of women and the eucharist, two of the five Apostolic halakhot explicitly mentioned in First Corinthians. In other words two elements of the Jewish-Christian, Apostolic tradition are referred to with the technical term παράδοσις.

Moreover the formal significance of παράδοσις as used here is evidenced in associated terminology: '...the traditions as I handed them down to you (ὡς παρέδωκα ὑμῖν', 1Cor 11:2). Similar words appear in the formula introducing the eucharist tradition, 'I received (παρέλαβον) from the Lord what I also handed down to you (παρέδωκα ὑμῖν, 11:23), and the resurrection tradition: 'I

---

[273] See παράδοσις τῶν πρεσβυτέρεων Mark 7:3, 5; Matt 15:2; παράδοσεις τῶν πατέρων (not kept by Sadducees) Josephus, Ant 13:297.

[274] Cf literally, παράδοσις τῶν ἀνθρώπων Mark 7:8, 13. The link is also explicit in the allusion to Isa 29:13 LXX in Col 2:22, Mark 7:6f and Matt 15:8f.

[275] SER 24 [26] p134, juxtaposing shabbat to the honour of father and mother and denouncing formalism with reference to Isa 29:13. On the relation of SER to hasidism see Safrai, 'Mishnat hasidim'.

[276] 2Thess 2:15 is similar both in form and content; see below.

handed down to you ...what I also received' (παρέδοκα ὑμῖν... ὃ καὶ παρέλα-βον; 15:3).[277] While παράδοσις in the affirmative sense is used only in 1Cor 11:2, the corresponding verbs παραδίδωμι and παραλαμβάνω as well as other terms which appear both here and elsewhere in Paul's letters similarly indicate authoritative, Apostolic tradition.[278]

This transmission terminology has its immediate backgound in Jewish tradition.[279] The verbs 'to hand down' and 'to receive' are technical terms specific to the transmission of oral tradition in Rabbinic Judaism; they suggest authority and accuracy. The precise Hebrew parallels are קיבל and מסר.[280]

In view of this information these passages in Paul not only indicate that he refers to Apostolic tradition but that he also uses formal Jewish terminology indicating trustworthiness and authority. Moreover one may conclude that in Corinth at least he initiated instructional frameworks not unlike those found in later Apostolic tradition.[281] It is obvious to think of forms of a baptismal catechism.[282]

The other terminological cluster evolves around the word ἀποστολή, apostleship. Paul establishes his apostleship in 1Cor 9:1-3 with the following words: 'Am I not free? Am I not an Apostle? Have I not seen Jesus our Lord? If to others I am not an Apostle, at least I am to you; for you are the seal of my apostleship in the Lord.' Proof for his apostleship are his apocalyptic vision of Jesus and the church he founded in Corinth, a church recognized by visits of other Apostles (cf v5). The appeal to the freedom ἐλευθερία and authority (ἐξουσία v4ff) involved in his apostleship creates the link with the chapters on idol offerings which precede and follow and are dealt with elsewhere in this book. Paul's apostleship is compareble to that of Cephas and the brothers of Jesus (v5), in other words authoritative leaders of the Jewish church. There follows an exposition of the Apostles' rights based on the Apostolic, Jewish-

[277] Cf 15:1 παρελάβετε. Significantly Marcion and some Latin versions delete 15:3 ὃ καὶ παρέλα-βον, suggesting resentment of Paul's dependence on apostolic tradition. Similarly Bultmann, *Theologie*, 473 thinks it clear beyond doubt that these are Hellenistic Christian cult traditions; cf above p13.

[278] Rom 6:17 ὃν παρεδόθητε τύπον διδαχῆς (cf 1Cor 6:11 for a material parallel); 1Thess 2:13 παραλαβόντες λόγον ἀκοῆς; ib 4:1 παρελάβετε παρ' ἡμῶν; Gal 1:9 εὐαγγελίζεται παρ' ὃ παρελάβετε; Phil 4:9 ἃ καὶ ἐμάθετε καὶ παρελάβετε καὶ ἠκούσατε καὶ εἴδετε ἐν ἐμοί; Col 2:6f παρελάβετε ...ἐδιδάχθητε. See also Rom 16:17 διδαχὴν ...ἐμάθετε; Col 1:7 (τον εὐαγγέλιον) ἐμάθετε.

[279] Conzelmann p238 also adduces Greek parallels, which in my view are more remote. He falls victim to the *interpretatio Graeco-Lutherana* when interpreting ἀπὸ τοῦ Κυρίου 1Cor 11:23 as indicating independence from human authority. n34 refers to Gal 1:12, not 1Cor 7:10; 9:14!

[280] See programmatically mAvot ch 1. Cf Safrai, 'Oral Tora', 42; Bacher, *Terminologie* 1, 106f, 165; Davies, *Setting*, 353-5. Another Tannaic term is שמע, 'to hear', and cognate שמועה, 'tradition, halakha'.

[281] Cf 2Thess 2:15 and 3:6 παράδοσις (see below); 2Pet 2:21 ἡ παραδοθεῖσα ...ἐντολή; Jude 3 ἡ παραδοθεῖσα πίστις; 1Klem 7:2 παραδόσεως ἡμῶν κανών; Pol 2Fil 7:2 ὁ παραδοθεὶς λόγος.

[282] Did 4:13 and Barn 19:11, φυλάξεις δὲ ἃ παρέλαβες μήτε προστιθεὶς μήτε ἀφαιρῶν, indicate the relationship to the formalized practical instruction of the baptismal catechism. Both are in longer sections reflecting the traditional instructional scheme consisting of 'the Two Ways'. Baptism seems implied in 1Cor 6:11 and Rom 6:17.

Christian tradition.

The terminology involved shows that Paul's 'apology' (v3) was not superficial but had an inner connection with Jewish-Christian tradition. Ἀποστολή, 'apostleship' is the equivalent of mishnaic Hebrew שליחות: agency, embassy, commission. It involves a שליח or שלוח, 'envoy', 'agent'; or in Greek an ἀπόστολος. He is 'sent' to act in the sender's name and for that aim he receives רשות, 'power', 'authority', in Greek best translated as: ἐξουσία.[283] Thus in mishnaic usage 'one's agent is like one's own person';[284] the agent can contract legal obligations for the sender such as marriage;[285] and the sender is liable for any faults committed within the limits of the commission.[286] This usage is reflected in the synoptic despatch narrative. Jesus 'sends' his 'apostles' to preach the Kingdom and gives them 'power' to heal and exorcize.[287] They are sent 'in his name';[288] and 'he who receives you receives me, and he who receives me receives him who sent me'.[289] The conclusion is that early Christian apostleship was rooted in this Jewish concept and its halakhic implications.[290]

This is not to deny that there is a difference, mishnaic usage being more strictly legal as against the messianic-apocalyptic emphasis of Apostolic usage. The problem is that this gives us no certainty about the degree of coexistence of halakha and apocalyptic tradition within Pharisaic-Rabbinic tradition in Paul's day. At any rate Paul's understanding of his apostleship does embrace both aspects. While it is based an an apocalyptic vision (1Cor 9:1; cf Gal 1:12) it involves 'authority' with halakhic implications. This authority is based on an 'instruction' of the Lord (1Cor 9:14)[291] which relates both to Rabbinic tradition and to the synoptic gospels. As we saw, Paul's apostleship also involves the authority to 'hand down' Apostolic 'tradition'. Moreover he has the authority to teach in Jesus' name, and with his own life style he presents the Corinthians with the Lord's example (11:1; 4:16).

---

[283] רשות also has the connotations 'dominion', '(foreign) government' (e.g. mAv 1:10, Shemaya; ib 2:3) and 'heavenly power', e.g. in שתי רשויות for radical dualism (e.g. Mekh Beshallah Shira [p130]; MekhRSbY p80; GenR 1,7 [p4]). Hence the ἐξουσίαι as 'heavenly powers', 1Cor 15:24, cf 11:10; 1Pet 3:22 etc; and ἐξουσία as command, (Roman) government: e.g. Luke 7:8; Rom 13:1-3. רשות as 'authority', 'title': see Str-B 3, 400f. Ἐξουσία as legal power: Acts 9:14 (cf 9:2!). See also Daube, *New Testament*, 205-23.

[284] E.g. mBer 5:5; derived from Exod 12:6 in Mekh Bo 5 (p17), which midrash is ascribed to R. Yoshua ben Korha, bKid 41b. See long note in Albeck, *Mishna* 1, 333-5.

[285] E.g. mKid 2:1.

[286] E.g. mKer 6:1.

[287] Mark 6:6-13; Matt 10:1-15; Luke 9:1-6, 10:1-20. Interesting is also the question about Jesus' and John the Baptist's ἐξουσία, Mark 11:27-33; Matt 21:23-27; Luke 20:1-8.

[288] Mark 9:37; Matt 18:5; Luke 9:48.

[289] Matt 10:40; Luke 10:16; John 13:20. Cf Mark 9:37 and Luke 9:48; John 13:16 and Matt 10:24. The large spread and variation of the saying indicates its authority.

[290] Thus already Harnack, *Mission*, 340ff, referring to Jerome and Epiphanius. Unconvincingly this is rejected by Lake, *Beginnings* 5, 46-52. Opinion converges again towards consensus here; see bibliographical survey by Agnew, 'Origin'. See also Ellis, *Paul*, 29-31; and especially the admirable article by Barrett, 'Shaliah and Apostle'.

[291] Διατάσσω is the word used here, as in Matt 11:1 (cf Dodd, 'Ennomos', 103).

Paul's positive relationship to Apostolic tradition also appears in other letters than First Corinthians. It is historically important that these include First Thessalonians, Paul's earliest letter. In the previous chapter the parenetic part of this letter was briefly reviewed. It includes three Apostolic commands in a framework of 'sanctification' language reminiscent of a baptismal setting (4:1-8) and reiterates another 'instruction' delivered earlier by the Apostle (4:9-12). What is important here is the similarity of these four commandments to some of the material in First Corinthians. The prohibition of πορνεία and the institution of an orderly married life (1Thess 4:3-5) is prominent in 1Cor 5-7; the order 'to work with your own hands' and 'be dependent on nobody' directly relates to Paul's own example in renouncing his Apostolic rights, which is elaborated on in 1Cor 9:1-18. The Jewish-Christian character of these traditions has been pointed out in the present chapter.

These traditions in First Thessalonians involve the same characteristic terminology. Paul adhorts the Thessalonians '...in the Lord Jesus, that as you received παρελάβετε from us how you ought to walk... you do so more and more; for you know what instructions we gave you (τίνας παραγγελίας ἐδώκαμεν ὑμῖν) through the Lord Jesus' (4:1f).

The author of Second Thessalonians felt that Paul's Apostolic commandment 'to work with your own hands' needed additional emphasis. He refers to it even more emphatically as 'the tradition that you received from us' (2Thess 3:6-12)[292] and connects it with another exhortation to follow the Apostle's own example (v7, 9). While this is strongly reminiscent of 1Cor 9 and does not give too great an impression of authenticity, it helps us to trace both the Apostolic, Jewish-Christian background of this commandment and its further development in the Pauline tradition.

It follows that from his earliest letter onwards, Paul appeals to Apostolic tradition without hesitation and refers to it by means of terminology which is both characteristic of that tradition and directly related to Jewish halakhic usage. In other words he not only asserts himself as an Apostle of Jesus but explicitly draws on the Jewish-Apostolic tradition.[293] The formal and material parallels with Rabbinic tradition make it likely that the Apostolic tradition Paul knew was also oral.[294]

At several points, we have seen, the Apostolic halakha Paul appears to be following deviates decisively from what may be supposed to have been the Pharisaic tradition he shared. The outstanding example is his marriage halakha, but the eucharist tradition should also be included here. When viewed in the context of the information assembled in this section, this all goes to enhance the view of his dependence on the basic Apostolic tradition as an authoritative

---

[292] κατὰ τὴν παράδοσιν ἣν παρελάβοσαν παρ' ἡμῶν (2Thess 3:6). Cf also 2:15, κρατεῖτε τὰς παραδόσεις ἃς ἐδιδάχθητε εἴτε διὰ λόγου εἴτε δι' ἐπιστολῆς ἡμῶν.

[293] Bultmann's hesitations, *Theologie*, 475ff reflect the theological inhibition inherent in the common Tübingen tradition (see Harnack, p10 n44!); cf Conzelmann, above n279.

[294] See discussion by Fjärstedt, *Synoptic Tradition*, 29-39. He does not elaborate on the material parallels.

code. This corresponds with the description Paul gives of his relationship with the Jerusalem Apostles in Gal 2:1-10,[295] which we shall discuss in chapter 6. Paul's mission to the gentiles involved a responsibility of his own and, as we shall also see, the readiness to oppose his fellow-Apostles firmly on issues vital to that mission. It is likely that these were novel issues on which there was as yet no Apostolic tradition. We have also met with instances of independent teaching by Paul, such as on marriage with unbelievers and celibacy. We may add his teaching on pagan food of doubtful provenance (chapter 5). But apart from these new questions Paul's Apostolic teaching was based on faithful obedience to the teachings of Jesus and his disciples.

The question why Paul shows so little of this dependence in other letters can only be answered by studying the purpose and occasion of those letters as compared with First Corinthians. As long as First Corinthians is considered an authentic Pauline letter, Paul's relationship to Apostolic tradition would seem to be undeniable.

A more general consideration is that for a Jew in antiquity dependence on an authoritative code did not preclude assimilation of various motifs from quite different Jewish or non-Jewish traditions. Philo is our prime example here: a deep-rooted loyalty to his local halakha was no impediment to his development of a philosophic-exegetical system incorporating a wealth of elements from Hellenistic thought. By analogy Paul's parenesis in which he develops mystic-apocalyptic and humanistic moral elements need not deny his faithfulness to the authoritative Apostolic tradition. We elaborate on these matters in the Conclusion.

Chapter Four

Laws concerning Idolatry in Early Judaïsm and Christianity

The subject of food offerings to idols, dealt with in 1Cor 8-10, is crucial to understanding Paul's practical and theoretical relationship with the Jewish Law. This is why it was excluded from the discussion of First Corinthians and here receives a separate chapter. On the other hand a correct appreciation of the subject requires insight in the significance of idolatry in early Judaism and Christianity, and the practical attitudes developed towards it. In other chapters this information is provided in the course of our study of Paul. Not so here. The present chapter provides a survey of ancient Jewish idolatry laws and of the early Christian attitudes towards idol offerings, while the next chapter will be devoted to Paul himself.

Biblical and Early Post-Biblical Law

For Second Temple Jews, the Tora was the source of prime authority both for the rules which shaped life and for the theological value these had. Discussion will therefore start with the laws concerning idolatry and their significance within the biblical narrative. Following this the embodiment of these biblical conceptions in practical life of the earlier Second Temple period will be discussed.

In the Tora, the prohibition of idolatry has an axiomatic absoluteness. This is evident from the fact that it is the first commandment of the Decalogue following the solemn opening statement: 'I am the Lord your God... You shall have no other gods before Me; you shall not make for yourself a graven image, or any likeness of anything that is in heaven above, or that is in the earth beneath or that is in the water under the earth; you shall not bow down to them or serve them' (Exod 20:3-5). When read with halakhic precision,[1] the passage appears to contain four distinct prohibited actions: not to have, not to make, not to serve idols and not to bow down for them. These prohibitions are repeated elsewhere, especially in the two covenant sections in Exodus 21-22 and 34 and in Deuteronomy,[2] with further commandments being added: not to

---

[1] Mekh Yitro 6 (p223-5); MekhRSbY p146f.

[2] See, in addition to the passages mentioned below, Lev 19:4; 26:1; Deut 4:15-20; 13:6-18; 17:2-7; 27:15. Cf arrangement of texts by Albeck, *Mishna* 4, 319f and 321 n1.

partake in the sacrifices to other gods (Exod 22:19; 34:16), not to adopt customs typical of their worship (Lev 18:21; 20:2-5; Deut 12:30f; 16:21f), not to mention their names (Exod 23:13), to destroy their images, altars and similar structures when found in the promised Land (Exod 23:24; 34:13; Deut 7:5; 12:2f), and not to compromise or make marriage agreements with their adherents (Exod 34:15f; Deut 7:2f). The Tora commandment to 'utterly detest and abhor' the heathen gods (Deut 7:25f) is specified in prophetic texts in the sense that the idols must be considered impure and also rendering the Israelites and their houses and utensils impure (Isa 30:22; Jer 19:13; Ezek 22:3f; 36:25).

The simple reason given for these prohibitions is that the Lord is 'a jealous God' who cannot bear Israel's devotion to other gods (Exod 20:5; 34:14). As such, it is the obverse side of Israel's election into the covenant that 'you shall be my own possession among all peoples, for all the earth is mine, and you shall be to me a kingdom of priests and a holy nation' (Exod 19:6; cf Deut 7:6). Israel is called to be God's own people and to carry out his commandments; the prohibition of idolatry is to safeguard that calling. Hence the ultimate crisis in Israel's existence is not its servitude to Pharao or other idolatrous rulers, but its almost complete self-degradation into a nation of idolaters: the episode of the golden calf (Exod 32). Were it not for Moses' faithfulness and intercession on behalf of Israel, and for his main argument: God's faithfulness to the promise he gave to the Patriarchs (Exod 32:13), God would have had no grounds on which to uphold Israel's election. Thus the ultimate crisis turns into the final revelation of God's divine Name, or in other words the attributes spelling out his relationship towards man: 'YHWH, The Lord, a God merciful and gracious, slow to anger, and abounding in steadfast love and faithfulness...' (Exod 34:6).

The golden calf narrative in Exodus has its counterpart in Numbers 25, the illicit alliance of the Israelites with the Moabites and their Baal-Peor. It is noteworthy that there is a direct and explicit connection here between sexual immorality and idolatry. A tradition preserved in Rabbinic literature likewise associates the 'playing' of Exod 32:6, the verse quoted extensively by Paul, with sexual orgiasm.[3] The same is pithily expressed in Exod 34:15f, 'play the harlot after their gods', and it is a basic ingredient in prophetic idiom.[4] The lesson is that sexual relations with the Canaanite peoples inescapably lead to involvement in their idolatry. Hence the prohibition on marriages with Canaanites is understood as an extension of the prohibition on idolatry (Exod 34:15f; Deut 7:2f). The Baal-Peor event figures in the didactic Psalm, 106:28, 'They joined together with Baal-Peor and ate sacrifices to the dead',[5] and is also referred to as a revealing experience at the beginning of the long prophetic admonishment presented by the book of Deuteronomy (3:29-4:4). Indeed that book as a whole, both in overall structure and in its details, continuously stresses the

[3] tSot 7:7 (R. Eliezer son of R. Yose ha-Gelili); GenR 53,10 (p567; R. Akiva); Tanh, ki tisa 20 (123a); TanhB, ki tisa 13 (57a); cf Rashi ad loc and TgPs-Yon. Str-B 3, 410 overlooks this. Cf מצחק in Gen 26:8 and the interpretation GenR 64,5 (p704f).
[4] Cf also Lev 17:7. For the prophets see Hos 1-4; Jer 3-5; Ezek 16; 23, etc.
[5] The latter expression also Jub 22:17, see below p153, 157.

urgency of the commandment against idolatry for the Israelites especially in connection with their imminent entry into the promised Land.[6] The same connection is found in the prophets.[7] It is obvious to read this sustained emphasis as a reflection of the hard struggle against the deep-rooted practice of idolatry in Old Testament times. On the other hand there is also a tendency towards universalism in the biblical prophets, which includes the idea that eventually all mankind shall worship the one true God.[8]

Post-exilic law on idolatry and gentile relations was more severe in several respects when compared with biblical law. The prohibition on marriage with Canaanites was extended to include all non-Israelites.[9] Further restrictions were introduced, as formulated in the book of Jubilees (22:16f): 'Separate yourself from the nations, and eat not with them; and do not perform deeds like theirs; and do not become associates of theirs; because their deeds are defiled, and all of their ways are contaminated, and despicable, and abominable; they slaughter their sacrifices to the dead and to the demons they bow down; and they eat in tombs.' The point is that idolatry, here called 'sacrifices to the dead', caused gentiles to be impure in 'all their ways' and hence forbidden to eat with for a Jew observing the laws of purity. The halakha of the book of Jubilees may be considered extreme in many respects,[10] as possibly also in this. But even if it was not observed by all, or not with equal strictness at all times, the concept of impurity caused by idolatry was a major theme both in the early and, through various transformations, in the later halakha governing relations with gentiles. Correspondingly early post-exilic sources mention Jews, either in Palestine or in the diaspora, abstaining from wine, oil, bread and other food deriving from or prepared by gentiles.[11] Likewise the idea of the impurity of gentile territory and dwellings must date back to somewhere early in the Second Temple period.[12] Finally, the Damascus Covenant (12:9-11) contains halakhot which

---

[6] See the connection as expressed in the introductory adhortation as a whole, chs 4 – 11; in ch 11, on the condition of living in the Land; in the immediate continuation in chs 12 – 13, on idolatry, as the beginning of the legislative middle section of the book; in the prominence of the commandment in the oath ceremony closing the middle section (27:15); and in the closing adhortatory section on life in the Land and exile and the prophetic song of Moses, chs 28 – 32 (29:17f, 30:17f, 31:16, 32:16f!).

[7] Elijah's ordeal on Mt Carmel, 1Kgs 18, is paradigmatic. See also Hoseah; Jeremiah 7ff; Ezek 36f.

[8] Isa 2:2-4 = Mic 4:1-3; Isa 40ff (esp 45:23, 'To Me every knee shall bow, every tongue shall swear'); Isa 56; 66; Zech 2:11; 8:20-23; 14 (esp 14:9, 'And the Lord will become king over all the earth; on that day the Lord will be one and his name one').

[9] Jub 30:7-17; TLevi 9:10; cf Ezra 9f; Neh 13. Jub 30:10 connects the prohibition with Lev 18:21, 'You shall not give any of your children *to make them pass* to Molech'. This interpretation of Lev 18:21 is also found in TgPs-Yon לציד בת עממין; Peshitta בנוכריתא; and mMeg 4:9 למעברא בארמיתא [ms K], quoted disprovingly; and see Albeck, *Mishna* 2, 505). LXX λατρεύειν ἄρχοντι is based on the reading להעביד למלך.

[10] Cf Safrai, 'Halakha', 140-5.

[11] The impression of exceptional and exemplary behaviour is created in Dan 1:8-16; Tob 1:10-12; Jdt 12:1f, 19; Add Esth 4:17x [14:17]. That a whole community was involved appears from Josephus Ant 12:120, referring to the time of Seleucus Nicator, 312-281/280 BCE (cf War 2:591, Life 74). Cf also 3Macc 3:4, 7; Jos Ant 4:137.

[12] A baraita relates that 'Yose(f) ben Yoezer, the man from Tsereida and Yose ben Yohanan, the man from Jerusalem, decreed impurity on the territory of the nations...' (yShab 1, 3d; yPes 1, 27d;

prohibit selling fowl and cattle to gentiles 'lest they sacrifice them', and of corn or wine. While the Essene position was undoubtedly extreme, it nevertheless implies that a general restrictive attitude existed towards selling to gentiles because of their idolatry and the impurity it entails.[13]

Jewish strictness on idolatry and relations with gentiles has often been the subject of non-Jewish disapproval, in both ancient and modern times.[14] In reaction to biased modern historiography, Jewish authors have tended to be apologetic on this topic.[15] A fair understanding cannot be gained without an appreciation of its context in biblical literature.[16] It reflects the idea of Israel's calling to be a nation devoted to a unique Deity which, though not depicted in images to ge grasped by everyone, is put forward as the God of all mankind. In other words, the laws of idolatry and gentile relations govern the relative isolation involved in that devotion. The complexity of this religious tradition is expressed in the fact that it also developed a markedly humane anthropology and on that level shows affinity with certain trends in gentile philosophy.[17]

Tannaic Halakha

The distinction between idolatry committed by Jews and by gentiles is basic to Rabbinic halakha.[18] A prohibition of idolatry for Jews was axiomatic, in line with biblical tradition.[19] In the Mishna it is mentioned only in order to define the exact culpability and punishment (mSanh 7:4, 6f, 10; 11:1, 6). According to the majority opinion, punishment for idolatry was of the severest category: stoning.[20] Correspondingly the prohibition of idolatry came first among the ancient tradition of three main commandments never to be transgressed by a Jew, even at the cost of his life: idolatry, illicit sexuality, and bloodshed.[21] All of this appears to reflect the historical situation of ancient Judaism. The evidence both of external and internal literary sources and of archeology indicates that Jewish idolatry was extremely rare, either in Palestine or in the diaspora.[22] This is the

yKet 8, 32c; bShab 14b). They were active in the early 2nd cent BCE.

[13] On these halakhot cf Schiffman, 'Legislation'; Blidstein, 'Sale'.

[14] For a summary of ancient views on Jews and Judaism see Stern, 'The Jews'; Tcherikover, *Civilization*, 357-77.

[15] E.g. Guttmann, *Judentum* (1927). A new approach was intimated by Alon, 'On the Impurity of Gentiles', in *Jews, Judaism*, 146-89, correcting an apologetic study by Büchler. A comprehensive re-assessment of the sources is given by Cohen, *Ha-yahas*, though somewhat 'anti-apologetic'.

[16] Cf the section on 'Nationality and Universality' in Moore, *Judaism* 1, 205-34.

[17] On anthropology see Flusser, 'Sensitivity'; Safrai, 'Oral Tora', 111-5; on affinity with the Cynico-Stoic universalism and pluralism cf below ch 6.

[18] See introduction to Avoda Zara in Albeck, *Mishna* 4, 321-3.

[19] Cf the tradition of 'the school of R. Yishmael' bHor 8a-b; 'Which is the commandment that was said first? None but the one on idolatry'. And see below, n31.

[20] mSan 6:1-6 deals with the procedure for stoning and then, before proceeding to 'lesser' capital punishments (7:2-3), summarizes its severity with a majority rule disputed by R. Shimon (7:1, cf 9:3). Cf the same order 7:4ff; 9:1ff; 11:1ff.

[21] Above p50.

[22] See review of sources by Urbach, 'Rabbinical Laws', 154-6. On the diaspora situation see

view of R. Yohanan ben Torta who said that the first Temple was destroyed because of idolatry, illicit sexual relations, and bloodshed; but at the time of the Second Temple they were punctilious in these and other commandments, and it collapsed due to greed and groundless hatred.[23]

On the other hand an entire tractate in the Mishna, as also in the Tosefta and the Talmudim, was devoted to the halakhot concerning idolatry by gentiles and the consequences of having social and economic relations with them: tractate *Avoda Zara*. The name refers to idolatry but literally means 'alien cult'. Related halakhot are scattered across other tractates. Common to all is that Jews should avoid contact with the sphere of 'alien cults' and try to diminish, or at least avoid to reinforce, their position in the Land of Israel.[24] By this territory the Sages meant the areas of Jewish settlement within what was understood as the biblical promised land: Judea, Galilee and the Perea across the Jordan.[25] Thus these halakhot expressed the ancient struggle against the power of alien cults and their presence in the Land. Jews took action to destroy pagan cult centres in the Land, not only during the Maccabean conquest but apparently already in the early Hellenistic period and also during the great war against Rome.[26] The Mishna even preserves a benediction to be said upon seeing a locality where a place of idolatrous worship has been destroyed.[27]

According to some Sages a similar benediction should be said upon seeing a ruined pagan sanctuary outside the Land.[28] This reflects the idea, inherent in prophetic universalism, that idolatry will ultimately be eradicated from all the earth.[29] The same idea is expressed in the tradition of the 'commandments of the sons of Noah' which counts the prohibition of idolatry as foremost among the commandments incumbent upon all mankind.[30] Indeed not only did the

Tcherikover, *Civilization*, 344-57.

[23] tMen 13:22; yYom 1, 38c; bYom 9a-b.

[24] For the territorial emphasis see mAZ 1:8f; tAZ 2:8f; 3:18-4:6. And cf bGit 88a, 'R. Yoshua ben Levi said, The Land of Israel was not laid waste until there were seven courts where they worshipped idolatry'.

[25] On its boundaries see mShev 9:2, cf 6:1; tShev 4:6-11; SifD 51 (p116-8); yShev 6, 36c; and the Rehov inscription (literature: A. Goldberg in *Compendia* II/3a, 317). For a historical discussion see Alon, *The Jews in Their Land* 1, 132-51; Schürer, *History* 2, 85-198.

[26] See Urbach, 'Rabbinical Laws', 156 for references. The warning of R. Yohanan ben Zakkai not to destroy pagan altars lest they be rebuilt under force (ARN b 31, p66) seems to reflect efforts to that effect during the first revolt. On pre-Maccabean times see Goldstein, 'Jewish Acceptance', 74f.

[27] mBer 9:1; tBer 7:2. For a survey of Jewish attitudes towards gentile idolatry see also Flusser, 'Paganism', 1088-98.

[28] tBer 7:2 (R. Shimon); yBer 9, 13b (Vatican ms: R. Shimon ben Gamliel); bBer 57b (R. Shimon ben Elazar). Others disagree 'since the majority of gentiles are idolaters'. R. Yohanan, yBer ib, says still they have hope (to repent) as long as they live; bHul 13b has him say, 'Gentiles outside the Land are no idolaters but continue the tradition of their ancestors'. On the later history of this saying see Katz, 'Shelosha mishpatim'.

[29] Cf R. Elazar, MekhRSbY p126 (R. Eliezer, Mekh p186f), commenting on Exod 17:14 (Amalek): 'Their name shall wiped out from the world, idolatry and its worshipers shall be eradicated, and the Omnipresent shall be the Only One in the world'. Cf also the *Aleinu* prayer, with reference to Isa 45:23 (cf Elbogen, *Gottesdienst*, 80f, 143).

[30] tAZ 8:4; GenR 34,8 (p316f); bSan 56a-59b (esp the versions of 'the school of Menashe' and of R.

Sages state that 'Whoever professes idolatry denies the Ten Words, the commandments of Moses and those of the prophets', they also said that 'Whoever denies idolatry, professes all of the Tora'. The universalist intention is evident.[31]

The power of idolatry itself was viewed by the Jewish Sages with a realistic eye.[32] The question before them was always to what extent in a given situation should gentiles be understood to be associated with the sphere of 'alien cults'. This realistic and rational attitude can be inferred from Tannaic halakha and it is also made explicit in several narratives. A gentile is said to have asked R. Akiva how he explained the apparent healing power of idols, since 'you know as well as I do that in the idol there is nothing real'.[33] The answer is that illnesses are decreed from heaven at which moment they should come and go, whether one prays to the idol or not. A similar mood is expressed in the answer which the Sages, one of whom again may have been R. Akiva, gave when on one of their visits in Rome they were asked why God, if he condemns idolatry, does not destroy the idols. They replied that since people also worship the sun, moon and the stars, he would have to destroy the whole world; and destroying only the man-made idols would plainly support the belief of those who worship elements of nature.[34] The element of irony is unmistakable and represents a wide-spread tradition, as we shall see below.

It is important to note that there was also a different, non-rational view of idolatry in ancient Judaism. This is the view of idolatry as dominated by demons, in opposition to the world of angels. It is found especially in circles associated with Essenism and apocalyptic literature,[35] including the Apocalypse of John in the New Testament.[36] The demons prominent in the synoptic tradition, as well as their exorcism by Jesus, must be seen in the same perspective.[37] As we shall see, Paul is divided. On the one hand he calls the Christian community 'light' and 'the Temple of God' against the idols as 'darkness' and the lot of 'Belial' (2Cor 6:14-16), but elsewhere he shares the rational view.[38] This is not fundamentally different from Rabbinic literature. In contrast to the Babylonian Talmud, demons, miracles, sorcery and magic, are hardly ever

Yehuda, 56b); GenR 16,6 (p149f). The Tora verse functioning as a peg in many of these universalist traditions is Gen 2:16, 'And the Lord God commanded the man'.

[31] SifNum 111 (p116), referring to Num 15:22 ('all these commandments', thought summarized in the idolatry prohibition; similarly bHor 8a), Exod 20:1ff (supposedly spoken 'in one word', Ps 62:12) and Gen 2:16. (And cf the tradition of 'the school of R. Yishmael' above n19). The saying is found also bNed 28a (= bShevu 29a); bKid 40a; bHul 5a.

[32] Cf Lieberman, *Hellenism*, 115-38.

[33] לית בה משש bAZ 55a; cf bSan 63b.

[34] mAZ 4:7; tAZ 6:7; bAZ 54b. On the travels of the Sages to Rome see Safrai, 'Visits'.

[35] Jub 1:11, 'they will sacrifice their children to the demons'; 1En 99:7, 'those who worship evil spirits and demons, and all kinds of idols...'; TJud 23:1, '...witchcraft and idolatry ...following ...demons of deceit'. In Qumran, all negative behaviour was directed by the Spirit of Darkness, 1QS 3:13ff.

[36] Rev 9:20, '...worshipping demons and idols of gold and silver'; cf previous n.

[37] On Jesus' dualism cf Flusser, 'Two Masters'.

[38] See below p202.

mentioned in Tannaic literature. But there are some mentions,[39] and they remind us that Judaism in Tannaic times was not quite as rational as the main collections suggest.[40] After all, mysticism, which hardly surfaces in these collections, was an important element in the lives of prominent Sages such as R. Akiva.[41] Miracles also were wrought by the early *hasidim*, who were something of a fringe movement of Pharisaic-Rabbinic Judaism.[42] Thus it is likely that the non-rational view of idolatry also existed among the Tannaim. A reflection may be seen in the biblical expression 'sacrifices to dead gods' (Ps 106:28) for idolatry commonly used in Tannaic tradition,[43] which in other writings indicates 'evil spirits',[44] and reflects ancient piety towards the dead.[45]

Nevertheless the rational, ironical attitude towards idolatry predominates in Tannaic literature. Interestingly, this not only reflects an authentic Jewish tradition but also coincides with a common pagan Hellenistic tradition.[46] Iconoclastic sarcasm is a well-established genre in ancient Jewish literature. It is prominent in (post-)exilic biblical prophecy,[47] and it is widespread both in later Second Temple Jewish writings[48] and in Rabbinic literature.[49] The Rabbis openly expressed this sarcastic attitude, as appears from the phrase, 'ridiculing the idols' ליצנותא דעבודה זרה.[50] On the other hand this Rabbinic rationalism coincides with the Cynico-Stoic criticism of idolatry which circulated in the Hellenistic world, especially in the first century BCE and the first and second centuries CE.[51] While in the past claims have been made for the Jewish or

[39] Idolatry is identified with the worship of שדים (demons) in association with Deut 32:17 (cf 1Cor 10:20!) in SifD 318 (p364) and MidrGad Deut p713. With reference to Lev 17:7 it is found in Sifra Aharei 9 (84a) and LevR 22,7 (p517). See also SifN 131 (p171) and other sources adduced by Lieberman, *Hellenism*, 121 n33. Cf the 'angels of Satan' tAZ 1:17f; and the elaboration on the 'ways of the Amorites' tShab 6-7.

[40] Urbach, 'Rabbinic Laws', 154 and n19 takes issue with Lieberman and maintains that there is only 'scarce and slight evidence' of this view in 'all the sayings of the Sages'.

[41] Cf above p48.

[42] See Safrai, 'Teaching'; id, 'Hasidim'.

[43] mAZ 2:3 (below p161); mAv 3:3 (below p205, 255); tAZ 4:6 (below p233f); SER 9 (p48).

[44] Jub 22:17 (above p153; and see Büchler, 'Traces', 324); cf Sir 30:18; Ep Jer 27, 32; Wis 14:15; Or Sib 8:382-4, 393; and cf Did 6:3 (below p180).

[45] Deut 26:14; cf Sir 7:33 and, strikingly positive, Tob 4:17. Anne Marie Reynen refers me to Augustine who in Conf 6:2 touchingly relates the same usage by his mother, as well as the disapproval of the hierarchy.

[46] See discussion, involving also the Christian apologetes, by Lieberman, *Hellenism*, 115-27; cf material in Horsley, 'Gnosis', 36-40.

[47] Especially Deutero-Isaiah (Isa 40:19f; 42:17; 44:9-20; 45:16, 20; 46:1-7; 48:5); also Jeremiah (10:1-16), some Psalms (115; 135:15-18), and Hab 2:18f.

[48] Thematically in the Epistle of Jeremiah; Bel and the Dragon; Wisdom chs 13-15; Apocalypse of Abraham chs 1-8. Cf also Josephus, Ag. Ap. 2:237-254.

[49] Motifs of iconoclastic sarcasm as opposed to trust in God's salvation, closely related to the Apocalypse of Abraham, are widespread in Rabbinic literature: GenR 38 (p361-4, and see Theodor's extended note ib); SER 6 (p27f); SEZ 25 (p47f); MidrGad Gen 11:28 (p202-7, and see further parallels noted by Margulies); ib 15:7 (p252f). See also Ginzberg, *Legends* 5, 218 nn50-51.

[50] bMeg 25b; bSan 65b; referring to the sarcasm of Isa 46:1f. Lieberman, *Hellenism*, 115.

[51] Heinemann, 'Briefe des Herakleitos', 232: 'Die Briefe geben ein lehrreiches Beispiel ...für die innerhellenistische Religionskritik, an welche die Angriffe des Judentums und des Christentums anknüpfen konnten.'

Christian origin of some of the relevant sources, recent study indicates that their criticism of idolatry in the name of enlightened religion would have been equally at home in the pagan world of that period.[52] This remarkable convergence may be seen as another example of parallel autonomous developments within Rabbinic Judaism and popular Greek thought, which interconnected at a later stage of the process and began to influence each other.[53]

A perusal of the halakhot as laid down in the Mishna tractate *Avoda Zara* reveals that the coexistence with gentiles was accepted as a fact of life, and that the problem was at precisely what moment did dealings with them or their possessions imply association with the sphere of idolatry. Thus rules were formulated giving days on which gentiles were supposed to be celebrating their festivals and hence when dealings with them were forbidden (mAZ 1:1-4). Prominent among these are such Roman and Hellenistic festival names as the *Calendae* and *Saturnalia*, κρατήσεις and γενεσίαι (1:3). The latter two categories commemorated the ascension to power and birth days, which were directly connected with the emperor cult.[54] Other rules laid down which things or services may not be rendered to gentiles since they are likely to serve their cults (1:5-9),[55] and which of their food stuffs may not be touched at all or, alternatively, may be handled but not eaten (2:3-7).[56] Another set of rules regulated the nature or condition of certain objects such as images, structures, hills or trees, indicating when they were associated with idolatry and when not (3:1-4:7). These objects may be used for one's profit if they do not appear to serve idolatry. In the same way other halakhot outline the circumstances in which wine may or may not be produced, handled or consumed together with gentiles or in their service (4:8-5:10). The problem was that gentiles were known to use their wine for libations to their gods, and use of gentile libation wine was forbidden in any quantity or dilution whatsoever (5:9). But as long as the impression was that no libation wine was involved, one may derive enjoyment or profit from gentile wine (2:6), or drink one's own wine in his presence (5:5).

---

[52] Attridge, *Cynicism*, esp 13-23, rebutting Bernays' theory of the pertinent sections of the letters of Pseudo-Heraclitus as Jewish or Christian interpolations. Note the text on a sherd found in Egypt which rejects image worship in the name of Isis and Osiris (ib 23), and the admiration expressed by Varro and Seneca for the purity of Jewish worship (ib 19).

[53] On a similar congruency in the field of fables and parables, involving the letters of Ps-Heraclitus, see Flusser, 'Lion as Porter'; and important theoretical remarks in id, *Gleichnisse*, 156-8. One should add the universal matrix of the more ancient Near Eastern tradition of wisdom proverbs and narratives.

[54] Cf Deissmann, *Licht*, p293 and p317 plate 69 for the Priene calendar inscription (9 BCE) which lists August's birthday as that of a deity ἡ γενέθλιος τοῦ θεοῦ. See also ib 291-6 on the emperor cult. The γενεσία of Herod (Antipas) is mentioned in Matt 14:6; Mark 6:21. See Schürer, *History* 1, 246ff n26.

[55] 2:1-2 formulates why and when animals or humans may not be delivered into the power of gentiles. Although originally idolatry may have been involved (Alon, *Jews, Judaism*, 182f), the emphasis is on suspected bad morals: illicit sexuality and bloodshed.

[56] These food laws relate to the Decree of Eighteen Things, see below.

Clearly, the power of idolatry was not perceived in the nature of things themselves, but in the way people treated them.

> An idol belonging to a gentile is forbidden (to have profit from) at once, but that of an Israelite not until it has been worshipped; a gentile can invalidate a gentile's or an Israelite's idol,[57] but an Israelite cannot invalidate a gentile's idol. (mAZ 4:4)

Apparently the situation was such that a Jew could possess images which he did not worship. In any case, what was decisive was the significance the gentile attached to the statue. This could be seen from its outward state or the way it was handled by gentiles:

> How does he invalidate it? If he broke the tip of its ear, its nose or its finger, or even if he beat it without breaking anything off, he invalidated it; but if he spat or urinated before it, dragged it away or trew filth at it, he did not invalidate it. (mAZ 4:5)

The implication of the latter case is that the invalidation was only temporal; the gentile may come back on his rage and restore the idol to its honour.[58]

It was different when a statue appeared to be in a state of being disrespected by the gentiles. This can be seen, among other things, from an interesting story told in the Mishna (mAZ 3:4).

> Proklos the son of Pelaslos[59] asked the following question of Rabban Gamliel in Acre because he bathed in the bath house of Aphrodite: 'It is written in your Law, "And nothing of the banned things shall cleave to your hand" (Deut 13:17) – then how can you bathe in the bath house of Aphrodite?' He answered: 'One may not answer (in matters of Tora) in the bath house.' When he came out he told him: 'I did not come in her territory, but she came into mine; (furthermore) they do not say,[60] "let us make a bath house for Aphrodite", but, "let her, Aphrodite, be made into an adornment for the bath house"; yet another reason: Even if they offer you much money, would you enter before your idol naked, having had a pollution or urinating before her? But this one stands above the gutter and everyone urinates before her! It was only written: "(You shall hew down the graven images) of their gods" (Deut 12:3) – that which is treated as representing a deity is forbidden, but what is not treated as representing a deity is allowed.

First of all the gentile expresses wonder at the Sage's tolerant attitude towards the statue of the goddess; apparently there were Jews at that time who were more strict.[61] Secondly, the gentile appears to know the scriptural basis of the

---

[57] The reading ושלישראל (mss K, P, C) was the version of R. Yehuda the Prince's youth; later he taught otherwise. See Epstein, *Nosah*, 22f.

[58] Thus Albeck a.l. Archeological finds confirmed the actual relevance of these halakhot; see Yadin, *Bar Kokhba*, 93-110 for vessels with defaced images.

[59] Thus the *lectio difficilior* in mss K, P, C, Parma C. In the Bavli (mss M, NY, ed princ) the Mishna version is פלוספוס i.e. φιλόσοφος, which yields 'Proklos the philosopher'.

[60] The following sentence read with mss K, C.

[61] Cf tMikw 6:3, where Rabban Gamliel is said to have bathed in the bath house at Ascalon, while

159

commandment, which according to the plain meaning would seem to condemn the Sage's behaviour. In other words, the question was about the interpretation of Scripture in view of Jewish-gentile relations, and our Sage advocates a tolerant line. Thirdly, his threefold answer reveals a very rational view of the power of idolatry: the statue was introduced into his dominion and not the reverse; it functions merely as an ornament in a public utility; and general behaviour makes it clear that it is not viewed as a real idol. Fourth, another scriptural verse offers support. Only 'the graven images *of their gods*', which is interpreted as '*actually dedicated* to their gods', must be destroyed, not just all 'their images'. Finally, this tolerant attitude is expressed in a rational principle: only that which is treated by men as representing the deity constitutes a sphere of idolatry.[62] This principle will appear to be very important for Paul's discussion on food offered to idols.

As suggested already, not all Tannaim shared Rabban Gamliel's attitude of inner strength and outward tolerance. Another opinion was that all gentiles must always be suspected to be intent on idolatry.

> (A Jew) who slaughters for a non-Jew: what he slaughters is valid. But R. Eliezer declares it invalid. Said R. Eliezer: Even if he slaughtered it in order that the non-Jew should eat (only) the lobe of its liver, it is invalid, since the unspecified intention of a non-Jew is towards alien cults סתם מחשבת נוכרי לעבודה זרה. (mHul 2:7)

In his generation, R. Eliezer was the main representative of the more conservative Shammaite school, and was therefore called שמתי *shammati*.[63] That his opinion on the slaughter of animals for non-Jews was connected with intolerance towards them is confirmed by his view, expressed elsewhere, that 'none of the gentiles have a share in the world to come'; as opposed to the Hillelite, R. Yoshua, who held that 'there are righteous among the nations who have a share in the world to come'.[64] It is noteworthy that R. Eliezer also defended the right to carry a sword on the Shabbat (mShab 6:4), which is remarkable in view of the general Shammaite strictness on Shabbat prohibitions. This points to the proximity of the Shammaites to the anti-gentile Zealot movement. In this connection, great importance must be attached to the so-called 'Decree of Eighteen Things', a set of prohibitions relating to gentiles, which were issued by a Shammaite majority in a Zealot atmosphere and were afterwards welcomed by R. Eliezer; they will be dealt with below. Thus R. Eliezer seems to represent a

---

the more pious Onkelos the Proselyte (tHag 3:3) preferred to bathe in the sea. For related Rabbinic stories on bath houses and sacred sources with Hellenistic parallels see Lieberman, *Hellenism*, 122-6, 132-4; and the parallel on sacred sources in Tertullian (De idol 15, CSEL 20, 48) quoted by Lieberman, *Texts*, 305.

[62] tAZ 5:6 gives both the rule and the fuller exposition. See also below n74 on the related passage yShev 8, 38b-c.

[63] See Safrai, 'Halakha', 198-200.

[64] tSan 13:2; ARN a 36 (54a). For the connection with idolatry see yBer 9, 13b bottom.

strictness on relations with idolatry and gentiles typical of the Shammaite school.[65]

Apart from the 'ideological' motive involved here, there is also a matter of logic. The Shammaites adhered to the stricter sense of Scripture and tended to judge by the outward quality of an act rather than the intention of the person. In contrast the Hillelites tended to reckon with the intention of the acting person and to explain Scripture in more imaginative ways.[66] This throws more light on R. Eliezer's opinion that since 'the implicit intention of a non-Jew is towards alien cults', the slaughter of animals on his behalf by a Jew is invalid. Significantly the same mishna adds a comment by a later Sage who obviously expresses the Hillelite view. R. Yose argued from the case of sacrificial slaughtering, where not the intention of the owner of the sacrificial animal, but only that of the slaughterer counts.[67] Likewise, 'in the case where intention does not make invalid, as with non-sacrificial meat, is it not logical that what counts is only the slaughterer?' (mHul 2:7). The Hillelite emphasis on the significance of intention allowed a Jewish slaughterer to distinguish between the aim later to be given to an object by the gentile and his apparent intention at the moment of slaughtering. The implication is that in the case discussed here the gentile did not express an intention towards idolatry; if it were otherwise, all would agree with R. Eliezer that the slaughtering was invalid (cf mHul 2:8).

In other words, the Shammaite R. Eliezer systematically supposed the unspecified intention of the gentile to be directed toward idolatry. The Hillelites approached the unspecified intention of a gentile differently. This is reflected in the important ruling by R. Akiva, which resembles the rule attributed to Rabban Gamliel cited above:

> Meat under way to an alien cult (location) is permitted (for a Jew to derive profit from), but when returning from it, it is forbidden, for it is like "sacrifices to the dead"; thus R. Akiva (mAZ 2:3).

The Palestinian Talmud notes that this opposes R. Eliezer's principle.[68] In addition, R. Akiva's rule is further specified, it being stated that only meat that entered 'behind the partition fence' demarcating the sanctuary proper is forbidden, while if it stayed outside, even in the vicinity of the alien cult centre, it may be handled by a Jew for his own profit.[69] What counts is the actual intention of the gentiles as apparent from their actions. The principle applied also in other situations:

> Those walking in a procession (תרפות lit. obscenity): it is forbidden to deal with them, but when they return it is permitted. (mAZ 2:3).

---

[65] See Gilat, *Eliezer*, 300-5; Cohen, *Ha-yahas*, 250; Safrai, 'Halakha', 192f.

[66] On Beit Shammai see Safrai, 'Halakha', 185-94.

[67] cf mZev 2:2f; 4:6.

[68] yAZ 2, 41b.

[69] yAZ 2, 41b. קנקלין = *cancellus*, κιγκλίς: fence, grid. Cf ib 42d bottom, where the same rule is applied (R. Yohanan in the name of R. Yannai) to non-edibles such as a purse of money. Krauss, *Lehnwörter* sv, explains it ySan [10,] 28d *coenaculum*.

A city in which an alien cult festival is going on, and some shops have wreaths while others have not – such was the case in Beit Shean, and the Sages said: those with wreaths are forbidden (to buy from), and those without are permitted. (mAZ 1:4)

By such outward showing, the gentile shopkeepers were taken to demonstrate their participation or non-participation in idolatrous rites.

Similarly, the Mishnaic rule is that it is forbidden to sell to gentiles matters which they are known to use for idolatrous cults, such as specific vegetables, frankincense and a white cock (mAZ 1:5). But this is further specified. Thus the Tosefta adds (1:21) that it is permitted to sell these goods in larger quantities, or to merchants, since in those cases it is not clear that the gentile buyer intends any specific item for idolatry. The same Mishna formulates the rule: 'As for (the selling of) all other goods, if they are unspecified סתמן, it is permitted, but if specified פירושן, it is forbidden'. And the Tosefta explains: as long as the purpose of the goods is not specified, even if it concerns swine or wine, they may be sold, in the characteristic phrase, 'without anxiety' ואינו חושש; 'but if he specified to him (their destination for idolatry), even water and salt are forbidden (to be sold)'. Thus foods otherwise forbidden may be sold if the destination remains unspecified; foods otherwise allowed may not be sold if the intention towards idolatry is specified.[70] The gentile's specification of his intention is another element which will appear to be very important in Paul's reasoning. In contrast, as noted above (p153f), Essene halakha prohibited selling any animals to gentiles whatsoever.

However we should be on guard against exaggerated systematization of the Shammaite strictness on idolatry and relations to gentiles. Precisely because of his anti-gentile tendency, R. Eliezer shows a strikingly rational attitude in two other halakhot. As opposed to his colleagues, he permits the earning of income from the production of ornaments known to be used later for idolatry.[71] Likewise he permits the use of wood from a tree formerly associated with idolatry provided the equivalent of the derived value is 'thrown into the Dead Sea'.[72]

There are two sides to each transaction between a Jew and a gentile. So far we have reviewed only halakhot pertaining to the gentile's intention towards the alien cult. The other side is the intention the gentile supposes the Jew to have, the supposition always being that the Jew's real intention is never towards idolatry. A term for how a gentile regards a Jew's actions is the phrase נראה, 'he is seen', 'he creates the impression'. Thus one should not bow down towards a pagan temple in order to collect a coin from the ground or drink from a

[70] As regards the white cock, R. Yehuda seemingly takes a more liberal position. But the correct version in the Mishna, which is closer to the Tosefta, shows that he is only quoting a general rule ('one may sell [unspecified] a white cock from among other cocks') and adding a specific comment on a single white cock. mAZ 1:5; tAZ 1:21. See Epstein, *Nosah*, 1104 on the text.

[71] mAZ 1:8; see discussion of text and contents by Urbach, 'Rabbinic Laws', 158f.

[72] mAZ 3:9, see Albeck a.l. Objects like coins (cf mAZ 3:3) which cannot be left to decay in time or burnt, as other forbidden materials which must be destroyed, were destined to be thrown into the Dead Sea. Cf also mNaz 4:4, 6; mTem 4:2f; mMeila 3:2.

fountain, 'since that creates the impression he is bowing before the idol'; what he can do is turn his back to the temple and do the same, and if he is not 'seen' at all, he can quietly do it the normal way (tAZ 6:4-6).[73] Once again, the pagan sanctuary itself has no special meaning to the Jew, and his own intention is in no way towards idolatry. What counts is the significance attached to his action by the gentiles.

This same principle is formulated with the help of the passive form מתחשב, 'drawing attention'. Thus it is ruled that in certain exceptional circumstances a Jew may visit Roman theatres and stadiums which were normally considered places of idolatry and bloodshed; 'but if he draws attention,[74] this is forbidden' (tAZ 2:5-7). Similarly, the rule that on festival days dealings with gentiles are forbidden to a Jew is said to apply only 'in places where this *draws attention*; but if he meets him in his regular way, he may greet him discreetly' (tAZ 1:2). A Jew may greet a gentile friend as long as that does not draw special attention and create the impression that he intends to welcome idolatry. In other words, a distinction is made between the human relationship to the gentile himself and his idolatrous connections.

This connects with two important moral principles in mishnaic halakha. The first implies that if a person is actually involved in a forbidden action, friendly human relations should be restrained: 'One does not strengthen the hands of the tresspasser'.[75] But if that is not clearly the case, human relations may be fostered, and this is summarized in a second principle: '...in view of the ways of peace'. These principles are complementary. Thus on the basis of the fact that gentiles, as opposed to Jews, are not under the obligation of the commandment of the Seventh Year, the Mishna can state: 'One strengthens the hands of gentiles (who work their fields, by wishing them well) in the Seventh Year, but not the hands of Israelites; and one greets them (the gentiles); in view of the ways of peace' (mShev 4:3).[76] The explanation of the latter rule is given in the Tosefta. Even if commercial dealings are forbidden, 'one greets gentiles *on their festival days* in view of the ways of peace' (tAZ 1:3). The expression 'in view of the ways of peace' מפני דרכי שלום is founded on Prov 3:17, 'Her (Wisdom's) ways are ways of pleasantness, and all her paths are peace'. It embodies the human element which increasingly came to govern the laws about gentile idolatry.

---

[73] Cf also tAZ 1:5f.

[74] במקום שמתחשב. yAZ 1, 40a erroneously reads מתחשד; bAZ 18b gives the explanatory expansion מתחשב עמהם. The correct meaning of the expression appears from its use in a similar situation (behaviour in a public building) mShev 8:11; cf Albeck, *Mishna* 1, 162 and 381. Commenting on that passage yShev 8, 38b-c gives two explanations: (1) it concerns an אדם של צורה, a remarkable person; (2) it concerns *privata* instead of δημοσία (βαλανεῖα), private rather than public baths. Note the mention of Aphrodite in this connection, cf above on mAZ 3:4.

[75] mShev 5:9; mGit 5:9. See next n.

[76] See Albeck a.l. The halakha is also quoted in the collection of halakhot מפני דרכי שלום listed mShev 5:9 and more completely mGit 5:8f.

We shall now discuss the historical perspective in which the halakha on idolatry should be viewed. During the period we are concerned with, a complex development took place in which various internal processes and external influences may be discerned. An overall tendency was from post-exilic strictness towards the more flexible attitude of the Amoraic period. But this development was certainly not homogeneous or synchronic in all quarters of Jewish society. Furthermore at various times there were movements in the opposite direction, in which the political dimension of the Jewish people as a religious-ethnic entity was stressed. Obviously the laws of idolatry not only governed personal relations with gentiles but regulated the concept of a nation devoted to the one true God. One such episode was the zealous defense of the Tora demanded by the so-called Hellenistic crisis and the religious persecution by Antiochus Epiphanes (167-164 BCE). All indications are that the Maccabean zeal against paganism was not new but arose from religious convictions deeply rooted in early Second Temple Judaism.[77] What was new was its re-affirmation in an unprecedented political and cultural setting, as was the religio-political structure which emerged. The task of historical interpretation regarding crises such as these is precisely to estimate the correct proportion of internal and external factors and the amount of change resulting from the upheavals in the short and long term. Quite another aspect is the development of pagan religion in our period, on which the last word has not yet been said.[78]

Since the work on an adequate overall re-interpretation of our period is still in full swing, a historical presentation of the ancient Jewish laws of idolatry must of necessity remain fragmentary and inconclusive. Moreover the present study only needs to focus on aspects relevant to Paul. First, two general trends are discussed: the overall development of idolatry laws towards rationality and leniency, and the tendency to detach them from the system of purity rules. Further sections deal with the complex issue of the laws on gentile food and the episode of the 'decree of eighteen things' connected with the Roman War. Our starting point is with a striking phenomenon: the liberality of Amoraic Judaism towards images of pagan origin.

It is only in the esthetic perfection of its nude human figures that the mosaic floor of the fourth century synagogue discovered at Hammat near Tiberias, where leading Sages are said to have been praying, is really unique.[79] Alongside that unabashed portrayal of the personified signs of the Zodiac, with the Four Seasons at the corners and sun god Helios prominent in the centre, discoveries of similar mosaics and frescoes from ancient Palestinian synagogues have

---

[77] Thus the thrust of Millar, 'Background'.

[78] For an impressive and stimulating contribution to the discussion see Fox, *Pagans*.

[79] For some discussion and literature see Naveh, *On Stone and Mosaic*, 47-50; M. Avi-Yonah, in *EJ* 7, 1242-4.

stunned archeologists and historians. How can this liberality in the portrayal of the human figure and the adoption of pagan motifs – not for trivial enjoyment but for decorating synagogues! – be sqared with the biblical prohibition of images and the Rabbinical laws of idolatry? Is it not mere pious rhetoric, when the Greek votive inscription identifies one of the founders of the Hammat synagogue as 'Severus, a pupil of the most illustrious Patriarchs'?

E.R. GOODENOUGH advanced the theory that the receptivity of Amoraic Jewry vis-à-vis pagan Hellenistic symbols indicates a decline in the position of Rabbinic tradition.[80] This theory is very questionable. The information about the inner developments of Rabbinic Judaism in late Tannaic and Amoraic times, especially in the halakhic field, points to a process of consolidation rather than of disintegration. Other explanations must be sought.

Basing himself mainly on an analysis of Rabbinic sources, E.E. URBACH squarely rejects Goodenough's theory.[81] The openness towards pagan symbols, Urbach posits, testifies not to the weakness but to the inner strength of Amoraic Rabbinism. A trend towards leniency is visible from the second or third generation of Tannaim onwards, which in Urbach's view was the resultant of two concurrent developments. In the first place the two successive wars against Rome entailed forced migration and urbanization of the rural population. This resulted in greater economic interaction and interdependence of Jews and gentiles. Out of necessity Jewish artisans would also turn to manufacture figurines and similar ornaments and sell them to gentiles, or buy and re-use them. A second development posited by Urbach consists of an increasing shallowness of pagan devotion during the Amoraic age, as ever more gentiles showed themselves ready to desecrate idols.[82] This part of the theory is disputable; Urbach only supports it with evidence from Rabbinic sources. Moreover a recent large-schale study of paganism and Christianity found that there was actually a revival of pagan cult-activities during the 2nd-3rd centuries CE, including in the Eastern parts of the Empire.[83] On the other hand Urbach points out the absence of any compromise on the emperor cult which grew especially important in the eastern parts of the Empire. This indicates clear limits to the practical compromise with idolatry; a stand-point evidently shared by early Christianity.

As stated, the external support for this theory does not appear convincing. Urbanization is not a sufficient cause, certainly not if it did not respond to an inner dynamic. Urbach adds the assumption that increased Jewish-gentile

[80] See *Symbols* 4, 3-24, 'The Relevance of Rabbinic Evidence'. The thesis of Rabbinic 'weakness' vis-à-vis surrounding culture has an irrational component correlate to an overrating of Hellenistic influence; see discussion on Hellenism and Judaism, above ch 1, on Goodenough p40-2. Information on the Hammat mosaic reached G. at a late stage, see vol 12, 185-8; p185 expresses misunderstanding of the distinct significance of halakha and religious thought.

[81] Urbach, 'Rabbinical Laws'.

[82] Urbach ib 162-4, 236f.

[83] Fox, *Pagans*, 64-101. Flusser, 'Paganism', 1098f concurs as regards Palestinian paganism from 200 CE onwards.

co-existence also necessitated greater stringency in the halakhot regulating social isolation, especially regarding gentile wine and food; this is inexact, to say the least.[84] Nevertheless a process towards practical compomise with gentile idolatry during the second half of the Tannaic era seems undeniable and fits in with the rational attitude of the Tannaim which we discussed above.

However the causes behind the development have still to be explained. Apparently they relate to complex changes set in motion by the wars against Rome. Intensified interaction with gentiles does not automatically lead to greater leniency vis-à-vis their religious systems; the opposite is just as likely to be true, as our considerations on diaspora Judaism showed (above p46). Thus there must have been an inner change within the Rabbinic movement, an ideological shift of balance which followed the destruction of the Temple.[85] It is possible that it related to the concurrent gradual take-over by the Hillelites who as we saw had much more moderate views regarding gentiles.[86] Significantly the Patriarch R. Yehuda the Prince had very positive relations with the Severan emperors,[87] and he was remarkably lenient toward gentiles. We have noted his willingness to go further than his colleagues in the question of desecration by sale. A similar lenience of his and his grandson's is visible in connection with the 'Decree of Eighteen Things' (below p176). These leading figures obviously express a type of Judaism very different from the one reflected in the earlier Second Temple sources. Of quite a different nature was the increasing and eventually decisive influence of Christianity on the decline of paganism, since it was concurrent to a deterioration of the position of Judaism.[88]

Confirmation for Urbach's overall theory is found in an eighth-century Palestinian halakhic source which declares that 'today, the smell of idolatry has been extinguished', whence liturgical acts are permitted in decorated locations hitherto forbidden.[89] This late source apparently preserves the rational attitude of the Amoraic Sages who concluded that idolatry no longer presents any danger and that pagan ornamental motifs did not harm the atmosphere of devotion in the synagogue.

A second aspect of the development of idolatry laws concerns the tendency to detach them from the system of purity rules. In order to examine this issue, let

---

[84] Urbach, 'Rabbinical Laws', 241-4; a traditional approach (cf Maimonides, below n116). This contradicts both his main theory and the sources. Developments as regards bread, oil and wine recorded in the Talmudim (below n104, 112f) reflect increasing leniency in Amoraic times. tAZ 4:6 notwithstanding (Urbach 242) Rabbinic sources confirm the presence of important Sages at gentile banquets; below p232f.

[85] Alon, *The Jews* 2 pinpoints the shift between the two great wars.

[86] On the process towards a Hillelite majority see Safrai, 'Decision'.

[87] See Gafni, 'Background' (in *Compendia* II/3a) 23.

[88] As noted by Urbach ib 244f.

[89] See Margulies, *Hilkhot Erets Yisrael*, 135 (T-S N.S. 135 fol 49a lines 8ff). Admittedly, the same source, a Palestinian *siddur* and the earliest of its kind, also mentions that it is forbidden to bow down in prayer on a 'table of images' (ib 49b line 4). But the reason is not idolatry but erotic associations. For a short discussion of the *siddur* see *Compendia* II/3a, 407f written by Dr Zeev Safrai, who also kindly drew my attention to the passage years ago.

us focus on the the early Second Temple stage of the process. In a ground-breaking study Gedalyahu ALON posited that the idea of impurity emanating from the idol was the original basis for all halakhot regarding idolatry and gentile relations.[90] In line with the biblical commandments, the sphere of idolatry was conceived as fundamentally impure and making a Jew unfit for his own ritual obligations. The impurity extended from the idol itself to anything touching it, its cultic attributes, sacrifices, buildings, its worshipers and, ultimately, all gentiles. Likewise areas of gentile settlement were considered impure and rendering impure any persons and objects deriving from them; this was formulated in the halakhot about the so-called 'impurity of gentile territory'.[91] The intention of these basically ancient laws was to prevent contact of Jews with its influence and to combat it in the Land of Israel.[92]

It is not true, Alon maintains,[93] that impurity was decreed on gentiles only on the occasion of the Decree of Eighteen Things; nor was it based on specific sources of impurity, and neither did it apply only to matters relating to the Temple service. Insofar as levitical purity was apparently observed in daily life by a reasonable number of Jews,[94] the idolatry laws had a great influence on the life of the population in Second Temple times. Examples of important halakhot deriving from this concept are the obligation of ritual immersion for proselytes after conversion and the prohibition against gentiles entering the sanctuary. On the other hand, the scope of the impurity issuing from idolatry in the varying circumstances of daily life was not fixed,[95] nor did all Jews always observe the purity laws. Hence the personal differences of opinion and the more general oscillations in attitude, as well as the incidental need felt for a formal reaffirmation of some of these laws in the Decree of Eighteen Things.

A crucial conclusion Alon draws from the sources is that according to the halakha, fundamentally gentiles were not liable to the laws of purity. Unlike 'regular' impurity deriving from physical sources such as bodily excretions or a corpse, the impurity of gentiles only resulted from their association with idolatry.[96] Hence the impurity of idolatry and gentiles was of a special type; it derived from spiritual rather than physical factors.

According to Alon this must have been the background of a remarkable development. In addition to changing historical circumstances, the peculiar nature of gentile impurity led to the removal of laws governing relations to gentiles from the developing system of purity rules and their integration into other halakhic subject areas. But remains of the original grounds were also

---

[90] Alon, *Jews, Judaism*, 146-89.
[91] טומאת ארץ העמים; see mOh 18:6b-10 and tAh 18:1-18. For their antiquity cf mOh 17:5; tAh 17:6; mToh 2:3.
[92] See above n12 and n24.
[93] On these points, Alon corrects the position taken by Büchler, 'Levitical Impurity'.
[94] This conclusion is worked out by Alon in his other fundamental article in this respect, *Jews, Judaism*, 190-234 ('The Bounds of the Laws of Levitical Cleanness').
[95] Alon (ib 168-72) discerns three opinions regarding the precise degree of impurity of the idol: impurity equalling that of a dead reptile, that of a menstruate woman, or that of a corpse.
[96] Alon ib 154-6, 159-68, in discussion, respectively, with Schürer and Büchler.

preserved, and characteristic contradictions were the result. Thus the impurity of gentile territory came to be grounded on doubt about the presence of corpses, although according to the halakha gentile corpses do not defile; and on the other hand gentile territory could not be purified from suspected 'grave impurity' as opposed to similar suspected areas within Jewish territory. Similar secondary and unsatisfactory explanations were sought for the laws prescribing ritual immersion of proselytes and of gentile utensils and those prohibiting gentile wet-nurses to suckle Jewish babies.[97] According to Alon, this development gained momentum especially after 70 CE, due to the changed historical circumstances; probably, this had to do with the more lenient Hillelite majority which emerged after the war.[98]

LAWS ABOUT GENTILE FOOD

One set of halakhot which is important for the present study is dealt with only summarily by ALON, and must be elaborated on here: the laws relating to gentile food in Mishna *Avoda Zara* chapter two.[99] Three categories are listed: foods prohibited in any respect; foods not sacrificed and prohibited only for consumption, and foods permitted in all respects.

(1) These things of gentiles are prohibited, which includes the prohibition to have profit from them: wine and vinegar of gentiles that at first was wine, Hadrianic sherds, and hides pierced at the heart... Meat under way to an alien cult is permitted (for having profit from), but when returning it is forbidden, for it is like "sacrifices to the dead"; thus R. Akiva... (2:3).

(2) These things of gentiles are prohibited, which does not include a prohibition to have profit from them: milk which a gentile milked when no Israelite watched him, their bread and their oil,[100] stews, pickles to which they add wine or vinegar, ...brine in which there is no fish... (2:6).

(3) These are permitted to be eaten: milk which a gentile milked while an Israelite watched him, honey, juicy grapes[101] – even though they are dripping, this does not count as moisture making them fit (for impurity) –, pickled food to which they do not add wine or vinegar... (2:7).

The first category contains foods sacrificed to idols. Gentile wine was plainly supposed to be sacrificed to idolatry by libation; and 'libation wine' יין נסך was forbidden in all respects in any quantity or dilution (mAZ 5:9-10). This also applied to 'Hadrianic sherds', sherds soaked in strong wine and used by soldiers

---

[97] See sources quoted by Alon ib 180-6.

[98] ib 149, without specifying the historical details; but cf above n85.

[99] Alon, *Jews, Judaism*, 181f. See tAZ 4:7-13; yAZ 4, 41a-42a (yShab 1, 3c-d); bAZ 29b-40b. The term 'food laws' used here and further on must be understood to include the leather wine skins also involved, mAZ 2:3f; tAZ 4:9f.

[100] 'Rabbi (Yehuda Nesia) and his court permitted oil' is a baraita crept into the Mishna, see tAZ 4:11; yAZ 2, 41d (yShab 1, 3c); bAZ 36a. Ms K, P, C and Mishna in Bavli ms M place it between 'stewed food' and 'pickled food'.

[101] Thus Albeck's explanation.

to flavour their drinking water.[102] A hole in a hide at the place of the heart indicated that the heart was taken out alive for a sacrifice. No dealings whatsoever with these goods were allowed; they were a source of impurity.[103] It is to be noted, however, that the Amoraim sought different reasons for these prohibitions and also modified them. Among other things they differentiated between actual libation wine and unspecified gentile wine.[104]

The second and third categories include foods not used for idolatrous ritual. Those of the second category may be bought, sold, or carried for wages, but not consumed. The precise reasons are unclear and disputed in the sources. If wine or vinegar was added the reason seems simple: libation wine. But as we saw libation wine is prohibited in any quantity and in any respect, which would exclude use for one's profit.[105] Indeed, the Tosefta preserves R. Meir's ruling to that effect, as opposed to the Sages: 'Stewed and pickled foods to which they add wine or vinegar, and Hadrianic sherds – their prohibition includes the prohibition to have profit from them.'[106] As for the reason for the prohibition of milk milked by a gentile, the Talmudim are divided,[107] which indicates that the original reason was lost. The reason for prohibiting gentile bread is also disputed. One of the reasons suggested is that buying gentile bread leads to intermarriage.[108] A more accurate guess would be that bread falls under the category of תבשילי גוים, tavshilei goyim, i.e. foods prepared by gentiles.[109] But even that is a secondary reason, for it would have been more efficient to mention that general category from the start and not mention bread specifically; 'stewed food' is in the same category.[110] Moreover, the Palestinian Talmud calls the prohibition of bread one of the 'halakhot of disregard' הלכות עימעום,[111] since in many situations it was not obeyed. It is also reported that

[102] bAZ 32a. This is an addition to the list; cf mAZ 5:9 and tAZ 4:8.

[103] 'Sacrifices to the dead' suggests impurity; cf Jub 22:17, mAZ 2:3; and sources quoted by Alon, *Jews, Judaism*, 170f. On wine see following n.

[104] See yAZ 2, 41a-b; bAZ 29b-32a. R. Yohanan differentiates between three types of wine: gentile wine explicitly devoted to an idol, which is forbidden and a source of impurity comparable to a dead reptile; gentile wine of unspecified status which is forbidden for profit but does not render impure; and Israelite wine which was under gentile custody and is permitted for profit (yAZ 2, 41b top, cf different version bAZ 30b-31a).

[105] mAZ 5:9-10; cf 5:2; tAZ 7:16.

[106] tAZ 4:8. R. Meir's opinion is held also by R. Lazar, yAZ 2, 42a: 'Thus fresh food to which he added (wine or vinegar) is prohibited even for deriving profit'. The reverse is taught by R. Yohanan bAZ 38b: 'Hizkia said, they taught this only about stews in which it is merely their custom (to add wine or vinegar), but if this is known for sure, they are prohibited. ...But R. Yohanan said: even if known for sure, they are permitted.'

[107] yAZ 2, 41d (yShab 1, 3c-d) proposes either גילוי, 'leaving it uncovered' (so that a snake can poison it, mTer 8:4) or 'mixture with (milk of) unclean cattle'. Cf tAZ 4:11. Similarly bAZ 35b: 'whispering on it' (incantations), mixture or confusion with unclean cattle; similar arguments are used for the prohibition of מורייס, bAZ 34b.

[108] bAZ 35b. This is a blanket argument also used for other prohibitions, e.g. bAZ 31b.

[109] yAZ 2, 41d (yShab 1, 3c).

[110] bAZ 37b-38a; yAZ 2, 41c (114) counts מורייס among this category.

[111] Collected yMSh 3, 54a; yShev 8, 38a.

R. Yehuda the Prince once appeared to permit gentile bread.[112] The same applies to oil; but here indeed the disregard eventually led to the formal annulment of the prohibition by the court of R. Yehuda the Prince's grandson, R. Yehuda Nesia. The explanation given is that 'Any decree imposed by a court on the community, which the majority of the community cannot bear, is no decree'.[113] – The conclusion must be that as long as no direct relation to idolatry is involved, the status of these gentile foodstuffs is far from clear in Rabbinic halakha.

The third category opens with three types of liquid from gentiles: milk, honey and juice dripping from grapes. Just as with the foodstuffs in the second category, these bear no direct relation to idolatry, but unlike them, they may be consumed. The explanation, however, which the Mishna adds in the third case differs completely from those given in the Talmudim in the second category: 'Even though they are dripping, this does not count as moisture making them fit (for impurity)'. Hence the issue here is purity. As implied in the Tora (Lev 11:38), food cannot be made impure until water is brought on it; but as soon the food is moistened, contact with a source of impurity renders it impure. The halakha extended this to be effected by other liquids such as wine, milk and honey (mMakh 1:1; 6:4). By implication, the problem in the first two cases is also food made susceptible of impurity by contact with liquid. Now our mishna rules that these three liquids do not cause susceptibility of impurity; one might apparently have expected otherwise. Susceptibility of impurity through moisture is involved in more halakhot about gentile foods which are not in direct contact with idolatry:

> Grape stones and grape skins from gentiles are prohibited, and this includes a prohibition to have profit from them – thus R. Meir; but the Sages say: when moist, they are forbidden, but when dry, permitted. (mAZ 2:4)[114]
>
> One may buy from the gentiles grain, peas, dried figs, garlic and onions in any case, *without fear for impurity*; sumac-tree berries in any case are pure;[115] rice in any case is pure. (tAZ 4:11)

In the latter list dryness is essential for the quality of the goods and hence in the interest of the gentile selling them. Thus there is no fear for impurity. Consequently the intention underlying these halakhot indeed was to avoid impurity of

---

[112] yMSh 3, 54a (yShev 8, 38a; yAZ 2, 41d): 'The Rabbis of Caesarea agree with him who permits (where no Jewish bread can be obtained), if only from the shop; but we do not act so'. bAZ ib: R. Yehuda the Prince saw a magnificent loaf of gentile bread and said: 'What reason had the Sages to forbid it?' etc. Cf also bAZ 37a: R. Simlai, of the more permissive Lyddans (bAZ 36a; yAZ 2, 41d), proposes to R. Yehuda Nesia also to permit gentile bread.

[113] yAZ 2, 41d (yShab 1, 3d). The (secondary) positive formulation bAZ 36a: 'One does not impose a decree on the community unless the majority can bear it'. It is also reported that Shmuel accepted the permission, while Rav initially kept to the prohibition (ib, ib).

[114] yAZ 2, 41c adds (Rav Sheshet in the name of Rav): 'When moist, they are prohibited even for profit; when dry, they are permitted even for consumption'. The same in the name of R. Yohanan bAZ 34a.

[115] With the Vienna ms and ed princ. But see tMakh 3:9.

170

goods deriving from gentiles. As long as the goods are dry or the moisture on them is not counted as making them susceptible of impurity, there is no impediment. Impurity here can only derive from the apparent involvement in idolatry of gentiles.

At this point, it is well to recall that the prohibition of gentile wine, bread and oil is well attested in the early Second Temple period. At root, it reflects the avoidance of idolatry and impurity. Precisely this basic explanation is cited by the Babylonian Talmud (AZ 36b) in the name of Rav: 'All of these were decreed on because of idolatry'. The severity of the prohibition of the first category (wine, idol meat) was caused by the fact that they were sacrificed to the idol and hence forbidden in any respect and a primary source of impurity. Non-sacrificial foodstuffs, however, were impure in a remote degree and only insofar as they were moistened and touched by the gentile, who himself was considered impure because he was involved in idolatry. But the inexact degree of this impurity, the change in social and economic circumstances and the decrease in gentile devotion to idolatry must have caused the halakhot in part to be reduced in force and in part to be based on other grounds. These included: the avoidance of forbidden animals, of gentile wine, and of the general category called תבשילי גוים, foods prepared by gentiles. A more general secondary motive was the avoidance of too much contact with gentiles. But as we saw, the original basic intention, avoidance of idol impurity, was retained in some cases. Hence the incoherence of these prohibitions regarding gentile food.[116]

An interesting narrative included in the same chapter of Mishna tractate *Avoda Zara* is illustrative of this unclarity. It contains a discussion on the prohibition of gentile cheese between R. Yishmael and his teacher, R. Yoshua. The narrative comes in the middle between the first and second categories of forbidden gentile foods, and functions as a literary transition illustrating an intermediary halakhic category of disputed character. The preceding mishna (2:4) prohibits cheese along with מורייס (*muries*, a fish brine),[117] but the scope of the prohibition is disputed. R. Meir appears to assume that they contain ingredients deriving from wine or meat sacrificed to idols and rules that

---

[116] Maimonides feels the need for a systematic explanation of all the halakhot mentioned in mAZ 2:6, and seeks it in the intention to avoid too much contact with gentiles, as expressed in the talmudic saying 'because of intermarriage'.

[117] המורייס וגבינה ותנייקי. Thus ms C, corrected ms K (filling in a *homoioteleuton*), and further versions mentioned by Epstein, *Nosah*, 1104f. The Bavli (Mishna and Gemara in mss NY, M), Maimonides and printed Mishna editions read: המורייס וגבינת בית אונייקי, 'muries and Bithynian cheese'. A similar variant is found in the Tosefta (AZ 4:13), but in a different halakha, teaching that one can buy the cheese in question: 'One buys [Bithynian] cheese only from the expert'. Ed. princ. here reads גבינת בית היניקאי; and ms Erfurt גבינה ובית היניקי, a composite reading. But ms Vienna accords with the better Mishna text: גבינה. Epstein proposes to read in the Mishna תרניקה or תרינקה, milk serum (cf ms P and Mishna in the Yerushalmi, ותירייקי, see Jastrow sv). The apparently Babylonian version 'Bithynian cheese' is restrictive; cf the explanation by Resh Lakish (Bavli) or R. Yoshua ben Levi (Yerushalmi): '…because of [*the majority of* – Geniza ms and Bavli] the calves they slaughter there in the name of idolatry'. This seems to reflect a later softening regarding gentile cheese.

they are prohibited in all respects (category one); but the Sages allow these products to be handled for profit (category two).[118] Thereupon R. Yehuda, R. Meir's usual partner in discussion who may represent 'the Sages' also in this case, is cited telling the story:[119]

> Said R. Yehuda: R. Yishmael asked a question of R. Yoshua while they were on a journey: Why did they prohibit the cheese of gentiles? He answered: Because they curdle it with (rennet from) the maw of un-properly slaughtered (calves). Then he said to him: But is not the maw from (a calf slaughtered for) a Whole-offering forbidden more strictly than that of an unproperly slaughtered calf, and yet they have said: A priest who is not squeamish may suck out (milk in its maw) raw?[120] ...He gave a second answer: Because they curdle it with (rennet from) the maw of (calves sacrificed to) alien cults. He said to him: If so, why did not they prohibit (cheese) also for profit? Then he led him to another matter, and said to him: Yishmael, my brother, how do you read, "Your love is better than wine"...?[121]

The Talmudim explain R. Yoshua's reticence from the fact that the prohibition of gentile cheese was only recent, and he did not want to have it criticized.[122] This refers to the prohibition as one of the Eighteen Things, which will be investigated below. It will appear that R. Yoshua himself was not happy with the decree, and his reticence may mean that he kept his mouth shut only because he was bound by it, even though he did not support it. At any rate the ambiguous explanation he gives of the prohibition is most revealing. Rennet from idol sacrifices would prohibit gentile cheese in any respect, just like brine containing libation wine. But the decree apparently prohibited eating only, not handling them for profit. The same contradiction, we saw, regards 'stewed and pickled foods to which they add wine or vinegar'; and there it was also R. Meir who, in contrast to the Sages, prohibited use for profit.[123] The explanation appears to be that the prohibition of cheese of gentiles, as the general prohibi-tion of their wine, bread and oil, was originally based on the impurity of gentiles

---

[118] yAZ 2, 41c; bAZ 34b-35c; *muries* usually contained wine, and the rennet used to curdle cheese could well derive from sacrificed calves.

[119] mAZ 2:5, quoted with some variants CantR 1,17.

[120] Thus Albeck's explanation. There follows an inserted comment rejecting the halakha quoted here by R. Yishmael, which is absent in CantR.

[121] The quotation is from Cant 1:2, the issue being whether to read דודיך *dodeikha* (masc, 'your love') or *dodayikh* (fem, 'your breasts'). The distraction would have been seductive (milk, sucking!). The section starting with 'then he led him to another matter...' is also contained in a parallel narrative about both travelling Sages, where R. Yishmael's question regards a purity law: tPara 10:3.

[122] bAZ 35a; yAZ 2, 41c bottom, adding 'R. Yishmael was still young'.

[123] In mAZ 2:4 R. Meir pursues R. Yishmael's argument that cheese should be forbidden for profit; and R. Yehuda may be understood to bring the story 2:5 in order to this argument. R. Meir's stringency in these halakhot may be explained from his tendency towards severity in purity laws. Cf yAZ 5, 44d bottom: 'R. Meir is stringent as regards purity but lenient as regards libation wine'; the issue is custody over a wine-shop by a gentile, where R. Meir is not reported to be stringent, mAZ 5:4; while in the case of custody over a house by an *am ha-arets* R. Meir is stringent, mToh 7:1-3 (tToh 8:1).

172

caused by contact with the idol. Either this contact or the impurity deriving from it apparently had come to be felt less clearly, and the prohibition had to be based on other grounds.

THE DECREE OF EIGHTEEN THINGS

As stated the Talmudim explain the episode by pointing out that the prohibition of gentile cheese was of recent date at the time when R. Yishmael asked his teacher. This indicates an origin somewhere in the second half of the first century CE. Hence there seems to be a connection with an enigmatic yet important episode in the history of halakha: the promulgation of the 'Decree of Eighteen Things'. All indications are that it happened at the very close of the Second Temple period, in connection with the war against Rome, and that it involved a bloody clash between Shammaites and Hillelites.[124]

The enigma is in the fact that while the decree is mentioned in Mishna and Tosefta, its contents are not. The Talmudim are uncertain and give various alternative explanations.[125] Explicit mention of the decree is made in mShab 1:4. Reflecting on the preceding halakhot about preservative limits to activities on Friday afternoon, this mishna also mentions eighteen 'things' which the Sages decreed on 'on that very day'. The day was when they went up to visit Hanina ben Hizkia ben Garon in his upper room, and when, we are also told, the Shammaites outnumbered the Hillelites in a vote. But as we said, we are not told what these things were. Other reports inform us that the session took place in a violent atmosphere in which the Shammaites even killed a number of Hillelites. Interestingly, the reports about casualties among the Hillelites are confirmed by much later Palestinian Jewish traditions of a fast day reminiscent of a similar sad occasion.[126] All of this points to the beginning of the Great War against Rome.

This date receives confirmation from the very plausible identification of one of the protagonists of the rebellion in Josephus' account,[127] 'the Temple-commander Eleazar, son of the (former) high-priest Ananias', as Elazar, the son of Hanina ben Hizkia ben Garon mentioned above. Josephus notes the tumultuous decision, taken at Eleazar's initiative by a majority of Temple functionaries, 'to accept no gift or sacrifice (δῶρον ἢ θυσίαν) from a foreigner' and to

---

[124] Graetz, *Geschichte* III/2, 470-2, and notes 24, 26 and 27 (p795ff). For full discussion of the passages involved see Goldberg, *Shabbat*, 15-22 (basically adopting Graetz' view); Lieberman, *Tosefta ki-Fshutah* 3, 13-20. See also Lerner, 'Die achtzehn Bestimmungen'; Zeitlin, 'Les dix-huit mesures'; Hengel, *Zeloten*, 204-11, 365-8; Urbach, *Sages*, 594-6; Rappaport, 'Yahasei Yehudim'.

[125] tShab 1:11-21; yShab 1, 3c-d (in part paralleled by yAZ 2, 41c-d); bShab 13b-17a (confusing chronology).

[126] The bloody confrontation between Shammaites and Hillelites referred to can hardly be a different one. According to 'Megillat Taanit Batra' the day is 9 Adar (Lurie, *Megillath Taanith*, 201). The 'Megillat ha-Tsomot' found in the Cairo Geniza mentions a fast on 4 Adar on which 'there occurred a confrontation between the disciples of Shammai and Hillel on which many were killed'; see Margulies, *Hilkhot Erets Yisrael*, 142 (T-S N.S. 235/10 1A).

[127] Josephus, *War* 2:409f.

173

discontinue the sacrifices offered on behalf of Rome and its emperor.[128] This, Josephus comments, was a direct *casus belli*. Rabbinic sources identify Elazar as a leading Shammaite.[129] In particular the responsibility ascribed to him for the 'writing', i.e. the updating and re-issuing, of *Megillat Taanit* (the Scroll of Fasting) is important. This document consists of a list of days of national rejoicing on which no fasting is allowed. Days from Hasmonean times are prominent, but the latest additions, apparently made by the final editors, relate to the first century CE.[130] The re-issuing of the Scroll was a clearly nationalist and Zealot activity.

In this light, an evaluation of the sources leads to the conclusion that the Eighteen Things are contained in a baraita in the name of R. Shimon ben Yohai in the Yerushalmi.[131] It lists eighteen comestibles and other matters connected with gentiles:[132]

> On that very day they decreed on their bread, their cheese, their wine, their vinegar, their brine, their *muries*, their pickles, their stews, their salted foods, their חילקה (*hilka*),[133] their pounded spices, their טיסני (*tisni,* barley groats), their language, their testimony, their offerings, their sons, their daughters, their first fruits.

Most of these are contained also in the food prohibitions enumerated in Mishna *Avoda Zara*, and it is clear that we are dealing with the same set of prohibitions: wine and vinegar (2:3), *muries* and cheese (2:4-5), bread, stews, pickles, and *hilek* (2:6-7). Oil, while being mentioned in the other lists in the Talmudim, is lacking here; as mentioned above, the oil prohibition was the only one to be formally rescinded at a later date. We have also seen that the prohibition of gentile wine, bread and oil, as also of 'their sons, their daughters', was well established long before the probable date of the decree. For the rest the prohibition of these Eighteen Things fits the inimical atmosphere of the war against Rome.[134]

---

[128] Graetz identified this with the מתנותיהם from the 18 things, but this contradicts regular mishnaic halakha; see Safrai, *Wallfahrt*, 287.

[129] In Mekh Yitro 7 (p229) he gives an opinion on the Shabbat elsewhere attributed to Shammai: MekhShbY p148; bBeitsa 16a; PesR 23 (115b). The Bavli (ib) also credits him with explaining away the contradictions between the book of Ezekiel and the Tora, which may well have been connected with the Temple ritual; his interest in explaining the Temple ritual in Ezekiel is confirmed in SifDeut 294 (p313).

[130] See Lichtenstein, 'Fastenrolle'. The attribution is made at the end of the scholion to the scroll, in Lichtenstein's ed p351; cf bShab 13b.

[131] This is the solution proposed by Graetz and followed, with more documentation, by Goldberg. Cf the tradition ascribed to Rav (bAZ 36a and b), below n136. On further literary and historical problems see my 'Zavim'.

[132] yShab 1, 3c.

[133] Cf mAZ 2:6 חילק, *hilek*; Latin *alec/halec* etc, a kind of fish(-brine). Cf also Latin *alica*, spelt(-drink), see Jastrow. And see Lieberman, *Hayerushalmi kiphshuto*, 44.

[134] A prohibition of 'non-Jewish' languages is difficult to imagine in actual life (Aramaic, like Greek, being spoken by many Jews including Sages) but reflects general resentment. Cf R. Yoshua on reading Greek, tAZ 1:20. Testimony of gentiles is declared invalid mYev 16:5 but was actually accepted according to tYev 14:7; bYev 122a. The prohibition of first fruits and 'gifts' may seem to

The publication of the Decree was essentially a re-enforcement of ancient halakhot. As we have seen Jewish abstainment from gentile wine, oil and bread is known from earlier Second Temple sources (above p153). Such was the nature of more public 'editions' made by the Sages. Another example is the re-issuing of the Scroll of Fasting we have mentioned above. Apparently it happened at exactly the same period and was another initiative of the Shammaites and also indicative of their anti-gentile, Zealot sentiment.[135] In this light ALON seems correct in assuming that the original reason for these anti-gentile prohibitions was gentile idolatry and the concomitant impurity of gentile goods. This is confirmed in two interrelated traditions ascribed to Rav (mid-third century), one of which has been quoted already: 'Their bread, their oil, their wine and their daughters were all among the Eighteen Things'; 'They were all decreed on because of idolatry'.[136] For some of the prohibited items there may not yet have been a clear-cut halakha at the time of issuing, but underlying them was the same general idea of the avoidance of contact with gentiles, with the sphere of idolatry and with the impurity emanating from it. In any case the issuing of the Decree indicates that towards the end of the Second Temple period not all of the prohibitions were observed by all Jews, and that many of the Sages at that time saw this as an unforgiveable laxity.

In this light it is important to reiterate that the Shammaite R. Eliezer is reported to have welcomed the Decree, while his Hillelite colleague R. Yoshua deplored it.[137] This concurs with reports that the Decree was issued on a day when the Shammaites outnumbered the Hillelites, and that they even used violence and killed a number of Hillelites. The Zealot connections of the Shammaites is an obvious factor at work here.[138] It may be that the sudden change of atmosphere at the beginning of the War presented a welcome opportunity to re-inforce ancient anti-gentile prohibitions and to add new ones, which the Hillelites thought inopportune, to say the least. And finally, this may explain R. Yoshua's later reticence when asked about the reason behind the prohibition of gentile cheese – one of the Eighteen Things and apparently a new item on the list.

When viewed from a distance the Decree of Eighteen Things is another illustration that there was no linear development from stringency to leniency in the laws concerning idolatry and gentile food. Although they did not think it opportune, the Hillelites respected the Decree once it was there, and even if R. Yoshua failed to explain the cheese prohibition to his pupil, neither did he utter a word of criticism against it.[139] One may speculate that the tragic outcome of

refer to gentile offerings for the Temple, but see above n128.
[135] Yet another example is the 'fixing' in number and rough formulation of the Eighteen Benedictions for the daily prayer on the initiative of Rabban Gamliel well after the war, mBer 4:3. See Safrai, 'Synagogue', 922-6.
[136] bAZ 36b (36a); cf bShab 17b.
[137] tShab 1:17; yShab 1, 3c. See my 'Zavim'.
[138] See Graetz (above n124).
[139] Hence the explanation in the Talmudim that he remained silent on the actual reasons because he

the War contributed to this change of mind. Another, more plausible reason is that the Sages, and certainly the Hillelites, accepted majority decisions in principle as binding.[140]

Later days and changed circumstances saw the abrogation of the prohibition on gentile oil and the softening of the prohibition on bread and, possibly, also cheese. In this connection the names of R. Yehuda the Prince and his grandson, R. Yehuda Nesia, are important.[141] We saw that the cause which was indicated is the change in attitude of majority of the people. Apparently outside conditions determine the degree and the form in which the ancient basic religious-national conceptions are realized in actual practice.[142]

SUMMARY

A general development is in evidence, from early Second Temple strictness on gentile idolatry to leniency in the Amoraic period. A concurrent process involved the decreasing awareness of gentile impurity and the trend towards removing idolatry laws from the purity system to other halakhic areas. This has been illustrated in the case of halakha on gentile food. For both processes the destruction of the Temple was a turning point. The complexity of the situation is indicated by the Decree of Eighteen Things which was issued at the same time and signalled a forced return to ancient strictness. Its influence is visible especially in the halakha on gentile food. On the other hand later generations redressed parts of the Decree, thus continuing the main tendency towards leniency.

We have ventured the assumption that the turning point which in spite of complications occurred around the time of the destruction of the Temple had to do with the gradual take-over of the Hillelites. Mishnaic halakha is Hillelite, and probably also its rationality towards gentile idolatry. A strong indication in that direction is the subdued Hillelite discontent with the Decree of Eighteen Things. Furthermore this fits in with the general character of the Hillelite tradition, which was more rational and gave priority to a person's conscious intention. By contrast the Shammaites were closer to zealotism and more conservative. However we have noted the exceptions of the two 'rational' halakhot of the Shammaite R. Eliezer. The relation between the schools eludes schematization, probably because of their constant inter-communication.

A central question to the present study concerns opinions presumably circulating around the middle of the first century CE. Events surrounding the Decree of Eighteen Things indicate that the Shammaites were in the majority at the

did not allow the new prohibition to be criticized (above n122).
[140] See mEd 1:5 and the following mishnayot; and the exemplary story of R. Eliezer the Shammaite, bBM 59b. Safrai, 'Halakha', 199f points out that he was banned solely for his unwillingness to accept the majority view in one point, while his other halakhic opinions were not contested at such.
[141] On bread see above n112; on cheese n117.
[142] Thus the final analysis of Alon's study on the 'Levitical Uncleanness of Gentiles', *Jews, Judaism*, 187-9.

outbreak of war. This also appears to have been the case two decades earlier.[143] On the other hand the subsequent prominence of R. Yohanan ben Zakkai signals the fact that the more moderate Hillelite tradition, even if in a minority, was very alive before the war.[144] If we add the open-mindedness towards gentiles attributed to Hillel, on which more later, we may confidently assume that in Paul's day a wide range of opinions existed in circles associated with the Pharisaic movement.

Idol Offerings in the Early Church

Idolatry, or the worship of 'other gods' than the Creator of heaven and earth, presented a challenge not only for Jews but also for the adherents of the other religious tradition which issued from this Jewish background: Christianity. In the following pages we focus on only one practical detail of the relationship of rising Christianity with paganism: food sacrificed to the gods, rather than taking a more general view. Not only is the development of Christian belief and ethic on the borderlines between Judaism and paganism of intriguing complexity; its study is in need of much further detailed analysis with an integration of scholarly traditions.[145] Even so, a survey of early Christian literature on the question of pagan food offerings will yield information which, in addition to our survey on Jewish attitudes towards paganism, sufficiently illuminates Paul's stance in this matter.

In order to quicken imagination let us first remember that until the fourth and fifth centuries pagan cults were still common in the Greco-Roman world. There were temples everywhere, as well as theatres and circuses where the cultic element, especially focusing on the emperor, was always prominent. As is well known both Jews and Christians had great difficulty with these practices and avoided getting involved in them at great cost. In fact this represents one of the essential points of agreement between Christians and Jews. Thus it is no surprise that, as we shall now see, the early Church was unanimous in its fundamental prohibition of idol food offerings.

A well known and fundamental discussion on the matter is contained in the Acts of the Apostles. We are told how the Apostles gathered in Jerusalem to discuss the question of the Law with regard to Christ-believing gentiles: what commandments should they keep? The decision was laid down in a letter addressed to the Churches in Antioch, Syria and Cilicia containing the following instruction: 'It has seemed good to the Holy Spirit and to us to lay upon you no greater burden than these necessary things: to abstain from food sacrificed to idols, from blood, from what is strangled and from unchastity'

---

[143] This was already maintained by Büchler, 'Halakhot le-maase'.
[144] For his position cf the baraita on bBB 10b.
[145] Fox, *Pagans* is brilliant and inspiring. See p30-33 for fundamentals on 'paganism' and 'religion'. The work displays striking intuition in complicated 'borderline' issues such as on God-fearers (318f) or divorce and celibacy (352f). Yet I think that a next generation may attain greater refinement in such issues, and a more adequate synthesis, by means of full integration of Jewish studies.

(Acts 15:28f). According to the narrative Paul was present at the meeting, but not in the foreground. He related about his journeys, kept silent during the actual discussion, and was then commissioned along with Barnabas to carry the letter to Antioch (v22-35). The author further emphasizes the importance of the decree in the story of Paul's stay in Jerusalem in chapter 21. During this visit, Paul observed the halakha along with the other Christ-believing Jews, while for the gentiles – according to the Jerusalem church in Acts – only the commandments mentioned in the Apostles' decree were binding (21:25).

It is obvious that this presentation clashes with Paul's own letters in several respects. Indeed since the work of F.C. BAUR, scholars are aware of the fundamental differences between the Acts account and Paul's own letters. The relationship between Paul and Acts, certainly where the Law is concerned, can be adequately assessed only on the basis of an independent evaluation of Paul, which is our objective here. The comparison between Paul and Acts goes beyond the scope of this study; we shall merely draw some preliminary conclusions in the final chapter. But that does not prevent us from studying Acts, as separate from Paul, as the oldest Christian document to discuss this problem.

Thus we read that Acts, amongst other things, records a plain and unambiguous prohibition against idol food offerings. As stated this is by no means an isolated position in the early Church. Acts is first and foremost in a long series of Christian writings reiterating this prohibition and in this respect it even acquired a position of unchallenged authority. Surprisingly this influence extended through the Middle Ages and well into the days of the Christian Hebraists in the seventeenth and eighteenth centuries. This whole development was the subject of a monograph by BÖCKENHOFF, *Das apostolische Speisegesetz in den ersten fünf Jahrhunderten* (1903).[146] The following survey of Patristic literature is based on the coverage of material presented in this work.[147]

As we noted, other prohibitions are contained in the Apostles' decree. Here however we are confronted with an intriguing divergency.[148] It should not be seen as a mere textual problem but as reflecting a serious practical divergency in the early Church which from the perspective of Judaism is really a halakhic dispute. According to the majority text quoted above it involves a prohibition of idol food (εἰδωλόθυτα), blood (αἷμα), strangled meat (πνικτά), and unchastity (πορνεία). This list is dominant in extant New Testament manuscripts and reflects the remarkable severity in food laws of the Eastern Churches; this is why it is called the Eastern text. Besides 'blood' this version of the decree also prohibits 'strangled meat' i.e. meat from animals not slaughtered by

---

[146] The author's intention is to find out whether the food laws of the Apostles' Decree, especially the blood prohibition, are to be considered binding in Roman Catholic canon law. The long list (3-7) of ancient and modern authors dealing with these questions, particularly the 17-18th cent Hebraists (Grotius!), is impressive. On the Apostles' decree he follows Harnack's view of the Western text as an anti-ritualist adaptation; this is understandable in view of his interest in Christian dietary laws.

[147] Cf presentations by Barrett, 'Things', 40-5; Brunt, *Attitude*, 266-74.

[148] See Flusser-Safrai, 'Aposteldekret', with references to important previous studies; Flusser, 'Paul's Jewish-Christian Opponents'.

pouring out their blood, in conformity with biblical and Jewish practice. This prohibition is absent in the so-called Western text which knows only three items, 'idol offerings, blood and unchastity'.[149] This appears to imply the interpretation of 'blood' not as a dietary law but as the moral prohibition of 'bloodshed' i.e. homicide, especially since the triad is practically identical to the three cardinal sins of Judaism, 'idolatry, illicit sexuality and bloodshed'.[150] But it need not be considered the secondary moralizing emendation of an originally ritual code, as was proposed by HARNACK and G. RESCH.[151] Plainly, idolatry is not a moral but a cultic issue, and hence in both versions the moral and ritual go together. Rather the Western text seems to be an authentic version.[152] Remarkably, the Western Church also largely abstained from eating blood on the basis of the commandment to Noah (Gen 9:4-6),[153] and as we shall see the Western text of the decree was often understood to imply a prohibition against the consumption of blood.

Our digression about the contents of the Apostles' decree illustrates the importance attached to dietary laws by Christians in the ancient East and, to a lesser degree apparently, in the West. This phenomenon is not widely recognized in modern research, and when fully taken into account may lead to a rather different and more subtle appreciation of the relations between ancient Judaism, Christianity and the various intermediary movements.[154] Incidentally, this may also have been one of the factors which made many Eastern Christians willing to accept Islam and its very similar dietary laws.[155] In any case dietary laws were not uncommon in the early Church and this throws light on the remarkable fact that the idol food prohibition was observed by all in the early Church, whether or not in explicit relation to the Apostles' decree from Acts.

[149] The absence of καὶ (τοῦ) πνικτοῦ is attested in 15:20 (D, Gigas, Irenaeus lat), 15:29 (D, Irenaeus lat, Tertullian, Ambrosiaster, Jerome mss) and 21:25 (D, Gigas).

[150] Above p50. A triad involving not 'idol meat' but 'idolatry', thus identical with the ancient Jewish triad, is attested both by Tertullian and Ambrosiaster, see Flusser-Safrai, 'Aposteldekret', 181. This may relate to the ambiguous expression in Acts 15:20, ἀλισγήματα τῶν εἰδώλων, 'pollutions of idols'.

[151] Harnack, 'Aposteldekret' and Resch, Aposteldecret (with full and accurate documentation) consider the Eastern text to be original because of its contents, and the Western text a later emendation copying the Jewish-Christian moral code reflected also in the Didache.

[152] Flusser-Safrai, 'Aposteldekret', 178, 186 invert the argument of Harnack and Resch and posit a secondary ritualization (Eastern text) of the original moral code (Western text). In view of the plurality of Noachian codes I would suggest to drop the opposition of ritual and morals and consider the Eastern text an alternative, stricter version which shortly after the Jerusalem meeting rose to acceptance in Asia minor (cf below, Conclusion).

[153] Harnack, 'Aposteldekret', 162f n2 points out that although Tertullian interprets 'blood' in the Decree as homicide, he observes the prohibition of blood, which he elsewhere grounds on Gen 9, not the Decree; similarly Resch, Aposteldecret, 148 regarding Irenaeus.

[154] See next n and n166f.

[155] For the rise of Islam among the tensions between Eastern and Western Christianity see Van Leeuwen, Christianity, 206-51. Islam developed in the overlap between Judaism and Eastern Christianity; its dietary laws enumerated Sura 5:3 equal those of the Pseudo-Clementine circles (Hom 7:8; Rec 4:36; cf Ps-Phoc 147) except apparently the prohibition of pork. Cf Flusser-Safrai, 'Aposteldekret', 184 n45.

179

Besides Acts the prohibition of idol food also figures in other Apostolic writings. Apart from the Didache, about which more later, it is found twice in the Revelation of John: 'I have ...against you ...the teaching of Balaam, ...that they might eat food sacrificed to idols and practise unchastity' (Rev 2:14); 'I have against you that you tolerate the woman Jezebel who ...is teaching ...my servants to practise unchastity and eat food sacrificed to idols' (Rev 2:20). The immediate association of idolatry and unchastity reminds one of biblical and early post-biblical usage and also of the three Jewish capital sins which in turn are central to the Noachian commandments (above p152). As such it also functions under the surface of Paul's argument (compare 1Cor 6:18 on 10:14) and is of course basic to the Apostolic decree itself. If Revelations does not depend on the decree, at least it displays a common tradition.

Dependence on some version of the Apostles' decree becomes somewhat more likely in view of the continuation in Revelation: '...But to the rest of you... who do not hold this teaching (of Jezebel) ...I do not lay upon you any other burden...' (Rev 2:24). The latter formulation is reminiscent of the letter containing the decree which Acts purports to quote, 'For it has seemed good ...to lay upon you no greater burden than these necessary things...'[156] Significantly a similar formulation appears in a reference to the idol food prohibition in the Didache: 'As for food, take upon you what you can bear, but keep away from food offered to idols, for it means worship of dead gods' (Did 6:3).[157] This formulation in its various forms is an indication of the diversity as to the number of commandments to be observed, obviously by non-Jews, while 'idol food' and 'unchastity' are the minimum requirement.[158] The absence of a real formal similarity with the decree in Acts indicates the circulation of independent alternative versions of the same tradition. Obviously this is of extreme importance for Paul's place in Apostolic Christianity; but we should not burden our argument by elaborating on this issue here.[159] Suffice it to say that in Apostolic Christianity there were several concurrent versions of the basic code of commandments for all mankind, and that the idol food prohibition was included.

Let us now move on to post-Apostolic times, here following the outline of BÖCKENHOFF's survey. Around the end of the second century the idol food prohibition is found in the East in Aristides of Athens, Justin, and Clement of Alexandria, and in the West in Irenaeus, Tertullian, and Minucius Felix.[160] This reflects a fundamental rejection of any association with idolatry, both ex-

---

[156] Rev 2:24, οὐ βάλλω ἐφ' ὑμᾶς ἄλλο βάρος πλήν; Acts 15:28, μηδὲν ...ἐπιτίθεσθαι ὑμῖν βάρος πλὴν. See Flusser, 'Paul's Jewish-Christian Opponents', 77. On the implications of Balaam and Jezebel see Barrett, 'Things', 41f.

[157] ὃ δύνασαι βάστασον; thus ms Jerusalem. On the expression 'sacrifices to dead gods' see above n5. The parallel in the Apostolic Constitutions reads, ἀπὸ δὲ τῶν εἰδωλοθύτων φεύγετε, ἐπὶ τιμῇ γὰρ δαιμόνων θύουσιν ταῦτα. This seemingly Pauline wording (1Cor 10:14, 20) contrasts with the anti-Pauline mood of the Constitutions and hence points towards a tradition independently shared by Paul and the Constitutions.

[158] Cf Flusser, 'Paul's Jewish-Christian Opponents'.

[159] On Paul cf Flusser ib 80f.

[160] Sources in Böckenhoff, *Speisegesetz*, 33-52.

180

pressed in an absolute prohibition of foods involved and in other prohibitions. Tertullian adds the interesting detail that for a Christian visiting pagan theatres, where idolatry and homicide are daily practice, would mean associating himself with idolatry in a degree similar to eating idol foods. Similarly Christians refrained from adorning themselves with wreaths as in pagan worship.[161] Significantly both Justin and Irenaeus remark that it is the Gnostic heretics who eat idol meat and visit the theatres in order to display their inner freedom.[162] A general prohibition against visiting pagan theatres and circuses is another common element among Christians and Jews in the ancient period.[163]

In the third century the prohibition of idol food is attested first and foremost by Origen. His development of the explanation of the prohibition on the grounds of pollution by demons is remarkable. The idea existed before, as we have seen in Paul, but Origen extended it to explain the prohibition against blood and strangled meats. Interestingly a similar abstention, in which both Jewish and neo-Platonist elements converged, was advocated by Origen's opponent, the pagan philosopher Porphyry.[164] Further third century evidence for the prohibition is found in a work by Methodius of Olympos.[165] More or less at the same time it is also found in the Pseudo-Clementine writings,[166] and in a Christian interpolation in the Sentences of Pseudo-Phocylides which in turn re-appear in the Christian-edited second book of Sibylline Oracles.[167]

In the third century Western Church, we have a quite remarkable testimony in the letter 'On Jewish Meats' written by the schismatic Roman theologian, Novatian. While emphatically declaring all levitical food laws obsolete, apparently including the blood prohibition, he made an exception for idol food. He gave a rational explanation of the idol food prohibition. Referring to Paul's exposition in 1Cor 10:25ff, he seems to imply that as soon as idol food is sold at the market, it is no longer defiled.[168]

The fourth century pagan philosopher and short-lived Roman emperor Julian (361-363 CE) was known for his struggle against the power of the Church

---

[161] Tertullian, De spectaculis (esp 13:4f); id, De corona. Similarly Minucius Felix, Octavius cap 38.

[162] Böckenhoff, *Speisegesetz*, 35; Brunt, *Attitude*, 270, 274.

[163] See tAZ 2:5-7; yAZ 1, 40a; bAZ 18b. The first stratum of these conditions seems to be late Tannaic (R. Meir), which hints at a novel situation after the Bar Kokhba war.

[164] Böckenhoff, *Speisegesetz*, 53-8.

[165] ib 58f.

[166] ib 60-63. For dating and literary problems, as well as a discussion of their Jewish-Christian character, see Molland, 'Circoncision'; and criticism by Klijn, 'Pseudo-Clementines'. The term 'Jewish-Christian' is inexact here, since circumcision seems to have been abrogated and replaced by baptism, see Molland ib 8-25, in discussion with Schoeps. And see next n.

[167] Ps-Phoc 31 (one ms only); Or Sib 2:96. See Van der Horst, *Sentences*, 84f, 135f. In the light of the evidence reviewed here, the combination of 'blood' and 'idol food' indicates a Christian rather than Jewish origin, but this need not be the Acts version of the apostolic decree. The prohibition of θηρόβορον (= θηριάλωτον, meat torn by wild animals) Ps-Phoc 147 (and Ps-Clem Hom 7:4, 7:8; Rec 4:36) may, but need not be, Jewish or Jewish-Christian; see below n186 on Jerome. Cf Van der Horst ib 209f.

[168] Böckenhoff, *Speisegesetz*, 66-70.

and his concomitant sympathy, albeit ambivalent, for the Jews.[169] He took a great interest in dietary laws – pagan, Jewish and Christian – and was keen on the Christians' abstention from idol food. Various sources report the trials he set up by contaminating market ware and springs with idol food.[170] When this was done in Constantinople, the Christians refused to eat anything polluted with sacrificial blood, extending the prohibition to eating polluted food unwittingly. A similar severe ban on food which might possibly have derived from idolatry was voiced at about the same time by Cyrill of Jerusalem.[171] On the other hand, the Antioch Christians did not go this far when tested by Julian. They bought and ate foods from the market that might have been contaminated by idol meat, on the grounds, it is reported, of a rational explanation of the Apostle's instruction in 1Cor 10:25.[172] This leniency appears not to have been an exception. In his apology against Julian's writings, Cyril of Alexandria (early fifth century) expressed a far-reaching rational explanation of the idol food prohibition which is reminiscent of the Antioch case.[173]

More explicitly and highly relevant to our study, a similar position was taken by the Antioch rhetor, Chrysostom, at the end of the fourth century. In spite of his violent adhortations against judaizing tendencies among his parishioners and his view that Jesus and the Apostles intended the abrogation of the Jewish Law, he maintains the prohibition of blood, non-slaughtered meat, and idol food. The reasons given for the prohibition, which is emphasized with impressive severity, are the weaker brother, the communion with the demons, and the incorrect judgment by the pagan.[174] Nevertheless, following the Apostle's instruction one can eat anything bought at the market or offered in a private home, as long as others on their own initiative do not indicate that it is idol food. For the uncleanness is not in the nature of the food, but in the idolater's consciousness (διανοία).[175] For that reason one should not inquire about the food; the other person's consciousness is decisive, not one's own.[176] The same line seems to have been followed by Chrysostom's pupil, Theodoret of Cyrus.[177]

Thus it seems that the decision of the Antioch Christians to eat food from the market that might have been polluted by the imperial order was not an emer-

---

[169] See Avi-Yonah, *Geschichte*, 188-208 on the dramatic history of Julian and the Jews.

[170] Böckenhoff, *Speisegesetz*, 71-5, referring for the Antioch case to Theodoret, Hist eccl 3:11 (MPG 82, 1104f) and for Constantinople to Nectarius, Enarratio in fest S Theodori 8-13 (MPG 39, 1828ff).

[171] Böckenhoff, *Speisegesetz*, 75-77.

[172] Source see n170.

[173] Böckenhoff, *Speisegesetz*, 106f (MPG 76, 856). Böckenhoff treats Cyrill of Alexandria and Augustine (see below) as the two fifth century authorities who first denied lasting formal validity of the 'Apostolic Food Law' (p98, 109; cf p1). This reflects his interest in canon law and his timeless conception of this Apostolic 'Law'. As for the actual eating of blood and idol meat, the difference between Cyrill and Chrysostom seems to be less than Böckenhoff suggests.

[174] I. Ep ad Cor homil 25:2 (MPG 61, 159ff). Böckenhoff, *Speisegesetz*, 84-9.

[175] "Ὥστε ἔστι καὶ φαγόντα ἀγνοοῦντα ἀπηλλάχθαι· τοιαῦτα γὰρ μὴ φύσει πονηρά, ἀλλ᾿ ἀπὸ τῆς διανοίας ποιοῦντα τὸ ἀκάθαρτον.

[176] ib 25:1. Böckenhoff overlooked Chrysostom's rationalism.

[177] Böckenhoff, *Speisegesetz*, 89 (MPG 80, 420; 82, 292).

gency decision. Indeed, an emergency situation might call for a tough stand and readiness to suffer for one's faith, as was the case with the Constantinople Christians. Antioch Christianity had some shining examples of that readiness: the memory of the Jewish martyrs of the persecution by Antiochus Epiphanes was honoured in Antioch, not only by Jews but also by Christians.[178] Their decision to buy and eat unspecified food must have been based on local Antiochcustom, which therefore differed from the tradition of the Constantinople Church. Some implications of this interesting phenomenon are discussed below.

The prohibition of idol food as contained in the Eastern version of the Apostles' decree became canon law at the synod of Gangra, c. 343 CE, and was therefore incorporated in the codification of Church law. It may also be supposed to have been implied in the food laws ratified at the 'Apostles' synod' of Antioch somewhere towards the end of the fourth century.[179]

We devote the last part of this section to three prominent exegetes of the Western Church in the late fourth and the fifth centuries. The unknown author of extensive Pauline commentaries, formerly incorrectly identified as Ambrose and hence called Ambrosiaster, was the first to draw attention to the difference between his traditional text of the Apostles' decree and the Eastern text. He rejects the item 'strangled meat', and instead of 'idol meat' reads 'idolatry'. This version of the Apostles' decree is almost identical to the ancient Jewish tradition of three cardinal sins: εἰδωλόθυτα, αἷμα, πορνεία; it may also be the Western version in its purest form.[180] Protesting against the Greek addition of 'strangled meat', Ambrosiaster nevertheless maintains the meaning of 'blood' as a dietary law in view of Gen 9:4-6.[181] As far as idol food is concerned, the prohibition is clear enough.[182] But regarding food bought at the market or offered at home Ambrosiaster offers an exposition similar to Chrysostom's. If bought or offered without its use being specified, it may always be eaten; eating a prohibited foodstuff unwittingly is not a sin.[183] But if the presence of an idolater could give one the impression that one joins in worshipping the idol, one is to abstain from eating.[184]

The erudite scholar Jerome, while rooted in Western Christianity, preferred

---

[178] See D. Flusser, 'Antioch', 71. On the use of 4Maccabees, the work directly involved here, by Chrysostom and other Church Fathers see Gilbert, 'Wisdom Literature', 318f.

[179] Cf Böckenhoff ib 78f, 82. The author hastens to add that the Gangra canons were used, and were not approved at the Council of Chalcedon 451 CE; cf n146.

[180] It is also attested by Tertullian, see Flusser-Safrai, 'Aposteldekret', 181 n30.

[181] Ad Gal 2:1 (MPL 17, 346); Böckenhoff, *Speisegesetz*, 90f.

[182] *Uxorem certe licet habere; sed si fornicata fuerit, abjicenda est; ita et carnem licet edere, sed si idolis oblata fuerit, respuenda est* (I. ad Cor [8:13], MPL 17, 241); *licet omnia edere, sed quod idolis immolatur, non aedificat* (ib 251; 1Cor 10:23).

[183] *Licet enim aliquid pollutum sit per accidentiam i.e. oblationem idoli; cum hoc tamen nescit qui emit, nullum patitur scrupulum et apud Deum immunis est* (ib, 1Cor 10:25).

[184] *Sed quia alius qui idolis servit gloriabitur te edente de sacrificatis quasi venereris idola, ideo non debet edi. ...Quid opus est ut putetur quia venerationis causa edat idolis immolata?* (ib, ad 1Cor 10:28, 29).

183

the Greek text of the Apostles' decree and thus introduced it in his Latin translation of the Bible. In addition, living in the East, he also appears to have observed it, differing in this respect with his usual partner in discussion, Augustine. Jerome applied what is said in the verse, 'Nothing that has died of itself or is torn, whether bird or beast, the priests shall eat' (Ezek 44:31) to the Christians.[185] He interpreted these as being a further specification of the prohibition of the items 'blood' and 'strangled meat' in the decree, thus even including the proper slaughtering of such Roman delicatessen as thrushes, hedge-sparrows or dormice.[186] Apparently reacting to this interpretation, Augustine declares that he sees no problem in eating thrushes or little mammals like hares when not properly slaughtered. In his view the Apostolic prohibition of blood aimed at the abstention from strangled meat (*praefocatis carnibus*), which was a temporal measure in view of the presence of Jews in the Church. But since the Church had now passed that initial stage of her history and 'no Israelite according to the flesh appears in her', there is no longer any need for the prohibition.[187] By this ingenious explanation, Augustine apparently seeks to rule out the item 'suffocated meat' from the Apostles' decree as advocated by Jerome, always his superior in erudition, and *de facto* to maintain the Western version.[188]

The contrast with Augustine's attitude towards the idol meat prohibition is striking. Although 'what enters through the mouth does not make one unclean' (Matt 15:11), food is made unclean by consecration to idols or demons. To be sure demoniacal uncleanness is not physical, as Porphyry and others erroneously thought, but it consists of a spiritual pollution of one's 'conscience' (*conscientia*) by communion with the demon. Thus Augustine maintains the prohibition against eating idol meat in any circumstances. He illustrates this with the interesting example of a hungry Christian traveller who sees some food in front of an idol while no one is around. In circumstances where it appears certain that the food is consecrated to idolatry, Augustine rules, it is better to die a good Christian than eat and sin. But in situations in which food is known not to have been consecrated or of which the status is unknown 'may be eaten out of

---

[185] In Rabbinic tradition, the statement that the priests shall abstain from נבילה and טריפה raises the question whether the prophet supposed Israelites to eat them. This is one of the difficult verses of Ezekiel about which the rationalist R. Yohanan remarks: 'This verse will be explained in the future by Elijah', bMen 45a. Jerome seems to draw on a different tradition, calling all Christians *sacerdotali ...qui uncti sunt oleo spirituali*, as it is said in Ps 45(44):8, 'God has anointed you with the oil of gladness above your fellows'.

[186] Jerome subsumes *morticinum et captum a bestia* (= θνησιμαίον καὶ θηριάλωτον, Ezek 44:31) under *suffocata* (= πνίκτα, Acts 15:29), and hence Ezekiel *condemnat sacerdotes qui in turdis, ficedulis, gliribus et caeteris huiusmodi haec aviditate gulae non custodiunt*. See Böckenhoff, *Speisegesetz*, 95-7 (quotation p96 n1), referring to Jerome's Ezekiel commentary.

[187] In his anti-Manichean polemic, Contra Faustum 33:13. Characteristic is the sentence, *...ubi ecclesia gentium talis effecta est ut in ea nullus Israelita appareat, quis iam hoc Christianus observat ut turdos vel minutiores aviculas non attingat nisi quarum sanguis effusus est?*

[188] Böckenhoff, mechanically operating with the Eastern text as the original decree, fails to see through Augustine's *philologia sacra*. Incorrectly (cf on idol meat) he sees Augustine as the first Western Church Father to declare the decree temporal and dispensable in canon law (cf ib p1).

necessity without any scruple of conscience'.[189] Thus it appears that Augustine has an attitude towards the idol food prohibition which is comparable to that of Chrysostom and Ambrosiaster. Eating food of unspecified origin is not blameworthy, but to eat food known to have been consecrated is a capital sin.

Some general features in concluding.

First of all the unanimity of the ancient Christian prohibition of idolatry and of food consecrated to idols is clear and convincing. Discussion exists only on doubtful cases, as with food sold in the market or found in ambiguous circumstances. Such situations are also well known in the halakha, and indicate agreement on the principle itself.

The early Christian unanimity on the prohibition of idol food makes the accepted scholarly view that Paul condoned it seem quite unlikely. If he did he would not just have been the first, but in effect the only early Christian authority to defend this position.[190] Indeed it would have been a miracle, resulting from pure misunderstanding, that First Corinthians was preserved at all by the early Church in its extant form. To say the least, our review of Patristic opinion once again offers a stimulus for a closer look on Paul.

A second general feature is the ambivalence toward the 'reality' of the pollution of idol food by demons. Some, like Origen or Cyrill of Jerusalem, maintain that real contamination is caused by the 'bloodthirsty' demons. Such physical demonology corresponds with certain Jewish and pagan traditions, see Porphyry.[191] Others deny it and see only a spiritual contamination, or as Augustine put it, a contamination of 'conscience'.

It seems that this ambivalence relates to a third general feature: an oscillation between an absolute prohibition or one dependent on circumstances. The probability of local differences in this matter, as between Constantinople and Antioch in the fourth century, must be taken seriously into account. In Antioch food of unspecified provenance bought in the market could freely be eaten, even if some items (though which was not known) may be contaminated by idol food. There was no physical contamination. Not so in Constantinople. Differences between local customs are a well known and accepted phenomenon in Rabbinic halakha.[192] It is interesting to note that a similar phenomenon existed

---

[189] Sources in Böckenhoff 101-3 [Contra Faust 33:13, MPL 42, 503f; De civ Dei 10:19, MPL 41, 298; De bono conjugali 16, MPL 40, 385; Ep 47:6, MPL 33, 187]. In the last mentioned passage cf the ruling: *Si ergo certum est esse (sc idolothytum) melius christiana virtute respuitur. Si autem vel non esse scitur vel ignoratur, sine ullo conscientiae scrupulo in usum necessitatis assumitur.* This extremely important formulation will receive more detailed attention in the next chapter.

[190] This position is defended by Brunt, *Attitude* and 'Rejected, Ignored, or Misunderstood?'

[191] Cf Böckenhoff, *Speisegesetz*, 64. With Bousset, *Religion*, ch 17 (331-42) he refers to the demonology patent in sectarian works such as 1Enoch and Jubilees. The similarity with Essene demonology is evident.

[192] A collection of halakhot pertaining to such differences is preserved in mPes 4:1-5 and tPis 3:14-19. And see the Talmudim ad loc. Regarding gentile idolatry mAZ 1:6 must be added. Another example concerns R. Simlai, a resident of the Judean town Lydda, whose residents are viewed by the Galilean colleagues as permissive (above n112).

in ancient Christianity, not only in the liturgy, where such is well known, but apparently also in such unexpected aspects as dietary laws.

Food from the market brings us back to Paul. A question not dealt with in the preceding survey is how the Church Fathers explained Paul's ruling 1Cor 10:25, 'All that is sold in the market place, you can eat without questioning on the ground of conscience'. Two clear alternatives appear to have existed, and very likely they relate to local custom and/or religious taste. Paul's permission to buy and eat without distinction is explained by a number of authorities as implicitly excluding idol food. Thus, plainly, Clement of Alexandria,[193] and similarly Tertullian: '(The Apostle) handed the keys of the market hall to you with the permission to eat everything, while maintaining the exception of idol food'.[194] The alternative explanation was proposed by Chrysostom, Ambrosiaster, and apparently Novatian and Augustine: what Paul meant was that food of un-specified provenance is permitted without questioning, but if specified by others as consecrated food it is prohibited. These alternatives will occupy us further in the next chapter, when studying Paul's own teaching.

---

[193] Böckenhoff, *Speisegesetz*, 41 (Strom 4:15).
[194] ib 47 (De jejun 15).

Chapter Five

1Cor 8-10: 'On Idol Offerings'

First Corinthians 8-10 is crucial for understanding Paul's practical teaching on the Law. For that reason two entire chapters are devoted to the subject. The previous chapter offers a survey of ancient Jewish and Christian attitudes towards idolatry as a necessary backgrond to the present chapter, which deals with Paul's own teaching.

We have seen that the prohibition of idolatry is firmly anchored in the Old Testament and Jewish tradition. It represented one of the commandments most vital to the existence of the Jews as a religious-ethnic community. The prohibition of food sacrificed to idols was obviously included. This meant that Christ-believing gentiles were forced to take a stand vis-à-vis a cornerstone of the Law of the Jews when confronted with the issue of idol food offerings. Moreover, inasmuch as for Jews the prohibition against contact with idolatry included communication with those eating sacrificial food, the attitude of non-Jewish believers would directly affect Jewish-gentile relations, both within the Church and outside it. This practical issue would be crucial for the validity of the Law and the unity of the Jewish-gentile Church – two prominent topics, especially in other letters of Paul. In that sense the issue of idol food may be perceived as a test-case for Paul himself.

Whether this is correct or not, the issue is at the very least a touch-stone for the present undertaking. Our text serves as the *locus classicus* for the near-consensus in New Testament scholarship that Paul no longer attached positive significance to the commandments of his Jewish past. As one scholar commented: 'The Law ...no longer had a salvific function: τέλος γὰρ νόμου Χριστὸς [for Christ is the end of the Law]; it had been superseded and its precepts were no longer binding, since obedience was owed only to Christ'.[1] Although more attentive to the intricacies of the question, C.K. BARRETT nevertheless agrees with this interpretation of the text. Referring to the rule that anything sold at the market can be eaten 'without inquiring' (1Cor 10:25), he concludes that 'Paul is nowhere more un-Jewish than in this μηδὲν ἀνακρίνοντες'[2] – a statement considered authoritative by others.[3] On this basis Barrett goes on to

---

[1] O'Connor, in a study bearing the ominous title, 'Freedom or the Ghetto'.
[2] Barrett, 'Things', 49; cf his Commentary a.l.
[3] Willis, *Idol Meat*, 231.

187

take issue with DAVIES and others who emphasize Paul's 'essential Jewishness', concluding that such views must be seriously modified.[4] We have noted that Davies in stressing Paul's faithfulness to the Law follows SCHWEITZER, who based this view on the *status quo* theory expressed in 1Cor 7:17-20. It appears that on this issue the ancient Patristic assumption still obtains:[5] for Paul, the Jewish Law would have ceased to have any practical significance.

Accordingly, the modern assumption about Paul and the Law also predominates in scholarship: halakha is hardly taken into account as a positive source for Paul. Although far-reaching judgments are pronounced on Paul's practical attitude towards Jewish Law, nowhere is a comparison made with the essential materials: the halakha on idolatry.[6] Of three monographs devoted to our passage only one makes any comparisons with the Jewish Law, but unfortunately this was focused on food laws.[7] According to this interpretation, the 'weak' in 1Cor 8 were Jewish Christians, from which category Paul is excluded, thus reviving BAUR's theory of a 'Petrine' party at Corinth.[8] It follows of necessity that Paul was steering a middle course between 'Petrinists' and 'radical Paulinists'.[9] This interpretation is based on confusion with Rom 14f, a problem we shall deal with in the next chapter. Moreover the text resists this: Paul calls the weak 'hitherto accustomed to the idol' (1Cor 8:7) which excludes Jews. The other two monographs on 1Cor 8-10 simply consider the Jewish Law the 'negative backdrop' to Paul's teaching,[10] or, as compared with non-Jewish Hellenistic cult traditions, not relevant at all.[11]

We have other weighty indications that the general interpretation is inadequate. In the previous chapter it appeared not only that early Christian literature was firm on the prohibition of idolatry but unanimous on the inclusion of idol food offerings.[12] Furthermore in chapter 3 we have seen that from the

[4] Barrett, 'Things', 50f. He sees the later universal Christian prohibition of idol meat as a triumph of Jewish Christianity, although, paradoxically, 'Jewish Christians became less important in the church' (ib 56).

[5] Similarly Sanders, *Paul, the Law*, 101; see next chapter. Flusser, 'Christenheit' shared the consensus, but he later appears to have abondoned it: Flusser-Safrai, 'Aposteldekret'. For other opinions see below n95.

[6] Barrett, 'Things', who pays more attention to Jewish material (see 'Shaliah and Apostle'), thinks 'a quick reading of Abodah Zarah' sufficient to see the difference with Paul's μηδὲν ἀνακρίνοντες (49). Von Soden, 'Sakrament', 352f recognizes a halakhic parallel from Str-B 3, 422 (mAZ 1:5), but cannot resist the urge to oppose that 'Gesetzeskasuistik' to Paul's gospel.

[7] Sawyer, *Problem*.

[8] Ib 122-30; 134-40.

[9] See Sawyer, ib 178-80: 'mediating position'.

[10] Brunt, *Paul's Attitude*, 250-4. This study into Paul's teaching regarding dietary practice also covers Rom 14f, but ignoring the specific differences concludes that 'the overall thrust of both passages is the same' (183). See also n12.

[11] Willis, *Idol Meat*, criticizing Sawyer for overstating 'the influence of Jewish food customs and regulations' and neglecting 'the very significant Hellenistic background' (p3). Willis provides much information on Hellenistic cults (7-64) but fails to explain its importance in understanding Paul's prohibition to participate in them (cf 62-4, 218-20, 265-7), as opposed to Jewish traditions (cf 133ff!).

[12] Brunt, 'Rejected, Ignored' takes the unanimous early Christian prohibition of idol food into account and comes to the incredible conclusion that in dietary matters Paul was not only unique vis-à-vis the Hellenistic world and Judaism but also vis-à-vis early Christianity.

remaining and largest parts of First Corinthians it appears that the halakha was of direct practical importance for Paul. Finally in our passage there is a section which contains both an unequivocal denunciation of participation in pagan cults and of eating idol food (1Cor 10:1-22). As in earlier chapters we shall therefore hypothesize that the Jewish Law did have practical significance for Paul's teaching on idol offerings and that halakhic literature is an important historical source for explaining it.

The Argument of 1Cor 8-10

The question centres on εἰδωλόθυτον, literally 'something offered to idols'. The word, which is also found elsewhere in the New Testament,[13] has an intrinsic polemical significance, naturally to be used by those who reject idolatry, i.e. Jews or Christians.[14] A pagan worshiper would call it ἱερόθυτον, 'sanctified food', as Paul indicates with socio-linguistic sensitivity (1Cor 10:28).[15]

As to the items covered by the term, these were apparently understood to include more foods than just meat. The verb θύω means not only 'slaughter', but also 'offer' (ceremoniously), 'celebrate'.[16] Hence bloodless offerings to the gods such as wine, corn or bread could be included. Correspondingly, it seems, Acts 15:20 describes the forbidden categories of food as 'that which is polluted by the idols'.[17] We have seen that for Jews, wine offered to idols was as strongly forbidden as meat. Paul's reference to 'the cup of demons' (1Cor 10:21) is clear enough.[18] Likewise, Patristic reports reflect the severity of the prohibition against libation wine.[19] 1Cor 8:13 refers to meat, but then how important was meat in the ancient diet?

In 1Cor 10:25 we read that the problem concerned food sold at the *macellum*,[20] the market hall. Apparently meat was just one of many articles for sale there. In antiquity meat was expensive and very difficult to keep. As is still the case in many third world countries, it was eaten only at special events such as festivals and ceremonies, certainly by the lower classes. As appears from literary and archeological sources, fish, bread, vagetables, cakes and fruit were the regular diet.[21]

---

[13]   Acts 15:29; 21:25; Rev 2:14, 20.
[14]   Cf 4Macc 5:2.
[15]   With P46, Sinai, A, B, etc; majority text εἰδωλόθυτον. On the word see Bauer, *Wörterbuch* s.v.
[16]   Bauer, *Wörterbuch* s.v. θυσία, θύω.
[17]   A similar circumscription is found in the anti-Pauline Pseudo-Clementine writings: 'sacrificial slaughterings ...and anything offered to demons' (Rec. 4:36); see Molland, 'Circoncision', 26, 34.
[18]   Cf the abstention from wine and meat, Rom 14:21.
[19]   Cyprian, De lapsis 25 (MPL 4, 499f), referred to by Böckenhoff, *Speisegesetz*, 119f.
[20]   Schneider, 'Macellum' thinks of a Semitic origin of the Latin word. The word מקולין is common in Rabbinic usage.
[21]   See Schneider, 'Macellum', 133; Cadbury, 'Macellum', 141; Barrett, 'Things', 47-9. Meat was exceptional in Jewish families in antiquity even on festivals, see Safrai, 'Home', 747 and sources cited there.

A question which is of great importance for our awareness of the actual situation is the connection between food bought in the market and idolatry. A number of studies, as well as archeological investigations, make it clear that this connection was by no means imaginary. At Pompei, a chapel for the emperor worship was right next to the *macellum*, although it is not clear whether this implies an immediate relation. Similarly around the *macellum* of Corinth, idolatry must have been present everywhere and for many people it was part of their daily routine.[22] Religion was an integral part of ancient society at all levels and in all their relations.[23] Jews, as one can well imagine and as is confirmed by ancient sources, had their separate religious and social organization and this must have included the supply of wine, grain or flour, oil and meat.[24] The dilemma for gentile Christians at Corinth and elsewhere was: how to live in gentile society and not get involved in idolatry? They would have to think carefully if they were to avoid partial integration in Jewish social networks.

From the head of the passage (1Cor 8:1, above p57) it appears that the Apostle is responding to a question written by the Corinthians. This implies that it represented an important issue involving a difference of opinion in the Corinthian church. A connection with Paul's earlier teaching, either orally or in his previous letter, seems obvious.[25] Such an important issue could not have been omitted in the Apostle's initial instruction to the church of his founding. But during his absence problems appear to have arisen. This partly explains his cautious approach. The complexity of the section has given rise to doubts about its unity. Indeed, 1Cor 8-10 has been 'the keystone in the various attempts to divide First Corinthians into two or more letters'.[26]

The section readily divides into four units:
(1) 8:1-13, on idol food offerings and 'the weak';
(2) 9:1-27, on the principles of Paul's Apostolic behaviour;
(3) 10:1-22, on the prohibition of idolatry;
(4) 10:23-11:1, on the consumption of pagan food bought at the market place or offered in private homes.

---

[22] See Schneider, 'Macellum' for a general survey. Cadbury, 'Macellum', discussing a Corinthian inscription mentioning the 'Macellum', warns against hasty conclusions from the Pompei situation in view of the general proximity of public buildings in the ancient town centres. Lietzmann, *Korinther*, 49-51 adduces further evidence, stressing the natural relation between the market and idolatry especially in view of Pompei; but in that situation, 'Paulus urteilt freier'. Hurd, *Origin*, 144f n1 summarizes Lietzmann and further research and concludes that most commentaries follow Lietzmann. Conzelmann, *Korinther*, 215f is more cautious here.

[23] See description of pagan cults in Lane Fox, *Pagans and Christians*, 64-101.

[24] See data on the Jewish community at Sardis in Applebaum, 'Organization', 477-80. 'Their bread, their wine, their oil' were among the 18 decreed articles (above p174) well rooted in ancient use; 'their meat' needed no mention.

[25] Hurd, *Origin*, 225f. Hurd's book is an invaluable study on the composition of 1 Corinthians and the possibly preceding history between Paul and the Corinthians.

[26] Hurd, *Origin*, 115; see ensuing discussion, 115-42.

The *inclusio* created by units (1) and (4), with prominent key words συν-είδησις and εἰδωλόθυτα gives the section its coherence, leaving units (2) and (3) as a digression. Similar structures with a digressive *inclusio* can be discerned in First Corinthians, which points to a common rhetorical feature.[27]

Unit (1) opens with things 'we all know': 'We know that all of us possess knowledge' (8:1); 'We know that an idol is nothing in the world' (8:4). Then, the restriction comes: 'However, not all have this knowledge; for some, being hitherto accustomed to idols, eat as though it is idol food, and their conscience, being weak, is defiled' (8:7). After more reasoning, the first unit concludes with a personal exclamation much like a vow of self-restraint: 'Therefore, if food is a cause of my brother's falling, I will never eat meat in eternity' (8:13).

Unit (2) continues to focus on Paul himself: 'Am I not free? Am I not an Apostle?' (9:1). 'Do we not have the right to our food and drink?' (9:4). 'But I have made no use of any of these rights' (9:15). 'For though I am free from all, I have made myself a slave of all, that I might win the more. To the Jews I became [as] a Jew... to the weak I became weak, that I might win the weak; I have become all things to all, that I might by all means save some' (9:19-22). 'Every athlete exercises self-control in all things'; 'I pommel my body and subdue it, lest ...I should be disqualified' (9:25f).

In unit (3) the focus first swerves to the example of biblical Israel and then gradually to Corinth. 'I do not want you to be without knowledge, brethren, that our fathers ...all were baptized into Moses ...and all ate the same spiritual food ...nevertheless with most of them God was not pleased... Now these things are examples for us' (10:1-6). 'Therefore, my beloved, flee idolatry' (10:14). 'You cannot partake of the table of the Lord and the table of demons' (10:21).

Finally unit (4) focusus completely on the situation under discussion: Corinth. 'All things are lawful, but not all things edify... Let no one seek his own good, but the good of his neighbour. All that is sold in the market place, ...all that is set before you, you can eat without questioning on the ground of consciousness. But if someone says to you, This is sacrificial food, do not eat for his sake... All things do to the glory of God. Give no offence to Jews, or to Greeks, or to the Church of God' (10:23-32).

There is a remarkable shift in focus between the four units. Unit (1) starts at Corinth and ends with Paul. Unit (2) continues with Paul's example. Unit (3) starts with biblical Israel, 'an example for us', and then returns in two stages to the Corinthian situation. Unit (4) focuses wholly on Corinth, including the market and private houses. Finally the whole tract culminates in the example of Christ. This larger movement shows Paul's rhetorical skill, and argues for the integrity of these chapters.[28]

---

[27] Notably chs 12-14 on spiritual gifts, with the digression of ch 13 on love; ch 7 on marriage and celibacy, with v17-24 on Paul's basic rule; chs 5 – 6 on unchastity, with 6:1-11 on gentile courts. See Wuellner, 'Greek Rhetoric'; Hurd ib 178.

[28] Similarly Willis, *Idol Meat*, 270-4.

Next to be observed is the recurring use of the word 'all': 'All have knowledge'; 'I have become all things to all, that I might by all means save some'; 'All were baptized into Moses, ...all ate the same spiritual food'; 'All things are lawful'; 'All that is sold in the marketplace... all that is set before you...'; 'All things do to the glory of God... just as I try to please all men in all things'. But there is also always a restriction: 'But not all have knowledge'; 'But I have made no use of any of these rights'; 'But with most of them God was not pleased'; 'But not all things are helpful'; 'But if some one says... do not eat'. This sustained rhetorical use of the word 'all' and its corresponding opposites is another common feature arguing for the unity of these chapters. Its effect is ambivalent: it expresses both an overwhelming and all-embracing movement and a repeated particularization and stressing of exceptions.

When viewed in the perspective of the chapters as a whole, the restrictive tendency seems to be more prominent. It is enhanced by the rhetorical figure of 'all ...but not all', noted above. The following examples and adhortations of self-restraint are heard: 'Therefore, if food is a cause of my brother's falling, I will never eat meat in eternity'; 'I have made myself a slave of all'; 'Every athlete exercises self-control in all things'; 'Therefore, my beloved, flee idolatry'; 'You cannot partake of ...the table of demons'; 'Let no one seek his own good, but the good of his neighbour'; 'Do not eat for his sake'.

In this light the digression contained in unit (2) appears to have a very clear function. It reminds the readers that although Paul possessed all the powers of an Apostle of the Lord, he decided not to use them while at Corinth. Similarly, he tries to be 'everything to all men', making himself 'a slave of all', apparently again renouncing things he is entitled to for the sake of the Gospel. The unit culminates in the image of the athlete who trains his body to exercise self-restraint. Thus Paul, by his own example, teaches that the Corinthians, too, should be willing to renounce rights and restrain themselves.

It seems that Paul felt the need to use all the means at his disposal to tell the Corinthians *not* to do something. What they should not be doing is revealed in unit (3): 'Flee idolatry... do I say then that idol food is anything? No, but ...they sacrifice to demons and not to God. You cannot partake of ...the table of demons'. In short: do not eat idol food. But then comes unit (4) to give practical instruction in difficult situations which may well have been very important to the whole issue. Here the restrictive moment is counterbalanced by the repeated statement that 'all... you may eat without inquiring'. We will discuss the intricacies of this balanced instruction below.

Previewing these chapters, one gets the impression that Paul is skillfully reiterating or further explaining something he has been saying before. The idol meat issue was raised by the Corinthians, and apparently this was in response to Paul's earlier instruction. Unit (3) appears to restate his basic position, and unit (2) connects it with the selfless example of his own life as an Apostle. But there was apparently reason to take recourse to a sophisticated argument, as developed in units (1) and (4). Crucial in both, and hence in the whole of 1Cor 8-10, is the concept of the other man's συνείδησις, usually translated as 'conscience', but, as will be explained below, better rendered as 'consciousness'.

1Cor 8 – 'Knowledge' and the 'Delicate'

The first unit, and therefore the passage as a whole, evidently addresses those who somehow doubted the use of the prohibition of food offered to idols. Their position may well have been reflected in the formulation of the written question from Corinth. It is apparent in three subsequent statements, to each of which the Apostle subtly responds with initial affirmation and subsequent correction: 'We know that we all have knowledge' (8:1); 'We know that an idol is nothing in the world' (8:4); 'Food will not commend us to God' (8:8). These might be actual quotations from their letter,[29] but at any rate they are insights we can well imagine in their minds. The three corresponding corrections are the following: 'Knowledge puffs up, but love builds up' (8:1); 'Not all share this knowledge' (8:7); 'Take care lest your liberty become a stumbling block to the weak' (8:9). Paul apparently refers again to their letter further on in his argument: 'I speak as to sensible men; judge for yourselves what I say' (10:15); 'What do I say then, that idol food is anything [or that an idol is anything]? No, but what they offer, "They offer to demons and not to God"' (10:19f); 'Let no one seek his own good, but the good of his neighbour' (10:24).[30]

It must be noted that Paul never uses the term 'strong' in this chapter, especially since it does occur in other contexts in his letter (1:27; 4:10; see below). Therefore it would not be justified to speak of a definite 'party of the strong' in chapter 8.[31] The position Paul addresses is explicitly characterized by another word: γνῶσις, knowledge. Its use here may or may not imply the existence of 'proto-Gnosis' in the city of Corinth,[32] but does not inform us about its existence within the church founded by Paul. We saw that Revelation, Justin and Irenaeus accused heretics, who may well represent various sorts of early Gnostics, of eating idol food as a sign of strength (p181). But this similarity must not be overstressed. A real Gnostic teaching in the sense of 'Balaam' or 'Jezebel' (Rev 2:14, 20) would certainly have provoked a very different reaction from Paul. Their 'knowledge' was in the rational insight that idols are nothing and that dedication to the gods does not make food any different.

Paul's remarkably cautious response need not be taken for weakness,[33] but points towards a more complex situation. As we have seen in the previous chapter there existed in the Hellenistic world a climate of rational criticism towards idolatry shared by the Pharisaic-Rabbinic and Cynico-Stoic traditions.

[29] Thus concisely Jeremias, 'Gedankenführung', 151f.
[30] Cf Hurd, Origin, 126-31 for the coherence between chs 8, 9 and 10 as against the background of the slogans of the strong.
[31] Thus also Hurd, Origins, 117-25; following him Fee, 'Eidôlothuta', 176.
[32] Cf Horsley, 'Gnosis', with further literature.
[33] Cf Räisänen, Paul, 48f: Paul had no defense against these slogans since they derived from his own teaching.

More specifically, the idea of 'liberty' as regards food was typical of the Cynics.[34] Evidently the 'knowing' at Corinth shared this view, whence the expressions ἐξουσία, 'power', and ἐλευθερία, 'freedom' in their attitude regarding idol offerings (8:9; 10:29).[35] But it appears that basically Paul also shared it, though not without qualification. Hence he was able to write, 'We know that an idol is nothing in the world' (8:4); 'idol meat is nothing' (10:19); and 'food will not commend us to God; we are no worse off if we do not eat, and no better of if we do' (8:8).

A basic affirmation of the rational view on idolatry combined with a subtle awareness of its power is found in the Tannaic Sages. While in the main they shared the view that 'in the idol there is nothing real', they would never even have thought of participating in its cult. The problem was in communication with gentiles. Here they were always on their guard not to 'strengthen the hands of the tresspasser': not to lend a hand to the practice of idolatry and support its power in society. Likewise Paul, while sharing the rational view that idolatry is 'nothing', thinks it inconceivable for someone who as a member of the body of Christ is a spiritual heir of 'our fathers' in the desert (10:1-13) to participate in their cult and thus communicate with demons (10:20f). But these theological concepts only appear in the second part of the digression. In chapter 8 Paul's argument moves on another level, which reappears after the digression in 10:25ff.

From 8:7 onwards another position is revealed: that of the 'weak'. It is to them that Paul now directs the attention of the 'knowing'. This shift is crucial in Paul's argument, as we will understand more fully later. A glance in the concordance shows that the word ἀσθενής is rather typical of First Corinthians and has a general emotional-ethical appeal, in occasional opposition to ἰσχυρός.[36] The Gospel of Christ crucified which Paul preaches is 'weak', while the world is 'strong' (1:25, 27); Paul came to Corinth 'in weakness' (2:3); he and the other Apostles are 'weak', while the Corinthians are 'strong' (4:10); 'Those parts of the body which seem weaker are indispensable' (12:22). The word appears with a similar emotional function in 2Cor 10-13, in yet another context: a moving apology directed against the Apostle's rivals and opponents.[37] But it seems that its use in 1Cor 8 is more specific. Similarly in Rom 14-15, the words 'weakness' and 'being weak' are used in relation to an issue regarding food;[38] although as we said the precise situation is different.

This specific connotation is confirmed in Rabbinic literature. Not only was the Greek word ἀσθενής among the relatively few to be assimilated into

---

[34] Stanley Jones, "Freiheit", 38-61, esp 59f.

[35] Stanley Jones ib 46 points out that 1Cor 9:19 ἐλεύθερος reflects the Socratic-Cynic ideal of economic αὐτάρκεια.

[36] 11 out of 25 mentions in all of the New Testament. Twice ἀσθένεια and twice ἀσθενέω must be added.

[37] 10:10, 'They say, his letters are weighty and strong, but his bodily presence is weak'! Further 6 x ἀσθένεια, 6 x ἀσθενέω.

[38] 3 x ἀσθενέω, once ἀσθενήμα. But a different category is meant.

Tannaic usage, but it was used specifically in matters of bodily constitution and diet. A mishna dating from the end of the first century CE at the latest,[39] informs us of the following detail regarding the ritual bath the High Priest had to take in the early morning of Yom Kippur: 'If the High Priest was aged or infirm אסטנס, *astneis*,[40] they made hot water for him...' (mYom 3:5). The word is more widely attested in later usage.[41] In view of its context in Paul it is quite likely that for him the word had a similar specific connotation: 'infirm, delicate', stressing a restrictive diet rather than a defective faith.[42] We shall translate it here as 'delicate'.

The shift in 8:7 not only brings the 'delicate' within view, but also their decisive attribute: their συνείδησις or consciousness. Paul explicitly directs the attention of the 'knowing' to the consciousness of the 'delicate' who have only recently been added to the church: 'For some, being hitherto used to the idol, eat (what they eat) as idol food, and their consciousness which is delicate is being defiled' (8:7). Paul wants the 'knowing' to have consideration for the difficult position of the delicate. The question is, why? One explanation which as stated is based on confusion of 1Cor 8-10 with Rom 14f, is that the delicate were Jewish Christians who had 'scruples' about eating idol food. But this is absurd, since Jews could not possibly be referred to as 'hitherto used to the idol' (cf also 12:2). Moreover this assumes that Paul basically allowed the eating of idol food, which conflicts with 10:1-22. The plain meaning is that the 'weak' were pagan neophytes who had difficulties with the power of idolatry: 'their delicate consciousness is being defiled'. What this means depends on the meaning of the crucial word συνείδησις.

A full discussion of συνείδησις is postponed until our discussion of its appearance in 10:25-28. However at this point a negative distinction must be made. Explanations which take either the word itself or its implication in the sense of 'conscience' or other moral connotations are bound to become unclear and inconsistent.[43] While in chapter 8 it is the consciousness of the delicate member of Christ which restricts the Christian's liberty, in chapter 10 it concerns a 'non-believer' (10:27). Translating συνείδησις there in the moral sense of 'conscience' would be absurd: why should the conscience of a non-believer, or even of a believer, be impaired by another person's eating idol food? Surely it would only please a pagan to see a Christian eating idol meat. And as for the delicate brother, if we explain that he would be induced to doubt the correctness of his own abstinence from idol food, we must either presuppose

[39] The main body of chs 1-7 of mYoma, to which 3:5 certainly belongs, must have been formulated in the first post-destruction generation. See Epstein, *Tannaitic Literature*, 36f.
[40] Thus the vocalizer of ms K which is in *scriptio defectiva*. The usual vocalization of the word, applied here by Ch. Yalon in Albeck's Mishna ed, and usually written *plene*, is איסטניס. The same situation, mBer 2:6.
[41] yBer 8, 12a (see ms Vatican); cf bHul 107b; bSanh 100b (opposite שדעתו יפה, cf mAZ 2:5!); GenR 11,3 (p90, with the connotation 'spoiled'); bPes 108a.
[42] On Rom 14:1 see below p243.
[43] Similarly Coune, 'Problème'; Eckstein, *Begriff*. Willis, *Idol Meat*, 89-92 wavers.

195

that Paul, in stating that his 'conscience' is impaired, actually advocated eating idol food, which cannot be reconciled with 1Cor 10:1-22,[44] or that he wanted to protect him against psychological stress, which is equally improbable. The only coherent way to explain chapters 8 and 10 seems to be to avoid any moral connotation in the word συνείδησις. We can avoid it with the translation 'consciousness'.

What bothers Paul, and what he asks the 'knowing' to consider, is the significance of their behaviour in the consciousness of the delicate, the new church member. The obvious object of the latter's consciousness is the reality of the pagan deities, represented in the idols and the food offered to them. Certainly, Paul agrees with the knowing, 'the idol is nothing', in itself. But it is something in the consciousness of the delicate. This concurs with the attitude of the Tannaim: the reality of idolatry is in man. Hence Paul warns the 'knowing': 'Take care lest this liberty of yours become a stumbling block for the delicate' (8:9).

The next question asked by Paul is clearly rhetorical: 'For if someone would see you,[45] with your knowledge, reclining in an idol temple, would not the consciousness of him that is weak be built towards eating idol food?' (8:10). In view of 1Cor 10:1-22, it is very hard to imagine how Paul could think of any Corinthian Christian merely being present in an idol temple.[46] The rhetorical question must be intended to make the 'knowing' realize the effect of their behaviour on the consciousness of the delicate. The real issue here is not visiting temples but eating sacrificial food (8:1, 4) and its effect on the consciousness of the delicate.

This is also indicated in the concluding sentence. If the condition of the delicate's consciousness should require it, the Apostle would abstain from eating meat altogether: 'If food causes my brother to stumble, I will never eat meat in eternity!' (8:13). This last sentence sounds like an exclamation in-dicating a voluntary vow of abstention as mentioned in tractate Nedarim of the Mishna. Voluntary abstention from meat is one of the obvious possibilities.[47] The imaginary vow indicates the seriousness of the matter for Paul. Incidental-ly, it would also seem to exclude the possibility that he ever ate idol meat at Corinth, since the delicate would be always at hand – though of course for a Jew it would have been out of the question to start with.

Let us now hear the chapter in full:

---

[44] Thus, for example, Murphy O'Connor, 'Freedom' (who simply ignores 1Cor 10:1-23); Willis, *Idol Meat*, 234ff (who joins the explanation that 1Cor 10:1-23 forbids temple visits but v24-29 permits eating idol food).

[45] σὲ is left out by in P46 and some others, which may be read as reflecting the impossibility of Paul's rhetorical example.

[46] Similarly Hurd, *Origin*, 142f. Hence the improbability of the explanation (popular among the commentaries, below n95) that 8:1-10:22 is about the prohibition of actual participation in cult meals, while 10:23ff is about eating idol food apart from such celebrations.

[47] mNed 6:6, הנודר מן הבשר. The Mishna accepts this practice as basic and is concerned with defining the degree to which such vows are binding or can be undone.

(1) Now about food offered to idols: We know that we all have knowledge. – Knowledge puffs up, but love builds up. (2) If someone deems himself knowing,[48] he has not yet come to know as one should know. (3) But if someone loves,[49] he is being known.[50]

(4) Hence, about the eating of food offered to idols: We know that an idol is nothing in the world and that there is no God but One; (5) for although there are those called gods either in heaven or on earth, as indeed there are many gods and many lords, (6) "For us[51] there is One God the Father, out of Whom all things are as we are towards Him, and One Lord Jesus Christ, through Whom all things are as we are towards Him". (7) But not in all is this knowledge; for some, being hitherto used[52] to the idol, eat (it) as offered to the idol, and their consciousness which is delicate is being defiled. (8) Food will not commend us to God: if we do eat we are no worse off, nor are we better off if we eat. (9) Take care lest your liberty become a stumbling block to the delicate: (10) for suppose someone would see you,[53] with your knowledge, reclining in an idol temple, would not his consciousness since he is delicate be edified towards eating idol food? (11) And so this delicate one would be lost – a brother for whom Christ died. (12) Thus, sinning against your brethren and wounding their delicate[54] consciousness, you sin against Christ. (13) Therefore, if food causes my brother to stumble, I will never eat meat in eternity, lest I cause my brother to stumble!

What Paul tries to establish in answering the Corinthians is that the reality of idolatry, which they agree is not contained in objects, is in man. Hence the problem is not with the 'weak in faith'[55] who have not yet attained to the enlightened insight that food is 'indifferent' and must be educated to that insight as soon as possible.[56] The problem is with the delicate consciousness of the

---

[48] τι is absent in P46 and Ambst.

[49] Τὸν θεόν absent in P46 and Cl. See next n.

[50] ὑπ'αὐτοῦ absent in P46, Sinai˙ and a minuscle. This can be understood as an addition which, correctly, explains the impersonal ἔγνωσται form as referring to God, a normal construction in Hebrew and Hebrew-influenced usage, cf Matt 7:1-5, 7-11; 5:3-10. The previous addition must have been inspired by this one but is less adequate: loving one's neighbour is loving the Creator. Cf 1John 2:3-11; Rom 13:8-10.

[51] ἀλλ' absent in P46, B, a minuscle, two ancient versions, and an Irenaeus ms.

[52] συνηθείᾳ Sinai˙, A, B, P, Athos, etc. Corrected Sinai, D, F, G, Koine, old Latin, Syriac and Ambst have συνειδήσει which, in view of our discussion below, may be better; it is left out here for the clarity of the discussion. Cf 2Pet 2:19 διὰ συνείδησιν θεοῦ, which according to Eckstein, *Syneidesis*, 308 is 'schwierig einzuordnen' but which he after much discussion (308-10) agrees to translate 'Gottes eingedenk' (Jerusalem and Zurich Bible). The most simple explanation confirming this translation is that it reflects the Hebrew דעת אלוהים. Hence 1Cor 8:7, συνείδησει ἕως ἄρτι τοῦ εἰδώλου, 'their consciousness hitherto being directed to the idol'. Thus also Coune, 'Problème'.

[53] See above n45.

[54] ἀσθενοῦσαν absent in P46 and Cl. This may be another explanatory addition, reflecting uncertainty about the term συνείδησις.

[55] The expression is alien to 1Cor and derives from Rom 14:1.

[56] As supposed by O'Connor, 'Freedom', 566-71 ('The Education of Conscience' – 'Transforming the Weak' [!]). Similarly C.T. Craig, quoted by Hurd, *Origin*, 125. This is the interpretation of Cyrill:

gentile neophyte, who is still under the influence of idolatry. In the awareness of the 'knowing', the 'delicate' represent the reality of idolatry in man.

1Cor 10:1-22 – On Idolatry

This unit is essential to the chapters on idol food in more than one way. It concludes the digression in the middle of the larger argument; it adduces the authoritative example of biblical Israel in the desert, connecting it with the vital existence of the church in the eucharist; and it gives a highly outspoken view on idolatry and idol food. Some consider it a 'difficult' passage because it does not support the commonly held view that Paul condoned the eating of idol food.[57] Its vigourous rejection of idolatry has been identified as 'Jewish' and representive of a different letter or a different Paul altogether, reminiscent of the 'zealous' emphasis of 2Cor 6:11-7:1. Naturally, this 'different, Jewish' Paul was supposed to be the earlier Paul. Thus the difficulty is 'solved' by construing one unwarranted hypothesis on top of another: (1) the unit is an interpolation from another letter, and (2) that other letter was stricter or more 'Jewish' about idolatry.[58] There is no textual support whatsoever for such theories. Moreover, literary features not only connect the unit with more remote chapters but also with the surrounding units on idol food (see below). Hence, the integrity of chapters 8-10 is most plausible and they should be read as Paul's prudent response to a complicated situation.[59]

Let us start by reviewing some central sentences of 10:1-22.

> Therefore, my beloved, flee from idolatry. ...Consider Israel according to the flesh; are not those who eat the sacrifices partners in the altar? ...You cannot partake of the table of the Lord and the table of demons (1Cor 10:14, 18, 21).

The parallel of these words with 2Cor 6:11-7:1 is enlightening and helps us understand the fundamental significance of 1Cor 10:1-22 in the larger argument on idol offerings.

> Do not be mismated with unbelievers. For what partnership have righteousness and iniquity? Or what fellowship has light with darkness? What accord has Christ with Belial? Or what has a believer in common with an unbeliever? What agreement has the temple of God with idols? For we

Christians should educate anyone weak in faith to be strong enough to eat idol meat (Böckenhoff, *Speisegesetz*, 106; MPL 76, 856). For Cyrill the presence of idolaters or recent converts seems to have become pure theory. – At another level, the Cynico-Stoic view that food is 'indifferent' certainly plays a role in Paul; see below, ch 6 and Conclusion.

[57] Cf Brunt, *Attitude*, 100: 1Cor 10:1-13 is 'the most difficult to fit into the course of the overall argument'. O'Connor, 'Freedom', 544 (cf above n15) thinks Brunt 'exaggerate(s) the import of x, 1-22', but he himself simply ignores that passage. Barrett, 'Things', 52 concludes on Paul's 'confused and inconsistent treatment of idolatry'.

[58] See discussion of the classic theories by Hurd, *Origin*, 43-6.

[59] The integrity is concluded on after prudent analysis by Hurd, *Origin*, 126-42. Similarly Sawyer, *Problem*, 160-4; Brunt, *Paul's Attitude*, 53-62; Wuellner, 'Greek Rhetoric'; Stanley Jones, *'Freiheit'*, 38-42. Willis, *Idol Meat* accepts the integrity as an established fact; see also his 'Apostolic Apologia'.

are the temple of the living God; as God said, "I will live in them and move among them, and I will be their God, and they shall be my people" (Ezek 37:27; cf Lev 26:12); "Therefore come out from their midst, and be separate from them, says the Lord, and touch nothing unclean" (Isa 52:11); "Then I will welcome you" (Ezek 20:34), "and I will be a father to you, and you shall be my sons and daughters, says the Lord Almighty" (cf 2Sam 7:8, 14). Since we have these promises, beloved, let us cleanse ourselves from every defilement of body and spirit, and make holiness perfect in the fear of God. (2Cor 6:14-7:1)

This is not the place to go into the literary problems surrounding Second Corinthians,[60] nor to elaborate on this brilliant concatenation of biblical verses into one coherent exposition.[61] We have already given attention to yet another aspect, the inclusion of women in the community (p134). What interests us here is the similarity to Essenism. The passage exudes a stark dualism expressed in sacramental and purificational language, which has even led to the hypothesis of a direct relationship with Essene literature.[62] The basic idea, connected with 2Sam 7, of the congregation of the chosen as a spiritual temple and as opposed to the 'sons of Belial' is also found in the Qumran scrolls.[63] But the expositional insertion of 'daughters' into 2Sam 7:14 should open our eyes to the fact that, although dualistic, Paul is remote from Essenism here. While women do figure in the Damascus Covenant and were to some extent present at Qumran,[64] their part in Essene salvation history was negligible. This emphasis on the 'daughtership of God' connects Paul with common Judaism.

At any rate, the Jewish-Christian view on the church and idolatry expressed in 2Cor 6:14-7:1 enhances the special atmosphere of 1Cor 10:1-22 and colours the argument on idol offerings of which this section is an integral part. Several other features stand out: the appeal Paul makes to the Tora as a source of authoritative teaching, the use he makes of midrash traditions, his insistence on the relationship between idolatry and illicit sexuality, and his theological conception of the nature of idolatry.

The remarkable use our passage makes of the Tora as a source of authority has already been noted (p70). This can now be discussed more fully. In the first place, the passage is full of allusions and references to the narrative of Israel's sojourn in the desert: the miraculous food and drink (Exod 15f), Israel's grumbling and putting God to the test, the water from the rock and the punishment of the snakes (Exod 17; Num 20f), and finally, the grave sin of

---

[60] For discussion see Thrall, 'Problem'; and, with reference to our problem, Fee, 'II Cor'.

[61] As in Rabbinic literature, the contexts of the verses quoted should be taken into account. They create a unity on a deeper level. Ezek 37:23-28 speaks of David, of God's sanctuary among the people of Israel, and of an end to idolatry; Isa 52:1-12 deals with Jerusalem as a sanctuary city free from impurity; and 2Sam 7 is about the future sanctuary to be built by David's son.

[62] Fitzmeyer, 'Qumran'.

[63] 4Qflor 1:1-13; see Dimant, 'Qumran', 518-21 and Flusser, 'Two Notes'. For broader discussion see Flusser, 'Dead Sea Sect', 227-36.

[64] On female remains found at Qumran see above p105 n55.

idolatry with the golden calf (Exod 32) and with Baal-Peor (Num 25). Evidently applying Greek expositional terminology, Paul also tells us what the implication is: 'Now these things are examples (τύποι) for us... they happened to them "typically", and were written down for our instruction, upon whom the end of the ages has come' (1Cor 10:6, 11).

As we have observed in other cases, Greek ideas blend perfectly together here with ancient biblical and midrash traditions. The idea of the spring and of the spiritual rock which travelled along with the children of Israel and so was able to quench their thirst in various locations has a remarkable diffusion over ancient Jewish literature.[65] The ancient tradition has roots in the biblical narrative, since it connects the gifts of water and of heavenly bread with God's testing and teaching Israel;[66] furthermore, the 'rock' is mentioned in a number of different places.[67] The fountain of life and the rivers of living water derive from the prophets.[68] All these traditions are woven together into the texture of Paul's exposition.

Thus the first part of the passage (1Cor 10:1-5) offers a simple exposition of these biblical and midrashic motifs, without yet referring to the Corinthians:

> I want you not to be ignorant, brethren, that our fathers were all under the cloud, and all passed through the sea, and all were baptized into Moses in the cloud and in the sea, and all ate the same spiritual food and all drank the same spiritual drink – for they drank from the spiritual rock which followed them, and the rock was the Christ –; nevertheless with most of them God was not pleased; for they were overthrown in the wilderness.

The second part (10:6-13) adds more biblical examples, explicitly called 'types', but subtly applies them to the situation of the Corinthians.[69] In particular, it stresses the close relationship between idolatry and illicit sexuality. This connection, as we have seen above, is evident from the Baal-Peor narrative (Num 25) and is pervasive in the prophets. This is the narrative to which Paul alludes, along with the other incisive case of idolatry in the Tora, the episode of the golden calf (Exod 32). In Paul's mind, the connection between idolatry and illicit sexuality applied particularly to the Corinthian situation. This becomes

---

[65] One is forced to be selective here. See CD 6:3-10, referring to Num 21:17 ('The Spring is the Tora'); CD 3:16; 19:34 ('the spring of living waters'). In Rabbinic literature: tSuk ch 3, esp 3:11 connecting the spring of Num 21:17 with the rock; GenR 70 (p806; the Holy Spirit 'drawn' from the Spring); ySuk 5, 55a (connecting with Isa 12:3, 'joy' and 'the wells of salvation'). These passages relate to the Sukkot festival and its popular water ceremony in which 'hasidim and men of holy deeds' were prominent (mSuk 4:9-5:4). See all parallels and related passages indicated by Theodor (GenR ib) and Lieberman (*Tosefta ki-Fshutah* 4, 876ff). And cf John 7:37-39 ('on the last day of the feast', the Spirit and living waters); 1Hen 48:1; WisSol ch 11 (Wisdom quenching their thirst); Philo, Leg all 2:86; Quod det 115-118.
[66] See Exod 15:25; 16:4 (cf Deut 8:3). This was made explicit by the דורשי רשומות of old who equated water and wood with Tora: Mekh Bashallah 1 (p154, 156).
[67] Exod 17:6; Num 21:8; Deut 32; and cf all those places in the Psalms where God is called Rock.
[68] E.g. Ezek 47; Zech 14:8. Cf Jer 17:8; Ps 1; and cf Sir 24:23-33.
[69] On these verses see Meeks, '"And Rose up to Play"'.

evident in the structural similarities between the next part of this unit, 10:14-22, and 1Cor 6:12-20 (see below). The second half of this part expounds the concept of πειρασμός, נסיון, inherent in Exod 15f, both referring to God's tempting Israel and Israel's tempting God and applying it to the Corinthian situation, in line with the intermediate character of the section:

> Now these things are examples for us, that we should not be covetous of evil things as they were covetous. And do not become idolaters as some of them were, as it is written, "The people sat down to eat and drink and rose up to play". And let us not commit illicit sexuality as some of them committed it, and twenty-three thousand fell in a single day. And let us not tempt the Christ,[70] as some of them tempted and they were destroyed by serpents. And do not grumble, as some of them grumbled and they were destroyed by the Destroyer. These things happened to them "typically", and they were written down for our instruction, upon whom the end of the ages has come. Therefore let him who thinks to be standing take heed lest he fall. No temptation has overtaken you that is not human. God is faithful, and he will not let you be tempted beyond your strength, but with the temptation will also create the way out by being able to endure. (1Cor 10:6-13)

The third part (10:14-22/23)[71] clearly represents a climax. Here Paul addresses the Corinthians directly. He is very explicit in his rejection of idolatry and reveals its abject nature. Opening with his emphatic appeal, he continues with the fundamental opposition between the communion with the body of Christ, realized in the Eucharist, and communion with the table of idols. This strong religious-moral dualism has already been stressed. We have also hinted at the structural similarities between this part and 6:12-20. In both passages a similar passionate appeal is made: 'Flee from illicit sexuality' (6:16); 'Flee from idolatry' (10:14). Furthermore, the same wisdom saying is applied: 'All things are lawful for me, but not all things edify; ...food is meant for the stomach and the stomach for food...; the body is not meant for illicit sexuality...' (6:12f); 'All things are lawful, but not all things edify...' (10:23).[72] Finally, in both passages the communion with the body of Christ plays an important role: 'Do you not know that your bodies are members of Christ? ...Do you not know that your body is a temple of the Holy Spirit...?' (6:15, 19); 'The bread which we break, is it not a communion in the body of Christ? Because there is one bread, we who are many are one body...' (10:16f). These literary elements and their varied cultural backgrounds have been discussed earlier. Their occurrence in both separate chapters once again demonstrates the extent to which 1Cor 10:1-22 is integral to the epistle.

---

[70] Thus P46, D, and many others; Sinai, B et al κύριον. Χριστόν is more surprising, but fits in better with v4 and 15ff.

[71] The Apostle's rhetoric defies neat division: v23 is a transitional phrase which belongs to the preceding section in its literary structure and to the following in its atmosphere.

[72] See preceding n.

The theological argument supporting Paul's denunciation of idolatry is especially interesting. It contains two conceps which do not appear to agree. On the one hand he appeals to the rational criticism of idolatry: 'What do I say then? That idol food is anything [or that an idol is anything]?' (10:19).[73] More explicitly, the idea appears in 1Cor 8:4, 'As to the eating of idol food, we know that an idol is nothing in the world and that none is God but One'. Paul is also able to express plain sarcasm, as in the phrase, 'the dumb idols' in 1Cor 12:2.[74] Here however Paul equates idolatry in the same breath with demon worship: 'No, but what the gentiles sacrifice,[75] they sacrifice to demons and not to God; I do not want you to communicate with the demons' (10:20). It is significant that this statement is based on a Tora verse which is quoted with the same implication in Tannaic literature: 'They sacrificed to demons, not God' (Deut 32:17). The continuation of the verse reappears further on in Paul's argument: 'They have provoked me to jealousy with what is no god, they have provoked me with their idols' (Deut 32:21); and seems to reverberate in 1Cor 10:22, 'Shall we provoke the Lord to jealousy?'[76] Thus a longer Tora passage underlies Paul's exposition, but it is nevertheless clear that it expresses his own view.

Apparently Paul is able to combine the two world views, in which the idol is either 'nothing' or represents a demon. As we saw earlier (p156f), the identification of idolatry with demon worship is hardly found in extant Tannaic literature; the rational approach dominates here, expressed in the view that 'in the idol is nothing real'. We have noted that this attitude converges with the Cynico-Stoic criticism of idolatry. On the other hand, demonology was prominent in Essene and apocalyptic thought, as also among Jesus and his disciples. We inferred that it must also have existed among the Pharisees. It follows that Paul, in using arguments from both cultural traditions, strikingly reflects the various trends in late Second Temple Judaism.[77] It remains open whether or not he was conscious of any tension. In view of similar reflections of demonology, angelology and apocalyptic throughout Paul's letters, this view of idolatry as demon worship cannot be dismissed as mere rhetoric.

The main issue of these chapters as a whole, idol food, is conspicuous here. Paul asks the rhetorical question: 'Do I say then that idol food is something?' (10:19). No, he wants to say, it is nothing; but partaking of it is communicating with demons. Despite his dual world view, Paul allows only one conclusion: idol food should not be eaten: 'You cannot partake of the table of the Lord and of

[73] The sentence 'or that an idol is anything' is lacking in P46, Sinai, A, C, Athos, et al. It can be read as a mitigating gloss.
[74] The expression is from Hab 2:18. The idea was common in Hellenistic Judaism; see Wolfson, *Philo* 1, 15 who refers to 3Macc 4:16; OrSib 4:7; 3:30. Add ib 8:379.
[75] Thus (P46, seemingly), Sinai, A, Athos, and many others. B, D and some others do not have τά ἔθνη, as in Deut 32:17, and are friendlier towards 'gentiles'.
[76] Pointed out by Von Soden, 'Sakrament', 348.
[77] In early Christian literature, demonology plays an important role in the observance of the prohibition of idol food. Cf Did 6:3 (mss C, A) and see below. Significantly, Paul's expression μετέχειν τραπέζης δαιμονίων is found several times in the anti-Pauline Pseudo-Clementine writings. See Molland, 'Circoncision', 32.

the table of demons' (10:21). Evidently, Paul felt the need to couch his prohibition in diplomatic wrapping. This is expressed in the wisdom saying which closes the section and at the same time leads in to the next. Let us listen to the entire third part:

> Therefore, my beloved, flee from idolatry. I speak as to sensible men; judge for yourselves what I say. The cup of blessing which we bless, is it not communion with the blood of the Christ? The bread which we break, is it not communion with the body of the Christ?[78] Because there is one bread, we who are many are one body, for we all partake of the one bread.[79] Consider Israel according to the flesh: are not those who eat the sacrifices partners in the altar?[80] What do I say then? That idol food is anything [or that an idol is anything]? No, but what the gentiles sacrifice, they sacrifice to demons and not to God; I do not want you to communicate with the demons. You cannot drink the cup of the Lord and the cup of demons; you cannot partake of the table of the Lord and the table of demons. Shall we provoke the Lord to jealousy? Are we stronger than he? (1Cor 10:14-22).

1Cor 10:23-11:1 – On Pagan Food

AN EXEGETICAL CRUX

We now turn to unit (4), and we must first reconsider its purpose in relation to the preceding. Unit (1) introduced the problem of idol food and pointed out that idolatry is real, not in the food but in the consciousness of the delicate brother, so that eating idol food is wrong for his sake. Then a long supporting digression followed, consisting of unit (2), a statement of Paul's life of self-denial for the sake of others, and unit (3) which gave theological arguments against idol food. That would be enough for a prohibition of idol food. But apparently there are practical questions still to be answered. These are dealt with in unit (4). They have to do with food bought at the market or eaten in private homes. The key word in unit (4) is 'consciousness', as in unit (1), and both units also relate to each other on a practical level. The Apostle reintroduces the problem in the following way:

> (10:23) All things are lawful, but not all things edify; all things are lawful, but not all things build up. (24) Let no one seek his own good, but the good of his neighbour.
> (25) All that is sold in the market place, you can eat without questioning for the sake of consciousness, (26) for "The earth is the Lord's and its fullness". (27) If anyone of the unbelievers invites you [to dinner][81] and

---

[78] The order wine-bread here is remarkable in view of 1Cor 11:23-26. See above p141f.

[79] The formulation is reminiscent of Did 9:4.

[80] The 'altar' as an almost personified entity is common in aggada and halakha, cf mShek 4:4, 9; mSuk 4:5; bSanh 22a.

[81] ms D and others explain and add, εἰς δεῖπνον.

you desire to go, all that is set before you, you can eat without questioning for the sake of consciousness. (28) But if anyone says to you, This is
sacrificial food! do not eat for his sake [- the one who warned you, and
consciousness].[82] (29) By consciousness I mean not one's own but that of
the other; for why should my liberty be liable to judgment on the ground
of another's consciousness?

The opening verses create an atmosphere of wisdom and peace.[83] As has been
indicated (p75f) the first verse reflects the wisdom saying from Ben Sira: 'Not all
things are helpful for all, nor do all souls prefer all foods' (Sir 37:28). It is also
applied in 6:12 where the issue is illicit sexuality; here it concerns food and the
saying is entirely appropriate. Together with the second verse, which seems to
be some paraphrase of the Golden Rule and hence connects with the biblical
commandment to 'love your neighbour as yourself',[84] this verse relates to the
humane Cynico-Stoic trend of thought which would be familiar to the Corinthians. As has been pointed out above, the recurrent use of the word 'all'
creates a rhetorical unity characterized by a continuous interplay of inclusive
and restrictive moments. This ambivalent rhetoric connects v23 with v25 and
27, and hence with the restriction given in v28f.

Nevertheless from v25 onwards a different language is used, not that of
ethical sayings but of clear and distinct rules. Even more explicitly than in
chapter 8, the decisive factor pointed out is the other person's consciousness.
But we are in a different situation here. In contrast to chapter 8 this concerns
someone who uses the term ἱερόθυτον, 'sanctified food'. This indicates he is a
pagan; a Jew or Christian would have used the term εἰδωλόθυτα. Indeed the
actual situations to which Paul refers are in pagan surroundings: the market
place and the home of an 'unbeliever'. Taken at face value this excludes the
possibility of the 'informant', whose consciousness is decisive, being a 'delicate'
fellow-Christian as in chapter 8.[85] Indeed the very word ἀσθενής is not mentioned in this chapter. The identity of the informant is not, and apparently need
not be, specified. It is simply someone involved in either of the settings Paul
mentions, i.e. someone at the market (v25) or one of the household of the
'unbeliever' who has invited the Christian (v27).[86] This person discloses a fact
about the food which was not indicated before: it passes for a pagan sacrifice.
This mere statement is sufficient reason not to eat; without it, eating would have

[82] Τὸν μηνύσαντα καὶ τὴν συνείδησιν is absent in P46. This may be caused by *homoioteleuton*
(from συνείδησιν). But the phrase may also be a gloss: stylistically it is awkward (καὶ τὴν
συνείδησιν), and it is halakhically unnecessary (see below).
[83] About the division see above n71.
[84] For the connection with Lev 19:18 see the testament of Isaac contained in Jub 36:4, 'Be loving of
your brothers as a man loves himself, with each man seeking for his brother what is good for him.'
[85] As against the most common opinion, voiced by O'Connor, ib (n44), and see list in Brunt, *Paul's
Attitude*, 109-12.
[86] The separation proposed by Willis, *Idol Meat*, 240-5 between vv25-27 and 28-29 is artificial; cf his
somewhat tortuous arguments (ib) in deciding on the identity of the informant and his speech (τις,
ἱερόθυτον). More adequately Stanley Jones, *"Freiheit"*, 54 proposes to leave τις as unspecified as
it is.

been permitted 'without enquiring'. How can we explain this? Why is the warning so important?

But we must interrupt our argument and consider the probability of a quite different explanation, i.e. that it concerned food laws. It has been suggested that Paul meant the fundamental nullity of Jewish food laws when he stated that, 'All that is sold at the market you can eat without questioning for the sake of consciousness, for "The earth is the Lord's, and its fullness"' (10:25). This assumption might gain inspiration from the philosophical words of King Antiochus when the priest Eleazar refused to eat pork: 'Why should you abhor eating the excellent meat of this animal which nature has freely bestowed on us?' (4Macc 5:8). The notion that food is religiously indifferent and the appeal to nature once more refer us to Cynico-Stoic tradition. Indeed the declared aim of Four Maccabees is to justify Judaism on a rational basis.[87] But again the question before us is whether Paul – and the author of Four Maccabees, for that matter – is to be fully identified with this tradition, or is also dependent on other traditions which limit its application.

The quotation is from Ps 24:1. In Rabbinic literature this verse serves to support the duty of blessing God at meal; hence we must find out whether that connection is relevant to Paul. The answer is positive. The theme of 'blessing', which we explored in chapter 3, becomes explicit in the continuation here: 'If I partake with thankfullness, why should I be denounced because of that over which I say a blessing (εὐχαριστῶ)?' (1Cor 10:30f). The halakha that God must be blessed upon enjoying food or anything else from his creation has been formulated in various ways. The Mishna formulates it positively: 'If three have eaten together, they are obliged to summon (each other to say grace after meal together)' (mBer 7:1). A negative formulation with reference to Scripture is given in the Tosefta: 'One should not savour anything until one has blessed, as it is said, "The earth is the Lord's and its fullness"' (tBer 4:1). Paradoxically. it was precisely on the strength of these data that some scholars concluded that Paul intended to point out the obsolescence of the food laws in quoting Ps 24:1.[88] They must have used the Rabbinic parallels on the basis of premises the Sages did not share. Blessing the Creator for all his diverse creatures does not oblige to eat of all of them.[89]

On the other hand the commandment to bless the Creator at table somehow has to do with the prohibition of idolatry. This is expressed in the saying of R. Shimon ben Yohai:

> If three have eaten at one table and not spoken words of the Tora on it, they are like those "eating sacrifices of the dead"... But if three have eaten at one table and spoken words of Tora on it, it is as if they have eaten from the table of the Holy One, blessed be He. (mAv 3:3)

---

[87] Cf below p249.

[88] Barrett, 'Things', 52; Lohse, 'Zu 1. Kor'. Lohse patently studies Paul and Judaism from Lutheran prejudice: '(Paulus) befreit ...das Gewissen des Christen von den kasuistischen Bestimmungen der Halaka und gibt dem Christen alles frei, weil alles Gott gehört' (279).

[89] Cf the irony inherent in the expression 'all things of the six days of creation', below p232.

It appears that the same profound connection is central to Paul's argument here. We shall explore it further at the end of the next chapter below. The conclusion relevant for us now is that it is by no means necessary to assume that Paul when quoting Ps 24:1 had the food laws in mind, let alone that he declared them void.

We can reject this possibility if we recall two fundamental observations made earlier. In First Corinthians Paul is addressing a church of gentiles, and he might be expected to deal only with those commandments he thinks relevant to them. Almost explicitly this is what is stated in an important passage in the same letter: 'Let every one live as the Lord has assigned to him, as God has called every one; this is what I order in all churches. Was someone called in the circumcision, let him not have it undone; was another called uncircumcised, let him not seek circumcision. ...Everyone should remain in the calling in which he was called' (1Cor 7:17-20). We shall study this passage in detail in the concluding chapter. But one thing is evident and undisputed among exegetes: Paul wants the 'uncircumcised' to remain as they are: gentile Christians. Thus when writing, 'All that is sold in the market hall you can eat without questioning', he never touches on Jewish dietary laws and can wholeheartedly allow gentiles to enjoy all the blessings of creation at liberty.

Incidentally one implication is that Paul did not prohibit non-slaughtered meat for gentiles. Passing over the weighty issue of Paul's relation to the Apostles' Decree here (for some observations see the Conclusion) we may conclude that he did not 'burden' the gentiles with any dietary restrictions except against food sacrificed to idols. This is the message of the preceding section, 1Cor 10:1-22.

Let us now return to where we left off. Everything offered at the market or in a pagan home may be eaten, except if a person warns that it concerns sacrificial food. What does this mean exactly? The possibility could never be excluded that meat sold on the market had previously been sacrificed to pagan deities, just as wine, of which a symbolical part may have been poured out in honour of the gods.[90] Does Paul therefore permit the gentile Christians to eat sacrificial food? If so, how does that fit with his preceding and, by all indications, unequivocal condemnation of idolatry? How can we explain this apparent contradiction?

Four possible solutions of this exegetical *aporia* offer themselves.

(1) *The contradiction is fundamental.* No further explanation is possible: Paul prohibits in one passage what he permits in the other. Hence we must suppose that either Paul or his letter was confused. The first possibility was suggested in recent years,[91] but appears to have been advocated already by the pagan critic of Christianity, Porphyry.[92] As we have seen the second possibility was suggest-

---

[90] Thus Barrett, 'Things', 49f, joined by Conzelmann, *Korinther*, 216.

[91] Barrett, 'Things'. Räisänen, *Paul*, 2f makes a point of signalling contradictions in Paul (see above ch 1) and in that context mentions Porphyry with admiration. He does not mention the fragment referred to in the next n.

[92] Böckenhoff, *Speisegesetz*, 57f refers to a passage quoted, and unconvincingly refuted, by Maca-

ed in critical scholarship, which supposed the letter to be composite and reflecting a development in Paul. We have also mentioned the objections to this explanation: in the rest of the letter Paul appears to be faithful to Jewish and Jewish-Christian halakhic tradition; all early Christian authorities unanimously rejected both idolatry and idol food; and the evidence in support of the unity of 1Cor 8-10 is strong.[93]

(2) *Paul expressed himself unclearly.* When writing that the Corinthians could eat 'all that is sold' and 'all that is set before you', Paul intended to exclude idol food. This explanation, as we have seen, was voiced by several Church Fathers.[94] There are two objections. It simply ignores the whole question Paul is taking so much pain to answer. It is also an impossible solution, for in 10:28 Paul mentions the possibility that one may buy food which a pagan tacitly considers consecrated; hence as long as he keeps silent, one would unknowingly be buying idol food. Meanwhile, this explanation vividly illustrates both the severity of the early Christian idol food prohibition and the impossibility, at a time when idolatry was still very real, of imagining Paul actually condoning the eating of idol food.

(3) *Paul discusses two different situations.* This is similar to the preceding explanation but more subtle. In 8:1-10:22 Paul speaks about idol food during actual participation in cult meals (cf 8:10, 10:21), while in 10:25-28 he deals with it as being separate from an actual cult ceremony. – This explanation is the most popular among modern commentators.[95] It has the advantage of reading the section as a whole and trying to understand the various parts on their own terms. The difficulty is the same as with the preceding solution: in 10:28, the question of idol food appears to be involved just as in 8:1ff and 10:19. Fundamentally, this approach underestimates the weight of the idolatry prohibition not only in ancient Judaism but also in Christianity. After all, how many Christians were willing to die rather than acknowledge the power of pagan deities by eating food offered to them?

In view of these difficulties, and on the basis of the evidence of First Corinthians as a whole and of the ancient Jewish laws about idolatry reviewed in the previous chapter, a new explanation is proposed here.

rius of Magneta (ed C. Blondel, *Jahrbücher f. deutsche Theol.* 23, Gotha 1878, 269ff, 303ff). According to one Wagenmann and O. Bardenhewer (ib n3) the fragment must come from Porphyry's work 'Against the Christians'. In the fragment, Paul is accused both of prohibiting idol food and calling it indifferent; saying that one can eat it as long as someone else does not tell one, and also stating that it is communication with demons. Paul is a funny archer whose arrows hit himself.

[93] Above p190-2.

[94] Explicitly so: Clemens of Alexandria, Strom 4:15 (Böckenhoff, *Speisegesetz*, 41), basing himself on Paul's support for the Apostolic Decree according to Acts; Tertullian, De ieiun 15 (ib 47).

[95] It was explored separately in Fee, '*Eidôlothuta*'. See also the commentaries on 1Cor by Robertson-Plummer; Lietzmann; Allo; Schlatter; Bruce; Pop; Wolff; Klauck. Basically the same Conzelmann; and Barrett. Following the commentaries, Sawyer, *Problem* distinguishes further between 'buying or using sacrificial meat' and 'eating with an unbeliever'; Brunt, *Paul's Attitude*, 118 wishes 'a sharp distinction (to) be drawn between idol meat and idolatry'; and Willis, *Idol Meat* elaborates the concept of κοινωνία in festive pagan meals.

(4) *Paul defines what is idol food in doubtful cases.* While 1Cor 8 introduces the problem and 10:1-22 reiterates the general prohibition of food known to be consecrated to idols, 10:25-29 deals with food of unspecified nature in a pagan setting. This explanation has several advantages:

(a) It reads 1Cor 8-10 as a natural unity with a common chiastic rhetorical pattern.

(b) It gives a natural explanation of the verse generally considered a *crux*, 1Cor 10:29.

(c) It gives the term συνείδησις a clear, specific significance which discloses the meaning of the whole passage.

(d) It explains Paul's diverse teaching in all sections of our passage as being an application of halakhic principles regarding gentile idolatry.

(e) It parallels explanations by some prominent Patristic authors.

The difficulty about our explanation is that we have no exact contemporary parallels in the extant halakhic documents. What we have are later parallels, analogies, and a reflection in an ancient non-halakhic text.

However this difficulty should be viewed within the framework of the historical study of halakha in ancient Jewish literature and the New Testament, as described in chapter 1 above. In itself it is no different from the problems concerning the halakha in Philo or in Jubilees. Historical study operates by accumulation of corroborative data from various sources, which when isolated may not seem all that convincing but in combination produce mutually enhanced probability. It all depends on our ability to perceive a pattern which integrates the various data in the most natural way, rather than limit ourselves to scrutinizing isolated details from the card index.

INTENTION (συνείδησις) AND IDOLATRY

In the last unit of his section on idolatry Paul gives practical instruction on what to do in doubtful cases, where food of unspecified nature is found in a pagan setting. It is likely that this problem was included in the question written in the letter from Corinth. At any rate Paul mentions it as a practical specification in the concluding part of the chiastic structure.[96] This gives us a good view on the effect of this rather sophisticated rhetorical technique: a practical problem is introduced in a general way, it is then approached from various illustrative and theoretical sides, and finally the practical problem returns and is settled by giving direct instructions.

There is also a specific parallel here with halakhic procedures. The formulation of decisions for doubtful cases which arise from the application of accepted rules is a common feature in Rabbinic halakha. An example similar to our problem deals with lost objects. It is a long-established principle that one should restore lost objects to their owner (cf Deut 22:1-4). But if the owner should be unknown, there are halakhic rules which define whether the owner can be

---

[96] Above p190f. Similarly Willis, *Idol Meat*, 271.

identified by the quality of the object or the conditions in which it was found.[97] The problem of unspecified food in a pagan setting is similar: what should a Christian who subscribes to the prohibition of idol food do with food of which he does not know the status in a pagan environment? If he has heard with certainty that it came from a pagan temple or celebration, he would consider it prohibited. But what if this is not clear and nobody is there to ask?

In addition to Rabbinic halakha, an answer is given by one of the Church Fathers. We referred earlier to the example given by Augustine (above p184) of a hungry traveller who finds food in front of a statue or altar with nobody around. The fact, Augustine explains, that it is left where it is, indicates that it is intended as an offering and therefore it is prohibited. But if there is no such indication, it is not prohibited. This way of reasoning resembles the principles of the halakha on idolatry. The irony is of course that when faced with in Jewish texts, Christian interpreters are tempted to call this 'casuistry'.[98]

A passage in the Mishna corresponds exactly to Augustine's example. This is surprising but no actual coincidence. It shows that this particular situation was very common in the ancient world and that Jews and Christians aproached it similarly. The mishna deals with objects found around what was called a מרקוליס, *merkolis*, i.e. *Mercurius* or Ἑρμῆς.[99] This was a rectangular column crowned with the head of the deity, the patron of travellers and merchants, and was used by the Romans as a road mark. Passers-by would throw stones or deposit food on top or in front of to express their devotion.[100] The underlying question in the mishnaic discussion is how one can know if objects found in its vicinity are intended for the idol or not. If not, the stones could be used and the food could for example be sold to a gentile.

> R. Yishmael says: three stones in a row next to the *merkolis* – these are forbidden, but two (stones) are permitted. But the Sages say: what appears to belong to it is prohibited, and what does not so appear is permitted. If one finds coins, clothes or utensils on top of it, they are permitted; but strands of grapes, wreaths of corn, wine, oil or flour – anything that is offered on the altar – are forbidden. (mAZ 4:1f)

Coins, clothes and household utensils are not likely to be ceremonially offered, but the other objects are. Similarly, two stones next to the column may lie there by accident, but three in a row signify human intention. The rule of the Sages gives a clear principle, although of course it leaves a margin of doubt: 'What is seen as belonging to the idol is forbidden, what is not so seen is permitted'. The important term is נראה, 'be seen', 'appear' (above p162). It all depends on the apparent significance given to the object by the gentile. For the reality of idolatry is not in objects, it is in the human consciousness. And the intention of

---

[97] mBM 2. Another example is mToh 4:7-13, a list of 'doubtful cases regarding purity laws'; cf mMikw chs 1-2. The systematic formulation of ספיקות, doubtful cases, may have been initiated by R. Akiva and developed by his pupils.

[98] E.g. von Soden, above n6.

[99] See Flusser, 'Paganism', 1087f.

[100] mSan 7:6.

this consciousness can only be judged by external signs. In the same way Augustine and other Church Fathers judge by the apparent intended significance.[101]

This allows us to discuss the implication of the term συνείδησις, which we have been translating as 'consciousness'. This Pauline anthropological term is generally recognized as crucial here and a lot of energy has been spent in trying to establish its significance.[102] However this has not yet resulted in a convincing, coherent explanation of the whole passage. In particular Paul's sentence, 'Of consciousness I speak, not one's own but that of the other person', is found to be a *crux interpretum*.[103] We have already pointed out that a moral interpretation of συνείδησις completely obscures its meaning in our passage.

The problem is apparently of ancient date and may be due to the fact that the Latin equivalent, *conscientia*, acquired a predominantly moral meaning.[104] At any rate, a set moral interpretation was given to the passage by the Augustine, who knew no Greek. Although his example of the hungry traveller is enlightening, he misunderstood the crucial concept in Paul's argument. Incidentally this shows us that he had not invented the example but that it came from actual life. In any case Augustine explained that if the food is consecrated to the idol with certainty, one may not eat *propter conscientiam, ne daemonibus communicasse videatur*, 'for reasons of conscience, so as not to appear to be communicating with demons'.[105] One could still try save Augustine by stressing the word *videatur*, but the thing is that he introduced the word *conscientia* while commenting on 1Cor 10:20 where the word is never used. And on the other hand, Augustine goes on to say, if it were certain that the food had not been consecrated to the deity, one could eat *sine ullo conscientiae scrupulo*.[106] Thus Augustine switched the focus from the consciousness of the delicate brother or the pagan to the scruples of conscience of the Christian himself, thereby distorting Paul's argument: 'Consciousness I say, not yours but the other person's' (1Cor 10:29). Instead of Paul's factual discernment of the 'intention towards idolatry', it was the scruples of Augustine's 'introspective conscience' which became decisive. And it was apparently through the radicalization of his view by the ex-Augustine monk, Luther, that this very un-Pauline interpretation became dominant in (Protestant) Western Christianity.[107] As a result modern Bible translations render 'conscience'.

---

[101] Cf Ambrosiaster, above p183 n184: the expressions *quasi venereris idola* and *ut putetur quia venerationis causa edat*.

[102] For full discussion see Eckstein, *Syneidesis* (previous research, 13-33). The most adequate interpretation was proposed by Coune, 'Problème'.

[103] Eckstein, *Syneidesis*, 262; O'Connor, 'Freedom', 567.

[104] See Eckstein, *Syneidesis*, p80ff for this conclusion.

[105] Contr Faust 33:13, MPL 42, 503f; quoted in Böckenhoff, *Speisegesetz*, 103.

[106] Ep 47:6, MPL 33, 187; Böckenhoff ib 102. Augustine is seemingly justified in this interpretation by 1Cor 8:7, ἡ συνείδησις αὐτῶν ...μολύνεται; but see below.

[107] Cf Stendahl's epoch-making paper, 'Paul and the Introspective Conscience' (above p15). As to Luther Eckstein, *Syneidesis*, 4f reports that it was he who coined in effect the fateful religious concept, 'Gewissen'. For the far-reaching psychological aspects of this novel 'negative conscience' cf Erikson, *Luther*, ch 6.

Much more philological sense is shown in the comments of Augustine's Greek-speaking contemporary, Chrysostom, on Paul's words about idol offerings: 'These things are not physically evil, but through the intention (διανοία) effectuate the unclean... It is no longer (a) physical (matter), but the disobedience and love of demons which makes me unclean, and the mental aim (προαίρεσις) effectuates the pollution'.[108] It is striking how Chrysostom avoids the word συνείδησις, used by Paul. Apparently in his vocabulary it did not, or no longer, express what he understood to be meant and described it using more appropriate words: intention, mental aim. The interesting thing is that the Antiochene deacon, whose respect for the traditions of his Jewish co-citizens was not impressive, offers a philologically precise explanation of Paul which, as we shall see below, closely resembles the meaning of the concept when compared with the halakha. This would seem to indicate that he shared a tradition which disclosed the meaning of this Pauline concept which has become so obscure to modern exegetes. We have already suggested the existence of such a tradition in view of the incident at Antioch under Julian (above p182).

The primary meaning of συνείδησις, as of *conscientia*, is 'knowing together', i.e. together with someone else, or, more often, with oneself. Hence the meaning 'knowing about one's conduct', or, as proposed in the above, 'consciousness, being con-scious'.[109] From this basic meaning, two further connotations can be developed, which appear both in general Greek usage and in the New Testament: 'conscience' in the moral sense, and 'intention'.[110] Incidentally, in modern French 'conscience' still combines both connotations. A further development is the meaning 'conscientiousness'.[111] The word has a general Hellenistic background. The connection with Stoic thought seems obvious, although it does not explain the origin of the concept.[112] As for the New Testament, the word is never used in the gospels. Out of the thirty times it is found, fourteen are in Paul, of which seven (or eight)[113] in our passage. In Paul, the moral meaning is found, but this is by no means everywhere the case.[114]

Luther, ch 6.

[108] Hom in I. Ep ad Cor 25:1-2 (MPG 61. 159ff). Above p182f.

[109] Thus Bultmann, *Theologie*, 217; but in the continuation he could not steer free from Augustinian-Lutheran moralism (enhanced by existentialist anthropology) and completely surrendered to the traditional meaning, 'conscience'.

[110] Eckstein, *Begriff*, 5-11 discerns the phases 'Mitwissen, Bewußtsein, Gewissen, Inneres'. Especially in view of the correlation with one's outward actions, the last word is more effectively rendered 'intention'.

[111] Bauer, *Wörterbuch* s.v. (literature!).

[112] Eckstein, *Begriff*, 65f. A general discussion is given by Davies, 'Conscience', without being aware of our problem.

[113] One is in the phrase in 10:28 missing in P46 (above n82); another in a variant reading in 8:7 (n127).

[114] The moral sense is obvious in Rom 2:15 (cf Wis 17:11!), but not so in Rom 9:1 and 2Cor 1:12. Eckstein, *Begriff*, taking his starting point in Rom 2:15, comes to the general circumscription, 'die Instanz ...die die Übereinstimmung zwischen den ihr vorgegebenen Wertnormen und dem Verhalten prüft' (190). This is hardly more than a de-Lutheranized definition of conscience. Correspondingly he renders διὰ τὴν συνείδησιν (also Rom 13:5) as 'aus der Verantwortung Gott und seinem

While the verb σύνοιδα and its cognates συνειδός and συνείδησις are in evidence from the fifth century BCE onwards,[115] the rise of the popular use both of συνείδησις and *conscientia* can be pinpointed in the first century BCE. This stamps the word as post-biblical. Indeed while first century Hellenistic Jewish authors like Philo and Josephus use the word, there is no direct equivalent in the Pentateuch and the prophetics books of the Hebrew Bible and their Greek translations. The word which comes closest is לבב/לב, 'heart'. In accordance with this usage, the Greek Hagiographa, Apocrypha and Pseudepigrapha use καρδία. However, the rare occurences of συνείδησις give us a clue. The word is used here twice in the moral sense: 'moral consciousness, conscience'.[116] But significantly, two other instances from the Septuagint, where we possess also the Hebrew parallels, do not fit in. In Eccl 10:20, 'Even in your thought do not curse the king', the Septuagint gives συνείδησις for מדע, a derivative of דעת 'to know'. And the version συνείδησις found in some manuscripts in Sir 42:18, 'The most High knows all consciousness' in the Hebrew, attested in the Masada fragments,[117] parallels the word דעת. Both wisdom sayings reflect the same general idea: hidden thoughts are known in Heaven.[118]

Here we are confronted with the interface between the Greek and Hebrew language spheres. While in biblical Hebrew the word דעת generally means 'knowing, knowledge', a later development tends toward 'discernment, under-standing'. There would seem to be a link with the wisdom tradition.[119] This development, of which the cited passage in Ben Sira is a somewhat later instance, resulted in a very wide expansion of the connotations of דעת in Rabbinic literature, involving such meanings as 'thought, reason, insight, con-sent, mentality, disposition'.[120] An apparently ancient Rabbinic tradition con-tains the expression, again related to the wisdom tradition but here referring to mystic knowledge, מבין מדעתו, 'he understands from his own insight'.[121] Another interesting example is the saying, found in the Babylonian Talmud,[122] which involves the admonition to 'direct one's heart לב towards heaven', but

Gebot gegenüber' (299); cf Bultmann, *Theologie*, 218. But the opposition διὰ τὴν ὀργὴν – διὰ τὴν συνείδησιν in Rom 13:5 suggests a less moralistic translation: '...one needs be subject, not only out of (fear for) the wrath (of the government carrying the sword out of God's mandate) but out of inner resolution'. Paul has something other in mind than the Lutheran teaching of two domains.

[115] For lexicographical data see Eckstein, *Begriff*. Coune, 'Problème', developing the thesis of Spicq, 'Conscience', stresses biblical דעת (אלוהים).

[116] Wis 17:11 and TestRub 4:3.

[117] Yadin, *Ben Sira Scroll*, 27.

[118] Cf Tg Eccl 10:20. A further development of this wisdom tradition is found in the teaching of Jesus, Luke 12:2-f; Matt 10:26f; cf Matt 6:4, 6, 18. A complex elaboration is 2Cor 4:2 (συνείδη-σις!). In the background may be the intriguing verse, Deut 29:28, cf TgPs-Yon.

[119] Job 34:35, 35:16, 36:12, 38:2, 42:3; Ps 139:6; all typical wisdom utterances. A different connota-tion, approaching דעת אלוהים, is found in the absolute דעת Isa 5:13; Ps 119:66.

[120] Safrai, 'Oral Tora', 88f. Eckstein, *Syneidesis*, 117-9, being dependent on Str-B, overlooks this connection; Coune, 'Problème' restricts himself to biblical Hebrew.

[121] mHag 2:1; cf Epstein, *Tannaitic Literature*, 46-52 on the tractate.

[122] bBer 17a; bSan 96a; bYom 42a; bShevu 15a; bMen 110a.

which in the Tannaic collections reads 'direct one's דעת towards Heaven'.[123] This illustrates strikingly the congruence of the older לב with the new דעת.

It does not seem correct to speak here of dependency one or the other way. Rather we seem to be faced with with a converging, synchronic development in Greek, Latin and Hebrew, in which formally equivalent words (דעת, συνεί-δησις, conscientia) came to embody a new anthropological concept denoting individual responsibility. On a broader level we may speak of a general cultural development in the Hellenistic world.[124] Further confirmation is found in the fact that other Hebrew equivalents exist, notably מחשבה (lit. 'thinking') and כונה (lit. 'direction'). The affinity of συνείδησις to Stoicism is important since, as we shall see especially in the next chapter, there is a level of open communication between the Cynic-Stoic tradition, Hellenistic Jewish thought and, most important, Hillelite Judaism.

But there is more. The cultural development just indicated received a specifically Jewish expression in the halakha. Not only the word דעת, but also מחשבה and כונה gained a specific significance in halakhic terminology.[125] This reflects a characteristic development of later Second Temple Judaism. The concept of individual responsibility came to constitute an important and independent factor in the evaluation of human actions. This implied that the halakhic quality of ceremonial acts and legal or economic transactions, as well as the halakhic status of objects involved, depended to a large extent on the conscious intention of the acting person. In this respect, significantly, there was a difference in emphasis between the schools of Shammai and Hillel. The basic attitude of the Hillelites was more rational and less conservative, and it was they who attached more importance to the factor of intention.[126]

One clear example of the importance of intention is the rule that in the case of 'deaf-mutes, imbeciles and minors', the halakha does not reckon their 'intention' מחשבה sufficient to determine the quality of the act or object; and this also excludes them from performing acts in which this is required. In other words, they have a limited responsibility.[127]

Most important for the present discussion is the inference that conscious intention is a decisive halakhic factor especially in the area of laws concerning idolatry. One example is the story about Rabban Gamliel who saw no problem

---

[123] mMen 13:11; Sifra Wayikra 9 (38b). Cf on the other hand mBer 5:1, שיכונו את לבם למקום.

[124] The development of an individualized personality concept in Judaism during the Hellenistic age is described by Bousset, *Religion*, 289-301. Another novel concept which embodied this anthropological change is תשובה (Safrai, 'Oral Tora', 108-111), which in the Greek form μετανοία plays a crucial role in the gospels. For other evidence see Flusser, 'New Sensitivity'; Safrai ib 88-100.

[125] There appear to be subtle nuances in emphasis. כונה seems to be specific to ceremonial settings, tending towards 'intentionality', while מחשבה may have a typically technical connotation in sacrificial and juridical contexts; דעת seems least specific. For a discussion of כונה and מחשבה see Urbach, *Ha-halakha*, 124, 130-8.

[126] Safrai, 'Halakha', 185-94.

[127] mKel 17:15; mToh 8:6; mMakhs 3:8. Cf mMakhs 3:1-3 which defines foods requiring not only הכשר, 'being made fit' (for impurity, by shedding liquid on them), but also מחשבה, conscious intention in doing so, and other combinations of both factors.

213

in visiting a bath house featuring a statue of Aphrodite, explaining himself with the rule, 'What is treated as a deity is prohibited, but what is not treated as a deity is permitted' (mAZ 3:4). As already noted in the previous chapter, he concluded from the apparent intended significance that the statue was not considered representative of the goddess but was a mere ornament. We met a similar rule in connection with the case also cited by Augustine: 'What appears to belong to (the idol) is forbidden, but what does not so appear is permitted' (mAZ 4:1). The importance of intention as a factor in the halakhot about idolatry can be easily understood. The Rabbinic view of idolatry is not so much concerned with material objects or actions as with the spiritual attitude with which these are approached by the gentiles. Correspondingly, the essence of idolatry is a ceremonial act of consecration, most typically expressed in slaughtering 'in the name of the deity'.[128] It is in this specific context that the word מחשבה is typically used.[129] We find it in R. Eliezer's rule about slaughter for a non-Jew: 'The unspecified intention סתם מחשבה of a gentile is towards idolatry' (mHul 2:7).

The problem was of course how one could tell whether a gentile's intention was towards idolatry or not. In the behavioural system of the halakha intention, either explicit or implicit, was read from significant details or circumstances. Three stones in a row could be taken as signifying an intention, but two could not. Grapes or corn ears made into an ornament signified a ceremonial intention, but coins, clothes or utensils might well have been left for other purposes and were considered unspecific. The same with things bought by a gentile. If he specifically wanted to buy a white cock, he was taken to have a ceremonial intention in mind, but if he wanted just any cock, it was indifferent and one may even sell him the white cock (above, p162). This difference was expressed in the rule: 'As for (the selling of) all other goods, if they were unspecified they are permitted, but if specified they are prohibited' (mAZ 1:5). In other words if the articles were unspecified, not singled out but sold in a larger quantity or at random, this yielded sufficient information that there was no intended sacrificial purpose. With the characteristic phrase of the Tosefta we have noted, he may sell 'without anxiety', ואינו חושש.

In view of the above, it is here formally proposed that the specific meaning of the term συνείδησις in these chapters of Paul is someone's 'consciousness' or 'intention', which is either directed toward idols or toward the Creator.[130] As we have seen, the connotation 'consciousness' existed in first century Greek and, *mutatis mutandis*, Hebrew and Latin. It seems that in the late fourth century CE a philological distinction was perceived by Chrysostom, for which reason he employed the more appropriate equivalents διανοία and προαίρεσις. In addition to the general usage of the Greco-Roman age, Paul's use of the word

---

[128] See the expression 'slaughter in the name of', 'for the sake of': tHul 2:18, השוחט לשום חמה לשום כוכבים... (cf mHul 2:8); כל הזבחים שנזבחו שלא לשמן, mZev 1:1; and see mZev chs 1-4.
[129] Above n125.
[130] Similarly but more theologically Coune, 'Problème', 529-32 proposes 'conviction réligieuse', viewing its background in biblical Hebrew usage and Christian soteriology.

214

here is informed by the connotation of individual responsibility specific of Jewish halakhic thinking. In particular, the halakhic significance of the term in 1Cor 8-10 concerns the conceptional intention with which food is being handled – either vis-à-vis pagan deities or the Creator.

Although the translation 'consciousness' applies in many other cases both in Paul and elsewhere, we have not yet found another instance of this specific halakhic application of the word. However it need not have been exclusive to our text here on principle. If Greek halakhic texts or traditions were in existence in written or oral form, as we have reason to suppose they were, there must have been cases where Greek equivalents of מחשבה, כונה or דעת were needed. Συνείδησις would have been a perfect term.

One could also think of γνῶσις, which is another equivalent of the Hebrew דעת. We have seen that Paul applies γνῶσις to those who were proud to have the insight that 'an idol is nothing, and there is no God but One' (1Cor 8:4). He does not use the word in a positive sense here: 'knowledge puffs up' (8:1), and 'by your knowledge the delicate is destroyed' (8:11). But in other contexts he does use it positively, in the sense of 'knowing' God or Christ.[131] Hence γνῶσις denotes religious or mystical knowledge, a category rather remote from human action which, as Paul indicates here, may even have a negative ethical effect. In contrast συνείδησις is directly associated with human action, both in the sense of 'conscience' or 'consciousness'. It would certainly be a good choice for the description of intention in human actions, certainly as long as the connotation 'conscience' stayed in the background.

Before applying this interpretation of συνείδησις to the passage under discussion, let us return to 1Cor 8:7-12 for a moment and see how well it fits in the relevant passages there.

> For some, being hitherto used to the idol, eat (what they eat) as idol food, and their consciousness which is delicate is being defiled. ...Take care lest your liberty become a stumbling block to the delicate: for suppose someone would see you, with your knowledge, reclining in an idol temple, would not his consciousness since he is delicate be edified towards eating idol food? ...Thus, sinning against your brethren and wounding their delicate consciousness, you sin against Christ.

We see now that the concept of halakhic intention discloses the very meaning of the first, essential sentence. The minds of the neophytes are still dominated by their awe of pagan deities. This is their 'delicate consciousness'; it comes to the fore during meals. In view of the close relation with 1Cor 10:23-29, where the practical aspect argument becomes more specific, it is likely that unspecified pagan food is involved here too. Thus when eating pagan food which they know may well have been consecrated to the gods, the 'delicate', whose consciousness is still dominated by idolatry, eat it ὡς εἰδωλόθυτον, 'as idol food'. (We shall later see Paul's views on the 'knowing', who have no such consciousness, eating

---

[131] 1Cor 1:5; 12:8; 13:2, 8; 14:6; similarly in 2Cor. It parallels דעת אלוהים, see above n119.

the same food.) To these delicate, and these alone, Paul is ready to apply R. Eliezer's principle: 'The unspecified intention of gentiles is towards idolatry.'

The consciousness of the delicate is 'defiled', i.e. it is not yet pure and directed towards the Creator.[132] By inconsiderate behaviour, the 'knowing' can 'edify' the 'delicate consciousness' towards idolatry, and 'wound' its relation to Christ.

Apparently Paul's argument in 1Cor 8 turns on the specific halakhic implication of συνείδησις. He even seems to utilize the delicate position of the new church members as an example in order to explain the essence of idolatry and its social dynamics, which is the real issue directly faced in 10:23-29. With these insights we now return to that passage.

HALAKHA ON PAGAN FOOD FOR GENTILES

The subject of 1Cor 10:23-29 is the dilemma of gentile Christians who buy food at the market where pagans abound, or have it offered as a guest at table with a pagan friend. Jewish dietary laws would not be the issue, since neither the halakha nor Paul considered these relevant for them. Their problem would be in the likelihood that somewhere along the line the food had been devoted to the gods. What should they do in this uncertain situation? Refrain from eating altogether? Inquire about the provenance of the food? Or was it all indifferent, as the cynicizing 'knowing' seemed to be thinking?

The last option, commonly thought to be Paul's basic opinion, is ruled out by the condition stated in v28: 'If someone says, "This is sanctified food," do not eat for his sake.' Since the issue is about idol food offerings, Paul's command not to eat implies that in this case he thinks the food represents idolatry. We can now understand that the reason is that the intention of all or some pagans present was apparently directed towards the idols. Eating with them would reinforce the position of idolatry on earth – and *de facto* renounce the belief that 'For us there is One God the Father' (8:6). It is now evident what interpretations ignoring the cruciality of the idolatry prohibition and stressing moral implications for 'conscience' have never been able to explain: 'Of συνείδησις I speak, not yours but the other one's' (v29). The pagan's intention towards idolatry prohibits the Christian's eating.

Nor should the continuation of the verse be taken in a moral sense, however much this is ingrained in exegetes' minds. It is prefectly possible and indeed enlightening to read: 'Why should my freedom be found guilty as a result of someone else's intention?' (1Cor 10:29b). Freedom, ἐλευθερία, here is not freedom from the Law, but from the power of idolatry; we saw that there is an affinity with the Cynic tradition.[133] In a paraphrase: my freedom, my attitude towards food which as far as I am concerned is uninhibited by the power of

---

[132] Cf Ps 24:4; below p256.

[133] Stanley Jones (above p194). Cf Willis, *Idol Meat*, 248, 98-104. The synonymity with ἐξουσία is clear from the common Hebrew equivalent, רשות; see above p147 n283.

idolatry, can be found guilty of idolatry as a result of someone else's behaviour. Eating what a pagan appears to consider an offering to his deity signifies cooperation in idolatry. The power of idolatry is not in the food, but in the pagan's mind.

But Paul also rejects the first and second options: inquiring about the nature of the food, not to mention total abstention. As Paul states, as long as no one raises the issue of idol offerings, 'you can eat anything ...without inquiring because of the intention' (v25, 27). Paul proposes a fourth option, which is based upon the apparent intention of those pagans present. He does not teach a partial permission to eat idol food. He teaches a rational, halakhic definition of what should be considered an idol offering in uncertain cases and what should not. Another review of the relevant halakha may help explain.

As we have seen, in the halakha about gentile idolatry the function or condition of the object can signify the intention of its owner. A statue damaged in the face or placed above the toilets in a bath house is evidently non-ceremonial; but grapes placed in front of an idol are seen as an offering. A single white cock bought by a gentile signifies idolatry, but not so if it is bought along with other cocks. We have seen the same phenomenon at work in relation to a gentile's apparent intention regarding meat. A Jew may derive income or other profit from this meat as long as it is still under way to a pagan temple, but when coming from a temple it is forbidden. Similarly, in the early Amoraic period a distinction is made between wine with certainty consecrated to idolatry and 'unspecified' gentile wine.[134]

Another condition which can signify the intention of an object, to which we have not yet referred, is sale. According to the Tannaim, by the sale the owner may signify that he no longer attaches ceremonial significance to the object: 'If a gentile sold an idol to worshipers, it is forbidden (to derive profit from), but if not to worshipers, it is allowed' (tAZ 5:5). Selling to a non-worshiper signifies the non-ceremonial intention of the seller: at the moment of selling, the object has a monetary, not a spiritual value. R. Yehuda the Prince wished to go even further and rule that selling in general signifies the non-sacral status of the object: 'If he sold it or gave it in pledge – Rabbi says, he made it invalid; but the Sages say: he has not made it invalid' (mAZ 4:5). This may be one of those individual leniencies for which R. Yehuda the Prince is known.[135] However according to leading Amoraim all agreed on the principle that sale to a non-worshiper such as a Jew, who would have the object defaced in order to be able to use it, effectively amounts to desecration.[136]

The evidence of these halakhot may not seem compelling in themselves. They come from at least a century after Paul. Furthermore they are about the sale of non-edible objects, whereas food was always a more complicated matter in this respect. Yet it appears that Paul must have known similar principles

---

134 Above p169 n104.
135 Above p169f. Cf his leniency on the Seventh Year, on which see Safrai, 'Sabbatical Year', part 2.
136 yAZ 4, 44a; bAZ 53a; see Urbach, 'Rabbinical Laws', 231 esp n70.

applying to food. We noted R. Akiva's halakha about meat (mAZ 2:3), in which the apparent intention of the gentile owners is decisive; it brings us back half a century at least. In fact, the idea that selling or giving away sacrifices indicates desecration is already found in a passage in the Epistle of Jeremiah. This pseudepigraphon dates back at least to the second century BCE and is entirely devoted to a sarcastic critique of idolatry. Among the indications that idols are nothing, the work lists the callous behaviour of their devotees, including the following: 'The things that are sacrificed to them, their priests sell and spend... knowing therefore by these things that they are no gods, fear them not.'[137] Moreover the idea that offerings are desecrated by giving or selling them to non-worshipers or non-initiated is universal. Not only is it found in biblical law (Exod 12:43-45; 29:33; Lev 22:10-15) but also in present-day pagan cults,[138] and even in the attitude of the Roman Catholic hierarchy toward communion for non-Catholics.

We can imagine that the pagan butcher who sold meat to a Christian at the Corinthian market could know he was selling to a 'non-worshiper' and thus be *de facto* desecrating the offering; moreover he apparently did not care either. It would be known that the Christian's religious sense was directed to the Creator and no longer considered pagan gods real. Certainly the Christian's friends would know, and given the fact that religion was prominent at all levels of society this would hardly remain a secret. Non-participation in pagan ritual would immediately be noted at the numerous festive occasions or banquets. Meat sold to such a person at the market could quietly be considered desecrated.

No inquiring was even needed, Paul teaches. This can be understood better when compared with the halakhic terminology used in relation with sale to gentiles. Goods of specified intention פירושן, i.e. which by quality or condition are evidently meant for idolatry, are forbidden. But if unspecified סתמן, i.e. not in this sort of quality or condition, they are permitted and one may sell 'without anxiety'; and there is no need to inquire. Even if there are idolatrous intentions, they were not openly uttered and did not represent the power of idolatry. 'But if (the pagan) specified, even water and salt are forbidden' (tAZ 1:21).

Even more characteristically the same terminology is used in the principle R. Eliezer advanced against slaughter for a non-Jew: 'The unspecified intention סתם מחשבה of a gentile is towards idolatry' (mHul 2:7). The question here is, when is slaughter for a gentile for the sake of idolatry? As we saw (above p214), the essence of idolatry is expressed in slaughtering 'in the name' of some deity, or in other words with intention towards it. Unless the opposite is explicitly specified, R. Eliezer assumes a gentile's intention to be directed towards

[137] Ep Jer 28f. On dating see G.W.E. Nickelsburg in *Compendia* II/2, 148; Schürer, *History* 3/2, 744. For the genre see above p157.
[138] The Rev. H.J. Visch tells me that for Balinese Hindus selling sacrificial food is a major sacrilege indicative of a complete lack of devotion.

idolatry. But the other Sages held a more moderate view on a gentile's implicit intention. The same opinion is shared by Paul: there are gentiles of whom one knows that they do not worship idols.

According to the latter opinion, in questions of 'implicit intention' it was unnecessary 'to inquire further' and have the gentile make his intention explicit. This means that Paul's μηδὲν ἀνακρίνοντες, 'without questioning', is not un-Jewish at all, but on the contrary reflects the humane, rational Rabbinic attitude towards idolatry we have come to know.

Thus Paul does not consider food to be actually consecrated to idols when sold without specification to a Christian at the market or when offered to him in a private pagan home. The reality of idolatry is not in food, but in people's minds. Paul teaches the Corinthians who apparently had problems with this that the circumstances indicate the pagan's mind.

As we have seen a similar interpretation is advanced by Chrysostom, Ambrosiaster and, apparently, some other Church Fathers.[139]

This conclusion has important implications, some of which must be made explicit here.

The Sages who opposed R. Eliezer's opinion that the implicit intention of a gentile is towards idolatry were more than likely of Beit Hillel, the school which showed more lenience towards gentiles. During the last decades of the Second Temple period, however, the Shammaites represented by R. Eliezer were in the majority. It was they, or at least a majority of them, who enforced the Decree of Eighteen Things and probably they who started the war against Rome. In the second place, R. Yehuda the Prince's opinion that selling in general signifies desecration of an idolatrous object was not accepted by a majority even at the beginning of the third century. We may cautiously conclude that Paul may well have faced fundamental opposition, not only from certain Pharisaic quarters but also from within the Apostolic Church. It is quite likely that other Jewish Christians were not as lenient about the pagans' unspecified intention. The next chapter will show us how. On the other hand, it seems quite likely that some at least of the Hillelite Sages would have been able to share Paul's reasoning about gentiles and pagan food.

It follows – and this is a second implication – that the question of idol food was not at all a test case for Paul. Consumption by gentiles of known idol food offerings was out of the question for him. Discussion was about gentile food of unspecified nature. In this there may have been a difference of opinion with other Apostles, which may well be reflected in Gal 2:11-14. Likewise one does not get the impression that the idol food issue was a test case in the early church. What is certain is that it has been a test case for historical criticsim, in other words for the adequacy of the ideas and methods with which Paul's letters are

---

[139] Chrysostom, Hom in I. ad Cor cap 25 (MPG 61, 159ff); Ambrosiaster (Comm in Cor, ad 8:13, 10:23, 25, 29; Migne PL 17, 249-51; cf Böckenhoff, *Speisegesetz*, 93). Apparently also Novatian, De cib judaic 7 (Böckenhoff ib 69) and Minucius Felix, Octavius ch 38 (Böckenhoff ib 49).

approached. The above interpretation once again confirms our hypothesis that the traditional asssumptions on Paul and the Law are inadequate. The Law does have practical significance for Paul, the polemic on its validity is by no means central to his thought, and the ancient halakha is invaluable for studying his practical instruction.

A final, quite surprising conclusion is that 1Cor 10:25-28, far from being Paul's unprincipled compromise with paganism, can well be seen as being another instance of halakha formulated in Greek. More examples of this extinct literary genre were found in 1Cor 7:39, the halakha about the remarriage of widows, and 1Cor 14:16, where halakhic terminology is used in connection with community benedictions. We also noted evidence for such 'Greek halakha' in other sources (above p143f). A little while ago we pointed out that the clear, practical language of 1Cor 10:25-28 differs from the preceding verses which have an air of suave wisdom. Similarly from v29 onwards the language is expositional and adhortative rather than exact and prescriptive. In short what we have here is a halakhic fragment, formulated in Greek and regarding gentile believers in the Creator:

> All that is sold in the marketplace you can eat without inquiring about intention; "For the earth is Lord's and its fullness". If one of the unbelieving calls you and you want to go, all that you are offered you can eat without inquiring about intention. But if someone says, "This is sacrificial food", do not eat for his sake.[140]

Speculation about possible authorship leads us no further than to Paul himself. As documented in Gal 2:1-14, not only did Paul consider the practical question of the food of gentile Christians to be under his jurisdiction, but he took a clear stand against the other Apostles. Furthermore Paul is writing here as an authorized Apostle to the church he founded, and in the preceding section he has cited more practical rules based on his own authority (1Cor 7:8, 12, 25, 40). Finally as we have seen the issue must have been discussed with the Corinthians on several earlier occasions, certainly the main principle, and here Paul formulates specific rules for borderline cases.

It would be enticing, though beyond the limits of this chapter, to speculate further about where this 'Hellenistic halakhist' received his education. Jerusalem might not be a bad guess.

---

[140] In this connection the words, '...him who warned you, and the intention', lacking in P46 (above n82), clearly appear superfluous. But this is not important to our argument. Moreover it may be that Paul himself added them in order to make his intention clear.

Chapter Six

Table Fellowship of Jews and Gentiles

Table fellowship of Jews and gentiles must have been an important issue in early diaspora Christianity. It features prominently in two Pauline letters, Romans and Galatians. These are also the letters in which 'justification by faith' plays an important role. This can hardly be incidental, but the question is what this means for the precise relationship between these two elements. As indicated in chapter 2, we shall study the practical issues and their halakhic background on their own merits. And incidentally, it may well be that the subtleties of Paul's theology of the Law are better understood from his practical position on food and table manners than the reverse.

Dietary laws have many functions in Judaism, a fact which may not be clear to the average reader of Paul. They have a fundamental significance both in religious and social sense. From the point of view of structural anthropology this is self-evident: dietary customs and table manners embody the specific human or 'rational' value system of any given culture.[1] The application of this anthropological approach to Jewish religion would seem obvious:[2] the halakha is a system of consciously guided practical conduct, in which all human acts and functions have a specific significance. In connecting values and beliefs to the basic acts of daily subsistence, dietary laws structure religious experience, inform ethical conduct and define corporate and individual identity. In terms of the normative framework of Jewish tradition their significance is governed by the central concept of קדושה sanctification, i.e. ritual or behavioural distinction of objects and persons for the sake of a specific ceremonial function.[3] Sanctification implies that a person or object is consciously distinguished and imbued with value and significance. The main operational concepts in the sphere of food are 'clean' and 'unclean'. Intention, or in other words consciousness of the implied significance, is an essential ingredient of sanctification.[4] It is an elementary concept in Judaism that it matters what you eat.

---

[1] See the work of Claude Lévi-Strauss, especially the 'Mythologiques' with such titles as *Le Cru et le cuit* (1964), *Du Miel aux cendres* (1967) and *L'Origine des manières de table* (1968).
[2] For the merits of an anthropological approach on Judaism including the halakha see Goldberg, *Judaism*, 1-43.
[3] For a description from this perspective, though not touching on dietary laws: Kadushin, *Worship and Ethics*, esp last chapter.
[4] Kadushin ib 219f. On intention see above ch5.

It is hard to imagine how Paul could have been 'indifferent' to Jewish dietary laws as such, as many suppose. He would either have had to reject them and Judaism with them, or accept them as a central fact in the life of his 'brothers according to the flesh'. In the first case Paul would then indeed have been the person who severed Christianity from Judaism; in the second he would have had to construct some joint Jewish-gentile modus vivendi within the church. The second is the more likely, and we shall see that indeed there is reason to speak of 'indifference' of dietary laws, but in a very specific sense.

Nor should the importance of table fellowship be underestimated. Eating together is a basic expression of social belonging rooted in earliest childhood experience. Conversely the highest sanction a religious movement can implement is excommunication i.e. exclusion from social contact; the ban pronounced on R. Eliezer by his colleagues may be cited as a proverbial example.[5] Excommunication specifically implies exclusion from table fellowship, as Paul explains in 1Cor 5:11, 'Now I write you not to associate with someone, even if he is called a brother, who is a debaucher, greedy, an idolater... and therefore[6] not to eat with such a one.' In antiquity the significance of table fellowship was even greater in that the etiquette of offering and accepting hospitality was full of significance; its violation was the proverbial sin of Sodom and Gomorra.[7] Hence the integration or segregation of Jews and gentiles within the church would to a large extent be decided by the degree to which they had common meals. It would have been a vital issue not only at the eucharist but at any meal during which blessings would be said – in other words at all communal meals.

Jewish-gentile table fellowship figures in Gal 2:11-14 and Rom 14:1-15:13. Let us begin with the passage in Galatians, outlining the halakhic situation it presupposes. We will try to elucidate it by studying halakhic sources on Jewish-gentile table fellowship. We will then go on to describe Paul's practical teaching on common meals of Jews and gentiles in Rom 14. We will also pay attention to the theological and philosophical motifs involved. Finally we will consider the liturgical implications of Rom 15:7-13.

The Antioch Incident (Gal 2:11-14)

But when Cephas came to Antioch I opposed him to his face, because he stood condemned. For before certain men came from James,[8] he ate with

---

[5] bBM 59b. See Safrai, 'Halakha', 194-200 for its background.

[6] RSV and other modern translations translate μηδὲ with 'even', although eating together obviously goes a great deal further than just talking. Cf Bauer, *Wörterbuch* s.v.

[7] Two random examples: hospitality towards apostles and their accepting or rejecting it (Matt 10:11-15 and parallels, mentioning Sodom and Gomorra!); the embarassment of R. Yannai when he offered hospitality to a well-dressed person who appeared to be uncultured but nevertheless saintly (LevR 9,3; p176-8).

[8] P46, three old Latin mss and Irenaeus: τινα ἀπὸ 'Ιακώβου, 'a man from James'. David Flusser drew my attention to this variant (see also his 'Paul's Anti-Jewish Opponents'); it must be weighed together with the evidence of the next n. Without this consideration Betz p107 rejects it.

the gentiles; but when they came[9] he drew back and separated himself, fearing those of the circumcision. And the other Jews joined him in this pretense, so that even Barnabas was carried away by their play-acting.[10] But when I saw that they did not walk straight in the truth of the gospel, I said to Cephas before them all: If you, being a Jew, live in a gentile [and not a Jewish][11] way, how can you compel the gentiles to judaize? (Gal 2:11-14)

Paul's account of the public confrontation which occurred between Peter and himself in the Antioch church has a shocking directness which has been occupying exegetes through the centuries. This is a blatant contradiction to the harmonious relation between both Apostles presented in Acts. Understandably, the Antioch incident became the Archimedean point for historical criticism of Paul and especially for BAUR and his theory of the opposition between Petrine and Pauline Christianity.[12] Traditional exegesis, which viewed the canon of Scripture as reflecting unitary, infallible truth, was unable to imagine a serious difference of opinion between two of the foremost Apostles and was forced to explain the Antioch incident in other ways. Franz OVERBECK wrote a biting essay on the efforts at harmonization of the Church Fathers: *Über die Auffassung des Streits des Paulus mit Petrus in Antiochien ... bei den Kirchenvätern* (1877). He pursues the aims of historical criticism but appears to be motivated among other things by a preference for the interpretation of Galatians by Augustine and especially Luther.

The brief but penetrating discussion of the context of Gal 2:11-14 at the start of Overbeck's analysis (6f) is enlightening. Paul cites the Antiochene incident as the last in a series of 'autobiographical' events which must be looked at in the context of the letter as a whole. His 'rhetorical' interest (the term is not used by Overbeck)[13] does not oblige Paul to give a full account. What he wants to prove is his independent authority as an Apostle. For Overbeck the point is that any theories about what Peter might have thought or said – the Church Fathers' refuge in explaining the conflict away – remains pure guesswork.

Unlike the Church Fathers, non-orthodox outsiders did perceive a fundamental divergence in Apostolic opinion. In the first place Marcion, the 'ultra-Paulinist', concluded that the other Apostles had corrupted the original law-free gospel. Secondly, at the other end of the spectrum, the anti-Pauline Jewish

---

[9] ἦλθεν P46, Sinai, B, D*, F, G, 33, b – an 'impressive attestation' according to Bruce p130, who nevertheless prefers the generally accepted ἦλθον of A, C, D² and many others.

[10] With Bruce p131, avoiding the pejorative moral sense of modern 'hypocrisy'. The moral note is again introduced by... Augustine, see below!

[11] καὶ οὐχὶ ᾽Ιουδαϊκῶς is uncertain, see below.

[12] See above p10 n44. Cf Lüdemann, *Paulus*, 13-23. This work of grand design is disappointing as to our problem: the importance of halakha for Jewish Christianity is not noticed (54f) and information on it is minimal (p65 n28: Str-B 4/1, 374ff; see below!). By contrast see Dunn, 'Incident'.

[13] For rhetorical analysis of Galatians see Betz, *Galatians*; Smit, *Opbouw*. Ironically Overbeck, who elsewhere rejected comparison of Paul with Greek rhetoric (Betz p14 n100), in headlines arrived at the same analysis.

223

Christians of the Clementine Homilies stressed the injustice Paul did to their main Apostle, Peter. In the third place pagan contenders of Christianity such as Porphyry did not leave this opportunity to prove its incoherence unused.[14]

The hermeneutic principle of Patristic exegesis was unity and its method harmonization, notably between Paul and Acts. Their explanation was therefore that of Apostolic accomodation. This is especially seen among the Eastern Fathers such as Origen[15] and Chrysostom.[16] They developed the idea of a tacit strategy agreed on between Paul and Peter, to the effect that Paul would publicly reproach Peter while the latter would keep silent, in order to win the Antioch Jewish Christians over to the 'truth of the gospel'. This idea was introduced in the West by Jerome,[17] where it was vigorously opposed by Augustine. Siding with Paul and condemning Peter for his fear of the Jewish Christians, Augustine was, according to Overbeck, the Church Father who came closest to understanding Gal 2.

Augustine also grasped the underlying problem: 'How could the Old Testament Law in its literal sense be suspended without encroaching upon the pre-Christian reverence for it which Christianity adopted along with the Old Testament itself?'[18] Augustine's solution is in a 'historization' of the abolition of the Law: although fundamentally the Law deserved respect it had become superfluous with the advent of Christ's gospel. Since then 'works of the Law' have become indifferent and could be performed *sine ulla salutatis necessitate*, as the Apostle demonstrated in Acts and stated in 1Cor 7:18-20 and Gal 6:15.[19] Peter's fault was not that he followed Jewish custom as such,[20] but his 'hypocrisy', the result of fear for the Jewish brethren, which in turn encouraged gentile judaizing. But his silent humility toward Paul was a model of Christian conduct and here Augustine too managed to maintain Apostolic harmony.[21]

Meanwhile Overbeck also notes other Patristic opinions. The fourth century Latin Father Victorinus is mentioned who, viewing Gal 2:11-14 as the climax of a 'rhetorical autobiography' proposed to prove Paul's Apostolic independence,

[14] Overbeck p8, referring to Marcion *apud* Tertullian, Adv Marc (1:20; 4:3; 5:3); Clem Hom 17:19; Porphyry *apud* Jerome, Ep 112 ad August 11 and Comm ad Gal, praefatio 1.

[15] Overbeck 19-24, referring mainly to Contra Cels 2:1-2 and Comm in Matt on Matt 15:2 where Origen demonstrated the nullity of the Jewish Law after Christ.

[16] Overbeck 29-36, mainly referring to Comm in Gal and Hom in Gal. For Chrysostom it was evident that the apostles, while living according to Judaism in Jerusalem, upon arrival in Antioch abandoned this observance and 'lived indiscriminately (ἀδιαφόρως ἔζων) with the believing gentiles'. In Peter's opinion this was also Jesus' attitude: ὅτι καὶ αὐτὸς Ἰουδαῖος ὢν ἐθνικῶς ζῇ (Gal 2:14, see below! – Hom in Gal 2:4 and 2:14).

[17] Comm in Gal 1:2. In order to appease the Jewish Christians Peter momentarily transgressed the apostolic *evangelium libertatis*; Paul would basically agree but opposed him *secundum faciem* i.e. in outward appearence' (for κατὰ πρόσωπον!).

[18] Overbeck 50; Augustine's fundamental position was outlined in his anti-Manichean treatise Contra Faustum; it was elaborated in his letter no. 82 to Jerome and in De mendacio ch 8.

[19] Overbeck 51f, although rejecting (p59) Augustine's interpretation of 1Cor 7:18-20 and Gal 6:15 as a harmonization!

[20] Cf the expression, *tunc fuit adprobanda nunc detestanda* (Ep 82).

[21] Overbeck 57.

and saw as Paul's real opponents James and his representatives. However according to Overbeck, Victorinus submerged this correct viewpoint under a layer of harmonization by stressing the Apostolic agreement in Gal 2:1-10.[22]

The position of the earlier Fathers, which Overbeck terms 'naive' and 'antique', is remarkable. The Greek solution of Apostolic accommodation was unknown not only to Western Fathers prior to Jerome, but also to late second century Apologetes such as Justin and Irenaeus. Polemicizing against Marcion, Irenaeus 'naively' emphasized the faithfulness of the Apostles to the Old Testament Law as revealed by the same God. Peter's conduct in Gal 2:11 was no different to that reported of Paul in Acts. The same view is found in Justin and Acts. Irenaeus and Justin read Paul from the point of view of Acts and completely ignored his position in Gal 2:14 – as in fact they do his whole 'gospel'.[23] Similarly Tertullian 'naively' blamed Paul for making a point about life style, incorrectly and from inexperience, while the Apostolic agreement (Gal 2) was about the gospel; moreover Paul advocated the same flexibility in life style in 1Cor 9:22.[24]

Let us sum up Overbeck's study. With Augustine's promising start and Luther's successful continuation, the Protestant view of the centrality of the Law polemic is clearly Overbeck's hermeneutical key. In addition to being preoccupied with the Patristic harmonization of the canon, this leads him to underestimate the 'naive' position of the Apologetes. Their tradition of the Apostles' own faithfulness towards the Law while leaving the gentiles free offers a highly important option as to the interpretion of Gal 2:11-14. In the same way Victorinus' emphasis on the radicality of James' attitude and the tension with Gal 2:1-10 is remarkable. Overbeck's view on Augustine is enlightening. Augustine grasped the fundamental problem: how should the Church view the Jewish Law, when considering the Old Testament as being holy scripture? Our question is: how close was Augustine to Paul when explaining that after Christ the commandments could in principle be observed 'without any necessity in view of salvation'?

Turning now to Paul, let us first look at the context of the incident narrative. As Overbeck noted, it concludes a series of events from Paul's own life which forms the introduction of the letter. It argues that Paul's gospel has been authentic from the start and needs no 'other gospel' (Gal 1:6-12). His 'preceding life in Judaism', presumably in Jerusalem, was one of 'violent persecution of the church of God' and 'excessive zeal for the ancestral traditions' (1:13f). An 'apocalypse of (God's) son' singled him out 'to preach him among the gentiles'; he did not confer about this calling with the Jerusalem Apostles (15-17). Only three years later did he spend two weeks in Jerusalem with Peter, and for the rest only ever saw James (18-14). Another fourteen years later there was an important meeting in Jerusalem where Paul's 'gospel to the gentiles' was

---

[22] Overbeck 40-43; Victorinus, In Gal. See below.
[23] Overbeck 8-10, referring to Irenaeus, Adv haer 3:12-15; Justin, Dial 47.
[24] Overbeck 10f, referring to Tertullian, Adv Marc 5:3 and In Gal 2:2.

discussed; the outcome was a full endorsement of his authority by James, Peter and John (2:1-10). Then the Antioch incident occured, at which Paul saw his gospel endangered and publicly stood up to Peter and the 'men of James' (2:11-14). It is immediately followed by a brief sermon which states that even Jews 'are saved not by works of the Law but by faith in Christ' (2:15-21). The sermon sets the stage for the main argument of the letter: 'If justification were through the Law, then Christ died in vain' (2:21b). The argument of Galatians is against forced circumcision of gentile Christians.

It follows that Gal 2:11-14 cannot possibly be taken as an impassive historical report. It would seem that SMIT is correct in concluding that the incident narrative should be read together with the 'sermon', 2:15-21.[25] This means that both passages are equally designed for Galatian readers. One gets the impression that people had come to Galatia from Jerusalem, preaching salvation in Christ through circumcision, and that this is what makes the narrative about the Antioch incident so violent. At any rate it is not possible to see the Antioch incident as isolated from the Galatian conflict.

This only underlines the seriousness of the Apostolic conflict concerning the attitude towards gentiles.[26] The historical question is about the precise relationship between the Antioch incident and the Galatian struggle. A fundamental consideration is that the conflict undermines the argument of the Apostolic agreement in Gal 2:1-10. If Paul wanted to demonstrate his authority vis-à-vis Jerusalem, he would have been better off with the endorsement of James and Peter. The Antiochian conflict makes his position more vulnerable, which adds to its historical value. In the second place we have ancient testimonies about Apostolic conflict in Antioch. A remote Jewish-Christian tradition about Apostles sent from Jerusalem to Antioch appears to be contained in a tenth century Arabic manuscript.[27] Furthermore the ancient witnesses cited by Overbeck all saw a real conflict in Antioch: Marcion, Porphyry, the Clementine Homilies and the Church Father Victorinus. It therefore seems quite likely that whatever the exaggeration caused by rhetorical expedience, Gal 2:11-14 reflects a historical event. Paul had a confrontation with Peter about table fellowship with the gentile brethren in Antioch triggered by representatives of James. While Peter was caught in the middle, along with Barnabas and the other Jewish Christians in Antioch, the real clash was between Paul and the men of James.

[25] Smit, *Opbouw*, 53f. Betz p62 thinks Gal 2:11-14 concludes the *narratio*.

[26] For a theory of the historico-political setting both of the conflict at Antioch and the (south-) Galatian trouble connected with Antioch see Dunn, 'Incident', 4-11; cf Jewett, 'Agitators'. I add the observation that political factors can never fully explain religious attitudes but only the circumstances in which they attain to expression; cf remarks on the Decree of 18 Things (ch 4), which incidentally may also relate to this. The religious motivation explored further below is at least as important.

[27] Abd al-Jabbar, Tathbit etc., fol 70a, in Pines, 'Jewish Christians', 261f; cf 245 n24. The report seems to derive from some Jewish-Christian version of Acts and tells of Apostles instructing gentile Christians to observe Jewish commandments such as the sabbath and circumcision (cf Acts 15f!). The references to subsequent Apostolic measures suggest an amalgamation of various sources (Acts, Paul, and unknown Jewish-Christian documents).

Let us now consider what the Apostolic conflict in Antioch may have been about.[28] In Paul's judgment it evidently violated the Apostolic agreement mentioned earlier. Hence we must first look at the report about the Jerusalem meeting, Gal 2:1-10. Like the Antioch incident, it cannot be viewed separately from its rhetorical function in Galatians. However Paul's report of a fundamental agreement with James and Peter does not lack historical support. Our study of First Corinthians showed that Paul accepted the Apostolic tradition as authoritative, even when it contradicted the halakhic tradition of his Pharisaic past. This implies that he respected the Apostolic authority of James and Peter, even if this did not exclude his right to disagree on certain issues. We also noted (above p88f) that Paul in Gal 5:3 adduced a proselyting halakha in defense of his Law-free gospel for gentiles; in this halakha he would have been in full agreement with the other Apostles. Furthermore the 'division of labour' between Paul's mission to gentiles and that to Jews entrusted to other Apostles is reflected in the fact that Paul's letters all seem to be addressed to 'churches of the gentiles' (above chapter 2). In this light Paul sounds historically trustworthy when writing:[29]

> When they saw that I had been entrusted with the gospel of the foreskin, just as Peter with that of the circumcision... and when they perceived the grace that was given to me, James and Cephas and John... gave to me and Barnabas the right hand of fellowship, that we be for the gentiles and they for the circumcision; only that we should remember the poor, which very thing I was eager to do. (Gal 2:7-10)

The agreement involved mutual trust and respect: neither party would interfere with the commission of the other. Paul could expect the others not to intervene in his 'Law-free gospel' for gentiles, just as James and Peter could count on his non-involvement with their Law-abiding gospel to Jews. This conclusion is utterly important: Paul implies here that his 'Law-free gospel' for Galatian gentiles was founded on his respect for Law-observance by Jewish Christians.[30]

All would be well as long as two separate domains remained. Problems might arise where they overlapped, or in other words where Jews and gentiles were living and eating together, as at Antioch. Thus the question was: can Jews and gentiles eat together without endangering either the Law-observance of the former or the freedom from the Law of the latter? James' representatives apparently thought they could not, but Paul and Barnabas, as well as the other Antioch Jews and Peter, thought they could. According to Gal 2:11-13 the majority of Jews of Antioch, as Peter and Barnabas and also Paul, thought it possible for Jews and gentiles to eat together without transgressing the Jewish Law. This conclusion agrees with what Overbeck termed the 'naive' conception of the Christian Apologetes and, for that matter, with Acts: the Jewish Apostles

---

[28] Cf for the following and the next section esp Dunn, 'Incident', 12-24.

[29] Significantly Paul's earliest letter, 1Thess 2:16a, mentions as Paul's task, in view of current obstruction by Jews in Judea, τοῖς ἔθνεσιν λαλῆσαι ἵνα σωθῶσιν.

[30] Cf Gaston, *Paul*, 107-115 on Paul's basically positive relationship with the Jerusalem church as expressed in Gal 2:1-10.

227

naturally kept the Jewish Law. As far as James and Peter are concerned this is generally accepted, but here it is also implied for Paul. This is another far-reaching conclusion from Galatians: when Paul ate with gentiles at Antioch, he would not be violating the Law in the eyes of the majority of Jews there.

Our next question is: what was it at table that endangered the Law in the eyes of James' emissaries, though not of Paul and most of the other Jews? This is obviously a halakhic question and it must be studied in close comparison with Jewish literature. But we will first turn to some of the more prominent Christian opinions. Chrysostom,[31] representing the *consensus ecclesiae* followed variously by modern scholars,[32] thought that the Jewish Law had become null and void with the coming of Christ and that the expression Paul addressed to Peter, ἐθνικῶς ζῆς, implies that both had done away with Jewish food laws. This interpretation does not do justice to the context since it ignores the report on the Jerusalem conference. If Paul really would have violated the food laws and induced others to do so in the presence of Barnabas, Peter and the Antioch Jews, he would have made the agreement null and void and his own apostolate impossible. But not only does this classical interpretation not respect the integrity of Paul's letter to the Galatians. It also portrays Paul as the Apostle who indeed severed Christianity from Judaism and hence excommunicated Jewish followers of Jesus. Chrysostom was conscious of this. As he wrote elsewhere, abrogating the food laws amounts to an abrogation of Judaism itself.[33] Modern commentators may be less familiar with Jewish Law than Chrysostom, but that is no excuse for not reading Paul according to his own intentions.

More moderately, other modern commentaries propose violation of purity laws.[34] The difference between purity and dietary laws will be discussed in the next section; here one decisive observation will suffice. Jewish purity rules could not possibly be kept outside the Land of Israel because of the impurity decreed on 'gentile lands' by the Sages.[35] The decree is traditionally ascribed to Yosef ben Yoezer of Tsereida and Yose ben Yohanan of Jerusalem, early

[31] Above n16.
[32] Traditionally Acts 10f is referred to in support of the hypothesis that the biblical food laws were void for Peter and Paul. See Lightfoot p112 (rather inexact). Burton p104, 130 hesitates. Lagrange p42 does not suppose food laws to have been violated, but Pharisaic purity laws. Betz p31, 107f inaccurately supposes *both* 'purity requirements' and 'Jewish dietary and purity laws'. Smit follows Sanders, *Paul, the Law* in supposing that Paul abrogates Jewish laws standing in the way of Jewish-gentile communication. More adequate to the halakhic questions is Dunn, 'Incident'.
[33] Hom in Matt 51:2-4, MPG 58, 512-5.
[34] See above n32. So especially Dunn, 'Incident', 14-16. The passages he refers to do not prove that purity rules were in force in the diaspora: Arist 305f and OrSib 3:592f explicitly refer to ablutions before prayer, which though related are not strictly a matter of purity; Josephus AgAp 2:198 mentions purity as a prerequisite for sacrifices, which implies Jerusalem; ib 203 refers to biblical marriage laws (as is known the laws of *nidda* are still held even though purity does not exist any more).
[35] Alon, 'The Levitical Uncleanness of Gentiles' and 'The Bounds of the Laws of Levitical Cleanness', in id, *Jews, Judaism*, 146-89, 190-234. The expression 'Jews outside the Land serve idols in purity' (see below p233) is merely rhetorical.

second century BCE.[36] As a result any Jew coming from abroad had to perform the seven day purification ritual before he could participate in sacrifices and other ceremonies requiring purity.[37] In short, while food laws could hardly have been the issue, purity rules were simply out of the question. The danger James' representatives perceived in eating together with gentile Christians at Antioch must apparently have had some other cause.[38]

But before passing to this halakhic question we must further study the meaning and function of the expression highlighted by Chrysostom: ἐθνικῶς ζῆς. It is in the beginning of Paul's words addressed to Peter: 'If you, being a Jew, live in a gentile [and not a Jewish] way, how can you compel the gentiles to judaize?' (Gal 2:14). As to text, the words 'and not in a Jewish way' are doubtful. They are absent altogether in the ancient papyrus, P46, in the Latin Fathers Ambrosiaster and Victorinus, and a few other versions.[39] In the Beza manuscript and the Byzantine majority the words follow somewhat clumsily in the rear: ἐθνικῶς ζῆς καὶ οὐχὶ [οὐκ] Ἰουδαϊκῶς. The great uncials are more sophisticated: ἐθνικῶς καὶ οὐχὶ [οὐκ] Ἰουδαϊκῶς ζῆς.[40] As to contents, the words καὶ οὐχὶ [οὐκ] Ἰουδαϊκῶς are tautological. But they present no logical difficulty and it is hard to imagine why they should have been dropped. It is logical that they were inserted after ἐθνικῶς ζῆς as a gloss. Thus the better version is the shorter one of P46 and the Latin Fathers; that of ms Beza and the Byzantine majority would be the poorly glossed text; and the uncials would represent the better edited and more 'official' text. Finally the shorter version is clear and coherent and even displays a chiastic symmetry: 'If you, being a Jew, live in a gentile way, how can you compel the gentiles to judaize?'

Thus understood the meaning of the sentence must be taken from its wording and context. As observed above, Gal 2:11-14 must be read together with the ensuing 'sermon'; or in other words v14b is the beginning of the sermon. Furthermore the passage as a whole is addressed to the Galatian Christians who do not know whether to accept circumcision or not. One aspect which certainly reflects this constellation is the recurrence of the key terminology: Ἰουδαῖος and ἔθνη in v14-15. The expressions ἰουδαΐζειν and ἐθνικῶς ζῆν (v14) are unique in the New Testament. They recall the word Ἰουδαϊσμός which in the whole of the New Testament occurs only twice in Gal 1:13f and there, at the beginning of the narrative exposition, underlines Paul's own former life in 'Judaism'. Ἰουδαϊσμός signifies the way of life according to the 'Law of the Jews';[41] correspondingly ἰουδαΐζειν means 'to live as a Jew', to adopt a

---

[36] See above ch4 n12.
[37] Num 19; an example seems to be found in Acts 21:26f. See Safrai, *Wallfahrt*, 142-4.
[38] Dunn, 'Incident', 15f also suggests tithing. Although formally restricted to the Land the commandment of tithing was also observed elsewhere. But it need not have been a problem since unlike defiled food, untithed food could be corrected (cf מתוקן, mDem 3:1) on the spot and made fit for consumption.
[39] 1881 pc a b d. Betz, *Galatians*, 112 n493 terms the words 'textually uncertain'.
[40] Sinai, A, B, C, F, G, H, P, Athos; plus a number of minuscles.
[41] See Amir, 'Ioudaïsmos'; and comment by Tomson, 'Names', 134 n53.

Jewish life style,[42] as opposed to ἐθνικῶς ζῆν.[43] This terminological complex reflects the central concern of the letter: the pressure exerted on Galatian gentiles to become Jewish proselytes.

These considerations further deminish the likeliness of Chrysostom's interpretation of the phrase ἐθνικῶς ζῆς as 'you, Peter, live like a gentile' i.e. without Jewish dietary laws.[44] The whole sentence is charged with rhetoric and functions as a power centre of Paul's argument against forced circumcision in Galatia. It does not describe Peter's diet but the liberal attitude towards the gentile brethren in which he used to be at one with Paul, vis-à-vis Antioch but more so Galatia. At this point the representatives of James disagreed, and Paul seems to rhetorically adopt their speech, 'live like a gentile'. The sentence may then be paraphrased: 'Before, you agreed to live and eat as a Jew together with the gentiles, and although some call that "living like a gentile", why do you now separate and wish to eat with them only if they become Jews?' This interpretation concurs with our analysis of Paul's report on the Jerusalem agreement: the agreement was based on mutual trust in view of Paul's Law-free gospel to the gentiles and Peter's Law-abiding one for the Jews. The conclusion is that here Paul does not urge Peter to join him again in a non-Jewish way of life. On the contrary: he urges for a Jewish life which does not force gentiles to judaize, in line with the agreement.

While the rhetoric has become clear, the halakhic problem at table in Antioch has not. We shall now turn to this issue.

Meals with Gentiles in Tannaic Halakha

The incident related in Galatians was apparently caused by the attitude of 'the men of James' towards eating with gentiles, an attitude more extreme than that of most Jews at Antioch, including Peter. Two halakhic questions emerge: (1) what degrees of Jewish-gentile table fellowship were possible according to the halakha, both in Palestine and the diaspora? (2) do the Jewish sources help understand the over-sensitivity of James' emissaries?

As to the first question, the suggestion offered by the *Kommentar* of STRACK-BILLERBECK is that the halakha made table fellowship of Jews and gentiles practically impossible. Excursus no. 15 on 'The Attitude of the Ancient Synagogue towards the Non-Jewish World' has a section on 'The Attitude of the Observant Jew towards Social Intercourse with Non-Jews', which in the main text states: 'Social intercourse of observant Jews with non-Jews was practically impossible... Only reluctantly, one would enter a non-Jewish house; and a Jew would feel even more uncomfortable when having a Goy in his own home. Hence table fellowship of Jews and Goyim was hardly possible, whether the Israelite was host or guest.'[45] There follows in fine print the usual accumulation

---

[42] See Dunn, 'Incident', 25-7.
[43] ἐθνικῶς ζῆν paralleling ἰουδαΐζειν indicates that there was no such expression as ἐθνίζειν; this is additional evidence against the reading καὶ οὐκ Ἰουδαϊκῶς ζῆς in v14b.
[44] Similarly Dunn, 'Incident', 28-30.
[45] Str-B 4/1, 374.

of Rabbinic and other traditions. However a number of those very halakhot and narratives cannot be reconciled with the opening statement. And curiously, the end of the same paragraph in the main text contradicts its highly negative start.[46]

In a more recent study titled *The Attitude towards the Non-Jew in Halakha and Reality in the Period of the Tannaim*, Yehezkel COHEN devotes a section to 'Hospitality in Jewish and Gentile Homes'.[47] Stressing, like Strack-Billerbeck,[48] the many restrictions and negative concepts which burdened Jewish-gentile relations both in the sphere of halakha and aggada, Cohen points to the remarkable fact that no halakhot actually prohibited mutual hospitality between Jews and non-Jews. Quite the reverse, there are convincing indications that in spite of the restrictions in the halakhic areas of idolatry, food and purity, marriage and sexual relations, Jews did not refrain from table fellowship with gentiles either in gentile homes or their own, and were even proud of their hospitality.[49]

Let us review some of the relevant sources. A mishna quoted also by Strack-Billerbeck reads:[50]

> If [an Israelite] was eating with [a gentile] at a table, and, leaving in his presence a flagon[51] [of wine] on the table and another flagon on the side-table[52], left him and went out – what is on the table is forbidden, but what is on the side-table is permitted (mAZ 5:5).

This halakha, which in view of its context seems to echo a possible situation in actual life, presupposes that it was perfectly possible to dine and have wine together with a gentile, even in the Jew's home.[53] The problem lay with the gentile's custom of pouring some of the wine to his deities and thereby consecrating the whole jar, thus spoiling it for the Jew. As long as the Jew is present he can make sure no libation is made. The gentile guest would not take wine from the side-table but would wait for his host to serve him.[54] The wine itself would have been 'Jewish' wine, i.e. prepared and treated according to the halakha. Similarly the food would be permitted for the Jew. These precautions having been taken, there appears to have been no reason for not having a drink with the gentile.

As observed in chapter 4 above, Tannaic halakha found a realistic modus

---

[46] This is one example of contradiction between the ideological framework of the work and the material it cites.

[47] Cohen, *Ha-yahas*, 291-7

[48] The prominence given to the hard line minority view (p291f!) reflects an anti-apologetic interest. Ironically, the approach Cohen opposes is itself a reaction against Christian presentations such as Str-B!

[49] Cohen 294-6.

[50] Str-B ib 378; reference is further made to mBer 7:1 which also presupposes joint dining by Jews and gentiles.

[51] לגין = λάγυνος, *lag[o]ena*.

[52] דלפיקי, δελφικὴ, Delphian (table).

[53] Sensitive to the implications for traditional Christian ideas Elmslie, *Idolatry*, 81 infers 'from this Mishna that these common meals must frequently have occurred.'

[54] Thus Albeck ad loc. The same principle goes for Jewish wine entrusted to gentiles: if the jars were stopped up and sealed or locked away, there was no impediment; mAZ 5:3-4; tAZ 7:7, 8, 12-14.

vivendi with gentile idolatry. Objects have no intrinsic idolatrous quality. As long as they were the object of adoration, contact with and profit from them was forbidden. But if the gentile did not treat them as representing the sphere of the deity, there was no danger. The same attitude seems to have been possible when dining with non-Jews. We have seen that in this area there were additional complicating factors: there were the dietary laws founded on the distinction between clean and unclean animals, slaughtering prescriptions and the prohibited combination of meat and milk; and inside the Land of Israel there were the purity laws. The dietary laws were easy to deal with: one could simply serve Jewish food or at least refrain from serving food forbidden to Jews. The requirement of purity was more complicated, both because of the uncertain status of the requirement and of the degree of impurity of the foods. But apparently it was no absolute barrier.

Cohen adduces several aggadic statements in which leading Tannaim display a tolerant view towards gentiles. In a tradition preserved in several places in Tannaic literature R. Yoshua and R. Tsadok extol universal love of mankind as practised by Abraham and by the Shekhina herself.[55] Since the narrative concerns two prominent Sages present in a gathering of 'all the great ones of the generation [of Yavne]', their opinion appears to represent the majority. It may be noted that the tradition emanates from the generation following the violent episode of the Shammaite anti-gentile decree of 18 articles (above p175). Furthermore, several additional halakhot refer to a situation of hospitality being offered to gentiles in Jewish homes.[56] Conversely several narratives report prominent Tannaic Sages attending non-Jewish parties.

In one tradition R. Meir is reported as saying:[57]

> A certain gentile living in our town arranged a banquet for all the town's dignitaries, inviting me too, and offered us of all that the Hole One, blessed be He, made on the six days of creation; nothing was lacking from his table but crack-nuts. What did he do? He took the beautiful table before him, worth six talents of silver, and smashed it. ...I applied the verse to him, "[The righteous has enough to satisfy his appetite, but] the belly of the wicked suffers want" (Prov 13:25).

Noticing the Sage's ironical self-restraint, we learn that R. Meir saw no problem in enjoying the gentile's hospitality. Certainly he would not try and taste everything created 'on the six days of creation'. The implication is apparently also that the libation ritual undoubtedly performed by his gentile host would not affect the Jewish wine he would be drinking.[58] Taking those considerations into account, R. Meir tells of his visit to a gentile banquet as if it were something normal.

[55] Mekh Amalek p195f; Mekh RSbY p131; SifD 38 (p74f).
[56] From tYT 2:6; Mekh RSbY p21; bBeitsa 21a-b Cohen, *Ha-yahas*, 294f concludes that it was acceptable to receive gentiles on non-festival days.
[57] PesRK 6 (p115); YalShim Prov no. 950. For more versions see Cohen p296. More stories are told of R. Meir (RuthR 2,14: in Gadara in the Peraea, i.e. Jewish territory?) and of R. Shimon ben Yohai and R. Hiya (EstR 2,4: both possibly near Tyre).
[58] This is to be inferred from the contrary instruction of his radical pupil R. Shimon ben Elazar, tAZ 4:6; see below.

A complicated halakhic question concerns the role the impurity decreed on gentiles as emanating from their idolatry played in this situation. R. Meir was not lax in the field of purity, on the contrary.[59] It could be that the story belongs to the time he was exiled from the Land of Israel, which was the only place where the purity laws applied.[60] But another story seems to refer to a visit he paid to a non-Jewish home in Gadara in the Peraea, i.e. within one of the three Jewish lands.[61] In any case, to the extent that from his perspective the observance of ritual purity was obligatory on principle, R. Meir was apparently willing temporarily to reliquish observance of that commandment for the sake of good relations. In the wider context of the mishna just quoted (mAZ chs 4-5) the possibility of defilement of Jewish wine and other foods is directly connected with a gentile's presence, and specific distinctions and precautions are given. The stories about R. Meir tell us that Jews and gentiles could find ways to get around halakhic difficulties and have good relations.

These considerations lead towards an answer to our first question. From aggadic traditions involving leading Tannaim such as R. Yoshua (second half of first century) and R. Meir (mid second century), as well as a number of explicit Tannaic halakhot, it appears to have been quite possible to enjoy table fellowship with gentiles, either in Jewish or gentile homes. While in diaspora locations this was simpler, given the ineffectiveness of purity rules, it was apparently also possible in the Land of Israel. Even in the case of meals where halakhic prescriptions were more complicated, the danger of cooperation with idolatry could be handled rationally. Thus we can quite well imagine a Jew like Peter dining at Antioch with his gentile brothers and sisters. We may add Paul and Barnabas, and in fact the majority of Antioch Jewish Christians, realizing that this was apparently the prevailing view in Tannaic Judaism. The reports about close co-existence of Jews and gentiles at Antioch (above p2f) justify the assumption that joint meals were no exception and went hand in hand with Jewish and gentile life.

However the Tannaim were not unanimous in this matter. An outspokenly negative view on table fellowship with gentiles is attributed to R. Meir's outstanding pupil, R. Shimon ben Elazar.[62]

> R. Shimon ben Elazar says: Israelites outside the land worship idols in purity. How? If a non-Jew prepared a wedding feast for his son and sent out to invite all Jews in his town – even if they have food and drink of their own and have their own servant waiting at them, they worship idols.[63] Thus it is said: "[...Lest you make a covenant... when they sacrifice to their gods and] when one invites you, you eat of his sacrifice" (Exod 34:15).[64]

[59] tToh 1:4; ib 1:6 (cf yHag 2, 78b; bHul 33b). And see below.
[60] See sources in Margalioth, *Encyclopedia* s.v. Meir. On purity outside the Land see above p228f.
[61] See above p155.
[62] On their relation see Safrai, 'Holy Congregation', 72-6.
[63] bAZ and ARN have the characteristic expression, אכלו מזבחי מתים; see below n68.
[64] tAZ 4:6; ARN a 26 (41b); bAZ 8a. See Cohen, *Ha-yahas*, 295 for text-critical remarks.

First of all, in posing a diaspora situation the narrative indicates that the problem was not with purity rules as such.[65] Furthermore the opinion is characteristic of R. Shimon ben Elazar since another tradition cites him as saying that a person caused exile to befall on his children 'if he ate with gentiles at table'.[66] This view on dining with gentiles strikingly contrasts with the attitude attributed to his teacher, R. Meir. It is even more curious that both Sages are known for their emphasis on piety and purity. In fact R. Shimon ben Elazar is mentioned in some connection with a specific group of pupils of R. Meir, who seem to have put their teacher's principles to practice in the form of a pious association living in Jerusalem at the end of the second century CE.[67] Thus R. Meir and R. Shimon ben Elazar seem to represent two divergent views on relations with gentiles within the same pious tradition.

Now a very similar tradition is quoted anonymously in Seder Eliahu Rabba: 'One should observe in his heart not to eat with a gentile at table... Thus they taught: anyone who eats with a gentile at table, worships idols and eats sacrifices to the dead.'[68] This work represents a specific brand of Rabbinic literature, basically rooted in Tannaic tradition and closely related to the 'early hasidim'; it emphasizes purity of heart and pious deeds.[69] The parallel with R. Meir's pious pupils is attractive, a major difference being that an emphasis on ritual purity, appraised by R. Shimon ben Elazar, was not typical of the early hasidim.[70] Remarkably, Seder Eliahu elsewhere contains the universalistic view that 'either gentile or Israelite' can count on God's grace without distinction.[71] Both passages clearly reflect the editor's touch, and they present us again with two possible options within one tradition.

It seems that if a direct relation between the pious tradition of Seder Eliahu and the circle of R. Shimon ben Elazar cannot be established, we now face a more general phenomenon. The special piety displayed by both circles could apparently express itself in two opposite attitudes to gentiles. On the side of R. Shimon ben Elazar and R. Meir, the duality is enhanced even further if we consider a teaching of the latter very similar in outlook to the universalistic tradition in Seder Eliahu Rabba. The Babylonian Talmud attributes R. Meir with the remarkable view that 'even a gentile who engages in Tora is like the high priest'.[72] Hence it seems that there was an ambivalent relationship between

---

[65] In consequence he uses the word 'purity' metaphorically.
[66] bSan 104a. Cf his outspoken stance on gentiles mAZ 4:11; tAZ 7:8, 13; 1:3; cf tAZ 6:18.
[67] Safrai, 'Holy Congregation'.
[68] SER 9 [8] p46-48; quoted in BerRabbati p206. On the last expression see above p157.
[69] See Safrai, 'Teaching of Pietists'; id 'Hasidim', esp p140, 149-51.
[70] tShab 1:14; yShab 1, 3b; see Safrai, 'Teaching of Pietists'.
[71] SER [6]7 (p36), cf also ib p34. This section is also quoted LevR 2,9 (p48, 51; see note Margulies ib p46). There is an important connection here with Paul; see below p273.
[72] bBK 38a; bSan 59a; bAZ 3a; thus also YalShim Lev no. 484 (p560); the contrast with R. Yohanan's saying immediately preceding is striking. In Sifra, Aharei (ed Weiss, 86b; not in ed princ) the attribution is to R. Jeremia. The attribution to R. Meir is supported by the consideration towards gentiles expressed in his version of the berakha, 'Blessed... who has made me an Israelite' (bMen 43b), as opposed to R. Yehuda's version '...who has not made me a gentile' (tBer 7:18; yBer 9, 13b).

piety and the attitude towards gentiles. R. Meir's piety resulted in a liberal attitude, as also reflected in the universalistic saying in Seder Eliahu. In view of the halakhic and aggadic traditions cited above, this more liberal attitude appears to have been dominant, certainly among later Tannaim.[73] The denunciation of table fellowship with gentiles of R. Shimon ben Elazar and the anonymous tradition in Seder Eliahu must have been a minority view.

The above necessitates some historical elucidation. R. Meir's positive attitude towards gentiles, while expressed in a specifically pious mood, coincides with that of R. Yoshua cited above. We have come to know this Hillelite through his positive view on gentiles, as opposed to the fundamentally negative view expressed by his Shammaite colleague, R. Eliezer. These two Sages were protagonists in the reports about the episode of the 'Decree of Eighteen Things' at the beginning of the great war against Rome (above p175). Here a basic difference in outlook between Shammaites and Hillelites came to light. Once more the Hillelite tradition appears to display more openness towards the outside world than that of the Shammaites. Inasmuch as the latter can also be characterized as the more conservative and rigid, we may suppose that this was an ancient, rather exclusivist world view. This connects with the general denunciation of social relations with gentiles in Jubilees and Essene literature (above p153f). These texts may be contrasted with ancient works such as Ben Sira or First Maccabees, works that are identifiable as thoroughly Jewish yet are open toward the outside world. Writings such as Aristeas or Second Maccabees, which display an openness typical of diaspora situations, may be ignored here for the sake of clarity. If we add that Seder Eliahu, while containing a basically Tannaic tradition, in extant form dates from the late fifth century at the earliest,[74] we have a range of data stretching over at least eight centuries.

It appears that ancient Judaism had a bi-polar reference system vis-à-vis its surroundings, one side being the prophetic calling of Israel, God's chosen people, and the other, the co-existence of Jews with other ethnic entities in the Persian and Greco-Roman world.[75] In certain socio-religious circles or in specific historical situations, or in a combination of both, either might gain ascendance over the other. Following the analysis of ALON (above p167f), the very conception of the impurity of gentiles and its vicissitudes in the development of the halakha serves to demonstrate this oscillating dynamic. The outbreak of the Roman war generated a polarization between both viewpoints, the Shammaites generally emphasizing the 'nationalist' side. It is worth noting that the Hillelite majority now emerging from the defeat may have been another factor in the process towards mitigation in this halakhic area.[76] In any case, both attitudes

---

[73] Thus the conclusion of Cohen, *Ha-yahas*, 296. But on the next page the author prefers to conclude the chapter with another adhortation against fellowship with gentiles from SER.

[74] See discussion in Strack-Stemberger, *Einleitung*, 306.

[75] Cf Tomson, 'Names', 123-9, 277-9 for similar observations on the basis of the function of the names 'Jew' and 'Israel'.

[76] The new Hillelite majority may also have influenced the development of purity rules, see Tomson, 'Zavim'.

toward fellowship with gentiles visible in late Tannaic pious circles can be seen as an authentic outgrowth of the bi-polar sense of Jewish identity.

We are now able to answer our second question and try to explain the 'Jacobine' side of the apostolic conflict in mid-first century Antioch. It appears that the traditions of R. Shimon ben Elazar offer us an illuminating parallel to the motivation of the men of James.[77] Even with such precautions as the majority of Jews thought effective in preventing cooperation with idolatry, R. Shimon pronounces a diaspora Jew dining with gentiles guilty of idolatry. His motivation appears to have been excessive fear of idolatry. Similarly, James' emissaries probably could not perceive the gentile Christians as being free from the sphere of idolatry. Unlike Peter and Barnabas, who were uncertain when it came to a crisis, Paul stood up for 'the truth of the gospel' (Gal 2:14). This is usually taken as a purely theological statement, but we can now understand that it had a halakhic basis. It was in the Tannaic tradition supported by most Sages in post-Temple times, and apparently already shared by the majority of Jews of first century Antioch.[78]

Pluriformity in Diet (Rom 14:1-15:13)

In a previous chapter we described Rom 14:1-15:13 as distinct from the remainder of Romans in that the passage is about a practical problem. While the letter as a whole deals with the relations of Jews and gentiles from a theological point of view – with occasional references to practical commandments or problems serving to underline the theological argument – these chapters address a problem which had to do with their relation in actual practice. The significance of this fact both for the interpretation of Romans and its place among Paul's letters has long been recognized. However the conclusions drawn were not based on a satisfactory analysis of the underlying halakhic problems.

Again it was BAUR who pioneered the approach of historical criticism.[79] In his view Rom 1-8 is only the theoretical introduction to the main issue, which is dealt with in Rom 9-11 and, on the practical level, in Rom 14-15. This position has been reiterated recently in more radical form by Francis WATSON, *Paul, Judaism and the Gentiles*. Updating Baur's analysis into what he calls 'a sociological approach', Watson views Rom 1-11 as a theoretical legitimization for the social re-orientation required of Christians in Rom 14:1-15:1. This is what Romans is about: 'The social reality which underlies Paul's discussions of Judaism and the law is his creation of Gentile Christian communities in sharp separation from the Jewish community. His theological reflection legitimates the separation of church from synagogue. ...Faith in Christ is incompatible with works of the law because the church is separate from the synagogue. ...The

---

[77] This possibility became clear to me long ago in conversation with Shmuel Safrai.

[78] Subsequent comparison of Paul and Acts in view of the halakhic basis could yield enhanced insight in this complex situation; see Conclusion below.

[79] See above p95.

Jewish Christians should realize that their future lies not with their fellow-Jews but with the Gentiles whom God has called.'[80] With these words Watson takes a stance which in effect is identical with that of Ignatius of Antioch.[81] The abandonment of the traditional Protestant view of justification as the heart of Paul has here resulted in the re-adoption of the Patristic hypothesis that Paul's main concern is the practical annulment of the Jewish Law. A somewhat similar return to Patristic views is proposed by another critic of traditional Protestant Paulinism, E.P. SANDERS. In his view Rom 14f signifies the fundamental indifference of Jewish dietary laws, and hence their abrogation, which underlies Paul's idea of the church as a 'third race'.[82]

Alternatively, we propose to adopt the approach of Krister STENDAHL, *Paul among Jews and Gentiles*.[83] As did Baur, Stendahl starts with the assumption that the actual issue in Romans was the conflict between Jews and gentiles within the church and that chs 9-11 are the climax of the letter. But rather than wishing to obliterate the differences between Jews and gentiles caused by the Law, Paul intended to reckon with them. This interpretation relates to what Albert SCHWEITZER called Paul's *status quo* theory, a solution also adopted by W.D. DAVIES: as long as we stay in the flesh the Law remains in force. In other words, we revert to our hypothesis that for Paul, as for other Jews, the Law was and remained valid for Jews, and in another way also for gentiles. Such, we have seen, was his position in First Corinthians and Galatians; such we may expect it to be in Romans too.

Our first duty is to outline the flow of the argument. 14:1 sets the scene for the whole section: 'Welcome him who is weak in faith, not for disputes over opinions.' The ensuing argument comes in three subsections, 14:2-12, 14:13-23 and 15:1-13, which introduce the details of the conflict and the conciliatory perceptions of the Apostle step by step.

14:2 gives a first statement of the conflict: 'One believes he may eat everything, but another is weak and eats (only) vegetables.' The next two verses plead for tolerance and mutual acceptance in view of this difference. v5 introduces another difference in similar wording: 'One distinguishes a certain day above the other, but another distinguishes every day.' But this seems to be a side issue, for the argument immediately returns to food and eating (v6b) which is also the main topic further on in the chapter. Again conciliatory language follows, this time more elaborate and extending to the conviction that 'none of us lives for himself or dies for himself' but '...whether we live or whether we die, we are the Lord's' – Christ's, who died and was risen (v7-9). The first subsection ends with the view that 'we shall all stand before the judgment seat of God', which is supported by a quotation from Isa 45:23 and summarized with the rule that 'each of us shall give account of himself to God' (v10-12).

[80]   ib 19, 47, 164.
[81]   See above p2 n11.
[82]   *Paul, The Law*, 100-105; 171-9. Sanders (p171 n1) is conscious of the definitely post-Pauline genesis of the term as showed by Harnack.
[83]   Watson consciously differs from Stendahl, see ib p20.

14:13 opens the second subsection by taking up the view that 'we should no longer pass judgment on one another' and adding another adhortation: 'not to put a stumbling block in the way of a brother or a hindrance'. The conflict now appears to be about food which some consider 'unclean' (v14). This sensitivity should be respected: although for the others this food is clean they should not by eating it 'cause the ruin of one for whom Christ died' (v15). After some more conciliatory words this adhortation is repeated in v20: 'everything indeed is clean, but it is bad for anyone who eats by way of a stumbling block.'[84] In order to prevent this the others should, if need be, '...not eat meat, drink wine, or anything by which your brother stumbles' (v21). The subsection ends by returning to the theme of 'judging': each one should act 'out of faith' and be convinced for himself (v22f). This is the link with the first subsection (judging, v10-12; faith, v1) and it provides the unity of the chapter.

The third subsection (15:1-13) appears to make the point in the wider context of the letter. The connection with the previous subsections is created by the expressions 'weaknesses of the powerless' (ἀσθενήματα τῶν ἀδυνάτων, 15:1) and 'welcome one another' (προσλαμβάνεσθε ἀλλήλους, 15:7); both revert to the introduction, 'Welcome him who is weak in faith' (τὸν δὲ ἀσθενοῦντα τῇ πίστει προσλαμβάνεσθε, 14:1). The theme is amplified here: 'We who are powerful ought to bear with the weaknesses of the powerless, and not please ourselves (ἑαυτοῖς); let each of us please his neighbour (πλησίον) ...' (15:1f). This appears to be an allusion to the commandment quoted as the summary of the Law in ch 13: 'You shall love your neighbour as yourself (τὸν πλησίον ὡς σεαυτόν)', (13:9). Indeed in this connection the whole of 13:8-14 appears to be an introduction to our passage. On this view 13:8 announces a new theme, 'To no one be anything indebted (ὀφείλετε) except to love one another (ἀλλήλους),' which in the ensuing section is gradually developed: 'Welcome him who is weak in faith (14:1)... If your brother is injured by food, you are no longer walking in love (14:15) ...We are indebted (ὀφείλομεν) ...not to please ourselves (15:1); ...therefore welcome one another (ἀλλήλους)' (15:7).

At this stage the partners in conflict appear to be those of 'the circumcision' and 'the gentiles' (15:8f) or in other words Jews and non-Jews. Paul's appeal is that they '...may seek unity among one another in the manner of (κατὰ) Christ Jesus, so that you may like-minded and with one mouth glorify the God and Father of our Lord Jesus Christ' (v5f). Christ welcomed both Jews and gentiles (v7) and both should praise the one God in unison, and this lofty vision is supported by Scripture quotations (v9-12). This idea concurs with the stated theme of the letter: the one gospel addressed 'to the Jew first and also to the Greek' (1:16); it also corresponds to the central position of chs 9-11, on Israel's continuing role in salvation history, and the elaboration on Abraham, the father of believers both gentile and circumcised, in chapter 4. Paul's moving

---

[84] RSV translates, 'make others fall by what he eats', but it is also possible to relate the προσκόμμα to the one who eats.

238

expression of concern for his 'kinsmen after the flesh' (9:3) gives a special ring to the repeated appeal, 'Welcome one another' (15:7; cf 14:1, 3). The appeal is to 'the powerful' (15:1) or in other words the gentiles.

Thus Paul pleads for pluralism: a united church in which Jews and gentiles lovingly accept each other, acknowledging differences about food and other matters. This implies the willingness of the 'powerful' to abstain from diets and other things which would present a 'stumbling block' for the 'weak'.

Next we must establish what the conflict was about. Rom 14:2 states that the weak eat only vegetables; 14:21 mentions meat and adds wine to the list of problematic articles. 14:5 mentions 'days' as a side issue; meanwhile this confirms the impression that Jewish sensitivities were at stake. The basic question then is: why do 'the weak' refrain from eating meat and have problems with wine? Explanations range from vegetarianism and asceticism to Jewish food or purity laws. Let us consider the possibilities against the background of the halakha.

Abstention from meat and wine might have a range of motives in ancient Judaism, as in other religious contexts. Philo reports that zeal for frugality induced the Therapeutes to abstain from meat and wine,[85] and the same goes for leaders of true character;[86] a connection with Hellenistic traditions seems implied here.[87] More specifically such abstinence might express spiritual concentration when mourning[88] or preparing for a divine revelation.[89] The tendency of Pharisaic-Rabbinic Sages to curb asceticism and vows of abstention apparently reflect to a marked disposition towards such pious behaviour in Second Temple Judaism.[90] This being so, abstention from meat and wine by a Second Temple Jew would nevertheless have signified exceptional behaviour when compared with his fellow Jews.[91] It would have influenced his relations with gentiles in a significant way.[92].

This was not the situation which Paul appears to have confronted. Although echoes of Hellenistic asceticism or Jewish vows of abstinence cannot formally be excluded, there are no indications that these were specific to the situation. On the other hand we took Rom 15:8f and 14:5 to indicate that Jewish as distinct from gentile custom was involved; this, we also pointed out, reflects the purpose of the letter as a whole which is to plead for one gospel both for Jew and

---

[85] Vit cont 73f.

[86] De prov 70; Spec leg 2:20.

[87] See note Colson, *Philo* 9, 159 (neo-Platonism). On the Greek background of Philo's attitude towards luxury and pleasure see Heinemann, *Bildung*, 431-46.

[88] Asc Isa 2:11; TJud 15:4; tSot 15:11 (פרושים, 'those who abstain').

[89] Dan 10:3; 4Ezra 9:24f.

[90] See Albeck, introduction to tractate Nazir, *Mishna* 3, 189-91. And cf R. Yoshua's response tSot 15:11.

[91] Abstention from wine and any grape products was one of the three characteristics of the *nazir*, see Num 6; mNaz 6:1f.

[92] Apart from grape products and the cutting of his hair a *nazir* need only avoid corpse impurity; Num 6:6f; mNaz 6:1; cf mNaz 1:2 and Albeck, *Mishna* 3, 195f, 371. See also the tradition of R. Natan, below p253.

Greek. Hence it is only by isolating 14:1f from 14:1-15:13 and from the letter as a whole that one can identify those who eat only vegetables in 14:2 as Pythagorean ascetes.[93] In contrast to this opinion, pioneered by Clement of Alexandria, the basic answer of the majority of Church Fathers appears best to interpret the evidence:[94] Jewish sensitivities relating to food and purity were the issue here.

This subject obviously requires more detailed study. There are decisive differences between food and purity laws which many exegetes ignore. The inherent 'uncleanness' of forbidden meats differs in character from the transferable ritual impurity emanating from a corpse, a leprous body or bodily excretion. Although the Tora uses the word טמא, 'unclean' i.e. 'ritually unfit', for both categories, it does seem to make an implicit distinction.[95] In post-biblical times the respective laws developed into two completely separate halakhic sub-systems.[96] Food laws, which consisted of the laws concerning forbidden meats (Lev 11; Deut 14), slaughtering (cf Lev 17:10-16) and 'meat and milk' (cf Exod 23:19), remained static for a long time and were accepted as basic.[97] In contrast the laws of Levitical purity (Lev 11 and 14f; Num 19) expanded greatly and were the subject of continuous controversy. *Toharot* or 'Purities' not only became the largest order of the Mishna but shows the traces of a continuous development throughout the Tannaic period.[98] Jesus' debate on the washing of hands illustrates the ongoing discussion in the earlier period.[99]

As a result of the failure to distinguish between purity and food laws many commentators confuse the situation referred to in Rom 14f with that in the synoptic debate on ritual purity. In particular Paul's statement, 'I know and am persuaded *in the Lord Jesus* that nothing is unclean in itself' (Rom 14:14), is associated with Jesus' saying that 'nothing which enters the mouth renders a

---

[93] Thus Barrett, *Romans*, 257.

[94] See discussion by Lagrange, *Romains*, 335-9.

[95] While Lev 11 deals with both categories at once, the one passage where contact impurity seems to derive from a living 'unclean' animal is v26, כל הנוגע בהם יטמא. But it is most natural to read this as the continuation of v25 where (as in v8, 11, 24, 27, 28, 31 and 32) 'their carcass' is meant. This is also the interpretation of the LXX (πᾶς ὁ ἁπτόμενος τῶν θνησιμαίων αὐτῶν) and Sifra shemini 52c: „במותם„ תלמוד לומר ? יכול בחייהם [v31]). See also Maimonides, Hilkhot avot ha-tuma 2:1; Ibn Ezra and Rashi on Lev 11:26. Moreover in contrast with Lev 11, Deut 14:3-21 mentions contact impurity just once (v8), which seems to reflect the development towards a conscious distinction.

[96] Significantly CD 12:11f forbids eating unclean animals with the expression אל ישקץ איש נפשו, 'one should not abominate his soul', i.e. the actual purity of the body is not involved.

[97] The principles of שחיטה are relatively independent of the Bible (Albeck, *Mishna* 5, 109-111) and do not seem to have involved fundamental controversy. The Essene requirements regarding forbidden meats and שחיטה for fish (CD 12:11-13) indicate a secondary extrapolation of established principles (cf mHul 3:6f; cf Ginzberg, *Jewish Sect*, 117, 126). The detailed development of בשר בחלב seems late; see mHul ch 8 and the Gemara.

[98] While Neusner's theory of an almost completely post-70 development is exaggerated (see Tomson, 'Zavim') the large proportion of later Tannaic innovations, both in form and content, is undeniable.

[99] For other examples see mEd 5:6; mZav 5:12 and related texts.

person unclean' (Matt 15:11; Mark 7:15).[100] However the halakhic implication of the terms 'clean' and 'unclean' is not unequivocal. Both in biblical and Rabbinic usage טהור and טמא refer to such contexts as levitical purity, food, and family and marriage relations. This is not to deny the possibility of any relation between Paul and Jesus on this subject. Granted the halakhic difference, there might still be a connection on the theological level. Actual traditions of 'the Lord' do play a role in Paul, and this may be suggested by his reference to 'the Lord Jesus'. We will return to this possibility in the next section, but first let us elaborate on the halakhic distinction.

When studied on its own terms the synoptic dispute narrative (Mark 7:1-23; Matt 15:1-20) appears not to be about dietary laws but about purity. Apparently the disciples did not wash their hands for a regular meal – obviously a matter of ritual purity. The Pharisees see this as an encroachment upon 'the tradition of the elders'. This is a technical term, not for a biblical commandment, as a reference to the food laws would require, but for a tradition of the Sages.[101] For Jesus this tradition, as the one regarding fictional vows, is secondary to a biblical commandment such as the duty to honour one's father and mother (Mark 7:10-13; Matt 15:3-5). Indeed the washing of hands is evidently a post-biblical innovation identified as such in Pharisaic-Rabbinic tradition.[102] Finally the saying which concludes Jesus' argument has to do with impurity contracted by eating impure food: 'Not what goes into the mouth defiles a man, but what comes out of the mouth, this defiles a man' (Matt 15:11). While the deeper message of the saying is that moral transgression overrules ritual failure,[103] it is obviously based on the halakhic opinion that impure food does not render a person to be impure. This reflects a more conservative opinion in early Tannaic discussions about derivative impurity.[104]

Nonetheless the view that the synoptic debate is about biblical food laws appears to have ancient antecedents. It is based on the secondary clause Mark 7:19b which is interpreted to mean: 'Thus he declared all foods clean'.[105] However the impression that this interpretation is supported by the major manuscripts[106] should be seen in the light of the fact that it is historically unimaginable that Jesus would have infringed upon the biblical food laws. His point is precisely that 'the commandments of men' are secondary to what is written in the Tora. This militates against the Pharisaic custom to wash one's

---

[100] The statement is presented as one of Paul's Jesus quotations by Dodd, 'Ennomos', 106; Davies, *Paul*, 138.

[101] See above p145 on the expression.

[102] See mHag 2:5; tDem 2:11 (Lieberman ad loc.); mZav 5:12; mYad 3:2 מדברי סופרים; yShab 1, 3d (baraita Shammai and Hillel); yHag 2, 78b מדבריהם. This subject is covered in my MA thesis, *Netilat yadayim li-seuda*.

[103] Luke 12:38-41, also about a Pharisaic purity law (mKel ch 25), has a similar jump from ritual to moral purity (cf Matt 23:25f).

[104] mZav 5:12 decrees a person eating impure food impure; mYad 3:2 reckons this among 'the words of the Scribes'. On the date see Tomson, 'Zavim'.

[105] Thus RSV and all modern translations I know.

[106] καθαρίζων πάντα τὰ βρώματα.

241

hands rather than against the biblical food laws. It is also possible,[107] and historically more plausible, to read the clause as a grammatically awkward apposition to the digestion process or to the privy 'cleaning all foods'. This interpretation was proposed by KLAUSNER,[108] who also pointed out that this is supported by its close similarity to another exposition relating to the natural functions which is preserved in Rabbinic literature. Significantly, a heretic called Yaakov from Sikhnin is quoted as ascribing it to 'Yeshua son of Panteri' or 'Jesus the Nazarene'.[109]

On the other hand purity laws proper are out of the question in Rom 14:1-15:13. In Rome as in Antioch, Jews could not maintain ritual purity because of the decree of impurity on gentile lands (above p228f). Indeed the details in our passage point towards food. 14:2 and 21 mention abstention from meat and wine. Moreover the vocabulary also points to food as the subject: 'eating' appears thirteen times (v2-6, 20-23) and 'food' four (v15, 17, 20). The latter word occurs in a passage on basic laws pertaining to food which also involves the terms 'clean/unclean'. Finally as pointed out in connection with 1Cor 8 (p194f) the verb 'being weak' (ἀσθενέω, Rom 14:1f; 15:1)[110] has the connotation of delicacy in dietary matters.

The relation to 1Cor 8-10 extends to other details too: in both passages Paul urges his readers not to pursue their own interests but to care for the 'weaker brother', so that it may be better 'not to eat meat' and not make him 'stumble'.[111] Therefore we must consider a third cause of the problem in Rom 14, idol offerings. This would mean that those whom Paul seems to call 'weak in faith' (14:1) would be those who only eat vegetables, while the others would be those 'strong' enough to eat meat offered to idols. But this is most unlikely for several reasons. A first, basic objection is that if Paul actually had prohibited idol offerings in the gentile church in Corinth, as we found he did, he cannot possibly have allowed it in Rome, especially not in view of the important position Jews held in that church. Furthermore the Patristic evidence we reviewed above makes it quite likely that the prohibition of idol offerings was firmly established in the Roman church in Paul's time. The same conclusion follows from the evidence in Romans itself, as we shall see now.

Let us first consider Paul's intention vis-à-vis the 'weak' in Rom 14f. We found that the emphasis of the whole passage is on respect for the Jewish brethren and their diet. This should be related to the opening phrase: 'Accept him who is weak in faith, not for disputes over opinions' (Rom 14:1). Whose faith is meant? The next sentence uses this word regarding the 'strong': 'One has faith to eat everything, but another is weak and eats vegetables' (Rom 14:2). The same seems to be implied at the end of the chapter: 'You have

---

[107] This interpretation is supported by the Byzantine majority reading καθαρίζον.
[108] *Jesus*, 50-52.
[109] bAZ 16b-17a; EcclR 1,8 [1,24]; cf tHul 2:24. On this important tradition cf Maier, *Jesus*, 130-81.
[110] v21 ἢ σκανδαλίζεται ἢ ἀσθενεῖ of the majority text seems to be a softening addition to the mere προσκόπτει of Sinai ms, A and some others.
[111] Rom 14:1f, 21; 15:1; 1Cor 8:9, 13; 10:24.

faith?[112] Have it for yourself [before God].[113] Happy is he who does not have to judge himself for what he approves. But he who is in inner conflict when he eats is condemned, for it is not out of faith; for all that is not out of faith is sin' (Rom 14:22f). Therefore it seems we must take the words that follow seriously and abandon the view that Paul considers the 'weak' imperfect in faith: 'Let him who eats not despise him who abstains... for God has welcomed him; who are you to pass judgment on the servant of another?' (v3f). Incidentally, this confirms the translation of ἀσθενής not as 'weak' but 'delicate', as proposed in the previous chapter; we shall henceforth use that translation.

What Paul calls for in Rom 14f is not a stronger faith on the side of the 'delicate' as to diet, and certainly not an effort to overcome their revulsion against idol offerings. What he calls for is faith on the part of the 'strong' in welcoming the 'delicate': 'We who are powerful are indebted to bear the delicacies of the powerless, and not to please ourselves' (Rom 15:1). As we saw (14:21) this 'faith' on the part of the strong involves tolerance of dietary restrictions. Confirmation is found in the connection of the verb 'to bear' (βαστάζειν) with dietary requirements as expressed in Did 6:3, 'As to food, bear what is in your power.'[114] The correspondence is striking precisely because this text is definitely not sympathetic to Paul.[115]

On the other hand there are decisive differences compared to 1Cor 8-10. Whereas εἰδωλόθυτα are the stated theme in 1Cor 8:1, they are mentioned nowhere in our passage. The theme stated in Rom 14:2 is that while some eat 'everything', the delicate eat 'vegetables' i.e. no meat. The reason is that they alone consider this meat 'unclean' (v14, 20), a category apparently connected with Jewish custom (15:8f). On the other hand in 1Cor 8-10 no Jews nor 'unclean' food is mentioned at all. On the contrary, the 'delicate' there are not Jews but people 'hitherto accustomed to idols' (1Cor 8:7; cf 12:2) i.e. gentile neophytes. Finally the key word in 1Cor 8-10, συνείδησις, which as we have seen indicates the consciousness dominated by idolatry, is never used in Rom 14f. Thus while in 1Cor 8-10 the issue is whether the 'knowing' may eat idol offerings in view of their 'delicate' gentile brethren, in Rom 14f it is about 'delicate' Jews and 'powerful' gentiles having different diets.

Actual consumption of idol offerings is also ruled out in specific expressions in our passage. Rom 14:6 states, 'Likewise he who eats, eats in the Lord, for he blesses (εὐχαριστεῖ) God; and he who abstains, abstains in the Lord and blesses God.' But for a gentile Christian to eat food which was considered to be consecrated to a pagan deity should prevent him from blessing his Creator, both within the perspective of Romans (cf 1:20-23) and other letters (1Cor 10:19-31). It would effectively prevent Jews from eating and saying grace with him (Rom 15:6, see below) and thus eventually destroy the stated purpose of Paul's letter

---

[112] Omitting ἦν with some uncials and the Byzantine majority.
[113] Omitted in Sinai*.
[114] Cf above p180.
[115] See Flusser, 'Paul's Jewish-Christian Opponents', esp p77.

to the Romans.

A final indication against the involvement of idol offerings is the quotation from Isa 45:23 in Rom 14:11, 'Why do you pass judgment on your brother? ...For we shall all stand before the judgment seat of God, as it is written, "As I live, says the Lord, every knee shall bow to me...".' The eschatological appeal to God's universal reign, which as Paul implies is now binding for Christ-believers both Jewish and gentile, excludes idolatry and as such is well-known in Jewish liturgy.[116]

If the problem in the Roman church was not about purity laws or idol offerings, we are left with two possibilities: Jewish food laws, or a 'sensitivity' such as that which we have seen in Gal 2. The truth is that the details are rather vague, and it is hard to decide. In the first sub-section (14:2-12) Paul urges mutual acceptance of dietary differences, but he had more to say about the conflict. Apparently the problem was not just Jews and gentiles each having their own diets but common meals. For in the second sub-section Paul calls on the gentiles to restrain themselves in their diet (meat, wine) for the sake of the Jews. Why? As for meat, it could have been meat of unclean animals, meat not properly slaughtered, or meat prepared with milk or cheese. Such meat was all right for gentiles but forbidden for Jews. Hence Paul may have meant that gentiles should not bring it to the common table so as not to embarrass the Jewish brethren.[117]

This possibility cannot be maintained regarding wine; yet this is also mentioned as a problem (14:21). From a halakhic point of view the only problem with gentile wine was its actual consecration to the gods, which we have already ruled out. Moreover we have seen that Tannaic halakha knew how to handle the difficulty with wine at a meal with a gentile. Thus it seems that among the Roman Jewish Christians there were indeed those who, like 'the men of James' at Antioch, refrained from eating with gentile brethren who had meat or wine, even though the latter did not consider these sanctified to the gods. Apparently as long as the gentiles did not abstain from meat and wine, these Jews were unable to accept that idolatry was really excluded.

Thus it seems that the food problem in Rom 14 was complex. At one level Paul's plea appears to have been for willingness on the part of gentile Christians to make allowances for basic Jewish food laws. On another level, he argued that gentile Christians should also bear with 'hyper-halakhic' anxieties regarding gentile wine and meat. As we have seen the details are not quite decisive and we have to leave both possibilities open.

Nevertheless this conclusion is astonishing. It means that in Romans and Galatians Paul argued diametrically opposed cases: at Antioch he would have openly withstood 'hyper-sensitive' Jews who made trouble for the gentiles, while in Rom 14 he appeals to gentiles to be tolerant towards such over-

---

[116] See the *Aleinu*-prayer, referred to above p155 n29.

[117] mHul 8:1 prohibits serving meat and cheese together; the Shammaite/Hillelite discussion on details indicates antiquity.

244

sensitive Jews!

Once again we are reminded of the extent to which Paul was not a 'systematic' thinker, apparently even in such 'practical' matters. However this is no reason to call him inconsistent. Two of his principles stand out in our explanation: nowhere does Paul argue abandonment of the commandments by Jews, and he always pleads for Jewish-gentile co-existence. The reason for the very different outcome of his arguments must have been in the difference between the situations in Rome in Antioch. The Jewish Christians at Antioch tended to shun communion with uncircumcised brethren out of 'delicacy' inspired by James. But their kinsmen in Rome were themselves in danger of being effectively excommunicated by gentile Christians out of disrespect for their 'delicacy'. His aim in both cases was co-existence of Jews and gentiles.

This complex interpretation is confirmed in one remarkable detail. In Rom 15:1 Paul includes himself among the 'strong': 'We who are powerful ought to bear the delicacies of the powerless.' While our interpretation allows that Paul was a Jew who observed the Jewish food laws, he clearly did not consider himself 'delicate'. As he acted out dramatically in the concrete situation at Antioch, he considered his gentile brethren free from association with idolatry and as an observant Jew felt no difficulty in eating and saying grace with them. Unlike the 'delicate', he would certainly do the same in Rome. But when the unity of the one church of Jews and gentiles was in danger, he urged tolerance – toward gentiles, or, in another situation, toward 'delicate' Jews.

If Paul's pluralist position in the issue of table fellowship has become clear, it is also clear that the later gentile Church did not follow him. Reference has been made to the view of Ignatius, bishop of Antioch two generations after Paul (above p2f), to the effect that the Law should not be observed by Christians. Consequently there was to be no communion between gentile Christians and Law-observant Christ-believers, leave alone, we may suppose, between Christians and non-believing Jews. This view rapidly developed into official Church doctrine. But thank Heavens, life is able to outwit doctrine. It appears that Jews and Christians kept enjoying common meals even at the high tide of community building on opposite sides. The synod held at Elvira in 305 CE saw need to decree: 'If any cleric or believer took a meal with Jews, be it advised to ban him from communion in order that he may mend his life.'[118] It is one instance in which hope for the future was in civil disobedience.

Paul's Pluralist Rationalism

In the previous section we only looked at the halakhic stratum of Rom 14. This was important, first, because the actual background of the issue needed clarification and second, because it gave us another look at Paul's attitude toward the halakha. But it is as least as interesting to analyse the intellectual background of the passage. Not only because halakha is not everyone's favou-

---

[118] Canon 50, quoted by Elmslie, *Idolatry*, 81.

rite (as the Talmud also knows) but because it helps us to see how halakha and theology co-exist in Paul's argument. We shall further pursue the observations made here in the concluding chapter.

First of all the parenthesis about 'days' is interesting: 'One distinguishes a certain day above the other, while another distinguishes every day. Let everyone be fully convinced in his own mind: he who observes the day observes it for the Lord...' (Rom 14:5-6a). Let us first isolate the clause, '...another distinguishes every day'. The expression is strange, since the very word κρίνει, 'judge' or 'distinguish', implies 'distinction'. It seems to indicate some special intention. This is confirmed by parallels in Rabbinic, pagan Greek and Hellenistic Jewish literature.

The Rabbinic parallel features in a controversy, and this is significant: 'From the First (day) after sabbath, Shammai the Elder used to buy wood for the sabbath; but Hillel the Elder had a different, greater criterium: "Let all your deeds be for the sake of Heaven"'.' The Babylonian Talmud adds another tradition: 'The Shammaites say, from the first (day) of your week (look forward) towards your sabbath; but the Hillelites say, "Blessed be the Lord from day to day" (Ps 68:19).[119] Shammaites continuously directed their attention towards the sacrosanct seventh day, but Hillel and his school somehow celebrated all the days of the week. The same behaviour as Shammai's is ascribed to Elazar ben Hananya, known from the Talmud and Josephus as a zealot leader in the great war against Rome.[120] As is well known, the Shammaites as a rule express the more conservative and literal interpretation.[121] In contrast, Hillel is famous for several liberal utterings. For example, he is portrayed as being open-minded towards gentiles interested in the Tora, here again in contrast to Shammai.[122] In another tradition he gives the surprising opinion that cleaning one's body even in a secular bath house is a divine task. Significantly this tradition is associated with the same saying, 'Let all your deeds be for the sake of Heaven'.[123]

Thus the saying, 'Let all your deeds be for the sake of Heaven', in two separate instances is associated with Hillel's proverbial broad-mindedness. In Avot (2:12), the Rabbinic wisdom tractate, the saying itself is attributed to R. Yose (mid-second century). This may or may not indicate retroactive attribution. As in other cases involving Hillel – and also Shammai as quoted here – the attribution may equally indicate a transmitter.[124] In any case the Hillelite saying is associated through interpretation with various wisdom proverbs such as:

---

[119] PesR 23 (115b); bBeitsa 16a.
[120] MekhSbY p148; above p173.
[121] See Safrai, 'Halakha', 185-94.
[122] ARN a 16; b 29 (11a-b); bShab 31a.
[123] ARN b 30 (33b); with another saying LevR 34,3 (p675-7).
[124] See Bacher, *Tannaiten* 1, 7f with examples. Add from ARN version b (not yet published in Bacher's day): ch26 (27a), R. Akiva // bShab 31a, Hillel; and ARN b 26 (28b), R. Yoshua // mAv 2:6, Hillel.

'Every work of the Lord is for his purpose' (Prov 16:4);[125] or, 'In all your ways know Him' (Prov 3:6). Indeed, 'wisdom' is an admirable description both of the feeling of the saying and of Hillel's behaviour.

In this light it is extremely important that both the saying and Hillel's attitude towards the sabbath appear to converge with popular Hellenistic motifs. First, both in form and content the saying seems to relate to a genre of brief sayings or narratives typical of Cynicism.[126] Second, Hillel's attitude itself relates to a Cynic concept which is also found in Philo. In the course of his 'Special Laws', Philo deals with the ten ceremonial festivals in the Jewish Law, and in introducing them states: 'The first, the mention of which may perhaps cause some surprise, is the feast of every day ...When the Law records that every day is a festival, it accomodates itself to the blameless life of righteous men who follow nature and her ordinances.'[127] Philo goes on to praise the true seekers of wisdom, found 'either among Hellenes or barbarians', who retreat from society and its sensuous pleasures and devote themselves every day to virtue and wisdom. HEINEMANN showed that the idea of a 'daily feast' derived from Cynic philosophy: the arch-Cynic Diogenes is attributed as saying, 'Does not a virtuous man greet every day like a feast?'[128] A Cynical atmosphere appears to be basic also to Philo's exposition of the nine other festivals in the 'Special Laws'. Heinemann goes as far as to identify a 'Cynic source', which in its explanation of ceremonial practice differs both from the allegorical and the literal interpretation: the festivals are actually celebrated, but in a very different and detached sense.[129] The continuous reference made to 'nature' and its basic 'ordinances' is typical of Cynicism, but in another sense it is also common to Stoic thought.[130]

Thus Paul's sympathetic statement that 'some distinguish every day' appears to relate to the universal atmosphere found in the Hillel traditions and in Philo, associated with biblical wisdom and expressed in the vocabulary of popular Cynico-Stoicism.

From here we can now address the main issue of the chapter, 'purity'. It is introduced with the well-known verses: 'I know and am persuaded in the Lord Jesus that nothing is unclean in itself, but for someone who reckons it unclean it is unclean. ...Everything indeed is clean, but it is bad for anyone who eats by way of a stumbling block' (Rom 14:14, 20). Traditionally these words are taken to signify Paul's theological annulment of Jewish dietary laws,[131] and hence to confirm or even directly quote what is understood as Jesus' radical disposal of the Jewish (food and) purity laws (Matt 15:11, above p241f). This radicalism is

---

[125] כל פעל ה׳ למענהו is read as ambiguous on two terms: the 'work' is God's or man's, and the purpose is God's or man's. Another association of the verse is with the blessing for food, see below.

[126] Fischel, 'Studies in Cynicism', esp 383 and 400f. The link with Hillel's saying about the body is not made.

[127] Spec leg 2:41f.

[128] Heinemann, *Bildung*, 106-110; referring to Plutarch, De tranquillitate animum 20. Further material in Fischel, 'Studies in Cynicism'.

[129] Heinemann ib 137-50.

[130] On φύσις in Philo see above p85 n119.

[131] Thus also Sanders and Watson, see beginning of the previous section.

very unlikely and we will now look for a more adequate explanation.

The view that 'nothing is unclean in itself' rather reminds one of the idea of the equality of all days and hence of a more general rational approach to ritual. Although the halakhic situation is different, there is indeed a correspondence with First Corinthians at the theological level: 'All that is sold in the market hall, eat without questioning about the intention, for "the earth is the Lord's, and its fullness" ' (1Cor 10:25f). Paul's message to the Corinthian 'church of gentiles' (Rom 16:4) is not that Jewish food and purity laws are void, but that gentiles may joyfully eat anything created, provided they do not cooperate with idolatry and honour the Creator of all. So we have in Rom 14, as in 1Cor 8 and 10, an unmistakable affinity to the Cynic view that food as such is religiously indifferent (above p204f).

We see that popular Cynic ideas are integral to Paul's pluralist rationalism both as to 'days' and 'food'. Once more this is reminiscent of the cynicizing rationalization of the festivals in Philo's 'Special Laws'. In both, it is a mitigated Cynicism which allows for actual observance by Jews, but by its rational spiritualization of their observance makes non-observance by gentiles equally acceptable. The comparison between Paul and Philo can be further elaborated on, but this will have to wait. Let us now follow the thread of rationalization of the commandments.

As we have seen, the quest for a rationale behind the precepts of the Jewish Law was a main objective of Hellenistic Jewish thought. And to a lesser extent, it was also an issue among the Tannaim and Amoraim.[132] It quite naturally emerged in conversation with non-Jews who inquired about Jewish religious customs, either with or without a sympathetical intention.[133] Apart from these confrontations the Sages also had their own interests. Especially noted for their moral symbolism, and at times their outright allegory,[134] are the explanations of the leading Hillelite and younger contemporary of Paul and Philo, Rabban Yohanan ben Zakkai.[135]

The question became especially pressing in relation to certain 'irrational' commandments. In a famous story a gentile rather maliciously questions Yohanan ben Zakkai about the reasons behind the purification ritual involving the ashes of a red heifer (Num 19). The Sage gives a defensive answer, concealing his own opinion. But when the disciples want a real answer after the man is gone, he says: 'By your lives! A corpse would not render impure, nor water

---

[132] See Heinemann, *Taamei ha-mitswot*, esp 22-35; and, in clear relation with Heinemann, Urbach, *Sages*, [321-47] 365-99.

[133] See Sifra Aharei 86a: '...those commandments questioned by the evil inclination and by the nations of the world, such as regarding pork, wearing mixed textiles...'; on which passage see Urbach ib [331 n30] 850 n40.

[134] Bacher, *Tannaiten* 1, 39. Urbach, *Sages*, [324f] 370-2 polemicizes and denies Yohanan's allegory; the motivation may well be traditional Paulinism, see ib [263, 228, n47] 296, 302, n53: Bultmann!

[135] tBK 7:2-9. See the exposition of Bacher, *Tannaiten* 1, 30-43. Note the enigmatic terminus technicus כמין חומר specific of Yohanan ben Zakkai and connected with this procedure; see ib 33-35; id, *Terminologie* 1, 61-3.

purify, were it not for the decree of the Holy one blessed be He.'[136] In a similar vein R. Elazar ben Azaria exclaims: '...One should not say, I do not wish to dress in mixed garments, I do not wish to eat pork, I do not wish to commit illicit sexuality – but I wish to and what can I do? For my Father in heaven decreed (the prohibitions) on me thus.'[137] Rather than the formalistic legalism which historians of religion recognized here in earlier days,[138] these traditions express an enlightened religious consciousness which subsumes irrational commandments under the irreducible uniqueness of Jewish existence, or in other words the divine election.[139]

Such abstract rationalism contrasts with Philo. In his non-allegorical commentary in 'On the Special Laws', the red heifer ritual is viewed from the start as part of a rationalist ethic.[140] While this has a didactic intention, his explanation clearly borrows from pagan Greek rationalizations of purity ritual.[141] It is not likely that this was all that Philo had to say on the matter, but it served the needs of a general apology vis-à-vis Jewish or gentile Hellenists. Ethical rationalization is also one of the motivations Philo produces for dietary laws, and here again a wide range of overlap with Hellenistic ideas is in evidence.[142] The idea that irrational commandments such as the dietary laws were given in order to teach Israel self-control is discussed extensively in philosophical garb, in 4 Maccabees.[143] A similar didactic rationalization of dietary laws is expressed in a Rabbinic tradition: 'The commandments were given in order to purify man; for what concern would the Holy One, blessed be He, have with one's slaughtering from the throat or from the neck? It is in order to purify man.'[144]

These comparisons help us appreciate the theological level of Paul's argument. He does not enter into pedagogic explanations, but neither does he introduce a theocentric view as Yohanan ben Zakkai did. Both decisions are quite understandable in view of the mixed Jewish-gentile situation he addresses. Paul's rationale of diet and purity laws is both anthropocentric and abstract:

---

[136] PesRK 4,7 (p74) and parallels indicated there. And cf the near-despair seemingly expressed in PesRK 4,1 (p54f).

[137] Sifra Aharei 93d; cf Sifra Shemini 57b.

[138] Bousset-Gressmann, *Religion*, 130: 'Die Inhalt der Bestimmungen ist... gleichgültig, es kommt auf die Form, die Unterwerfung an'; and echo in Bultmann, *Theologie*, 10-12: 'Der Gehorsam... (wird) als ein rein formaler verstanden ...der die Forderung der Buchstabens erfüllt ...ohne nach dem Warum, dem Sinn der Forderung, zu fragen'. This corresponds to the misunderstanding of Paul as intending a formal abrogation of Jewish ritual laws.

[139] Heinemann, *Taamei ha-mitswot*, 38f counts respect for the πάτριοι νόμοι, common in the Hellenistic world, among the irrational reasons Hellenistic Jews saw for such specific commandments.

[140] Spec leg 1:257-272.

[141] Heinemann, *Bildung*, 71-4, 507.

[142] Heinemann, *Bildung*, 154-66.

[143] Chs 1-2 (cf above p205). But note that no actual explanation is produced for the dietary laws.

[144] GenR 44,1 (p424f, attributed to Rav, early 3d cent CE); cf LevR 13,3 (p207) and parallels indicated there. See same tradition Tanh Shemini 7-8 (14b-15a); TanhB Shemini 12-13 (15b-16a), in the context of the food laws and the intriguing speculation about the Leviathan and the nullity of food laws both at the time of creation and in the world to come.

'Nothing is unclean *in itself*, but *for someone* who reckons it unclean it is unclean; ...everything indeed is clean, but it is bad for anyone who eats by way of a stumbling block' (Rom 14:14, 20). In this ingenious way Paul is able to treat both Jewish and gentile life styles with equal respect: purity or food laws are important for Jews, not gentiles. It is interesting to observe that since abstract theocentric and ethical anthropocentric motivations are known in Rabbinic tradition as in Philo, there is no reason to suppose that Paul could not adopt such views in other situations. However the situation here does not allow him to do so. What he needs here is a 'neutral' rationale which allows both gentile and Jewish diets.

Thus neither way of life should be considered devoid of significance before God. Paul's anthropocentric approach has a theocentric corollary: 'Let every one be fully convinced in his own mind'; 'for we shall all stand before the judgment seat of God' (Rom 14:5, 10). It is precisely this 'theocentric anthropo-centrism'[145] which offers the cue for Paul's actual message here. Because *both* ways of life are valid before God, gentiles can wholeheartedly accept Jews with all their ritual: 'As for the delicate, welcome him in faith, not for disputes over opinions. ...Therefore welcome one another, as Christ has welcomed you, for the glory of God' (Rom 14:1; 15:7). Thus both Jews with Jewish rites and gentiles without are acceptable before God: 'For I tell you that Christ became a servant to the circumcised because of God's faithfulness..., and in order that the gentiles might glorify God for his mercy' (15:8).

At this point it is interesting to refer back to a question we abandoned temporarily, the relationship between Rom 14 and the synoptic discussion on purity (above p241f). Paul, in pleading pluralism as to dietary delicacy, seeks recourse in universal rational ideas but does not actually state the nature of the dietary problems. This is very different from the synoptic discussion on the washing of hands. It revolves around the halakhic question of the purity of hands, and Jesus' final saying is based on the halakhic opinion that food does not transfer its impurity to persons. Moreover the intention of the saying is very different from Paul's anthropocentric rationalization of 'impurity'.[146] The say-ing is aimed at moral impurity, the source of which is in man's heart. It signifies a moral radicalization of the concept of 'impurity' which connects with biblical usage on a terminological level and is also found among the Essenes. In another sense, Jesus' attitude has some affinity with the hasidic fringe movement in ancient Judaism, which displayed a certain wariness towards Pharisaic purity rules but extra stringency in other halakhic areas.[147] Hence if Paul's testifying that 'in the Lord Jesus... nothing is impure in itself' would refer to the synoptic saying, he interpreted it very differently from its meaning in context. Whether this was the case, and if he was conscious of it, the sources do not allow us to

---

[145] The term (in reverse order) and its relation to the Hillelite tradition was introduced by Flusser, see his 'Hillel's Self-Awareness', 35; 'New Sensitivity', 121.

[146] The difference between Jesus and Yohanan ben Zakkai's rationalism was hinted at by Flusser, *Jesus*, 45f.

[147] Safrai, 'Teaching of Pietists'.

250

decide. What they show us is that Paul's rational attitude to ritual differs from that of the synoptic Jesus.

There are even more aspects to the background of Paul's pluralism. Although not widely recognized as such, pluralism was highly esteemed within the dominant Rabbinic tradition and was in a way essential to it. In the last few generations before the destruction of the Temple the Pharisaic-Rabbinic movement was divided into the schools of Shammai and Hillel.[148] They differed on such a large number of aggadic and halakhic issues, sometimes quite powerfully, that it may be justified to speak of two movements. According to Rabbinic tradition, this was accepted as a fact of life and both schools cultivated mutual relations.[149] Nevertheless we know of a dispute between these schools which was solved by force of arms during the time of the Great War against Rome. There were mortal casualties among the Hillelites, who were brutally overruled by the zealot Shammaites and mourned the event for centuries (above p175). In contrast with this violent solution, Avot, the Rabbinic wisdom tractate, praises discussion and diversity of opinion: 'Every dispute which is for the sake of Heaven will exist forever, but which is not for the sake of Heaven will not exist forever.'[150] One gets the impression this was a Hillelite view.

Confirmation for the Hillelite background of Rabbinic pluralism is found in Acts 5:34-39. The Sadducee high priest and his allies incriminate Peter and other Apostles, calling for the death sentence. Not so Gamaliel, 'a Pharisee' and 'teacher of the law held in honour by all the people'. This has to be the same Rabban Gamliel the Elder, well-known from Rabbinic literature as the grandson of Hillel and leader of the Hillelites. Gamaliel pleads tolerance towards the Apostles, pointing out that messianic pretensions usually peter out and moreover adducing a theological motive: 'If this plan or undertaking is of men it will fail, but if it is of God, you will not be able to overthrow them.' These words are very similar in mood to the saying in Avot we have quoted, and even more so in the parallel version found in the same tractate: 'Every congregation which is for the sake of heaven will exist forever, but which is not for the sake of heaven will not exist forever.'[151] Leaving aside the interesting questions regarding the relationship between Paul and Acts, we are now interested in the apparent Hillelite colouring of Rabbinic pluralism.

A verse in Rom 14 may directly relate to this. It sums up the preceding passage about diversity in life styles: 'So each of us shall give account of himself to God' (14:12). The verse immediately preceding cites Isa 45:23, emphasizing God's universal reign (see below). But the individual emphasis of v12 and of the passage as a whole rather reflects the mood, again, of the biblical wisdom tradition. There is affinity with the verse, 'Every way of a man is pure in his own eyes, but the Lord weighs the spirit' (Prov 16:2; cf 21:2). The word 'pure' (זך)

---

[148] For a survey see Safrai, 'Halakha', 185-200; for detailed discussion Safrai, 'Decision'.
[149] Cf tYev 1:10-13.
[150] mAv 5:17. On the value of dispute see Safrai, 'Halakha', 168-75.
[151] mAv 4:11. Both versions together ARN a 40 / b 46 (64b-65a).

251

offers a direct link with the subject of the chapter: purity. Indeed the Tosefta connects this verse from Proverbs with the narrative tradition that although Shammaites and Hillelites widely differed as regards purity they did not refrain from dining with one another;[152] the context is that of the divergencies between both schools mentioned here.

Apart from pluralism between the schools, Rabbinic tradition cherished the value of tolerance at the personal level; it was even turned into a halakha. This is the principle that 'in the presence of a brother one is not to treat as permitted what for him is forbidden'.[153] The principle is cited, for example, in connection with halakhic divergencies rooted in local custom.[154] At least in intention, the rule to tolerate a brother's stringency may have been another element of Paul's Jewish education.

There is a more explicit connection between another verse of Paul and the concept of tolerance as developed elsewhere in Rabbinic tradition: 'Do not let what you eat cause the ruin of one for whom Christ died; ...let us *pursue the ways of peace...*' (Rom 14:15, 19). The italicized expression not only develops biblical usage (Ps 34:15). It also appears in a saying, again, of Hillel which embodies many aspects of his humane attitude as reviewed earlier: 'Be of the disciples of Aaron, loving peace and pursuing peace, loving mankind and bringing them nigh to the Tora' (mAv 1:12). Possibly in connection with this saying, 'the ways of peace' developed into a practical principle, with a number of halakhot implying tolerance towards maladjusted behaviour for the sake of social harmony.[155]

There remains one last verse to be examined, which connects Paul's plea for pluralism with yet another circuit within his complex mind: that of midrash and eschatology. It concerns Rom 14:13, '...rather you must decide not to put a stumbling block (προσκόμμα) in the way of a brother or a hindrance (σκάνδαλον)'. This sounds like an allusion to two scriptural verses from different contexts. One is Isa 8:14, 'The Lord ...will become ...a stone of offence and a rock of stumbling to both houses of Israel...'[156] In the chapters on Israel's place in salvation history Paul explicitly quoted this verse (Rom 9:32f).[157] The other possible allusion is to Lev 19:14, 'You shall not ...put a stumbling block[158] before the blind.'

Lev 19:14 involves an appeal to mutual responsibility. This is the implied

---

[152] tYev 1:11, with a composite quote of Prov 16:2 and 21:2.

[153] bNed 15a (apparently quoted in the mss of SifD 104, p163; see Finkelstein a.l.); ib 81b; and next n.

[154] yBer 8, 12a, in the (Aramaic!) formulation דלא מפלג על בר נש באתריה; bPes 50b-51a, דברים המותרים ואחרים נהגו בהן איסור אי אתה רשאי להתירן בפניהם; cf bMeg 5b.

[155] The halakhot motivated מפני דרכי שלום, mGit 5:8f; mShev 5:9.

[156] LXX λίθου προσκόμματι ...πέτρας πτώματι; but Aquila, Symmachos and Theodotion agree with Paul; cf Baur, *Wörterbuch* sv σκάνδαλον.

[157] Λίθον προσκόμματος καὶ πέτραν σκανδάλου; the same 1Pet 2:8, a passage altogether related to Rom 9:32f (see Flusser, *Judaism*, 75-87). Cf also Rom 14:21 according to P46?, corr Sinai, B, D etc, and Byzantine majority: προσκόπτει ἢ σκανδαλίζεται ἢ ἀσθενεῖ.

[158] LXX οὐ προσθήσεις σκάνδαλον.

252

interpretation of the verse in Rabbinic literature in various contexts.[159] A particularly close parallel involving wine and meat is found in a Tannaic tradition: 'R. Natan says: Whence do we know that one should not reach a cup of wine to a *nazir* nor meat cut from a living animal to a Noahide? Scripture teaches, "You shall not put a stumbling block before the blind" (Lev 19:14).'[160] An explicit reference to Lev 19:14 in connection with offerings appears elsewhere in the New Testament.[161] The parallel with these passages does not extend to the halakhic specifics.[162] The implication is more basic, as appears from the recurrence of 'food' as a 'stumbling block' in Rom 14:20f. What is meant is the gentiles' responsibility towards the Jews. Elsewhere, Paul makes the same implicit allusion: 'Take care lest this liberty of yours somehow becomes a stumbling block to the delicate' (1Cor 8:9). Paul applies the same idea in different halakhic situations: as we have seen, the 'delicate' in 1Cor 8 are not Jews but gentile neophytes still susceptible to the power of idolatry.

The possible allusion in Rom 14:13 to Isa 8:14 is not that clear. The word σκάνδαλον appears to be tautological after προσκόμμα and follows strangely:[163] indeed it may be no more than a mechanical echo of the quotation in Rom 9:32f. But we cannot ignore the possibility that the prophetic connotation of that passage was present in Paul's multi-layered mind. A prophetic dimension becomes apparent in the reference to 'God's judgment seat' and the quotation from Isa 45:23, 'Every knee shall bow to Me...' In this case his words convey a shade of criticism vis-à-vis his 'delicate' kinsmen: '...a stone of offense and a rock of stumbling for ...Israel'. Paul is adhorting gentile Christians to respect their Jewish brethren, and this means that it is inopportune to criticize the 'delicate'. However as has been seen earlier the words 'we who are strong' (Rom 15:1) show that Paul did not identify with their position; this is also what he made quite clear in Gal 2:11-14. This actual opinion of Paul's may be reflected in his implicit allusion to Isa 8:14.

To summarize, Rom 14f pleads for tolerance and pluralism as to Jewish dietary delicacy. The argument draws on a wide range of intellectual sources. One is a popular Cynico-Stoic trend of thought also found in Philo and in traditions about Hillel; it allows ceremonial divergency within an atmosphere of rational pluralism. Another source, organically connected with the preceding one, is biblical wisdom and its continuation in the Rabbinic ethic of pluriformity. Here, the recurring affinity to the Hillelite ethics of 'the ways of peace' is particularly interesting. A third source is the sphere of midrash and eschatol-

[159] See Str-B 3, 310-2.
[160] bPes 22b; bAZ 6a; cf bNed 81a for the principle. On meat from a living animal for a Noahide cf yDem 3, 23b, where the term is not מכשול but תקלה.
[161] Rev 2:14, '...Balaam ...taught Balak to put a stumbling block before (βαλεῖν σκάνδαλον ἐνώπιον) the sons of Israel, that they might eat food sacrificed to idols and practise immorality'.
[162] R. Natan allows the others to have their own wine and only forbids offering it to the *nazir*, while Paul actually calls on the gentiles to abstain from their own wine. Nor is it evident that Paul would agree to the prohibition of אבר מן החי for gentiles.
[163] Apparently for stylistic reasons B omits προσκόμμα ...ἢ and retains only σκάνδαλον; but see B in v21!

ogy, reflected in the ethic of mutual responsibility and the idea of God's universal judgment. Finally, the dominant spiritual dimension always present in Paul must be mentioned: the body of Christ. The aim of the section may be summarized as, '...harmony with one another in accord with Christ Jesus' (Rom 15:5).

Jews and Gentiles Bless Their Creator

The passage on table fellowship in Romans ends in the mood of liturgy and benedictions. The same occurs 1Cor 10:30f, the passage which as we saw is related in topic although based on a different halakhic situation.[164] This does not seem to be incidental, and may reflect an intention of Paul's. Let us examine this matter and its relevance for the present study more closely.

Blessings over food are referred to earlier in the chapter: 'He also who eats, eats in honour of the Lord, since he blesses (εὐχαριστεῖ) God; while he who abstains, abstains in honour of the Lord and blesses God' (Rom 14:6). The halakhic issue, as we have seen, is the more restrictive diet of Jewish Christians. Similar language is used in 1Cor 10:30f, 'If I partake in thankfulness, why should I be denounced because of that over which I say a blessing (εὐχαριστεῶ)? So, whether you eat or drink, or whatever you do, do all to the glory of God.' Here the issue is about offerings; the Apostle prohibits undoubted offerings but permits food which to all appearances is not treated as such by pagans. We have also noted the Cynic trend of thought which enables one to imagine divergent life styles coexisting at one table. Now we shall see how this universal humane conceptuology blends together with Jewish halakha in the liturgical setting of the blessing at meals.

When arguing the admissibility of 'undesignated' pagan food Paul quotes the Psalm verse, 'The earth is the Lord's and its fullness' (Ps 24:1; 1Cor 10:26). In Rabbinic tradition, as we saw earlier (p205f), this verse is interpreted to support the commandment to bless God upon enjoying anything from his creation. Thus as a basic rule, 'One should not savour anything until one has blessed, as it is said, "The earth is the Lord's and its fullnes"' (tBer 4:1). The next question in the halakha is what specific blessings one should say on enjoying any particular kind of food in various circumstances, and this is what the Tosefta, paralleling Mishna Berakhot 6, proceeds to formulate.

The concrete relations between food, faith and blessings are essential both in the halakha and in the present context in Paul. It has been pointed out that the blessings which according to Rabbinic tradition are said upon eating or other enjoyments incorporate an attentive and positive relation both to these goods and towards their good Creator: 'A commonplace thing and ordinary events in daily life have now become a unitary entity full of significance'.[165] Under-

---

[164] The aspect of praise parallel in Rom 15 and 1Cor 10 is correctly elaborated by Willis, *Idol Meat*, 251-4, but without noting the link with the Jewish *berakhot* and the concept of creation.
[165] Kadushin, *Worship*, 63-78; quote p65.

standably then another verse cited by the Sages in this connection is, 'Every work of the Lord is for his purpose' (Prov 16:4; tBer 4:1). Secular events are perceived within a framework of sanctification. The latter verse is also interpreted in connection with the proverbial saying associated with Hillel the Elder, which we came across earlier: 'Let all your deeds be for the sake of Heaven' (mAv 2:12).[166] Indeed, it appears that Paul is actually referring to some version of this tradition when he writes, 'Thus whether you eat or drink, or whatever you do, do all to the glory of God!' (1Cor10:31). The last phrase may even be a paraphrase of the saying associated with Hillel.[167]

The sanctification of daily life, a central concern of the Pharisaic Sages, is admirably expressed in R. Shimon ben Yohai's saying, which refers us back to our main theme here at once:

> R. Shimon said: If three have eaten at one table and not spoken words of the Tora on it, they are like those "eating sacrifices of the dead", for it is written: "For all tables are full of vomit and filth, without (the) Place (i.e. God)" (Isa 28:8). But if three have eaten at one table and spoken words of Tora on it, it is as if they have eaten from the table of the Holy One, blessed be He, for it is written, "And he said to me, This is the table that is before the Lord" (Ezek 41:22). (mAv 3:3)

As we saw the realization of his lofty vision is not left to chance but formulated in a halakha (above p205).

Meanwhile everything appears to hinge on the concept of creation. Indeed Ps 24 is a 'Kingship' psalm which opens with the theme of creation; according to ancient tradition it was said in the Temple on the first day of the week, in remembrance of the first day of creation.[168] Furthermore, the concept of creation is essential to Jewish *berakhot* like the one for wine: 'Blessed ...who creates the fruit of the vine'; it dates back at least to the late Second Temple period.[169] It would not be far fetched to see this ancient blessing over wine as the Jew's counterpart to the pagan's libation formula 'in the name of' his own godhead.[170]

Thus we see how the benediction of the Creator confronts what is perceived as idolatry, 'alien cult', i.e. the estrangement of elements of creation from their created status into their deification. Paul makes this explicit in another connection: '...They exchanged the truth about God for a lie and worshipped and served the creature instead of the Creator,[171] who is blessed for ever! Amen'

---

[166] See above p246f.

[167] P46 et al read εἴτε τι ποιεῖτε πάντα εἰς δόξαν θεοῦ [...], apparently feeling the second ποιεῖτε to be superfluous. Indeed the formulation is curious and indicates a tradition being quoted. Cf also Willis, *Idol Meat*, 251.

[168] LXX Ps 23:1, τῆς μιᾶς σαββάτων; mTam 7:4 (on which baraita see Epstein, *Tannaitic Literature*, 30).

[169] tBer 4:3, a dispute of R. Eliezer and his colleagues developing more ancient rules relating to the dispute on table order between Shammaites and Hillelites, mBer 8 and tBer 6.

[170] cf Poland, *Geschichte*, 262f for the importance of the wine libation (σπονδή) at the beginning of festive pagan meals. For the votive phrase לשם see above p214 n118.

[171] For similar language see Wis 14:11.

(Rom 1:25). Incidentally the latter clause is not only standard in Paul's usage,[172] but is reminiscent of Hebrew liturgical phraseology and more specifically of the Rabbinic phenomenon of hymnic insertions in narrative or argumentative language.[173]

This reveals a profound connection between the topic of food offered to idols and the blessing of the Creator at meal, a connection which we already noted superficially when studying 1Cor 10. It also explains the meaning of the verses, 'But if someone says to you, This is sacrificial food, do not eat on his account. For why should my liberty be found guilty by another one's consciousness? If I partake with thankfulness, why should I be denounced (βλασφημοῦμαι) because of that over which I say a blessing?' (10:28-30). Eating food which a pagan considers to be sanctified to his godhead is cooperating in the deification of created things and hence a blasphemy to the Creator – who would be blessed over the same food! The pagan's idolatrous consciousness turns the benediction into a curse. But the reality of idolatry is in man's intention, not in the food. Where there is no idolatrous consciousness, one can 'partake with thankfulness' and 'bless' the Creator.[174] Surprisingly, this may be read in the continuation of the same Psalm: 'Who shall ascend the hill of the Lord? And who shall stand in his holy place? He who has clean hands and a pure heart, who does not lift up his soul to what is false' (Ps 24:3f). And we are strikingly reminded of the crucial significance of 'consciousness' συνείδησις in Paul's discussion of idol offerings when we note that the Targum here renders 'a pure heart' בר לבב in this passage as 'a clear intention' בריר רעיונא.

Incidentally our discussion on Paul also offers deeper insight into the saying of R. Shimon quoted above, 'If three have eaten at one table and not spoken words of the Tora on it, they are like those "eating sacrifices of the dead" '. Upon eating, the intention of loving worship of the Creator comes to life in the sharing of words of Tora and blessings. Without these, it is like partaking of the cold world of silent idols.

If idolatry is condemned in the hymnic peroration of 1Cor 10, so is the apartheid of Jews and gentiles in Rom 15. In Rom 14:11 Paul already intimated the theme of common Jewish-gentile worship by quoting Isa 45:23, '...Every tongue shall confess to God.' This liturgical expression of Jewish-gentile table fellowship comes to full fruition in Rom 15:5-9:

> May the God of steadfastness and encouragement grant you to live in such harmony with one another, in accord with Christ Jesus, that together you may with one voice glorify the God and Father of our Lord Jesus Christ. Welcome one another, therefore, as Christ has welcomed you, for the glory of God. For I tell you that Christ became a servant to the

---

[172] Also Rom 9:5 and 2Cor 11:31.

[173] One is reminded especially of the typical language of Seder Eliyahu, see ed Friedmann, introduction, p118f.

[174] 'With thankfulness', χάριτι, v30 reminds of words from the *birkat ha-mazon* like להודות חין, חסד, רחמים. On χάρις/χάρισμα see above p78 n97. In contrast 1Tim 4:3-5 μετὰ εὐχαριστίας 'with a benediction' implies the act of blessing.

circumcised to show God's truthfulness, in order to confirm the promises given to the patriarchs, and in order that the gentiles might glorify God for his mercy.

In chapter 3 we investigated the language of blessings used by Paul and its halakhic background. In that connection we mentioned a halakhic tradition to the effect that one must hear the whole blessing before responding 'Amen' (1Cor 14:16). Understandably, this halakha would apply especially in the case of people with a different religious background such as a non-Jew or a Samaritan, and this is what we find in connection with the same tradition. It is preserved in two versions:

> If a gentile blesses the Name one answers Amen; if with the Name, one does not answer.[175]

> ...The benediction is said over the food and then over the wine. One says Amen after an Israelite who says a benediction, but not after a Samaritan until he has pronounced the whole benediction.[176]

The first version is not only briefer but more basic and appears to be older; the second indicates that this halakha applied typically to Jewish-gentile table fellowship.

This is the setting of Paul's instruction in Romans, and once again we see the extent to which the Apostle to the gentiles has remained true to his halakhic background. It is tempting to associate the atmosphere expressed in these halakhot with the universal human trend shared by the Hillelite tradition, remembering that Paul showed affinity with it in other connections. The following eschatological dispute is illuminating, since it connects with the ancient Jewish belief that 'all Israel has a share in the world to come', except 'him who denies the resurrection of the dead and the giving of Tora from heaven, and the Epicurean':[177]

> R. Eliezer says: None of the gentiles has a share in the world to come, for it is said: "The wicked shall depart to the underworld, all the nations that forget God: (Ps 9:17[18]). "The wicked shall depart to the underworld" – these are the wicked Israelites; "all the nations that forget God" – these are the wicked of the gentiles. Said R. Yoshua to him: If Scripture would say, "The wicked shall depart to the underworld, all the nations" – and be silent, I would agree with your words. But now that Scripture goes on to say, "...that forget God" – you see that there are righteous among the nations who have a share in the world to come.[178]

---

[175] tBer 5:21; yBer 8, [12]c; ySuk 3, 54a; yMeg 1, 72a; GenR 66,6 (p751, not in London ms and main text). Blessing 'with the Name' reflects gentile theurgy; as is known, the name of the Jewish Godhead became popular ('Iao' etc) in pagan incantation.

[176] mBer 8:8; tBer 3:26; כותי is a common euphemism for גוי, but the text here seems firmly established and appears to be a stricter specification. Shmuel Safrai surmises that this halakha suspects the Samaritan's blessing to refer to Mt Gerizim instead of Jerusalem; cf John 4:20f. On the relation to Samaritans cf Alon, *The Jews* 2, 562-5.

[177] mSan 10:1. Its antiquity is apparent from the close parallel of the continuation with 1En 60:6. For Paul and the Pharisee belief in resurrection see Acts 23:6-9.

[178] tSan 13:2 (ms B); bSan 105a.

R. Eliezer, who was about a generation younger than Paul, is the main spokesman of the Shammaite tradition in Tannaic literature. Opposing his anti-pagan stance which was apparently typical for the Shammaites, the Hillelite partner in discussion envisages a future salvation in which Jews and gentiles partake alike. It is quite conceivable that R. Eliezer, as opposed to R. Yoshua, would refuse to agree with the halakha just quoted. But this is a mere educated guess.

Suffice it to say that Paul's discussion on the table fellowship of Jew and non-Jew follows the lines of the halakha and concludes in the language of Jewish benedictions. It is appropriate for us to quote from it at the end of this study: 'Therefore I will praise thee among the gentiles... Rejoice, o gentiles, with his people' (Rom 15:9f). True to Pharisaic-Rabbinic tradition, the quotations in this Jewish-gentile duet are fraught with midrashic allusions involving Israel's future among the nations and its Messiah.[179]

[179] 2Sam 22:50 = Ps 18:50, see next verse, 'he shows steadfast love to his Anointed, to David and to his descendants forever'; and Deut 32:43 (LXX), see e.g. the Targumim ad loc.

Conclusion

The Nexus of Halakha and Theology

In this concluding chapter we will pull the threads together and review the patterns that have emerged. That is to say, first of all we will summarize the evidence for the presence of halakha in Paul's letters and discuss the implications this has for his attitude towards Jewish tradition and his place in Judaism.

However there is an interesting subcutaneous relationship between halakha and thought. Having outlined the function of halakha in Paul it would be interesting to speculate on the form and content of his theology. But we will have to restrict ourselves to a sketch of the texture of Paul's thought and of two 'theological' passages of immediate importance for his practical attitude towards the Law. In passing we will also have occasion to make some remarks on the relationship between Paul and Acts.

Page references to the preceding chapters are omitted. They would be numerous and boring, and the reader can find his way using table of contents and indices.

The Presence of Halakha in Paul

In the introduction we discussed the appearance of halakha in ancient Jewish and Christian sources and designed a number of categories and sub-categories. Such schedules should of course never be considered to be absolute; they should aid an adequate approach of the documents. More specifically their aim is to enhance observation by distinction and association.

We distinguished between two main categories: halakhic sources, or those that are intended to formulate halakha, either in 'pure' or in midrash form; and non-halakhic sources such as narratives, apocalypses or adhortations, which contain or reflect halakha in an incidental or fragmentary way. Paul's letters, as all extant early Christian writings, belong to the second main category: they are non-halakhic sources.

Generally speaking letters, as distinct from narrative or other genres in the third person, are a more direct literary medium for expressing the author's views. Any positive or negative statement in an authentic letter relating to halakha can be taken to reflect Paul's own opinion.

259

Next, we distinguished between three different modes of the possible presence of halakha in early Christian literature. For clarity's sake we will repeat them here in brief:

(1) halakha reflected in behaviour or speech of Jews within a narrative;
(2) halakha cited in support of a hortatory argument;
(3) halakha quoted in a work based on the premise that Law observance is obsolete.

The distinct literary significance of these three modes is apparent in the relationship between an author's purpose and the halakha he utilizes. Mode (1) gives only indirect information on the author's own attitude towards the halakha he describes. Mode (2) by definition gives direct expression to the author's positive attitude. Mode (3) expresses a contrast between the author's attitude towards the halakha and the specific tradition he happens to utilize.

Consideration of the literary significance of each mode in a wider perspective yields their historical and theological significance. Pertinent conclusions here will be drawn in the course of our exposition.

Another aspect regards literary form, in particular the degree to which actual halakhic formulations are to be found. Mode (1) will contain few direct literary reflections, most of which will be technical terms. Mode (2) tends to be very direct, because the author supports his adhortation with the halakha he cites; while adaptation cannot be excluded, exact quotation is likely. In mode (3) the author shows no positive interest in the halakha he cites, but neither is he interested in distorting it; adaptation is possible but exact quotation more likely.

We will now arrange our findings about halakha in Paul according to these distinctions.

Mode (1) occurs in the narrative or personal passages in Paul's letters. Examples include what he relates about his own circumcision or that of others (Phil 3:5; Gal 2:3), the synagogal judiciary measures he underwent (2Cor 11:24), and his planned participation in festivals (1Cor 16:8). These instances underline his Jewish surroundings and provenance, just as with Jesus and his disciples in the gospels. They inform us about which halakhot were current in which circles and are therefore important sources for the history of the halakha. In themselves they offer only 'matter of fact' information on Paul's own attitude towards the halakha: he was circumcised, went to synagogue, and celebrated Shavuot. What they mean to Paul's attitude depends on their rhetorical function.

Thus we found ourselves dealing at length with one such indirect reflection of halakha, contained in a long narrative passage typical of the letter involved: the Antioch incident in Gal 2:11-14. Its significance is not in the amount of halakha reflected, for information on it is meagre and indirect. It lies in the rhetorical significance of the incident in the framework of the letter as a whole. Yes, and even more so: its importance is that it occurs in two chapters of narrative which are part of a letter wholly devoted to polemic on the Law. We have consistently maintained that the Law polemic was not central and that consequently Galatians was but one among many possible expressions of Paul's mind. Other letters and especially First Corinthians have confirmed this. Just so, the character of Galatians is remarkable in itself. Its sustained and vigorous polemic against forced judaizing and proselyting of gentile Christians is striking and creates a most unlikely setting for a specific report on a halakhic problem. The unexpectedness has deluded commentators and lead them to suppose that the report meant that the Apostle considered the halakha obsolete as such. A different explanation appeared plausible, according to which Paul's attitude towards the halakha remained unaltered even in the midst of Law polemic.

Another example in Galatians which we have not discussed at length supports this conclusion: the proselyting halakha cited in Gal 5:3. We may now try to get that remarkable instance in focus. Paul supports his plea against forced judaizing of gentile believers with an explicit appeal to a halakha which pertains to proselyting procedures: 'Every man who is circumcised is bound to keep the whole Law.' This means that one who is not circumcised is not obliged to do so. In other words Paul relies on the halakhic distinction between Jews and gentiles as to the obligatoriness of the commandments. His plea against forced observance of the Law is based on the halakha.

By this very contrast Galatians demonstrates that category (3) is not found in Paul: halakha cited by an author who himself takes a negative view on halakha. A quick reference to one passage suffices which in our evaluation, as opposed to the traditional view, failed to qualify for this category: the idol food passage in 1Cor 8-10. Here Paul does not reject halakha as such but follows a well identifiable halakhic tradition based on a positive relationship to the Jewish Law. Something similar holds true for Rom 14f. We found that Paul, rather than abrogating dietary and purity commandments, is calling here for forbearance with those who keep them. The contrast with the Letter of Barnabas is vast, precisely in view of the material similarities. While both authors cite halakha in the course of a 'letter' (Barnabas is a pseudepigraph) and thus directly express their own view on it, Pseudo-Barnabas argues the fundamental obsolescence of the Law while Paul pleads for freedom from the Jewish Law for gentiles on the basis of its validity for Jews.

Another case for comparison is the Didache, which incorporates a pre-Christian Jewish source containing halakha in the initial part and in the remainder formulates, *inter alia*, typically Christian halakhot not opposed to the Law as such but representing a dissenting type of Judaism.[1] While gentile Christians are addressed in Did 6:2f, the same passage implies that more of the Law may be done and that full observance is legitimate. This was not Paul's opinion,[2] but for the sake of the present argument we can view both sets of sources together. Both Paul's letters and the Didache are Christian writings which in their adhortation utilize Jewish and Jewish-Christian halakhot. A difference is that

[1] Thus Alon, 'Ha-halakha be-Torat 12 ha-Shelihim'.
[2] Flusser, 'Paul's Opponents'.

261

the Didache appears to contain a Jewish source *in toto* whereas in Paul we have only fragmentary quotations of Jewish documents or traditions.

Thus halakha appears to be specifically contained in Paul's letters in mode (2): halakha cited in support of Christian adhortation. We can distinguish the following types:

- *Dominical halakha*, or halakhic teachings of Jesus. While they are explicitly announced as such, they are apparently paraphrased in three of the four cases:
  - 1Cor 7:10f, on divorce;
  - 1Cor 9:14, on sustenance of Apostles (cf Gal 6:6; cf 1Thess 4:11);
  - 1Cor 14:34, on the silence of women during worship.
Only in the fourth case does Paul extensively cite a 'tradition of the Lord':
  - 1Cor 11:23-25, the eucharist tradition which contains halakhic elements on table order.
While the halakhot on Apostolic sustenance and the silence of women agree with Pharisaic-Rabbinic halakha, the ones on divorce and the table order are closer to Essene halakha and at any rate identify this halakhic tradition as non-Pharisaic.

- *Apostolic halakha*, or Apostolic rules not ascribed to Jesus:
  - 1Cor 7:39, the halakhic formula regarding the remarriage of widows; cf its homiletical utilization in Rom 7:2f;
  - 1Cor 11:2-16, the instruction concerning headcovering of women; although in essence a common Jewish usage, it is ascribed to 'the custom of the churches of God'.
- *General halakha*, or halakhot not evidently typical to Apostolic tradition:
  - Gal 5:3, the proselyting halakha which as we just reiterated supports Paul's theological argument against forced judaizing by gentile Christians.
  - 1Cor 14:16, the common Jewish liturgical functionary of 'deputy of the community';
  - 1Cor 5:1, the prohibition of 'unchastity', in this case sexual union with the step-mother; cf 1Thess 4:3;
  - 1Cor 7:2f; the duty of married partners to allow sexual intercourse; cf in this respect 1Thess 4:4;
  - 1Thess 4:6, the prohibition against wrongdoing in business;
  - 1Cor 9:9f, halakhic midrash which, in comparison with Matt 10 and parallels, appears to refer to the rights of field labourers and is applied to the Apostles' right of sustenance.
A fourth possible category is *halakha formulated by Paul himself*:
  - 1Cor 10:25-27, the rule defining behaviour of gentiles as regards 'undesignated food' in pagan surroundings.
This halakha is remarkable since it concerns the behaviour of gentiles. This must have been characteristic of the Christian churches, which may be supposed to have relied on Apostolic-Jewish traditions on the one hand and

262

included many gentiles on the other. The declared advocate of the inclusion of gentiles as gentiles was Paul (Gal 2:11-14!); that he had received a Pharisaic training in the Law we know from his own words (Phil 3:5; Gal 1:14).

We have not yet allocated the important passage on table fellowship in Rom 14f. It is a directly parenetic passage in which halakha is at stake. Yet it does not fit in mode (2) as defined above: it does not cite halakha to support the argument; nor does it belong in categories (3) or (1). It does refer to halakha, but not in a way which directly appeals to the reader: 'One believes he may eat everything, while the delicate one eats only vegetables'; 'One distinguishes a certain day above others, while another distinguishes all days'; 'Nothing is unclean in itself, but it is unclean for him who thinks it unclean'; 'It is right not to eat meat or drink wine or do anything that makes your brother stumble' (Rom 14:2, 5, 14, 21). We deduced from 15:8f that Jews and gentiles are involved. The passage did not give us enough information to decide which halakhic problems actually were involved; we surmised Jewish dietary laws and/or 'hyper-delicacy' vis-à-vis gentile idolatry. The reader has to decide on these halakhic matters. The message is on another level. It is a moral appeal for tolerance: 'We who are strong ought to bear with the delicacies of the weak' (15:1). It is obvious that the halakhic principle is implied, which is also present in Galatians, that gentiles are not obliged to keep Jewish commandments. The strong are called on to forbear with their delicate Jewish brothers and sisters.

These distinctions help us better to understand Rom 14f. It consists of practical parenesis; it refers to halakha; and it presupposes the halakhic priciple that gentiles are not bound to the Jewish Law. The message is: respect Jewish customs and delicacies of your fellow-believers. In other words: respect the halakha. This message coincides with the theological argument of Rom 9-11 on the practical level. It shows what HARNACK called 'Paul's Jewish constraints', and which we have got to know as his fundamentally positive relationship to the halakha.

Evidently, we should adapt our scheme to include a sub-category (2b) to accomodate Rom 14f: halakha presupposed *de facto* in a hortatory argument.

An important observation should be made regarding the history of the halakha. As we noted several times in passing, Paul is another witness to the one-time existence of halakha formulated in Greek. Outstanding examples where grecized halakhot or halakhic expressions are literally quoted are 1Cor 7:39; Gal 5:3; 1Cor 14:16; and, if the above assumption is correct, 1Cor 10:25-27. Traces of grecized halakha are few but some are found elsewhere: in the Aphrodisias inscription, in incidental details in Greek Jewish literature, and, the intentions of the author notwithstanding, in the Letter of Barnabas.[3] That halakha played an essential role in Hellenistic diaspora Judaism was pointed out in chapter 1. These data, Paul's included, indicate that Hellenistic Jews seem to have had

---

[3] Alon, 'Ha-halakha be-Iggeret Bar Nava'.

their own halakhic traditions, written or oral, and that they were closely related to the halakhic traditions of Palestinian Jewry.

Finally the dual significance of this evidence in Paul should not be missed. His letters contribute to our knowledge of an almost lost literary genre: grecized halakha. On the other hand this enhances his Pharisaic background, which as our study showed was not left behind after his 'conversion' on the Damascus road but accompanied him on his further travels, so much indeed that we actually find him formulating halakha for gentiles in Greek. Returning to a suggestion we made in the discussion of Paul's historical background, there appears to be every reason to call him a Hellenistic Pharisee.

That he was also a believer in Jesus the Christ does not seem to have been a contradiction. How the various elements were able to fit together may become clear from further consideration of the texture of his thought.

The Texture of Paul's Thought

When discussing the nature and purpose of Paul's letters we described his thought as un-systematic though not incoherent. In the first place he always focuses on the actual situation of the particular church he is addressing. In the second place his thought structures have a flexibility reminiscent of Rabbinical midrash, as well as of Philo's non-systematic 'eclecticism'. This description may be illustrated by a consideration of the various facets of his thought as well as of the way he elaborates certain specific themes in different contexts. Aspects of Paul's thought have been listed in chapter 2 under the heading 'Traditions in First Corinthians'; we enumerated the various sources of authority which support Paul's instruction in that letter. Our purpose here is more general: while incorporating our results there, let us now look at the main themes and trends of thought which appear in all the letters analysed above. What we want is to establish how Paul's complex and flexible thought operates, i.e. its texture.

Let us start with a general observation. The evidence as summarized in the preceding section shows that halakha was pervasive in Paul's thought. We are justified to suppose that it was always there, even if not made explicit. This is not the incorrect, traditional assumption of the pervasiveness of the Law polemic turned upside down. Our conclusion is based on critical analysis, whereas the traditional assumption resulted unwittingly from an unfounded generalization. Pervasiveness of halakha in thought logically implies observance of halakha in life. In the next section we will study 1Cor 7:17-24, a passage relating to Paul's Law theology which confirms this assumption. An observant life according to Paul's views would of course not be rigid and monolythic but presuppose pluriformity and mutual accomodation in view of gentile behaviour (Galatians) and Jewish sensitivities (Romans), always pursuing the unity of the church. This involves a dynamic which is expressed in another, more famous passage which we will also study below, 1Cor 9:19-23. But as appears especially from First Corinthians there is no justification to take this dynamic as arbitrariness vis-à-vis the Law 'in order to please men'. Here again we see the

264

importance of Paul's practical instruction in understanding his theology: it shows his sustained determination to guide his churches in the ways of truth,[4] and it is full of halakha.

Recalling Philo's example again we may infer that it is precisely this variegated structuring of life by means of halakha which enables and indeed requires the seemingly unlimited flexibility of theological thought in Paul. In other words the basic coherence of Paul's thought is not in any particular theological theme but in the organic structure of practical life. The actual life of the 'churches of God' as he calls them is basic, be they 'churches of gentiles', Jewish or mixed communities. Community meals and worship services represent the 'body of Christ' in visible form, and life is structured according to the Apostolic tradition as imparted by Paul. The various extant Pauline letters each reflect distinct momentary situations in the existence of the respective churches. First Corinthians shows us some of the basic instruction. Galatians shows what happens if the fundamental pluriformity is violated to the detriment of gentiles, and Romans if it concerns Jews. Second Corinthians, Philippians and Colossians all appear to address varying situations in which tension with Jewish or judaizing gentile Christians endangered Paul's pluriform ecclesiology. Paul uses a guiding concept which involves diversity while preserving unity: the one 'body of Christ'. This important theological concept, which relates significantly to the Cynico-Stoic tradition, at once embodies the organic unity of Paul's churches and the coherence of his dynamic thought. It is a concept with immediate practical implication (1Cor 6:15; 10:16; 11:27).[5]

This flexibility of thought on the basis of a life structured by halakha also explains the freedom in which Paul is able to utilize trends of thought from very different surroundings. Once again this reminds one of Philo, who in Heinemann's conclusion (above chapter 1) expressed a philosophical 'eclecticism' which on the surface seems arbitrary but reflects the interests and needs of his life as a member of the Jewish community in Alexandria. That Philo ended up with a very different theological superstructure than Paul does not refute our comparison, it confirms it.

The source of his teaching to which Paul would undoubtedly have given priority is *Apostolic tradition*. This tradition has an important halakhic segment which is prominent in First Corinthians and significantly contains Dominical halakha, i.e. halakha taught by Jesus. In a number of details the Apostolic tradition resembles Essene halakha, notably on divorce and the eucharist procedure. But it also contains essential non-halakhic elements. First and foremost we must consider the gospel tradition, which Paul as a trained Pharisee undoubtedly knew in oral form; incidental paraphrastic references to *logia* of Jesus seem to confirm this. Furthermore we have here traditions such as

---

[4] Chadwick, 'All Things' comments on 1Cor 9:22 by studying Paul's flexible ways of instruction in 1Cor 7, 1Cor 8-10 and Colossians and perceives a basic coherence in his concern for such divergent and intricate situations.

[5] See for this topic Meuzelaar, *Leib*.

those concerning the resurrection of Jesus and the future resurrection of all (1Cor 15), as well as other elements of eschatology (1Thess 4-5). Another important element is the concept of the church as a spiritual temple (1Cor 4:16f; 6:12-20; 10:14-23; 11:20-29) which stands opposite to the community of the wicked and again is reminiscent of Qumran (cf especially 2Cor 6:14-7:1).[6]

Another source of Paul's thought is *general Jewish tradition*. We have already listed the halakhic element, but let us now add *midrash* (1Cor 10:1-13 out of many possible examples); *apocalyptic* (cf 'mystery' in 1Cor 15:50 and Rom 11:25; the 'appointed time' 1Cor 7:29-31); *targum* (1Cor 15:54f); and *berakhot* formulae (Rom 1:25 = Rom 9:5 = 2Cor 11:31; cf 1Cor 10:26, 30f). All of this might be the subject of more elaboration, but the point is clear and we must restrict ourselves.

Of special significance for crucial elements of Paul's teaching are similarities with the *Hillelite tradition*. A foremost element is the attitude towards gentiles. In contrast to the Shammaites, the Hillelites display a proverbial openness towards gentiles, regarding social relations, proselytism and future salvation, and apparently also elements of popular gentile wisdom. We use the word 'proverbial' because this image is embedded in later Rabbinic views on Hillel and his followers and certainly involves simplification and idealization. On the other hand it is a fact that Rabbinic literature is predominantly Hillelite in outlook and halakhic opinion, so that this idealization would itself express a Hillelite attitude.

On idol offerings Paul seems to express a non-Shammaite and therefore probably Hillelite affinity. While R. Eliezer appears to be a typical Shammaite in stating that 'the unspecified intention of gentiles is towards idolatry' (mHul 2:7), Paul was of the opinion that gentiles who believed in the Creator could be counted on no longer to partake in idol worship; hence his stance in Gal 2:11-14. The significance of intention in the halakha was a Hillelite tenet, and we may see a combined expression of both elements in Paul's grecized halakha for gentile Christians concerning unspecified pagan food: they do not have to inquire 'in view of consciousness', since the pagan's consciousness when offering food to Christians indicates their non-worship (1Cor 10:25, 27).

Paul expresses a universalistic outlook especially in his tolerant teaching on the observance of 'days' and 'purity' in Rom 14. Similar ideas are also seen in his teaching on idol offerings on an 'ideological' level. Here we noted a most interesting convergence of Paul's teaching with Hillel's, Philo's and *popular Stoic-Cynic wisdom*. In other words the relative openness towards gentiles found among Hillelites points towards a wider, international trend of thought in which Paul, Philo and apparently many of the Hillelites each shared in their respective ways.

---

[6] See Flusser, 'Dead Sea Sect'. What is here called 'Apostolic tradition' may in effect coincide with most of these Essene-like topics which Flusser ascribes to the 'second stratum of Christianity' (a modification of the post-Jesuanic 'hellenistische Urgemeinde' of Bousset-Bultmann).

This allows us to place the *Hellenistic elements* in Paul's thought: his epistolary style and rhetoric, and especially the elements from popular Cynico-Stoic
tradition such as *exempla* and metaphors, the central concept of the 'body'
expressed at length in the fable in 1Cor 12:14-26, and the humane, egalitarian
emphasis which reappears in various contexts. These elements do not make him
any more 'Hellenistic' than most other Jews, certainly not Philo with his interest
in Greek philosophy. As noted the halakhic substructure is decisive in this
respect. The traces of grecized halakha we uncovered are typical of Paul's
Jewish Hellenism.

A striking example of Paul's 'eclecticism' is found in his teaching on the
nature of idolatry. In the same breath he calls idols and idol offerings 'nothing',
i.e. indifferent and harmless, and then goes on to depict them as the dwelling
place of demons (1Cor 10:19f; cf 8:4). The idea of idols as void and harmless
relates to the combined tradition of biblical prophecy and post-biblical wisdom
and the Greek Cynico-Stoic tradition. In contrast the view of idolatry as the
worship of demons and spirits has affinity with the atmosphere of apocalyptic
demonology found e.g. in Jubilees and the Qumran writings. Together with
angelology (1Cor 11:10, angels and women!) this complex seems to reflect the
influence of Persian religion dating back to the early Second Temple period.[7] In
a more general sense too Paul, the Hellenistic Pharisee, reflects both spheres of
influence: Persian-influenced apocalyptic and Greek-inspired humanism.
Nonetheless these influences seem to have been fully assimilated into the
Pharisaic-Rabbinic tradition and there is no reason not to call the respective
elements 'Jewish'. We need not repeat the simile of 'Jewish' food developed in
chapter 1.

The teaching on idolatry has yet another dimension, which again refers us to
the nexus of halakha and thought. Central in Paul's teaching there, as we have
noted, is the term συνείδησις which is well-known from Stoic usage. We have
argued that the emergence of this term, as of the Latin *conscientia*, coincided
with the rise of their Hebrew equivalents, כונה, מחשבה, דעת. We interpreted the emergence of these words as parallel expressions of an overall
cultural development. We can observe the interconnection between the various
aspects of this development in Paul. At the level of international cultural
exchange, he uses the Greek word which connects with Stoicism. Elsewhere in
his letters this 'international' connotation prevails. But in 1Cor 8-10 the word is
understandable only in the typically Jewish context of halakhic reasoning, as a
parallel to the Hebrew מחשבה or דעת. In this passage we can see how the
substructure of halakha is able to give the international concept a specific
meaning.

We see how careful one must be when dealing with foreign influences such as
the 'hellenization' of Judaism. On the one hand it is clear that Judaism here
shared a cultural development in the Hellenistic world, but on the other, this

---

[7] This connection is stressed by David Flusser, orally; and see especially Bousset, *Religion*, last
chapter.

development received a unique expression within the framework of the halakha. In other words we should always distinguish between foreign influences and the internal development of the halacha, which had its own dynamic. Paul offers an interesting case in point.

This also illuminates the flexibility of Paul's theological thought. It is flexible not only in the sense of his 'eclectic' borrowing from different traditions, but also in the dynamics of its reasoning. Paul is able to apply the same theological concepts in two halakhically different situations, as the case requires. We dealt with two important passages which relate to different practical problems although in their argument they use a number of common concepts: Rom 14 and 1Cor 8-10. The precise implication of 'delicacy', 'stumbling', 'eating meat' and 'loving one another' are not inherent in these concepts but are derived from the respective halakhic situation. Or in other words, the same theological imagery serves to elucidate different practical problems and their solutions. A significant difference, as we have noted, is that 'consciousness' is never used in Rom 14f.

Here we begin to see the contours of Paul's thought in the nexus of halakha and theology. In both passages there is a clear Cynico-Stoic emphasis on universalism and tolerance which is more than just another ingredient of Paul's thought. Precisely when taking into account the distinctive halakhic situations, we see that it is the Cynico-Stoic trend of thought which shapes the theological argument in both cases. It is true that both in relation to idol food offerings and Jewish-gentile dietary divergency, the combination of different tradition elements also creates a certain tension. The Cynico-Stoic tradition in itself tends to be indifferent to food and considers food laws irrational; yet Paul in the one case combines it with the biblical and apocalyptic verdict on idolatry and in the other with a plea for forbearance with Jewish hyper-sensitive fear of gentile idolatry. We are now able to understand both this tension and the underlying coherence. The coherence, we have been maintaining, is rooted in the substructure of the halakha; Philo is our case for comparison. Now we see that there is also a theological superstructure which, underlying all flexibility, has its own coherence. This, it seems, is provided by socio-theological elements from the Cynico-Stoic tradition. An important example may be seen, without making it into the centre of Paul's 'system', in the concept of the 'body of Christ' we have emphasized earlier. We will return to these considerations later, but first continue our discussion on the dynamics of Paul's thought.

Another facet is reflected in the table fellowship issue. Rom 14 is again involved but relates in this respect to Gal 2. In the latter passage Paul cites the Antioch conflict about table fellowship with gentiles in the framework of his sustained polemic on the Law, or in other words his defense of the right of existence of a gentile Christianity. But in Rom 14 not only does he give his practical instruction on the same problem quite independently of the Law polemic; he also takes a position which in a way is opposite to that which he took in Gal 2. In Romans he pleads for forbearance by the 'strong', particularly gentiles, with Jewish hyper-sensitivities; in Galatians he castigates Jewish separation which comes down to inacceptance of the gentile Christians. Moreover in Gal 2 he is quite clear about his own position, explaining it extensively by means of his Law theology, whereas in Rom 14 he is silent on his personal opinion and we only catch a glimpse of it in Rom 15:1, 'we who are strong'. What is constant is Paul's attachment to the practical situation in each case and his resolute commitment to a pluriform church of Jews and gentiles: the one body of Christ.

The latter comparison once again reminds us that the purpose of Paul's Law theology is not to answer practical questions regarding the Law. In fact the theology of Law and justification only has to do with observance in an absolute sense: observance of 'the whole Law', as incumbent on Jews and proselytes: 'Any one who is circumcised is bound to keep the whole Law' (Gal 5:3); but not gentiles: '...How can you compel the gentiles to judaize? ...For we know that a man is not justified by works of the Law but through faith in Jesus Christ' (Gal 2:14-16). Clearly 'the Law' means 'the Law of the Jews' i.e. the 'constitution' of the nation of Jews.[8] Belonging to it is no prerequisite for salvation, for: 'There is neither Jew nor Greek, there is neither slave nor free, there is neither male nor female; for you are all one in Christ Jesus' (Gal 3:28). This is Law theology, and it has nothing to do with practical commandments as such. Practical teachings on divorce, incest, idolatry, table fellowship or the worship service are on a different level. Law theology only supports the equal rights 'in Christ' of gentile believers and in fact it serves Paul's pluriform ecclesiology which is rooted in actual practice.

The aim of this study has not been to compare Paul with the Acts of the Apostles. Nevertheless we should not miss the opportunity to observe that the Hillelite affinities of Paul's thought converge with the Acts tradition of Paul as a disciple of the humane leader of the Hillelites, Gamaliel the Elder (Acts 5:34; 22:3). A further convergence with Acts which the reader will not have missed is with the importance of halakha in his letters. The basic Tübingen approach which as MUNCK wrote is still widely supported involves an antithesis between the revolutionary Paul of his own letters and the harmonizing Paul, who makes compromises with the Jews, created by Acts. In our discussion of Gal 2 we noted that the Apostolic Fathers were of the opinion, 'naive' in OVERBECK'S eyes, that the Jewish Apostles naturally observed the commandments, even if they themselves, gentile Christians, did not feel any need to do so. An echo of this 'naivety' is still seen in Augustine and his respect for the Law of the Old Covenant. The convergence we observe between the 'real' Paul of the letters and his portrait in Acts confirms this Patristic naivety. While the wording of Pauline motifs in Acts is unmistakably secondary, the basic correspondence between Paul and Acts on the significance of halakha constitutes a situation fundamentally different from the one presupposed by dominant post-Tübingen scholarship.

---

[8]   As in Hellenistic Jewish usage, νόμος τῶν Ἰουδαίων.

'My Rule in All the Churches' (1Cor 7:17-24)

In the midst of his practical instruction on celibacy, marriage and divorce, in what can be considered one of the most 'legal' chapters in Paul, the Apostle suddenly makes one of his digressions and states his 'rule for all the churches'. This passage shed light on our observations on the nexus of halakha and theology and is fundamental for understanding Paul's attitude to the Law both in theory and practice.

Significantly the digression, 1Cor 7:17-24, could be left out of the chapter without damaging the argument.[9] But not only is it accidental, it also complicates the argument. The issue is about celibacy for the sake of the Kingdom, which Paul personally encourages especially in view of the widowed, but advises against for those who cannot maintain moral purity, forbids for the married and dissuades for those living with a non-believing partner. As for virgins, he repeats his preference for virginity and supports this with the arguments of the brevity of the 'appointed time' and availability for the 'affairs of the Lord'. The 'rule for all the churches' however has nothing to do with all these themes but states Paul's pluriform ecclesiology. It introduces two issues which have nothing to do in the chapter: the relation of Jews and gentiles and slavery, and on the other hand does not touch on the subject under discussion: celibacy and marriage. Moreover the widowed may very well have been 'called' during their married state, which would complicate the argument. Conversely if μᾶλλον χρῆσαι in the passage means 'use the opportunity' (for slaves to get free) it flatly contradicts the argument of the chapter. Obviously the 'rule' comes from another context. It is a digression *par excellence* which actually clarifies one patent fact: the brilliant complexity of Paul's mind.

The 'rule' has to do with 'circumcised' and 'uncircumcised' and their respective status in the church. Obviously the primary context is Law theology. But the point of the argument, as far as we can judge from the fragmentary nature of the passage, differs from the theological polemics of the letter devoted to the theme, Galatians, and in another sense also from the balanced dialectics of Romans. The point of this rule is for practical life.

In our survey of Pauline research in the introduction we wrote that a central sentence in the passage (1Cor 7:19) was noted by E.P. SANDERS and Heikki RÄISÄNEN, who considered it 'one of the most amazing sentences (Paul) ever wrote', and respectively, a 'surprising' and 'very Jewish' statement. We also saw that Adolf von HARNACK took the passage as a major indication of the 'Jewish limitations' preventing the full development of Paul's theology of liberation from Judaism. The Jewish Paul which emerges here was a major anomaly in the face of the scholarly paradigm of Harnack and the traditional interpretation of Paul he represents.

---

[9] Weiss p183f calls this admirable 'Paulinische Kunstsatz' an insert and in truth a quotation of Hellenistic, particularly Stoic (187 n1) character.

In contrast we noted that Albert SCHWEITZER recognized the passage as crucial for Paul's apocalyptic theory of accomodation 'in the flesh' while awaiting this world's passing. According to Schweitzer this *status quo* theory of Paul included that while gentiles do not observe the Law, Jews may remain doing so until the Law is abolished in the spiritual world to come. Finally when discussing the Antioch incident we noted Augustine's opinion that in this passage Paul stated the principle he acted out in the Acts story of his Law-observant behaviour, and that he reiterated it in Gal 6:15: 'For neither circumcision counts for anything, nor uncircumcision, but a new creation'.

Let us now quote the relevant parts of the passage:

> (17) Only let every one walk as the Lord has assigned to him, every one as God has called him. For thus I ordain in all the churches. (18) Was someone called circumcised? – let him not have it operated on; was someone called in the foreskin? – let him not be circumcised. (19) For neither circumcision is anything nor the foreskin is anything, but keeping the commandments of God. (20) Let every one stay in that particular calling in which he was called. (21) Were you called a slave? – let it not worry you; but if you can gain freedom, use it all the more...

First to be noted is the expression, 'I ordain' (διατάσσομαι; in some manuscripts διδάσκω). As we saw in chapter 3 it introduces the authoritative teaching of the Apostle.

Next we observe that Paul explicitly states that this is what he ordains *in all the churches*. In other words this is a principle basic to his apostolate, and he teaches it as a rule of thumb wherever he comes.

We already inferred that the rule concerns Paul's Law theology, or in other words the respective place of Jews and gentiles in the church. Hence: 'neither circumcision is anything, nor the foreskin is anything'. The second part of this saying should be emphasized. The traditional assumption about Paul and the Law has been producing theological myopy for the fact that Paul *also* states that *not* being Jewish is 'nothing'.

The next surprise is in the saying in v19. It has three parallels in Galatians, but instead of a concluding clause such as, '...for you are all one in Christ' (Gal 3:28) or, '...but a new creation' (Gal 6:16), or even, '...but faith working through love' (Gal 5:6) – the statement that not being a Jew or gentile counts anything is here concluded with the clause, '...but keeping the commandments of God'. This is a Jewish Paul who stresses doing commandments yet states that being a Jew or gentile does not matter. How do we settle that?

The solution is simple but profound. Paul can only mean that gentiles should obey commandments also, although evidently not the same ones as Jews. He views gentiles as included in the perspective of the Creator which involves commandments for all. In other words: he envisages what elsewhere are called Noachian commandments. This connection appears also from the context of the passage: the chapter itself is about marriage and sexuality, it follows an adhortation about unchastity, and the next section is about idolatry. Idolatry and unchastity, we recall, are two of the three basic commandments belonging

271

to the universal or Noachian code, bloodshed being the third. The saying would then imply that whether or not one is a Jew does not matter before God, but whether one performs the commandments incumbent upon one does: Jews the Jewish Law, and gentiles the Noachian code – in the version to be propagated by Paul.

This is what is the message of the repeated appeal, 'Let every one walk as the Lord has assigned to him, every one as God has called him; …let every one stay in that particular calling in which he was called.' The *status quo* of every one's calling, either Jew or gentile, is to be maintained. SCHWEITZER explained this teaching from eschatology; an aspect which certainly plays a role. A tradition exists in ancient Jewish and Rabbinic literature that in the messianic age the Tora, or parts of it, will be abolished. As in Rom 7:2ff, this is associated with the redeeming effect of death.[10] Another midrashic connection of very ancient date is the myth of the messianic banquet where Israel will dine of the evidently non-kosher Leviathan.[11]

But there are other important strata to Paul's argument of the *status quo*. One is the distinctive position of Jews and gentiles (Noachians) vis-à-vis the Law – an axiom in the halakha, which as we saw apparently did not change in Paul's mind once he became an Apostle.

Another stratum in Paul's saying is his reference to the wisdom tradition implicit in the final clause, 'keeping the commandments of God' (τήρησις ἐντολῶν θεοῦ). One parallel is in Ben Sira: 'In all your acts guard your soul שמור נפשך, for he who acts thus guards commandments שומר מצוה.'[12] The Greek has for the latter expression, τοῦτό ἐστιν τήρησις ἐντολῶν.[13] Another parallel is in Proverbs: 'He who guards the commandment guards his soul'.[14] In both contexts the message is that one should fear God and be intent on what is fundamentally commanded.

Jewish and biblical wisdom tradition, as we also saw in the case of the critique on idolatry, relates to international, especially Cynico-Stoic, wisdom. In a different combination these connections surface in Rom 14:6, where Paul's teaching on 'days' exudes a pluralistic rationalism also found in Philo and Hillel. Furthermore we concluded that the Cynico-Stoic trend towards the relative equivalence of religious ritual, assimilated into Rabbinic and Hellenistic Jewish tradition, provided Paul with a structural framework for pluralism regarding the commandments. Now we are able to establish the structural function of Stoic-Cynic universalism in the summary rule of Paul's Law theology.[15]

[10] See Davies, *Setting*, 109-90. See above p94 n160.
[11] See 1En 60:7, 24; 2Bar 29:3-8; 4Ezra 6:47-52; TgPsYon Gen 1:21; Tg Ps 50:10; GenR 7,4 (p52-4); bBB 74b = YalShim Gen 434; bAZ 3b; TgSheni Est 3:7. For the halakhic aspect see LevR 13,3 (p277-80); ib 22,10 (p521-6) and parallels there indicated. Schäfer, 'Torah' correctly reminds us that this Rabbinic tradition is one among many others.
[12] Sir 32:23 (ed Segal p205).
[13] Cf Prov 19:16, ὃς φυλάσσει ἐντολήν; Eccl 8:5, ὁ φυλάσσων ἐντολήν.
[14] Prov 19:16, שומר מצוה שומר נפשו; cf Eccl 8:5 שומר מצוה לא ידע דבר רע.
[15] See Weiss p187 n1. A connection with Jewish piety is also present; see p234f.

272

In the case of 1Cor 7:17-20 this is all there is to be said; a christological element is not explicit. The same goes for most of the many parallels to the saying in Paul; they each stress the equivalence of Jewish and gentile life styles and in various combinations reflect the same background of wisdom, halakhic pluralism and apocalyptic.[16] Only a few have an explicit christological emphasis.[17] To these we must add the second part of our passage, which can actually be considered independently and contains a supporting verse which calls a slave 'free in Christ' and his master 'a slave of Christ' (1Cor 7:22); yet this is also one of the statements with an unmistakable Stoic-Cynic affinity.[18] This indicates that christology is one stratum among many in Paul's thought – at least as far as the *status quo* teaching of Jews and gentiles vis-à-vis the Law is concerned. In this connection christology, or the theological unfolding of the significance of the Christ, appears to be an additional superstructure in Paul's flexible, dynamic thought – even if he himself would undoubtedly have placed it, as we have said, above all others.

An important practical consequence is that Paul's 'egalitarianism' did not mean an eradication of all distinctions. This is another aspect of the nexus of halakha and theology. While the Cynico-Stoic trend of universalism and equality provides a conceptuological framework for christology and ecclesiology (which in Paul are intimately related), the halakhic substructure continues to govern actual life.[19] Though it 'is nothing' whether one is circumcised or not, Jews and gentiles have their distinct codes of behaviour. Similarly, women and slaves are not thought to be collectively emancipated when stating that 'you are all one in Christ' (Gal 3:28). Paul's teaching on female participation in worship is clear enough: patriarchy remains in force. The conception of civil emancipation is altogether modern and is possible only on the premises of the Enlightenment. Precisely so, the 'egalitarian' potential in Paul could inspire his modern readers.[20]

Let us conclude this section with a another few remarks – though with wide implications – on the problem of Paul and Acts. If 'keeping the commandments of God' for gentiles means to observe the universal or Noachian code in Paul's version, the obvious question is how this relates to the Apostolic Decree of Acts. We saw that the immediate context of the saying involves the prohibition of unchastity and idolatry.[21] Bloodshed is another obvious prohibition which hardly needs mention and in any case was not an issue in the Corinthian church; hence we may consider it tacitly included.[22] On the other hand we have noted

---

[16] Gal 3:28; 5:6; 6:16; 1Cor 12:13; Rom 2:25f; 3:28-30; 10:12.

[17] Gal 3:27-28; 1Cor 12:13, both with explicit reference to baptism.

[18] See Stanley Jones, *Freiheit*, 27-37.

[19] This view on Paul's 'egalitarianism' is also found in Falk, *Legal Values*, 112f with reference to Rabbinic literature and Stoic tradition.

[20] Stendahl, *Bible*.

[21] 1Cor 5-7, πορνεία; ib 8-10 εἰδωλόθυτα. The two sections have various literary connections, see especially the sayings 1Cor 6:18 // 10:14 and 6:12 // 10:23.

[22] Neither is homicide mentioned in the vice lists 1Cor 5:11 and 6:9f. In both, idolatry and unchastity are prominent, along with greed, theft and robbery, well-known from the 'second table' of the Ten

that Paul allowed the gentile Christians at Corinth to eat 'all that is sold in the market'. We rejected the assumption that he meant that idolatry was no real problem. What his statement does imply is that meat of animals which had not been slaughtered but 'strangled' could be eaten. It would follow that Paul's list of the 'commandments of God' for gentiles was identical with a basic version of the Western text of the Apostolic Decree and with the three capital commandments of ancient Judaism.[23]

These considerations lead us to a hypothesis which needs further documentation but is proposed here to keep things moving. Paul's 'rule for all churches' in 1Cor 7:17-20 included three 'commandments of God' for gentiles (no idolatry, unchastity and bloodshed) and may be considered as being his version of the Apostolic Decree which is basically identical to the Western text. Ignoring the tricky problem of chronology we can also infer that Paul's story in Gal 2:1-14 presupposes this version of the Decree. As HARNACK suggested,[24] the best argument for the authenticity of the Western version is Paul's silence on the subject in Gal 2. Had James disputed Paul's version during the Jerusalem meeting, Paul could not have used the meeting to argue his fundamental support from Jerusalem.[25] This is not a plain argument from silence, for Paul's apology in Gal 2 is based on the assumption that James did support him, and this must have included some agreement on the moral code for gentile believers. It would follow that the requirements forwarded at Antioch by James' emissary transcended that basic Apostolic agreement.[26]

'All Things to All Men' (1Cor 9:19-23)

Another related passage is that which since the Church Fathers has been considered the classic text for Paul's alternating 'accomodation' to Jews and gentiles, 1Cor 9:19-23. The passionate dialectic of this fragment of Law theology typically Pauline, and it has has drawn much attention in recent years.[27] Unlike 1Cor 7:17-24 textual variants are considerable here and in their own way indicate that difficulty was found with the passage early on.

Commandments in which murder comes first. Cf Gal 5:19-21 and Did 2.

[23] If Paul taught εἰδωλολατρία instead of εἰδωλόθυτα the question from Corinth (1Cor 8:1) is the more understandable: does it include sacrificial food also as apart from actual worship?

[24] 'Aposteldekret', 159.

[25] The 'standard' Acts version may have become accepted in Asia minor including Antioch some years after the Jerusalem meeting. In view of the plurality of Noachian codes it need not be considered as being 'later' but simply a competitive stricter version which gained preference in times of tension. The initiative may well have been taken by James, see next n. On the historical background see above p235f and Dunn, 'Incident', 4-11; and cf Jewett, 'Agitators'.

[26] A next step would be to suggest that the Eastern text of the Decree was James' version imposed in excess of earlier agreement, as argued e.g. by Catchpole, 'Paul, James'. If tenable this would be an alternative to the explanation of the halakhic issue of Gal 2:11-14 offered in ch 6 above. But as stated this needs further study.

[27] See Chadwick, 'All Things'; Dodd, 'Ennomos Christou'; Bornkamm, 'Paul's Missionary Stance'; Richardson, 'Pauline Inconsistency'; Willis, 'Apostolic Apologia'; Gaston, Paul, 29-31; Gager, Origin, 236f.

The passage is intriguing since it is the only one where Paul speaks about his actual behaviour regarding what has come to be considered the central issue in his thought: the Law.[28] There is no reason to suppose that in this case commentators would stop applying the assumptions otherwise underlying their interpretation of his Law theology. Neither is it likely that the traditional assumptions are more apposite here than elsewhere in Paul. Therefore we would do well to consider the passage in close relation to its immediate and wider context as described above.

These are Paul's words:

> For though I am free from all, to all I came to serve, that I shall win the most: Thus I became to the Jews [as][29] a Jew, that I shall win Jews;[30] to those under the Law as under the Law, [not being myself under the Law][31] that I shall win those under the Law; to those without the Law as one without the Law – not being without the Law toward[32] God but in the Law toward Christ – that I win[33] those[34] without the Law; I became [like][35] a delicate to the delicate, that I shall win the delicate. To all I have become all things, that I shall by all means save some; and all[36] this I do for the sake of the gospel, that I may become its participant.

As we noted when analysing the argument of 1Cor 8-10 the words πᾶς and πάντα are thematic in those chapters. This is also true in our passage, which is full of rhetoric. It expresses the passionate desire to embrace all but at another level also involves a characteristic use of the Cynico-Stoic concept of freedom.[37] In addition we saw that chapter 9 as a whole is a rhetorical digression designed to illuminate the argument in chapters 8 and 10.

Therefore the passage must be intended to support, not to contradict the argument it is part and parcel of. We found that in contrast to traditional explanations, in the surrounding chapters Paul does not teach that idol food is indifferent and the Jewish Law irrelevant. As in the whole of First Corinthians the Law is extremely relevant in those of its commandments which also concern

[28] As noted by Weiss p242.
[29] Absent in some late mss, among others in uncorrected G; but G adds ὡς in v22 which supports its original reading here.
[30] The whole clause is absent in P46, most probably by *homoioteleuton* (Kenyon, *Chester Beatty* ad loc).
[31] Absent in D², Athos, Byzantine majority, one Syrian version, Origen (part), Chrysostom's commentary as opposed to the *lemma* (!) and other Patristic sources; see Aland-Black-Metzger, *Greek NT* (but see below). In P46 the place of the clause is in two decayed bottom lines which leave enough space to have included it; see Kenyon, *Papyri*, p71 fol 48 recto.
[32] Θεοῦ, Χριστοῦ; but D², Athos and Byzantine majority θεῳ, Χριστῳ, an easier and probably explanatory reading.
[33] κερδάνω; but P46 , corrected Sinai, Athos and Byzantine majority, as before, κερδήσω.
[34] Not in some uncials and the Byzantine majority.
[35] In Sinai corrector, Athos and other uncials, Byzantine majority, etc; not in P46, Sinai, A, B, etc.
[36] πάντα; but Athos, Byzantine majority and Syriac τούτο, which curiously breaks up the rhetorical unity.
[37] See Willis, 'Apostolic Apologia', 37 ('stock-in-trade parallels' which Paul 'reverses ...in a paradoxical manner'); Stanley Jones, *Freiheit*, 46-48; cf conclusions 143-5.

275

gentiles, in this case obviously the prohibition of idolatry. This does not of course mean that an idol or food offered to it 'is anything' in itself, and eating 'unspecified' pagan food is all right for gentile Christ-believers. But if a pagan indicates it to be sacrificial or a Christian neophyte suspects it to be so, one should not eat because of their idolatrous consciousness. The message is to renounce the 'freedom' to eat in those situations. This message of renunciation illuminated by the Apostle's self-sacrifice of his Apostolic right to 'eat and drink' and – in our passage – his personal forbearance regarding Jews, those 'under' or 'outside' the Law, and the delicate.

These considerations make it quite unlikely that Paul intended the phrase, 'to all I have become all things', to mean that he behaved like an unprincipled, cameleontic missionary;[38] or as the joke has it: that in trying to be a Jew with Jews and a Greek with Greeks he ended up being a Greek for Jews and a Jew for Greeks. Instead he wrote things like: 'If food causes my (delicate) brother to stumble, I shall never eat meat in eternity!' (8:13), as indeed, 'I became delicate to the delicate'. In view of the whole section on idol food it is impossible that Paul would accomodate to the extent of eating idol offerings in order to win Corinthian pagans. Nor, in view of our analyses of Gal 2 and Rom 14, should we suppose he would suspend Jewish dietary laws in order not to lose the gentiles at Antioch.[39] Indeed our explanation of 1Cor 7:17-20 makes that wholly improbable.[40] What we can suppose he did in order to communicate with gentiles and pagans, is to take a moderate view on their supposed idolatrous intention and eat with them as far as the flexibility of his tradition allowed him to do. Taking the context into account, the passage rather reminds one of his plea for plurality in life styles and expresses his desire to embrace 'all' in his passionate vision of the one 'body of Christ'. The passage serves the propagation of this vision directly in its context, but also illustrates it with the behaviour of the Apostle. In short 1Cor 9:19-23 seems to express Paul's personal efforts to effectuate the 'rule for all churches' stated in 1Cor 7:17-24.

With this review of the context in mind let us now turn to two relevant textual problems. First is the variant omitting '*as*' in the phrase 'I became to the Jews as a Jew'. Ἐγενόμην ὡς could be read as 'I showed myself to be',[41] which would

---

[38] Cf Chadwick, 'All Things', 261. His is an interesting study on Paul's 'astonishing flexibility of mind' in dealing with tricky situations, mentioning 1Cor 7; 8-10 and Col as examples. Unprincipled accomodation is presupposed by Barrett p211: 'His Judaism was no longer of his very being but a guise [!] he could adopt or discard at will.'

[39] Richardson, 'Pauline Inconsistency' sees 1Cor 9:19-24 as Paul's missionary 'principle of accomodation' which however he did not apply towards the Jewish brethren (Gal 2:11-14), seeing himself forced to sacrifice 'certain Jewish customs' (354). Furthermore Paul's 'treatment of women, body, prophecy, tongues all suggest a less flexible and more structured view of things' (356). More adequate Willis, 'Apostolic Apologia', 36 sees the passage as the stated 'principle' underlying Paul's unselfish behaviour recounted in 9:4-18.

[40] Bornkamm, 'Paul's Missionary Stance', 196f correctly states that 'Paul's attitude must be understood in light of 1Cor 7:17-24', but complicates this by means of the traditional principle that (even though 'not explicitly discussed') justification theology is central also in 1Cor.

[41] Conzelmann p195: ὡς is 'entbehrlich doch ursprünglich' and means 'ich zeige mich als'. Weiss

276

make the variant insignificant. However this should not stop us questioning its authenticity. There is some manuscript support for dropping ὡς;[42] moreover in view of the progressive development of anti-Judaism it is much easier to imagine its being added than its suppression. As to contents, the word γίγνο-μαι is used in an identical sense in some remarkable passages: Gal 4:4, 'God sent his son, born (γενόμενον) of woman, born under the Law',[43] and Rom 1:3, '...his son who was descended γενομένου from David according to the flesh'. Γίγνομαι seems to indicate 'factual becoming', indeed 'being born', and if we follow that rendering we get a very specific meaning especially fitting in the first and last relative clauses, the latter being unanimously attested without ὡς: 'I was born the Jews a Jew, ...I was born the delicate a delicate...' Elsewhere Paul emphatically declares that indeed he is a Jew 'according to the flesh' (Rom 9:3), and that a 'weakness' was bestowed on him, a 'thorn in the flesh' which was there to remain (2Cor 12:5-10). This decides the case against ὡς in v20a.

The incisive variant omitting the restrictive clause, 'not being myself under the Law', requires more explanation. We will successively discuss the textual aspects, the literary aspects, and contents. The omission not only occurs in late manuscripts, including the majority of Greek minuscles which all follow one main tradition, but significantly also in a quote in the course of Chrysostom's commentary, whereas the clause does appear in the 'lemma' at the head of the commentary section.[44] This indicates that his copyist, who would be used to insert or at least correct the extensive quotations at the head of each section, faithfully copied the shorter version within the commentary. There are three possibilities: the phrase was omitted later on purpose; it was omitted by mistake (jumping from the second to the third 'under Law'); or it was added later. The second possibility can never be excluded. The first possibility is unlikely, but the third very likely, once again in view of the development of anti-Judaism. Since the longer version is well documented in Chrysostom's day, his use within the commentary of the shorter version is very significant – all the more so since he would otherwise never have missed an opportunity to express his unflattering views on the Jews and their Law. Thus although as stated we cannot exclude scribal failure, the case for a later insertion seems reasonable.

As to the literary aspect it has been argued that our passage displays a beautiful harmonic structure.[45] This criterion should not lead an independent

points to γίνεσθαί τινί τι (Rom 16:2; Col 4:11), 'to act as though'; ὡς is unnecessary here hence omitted by some; but regarding the Law it is necessary because he had 'long since cut any relations with it'. This projects modern secularized Jewish existence into antiquity.

[42] See n29.

[43] With von der Osten-Sacken, *Evangelium*, 162.

[44] Cf above n31.

[45] Weiss p242; Bornkamm, 'Paul's Missionary Stance', 194f; Willis, 'Apostolic Apologia', p37 and n30.

life.[46] Leaving out the clause also produces an interesting structure.[47] Further-more, by itself the clause 'not being myself under the Law' sounds rather pedestrian and tautological after the restrictive 'as under the Law' and could have been thought up by any scribe. In contrast, the double clause 'not being without the Law toward God, but in the Law toward Christ' is no tautology but adds a brilliant, unmistakably Pauline dialectic. Finally both clauses in combi-nation create a sophism alien to Paul's passionate thought. As we shall see ἔννομος means 'respecting the Law'. Hence Paul would be stating here that he is 'not under the Law', yet 'not without the Law' but 'respecting the Law'. That sounds rather much like the unresolved and unprincipled missionary he was turned into. In contrast omitting the first clause makes the passage coherent: Paul, being a Jew, can communicate with Jews and also with gentiles as one of them, although he is not actually a gentile.

The contents of the disputed clause in themselves are certainly Pauline and seem to favour maintaining it. In other contexts Paul states, 'If you are led by the spirit you are not under the Law' (Gal 5:18); 'we were confined under the Law ...so that the Law was our custodian... but now that faith has come we are no longer under the custodian' (Gal 3:23-25); and, 'Sin will not have dominion over you, since you are not under the Law but under grace' (Rom 6:14). In this sense the term 'under the Law' relates to Paul's apocalyptic Law theology in which on the one hand one is still 'in the flesh' and (as a Jew) consequently 'under the Law', but on the other already 'led by the spirit'.[48] We should also recall that according to all manuscripts Paul inserts the particle 'as under the Law' in the preceding clause, the suggestion being that he is not really or not in all respects 'under the Law'. Here we may indeed surmise a shimmering reflection of the apocalyptic Law dialectics. The clause 'not being myself under the Law' would make this apocalyptic potential explicit.

But it is not clear why this apocalyptic imagery should actually be relevant in our passage, any more than in the sense of a faint echo from some such other

---

[46] Bornkamm, 'Missionary Stance', 194f, taking v20a and b together to make three clauses referring to Jews (v20), gentiles (v21) and the 'weak' of 1Cor 8-10 (v22a), concludes that *all* sentences (v19, 20-22a, 22b-23) have 'a concessive participal clause' (involving ὤν) stating Paul's Apostolic right and conduct. But on the accepted reading Bornkamm's 'middle sentence' has two concessive clauses and the third (v22b-23) has none. Moreover the grouping 'Jews, gentiles, and the "weak"' (doubtlessly inspired by the parallel in 10:32, see below) breaks up the fourfold divison.

[47] With the phrases of 'carnal factuality' as corner pieces the highly dialectic parenthesis ends up in the middle:

I was born the Jews a Jew, that I shall win Jews;

those under the Law as under the Law, that I shall win those under the Law;

those without the Law as one without the Law

-not being without the Law toward God but in the Law toward Christ -

that I win those without the Law;

I was born the delicate a delicate, that I shall win the delicate.

[48] For the apocalyptic dialectics of 'in the flesh' see e.g. Phil 1:22f and Phlm 16, ἐν σαρκὶ – ἐν Χριστῷ/κυρίῳ as a 'naive' opposition; Rom 7 (v5 versus v14, 18, 25!) as a painful 'meta-historical' antithesis; 2Cor 5:1-8 and 1Cor 15:35-49 on the eschatological horizon.

context.[49] On the contrary, the reference here is to various 'real' human positions or classes; this also applies to the second clause (see below). If Paul was a 'Jew', he would by all standards of antiquity be 'under' the Jewish Law. Indeed, the expression 'under the Law' also has a 'realistic' connotation which seems rather more appropriate here: 'Tell me, you who desire to be under the Law, do you not hear the Law?' (Gal 4:21). The reference is to Galatian Christians who feel the urge to accept the Jewish Law or at least to observe a number of additional commandments.[50] In that 'realistic' sense it is difficult to imagine how Paul, besides saying he is 'not without the Law but respecting it', could also state that he himself is 'not under the Law'.

Comparison of the contents with Gal 4:4f strongly pleads against acceptance of the clause. That verse is actually a full and important parallel to our passage: Christ was 'born from woman, born under the Law, that he should redeem those under the Law'. In view of this parallel the clause in our passage may be seen as another instance of *imitatio Christi*, a common topos in Paul and related to Hellenistic rhetoric.[51] Indeed this reveals an important new dimension: our passage itself functions as an extended appeal to follow Paul's unselfish example (the digression between 1Cor 8 and 10), as Paul in turn follows Christ's example. This is made explicit at the end of the longer section of which our passage is a part, and which is directly related to it:

> So whether you eat or drink, or whatever you do, do all to the glory of God; give no offense to Jews or to Greeks or to the church of God, just as I try to please all in all things, not seeking my own advantage but that of many that they may be saved; be imitators of me, as I am of Christ. (1Cor 10:31-11:1)

We note the recurring key word, 'all', the desire to 'save' all, and the intention towards Jews, Greeks and others. The imitation topic implies self-sacrifice and suffering for the good of others, as Paul makes explicit.[52] It would follow that in our passage Paul, following Christ, understands himself to be under the Law to save those under the Law. The clause 'not being myself under the Law' disrupts this vital connection.

Thus there are good arguments to omit the first restrictive clause. In that form the passage is a coherent and profound statement of Paul's personal position towards the Law both in a theoretical and a practical sense.[53]

---

[49] As in the, more elaborate, targumic flare-up of Law theology in the eschatological chapter, 1Cor 15:54-57.

[50] Gager, *Origin*, 236f proposes God-fearers or judaizers, correcting Gaston, *Paul*, 29-31 who takes the phrase to mean the 'gentile situation'. Both think of a distinctive group, which seems to be making too much of the rhetorics. On the other hand Willis, 'Apostolic Apologia', 37 overstates rhetorics and underestimates halakha.

[51] See above p83 n116.

[52] Cf also Phil 2:1-11; Col 1:24.

[53] The message of ἔννομος Χριστοῦ remains even if the clause is maintained, but is complicated by artificial dialectic.

As we have said the parenthesis μὴ ὢν ἄνομος θεοῦ ἀλλ' ἔννομος Χριστοῦ involves brilliant dialectics in regard of the Law. The word ἀνόμως elsewhere in Paul denotes 'outside the Law', i.e. the gentile position, with the correlate ἐν νόμῳ, within the Law', the position of Jews.[54] Furthermore the word ἔννομος is well attested in Philo and means 'respecting the Law', as opposed to ἔκνομος, 'outlaw'.[55] We note that in all cases 'the Law' has a factual meaning and in particular it means 'the Law of the Jews'. Thus at surface level Paul is not 'outside the Law' like a gentile; he is a Jew 'respecting the Law'.[56]

These attributes however are qualified by the dual concepts 'of God' and 'of Christ'. If this is to be taken as more than sheer rhetoric, as must always be supposed in Paul, it must have to do with his general conception of the position of Christ. Theological discussions by later authorities notwithstanding, Paul's christology is subordinationist and, for lack of a better term, inclusivist: 'You are Christ's and Christ is God's'; '...His son ...the first-born among many brethren'.[57] Paul is not Law-less, not a non-Jew, 'of God' – aptly translated 'toward God' or more elaborately 'under the aspect of God'; he is Law-respecting 'under the aspect of Christ'. This makes Pauline sense. 'Under the aspect of God', before his judgment seat where Jew and gentile are not to judge each other (cf Rom 14:10-12),[58] Paul is not a gentile but a Jew and is not going to change that (1Cor 7:18!). And positively he is Law-respecting 'under the aspect of Christ': he does not observe the Law as an aim in itself and standing alone but as one among various members of Christ's body.[59]

Again this leads us to compare Paul with Acts. Paul's well-known participation in purification ritual (Acts 21:17-26) followed a suggestion of the Jewish brethren in Jerusalem, and today this is often thought to reflect the author's interest in portraying a judaizing Paul. It is clear that the author has a personal stake in the issue, since he explicitly cites the Apostolic Decree in this context which obviously expresses one of his main concerns. But our interpretation of Paul's Apostolic example shows that the Acts story nevertheless portrays an authentic Paul. As far as the halakha is concerned the Acts Paul does not seem to differ much from the writer of the authentic Pauline letters.

Paul was actually born a Jew and a delicate,[60] and he 'became' as one under the Law but also as one without the Law – although not really without the Law. As such, he was able to communicate with all, while both staying true to his

---

54 Rom 2:12; cf 3:19 τοῖς ἐν τῷ νόμῳ i.e. the Jews.
55 Philo, In Flac 102, 104, 106f, 146, 189; De bened 82 (Flaccus = ἔκνομος). Weiss p244 refers to Plato, republ IV 424E ἔννομος, a suggestion adopted by Barrett p214 who translates 'Christ's law-abiding one'.
56 Dodd, 'Ennomos', explores the 'legalistic' potential of ἔννομος Χριστοῦ in the sense of a lex Christi opposed to the Mosaic Law, but taking into account the Jesus traditions in Paul.
57 1Cor 3:23 (see also 11:3; 15:28; Rom 1:4) and Rom 8:29 (see also 1Kor 15:20; Col 1:15, 18).
58 Cf Weiss p243 'nach dem Urteile Gottes'.
59 I interpret ὃ δὲ νῦν ζῶ ἐν σαρκί ἐν πίστει ζῶ (Gal 2:20, rhetorically addressed to Cephas, a fellow-Jew, 2:15!) in the sense of Rom 4:12, οὐκ ἐκ περιτομῆς μόνον ἀλλὰ καὶ ...τοῖς ἴχνεσιν ...τῆς πίστεως.
60 Rom 15:1 shows that Paul could change his point of view even here.

basic life as a Jew and to his guiding vision, the one body of Christ. This involved a double membership: of the group of those 'respecting the Law', the Jews, and of the body of Christ. The same duality is borne out in Rom 9-11, where Paul seems to think in terms of two concurrent elections: that of 'all Israel'[61] and that of the 'people' of Jews and gentiles, the community of Christ.[62]

This interpretation reveals 1Cor 9:19-23 as being the example in the Apostle's person of the same 'rule for all the churches' he stated two chapters earlier. It also confirms our preliminary conclusion regarding the meaning of the passage in view of its context. Furthermore it underlines the coherence of First Corinthians as a whole in which as we saw the halakha plays a distinctive role also for gentiles. We do not have to look for words describing that situation. Paul formulated them: 'For circumcision is nothing and foreskin is nothing, but keeping the commandments of God.'

We have concluded this book were we began: with the inspiration drawn from Albert SCHWEITZER. His explanation of what he termed Paul's *status quo* teaching proved a seminal insight. Schweitzer can stand on his own, failures included, and has done so all along. But we should not overlook the connection he points out on the existential level between Paul's subtle teaching regarding the Law and his eschatologically-motivated ethics. Beautiful and simple, the last chapter of his *Mystik*, written on the steamer to Lambarene,[63] seems to catch the quintessence of Paul: the visionary power of his thought, his awareness that 'in Christ' the new age is dawning which transcends the distinction between Jew and Greek, his confidence that this wicked world and the Law as we know it are passing, his sense of frailty of the human body and his intense yearning to see face to face at last. Precisely so, human life 'in the flesh' must be honoured. The eschatological existence 'in Christ' is consummated in actual life.

---

[61] 9:4; 11:1; 11:25. The phrase is standard in view of Israel's salvation, see mSan 10:1.
[62] Rom 9:6-24; 10:4-13.
[63] Schweitzer, *Leben und Denken*, 160.

Abbreviations

Names of biblical books, Apocrypha and Pseudepigraha, Josephus and Qumran are abbreviated according to the JBL system, with exception of the prefixed numeral (1Cor) and omitting italics and full stops. Philo's works are indicated with the abbreviations of the Loeb edition. For Rabbinic works see list below.

In the transcription of Hebrew words and names, a simple Anglo-based phonetic system rendering Israeli pronunciation is followed.

New Testament mss are mostly indicated with the sigla used and explained in Nestle-Aland (26th ed), except for non-Latin characters: Sinai (= alef), Athos (= psi), Byzantine majority or Koine (= Gothic M).

Works referred to by mere author name are commentaries on the Pauline passage under discussion.

1. *Text Editions of Mishna, Tosefta, Talmud*

Mishna
K	ms Kaufmann (ed Beer 1929) repr 1968
C	ms Cambridge (ed Lowe 1883) repr 1967
P	ms Parma (De Rossi 138) 1970
Parma C	ms Parma C (De Rossi 984) 1971

Tosefta
Zeraim-Nashim:	ed Lieberman 1955-73
Nezikin-Toharot:	ed Zuckermandel 1880

Yerushalmi
Geniza fragments:	ed Ginzberg 1909
ms Rome	ib
ed princ	Venice 1523-4, facs repr Berlin n.d.

Bavli
M	ms Munich (ed Strack 1912) repr 1971
NY	ms New York, ed Abramson 1957
ed princ	Venice 1520-3, repr 1968

2. *Mishnaic Tractates and Midrash Collections*

Ah	Ahilut
Ar	Arakhin
ARN a/b	Avot de-R. Natan (ed Schechter) vers. A/B
AZ	Avoda Zara
Av	Avot
b	Bavli (Babylonian Talmud)
BB	Bava Batra
Bekh	Bekhorot
Ber	Berakhot
Bik	Bikkurim
BK	Bava Kamma
BM	Bava Metsia
CantR	Canticles Rabba
Dem	Demai
Ed	Eduyot
Er	Eruvin
GenR	Genesis Rabba (ed Theodor-Albeck)
Git	Gittin
Hag	Hagiga
Hal	Halla
Hor	Horayot
Hul	Hullin
Kel	Kelim
Ker	Keritot
Ket	Ketubbot
Kid	Kiddushin
LevR	Leviticus Rabba (ed M. Margulies)
m	Mishna
Maas	Maasrot
Mak	Makkot
Makhs	Makhshirin
Meg	Megilla
Mekh	Mekhilta de-R. Yishmael (ed Horovitz-Rabin)
MekhRSbY	Mekhilta de-R. Sh. b. Yohai (ed Epstein-Melamed)
Men	Menahot
Mid	Middot
MidrGad Deut	Midrash Gadol on Deuteronomy (ed Fisch)
MidrGad Gen	Midrash Gadol on Genesis (ed Margulies)
MidrPs	Midrash on Psalms (ed Buber)
Mikw	Mikwaot
MSh	Maaser Sheni
Naz	Nazir
Ned	Nedarim

Oh	Ohalot
Pes	Pesahim
PesR	Pesikta Rabbati (ed Friedmann)
PesRK	Pesikta de-R. Kahana (ed Mandelbaum)
Pis	Pisha
RH	Rosh Hashana
San	Sanhedrin
SER	Seder Eliyahu Rabba (ed Friedmann)
SEZ	Seder Eliyahu Zutta (ed Friedmann)
Shab	Shabbat
Shev	Sheviit
Shevu	Shevuot
Shek	Shekalim
SifDeut	Sifrei Deuteronomy (ed Finkelstein)
SifNum	Sifrei Numbers (ed Horovitz)
Sot	Sota
Suk	Sukka
t	Tosefta
Taan	Taanit
Tam	Tamid
Tanh	Tanhuma
TanhB	Tanhuma (ed Buber)
Tem	Temura
TevY	Tevul Yom
Tg	Targum
TgPs-Yon	Targum Pseudo-Yonathan = TgYer (Yerushalmi)
Toh	Toharot
Ukts	Uktsin
y	Yerushalmi (Palestinian Talmud)
Yad	Yadayim
YalkShim	Yalkut Shimoni (ed Hyman)
Yev	Yevamot
Yom	Yoma
YT	Yom Tov
Zav	Zavim
Zev	Zevahim

3. Periodicals, Reference Works and Related Abbreviations

ANRW	Aufstieg und Niedergang der römischen Welt (Berlin; ed W. Haase – H. Temporini)
ASTI	Annual of the Swedish Theological Institute
BAR	Biblical Archeological Review
BJRL	Bulletin of the John Rylands Library
CBQ	Catholic Biblical Quarterly
CII	Corpus inscriptionum iudaicarum (Frey)

DJD	Discoveries in the Judaean Desert
EJ	Encyclopaedia Judaica (1972)
EphTh	Ephemerides Theologicae Lovanienses
ET	English translation
EvTh	Evangelische Theologie
FS	Festschrift
GT	German translation
HTR	Harvard Theological Review
HTS	Harvard Theological Studies
HUCA	Hebrew Union College Annual
ICC	International Critical Commentary
IEJ	Israel Exploration Journal
JJS	Journal of Jewish Studies
JBL	Journal of Biblical Literature
JQR	Jewish Quarterly Review
JSNT	Journal for the Study of the New Testamenty
JThSt	Journal of Theological Studies
KS	Kirjath Sepher
MGWJ	Monatsschrift f. d. Geschichte und Wissenschaft des Judentums
MPG	Migne, Patrum graecorum cursus completus
MPL	Migne, Patrum latinorum cursus completus
NedTT	Nederlands Theologisch Tijdschrift
nF	Neue Folge
NovT	Novum Testamentum
ns	new series
NTS	New Testament Studies
PIASH	Proceedings of the Israel Academy of Sciences and Humanities
PW	Pauly-Wissowa (see Bibl.)
PWCJS	Proceedings, World Congress of Jewish Studies
RB	Revue biblique
REJ	Revue des études juives
RQ	Revue de Qumran
RSR	Recherches de science réligieuse
RSV	Revised Standard Version
SBL	Society for Biblical Literature
Scripta	Scripta Hierosolymitana
SNTS	Societas Novi Testamenti Studiosorum
ST	Studia Theologica
ThExH	Theologische Existenz Heute
TuU	Texte und Untersuchungen
ZNW	Zeitschrift für die neutestamentliche Wissenschaft
ZRGG	Zeitschrift für Religion und Geistesgeschichte
ZTK	Zeitschrift für Theologie und Kirche

Bibliography

AGNEW, F.H. 'The Origin of the New Testament Apostle-Concept. A Review of Research'. *JBL* 105 (1986) 75-96

ALAND, K. – BLACK, M. – METZGER, B. *The Greek New Testament*. 3rd ed [Münster] 1975

ALBECK, CH. *Introduction to the Mishna*. 4th pr Jerusalem – Tel Aviv 1974 (Hebr; GT Berlin – New York 1971)

-- *Shisha Sidrei Mishna* 1-6. Jerusalem – Tel Aviv 1952-8 and repr

ALLISON, D.C. 'The Pauline Epistles and the Synoptic Gospels: The Pattern of the Parallels'. *NTS* 28 (1982) 1-32

ALLO, P.E.-B. *St. Paul: Première Épître aux Corinthiens*. 2nd ed Paris 1956

ALON, G. 'Ha-halakha be-Iggeret Bar Nava', *Tarbiz* 12 (1940-41) 23-43, 223 (repr in *Studies* 1, 295-312)

-- 'Ha-halakha ba-Torat 12 ha-Shelihim', *Tarbiz* 11 (1939-40) 127-45 (repr in *Studies* 1, 274-94)

-- *Jews, Judaism and the Classical World. Studies in Jewish History in the Times of the Second Temple and the Talmud*. Jerusalem 1977

-- *The Jews in Their Land in the Talmudic Age* 1-2. Jerusalem 1980-4

-- *Studies in Jewish History in the Times of the Second Temple, the Mishna and the Talmud* 1-2. Tel Aviv 1958 (Hebr)

AMIR, Y. *Die hellenistische Gestalt des Judentums bei Philon von Alexandrien*. Neukirchen-Vluyn 1983

-- 'The Term Ioudaïsmos. A Study in Jewish-Hellenistic Self-Identification'. *Immanuel* 14 (1982) 34-41

APPLEBAUM, S. 'The Organization of the Jewish Communities in the Diaspora', in *Compendia* I/2, 464-503

ATTRIDGE, H.W. *First Century Cynicism in the Epistles of Heraclitus* (HTS 29) Missoula 1976

AVI-YONAH, M. *Geschichte der Juden im Zeitalter des Talmud in den Tagen von Rom und Byzanz*. Berlin 1962

AYALI, M. *Poalim we-omanim; malakhatam u-maamadam be-sifrut Hazal*. Jerusalem 1987

BACHER, W. *Die Agada der Tannaiten* 1-2. Strassburg 1884-90

-- *Die exegetische Terminologie der jüdischen Traditionsliteratur* 1-2 (1899-1905) repr Darmstadt 1965

BAER, Y.F. *Israel among the Nations*. Jerusalem 1955 (Hebr)

BAMMEL, E. – BARRETT, C.K. – DAVIES, W.D. (eds) *Donum gentilicum; New Testament Studies in Honour of David Daube*. Oxford 1978

BARRETT, C.K. 'Cephas and Corinth', (in *Abraham unser Vater. FS O. Michel* 1963) repr in *Essays*, 28-39

-- *A Commentary on the First Epistle to the Corinthians*. 2nd ed London 1971 and repr

-- *Essays on Paul*. London 1982

-- 'Paul and the 'Pillar' Apostles'; in Sevenster – Van Unnik, *Studia Paulina*, 1-19

-- 'Shaliah and Apostle', in Bammel, *Donum gentilicum*, 88-102

-- 'Things Sacrificed to Idols', (*NTS* 11 [1964-65] 138-53) repr in *Essays*, 40-59

BARTCHY, S.S. *Mallon Chrêsai: First-Century Slavery and I Corinthians 7:21* (SBL Diss Ser 11) Missoula 1973

BARTH, K. *Evangelium und Gesetz* (ThExH 32) München 1935
-- *Die kirchliche Dogmatik* 1/1-4/4. Zurich 1932-67
-- *Der Römerbrief.* 2nd ed (1922) repr Zurich 1967
-- 'Rudolf Bultmann – ein Versuch, ihn zu verstehen'; in id, *Rudolf Bultmann. Christus und Adam. Zwei theologische Studien.* 3d ed Zurich 1964, 9-65
BAUER, W. *Wörterbuch zu den Schriften des Neuen Testaments und der übrigen urchristlichen Literatur.* 5th ed Berlin 1963
BAUMGARTEN, J.M. 'The Laws of 'Orlah and First Fruits in the Light of Jubilees, the Qumran Writings, and Targum Ps. Jonathan'. *JJS* 38 (1987) 195-202
-- *Studies in Qumran Law,* Leiden 1977
BAUR, F.C. 'Die Christuspartei in der korinthischen Gemeinde, der Gegensatz des petrinischen und paulinischen Christentums in der ältesten Kirche, der Apostel Petrus in Rom'. *Tübinger Zeitschrift für Theologie,* 1831 fasc 4, 61-206 (repr in id, *Ausgewählte Werke in Einzelausgaben* 1, ed K. Scholder, Stuttgart – Bad Cannstatt 1963, 1-146)
-- 'Über Zweck und Veranlassung des Römerbriefs und die damit zusammenhängenden Verhältnisse der römischen Gemeinde. Eine historisch-kritische Untersuchung'. *Tübinger Zeitschrift für Theologie,* 1836 fasc 3, 59-178 (repr in id, *Ausgewählte Werke in Einzelausgaben* 1, ed K. Scholder, Stuttgart – Bad Cannstatt 1963, 147-266)
BEKER, J.C. *Paul the Apostle: The Triumph of God in Life and Thought.* Edinburgh 1980
-- 'Paul's Theology: Consistent or Inconsistent?' *NTS* 34 (1988) 364-77
BELKIN, S. *The Alexandrian Halakah in Apologetic Literature of the First Century C.E.* Philadelphia n.d.
-- *Philo and the Oral Law; The Philonic Interpretation of Biblical Law in Relation to the Palestinian Halakah.* Cambridge MA 1940
BETZ, H.D. '2 Cor 6:14-7:1: An Anti-Pauline Fragment?' *JBL* 92 (1973) 88-108
-- *Galatians; A Commentary on Paul's Letter to the Churches in Galatia.* Philadelphia 1979
BLAU, L. *Die jüdische Ehescheidung und der jüdische Scheidebrief; eine historische Untersuchung* 1-2. Strassburg 1911-12
BLIDSTEIN, G.J. 'The Sale of Animals to Gentiles in Talmudic Law'. *JQR* 61 (1970-1) 188-98
BOCKMUEHL, M. 'Matthew 5.32; 19.9 in the Light of Pre-Rabbinic Halakhah'. *NTS* 35 (1989) 291-5
BÖCKENHOFF, K. *Das apostolische Speisegesetz in den ersten fünf Jahrhunderten.* Paderborn 1903
BORNKAMM, G. 'The Missionary Stance of Paul in I Cor. 9 and Acts', in L. Keck – L. Martyn, *Studies in Luke-Acts* (in honour of P. Schubert) London 1966 (repr 1978) 194-207
BOUSSET, W. *Der Apostel Paulus.* Tübingen 1906
-- *Kyrios Christos. Geschichte des Christusglaubens von den Anfangen des Christentums bis Irenäus.* 2nd ed Göttingen 1921
BOUSSET, W. – GRESSMANN, H. *Die Religion des Judentums im späthellenistischen Zeitalter.* 3rd ed Tübingen 1926
BROOTEN, B.J. 'Jewish Women's History in the Roman Period: A Task for Christian Theology'. *HTR* 79 (1986) 22-30
-- 'Konnten Frauen im alten Judentum die Scheidung betreiben? Überlegungen zu Mk 10, 10-12 und 1 Kor 7,10-11'. *EvTh* 42 (1982) 65-80
-- *Women Leaders in the Ancient Synagogue. Inscriptional Evidence and Background Issues.* Chico CA 1982
BROWN, R.E. *The Semitic Background of the Term 'Mystery' in the New Testament.* Philadelphia 1968
BRUCE, F.F. *1 and 2 Corinthians.* London 1971
-- 'The Romans Debate – Continued'. *BJRL* 64/2 (1981) 334-59
BRUNT, J.C. *Paul's Attitude toward and Treatment of Problems Involving Dietary Practice. A Case Study in Pauline Ethics* (microf diss, Emory U) Ann Arbor 1978
-- 'Rejected, Ignored, or Misunderstood? The Fate of Paul's Approach to the Problem of Food Offered to Idols in Early Christianity'. *NTS* 31 (1985) 113-24
BUBER, M. *Zwei Glaubensweisen* (1950) repr in id, *Werke* 1, Munich 1961, 651-782
BÜCHLER, A. 'Halakhot le-maase ke-Veit Shammai bi-zeman ha-bait', in *FS M. Bloch* 2. Budapest 1905, 21-30

-- 'Hearot we-haarot al matsav ha-isha be-Sefer Yehudit' (in *FS Blau*, Budapest 1926) repr in id, *Studies*, Hebrew part 45-77

-- 'Igarot Rabban Shimon ben Gamliel ha-Zaken we-Rabban Yohanan ben Zakkai al biur maaser bi-zeman ha-Bayit' (in *Blau Memorial Vol.*, Budapest 1938) repr in id, *Studies*, Hebrew part 1-14

-- 'The Levitical Impurity of the Gentile in Palestine before the Year 70'. *JQR* ns 17 (1926-7) 1-81

-- *Studies in Jewish History*, Oxford 1956

-- 'Traces des idées et coutûmes hellénistiques dans le livre des Jubilés'. *REJ* 89 (1930) 321-48

BULTMANN, R. 'Christus des Gesetzes Ende'; in id, *Glauben und Verstehen* 2. 3d ed Tübingen 1961, 32-58

-- 'Zur Geschichte der Paulus-Forschung', (*Theol. Rundschau* ns 1 [1929] 26-59) repr in Rengstorf – Luck, *Paulusbild*, 304-37

-- *Theologie des Neuen Testaments*. 5th ed Tübingen 1965

BURTON, E. DEWITT *A Critical and Exegetical Commentary on the Epistle to the Galatians* (ICC) Edinburgh 1921

CADBURY, H.J. 'The Macellum of Corinth'. *JBL* 53 (1934) 134-41

CATCHPOLE, D.R. 'Paul, James and the Apostolic Decree'. *NTS* 23 (1977) 428-44

CERFAUX, L. *La Théologie de l'Église suivant St. Paul*. 3d ed Paris 1965

CHADWICK, H. ''All Things to All Men' (I Cor. ix. 22)'. *NTS* 1 (1954-5) 261-75

-- 'St. Paul and Philo of Alexandria'. *BJRL* 48 (1965-6) 286-307

CHARLESWORTH, J. *The Old Testament Pseudepigrapha* 1-2. Garden City / London 1983-5

COHEN, B. *Jewish and Roman Law; A Comparative Study* 1-2. New York 1966

COHEN, N.G. 'The Jewish Dimension of Philo's Judaism – An Elucidation of the Spec. Leg. IV 132-150'. *JJS* 38 (1987) 164-86

COHEN, Y. *Ha-yahas el ha-nokhri ba-halakha uba-metsiut bi-tekufat ha-Tannaim* (diss Hebrew U) Jerusalem 1975

COLSON, F.H. *Philo. With an English Translation* 1-10. *Supplement* (transl R.A. Marcus) 1-2. (Loeb Classical Library) London – Cambridge MA 1929-53 and repr

COMPENDIA I/1-2: see Safrai-Stern

COMPENDIA II/2: see Stone

COMPENDIA II/3a: see Safrai

CONZELMANN, H. *Der erste Brief an die Korinther* (Meyers Komm 5, 12th ed) 2nd ed Göttingen 1981

COUNE, M. 'La Problème des idolothytes et l'éducation de la syneidêsis'. *RSR* 51 (1963) 497-534

DAUBE, D. *The New Testament and Rabbinic Judaism*. London 1956

-- 'Onesimos', *HTR* 79 (1986) 40-43

DAVIES, W.D. *Christian Origins and Judaism*. London 1962

-- 'Conscience and Its Use in the New Testament'; in id, *Studies*, 243-56

-- *Jewish and Pauline Studies* (ed by D.C. Allison) London 1984

-- 'Paul and Judaism [since Schweitzer]' (in Hyatt, *Bible*, 17886) repr in Davies, *Paul*, vii-xv

-- 'Paul and the Law'; in Hooker-Wilson, *Paul and Paulinism*, 4-16

-- 'Paul and the People of Israel', (*NTS* 24 [1977] 4-39) in id, *Studies*, 123-52, 341-56

-- *Paul and Rabbinic Judaism* (1948) 3rd ed London 1971

-- *The Setting of the Sermon on the Mount* (1963) repr Cambridge 1966

DEISSMANN, A. *Licht vom Osten*. 4th ed Tübingen 1923

DIBELIUS, M. *Der Hirt des Hermas* (Ergzbd Hdb z NT, Die apostolischen Väter iv) Tübingen 1923

DIMANT, D. '4QFlorilegium and the Idea of the Community as Temple', in A. Caquot – M. Hadas-Lebel – J. Riaud (eds) *Hellenica et Judaica; Hommage à Valentin Nikiprowetzky Z'L*. Leuven – Paris 1986, 165-89

-- 'Qumran Sectarian Literature'; in *Compendia* II/2, 483-550

DODD, C.H. 'Ennomos Christou'; in Sevenster-van Unnik, *Studia Paulina*, 96-111

DONFRIED, K.P. (ed) *The Romans Debate*. Minneapolis 1977

DRANE, J.W. *Paul, Libertine or Legalist? A Study in the Theology of the Major Pauline Epistles*. London 1975

-- 'Tradition, Law and Ethics in Pauline Theology'. *NovT* 16 (1974) 167-78

DUNN, J.D.G. 'The Incident at Antioch (Gal. 2:11-18)'. *JSNT* 18 (1983) 3-57

-- 'The New Perspective on Paul'. *BJRL* 65/2 (1982) 95-122

ECKSTEIN, H.-J. *Der Begriff Syneidesis bei Paulus. Eine neutestamentlich-exegetische Untersuchung zum 'Gewissensbegriff* (WUNT 2/10) Tübingen 1983

ELBOGEN, I. *Der jüdische Gottesdienst in seiner geschichtlichen Entwicklung.* Frankfurt 1931, repr Hildesheim 1962

ELLIS, E.E. 'Pauline Studies in Recent Research'; in id, *Paul and His Recent Interpreters.* Grand Rapids 1961, 11-34

-- 'Traditions in I Corinthians'. *NTS* 32 (1986) 481-502

ELMSLIE, W.A.I. *The Mishnah on Idolatry.* Cambridge 1911, repr Wiesbaden 1967

EPSTEIN, J.N. *Introduction to Tannaitic Literature. Mishna, Tosephta and Halakhic Midrashim.* Ed by E.Z. Melamed. Jerusalem 1957 (Hebr)

-- 'Ha-madda ha-talmudi we-tsorkhav', in *Yediot ha-Makhon le-maddaei ha-Yahadut,* fasc 2, Jerusalem 1925, 5-22

-- *Mavo le-nosah ha-Mishna.* 1-2. Jerusalem 1948, rev ed 1964

ERIKSON, E.H. *Young Man Luther; A Study in Psychoanalysis and History.* New York 1958

FALK, Z.W. *Introduction to Jewish Law of the Second Commonwealth* 1-2. Leiden 1972-78

-- *Legal Values and Judaism; Towards a Philosophy of Halakhah.* Jerusalem 1980 (Hebr)

-- 'Jewish Private Law', in *Compendia* I/1, 504-34

FEE, G.D. 'II Cor. vi.14-vii.1 and Food Offered to Idols'. *NTS* 23 (1976-7) 140-61

-- 'Eidolothuta Once Again: An Interpretation of 1 Cor. 8-10'. *Biblica* 61 (1980) 172-97

FELDMAN, L. 'How Much Hellenism in Jewish Palestine?'. *HUCA* 57 (1986) 86-112

-- 'The Omnipresence of the God-Fearers'. *BAR* 12 (1986) 58-69

FINKELSTEIN, L. 'The Book of Jubilees and the Rabbinic Halaka'. *HTR* 16 (1923) 39-61

FISCHEL, H.A. 'Studies in Cynicism and the Ancient Near East; The Transformation of a Chria', in: Neusner, *Religions*, 372-411

-- *Rabbinic Literature and Graeco-Roman Philosophy; A Study of Epicurea and Rhetorica in Early Midrashic Writings.* Leiden 1973

FISCHEL, H.A. (ed) *Essays in Greco-Roman and Related Talmudic Literature.* New York 1977

FITZMEYER, J.A. *To Advance the Gospel; New Testament Studies.* New York 1981

-- 'Paul and the Law', in *To Advance the Gospel*, 185-201

-- 'The Matthean Divorce Texts and Some New Palestinian Evidence', in *To Advance the Gospel*, 79-111

-- 'Qumran and the Interpolated Paragraph 2 Cor 6:14-7:1'. *CBQ* 23 (1961) 271-80 (GT in Grözinger, *Qumran*, 385-98)

FJÄRSTEDT, B. *Synoptic Tradition in 1 Corinthians; Themes and Clusters of Theme Words in 1 Corinthians 1-4 and 9.* Uppsala 1974

FLUSSER, D. 'Antioch'; in *EJ* 3, 71-73

-- 'Blessed are the Poor in Spirit'. *IEJ* 10 (1960) 1-13

-- 'Die Christenheit nach dem Apostelkonzil'; in W.P Eckert – N.P. Levinson – M. Stohr (eds) *Antijudaismus im Neuen Testament? Exegetische und systematische Beiträge.* Munich 1967, 60-81

-- 'The Conclusion of Matthew in a New Source'. *ASTI* 5 (1967) 110-20

-- 'The Dead Sea Sect and Pre-Pauline Christianity'; in *Scripta* 4 (1958) 215-66

-- 'Have You ever seen a Lion as Porter?' in B. Uffenheimer (ed) *Bible and Jewish History. Studies in Bible and Jewish History Dedicated to the Memory of J. Liver.* Tel Aviv 1971, 330-40 (Hebr)

-- *Jesus; in Selbstzeugnissen und Bilddokumenten.* Hamburg 1968

-- *Jewish Sources in Early Christianity. Studies and Essays.* Jerusalem 1979 (Hebr)

-- 'De Joodse en Griekse vorming van Paulus', in *Paulus.* Becht: Amsterdam (no date; tr from the German, Herder: Freiburg i/Br) 9-37

-- *Judaism and the Origins of Christianity* (collected articles) Jerusalem 1988

-- 'The Last Supper and the Essenes'. *Immanuel* 2 (1973) 23-7

-- 'Melchizedek and the Son of Man'. *Christian News from Israel* 17 (1966) 23-9

-- 'Motsa ha-Natsrut min ha-Yahadut'; in *Sefer Yitshak Baer.* Jerusalem 1961, 75-98

-- 'A New Sensitivity in Judaism and the Christian Message'. *HTR* 61 (1968) 107-27

-- 'Paganism in Palestine'; in *Compendia* I/2, 1065-1100

-- 'Paul's Jewish-Christian Opponents in the Didache', in *Gilgul. Essays on Transformation, Revolution and Permanence in the history of Religions. Dedicated to R.J. Zwi Werblowski*. Ed by S. Shaked, D. Shulman and G.G. Strumsa. Leiden–New York–Copenhagen–Cologne 1987, 71-90

-- 'Pharisäer, Sadduzäer und Essener im Pesher Nahum', in Grözinger, *Qumran*, 121-66

-- *Die rabbinischen Gleichnisse und der Gleichniserzähler Jesus*. 1: *Das Wesen der Gleichnisse*. Bern– Frankfurt/M – Las Vegas 1981

-- 'Qumran und die Zwölf'; in C.J. Bleeker (ed) *Initiation. Contributions... International Association for the History of Religions*. Leiden 1965, 134-46

-- 'The Slave of Two Masters'. *Immanuel* 6 (1976) 30-33

-- 'Die Tora in der Bergpredigt', in H. Kremers (ed) *Juden und Christen lesen dieselbe Bibel*. Duisburg 1973, 102-113

-- 'Two Anti-Jewish Montages in Matthew'. *Immanuel* 5 (1975) 37-45 (also in *Judaism*, 552-60)

-- 'Two Notes on the Midrash on 2 Sam. vii'. *IEJ* 9 (1959) 99-109

FLUSSER, D. – SAFRAI, S. 'Das Aposteldekret und die Noachitischen Gebote'; in E. Brocke – H.-J. Barkenings (eds) *'Wer Tora vermehrt, mehrt Leben'. Festgabe für Heinz Kremers zum 60. Geburtstag*. Neukirchen/Vluyn 1986, 173-92

FOX, R.L. *Pagans and Christians in the Mediterranean World from the Second Century AD to the Conversion of Constantine* (1986) repr London 1988

FREY, J.B. *Corpus Inscriptionum Iudaicarum* 1-2. Rome 1936-52

GAFNI, I.M. 'The Historical Background'; in *Compendia* II/2, 1-31

GAGER, J.C. 'Jews, Gentiles and Synagogues in the Book of Acts'. *HTR* 79 (1986) 91-99

-- *The Origins of Anti-Semitism: Attitudes towards Judaism in Pagan and Christian Antiquity*. New York 1983

GAYER, R. *Die Stellung des Sklaven in den paulinischen Gemeinden und bei Paulus. Zugleich ein sozialgeschichtlich vergleichender Beitrag zur Wertung des Sklaven in der Antike* (Europ Univ Papers xxiii/78) Bern – Frankfurt/M 1976

GASTON, L. *Paul and the Torah*. Vancouver 1987

GERHARDSSON, B. 'I Kor 13 – Zur Frage von Paulus' rabbinischem Hintergrund', in Bammel, *Donum gentilicum*, 185-209

GILAT, Y.D. *The Teachings of R. Eliezer ben Hyrcanos and Their Position in the History of the Halakha*. Tel Aviv 1968 (Hebr)

GILBERT, M. 'Wisdom Literature'; in *Compendia* II/2, 283-324

GINZBERG, L. *A Commentary on the Palestinian Talmud* 1-4. New York 1941-61 (Hebr)

-- *The Legends of the Jews* 1-6. Philadelphia 1909-28; vol 7, index (B. Cohen) 1938; and repr

-- 'The Religion of the Jews at the Time of Jesus'. *HUCA* 1 (1924) 307-21

-- *An Unknown Jewish Sect* (integral publ of *Eine unbekannte jüdische Sekte*, 1922) New York 1976

GOLDBERG, ABR. *Commentary to the Mishna Shabbat*. Critically Edited and Provided with Introduction, Commentary and Notes. Jerusalem 1976 (Hebr)

-- 'The Mishna – A Study Book of Halakha', in *Compendia* II/3a, 211-44

-- 'The Tosefta – Companion to the Mishna', in *Compendia* II/3a, 283-98

GOLDBERG, H.E. (ed) *Judaism Viewed from Within and From Without; Anthropological Studies*. Albany NY 1987

GOLDSTEIN, J.A. 'Jewish Acceptance and Rejection of Hellenism'; in E.P. Sanders et al (eds) *Jewish and Christian Self-Definition*. 2: *Aspects of Judaism in the Graeco-Roman Period*. London 1981, 64-87

GOODENOUGH, E.R. *An Introduction to Philo Judaeus* (1940) 2nd ed Oxford 1962

-- *Jewish Symbols in The Greco-Roman Period* 1-13. New York 1953-68

-- *By Light, Light; The Mystic Gospel of Hellenistic Judaism* (New Haven 1935) repr Amsterdam 1969

-- 'Paul and the Hellenization of Christianity', in Neusner, *Religions*, 23-68

-- *The Politics of Philo Judaeus*. New Haven 1938

GRAETZ, H. *Geschichte der Juden von den ältesten Zeiten bis auf die Gegenwart* 3/2. Leipzig 1888

GRÖZINGER, K.E. et al (eds), *Qumran* (Wege der Forschung 410) Darmstadt 1981

GUTTMANN, M. *Das Judentum und seine Umwelt*. Berlin 1927

291

HAACKER, K. 'War Paulus Hillelit?' in *Das Institutum Judaicum der Universität Tübingen* 1971-72, 106-20

HAHN, F. 'Taufe und Rechtfertigung. Ein Beitrag zur paulinischen Theologie in ihrer Vor- und Nachgeschichte'; in *FS Käsemann*, 95-124

HARNACK, A. VON, 'Das Aposteldekret und die Blaßsche Hypothese', in *Sitzungsberichte der königlichen preußischen Akademie der Wissenschaften* 1, Berlin 1899, 150-76 (repr in id, *Studien zur Geschichte des Neuen Testaments und der alten Kirche*. Berlin – Leipzig 1931, 1-32)

-- *Beiträge zur Einleitung in das Neue Testament* IV: *Neue Untersuchungen zur Apostelgeschichte und zur Abfassungszeit der synoptischen Evangelien*. Leipzig 1911

-- *Marcion: das Evangelium vom fremden Gott; eine Monographie zur Geschichte der Grundlegung der Katholischen Kirche* (TuU 3/15) Leipzig 1921

-- *Die Mission und Ausbreitung des Christentums in den ersten drei Jahrhunderten*. 4th ed Leipzig 1924

-- *Das Wesen des Christentums*. Leipzig 1901

HEINEMANN, I. 'Herakleitos, Briefe des'; in *PW Suppl* 5, 228-32

-- *Philons griechische und jüdische Bildung; kulturvergleichende Untersuchungen zu Philons Darstellung der jüdischen Gesetze* (Breslau 1929-32) repr Darmstadt 1962

-- *Taamei ha-mitswot be-sifrut Yisrael* 1 (1942) 5th ed Jerusalem 1966

HENGEL, M. *Judaism and Hellenism. Studies in their Encounter in Palestine during the Early Hellenistic Period* 1-2 (ET of 2nd ed 1973) repr London 1981

-- *Juden, Griechen und Barbaren*. Stuttgart 1976

-- 'Zwischen Jesus und Paulus. Die 'Hellenisten', die 'Sieben' und Stephanus (Apg 6,1-15; 7,54-8,3)'. *ZTK* 72 (1975) 151-206

-- *Die Zeloten. Untersuchungen zur jüdischen Freiheitsbewegung in der Zeit von Herodes I bis 70 n. Chr.* 2nd ed Leiden 1976

HERR, M.D. 'Ha-hellenismus weha-Yehudim be-Erets Yisrael'. *Eshkoliot* ns 3-2 (1976-7) 20-7

-- 'Persecutions and Martyrdom in Hadrian's Days', in *Scripta* 23 (1972) 85-125

HOFFMANN, C. *Juden und Judentum im Werk deutscher Althistoriker des 19. und 20. Jahrhunderts*. Leiden 1988

HOFFMANN, D. *Midrasch Tannaim zum Deuteronomium* 2. (Berlin 1909) repr n. d., n. pl. (Hebr)

HOHEISEL, K. *Das antike Judentum in christlicher Sicht. Ein Beitrag zur neueren Forschungsgeschichte*. Wiesbaden 1978

HOOKER, M.D. 'Paul and Covenantal Nomism'; in Hooker-Wilson, *Paul*, 47-56

HOOKER, M.D. – WILSON, S.G. (eds) *Paul and Paulinism. Essays in honour of C.K. Barrett*. London 1982

HORSLEY, R.A. 'Gnosis in Corinth: 1 Cor. 8.1-6'. *NTS* 27 (1981) 32-51

HORST, P.W. VAN DER, 'Jews and Christians in Aphrodisias in the Light of Their Relations in Other Cities of Asia Minor'. *NedTT* 43 (1989) 106-21

-- *The Sentences of Pseudo-Phocylides. With Introduction and Commentary*. Leiden 1978

HÜBNER, H. 'Gal 3,10 und die Herkunft des Paulus'. *KuD* 19 (1973) 215-31

-- *Das Gesetz bei Paulus; ein Beitrag zum Werden der paulinischen Theologie*. 2nd ed Göttingen 1980

-- 'Paulusforschung seit 1945; ein kritischer Literaturbericht', in *ANRW* II/25.4, 2649-2840 [sic]

HURD, J.C. *The Origin of I Corinthians*. London 1965

HYATT, J.P. *The Bible in Modern Scholarship* (papers 100th SBL meeting 1964) London 1966

JASTROW, M. *A Dictionary of the Targumim, the Talmud Babli and Yerushalmi, and the Midrashic Literature* 1-2. Philadelphia 1903 and repr

JEREMIAS, J. 'Zur Gedankenführung in den paulinischen Briefen'; in Sevenster-van Unnik, *Studia Paulina*, 146-54

-- 'Paulus als Hillelit', in E.E. Ellis – M. Wilcox (eds) *Neotestamentica et semitica; Studies in Honour of M. Black*. Edinburgh 1969, 88-94

JEWETT, R. 'The Agitators and the Galatian Congregation'. *NTS* 17 (1970-1) 198-212

JÓNSSON, J. *Humour and Irony in the New Testament; Illuminated by Parallels in Talmud and Midrash*. 2nd ed Leiden 1985

KADUSHIN, M. *Worship and Ethics. A Study in Rabbinic Judaism*. Northwestern University Press 1964

KAPLAN, H. [HAYIM] 'Halakha be-Sefer ha-Yovelot', *Horev* 1 (1934) 92-99

KÄSEMANN, E. *Exegetische Versuche und Besinnungen* 1-2 (in one vol) 4th ed Göttingen 1965
-- 'Gottesgerechtigkeit bei Paulus'. *ZTK* 58 (1961) 367-78
-- *Paulinische Perspektiven*. Tübingen 1972
-- 'Paulus und Israel'; in *Versuche* 2, 194-7
-- 'Das Problem des historischen Jesus'; in *Versuche* 1, 187-214
-- *An die Römer*. 3rd ed Tübingen 1974
FS Käsemann: J. Friedrich – W. Pöhlmann – P. Stuhlmacher (eds) *Rechtfertigung. Festschrift für Ernst Käsemann zum 70. Geburtstag*. Tübingen/Göttingen 1976
KATZ, J. 'Shelosha mishpatim apologetiim be-gilguleihem'. *Zion* 23-24 (1958-9) 174-93
KENYON, F.C. *The Chester Beatty Biblical Papyri* (etc) III/1-4. London 1934
KIPPENBERG, H.G. 'Die jüdischen Überlieferungen als *patrioi nomoi*'; in R. Faber – R. Schlesier (eds) *Die Restauration der Götter. Antike Religion und Neo-Paganismus*. 1986, 45-60
KLAUCK, H.J. *1. Korintherbrief* (Die neue Echter Bibel) Würzburg 1984
KLAUSNER, J. *Jesus von Nazareth*. 3d pr Jerusalem 1957
-- *Von Jesus zu Paulus*. Jerusalem 1950
KLIJN, A.F.J. 'The Pseudo-Clementines and the Apostolic Decree'. *NovT* 10 (1968) 305-12
KNOX, W.L. *St. Paul and the Church of the Gentiles*. Cambridge 1939
KOESTER, H.H. 'Paul and Hellenism', in Hyatt, *Bible*, 18795
KRAABEL, A.T. 'Greeks, Jews and Lutherans in the Middle Half of Acts'. *HTR* 79 (1986) 147-57
KRAEMER, R.S. 'A New Inscription from Malta and the Question of Women Elders in the Diaspora Jewish Communities'. *HTR* 78 (1975) 431-8
KRAUSS, S. *Griechische und lateinische Lehnwörter in Talmud, Midrasch und Targum* 1-2 (1898-99) repr w add by I. Löw. Hildesheim 1964
KÜCHLER, M. *Schweigen, Schmuck und Schleier. Drei neutestamentliche Vorschriften zur Verdrängung der Frauen auf dem Hintergrund einer frauenfeindlichen Exegese des Alten Testaments im antiken Judentum*. Freiburg (Switz.) – Göttingen 1986
KÜMMEL, W.G. 'Zur Einführung'; in Schweitzer, *Mystik*, i*-xvii*
KUHN, T.S. *The Structure of Scientific Revolutions*. 2nd ed Chicago 1970
LAGRANGE, M.-J. *St. Paul: Épitre aux Galates*. repr Paris 1950
-- *St. Paul: Épitre aux Romains*. Paris 1922
LAKE, K. – JACKSON, FOAKES *The Beginnings of Christianity* 1-5. London 1920-33
LANGE, N.R.M. DE, *Origen and the Jews*. 2nd ed Cambridge 1976
LAUTERBACH, J.Z. '[Philo] – His Relation to the Halakah', in *Jewish Encyclopedia* 10. New York – London 1905, 10-18
LEEUWEN, A. TH. VAN, *Christianity in World History. The Meeting of the Faiths of East and West*. 4th pr London – Edinburgh 1966
LERNER, M. 'Die achtzehn Bestimmungen', *Magazin für die Wissenschaft des Judentums* 9 (1882) 113-44; 10 (1883) 121-56
LESZYNSKY, R. *Die Sadduzäer*. Berlin 1912
LICHT, J. *The Rule Scroll; A Scroll from the Wilderness of Judaea; 1QS – 1QSa – 1QSb; Text, Introduction and Commentary*. Jerusalem 1965 (Hebr)
LICHTENSTEIN, H. 'Die Fastenrolle; eine Untersuchung zur jüdisch-hellenistischen Geschichte'. *HUCA* 8-9 (1931-2) 257-351
LIEBERMA[N], S. 'The Discipline in the So-Called Dead Sea Manual of Discipline' (*JBL* 71 [1951] 199-206) repr in *Texts*, 200-7
-- *Greek in Jewish Palestine. Studies in the Life and Manners of Jewish Palestine in the II-IV Centuries C.E.* 2nd ed New York 1965
-- *Hellenism in Jewish Palestine. Studies in the Literary Transmission, Beliefs and Manners of Palestine in the I Century B.C.E. – IV Century C.E.* 2nd ed New York 1962
-- 'How Much Greek in Jewish Palestine?' (in A. Altmann, *Biblical and Other Studies*. Cambridge MA 1962, 123-41) repr in *Texts*, 21634
-- *Texts and Studies*. New York 1974
-- *Tosefta ki-Fshutah. A Comprehensive Commentary on the Tosefta* 1-8. New York 1955-73 (Hebr)
-- *Ha-Yerushalmi Kiphshuto. Shabbat, Erubin, Pesahim*. Jerusalem 1934 (Hebr)
LIETZMANN, H. *An die Korinther* I. II. (Handb z NT 9) 3rd ed Tübingen 1931

293

LIFSHITZ, B. 'L'Hellénisation des Juifs de Palestine'. *RB* 72 (1965) 520-38

LIGHTFOOT, J.B. *The Epistle to the Galatians* (1865) repr Grand Rapids 1969

LÖWY, M. 'Die paulinische Lehre vom Gesetz'. [I] *MGWJ* 47 (1903) 322-39, 417-33, 534-44; [II] ib 48 (1904) 268-76, 321-7, 400-16

LOHSE, E. 'Zu 1. Kor. 10,26. 31'. *ZNW* 47 (1956) 277-80

LÜDEMANN, G. *Paulus der Heidenapostel* 2: *Anti-Paulinismus im frühen Christentum* (FRLANT 130) Göttingen 1983

LURIE, B.Z. *Megillath Ta'anith. With Introduction and Notes*. Jerusalem 1964 (Hebr)

LUZ, U. *Das Evangelium nach Matthäus* 1 [Mt 1-7] (EKK) Zurich, Einsiedeln, Cologne / Neukirchen-Vluyn 1985

-- 'Rechtfertigung bei den Paulusschülern'; in *FS Käsemann*, 365-83

MACLENNON, R.S. – KRAABEL, A.T. 'The God-Fearers – A Literary and theological Invention'. *BAR* 12 (1986) 46-53, 64

MAIER, J. *Jesus von Nazareth in der Talmudischen Überlieferung*. Darmstadt 1978

MANN, J. 'Rabbinic Studies in the Synoptic Gospels'. *HUCA* 1 (1924) 323-55

MARCUS, R. *Law in the Apocrypha* (1927) repr (Columbia Oriental Studies) New York 1966

MARGALIOTH [MARGULIES], M.[M.] *Encycopedia of Talmudic and Geonic Literature; Being a Biographical Dictionary of the Tannaim, Amoraim and Geonim* 1-2. Tel Aviv 1973 (Hebr)

-- *Hilkhot Erets Yisrael min ha-Geniza*. Jerusalem 1974

MEEKS, W.A. ''And Rose up to Play': Midrash and Paraenesis in 1 Corinthians 10:1-22'. *JSNT* 16 (1982) 64-78

MEEKS, W.A. – WILKEN, R.L. *Jews and Christians in Antioch in the First Four Centuries of the Common Era* (SBL SBS 13) Missoula 1978

METZGER, B.M. *Index to Periodical Literature on the Apostle Paul*. 2nd ed Grand Rapids 1970

MEUZELAAR, J.J. *Der Leib des Messias* (diss Amsterdam) Assen 1961

MILLAR, F. 'The Background to the Maccabean Revolution: Reflections on Martin Hengel's 'Judaism and Hellenism''. *JJS* 29 (1978) 1-21

MOFFATT, J. *The First Epistle of Paul to the Corinthians*. 8th pr London 1954

MOLLAND, E. 'La Circoncision, le baptême et l'autorité du décret apostolique (Actes XV,28 sq.) dans les milieux judéo-chrétiens des Pseudo-Clémentines'. *ST* 9 (1955) 1-39

MOMMSEN, T. 'Die Rechtsverhältnisse des Apostels Paulus'. *ZNW* 2 (1901) 81-96

MOMIGLIANO, A.D. 'Hellenism'; in *EJ* 8, 291-5

-- 'Judentum und Hellenismus, etc' [review of Hengel, Judentum]. *JThSt* ns 21 (1970) 149-53

MONTEFIORE, M. *Judaism and St. Paul; Two Essays* (London 1914) repr New York 1973

MOORE, G.F. 'Christian Writers on Judaism'. *HTR* 14 (1921) 197-254

-- *Judaism in the First Centuries of the Christian Era. The Age of the Tannaim* 1-3. Cambridge MA 1927-30

MUNCK, J. 'Pauline Research since Schweitzer', in Hyatt, *Bible*, 166-77

-- *Paulus und die Heilsgeschichte* (Acta Jutlandica 26.1, theologisk serie 6) Copenhagen 1954

MURPHY O'CONNOR, J. 'Freedom or the Ghetto (I Cor. viii, 1-13; x, 23-xi, 1)'. *RB* 85 (1978) 543-74

MUUSSIES, G. 'Greek in Palestine and the Diaspora'; in *Compendia* I/2, 1040-64

NAVEH, J. *On Stone and Mosaic. The Aramaic and Hebrew Inscriptions from Ancient Synagogues*. Jerusalem – Tel Aviv 1978 (Hebr)

NESTLE-ALAND: Eb. Nestle – Erwin Nestle, *Novum Testamentum graece*. Rev printing of 26th ed by K. Aland et al, Stuttgart 1981

NEUSNER, J. 'The Fellowship (Haburah) in the Second Jewish Commonwealth'. *HTR* 53 (1960) 125-42

NEUSNER, J. (ed) *Religions in Antiquity* (Essays in Memory of E.R. Goodenough) Leiden 1968

OBERMAN, H.A. *Luther. Mensch zwischen Gott und Teufel*. Berlin 1982

-- *Wurzeln des Antisemitismus. Christenangst und Judenplage im Zeitalter von Humanismus und Reformation*. Berlin 1981

OLENDER, M. *Les Langues du paradis; Aryens et Sémites: un couple providentiel*. [Paris] 1989

OSTEN-SACKEN, P. VON DER, *Die Heiligkeit der Tora; Studien zum Gesetz bei Paulus*. Munich 1989

-- *Evangelium und Tora; Aufsätze zu Paulus*. Munich 1987

OSTER, R.E. 'When Men Wore Veils in Worship: The Historical Context of I Corinthians 11.4'. *NTS* 34 (1988) 481-505

PARKES, J. *The Conflict of the Church and the Synagogue. A Study in the Origins of Antisemitism.* (1934) repr New York 1977

PAULY-WISSOWA: *Paulys Real-Encyclopädie der classischen Altertumswissenschaft.* New ed by G. Wissowa et al. 1/1-24; 2/1-10; suppl 1-15. Stuttgart 1894-1978

PINES, S. 'The Jewish Christians of the Early Centuries of Christianity according to a New Source', in *PIASH* 2 (1968) 237-310

PLASKOW, J. – DAUM, A. 'Blaming Jews for Inventing Patriarchy / for the Death of the Goddess'. *Lilith* 7 (1980) 11-13

POHLENZ, M. *Paulus und die Stoa* (*ZNW* 42 [1949] 69-104) repr Darmstadt 1964; also in Rengstorf, *Paulusbild*, 522-64

POLAND, F. *Geschichte des griechischen Vereinswesens* (1909) repr Leipzig 1967

POP, F.J. *De eerste brief van Paulus aan de Corinthiërs.* Nijkerk 1978

QIMRON, E. – STRUGNELL, J. 'An Unpublished Halakhic Letter from Qumran', in *Biblical Archeology Today.* Jerusalem 1985, 400-7

RABIN, CH. 'Hebrew and Aramaic in the First Century'; in *Compendia* I/2, 1007-39

RABINOWITZ, L.I. 'The Halakha as Reflected in Ben-Sira', in *PWCJS* 4/1 (1967) 145-8 (Hebr; Eng summ 264)

RÄISÄNEN, H. *Paul and the Law.* Tübingen 1983

RAPPAPORT, U. 'Yahasei Yehudim we-lo-Yehudim be-Erets Yisrael weha-mered ha-gadol ba-Romi', (*Tarbiz* 47 [1978-9] 1-14) repr in A. Kasher (ed) *The Great Jewish Revolt. Factors and Circumstances Leading to its Outbreak.* Jerusalem 1983, 159-72 (Hebr)

RENGSTORF, K.H. – LUCK, U. (eds) *Das Paulusbild in der neueren deutschen Forschung.* Darmstadt 1982

RESCH, A. *Der Paulinismus und die Logia Jesu in ihrem gegenseitigen Verhältnis untersucht.* Leipzig 1904

RESCH, G. *Das Aposteldecret nach seiner außerkanonischen Textgestalt.* (TuU nF 13/3) Leipzig 1905

REVEL, B. 'Some Anti-Traditional Laws of Josephus', *JQR* ns 14 (1923-4) 293-301

REYNOLDS, J. – TANNENBAUM, R. *Jews and Godfearers at Aphrodisias.* Cambridge 1987

RICHARDSON, P. *Israel in the Apostolic Church* (SNTS MonSer 10) Cambridge 1969

-- 'Pauline Inconsistency: 1 Corinthians 9:19-23 and Galatians 2:11-14', *NTS* 26 (1980) 347-62

RIGAUX, B. *Saint Paul et ses lettres.* Paris – Bruges 1962

RITTER, B. *Philo und die Halacha; eine vergleichende Studie.* Leipzig 1879

ROBERTSON, A. – PLUMMER, A. *A Critical and Exegetical Commentary on the First Epistle of St. Paul to the Corinthians* (ICC) 2nd ed 1914, repr Edinburgh 1955

ROBINSON, J.M. *The Nag Hammadi Library in English.* Leiden 1977

ROSEN, H.B. 'Die Sprachsituation im römischen Palästina'; in G. Neumann – J. Untermann (eds) *Die Sprachen im römischen Reich der Kaiserzeit. Kolloquium 8.-10. April 1974.* Cologne – Bonn 1980, 215-39

RUNIA, D.T. 'Naming and Knowing; Themes in Philonic Theology with Special Reference to the *De mutatione nominum*', in R. van den Broek – T. Baarda – J. Mansfeld (eds) *Knowledge of God in the Graeco-Roman world* (Études préliminaires aux réligions orientales dans l'empire Romain, vol 12) Leiden 1988, 69-91

RUNIA, D.T. – RADICE, R. *Philo of Alexandria; An Annotated Bibliography 1937-1986.* Leiden / New York / København / Köln 1988

SAFRAI, S. *R. Akiva ben Yosef: hayyav u-mishnato; pirkei halakha we-aggada melukatim u-mevuarim be-tseiruf mavo.* Jerusalem 1970

-- 'And All is According to the Majority of Deeds'. *Tarbiz* 53 (1983-4) 33-40 (Hebr)

-- 'The Decision according to the School of Hillel in Yavneh'. *PWCJS* 7/3 (1981) 21-44 (Hebr)

-- 'Education and the Study of the Torah', in *Compendia* I/2, 94570

-- 'Halakha'; in *Compendia* II/3a, 121-209

-- 'Hasidim we-anshei maase'. *Zion* 50 (1984-5) 133-54

-- 'The Holy Congregation in Jerusalem'; in *Scripta* 23. Jerusalem 1972, 62-78

-- 'Home and Family'; in *Compendia* I/2, 728-92

-- 'Jewish Self-Government', in *Compendia* I/2, 377-419
-- 'Kiddush Ha-Shem in the Teaching of the Tannaim'; in *Sefer Zikkaron le-Yitshak Baer*. Jerusalem 1981, 28-42 (Hebr; ET in Th.C. de Kruijf – H.v.d. Sandt [eds] *Sjaloom. Ter Nagedachtenis van A.C. Ramselaar*. Hilversum 1983, 145-65)
-- 'Mishnat hasidim be-sifrut ha-Tannaim', in *We-hinei ein Yosef. Kovets le-zikhro shel Y. Amorai*. Tel Aviv 1973, 136-52
-- 'Oral Tora'; in *Compendia* II/3a, 35-119
-- 'The Practical Implementation of the Sabbatical Year after the Destruction of the Second Temple'. *Tarbiz* 35 (1965-6) 304-28; 36 (1966-7) 1-12 (Hebr)
-- 'Relations between the Diaspora and the Land of Israel', in *Compendia* I/1, 184-215
-- 'The Synagogue'; in *Compendia* I/2, 908-44
-- 'Tales of the Sages in the Palestinian Tradition and the Babylonian Talmud'; in *Scripta* 22 (1971) 209-32
-- 'Teaching of Pietists in Mishnaic Literature'. *JJS* 16 (1965) 15-33
-- 'The Visits to Rome of the Sages of Yavne'; in *Scritti in Memoria di Umberto Nahon*. Jerusalem 1978, 151-67 (Hebr)
-- *Die Wallfahrt im Zeitalter des Zweiten Tempels*. NeukirchenVluyn 1981
-- 'Was there a Women's Gallery in the Synagogue of Antiquity?' *Tarbiz* 32 (1962-3) 329-38 (Hebr)
SAFRAI, S. (ed) *The Literature of the Sages. First Part: Oral Tora, Halakha, Mishna, Tosefta, Talmud, External Tractates* (Compendia rerum iudaicarum ad Novum Testamentum II/3a) Executive editor: P.J. Tomson. Assen – Philadelphia 1987
SAFRAI, S. – STERN, M. (eds) *The Jewish People in the First Century. Historical Geography, Political History, Social, Cultural and Religious Life and Institutions* (Compendia rerum iudaicarum ad Novum Testamentum I/1-2) edited in cooperation with D. Flusser and W.C. van Unnik. Assen – Philadelphia 1974-6
SANDERS, E.P. *Paul and Palestinian Judaism. A Comparison of Patterns of Religion*. Philadelphia/ London 1977
-- *Paul, the Law, and the Jewish People*. Philadelphia / London 1983/85
SANDMEL, S. *The Genius of Paul; A Study in History*. New York 1970
-- *Philo of Alexandria; An Introduction*. New York / Oxford 1979
-- *Philo's Place in Judaism* (1956) augmented ed New York 1971
SAWYER, W.T. *The Problem of Meat Sacrificed to Idols in the Corinthian Church* (microf diss) Ann Arbor 1968
SCHÄFER, P. 'Die Torah der messianischen Zeit', *ZNW* 65 (1974) 27-42
SCHIFFMAN, L.H. *The Halakha at Qumran*, Leiden 1975
-- 'Legislation Concerning Relations with Non-Jews in the Zadokite Fragments and in the Tannaitic Literature'. *RQ* 11 (1983) 379-89
SCHNEEMELCHER, W. *Neutestamentliche Apokryphen; in deutscher Übersetzung* 2 (vol 1: E. Hennecke – W. Schneemelcher) 5th ed Tübingen 1987
SCHNEIDER, K. 'Macellum'; in *PW* 16/1, 129-33
SCHOEPS, H.J. *Paulus. Die Theologie des Apostels im Lichte der jüdischen Religionsgeschichte*. 2nd ed Darmstadt 1972
SCHRAGE, W. *Die konkreten Einzelgebote in der paulinischen Paränese*. Gütersloh 1961
-- 'Die Frage nach der Mitte und dem Kanon im Kanon des NT in der neueren Diskussion', in *FS Käsemann*, 415-42
SCHÜRER, *History*: E. Schürer, *The History of the Jewish People in the Age of Jesus Christ. A New English Version Revised and Edited by G. Vermes, F. Millar et al*. 1-3/2. Edinburgh 1973-87
SCHÜRER, E. *Geschichte des jüdischen Volkes im Zeitalter Jesu Christi* 1-3 (Leipzig 1907) repr Hildesheim 1964
SCHÜSSLER FIORENZA, E. *Bread Not Stone. The Challenge of Feminist Biblical Interpretation*. Boston 1984
-- 'Die Frauen in den vorpaulinischen und paulinischen Gemeinden', in B. Brooten – N. Greinacher, *Frauen in der Männerkirche*. München – Mainz 1982, 112-40
-- *In Memory of Her. A Feminist Theological Reconstruction of Christian Origins*. London 1983
-- 'Rhetorical Situation and Historical Reconstruction in 1 Corinthians'. *NTS* 33 (1987) 386-403

SCHWEITZER, A. *Aus meinem Leben und Denken* (1931) repr Frankfurt/M 1980

-- *Geschichte der Leben-Jesu-Forschung* (1913) 6th ed Tübingen 1951

-- *Geschichte der paulinischen Forschung von der Reformation bis auf der Gegenwart* (= *Geschichte*). Tübingen 1911

-- *Die Mystik des Apostels Paulus* (1930) repr with 'Einführung' by W.G. Kümmel, Tübingen 1981

SEGAL, M.H. *Sefer Ben Sira ha-shalem*. 2nd ed Jerusalem 1958 and repr

SELLIN, G. 'Hauptprobleme des Ersten Korintherbriefes', in *ANRW* II/25.4, 2940-3044 [sic]

SEVENSTER, J.N. *Paul and Seneca*. Leiden 1961

SEVENSTER, J.N. – UNNIK, W.C. VAN, (eds) *Studia Paulina in honorem Johannis de Zwaan septuagenarii*. Haarlem 1953

SIMON, M. *Verus Israel. Étude sur les rélations entre chrétiens et juifs dans l'empire romain (135-425)*. Paris 1948

SMALLWOOD, E.M. *The Jews under Roman Rule from Pompey to Diocletian; A Study in Political Relations*. 2nd ed Leiden 1981

SMIT, J. *Opbouw en gedachtengang van de brief aan de Galaten* (diss) Nijmegen 1986

SODEN, H. VON, 'Sakrament und Ethik bei Paulus. Zur Frage der literarischen und theologischen Einheitlichkeit von 1. Kor. 8-10' (*Marburger Theol. Stud.* 1, Gotha 1931, 1-40) repr in Rengstorf – Luck, *Paulusbild*, 338-79

SPERBER, D. *A Dictionary of Greek and Latin Legal Terms in Rabbinic Literature* (Bar Ilan U Press) 1984

SPICQ, C. 'La Conscience dans le Nouveau Testament'. *RB* 47 (1938) 50-80

STANLEY JONES, F. *'Freiheit' in den Briefen des Apostels Paulus; eine historische, exegetische und religionsgeschichtliche Studie*. Göttingen 1987

STENDAHL, K. *The Bible and the Role of Women; A Case Study in Hermeneutics*. Philadelphia (1966) repr 1979

-- *Paul among Jews and Gentiles, and Other Essays*. London 1977

STERN, M. 'Aspects of Jewish Society; The Priesthood and Other Classes', in *Compendia* I/2, 561-630

-- *Greek and Latin Authors on Jews and Judaism* 1-3. Jerusalem 1974-84

-- 'The Jewish Diaspora', in *Compendia* I/1, 117-83

-- 'The Jews in Greek and Latin Literature'; in *Compendia* I/2, 1101-1159

-- 'Hengel, M. Judentum und Hellenismus' [Review article]. *KS* 46 (1970-1) 94-9 (Hebr)

STONE, M.E. (ed) *Jewish Writings of the Second Temple Period. Apocrypha, Pseudepigrapha, Qumran Sectarian Writings, Philo, Josephus* (Compendia rerum iudaicarum ad Novum Testamentum II/2) Assen – Philadelphia 1984

STRACK, H.L. – BILLERBECK, P. *Kommentar zum neuen Testament aus Talmud und Midrasch* 1-4/2. Munich 1922-28

STRACK, H.L. – STEMBERGER, G. *Einleitung in Talmud und Midrasch*. 7th ed Munich 1982

STROBEL, A. 'Das Aposteldekret in Galatien: zur Situation von Gal. 1 und 2'. *NTS* 20 (1973-4) 177-90

STUHLMACHER, P. *Gerechtigkeit Gottes bei Paulus*. Göttingen 1965

TANNENBAUM, R.F. 'Jews and God-Fearers in the Holy City of Aphrodite'. *BAR* 12 (1986) 54-37

TCHERIKOVER, V.A. *Hellenistic Civilization and the Jews*. Philadelphia 1966

THRALL, M.E. 'The Problem of II Cor. vi.14-vii.1 in Some Recent Discussion'. *NTS* 24 (1977-8) 132-49

TOMSON, P.J. *Jewish Law in First Corinthians* (unpubl diss) Amsterdam 1988

-- 'K.H. Miskotte und das heutige jüdisch-christliche Gespräch'. *NedTT* 44 (1990) 15-34

-- *Mitswat netilat yadayim li-seuda; Het wassen van de handen voor de maaltijd, een rabbijns gebod* (unpubl MA thesis) Amsterdam 1978

-- 'The Names Israel and Jew in Ancient Judaism and in the New Testament'. *Bijdragen* 47 (1986) 120-40, 266-89

-- 'Paulus und das Gesetz: die konkreten Halachot über Ehe und Scheidung 1. Kor 7', in K. Ebert (ed) *Alltagswelt und Ethik; Beiträge zu einem sozial-ethischen Problemfeld; für Adam Weyer zum 60. Geburtstag*. Wuppertal 1988, 157-75

-- 'Zavim 5:12 – Reflections on Dating Mishnaic Halakha'; in A. Kuyt – N.A. van Uchelen (eds) *History and Form: Dutch Studies in the Mishnah; Papers Read at the Workshop 'Mishnah'*. Amsterdam 1988, 53-69

297

Tov, E. 'The Septuagint', in *Compendia* II/1, 161-88

Townsend, J.T. 'I Corinthians 3:15 and the School of Shammai', *HTR* 61 (1968) 500-4

Unnik, W.C. van, 'Tarsus or Jerusalem: The City of Paul's Youth', in *Sparsa Collecta. The Collected Essays of W.C. van Unnik* 1. Leiden 1973, 259-320

Urbach, E.E. *Ha-Halakha, mekoroteha we-hitpathuteha*. Givataim 1984

-- 'The Rabbinical Laws of Idolatry in the Second and Third Centuries in the Light of Archaeological and Historical Facts'. *IEJ* 9 (1959) 149-65; 229-45

-- *The Sages. Their Concepts and Beliefs* 1-2. 2nd enlarged ed Jerusalem 1979

Watson, F. *Paul, Judaism and the Gentiles. A Sociological Approach* (SNTS MonSer 56) Cambridge 1986

Weber, F. *System der altsynagogalen palästinensischen Theologie*. 2nd ed Leipzig 1880

Weinfeld, M. 'Pentecost as a Festival of the Giving of the Law'. *Immanuel* 8 (1978) 7-18

Weiss, J. *Der erste Korintherbrief* (1910) repr Göttingen 1970

Wilckens, U. 'Zur Entwicklung des paulinischen Gesetzesverständnisses'. *NTS* 28 (1982) 154-90 (summary: 'Statements on the Development of Paul's View of the Law'; in Hooker-Wilson, *Paul and Paulinism*, 17-26)

Willis, W.L. 'An Apostolic Apologia? The Form and Function of 1 Corinthians 9'. *JSNT* 24 (1985) 33-48

-- *Idol Meat in Corinth. The Pauline Argument in 1 Corinthians 8 and 10* (SBL DissSer 68) Chico CA 1985

Windisch, H. *Paulus und das Judentum*. Stuttgart 1935

Wolff, C. *Der erste Brief des Paulus an die Korinther* 1-2. Berlin 1982

Wolff, H.J. 'Hellenistic Private Law'; in *Compendia* I/1, 534-60

-- *Written and Unwritten Marriages in Hellenistic and Post-Classical Roman Law* (Monogr Amer Philol Ass no 9) Haverford (PA) 1939

Wolfson, H.A. *Philo. Foundations of Religious Philosophy in Judaism, Christianity and Islam* 1-2. Cambridge MA (1948) 3rd ed 1962

Wrede, W. *Paulus* (1904) repr in Rengstorf – Luck, *Paulusbild*, 1-97

Wuellner, W. 'Greek Rhetoric and Pauline Argumentation', in W.R. Schoedel – R. Wilken (eds) *Early Christian Literature and the Classical Intellectual Tradition; in honorem Robert M. Grant* (Théologie historique) Paris 1979, 177-88

Yadin, Y. *Bar-Kokhba: The Rediscovery of the Legendary Hero of the Second Jewish Revolt against Rome*. London 1971

-- *The Ben Sira Scroll from Masada*. Jerusalem 1965

-- *The Temple Scroll* 1-3. Jerusalem 1977 (Hebr; ET Jerusalem 1983)

Yarbrough, O.L. *Not Like the Gentiles. Marriage Rules in the Letters of Paul* (SBLDissSer 80) Atlanta 1985

Zeitlin, S. 'Les Dix-huit mesures'. *REJ* 68 (1914) 22-29 (= *Bitsaron* 25 [1964] 2-12)

-- 'The Halaka in the Gospels and Its Relation to the Jewish Law at the Time of Jesus'. *HUCA* 1 (1924) 357-73

Index of Sources

This index is selective as regards Paul. Bold print indicates extensive discussion of entire passages or letters; single verses from these on the intermediate pages are not listed. Neither are Pauline passages from the concluding chapter included.

Division:
1. *Hebrew Bible, Ancient Jewish Writings*. Hebrew Bible; Septuagint and Apocrypha; Pseudepigrapha; Qumran Scrolls; Philo; Josephus.
2. *Early Christian Documents*. New Testament; Apostolic, Patristic and Other Christian Writings.
3. *Classical Rabbinic Literature*. Halakhic Collections; Targum, Midrash Collections; External Tractates, Varia.
4. *Other Sources*.

1. Hebrew Bible, Early Jewish Writings

Hebrew Bible

Genesis		Exodus	
1:27	111, 114, 135, 137	3	28
2:7	82	4:31	66
2:16	156	12	28
2:18	82	12:6	147
2:18-23	137	12:42-45	218
2:24	75, 82, 99f, 102, 105, 107, 114f, 123	15f	199, 201
3:16	137	15:25	200
6:1-4	103, 106	16:4	200
9:4-6	179, 183	17	199
12:1-4	43	17:6	200
12:3	65	17:14	155
15:6	65-67	19:6	152
17:10	65	20:1ff	156
25:22	100	20:3-5	151
26:8	152	20:5	152
27:1	80	20:19	78
49:1	80	21-22	151
49:4	100	21:10	107
		22:19	152
		22:20	91
		23:13	152

300

301

Sir 6:18f	84, 129
7:33	157
19:2	123
24:23-33	200
25:29[25f]	123
30:18	157
32:23	84, 272
37:28	75, 84, 204
42:18	212
Ezek 44:31	184
Isa 29:13	145
Ep Jer	157
27	157
28f	218
32	157
Bel et Draco	157

Pseudepigrapha
(listed alphabetically)

Aristeas

305f	227

Apocalypse of Abraham

1-8	157

Apocalypse of Moses

19:3	106

Aristeas

144	128

Ascensio Isaiae

2:11	239

2Baruch

29:3-8	272

1Enoch

-	185
6-12	103
48:1	200
60:6	80, 257
60:7	272

60:24	272
69:4f	103
99:7	156

2Enoch

31:3-6	103

4Ezra

4:28-32	84, 130
6:47-52	272
8:41-44	84, 130
9:17	84, 130
9:24f	239
9:30-37	84, 130

Jubilees

-	185
1:11	156
3:3-7	115
4:21f	103
7:20	99
10:5	103
22:16f	153
22:17	152, 157, 169
30:7-17	153
30:10	153
36:4	204

Life of Adam and Eve

18:1-4	106

Pseudo-Phocylides

31	181
146	76
147	181

Sibylline Oracles

2:96	181
3:30	202
3:592f	228
4:7	202
8:379	202
8:382-4	157
8:393	157

Testaments of the 12 Patriarchs

TReub	212
4:6	99

Qumran Scrolls

Philo

Josephus

2. Early Christian Documents

307

308

309

Apostolic, Patristic and Other Christian Writings (listed alphabetically)

311

3. *Classical Rabbinic Literature*

Halakhic Collections

313

bMenahot	
43b	234
45a	184
110a	212

bHullin	
5a	156
13b	155
33b	233
107b	195

bBekhorot	
30b	89
47a	100

bNidda	
38a-b	105
61b	94f
69b	45

Targum, Midrash Collections

Targum Onkelos	
Exod 21:10	107
Exod 23:33	92
Deut 32:43	258

Targum Pseudo-Yonatan	
Gen 1:21	272
Exod 21:10	107
Exod 23:33	92
Exod 32:6	152
Lev 18:21	153
Deut 23:24f	127
Deut 29:28	212
Deut 32:43	258

Targum Yonatan	
Hos 13:14	71
Ps 68:19	78
Ps 88:6	95
Eccl 10:20	212

Targum Sheni Esther	
3:7	272

Mekhilta de-R. Yishmael (ed Horovitz-Rabin)	
p17	147
p97-100	66
p98	67
p99	66
p114f	66f
p130	147
p154	200

p156	200
p186f	155
p195f	232
p205	128
p223-5	151
p229	174
p258f	107

Mekhilta de-R. Shimon ben Yohai (ed Epstein-Melamed)	
p21	232
p57-59	66
p57f	67
p58	66
p70	66f
p80	147
p126	155
p131	232
p146f	151
p148	174, 246
p167f	107

Sifra (ed Weiss)	
Wayikra 9 (38b)	213
Shemini 52c	240
Shemini 57b	249
Kedoshim 8 (91a)	89
Aharei 9 (84a)	157
Aharei 85d	99
Aharei 86a	248
Aharei 86b	234
Aharei 93d	249

Sifrei Numbers	
111 (p116)	156
131 (p171)	157

Sifrei Deuteronomy (ed Finkelstein)	
38 (p74f)	232
48 (p111)	128
51 (p116-8)	155
104 (p163)	252
149 (p203f)	103
235 (p269)	134
259 (p282)	93
266f (p286f)	127
269 (p288)	110
269 (p289)	121
287 (p305)	127
294 (p313)	174
318 (p364)	157

Genesis Rabba (ed Theodor-Albeck)	
1,7 (p4)	147
7,4 (p52-4)	272

11,3 (p90)	195	Tanhuma, ed Buber	
13,3-6 (p115-7)	130	Wayehi 8 (108b)	80
16,6 (149f)	156	Shemot 22 (7a)	78
16,6 (p150)	99, 105	Ki tisa 13 (57a)	152
16,6 (p151)	99	Wayikra 3 (2a)	89
18,5 (p165)	100		
18,5 (p166)	99, 109, 115	Seder Eliyahu Rabba (ed Friedmann)	
18,6 (p167)	99	6 (p27f)	157
18,24 (p165f)	99	7 [6] (p34, 36)	234
34,8 (p316f)	155	9 (p46-48)	234
34,14 (p326f)	106	9 (p48)	157
38 (p361-4)	157	24 [26] p134	145
44,1 (p242f)	249		
53,10 (p567)	152	Seder Eliyahu Zutta (ed Friedmann)	
64,5 (p704f)	152	25 (p47f)	157
66,6 (p751)	257		
70 (p806)	200	Midrash Psalms (ed Buber)	
		68,5 (159a)	78
Leviticus Rabba (ed Margulies)		68,11 (160a)	78, 128
2,9 (p48, 51)	234		
9,3 (p176-8)	222	Bereshit Rabbati (ed Albeck)	
13,3 (p207)	249	p206	234
13,3 (277-80)	272		
22,7 (p517)	157	Yalkut Shimoni (ed Hyman)	
22,10 (p521-6)	272	Gen 2:6 (p77f)	99
24,6 (p559f)	98	Gen 2:24 (p88)	115
34,3 (p675-7)	246	Gen 2:25 (p86-88)	99
		Lev 18:5 (p560)	234
Canticles Rabba			
1,17	172	Yalkut Shimoni (trad)	
		Prov, no. 950	232
Ruth Rabba			
2,14	232	Midrash Gadol	
Eccl Rabba		Genesis (ed Margulies)	
1,8 [1,24]	242	2:6 (p83)	99
		2:24 (p91f)	99f
Esth Rabba		10:28 (p202-7)	157
2,4	232	15:7 (p252f)	157
Pesikta de-Rav Kahana (ed Mandelbaum)		Deuteronomy (ed Fisch)	
p54f	249	17 (p282-6)	103
p74	114, 249	23:15 (p522f)	110
p88-99	48	23:16 (p524)	92
p115	232	23:16 (p525)	92f
p203	79	23:24f (p533-5)	127
p450	95	23:25 (p533)	127, 129
		25:4 (p560)	125, 127
Pesikta Rabbati (ed Friedmann)		26:1 (p597f)	86
23 (115b)	174, 246	28:12 (p610-3)	130
		32:17 (p713)	157
Tanhuma			
Ki tisa 20 (123a)	152	Sefer Pitron Tora (ed Urbach)	
Wayikra 2 (1b)	89	p79f	95
Shemini 12f (15b)	249		

4. *Other Sources*

Index of Modern Authors

324